W9-BSH-651

# THE POLICE IN AMERICA

# THE POLICE IN AMERICA

## AN INTRODUCTION

### THIRD EDITION

## Samuel Walker
University of Nebraska at Omaha

Boston   Burr Ridge, IL  Dubuque, IA  Madison, WI  New York  San Francisco  St. Louis
Bangkok  Bogotá  Caracas  Lisbon  London  Madrid
Mexico City   Milan  New Delhi  Seoul  Singapore  Sydney  Taipei  Toronto

## McGraw-Hill College

*A Division of The* **McGraw·Hill** *Companies*

**THE POLICE IN AMERICA: AN INTRODUCTION**

Copyright © 1999 by The McGraw-Hill Companies, Inc. All rights reserved. Previous editions © 1983 and 1992. Printed in the United States of America. Except as permitted under the United States Copyright Act of 1976, no part of this publication may be reproduced or distributed in any form or by any means, or stored in a database or retrieval system, without the prior written permission of the publisher.

This book is printed on acid-free paper.

1 2 3 4 5 6 7 8 9 0 DOC/DOC 9 3 2 1 0 9 8

ISBN 0-07-067911-8

Editorial director: *Phillip A. Butcher*
Sponsoring editor: *Nancy Blaine*
Marketing manager: *Leslie Kraham*
Project manager: *Christina Thornton-Villagomez*
Senior production supervisor: *Madelyn S. Underwood*
Designer: *Kiera Cunningham*
Photo research coordinator: *Sharon Miller*
Photo researcher: *Elyse Rieder*
Supplement coordinator: *Carol Loreth*
Compositor: *GAC Shepard Poorman Communications*
Typeface: *10/12 Times Roman*
Printer: *R. R. Donnelley & Sons Company*

**Library of Congress Cataloging-in-Publication Data**

Walker, Samuel (date)
    The Police in America : an introduction / Samuel Walker. —
3rd ed.
        p.   cm.
    ISBN   0-07-067911-8
    Includes index.
    1. Police—United States.   2. Police administration—
United States.   I. Title.
HV8138.W3418 1998
363.2/0973—dc21                                        98-19785

http://www.mhhe.com

# ABOUT THE AUTHOR

SAMUEL WALKER is a professor of criminal justice at the University of Nebraska at Omaha. He teaches an undergraduate course, Police and Society, for which this book is designed, a graduate course on the administration of justice, and other courses. He is the author of nine books on the police, the history of criminal justice, criminal justice policy, and civil liberties. His primary research interests involve citizen complaints against the police and citizen complaint review procedures. In 1998 he was awarded the Bruce Smith Award by the Academy of Criminal Justice Sciences (ACJS).

# CONTENTS IN BRIEF

PREFACE                                                                 xxiii

**PART 1    FOUNDATIONS**

  1    Police and Society                                              3

  2    The History of the American Police                             19

  3    The Contemporary Law Enforcement Industry                      49


**PART 2    POLICE WORK**

  4    Patrol: The Backbone of Policing                               70

  5    Peacekeeping and Order Maintenance                             97

  6    The Police and Crime                                          125

  7    Policing Communities                                          156


**PART 3    POLICE PROBLEMS**

  8    Police Discretion                                             189

  9    Police–Community Relations                                    211

  10    Police Corruption                                            242

  11    Accountability of the Police                                 267


**PART 4    OFFICERS AND ORGANIZATIONS**

  12    Police Officers I: Entering Police Work                      293

  13    Policing Officers II: On The Job                             322

  14    Police Organizations                                         355

INDEX                                                                   377

# CONTENTS

PREFACE                                                                    xiii

## PART 1  FOUNDATIONS

### 1  Police and Society                                                   3

WHY POLICE?                                                                  4
    The Goals of This Book                             4
    Myths, Realities, and Possibilities                4
MYTHS ABOUT POLICING                                                        4
    Sources of the Crime-Fighter Image                 5
    Consequences of the Crime-Fighter Image            5
THE REALITIES OF POLICING                                                   6
    Factors That Shape the Police Role                 9
    The Authority to Use Force                         10
    The Police and Social Control                      10
    The Police and Social Control Systems              11
POSSIBILTIES                                                                12
    Functional Specialization                          12
    Problem-Oriented Policing                          13
    Community Policing                                  14
    Zero-Tolerance Policing                            14
    Honest Law Enforcement                             15
THE IMPLICATIONS OF CHANGE                                                  15
CONCLUSION                                                                  17
NOTES                                                                       17

2   **The History of the American Police**                           19

THE RELEVANCE OF HISTORY                                             20
THE ENGLISH HERITAGE                                                 20
    Creation of Modern Police: London, 1829                          21
LAW ENFORCEMENT IN COLONIAL AMERICA                                  21
    The Quality of Colonial Law Enforcement                          22
    The First Modern American Police                                 23
AMERICAN POLICING IN THE 19TH CENTURY                                24
    Patrol Work                                                      25
    The Police and the Public                                        25
    Corruption and Politics                                          26
    The Failure of Police Reform                                     26
    The Impact of the Police on Society                              27
THE 20TH CENTURY: THE ORIGINS OF POLICE
    PROFESSIONALISM                                                  27
    The Professionalization Movement                                 28
    The Reform Agenda                                                28
    The Impact of Professionalization                                29
    New Problems in Policing                                         30
    Police and Racial Minorities                                     30
    New Law Enforcement Agencies                                     31
THE NEW COMMUNICATIONS TECHNOLOGY                                    31
NEW DIRECTIONS IN POLICE ADMINISTRATION,
    1930-1960                                                        32
    The Wickersham Commission Report                                 32
    Professionalization Continues                                    33
    J. Edgar Hoover and the War on Crime                             33
THE POLICE CRISIS OF THE 1960s                                       34
    The Police in the National Spotlight                             35
NEW DEVELOPMENTS IN POLICING                                         36
    The Changing Police Officer                                      37
    Supervision and the Control of Discretion                        37
    Police Unions                                                    38
    Citizens Review of Complaints                                    39
    Community Policing                                               39
CONCLUSION:  THE LESSONS OF THE PAST                                 40
NOTES                                                                41


3   **The Contemporary Law Enforcement Industry**                    46

OVERVIEW OF LAW ENFORCEMENT                                          47
    Basic Features of American Law Enforcement                       47
    An Industry Perspective                                          47
    An International Perspective                                     47

A DEFINITION OF TERMS 49
What Is a Law Enforcement Agency? 49
Who Is a Police Officer? 49
SIZE AND SCOPE OF THE LAW ENFORCEMENT
INDUSTRY 50
The Number of Law Enforcement Agencies 50
The Number of Law Enforcement Personnel 50
Understanding Law Enforcement Personnel Data 50
Civilianization 51
The Police/Population Ratio 52
The Cost of Police Protection 52
MUNICIPAL POLICE 52
THE COUNTY SHERIFF 53
The Role of the Sheriff 54
OTHER LOCAL AGENCIES 54
NATIVE-AMERICAN TRIBAL POLICE 55
STATE LAW ENFORCEMENT AGENCIES 56
Roles and Responsibilities 56
FEDERAL LAW ENFORCEMENT AGENCIES 57
Roles and Responsibilities 57
THE PRIVATE SECURITY INDUSTRY 57
THE FRAGMENTATION ISSUE 58
Alternatives to Fragmentation 60
The Fragmentation Problem Reconsidered 61
MINIMUM STANDARDS: AMERICAN STYLE 61
The Role of the Federal Government 62
The Role of State Governments 62
Accreditation 63
CONCLUSION 63
NOTES 63


PART 2 POLICE WORK

4 Patrol: The Backbone of Policing 69

THE CENTRAL ROLE OF PATROL 70
THE FUNCTIONS OF PATROL 70
THE ORGANIZATION AND DELIVERY OF PATROL 71
Number of Sworn Officers 71
Allocation and Distribution of Officers to Patrol 72
Assignment to Shifts and Areas 74
Types of Patrol 74
Staffing Patrol Beats 75
Styles of Patrol 76

Organizational Styles                                          76
Type of Supervision                                           76
Summary                                                       77
CALLS FOR POLICE SERVICE                                      77
The Communications Center                                    77
Processing Calls for Service                                 78
THE SERVICE CALL WORKLOAD                                     80
ASPECTS OF PATROL WORK                                        82
Response Time                                                 82
Officer Use of Patrol Time                                    83
Evasion of Duty                                               84
High-Speed Pursuits                                           84
THE EFFECTIVENESS OF PATROL                                   85
The Kansas City Preventive Patrol Experiment                 85
The Newark Foot Patrol Experiment                            87
Summary                                                       87
IMPROVING PATROL                                              88
Differential Response to Calls                               88
Police Aides or Cadets                                        89
Directed Patrol and Hot Spots                                90
Beyond Traditional Patrol                                     90
CONCLUSION                                                    91
NOTES                                                         91

5   **Peacekeeping and Order Maintenance**                    97
THE POLICE ROLE                                               98
CALLING THE POLICE                                            98
Public Expectations                                           99
Police Response                                               99
POLICING DOMESTIC DISPUTES                                   100
Defining Our Terms                                           101
The Prevalence of Domestic Violence                          101
The Husband-Beating Controversy                              101
Calling the Police                                           102
Danger to Police?                                            103
Police Response to Domestic Disturbances                     104
Factors Influencing the Arrest Decision                      105
A Revolution in Policy: Mandatory Arrest                     105
The Impact of Arrest on Domestic Violence                    106
Impact of Mandatory Arrest Laws and Policies                 107
Other Laws and Policies                                       108
The Future of Domestic Violence Policy                       108
POLICING THE HOMELESS                                        109
The Homeless Problem: Old and New                            109
Police and the Chronic Alcoholic                             111

POLICING THE MENTALLY ILL                                        112
   Police Response to the Mentally Ill                       112
   Old Problems/New Programs                                113
POLICING PEOPLE WITH DISABILITIES                               113
POLICING PEOPLE WITH AIDS                                       114
POLICING JUVENILES                                              114
   Controversy over the Police Role                         115
   Specialized Juvenile Units                               116
   On-the-Street Encounters                                 116
   The Issue of Race Discrimination                         117
   Police Diversion Programs                                118
   Crime Prevention Programs                                118
CONCLUSION                                                      119
NOTES                                                           119

**6    The Police and Crime                                    125**

THE POLICE AND CRIME                                            126
   Crime Control Strategies                                 126
   Crime Control Assumptions                                127
   Measuring Effectiveness                                  127
PREVENTING CRIME                                                128
APPREHENDING CRIMINALS                                          128
   Citizen Reporting of Crime                               129
   Reporting and Unfounding Crimes                          129
CRIMINAL INVESTIGATION                                          131
   Myths about Detective Work                               131
   The Organization of Detective Work                       132
THE INVESTIGATION PROCESS                                       133
   The Preliminary Investigation                            133
   Arrest Discretion                                        133
   Follow-Up Investigations                                 133
   The Reality of Detective Work                            134
   Case Screening                                           134
MEASURING THE EFFECTIVENESS OF CRIMINAL
   INVESTIGATION                                            135
   The Clearance Rate                                       135
   Defining an Arrest                                       136
SUCCESS AND FAILURE IN SOLVING CRIMES                          137
   Eyewitness Identification                                138
   Criminalistics                                           138
   Officer Productivity                                     139
   The Problem of Case Attrition                            139
IMPROVING CRIMINAL INVESTIGATIONS                              140
   Targeting Career Criminals                               140

TRAFFIC ENFORCEMENT                                       141
    Drunk-Driving Crackdowns                          142
POLICING VICE                                             143
    Prostitution                                      144
    Gambling                                          144
DRUG ENFORCEMENT                                          145
    Drug Enforcement Strategies                       145
    Drug Crackdowns                                   146
    Minorities and the War on Drugs                   147
    Demand Reduction: The D.A.R.E. Program            148
    New Approaches to Drug Enforcement                148
TARGETING GUNS AND GUN CRIMES                             148
    The Kansas City Gun Experiment                    148
SPECIAL INVESTIGATIVE TECHNIQUES                          149
    Undercover Police Work                            149
    Informants                                        150
CONCLUSION                                                150
NOTES                                                     150

7   Policing Communities                                 156
THE ROOTS OF COMMUNITY POLICING                          157
PROBLEM-ORIENTED POLICING                                157
"BROKEN WINDOWS"                                          158
    Types of Disorders                                160
INITIAL EXPERIMENTS                                       161
    Fear Reduction in Houston and Newark              161
    Problem-Oriented Policing in Newport News         162
PRINCIPLES OF COMMUNITY POLICING                         163
COMMUNITY POLICING EXPERIMENTS:
    CAPS IN CHICAGO                                   164
    The CAPS Plan                                     164
    Obstacles to Change                               165
    CAPS in Action                                    166
    Evaluation of CAPS                                167
EIGHT INOP PROGRAMS                                       168
OTHER PROGRAMS                                            169
    COPE in Baltimore                                 169
    SMART in Oakland                                  170
NEW YORK CITY: FROM CPOP TO ZERO TOLERANCE               171
    Zero-Tolerance Policing                           172
PERSPECTIVES ON COMMUNITY POLICING                       173
    Team Policing                                     173
    Team Policing in Operation                        173
    The Failure of Team Policing                      174
    Police–Community Relations                        174

COMMUNITY POLICING: PROBLEMS AND PROSPECTS    175
  Rhetoric or Reality?    175
  Too Rapid Expansion    175
  A Legitimate Police Role?    176
  A Political Police?    176
  Changing the Police Culture    176
  Community Coproduction    177
  Decentralization and Accountability    180
  Conflicting Community Interests    180
  Policing Where "Community" Has Collapsed    181
SUMMARY: A NEW ERA IN POLICING?    182
NOTES    183

## PART 3    POLICE PROBLEMS

### 8    Police Discretion    189

EXAMPLES OF DISCRETION    190
A DEFINITION OF DISCRETION    190
ASPECTS OF POLICE DISCRETION    190
  Low-Level Decision Making    190
  Police Discretion and the Criminal Justice System    191
  Problems with Discretion    191
DECISION POINTS AND DECISION MAKERS    192
  Patrol Tactics Decisions    192
  Order Maintenance Decisions    192
  Investigative Decisions    192
  Law Enforcement Priorities    193
  Police Role    193
SOURCES OF POLICE DISCRETION    193
  The Nature of the Criminal Law    193
  The Work Environment of Policing    194
  Limited Police Resources    194
FACTORS INFLENCING DISCRETIONARY
  DECISIONS    194
  Situational Factors    194
  The Immediate Work Environment    196
  Department Policy    196
  Characteristics of the Individual Officer    196
THE CONTROL OF DISCRETION    197
  The Need for Control    197
  Bureaucracy and the Control of Discretion    198
  Strategies for Controlling Discretion    198
  Abolishing Discretion    199

Enhancing Professional Judgment 199
Written Policies 200
ADMINISTRATIVE RULE MAKING 200
Examples of Administrative Rule Making 200
Principles of Administrative Rule Making 201
The Advantages of Written Rules 201
The Impact of Administrative Rule Making 202
The Limits of Administrative Rule Making 203
Codifying Rules: The Standard Operating
     Procedure Manual 204
Making Rule Making More Systematic 205
Rule Making and Community Policing 205
CONCLUSION 206
NOTES 206

9   Police–Community Relations 211

A DEFINITION OF POLICE–COMMUNITY RELATIONS 212
RACE AND ETHNICITY IN AMERICA 213
Definitions of Race and Ethnicity 213
Discrimination and Disparity 214
PUBLIC OPINION AND THE POLICE 215
Racial and Ethnic Differences 215
Attitudes about Police Use of Force 216
Other Demographic Variables 217
Intercity Variations 217
The Impact of Dramatic Events 217
The Detroit Exception 218
The Police and the Larger Society 218
Comparisons with the Other Occupations 218
POLICE PERCEPTIONS OF CITIZENS 219
Sources of Police Attitudes 220
SOURCES OF POLICE–COMMUNITY RELATIONS
   PROBLEMS 220
LAW ENFORCEMENT POLICY 221
Inadequate Police Protection 221
POLICE FIELD PRACTICES 223
Deadly Force 223
Use of Physical Force 224
Arrests 225
Stops and Frisks 227
Verbal Abuse and Racial and Ethnic Slurs 228
Traffic Citations 228
Delay in Responding to Calls 229
Summary 229
ADMINISTRATIVE PRACTICES 229

POLICE EMPLOYMENT PRACTICES ..... 230
    Increasing Minority Employment in Policing ..... 231
IMPROVING POLICE–COMMUNITY RELATIONS ..... 232
    Special Police–Community Relations Units ..... 232
    Race Relations and Human Relations Training ..... 233
NEW APPROACHES TO IMPROVING POLICE–COMMUNITY
    RELATIONS ..... 234
CONCLUSION ..... 235
NOTES ..... 235

**10   Police Corruption** ..... **242**

A DEFINITION OF POLICE CORRUPTION ..... 243
THE COSTS OF POLICE CORRUPTION ..... 243
TYPES OF CORRUPTION ..... 245
    Gratuities ..... 245
    Bribes ..... 247
    Theft and Burglary ..... 247
    Internal Corruption ..... 248
    Corruption and Brutality ..... 248
LEVELS OF CORRUPTION ..... 248
THEORIES OF POLICE CORRUPTION ..... 249
    Individual Officer Explanations ..... 249
    Social Structural Explanations ..... 250
    The Nature of Police Work ..... 251
    The Police Subculture ..... 252
    The Police Organization ..... 252
BECOMING CORRUPT ..... 253
    The Moral Careers of Individual Officers ..... 253
    Corrupting Organizations ..... 254
CONTROLLING CORRUPTION ..... 254
INTERNAL CORRUPTION CONTROL STRATEGIES ..... 255
    The Attitude of the Chief ..... 255
    Rules and Regulations ..... 256
    Managing Anticorruption Investigations ..... 256
    Investigative Tactics ..... 258
    Cracking the Blue Curtain ..... 259
    Proactive Integrity Tests ..... 259
    Effective Supervision ..... 260
    Rewarding the Good Officers ..... 260
    Personnel Recruitment ..... 260
EXTERNAL CORRUPTION CONTROL APPROACHES ..... 261
    Special Investigations ..... 261
    Criminal Prosecution ..... 262
    Mobilizing Public Opinion ..... 262
    Altering the External Environment ..... 262

The Limits of Anticorruption Efforts                263
The Future of Police Integrity                      263
CONCLUSION                                          263
NOTES                                               263

11  Accountability of the Police                    267

POLICE ACCOUNTABILITY IN A DEMOCRATIC
    SOCIETY                                         268
BASIC ISSUES IN POLICE ACCOUNTABILITY               268
    A Historical Perspective on Accountability      269
SUBSTANTIVE ACCOUNTABILITY ISSUES                   269
    Traditional Issues                              269
    New Measures                                    270
THE POLITICAL PROCESS AS A MECHANISM
    OF ACCOUNTABILITY                               270
    The Dilemma of Democracy                        272
    Community Control                               273
THE SUPREME COURT AS A MECHANISM
    OF ACCOUNTABILITY                               274
    Impact of Supreme Court Decisions               275
LEGAL REMEDIES FOR POLICE MISCONDUCT                276
    Civil Damages                                   277
    Injunctions                                     278
    Criminal Prosecution                            278
INTERNAL MECHANISMS OF POLICE ACCOUNTABILITY        279
    Routine Supervision                             279
    Internal Affairs Units                          280
    Early Warning Systems                           281
CIVILIAN OVERSIGHT OF THE POLICE                    282
    Forms of Citizen Review                         282
    The Role of Citizen Review                      283
    Citizen Review: Pro and Con                     284
ACCREDITATION                                       284
BLUE-RIBBON COMMISSIONS                             285
THE NEWS MEDIA                                      286
PUBLIC INTEREST GROUPS                              286
A MIXED APPROACH TO POLICE ACCOUNTABILITY           286
CONCLUSION                                          287
NOTES                                               287

PART 4   OFFICERS AND ORGANIZATIONS

12  Police Officers I: Entering Police Work         295

THE CHANGING AMERICAN POLICE OFFICER                296

A Career Perspective                                         296
Beyond Stereotypes of Cops                                   296
The Personnel Process: A Shared Responsibility               296
RECRUITMENT                                                  297
Minimum Qualifications                                       297
The Recruitment Effort                                       300
Choosing Law Enforcement as a Career                         301
People Who Do Not Apply                                      303
SELECTION                                                    303
Oral Interviews                                              304
Background Investigations                                    304
THE PROBLEM OF SELECTING GOOD POLICE OFFICERS                305
EQUAL EMPLOYMENT OPPORTUNITY                                 306
Job-Related Qualifications                                   307
Employment of Racial and Ethnic Minorities                   308
Women in Policing                                            309
Employment Discrimination Litigation                         310
THE AFFIRMATIVE ACTION CONTROVERSY                           311
The Issue of Quotas                                          311
TRAINING                                                     313
Field Training                                               314
State Training and Certification                             314
Shortcomings of Current Police Training                      315
THE PROBATIONARY PERIOD                                      316
CONCLUSION                                                   316
NOTES                                                        316

13   Police Officers II: On the Job                          322

BEGINNING POLICE WORK: REALITY SHOCK                         323
Encountering Citizens                                        323
Encountering the Criminal Justice System                     324
Encountering the Department                                  324
The Seniority System                                         324
POLICE OFFICER ATTITUDES AND BEHAVIOR                        325
The Concept of a Police Subculture                           325
Criticisms of the Police Subculture Concept                  327
THE CHANGING RANK AND FILE                                   328
Gender                                                       328
Race and Ethnicity                                           329
Sexual Orientation                                           330
Patterns of Interaction                                      330
Intergroup Conflict                                          331
Education                                                    331
Cohort Effects                                               332
Summary                                                      332

THE RELATIONSHIP BETWEEN ATTITUDES
  AND BEHAVIOR                                              332
BACKGROUND CHARACTERISTICS AND BEHAVIOR                    333
  Race and Ethnicity                                       333
  Gender                                                   334
  Education                                                335
  Summary                                                  335
STYLES OF POLICE WORK                                      335
CAREER DEVELOPMENT                                         337
  Promotion                                                337
  Salaries and Benefits                                    337
  Assignment                                               338
  Lateral Entry                                            339
PERFORMANCE EVALUATION                                     339
JOB SATISFACTION AND JOB STRESS                            342
  Coping with Stress                                       346
THE RIGHTS OF POLICE OFFICERS                              347
OUTSIDE EMPLOYMENT                                         348
TURNOVER: LEAVING POLICE WORK                              348
CONCLUSION                                                 349
NOTES                                                      349


14  Police Organizations                                   355

THE QUASI-MILITARY STYLE OF POLICE
  ORGANIZATIONS                                            356
  Criticisms of the Quasi-Military Style                   356
POLICE DEPARTMENTS  AS ORGANIZATIONS                       357
  The Dominant Style of American Police Organizations      357
  Police Organizations as Bureaucracies                    357
  The Problems with Bureaucracy                            358
  Police Organizations as Bureaucracies                    358
PROBLEMS WITH POLICE ORGANIZATIONS                         359
  The Positive Contributions of Bureaucracy in Policing    361
  Informal Aspects of Police Organizations                 361
BUREAUCRACY AND POLICE PROFESSIONALISM                     362
CHANGING POLICE ORGANIZATIONS                              363
  The Team Policing Experiments                            363
  Task Forces                                              364
  Community Policing                                       365
  Creating Learning Organizations                          365
  Strategic Management of Police Organizations             367
CIVIL SERVICE                                              367
POLICE UNIONS                                              368
  Aspects of Police Unions                                 368

Collective Bargaining 369
Grievance Procedures 369
Unions and Shared Governance 371
Impasse Settlement and Strikes 371
The Impact of Police Unions 371
THE INSTITUTIONAL ENVIRONMENT OF
    POLICE ORGANIZATIONS 373
CONCLUSION 374
NOTES 374

**INDEX** 377

# PREFACE

*The Police in America: An Introduction* provides a comprehensive introduction to policing in America. Primarily descriptive, it is designed to offer undergraduate students a balanced and up-to-date overview of who the police are and what they do, the problems related to policing, and the many reforms and innovations that have been attempted.

The third edition has been completely rewritten. It incorporates extensive new material on community policing, problem-oriented policing, citizen oversight of the police, and other current developments. A special effort has been made to include the most recent research on each topic.

This book is designed primarily for undergraduate students enrolled in their first course on the police or law enforcement. It is not a police management text, or a book on criminal procedure.

## ACKNOWLEDGMENTS

Many people have contributed directly and indirectly to the completion of this book. I want to thank my colleagues in the University of Nebraska at Omaha Department of Criminal Justice who have helped maintain an extraordinarily pleasant and supportive working environment. Dean David Hinton also deserves credit for aggressively defending the department at every turn and supporting new initiatives. With respect to the actual writing and production of the book, my editor at McGraw-Hill, Nancy Blaine, has been very supportive and understanding about deadlines and my other commitments. My graduate assistant, Paula Kautt, was always available to track down missing data or a complete citation.

*Samuel Walker*

# THE POLICE IN AMERICA

# PART ONE

# FOUNDATIONS

# CHAPTER 1

# POLICE AND SOCIETY

## WHY POLICE?

More than 30 years ago, Jerome Skolnick posed the fundamental question: "For what social purpose do police exist?"[1] Why do we have police? What purpose do they serve? What do we want them to do? What do they do that other government agencies do not do? How do we want them to do these things? These are basic questions related to the police role in society.

Too often the answers to these questions are vague and simplistic. People say the police should "protect and serve," or "enforce the law." Such answers, however, avoid all the important issues. Policing is extremely complex, involving difficult questions about the police role; treating citizens fairly; police organizations; and the recruitment, training, and supervision of police officers.

### The Goals of This Book

The community policing movement has raised new questions about the police role. Community policing represents a different role for the police compared to the professional style of policing that prevailed as a result of the professionalization movement (1900–1980).[2] It reopens all of the basic questions about how we should organize and deliver police services, who we should recruit as officers, and how we should evaluate them.

The purpose of this book is not to argue for or against community policing. It is to provide the necessary background information about policing to help you, the reader, discuss American policing intelligently. It seeks to describe what police do (Chapter 4), the many problems that arise such as the exercise of discretion (Chapter 8), police–community relations (Chapter 9), who police officers are (Chapters 12 and 13), and how police organizations operate (Chapter 14). It seeks to describe what policing has been in the past (Chapter 2), what it is like today, and what it could be.

### Myths, Realities, and Possibilities

At the outset it is necessary to sort out the myths, realities, and possibilities of policing. The myths include the many erroneous ideas about what the police do and what they should do. The realities include what the police in fact do on a day-to-day basis, and the role they play in society. The possibilities include the ways in which policing could be different from what it is today.

### MYTHS ABOUT POLICING

Policing is surrounded by many myths and stereotypes.[3] One of the enduring myths is that the police are primarily crime fighters. According to this view, police devote most of their efforts to enforcing criminal law: patrolling to deter crime, investigating crimes, and arresting criminals. Some people believe that this is what the police *should* do. A lot of the rhetoric about the police reflects the crime-fighter image: the idea of the police as a "thin blue line," fighting a war on crime.[4]

The crime-fighter image, however, is not an accurate description of what the police actually do. Only about one-third of a patrol officer's activities involve criminal law enforcement (Chapter 4). The typical police officer rarely makes a felony arrest, and most officers never fire their weapons even once in their entire careers. Most police work is best described as peacekeeping, order maintenance, or problem solving (Chapter 5).

### Sources of the Crime-Fighter Image

The myth of the crime fighter endures for many reasons. The entertainment media play a major role in popularizing it. Movies and television police shows feature crime-related stories because they offer drama, fast-paced action, and violence. Think for a moment about the latest Hollywood cop movie: How many car chases were there? How many shoot-outs? The typical domestic disturbance, which in real life is a common police situation, does not offer the same kind of dramatic possibilities.

The news media are equally guilty of overemphasizing police crime fighting. A recent study of crime and the news media concluded, "Crime stories are frequently presented and prominently displayed" and the number of these stories is "large in comparison with other topics."[5] A serious crime is a newsworthy event. There is a victim who engages our sympathies, a story, and then an arrest that offers dramatic visuals of the suspect in custody. A typical night's work for a patrol officer, by way of contrast, does not offer much in the way of dramatic news.

The police perpetuate the crime-fighter image themselves. Official press releases and annual reports emphasize crime and arrests. Crime fighting is a way for the police to tell the public they are doing something and doing something important. Peter Manning argues that the police deliberately adopted the crime-fighter role image as a way of staking claim to a domain of professional expertise that they, and they alone, could control.[6]

### Consequences of the Crime-Fighter Image

Because it does not present an accurate picture of what the police do, the crime-fighter image creates a number of serious problems.[7] Most important, it ignores the order maintenance and peacekeeping activities that consume most police time and effort (Chapters 4 and 5). This prevents us from intelligently evaluating police performance. The emphasis on crime fighting also creates unrealistic public expectations about the ability of the police to prevent crime and catch criminals. Movies and TV shows strengthen the impression that the police are highly successful in solving crimes when, in fact, only 21 percent of all reported Index crimes are solved (Chapter 6).

The police suffer from this distorted self-image. Police chiefs cannot effectively manage their departments when so much attention is given to only one small part of their activities. The crime-fighter image also creates role conflict for individual police officers. Placing a premium on detective work and devaluing patrol work creates a contradiction between what officers value and what they actually do.[8]

## THE REALITIES OF POLICING

The reality of policing is that the police play an extremely complex role in today's society. This role involves many different tasks. Herman Goldstein warns that "anyone attempting to construct a workable definition of the police role will typically come away with old images shattered and a new-found appreciation for the intricacies of police work."[9]

Many studies of police work document the complexity of the police role. The Police Services Study (PSS), for example, examined 26,418 calls for service to the police in three metropolitan areas.[10] As the data in Table 1–1 indicate, only 19 percent of the calls involve crime, and only 2 percent of the total involve violent crime.

The data in Table 3–1 also illustrate how ambiguous so much police work is. The situations in the category of interpersonal conflict, for example, may involve a potential crime (e.g., assault), or pose a serious risk to the officer or another person (e.g., a mentally disturbed person with a gun), or merely be an argument and some noise.

One of the most important aspects of policing is that officers exercise enormous discretion in handling these situations (Chapter 8). Faced with a dispute, should a police officer warn the people involved, ask one of them to leave the premises, or try to mediate the dispute? These are difficult choices, requiring good judgment and human relations skills. It is not a simple matter of making an arrest, as the crime-fighter image suggests.

The American Bar Association's *Standards Relating to the Urban Police Function* illustrates the complexity of the police role by identifying 11 different police responsibilities (Figure 1–1).[11]

The ABA list illustrates three ways in which the police role is extremely complex. First, it involves a wide variety of tasks. Only a few deal with criminal law enforcement.

Second, many of those tasks are extremely vague. Resolving conflict, for example, raises a number of difficult questions. What kinds of situations represent conflicts that require police intervention? What is the best response to a conflict situation? Should officers always make arrests in domestic disputes, for example? If not, what should they do?

Third, different responsibilities often conflict with each other. Police are responsible for both maintaining order and protecting constitutional liberties. In the case of a large political demonstration, the police have to balance the First Amendment rights of the protesters and the need to maintain order and protect the rights of other people to use the streets and sidewalks.

As Goldstein points out, "The police, by the very nature of their function, are an anomaly in a free society."[12] On the one hand, we expect them to exercise coercive force: to restrain people when they are out of control; to arrest them when they break the law; and in some extreme cases to use deadly force. At the same time, however, we expect the police to protect the individual freedoms that are the essential part of a democratic society. The tension between freedom and constraint is one of the central problems in American policing.[13]

**TABLE 1–1**
CITIZEN CALLS FOR POLICE SERVICES, BY GENERAL PROBLEM TYPES
AND SUBCATEGORIES

| Type of problem | Number of calls | Percent of total | Percent of category |
|---|---|---|---|
| VIOLENT CRIMES | 642 | 2 | |
| 1. Homicide | 9 | | 1 |
| 2. Sexual attack | 26 | | 4 |
| 3. Robbery | 118 | | 18 |
| 4. Aggravated assault | 74 | | 12 |
| 5. Simple assault | 351 | | 55 |
| 6. Child abuse | 38 | | 6 |
| 7. Kidnapping | 26 | | 4 |
| NONVIOLENT CRIMES | 4,489 | 17 | |
| 1. Burglary and break-ins | 1,544 | | 34 |
| 2. Theft | 1,389 | | 31 |
| 3. Motor vehicle theft | 284 | | 6 |
| 4. Vandalism, arson | 866 | | 19 |
| 5. Problems with money/credit/documents | 209 | | 5 |
| 6. Crimes against the family | 29 | | 1 |
| 7. Leaving the scene | 168 | | 4 |
| INTERPERSONAL CONFLICT | 1,763 | 7 | |
| 1. Domestic conflict | 694 | | 39 |
| 2. Nondomestic arguments | 335 | | 19 |
| 3. Nondomestic threats | 277 | | 16 |
| 4. Nondomestic fights | 457 | | 26 |
| MEDICAL ASSISTANCE | 810 | 3 | |
| 1. Medical assistance | 274 | | 34 |
| 2. Death | 38 | | 5 |
| 3. Suicide | 34 | | 4 |
| 4. Emergency transport | 203 | | 25 |
| 5. Personal injury, traffic accident | 261 | | 32 |
| TRAFFIC PROBLEMS | 2,467 | 9 | |
| 1. Property damage, traffic accident | 1,141 | | 46 |
| 2. Vehicle violation | 543 | | 22 |
| 3. Traffic-flow problem | 322 | | 13 |
| 4. Moving violation | 292 | | 12 |
| 5. Abandoned vehicle | 169 | | 7 |
| DEPENDENT PERSONS | 774 | 3 | |
| 1. Drunk | 146 | | 19 |
| 2. Missing persons | 318 | | 41 |
| 3. Juvenile runaway | 121 | | 16 |
| 4. Subject of police concern | 134 | | 17 |
| 5. Mentally disordered | 55 | | 7 |
| PUBLIC NUISANCES | 3,002 | 11 | |
| 1. Annoyance, harassment | 980 | | 33 |
| 2. Noise disturbance | 984 | | 33 |
| 3. Trespassing, unwanted entry | 302 | | 10 |

**TABLE 1–1**
CONTINUED

| Type of problem | Number of calls | Percent of total | Percent of category |
|---|---|---|---|
| PUBLIC NUISANCES (continued) | | | |
| 4. Alcohol, drug violations | 130 | | 4 |
| 5. Public morals | 124 | | 4 |
| 6. Juvenile problem | 439 | | 15 |
| 7. Ordinance violations | 43 | | 1 |
| SUSPICIOUS CIRCUMSTANCES | 1,248 | 5 | |
| 1. Suspicious person | 674 | | 54 |
| 2. Suspicious property condition | 475 | | 38 |
| 3. Dangerous person or situation | 99 | | 8 |
| ASSISTANCE | 3,039 | 12 | |
| 1. Animal problem | 755 | | 24 |
| 2. Property check | 616 | | 20 |
| 3. Escorts and transports | 86 | | 3 |
| 4. Utility problem | 438 | | 14 |
| 5. Property discovery | 240 | | 8 |
| 6. Assistance to motorist | 154 | | 5 |
| 7. Fires, alarms | 112 | | 4 |
| 8. Crank calls | 114 | | 4 |
| 9. Unspecified requests | 425 | | 14 |
| 10. Other requests | 99 | | 3 |
| CITIZEN WANTS INFORMATION | 5,558 | 21 | |
| 1. Information, unspecified | 248 | | 5 |
| 2. Information, police related | 1,262 | | 23 |
| 3. Information about specific case | 1,865 | | 34 |
| 4. Information, nonpolice related | 577 | | 10 |
| 5. Road directions | 189 | | 3 |
| 6. Directions, nontraffic | 55 | | 1 |
| 7. Requests for specific unit | 1,362 | | 25 |
| CITIZEN WANTS TO GIVE INFORMATION | 1,993 | 8 | |
| 1. General information | 1,090 | | 55 |
| 2. Return of property | 156 | | 8 |
| 3. False alarm | 176 | | 9 |
| 4. Complaint against specific officer | 105 | | 5 |
| 5. Complaint against police in general | 350 | | 18 |
| 6. Compliments for police | 20 | | 1 |
| 7. Hospital report to police | 96 | | 5 |
| INTERNAL OPERATIONS | 633 | 2 | |
| 1. Internal legal procedures | 63 | | 10 |
| 2. Internal assistance request | 134 | | 21 |
| 3. Officer wants to give information | 298 | | 47 |
| 4. Officer wants information | 132 | | 21 |
| 5. Other internal procedures | 6 | | |
| Total calls | 26,418 | 100 | 1 |

*Source:* Eric J. Scott, *Calls for Service: Citizen Demand and Initial Police Response* (Washington, DC: Government Printing Office, 1981), pp. 28–30.

**FIGURE 1–1**

POLICE ROLES AND RESPONSIBILITIES

---

1 Identify criminal offenders and criminal activity and, when appropriate, apprehend offenders and participate in subsequent court proceedings.
2 Reduce the opportunities for the commission of some crimes through preventive patrol and other measures.
3 Aid individuals who are in danger of physical harm.
4 Protect constitutional guarantees.
5 Facilitate the movement of people and vehicles.
6 Assist those who cannot care for themselves.
7 Resolve conflict.
8 Identify problems that are potentially serious law enforcement or government problems.
9 Create and maintain a feeling of security in the community.
10 Promote and preserve civil order.
11 Provide other services on an emergency basis.

---

*Source:* American Bar Association, "Major Current Responsibilities of Police," *Standard 1-2.2 in Standards Relating to the Urban Police Function*, 2d ed. (Boston: Little, Brown, 1980), pp. 1-31 to 1-32.

### Factors That Shape the Police Role

Several factors contribute to the complexity of the police role. Most important is the fact that police services are available 24 hours a day. The telephone makes it possible to call the police at any hour and for any problem. The police, moreover, have encouraged people to call and have promised to respond to those calls. Goldstein argues that the police end up handling many problems "because no other means has been found to solve them. They are the residual problems of society."[14] Policing involves society's "dirty work": the tasks that no one else wants to do.[15] People call the police when everything else has failed.

The public wants a general-purpose emergency service, available to handle problems that arise. This job falls to the police. It would be extremely expensive to maintain a number of additional specialized agencies, for example, one that deals only with domestic disturbances, or one that responds only to mental illness situations. The 24-hour availability of the police gives them an extremely heavy workload. Many calls do not necessarily require a sworn police officer with arrest power. Also, some of these calls require someone with professional expertise (some mental health incidents, for example). As a result, the police are generalists, expected to handle a wide range of situations, but with only limited training and expertise in family problems, mental illness, or alcohol and drug abuse.

The complexity of the police role was not really planned. For the most part, it just happened. The police acquired many responsibilities simply because they were the only agency available. The telephone made it convenient for people to call the police, and so they did (Chapter 2). The debate over the police role today raises basic questions about whether we really want the police to do all these things.

## The Authority to Use Force

The authority to use force is one of the most important factors shaping the police role. In this crucial respect, the police are different from other professionals: teachers, social workers, doctors. In one of the most important essays on policing, Egon Bittner argues that this capacity to use coercive force is the defining feature of the police.[16] Force includes the power to take someone's life (deadly force), the use of physical force, and the power to deprive people of their liberty through arrest.

Bittner quickly adds that the authority to use force is not unlimited. First, it is limited by law. The police cannot lawfully shoot to kill anyone. The power to arrest is also limited by law. Second, officers may use force only in the performance of their job. They may not use force, for example, to settle a private dispute. Third, officers may not use force maliciously or frivolously. They may not arrest, harass, or abuse citizens for personal spite or amusement.

The authority to use force has implications that go far beyond its actual use. Bittner argues that it is latent and ever present, defining relations between officers and citizens. He observes: "There can be no doubt that this feature of police work is uppermost in the minds of people who solicit police aid. . . ."[17] People call the police because they want an officer to settle a problem: arrest someone, get someone to calm down, or have someone removed from the home. People generally defer to police authority. In the vast majority of situations, citizens comply with police officer requests, suggestions, or threats.[18]

## The Police and Social Control

The police are part of the system of social control. Morris Janowitz defines social control as "the capacity of a society to regulate itself according to desired principles and values."[19] Control, in this sense, is not the same as repression or enforced conformity. It refers to the shaping of behavior through a broad range of formal and informal mechanisms, only some of which use coercive force. The distinguishing feature of a democratic society is the existence of mechanisms for peaceful political change. Constitutional guarantees of freedom of speech, press, and assembly facilitate peaceful change by allowing new and controversial ideas to be heard. As the ABA list of police tasks indicates (Figure 1–1), preserving constitutional rights is part of the police role.

The police contribute to social control through both their law enforcement and order maintenance responsibilities. Their task is to preserve the norms of society by deterring crime and arresting people who violate the criminal law, which embodies those norms. The police presence in society is also intended to preserve order by serving as a deterrent to misconduct and by providing a quick-response mechanism for potential or low-level problems.

The capacity of the police to exercise social control is extremely limited, however. As we will learn in Chapter 4, routine patrol has only a limited effect on crime and, as we will see in Chapter 5, the ability of the police to identify and arrest criminal suspects is extremely limited.

Experts now recognize that the police are heavily dependent on citizens in carrying out their responsibilities. Police depend on people to report crimes, to provide information about suspects, to cooperate in investigations, and so on. For this reason, many experts refer to citizens as "coproducers" of police services.[20]

In the colonial era (1600–1840s), before we had the modern police, citizens were the primary agents of social control. Behavior was regulated by comments, warnings, or rebukes by family, friends, and neighbors.[21] The creation of the modern police, as a large professional bureaucracy, transferred that responsibility away from citizens [Chapter 2]. The community policing movement is an attempt to restore and develop the role of citizens as co-producers of police services.

The police are usually the last resort in the system of social control. We call the police when everything else has failed. The primary social control mechanism is the family. Peer groups, community groups, religious institutions, and the schools are also important. When these mechanisms fail and a person breaks the law, we call the police.

### The Police and Social Control Systems

The police are part of several different systems of social control. First, and most important, they are the "gatekeepers" of the criminal justice system. The decision by a police officer to make an arrest initiates most criminal cases. The decision not to arrest keeps the incident out of the system.[22] Thus, the police determine the workload for the criminal justice system. At the same time, police efforts are deeply affected by the actions of other criminal justice agencies.

Second, the police are an important part of the social welfare system. They are often the first contact that official agencies have with social problems such as delinquency, family problems, drug abuse, and alcoholism. The police often refer individuals to social service agencies. The police are also an important part of the mental health system. Patrol units are routinely called to situations where someone is believed to be mentally ill. The officer has the responsibility of determining whether the person is in fact mentally ill and requires hospitalization. Goldstein argues that we should develop alternatives to the criminal justice system for dealing with these situations.[23]

Third, the police are an important part of the political system. In a democratic society, the political system ensures public control and accountability of the police. The people, acting through their elected representatives, determine police policy: community policing, or not? aggressive enforcement of traffic laws, or not? In the case of the sheriff, the people directly elect the top law enforcement official (Chapter 3).

Political control of law enforcement agencies represents one of the central dilemmas of policing a democratic society. On the one hand, the people have a fundamental right to control their government agencies. At the same time, however, politics has histori-cally been the source of much corruption and abuse of law enforcement powers (Chapter 2). Striking the balance between popular control and professional standards is another one of the basic tensions in American policing. This problem is discussed in detail in Chapter 11.

In important respects, the police are symbols of the political system. They are the most visible manifestation of power and authority in society. The badge, the gun, and the billy club are potent visual reminders of the ultimate power of the police in main-taining the existing social and political system. As a result, attitudes toward the police are influenced by peoples' attitudes toward the political system generally. Arthur Niederhoffer describes the police officer as "a 'Rorschach' in uniform." People project upon the officer their attitudes about a wide range of issues.[24]

## POSSIBILITIES

The form of policing we currently have is not the only one that is possible. The idea that the police do not and cannot change is a myth. The history of the police indicates that they have changed dramatically over the years (Chapter 2).[25] In *Police for the Future*, David H. Bayley argues that we have a choice—a political choice about different possibilities for policing.[26] The real question is, What kind of policing do we want to create?

Bayley argues that we should take the crime prevention role of the police seriously. He believes that the police, as traditionally organized, cannot effectively prevent crime. But he does see the possibility of more effective crime prevention if we choose to decentralize police departments and give more responsibility to neighborhood police officers (NPOs). This approach takes police departments and stands them on their heads, giving more decision-making responsibilities to the officers at the bottom of the organization. Executives at the top of the organization would coordinate rather than command, as they do in the traditional quasi-military-style organization.[27]

Is Bayley's proposal sound? Would it achieve its goals without doing more harm to society? The purpose of this book is not to provide prescriptive yes or no answers to these questions. Instead, our purpose is to provide a factual, up-to-date description of policing today so that we can make informed decisions about the choices that are available.

Let's consider some of the alternative possibilities for the police.

### Functional Specialization

In 1967 the President's Crime Commission proposed dividing current police tasks among three different specialties within police agencies. Community service officers (CSOs), apprentices between the ages of 17 and 21, would work under the supervision of a regular police officer. They would be responsible for nonemergency calls for service. Police officers would perform most of the patrol, investigation, and enforcement tasks currently handled by the police. Police agents would concentrate on criminal investigation, with subspecialties focusing on homicide, rape, and so on.[28]

The Crime Commission's proposal represents a functional specialization approach. Most other professions operate in this way. Professional educators, for example, specialize in preschool, elementary, and secondary education, and college and university teaching. Within levels of education, moreover, there are area specialties: mathematics, biology, history, and so on. Lawyers specialize in criminal defense, tax law, personal injury, and so on. Also, most professions delegate less-critical tasks to paraprofessionals: teaching assistants, law clerks, nurses, and so on.[29]

Some police departments have experimented with part of the Crime Commission's proposal, using police cadets or aides for nonemergency tasks. An evaluation of a

CSO-type program in Worcester, Massachusetts, found it to be highly effective. The officers, called police service aides (PSAs), handled "cold" crimes—those that are not discovered or reported until after they have been committed. The PSAs took crime reports, transported suspects, and provided information and miscellaneous nonemergency services to the public. The evaluation found that the PSAs handled 24.7 percent of all citizen calls directly and assisted in another 8.2 percent. Citizens, PSAs, and regular police officers expressed satisfaction with their performance.[30]

The Crime Commission's full proposal has not been adopted by police departments, however. The basic problem is that it does not resolve the basic problems surrounding the complexity of the police role. Police officers would still be called to many situations where they would have to determine what is happening and make difficult discretionary decisions about the best response.

### Problem-Oriented Policing

Herman Goldstein's concept of problem-oriented policing (POP) represents a different approach to the complexity of the police role. He argues that the police should disaggregate their workloads, identify recurring problems, and develop strategies to reduce or eliminate those problems. Instead of thinking in terms of general categories of crime and disorder, the police should identify particular kinds of crime (drug dealing, drunk driving) and disorder (rowdy juveniles, chronic alcoholics in the neighborhood) and develop appropriate responses. POP represents a proactive approach, very different from the reactive approach of simply responding to 911 calls. It involves research and planning, and a shift from individual calls for service to a concern with underlying problems. The category of disorder, for example, would be disaggregated into separate problems: domestic disturbances, juvenile rowdiness, chronic alcoholism on the street. A different strategy should be developed for each problem.[31]

One of the first experiments in problem-oriented policing occurred in Newport News, Virginia, in the mid-1980s. The program focused on burglaries in the New Briarfield apartments, one of the worst low-income housing units in the city. The project began by analyzing crime patterns in the area and conducting an opinion survey of apartment complex residents. The survey discovered that deteriorated buildings contributed to many burglaries: windows and doors were easily broken into, vacant apartments created havens for criminals, and deteriorated conditions created an atmosphere of despair and powerlessness among the residents.[32]

Police officers assigned to New Briarfield responded by attempting to improve the physical conditions of the buildings. One officer negotiated the settlement of a dispute with the private trash hauler that resulted in the removal of accumulated garbage. Abandoned refrigerators and other dangers to children were also removed. The police department organized a meeting of government agencies that had some responsibility for the housing project: the fire department, the Department of Public Works, the Redevelopment and Housing Authority, and so on. The purpose of the meeting was to develop a coordinated strategy to improve conditions in the complex. One officer organized a tenants' group to pressure city officials into making short-term improvements in the apartments.

POP in Newport News represented a new role for the police. Officers functioned as community organizers and brokers of government services, mediating between citizens and other agencies. Problem-oriented policing is examined in greater detail in Chapter 7.

### Community Policing

The most popular new approach to policing today is community policing. Community policing is a philosophy of policing. It holds that the police should work closely with community residents, instead of being an inward-looking bureaucracy; that they should emphasize crime prevention, as opposed to law enforcement; and that they should decentralize the decision-making authority to rank and file officers, as opposed to a top-down military-style organization.[33]

Community policing programs take many different forms.[34] Some emphasize disorder and quality of life issues, whereas others focus on serious crime. Some primarily address drug-related crime. Chapter 7 examines some of these programs in detail.

In the New York City Community Patrol Officer Program, which has since been abandoned, CPOP officers did not answer calls for service (regular patrol officers assigned to the same neighborhoods handled those calls) but were expected to identify neighborhood problems and develop short-term and long-term strategies for solving them. CPOP officers have been described as planners, problem solvers, community organizers, and information exchange links.[35] CPOP officers, for example, helped neighborhood residents clear up abandoned lots that had become safety hazards. Although trash-filled lots and unsafe playgrounds are not crime problems in the traditional sense, they were perceived by residents as threats to their safety and the quality of their neighborhoods.

In Chicago, the CAPS (Chicago Alternative Policing Strategy) officers meet regularly with neighborhood residents to discuss problems in the community and develop strategies to solve them.[36]

In Oakland, California, the SMART (Specialized Multi-Agency Response Team) program involves many different government agencies working closely with the police to tackle drug-related problems. City housing inspectors, for example, cite suspected drug houses for building code violations, landlords are encouraged or coerced into cleaning up blighted properties, and the police engage in standard law enforcement tactics. Lorraine Green's evaluation of SMART found that it not only reduces drug activity, but also diffuses the positive benefits to surrounding areas.[37] SMART is an example of the community policing philosophy of the police working closely with other agencies and using noncriminal justice system strategies.

### Zero-Tolerance Policing

New York City adopted a policy of zero-tolerance policing in the 1990s. This approach concentrates on relatively minor quality-of-life issues, such as urinating in public and "fare beating" (jumping over the subway turnstiles to avoid paying the fare). George

Kelling and Catherine Coles argue that tough enforcement on minor crimes directly contributes to a significant reduction in serious crime. Some fare-beaters, for example, were found to be carrying weapons in violation of the law. The weapons were then seized and the person arrested on more serious gun charges. The crime rate in New York City began to fall dramatically in 1992, and by 1997 was at the lowest level in 30 years.[38]

Critics of the zero-tolerance policy, however, argue that it encourages police abuse of citizens. And, in fact, complaints against New York City police officers increased in the 1990s and, in 1997, officers were prosecuted for a particularly vicious attack on a Haitian immigrant.[39] These allegations raise the question of whether it is possible to have tough law enforcement while at the same time respecting the rights of citizens.

**Honest Law Enforcement**

One of the options identified by Bayley in *Police for the Future* is "honest law enforcement." Under this approach, the police would continue to do what they now do well, but be honest with themselves and the public about it. They would continue to patrol neighborhoods, answer calls for service, intervene in problem situations, and try to apprehend offenders, but they would not claim that they are preventing crime. This approach represents low expectations for what the police can do, but it does have the virtue of being honest about it. As Bayley points out, too much of contemporary policing involves "dishonest law enforcement," making unjustified claims for effective crime prevention.[40]

**THE IMPLICATIONS OF CHANGE**

It is easy to talk about dramatic changes in policing. Advocates of community policing believe that it represents a new era in American policing. Translating ideas into practice is extremely difficult, however. Consider, for example, the case of team policing. It was a radical innovation in the early 1970s, involving restructuring police operations along neighborhood lines and decentralizing decision-making authority. At one point a large number of police departments said that they were doing team policing.[41] And then, suddenly, the team policing movement collapsed and it vanished.[42] Obviously, something went wrong. Most analysts conclude that team policing experiments were poorly planned, with little attention given to important operational details.[43]

In retrospect, team policing offers a sobering lesson about the difficulty of making radical changes in policing No matter what a police department decides to do—community policing, problem-oriented policing, zero-tolerance policing, or traditional-style policing—a number of basic issues must be faced.

• **Mission.** What is the primary mission of the department? Law enforcement, order maintenance, service, crime prevention, or some combination of all four? How is that mission expressed? How do citizens know what it is? How do officers know what it is? Does the department have a written mission statement? If so, what does it say?

---

**POLICE ON THE WEB**

Many police departments have placed their mission statements on the web. Locate the web sites for several departments. Which ones have mission statements? How do they compare?

---

- **Patrol Operations.** What is the place of basic preventive patrol operations in the mission of the department? Is it the central aspect of departmental activities? Or is it only one part of a multiphased mission? If it is central, how efficiently is it currently being operated. What improvements need to be made? These issues are covered in Chapter 4.
- **Calls for Service.** Does the department respond to each and every call for service? Does the department attempt to the manage the call for service workload through differential response? These issues are also covered in Chapter 4.
- **Discretion.** How does the department maintain control of police officer discretion? Is officer initiative encouraged? In what areas? Within what limits? What kind of discretion is given rank and file officers? These issues are covered in Chapter 8.
- **Police–Community Relations.** How effective are the department's relations with racial and ethnic minority communities? Is there a high level of tension and conflict? What kinds of programs does the department maintain to improve police-community relations? These issues are covered in Chapter 9.
- **Corruption.** Does the department have a reputation for corruption? If it does, what evidence is there to support this reputation? Does the department have a specific anti-corruption program? These issues are covered in Chapter 10.
- **Accountability.** What accountability mechanisms exist in local law enforcement agencies? Is there a citizen review board? Does the police chief have civil service protection, or can he or she be fired at will? What kind of data are published in the annual report? Does this report provide information that allows you to make a meaningful judgment about the performance of the department? See Chapter 11 for a discussion of these issues.
- **Personnel.** What minimum recruitment standards are best? What level of education is needed for policing? What kind of preservice training should be offered? What is the proper racial, ethnic, and gender composition for police departments? Personnel issues are covered in Chapters 12 and 13.
- **Organization.** What is the organizational structure of the department? Is it consistent with recommended standards? If there is a community policing program, is it departmentwide or carried out by a special unit? Does a recognized police union represent the rank and file officers? How powerful is the union? What influence does it have over department policy? These issues are covered in Chapter 14.

## CONCLUSION

Why do we have police? Jerome Skolnick's question, with which we opened this chapter, cannot be avoided. As this chapter has indicated, we cannot be satisfied with simplistic answers like "protect and serve." The police role is extremely complex. First, we must decide which tasks we want the police to emphasize: law enforcement, crime prevention, order maintenance. Second, we need to decide how we want the police to carry out those tasks. Third, we need to decide what kinds of officers we want for these tasks, including what selection criteria we want to use, what kind of training they will receive, and how they will be supervised. We need to decide how we are going to hold the police accountable for the tasks we ask them to carry out.

All of these questions are extremely complex. This book is designed to provide a basic introduction to the police in America so that we can discuss policing in an informed manner.

## NOTES

**1** Jerome H. Skolnick, *Justice without Trial: Law Enforcement in a Democratic Society*, 3d ed. (New York: Macmillan, 1994), p. 1.

**2** George L. Kelling and Mark H. Moore, *The Evolving Strategy of Policing,* no. 4 of "Perspectives on Policing," (Washington: Government Printing Office, 1988); Samuel Walker, *A Critical History of Police Reform* (Lexington, Mass.: Lexington Books, 1977).

**3** David H. Bayley, *Police for the Future* (New York: Oxford University Press, 1994), chap. 1.

**4** Egon Bittner, *The Functions of the Police in Modern Society* (Cambridge, Mass.: Olgeschlager, Gunn, and Hain, 1980) pp. 120–132.

**5** Steven M. Chermak, *Victims in the News: Crime and the American News Media* (Boulder: Westview Press, 1995), p. 47.

**6** Peter Manning, *Police Work* (Cambridge: MIT Press, 1977).

**7** Herman Goldstein, *Policing a Free Society* (Cambridge, Mass.: Ballinger, 1977), pp. 29–31.

**8** J. Milton Yinger, *Toward a Field Theory of Behavior* (New York: McGraw-Hill, 1965), pp. 99–100.

**9** Goldstein, *Policing a Free Society*, p. 21.

**10** Eric J. Scott, *Calls for Service: Citizen Demand and Initial Police Response* (Washington: Government Printing Office, 1981), pp. 24–30.

**11** American Bar Association, *Standards Relating to the Urban Police Function*, 2d ed. (Boston: Little, Brown, 1980), 1–31 to 1–32.

**12** Goldstein, *Policing a Free Society*, p. 1.

**13** The classic discussion is Skolnick, *Justice without Trial*.

**14** Herman Goldstein, "Improving Policing: A Problem-Oriented Approach, *Crime and Delinquency* 25 (April 1979): 236–258.

**15** William A. Westley, *Violence and the Police* (Cambridge: MIT Press, 1970), pp. 18–19.

**16** Bittner, "The Capacity to Use Force as the Core of the Police Role," in *The Functions of the Police in Modern Society*, pp. 36–47.

**17** Ibid., p. 40.

**18** Stephen D. Mastrofski, Jeffrey B. Snipes, and Anne E. Supina, "Compliance on Demand: The Public's Response to Specific Police Requests," *Journal of Research in Crime and Delinquency* 33 (August 1996): 269–305.

**19** Morris Janowitz, "Sociological Theory and Social Control," *American Journal of Sociology* 81 (July 1975): 82–85.

**20** Wesley G. Skogan and George E. Antunes, "Information, Apprehension, and Deterrence: Exploring the Limits of Police Productivity," *Journal of Criminal Justice* 7 (Fall 1979): 217–241.

**21** Samuel Walker, *Popular Justice: A History of American Criminal Justice*, 2d ed. (New York: Oxford University Press, 1998), chap. 1.

**22** Wayne LaFave, *Arrest* (Boston: Little, Brown, 1965).

**23** Goldstein, *Policing a Free Society*, chap. 4.

**24** Arthur Niederhoffer, *Behind the Shield: The Police in Urban Society* (Garden City, N.Y.: Anchor Books, 1969), p. 1.

**25** Walker, *Popular Justice*.

**26** Bayley, pt. 2 of *Police for the Future*, "Possibilities," pp. 77–120.

**27** Bayley, *Police for the Future*, pp. 143–161.

**28** President's Commission on Law Enforcement and Administration of Justice, *The Challenge of Crime in a Free Society* (Washington: Government Printing Office, 1967), pp. 108–109.

**29** Wilbert E. Moore, *The Professions: Roles and Rules* (New York: Russell Sage Foundation, 1970).

**30** James N. Tien and Richard C. Larson, "Police Service Aides: Paraprofessionals for Police," *Journal of Criminal Justice* 6 (Summer 1978): 117–131.

**31** Herman Goldstein, "Improving Policing: A Problem-Oriented Approach," *Crime and Delinquency* 25 (April 1979): 236–258; Herman Goldstein, *Problem-Oriented Policing* (New York: McGraw-Hill, 1990).

**32** John E. Eck and William Spelman, *Problem-Solving: Problem-Oriented Policing in Newport News* (Washington: Police Executive Research Forum, 1987).

**33** Jack R. Greene and Stephen D. Mastrofski, eds., *Community Policing: Rhetoric or Reality* (New York: Praeger, 1991).

**34** Dennis P. Rosenbaum, ed., *The Challenge of Community Policing: Testing the Promises* (Thousand Oaks, Calif.: Sage, 1994).

**35** Jerome E. McElroy, Colleen A. Cosgrove, and Susan Saad, *Community Policing: The CPOP in New York* (Newbury Park, Calif.: Sage Publications, 1993).

**36** Wesley G. Skogan and Susan M. Hartnett, *Community Policing: Chicago Style* (New York: Oxford University Press, 1997).

**37** Lorraine Greene, "Cleaning Up Drug Hot Spots in Oakland, California: The Displacement and Diffusion Effects," *Justice Quarterly* 12 (December 1995): 737–754.

**38** George L. Kelling and Catherine Coles, *Fixing Broken Windows* (New York: Free Press, 1996). William Bratton and Peter Knobler, *Turnaround* (New York: Random House, 1998).

**39** Bob Herbert, "Good Cop, Bad Cop," *New York Times*, March 24, 1997; Dan Barry, "2 More Officers Held in Beating of Haitian Man," *New York Times*, August 19, 1997, p. 1.

**40** Bayley, *Police for the Future*, pp. 124–130.

**41** John F. Heaply, Police Practices: *The General Administrative Survey* (Washington, DC: The Police Foundation, 1978).

**42** Samuel Walker, "Does Anyone Remember Team Policing," *American Journal of Police*, XII (1993, No. 1): 33–55.

**43** Lawrence W. Sherman et al., *Team Policing: Seven Case Studies* (Washington: The Police Foundation, 1973).

CHAPTER **2**

# THE HISTORY OF THE
# AMERICAN POLICE

## THE RELEVANCE OF HISTORY

The history of the American police can help us understand policing today. The idea that the police do not change is a myth. In fact, American policing has changed tremendously, even in the last few years.[1] The study of its history helps us understand how and why these changes occur. It can illuminate the social and political forces affecting the police, as well as the impact of different reforms.

Many current police problems have long histories. Corruption, for example, is deeply rooted in police history, and it is useful to understand its origins and why it has been so difficult to eliminate. Some current problems, on the other hand, are the result of yesterday's reforms.[2] The patrol car was hailed as a great advance because it allowed efficient patrol coverage, but it isolated officers from the public and contributed to police–community relations problems. Other reforms have succeeded. Recent controls over police use of deadly force have significantly reduced the number of citizens shot and killed by the police. It is useful to analyze why some reforms succeed, and why other reforms fail.

## THE ENGLISH HERITAGE

American policing is a product of its English heritage. The English colonists brought a criminal justice system as part of their cultural baggage. This heritage included the English common law, the high value placed on individual rights, the court system, various forms of punishment, along with different law enforcement agencies.[3]

The English heritage contributed three enduring features to American policing. The first is a tradition of limited police authority. The Anglo-American legal tradition places a high premium on protecting individual liberty and, to that end, places limits on governmental authority.[4] In the United States, these limits are embodied in the Bill of Rights. Continental European countries, by contrast, give their law enforcement agencies much broader powers. German citizens, for example, are required to carry identity cards and report changes of address to police authorities.

The second feature inherited from England is a tradition of local control of law enforcement agencies.[5] Countries in Europe, Asia, Africa, and South America, by contrast, have centralized, national police forces.

Local control contributes to the third feature, a highly decentralized and fragmented system of law enforcement. The United States is unique in having about 18,000 separate

---

SIDEBAR 2–1

THE RELEVANCE OF HISTORY

The study of police history can
1 Dramatize the fact of change.
2 Put current problems in perspective.
3 Help us understand what reforms have worked.
4 Alert us to the unintended consequences of reforms.

law enforcement agencies, subject only to minimal coordination and very little national control or regulation.[6] This issue is discussed in detail in Chapter 3.

Formal law enforcement agencies emerged in England in the 13th century, and over the centuries evolved in an unsystematic fashion. Responsibility for law enforcement and keeping the peace was shared by the constable, the sheriff, and the justice of the peace. Private citizens, however, retained much of the responsibility for law enforcement, pursuing offenders on their own and initiating criminal cases. This approach was brought to America and persisted into the 19th century.[7]

### Creation of the Modern Police: London, 1829

By the early 19th century the old system of law enforcement in England began to collapse. London had grown into a large industrial city, with problems of poverty, disorder, ethnic conflict, and crime. The 1780 Gordon riots, a clash between Irish immigrants and English citizens, triggered a 50-year debate over the need for better public safety. Parliament finally created the London Metropolitan Police in 1829. The father of the London police was Sir Robert Peel, from whom the term "Bobbies" originated.[8]

The London police introduced three new elements that became the basis for modern policing: mission, strategy, and organizational structure.

The *mission* of the new police was crime prevention. This reflected the utilitarian idea that it was better to prevent crime than to respond after the fact. Crime prevention, or deterrence, was to be achieved through a *strategy* of preventive patrol. Officers would maintain a visible presence throughout the community by continuously patrolling fixed "beats." Peel borrowed the organizational structure of the London police from the military, including uniforms, rank designations, and the authoritarian system of command and discipline. This quasi-military style prevails in American police administration to this day.

In a comparative study of the development of policing around the world, David Bayley argues that the essential features of the modern police are that they are "public, specialized, and profession."[9] They are public in the sense that government agencies have primary responsibility for maintaining public safety. They are specialized in the sense that they have a distinct mission of law enforcement and crime prevention. Finally, they are professional in the sense that they involve full-time, paid employees. Bayley cautions that these characteristics did not appear all at once. Although the London police were formally established in 1829, in reality it represents a consolidation of features that had been developing for centuries.

The continual presence of the police throughout the community was part of a general growth of government regulation in all aspects of social and economic life. Allan Silver argues that this presence reflected a "demand for order" in the emerging urban industrial society.[10]

### LAW ENFORCEMENT IN COLONIAL AMERICA

The first English colonists in America created law enforcement institutions as soon as they established organized communities. Although borrowed from England, the sheriff, the constable, and the watch evolved in the new environment and eventually acquired distinctive American features.[11]

The sheriff, appointed by the colonial governor, was the chief local government official. In addition to criminal law enforcement, the sheriff's responsibilities included collecting taxes, conducting elections, maintaining bridges and roads, and other duties.[12] The constable also had some responsibility for enforcing the law and maintaining order. Initially an elective position, the constable gradually evolved into a semiprofessional appointed office. In Boston and several other cities, the office of constable became a desirable and often lucrative position.[13]

The watch resembled the modern-day police in some respects. Watchmen patrolled the city to guard against fire, crime, and disorder. At first there was only a night watch. Gradually, however, as towns grew larger they created a day watch. Boston created a watch in 1634. Following the English tradition, all adult males were expected to serve as watchmen. Many men tried to avoid this duty, either by outright evasion or by paying others to serve in their places. Eventually, the watch evolved into a paid professional position.[14]

The slave patrol was a distinctly American form of law enforcement. In southern states where slavery existed, it was intended to guard against slave revolts and capture runaway slaves. The slave patrols were probably the first modern police forces in this country. The Charleston, South Carolina, slave patrol, had about 100 officers in 1837 and was far larger than any northern city police force.[15]

### The Quality of Colonial Law Enforcement

Colonial law enforcement was inefficient, corrupt, and subject to political interference. There was never a "golden age" of efficiency and integrity in American policing.

The sheriff, the constable, and the watch had little capacity to either prevent crime or apprehend offenders.[16] The sheriff and constable were reactive agencies, responding to complaints brought to them, and did not engage in preventive patrol. Moreover, they did not have enough personnel to investigate many crimes. Crime victims had no convenient way to report crimes. Finally, officials were paid through a system of fees that reimbursed them for particular duties. As a result, they had greater incentives to work on their civil responsibilities, which offered more certain payment, than on criminal law enforcement.

Members of the watch patrolled city streets—checking taverns for drunks, for example—but were not much of a deterrent to crime. They were few in number, patrolled on foot, and had no way of communicating with one another in case of serious trouble.

For the same reasons, these agencies were ill-equipped to maintain order. There were simply too few watchmen on duty to be effective in the case of major problems. Disorder was a serious problem in colonial cities. Public drunkenness was a constant problem, particularly among sailors in seaport cities. Riots were common as well.[17] Citizens could not readily report disturbances, and neither the sheriff nor the constable could respond effectively. Providing emergency services, as today's police do, was not a regular part of the sheriff's or the constable's job.

In practice, official law enforcement agencies played a relatively small role in maintaining law and order. Ordinary citizens maintained social control through informal means: a comment, a warning, or a rebuke from friends or neighbors, or a "trial" by the church congregation for misbehavior. This system worked because communities were small and homogeneous; there was much face-to-face contact and people shared the same basic values. The system eventually broke down as communities grew into larger, diverse towns and cities.[18]

If policing was ineffective in cities and towns, it was almost nonexistent on the frontier. Organized government did not appear in many areas for decades. Even then, the courts operated only once or twice a year. Settlers had to rely on their own resources and often took the law into their own hands. This tradition of vigilantism persisted into the 20th century.[19]

Corruption appeared very early. The criminal law was even more moralistic than today, with restrictions on drinking, gambling, and sexual practices. But as is the case today, people wanted to engage in these activities and tried to bribe law enforcement officials to not enforce the law.

### The First Modern American Police

Modern police forces were established in the United States in the 1830s and 1840s. As in England, the old system of law enforcement broke down under the impact of urbanization, industrialization, and immigration. In the 1830s, a wave of riots struck American cities. Boston had major riots in 1834, 1835, and 1837.[20] Philadelphia, New York, Cincinnati, Detroit, and other cities all had major disturbances. In 1838, Abraham Lincoln, then a member of the Illinois state legislature, warned of the "increasing disregard for law which pervades the country."[21]

Many riots were clashes between different ethnic groups: Irish or German immigrants against native-born English Protestants. Other riots were economic in nature. During economic crises, for example, angry depositors often stormed and destroyed banks. Moral issues also produced violence. People objecting to medical research on cadavers attacked hospitals; residents of Detroit staged several "whorehouse riots," attempting to close down houses of prostitution. Finally, pro-slavery whites attacked abolitionists and free black citizens in northern cities.[22]

Despite the breakdown in law and order, Americans moved very slowly in creating new police forces. New York City did not create one until 1845, 11 years after the first outbreak of riots. Philadelphia followed a more erratic course. Between 1833 and 1854, it created and abolished several different forms of law enforcement before finally creating a consolidated, citywide police force on the London model.[23]

These delays reflected deep public uncertainty about how to maintain public safety. The idea of a continual police presence throughout the community was something radically new. For many Americans, it brought back memories of the hated British colonial army. Others were afraid that their political opponents would control the police and use them to their advantage. Finally, many people were not prepared to pay the cost of a public police force.

Many of the early American police departments were little more than expanded versions of the existing watch system. The Boston police department had only nine officers in 1838.[24] The first American police officers did not wear uniforms, but were identified only by a distinctive hat and badge. They also did not carry firearms. Weapons did not become standard police equipment until the late 19th century, in response to rising levels of crime and violence.

Americans borrowed most of the London model of modern policing: the mission of crime prevention, the strategy of visible patrol over fixed beats, and the quasi-military organizational structure. The structure of political control of the police, however, was very different. The United States was a far more democratic country than Britain. American voters—only white males with property in the early part of the century— exercised direct control over all government agencies. London residents, by contrast, had no direct control over their police. As a result, American police departments were immediately immersed in local politics, a situation that led to much improper political influence. The commissioners of the London police, freed from political influence, were able to maintain high personnel standards.[25]

In the United States, however, politics influenced every aspect of American policing in the 19th century. Inefficiency, corruption, and lack of professionalism were the chief results.[26]

## AMERICAN POLICING IN THE 19TH CENTURY

Personnel standards, for all practical purposes, did not exist. Officers were selected entirely on the basis of their political connections. Men who had no education, bad health, and criminal records were hired as officers. There were a few female matrons, but no female sworn officers until the early 20th century. In New York City, a $300 payment to the Tammany Hall political machine was the only requirement for appointment to the force.[27]

Only a few departments offered recruits any formal preservice training. New officers were generally handed a badge, a baton, and a copy of the department rules (if one existed), and were sent out on patrol duty. Cincinnati created a police academy in 1888, but it lasted only a few years. New York City established the School of Pistol Practice in 1895, but offered no training in any other aspect of policing until 1909. Even then, a 1913 investigation found that it gave no tests and all recruits were automatically passed.[28]

Police officers had no job security and could be fired at will. In some instances, almost the entire police force was dismissed after an election. Nonetheless, it was an attractive job because salaries were generally higher than those for most blue-collar jobs. In 1880 officers in most big cities earned $900 a year, compared with $450 for factory workers.

Jobs on the police force were a major form of patronage, which local politicians used to reward their friends. Consequently, the composition of departments reflected the ethnic and religious makeup of the cities. When Irish Americans began to win political power, they appointed their friends as police officers. When Barney McGinniskin became the first Irish-American police officer in Boston in 1851, it provoked major protests from the English and Protestant establishment in the city. Many German Americans served as police officers in Cleveland, Cincinnati, Milwaukee, and St. Louis, where German immigration was heavy. After the Civil War, some African Americans were appointed police officers in northern cities where the Republicans were in power.[29]

## Patrol Work

Police patrol was hopelessly inefficient. Officers patrolled on foot and were spread very thin. In Chicago, beats were three and four miles long. In many cities entire areas were not patrolled at all. The lack of communications systems made it impossible to respond to crime and disorder.

Supervision was equally weak. Officers easily evaded duty and spent much of their time in saloons and barber shops. Rain, snow, and extremely hot weather were powerful incentives for officers to avoid patrolling. Sergeants also patrolled on foot and found it nearly impossible to keep track of the officers under their command.

The first primitive communications system involved a network of call boxes which allowed patrol officers to call precinct stations. Officers learned to sabotage them: They left receivers off the hook, which took the early systems out of operation, or lied about where they were.[30]

The lack of an effective communications system made it difficult if not impossible for citizens to contact the police. In the event of a crime or disturbance, someone had to personally locate an officer who would then have to walk to the scene.

The police were a major social welfare institution in the 19th century. Precinct stations offered lodging to the homeless. The Philadelphia police, for example, lodged over 100,000 people a year during the 1880s. After 1900, care for the poor became the responsibility of professional social work agencies, and the police concentrated more on crime.[31]

## The Police and the Public

Many people today have a romanticized image of the 19th-century police officer. The myth is that officers were friendly, knowledgeable about the neighborhood, and helpful.

---

**SIDEBAR 2–2**

THE DIARY OF A POLICE OFFICER: BOSTON, 1895

We know very little about what police officers actually did in the early years. Most of the evidence comes from reformers or journalists seeking to expose corruption and inefficiency. Their reports are inherently biased. The recently discovered 1895 diary of Boston police officer Stillman S. Wakeman provides a revealing glimpse into actual police work 100 years ago.

Officer Wakeman was "an officer of the neighborhood." He spent most of his time on patrol responding to little problems that neighborhood residents brought to him: disputes, minor property crimes, and so on. He spent relatively little time on major offenses: murder, rape, robbery. Generally, he acted as a neighborhood magistrate, resolving problems informally.

Officer Wakeman's role was not that different from that of contemporary patrol officers. He was reactive and a problem solver. The major difference was the absence of the modern police technology: the patrol car and the 911 telephone system.

*Source:* Alexander von Hoffman, "An Officer of the Neighborhood: A Boston Patrolman on the Beat in 1895," *Journal of Social History* 26 (Winter 1992): 309–330.

---

If their methods were often rough, they did maintain order. This image is highly inaccurate. It is unlikely that police officers had close relations with many people on their beats. They were few in number, personnel turnover was high, and people moved more often than today. Official records, moreover, indicate that many police officers had serious drinking problems and frequently used excessive physical force. There is considerable evidence that police officers enjoyed little citizen respect and often faced open hostility from the public. Juvenile gangs, for example, made a sport of throwing rocks at the police or taunting them. People who were arrested often fought back.[32]

In a provocative study of the police in London and New York City, Wilbur Miller argues that in London a high level of mutual respect emerged between citizens and police. Through their restrained and civil conduct, the police overcame initial public hostility. The commissioners of the London Metropolitan Police maintained high personnel standards and exercised strict supervision. In the United States, however, the lack of adequate supervision allowed police officers to respond to public hostility with physical force. The result was a complete lack of professionalism.[33]

Citizen violence eventually caused American police officers to adopt firearms. As late as 1880 the police in Brooklyn (then an independent city of 500,000 people) were unarmed. In some cities weapons were optional or carried at the discretion of a sergeant. Firearms did not become standard equipment for police officers until the late 19th century, in response to rising levels of crime and violence.

### Corruption and Politics

Police corruption was epidemic in the 19th century. Historian Mark Haller argues that corruption was one of the main functions of local government, and the police were only one part of the problem.[34] The police took payoffs for not enforcing laws on drinking, gambling, and prostitution. The money was divided among officers at all ranks. Corruption extended to personnel decisions. Officers often had to pay bribes for promotion. The cost of obtaining a promotion was compensated for by the greater opportunities for graft. One New York City Police Officer, admitted in 1894 that he had amassed a personal fortune of over $350,000.[35]

Corruption served important social and political ends. Alcohol was an important symbolic issue in American politics. Protestant Americans saw sobriety as a badge of respectability and self-discipline. They sought to impose their morality on immigrant groups, especially the Irish and Germans, by controlling or outlawing drinking. For immigrant and blue-collar Americans, meanwhile, the neighborhood saloon was an important social institution and often the base of operations for political machines. Thus, the attack on drinking was also an attack on working-class political power. Working-class immigrants fought back by controlling the police through their political machines and effectively nullified laws intended to control drinking.[36]

### The Failure of Police Reform

Political reformers made police corruption a major issue during the 19th century, but their efforts were generally unsuccessful. They concentrated on changing the formal structure of control of police departments, usually by creating a board of police commissioners appointed by the governor or the legislature. This struggle for control reflected political, ethnic, and urban and rural conflicts. New York created the first state-controlled police commission in 1857.[37] In many cities, the battle for control of the police was endless. Cincinnati underwent 10 major changes in the form of police control between 1859 and 1910.[38]

Even when the reformers won, however, they did not succeed in improving the quality of policing. Their reform agenda emphasized replacing "bad" people (their opponents) with "good" people (their own). They did not have any substantive ideas about police administration, and made no significant changes in recruitment standards, training, or supervision.

Theodore Roosevelt's two-year term as New York City police commissioner between 1895 and 1897 illustrates the failure of the reformers. The future U.S. president made a vigorous effort to raise recruitment standards, discipline officers who were guilty of misconduct, and ensure enforcement of laws prohibiting the sale of liquor on Sundays. But most of his efforts were dramatic personal gestures, rather than institutional reforms: He would go out at night to catch officers not working. He made no lasting changes, however, and corruption and inefficiency continued long after he resigned in 1897.[39]

### The Impact of the Police on Society

Historians debate the impact of the police on society. Some argue that the police did help to maintain order. Cities became more orderly as the 19th century progressed, but it is not clear that the police were primarily responsible for this. Other historians argue that the police were so few in number that they could not possibly have deterred crime. Orderliness may have been the result of a more general adaptation to urban life. The daily routine of urban life—reporting to work every day at the same hour—cultivated habits of self-discipline and order. The police, according to this view, played a supporting role at best.[40]

The role of the police in labor relations during the 19th century is also a matter of debate among historians. Sid Harring and other Marxist historians argue that the police served the interests of business and were used to harass labor unions and break strikes.[41] American labor relations during these years were extremely violent. Management adamantly resisted unions, and many strikes led to violence. In some communities, particularly those with coal and steel industries, strikes were virtual civil war. In many cities, however, the police were friendly to organized labor, mainly because they came from the same blue-collar communities.[42]

The modern police were created to deal with the problems of crime and disorder, but they succeeded primarily in becoming a social problem themselves. The rampant corruption and inefficiency set in motion generations of reform efforts that continue today.

### THE 20TH CENTURY: THE ORIGINS OF POLICE PROFESSIONALISM

American policing underwent a dramatic change in the 20th century. There were three principal forces for change: an organized movement for police professionalism, the

**FIGURE 2–1**

THE REFORM AGENDA OF THE PROFESSIONALIZATION MOVEMENT

1 Eliminate political influence from policing.
2 Appoint qualified chief executives.
3 Define a mission of nonpartisan public service.
4 Raise personnel standards.
5 Introduce principles of scientific management.
6 Develop specialized units.

introduction of modern communications technology, and the civil rights movement's demand for equal justice.

## The Professionalization Movement

Around the turn of the century, a new generation of leaders launched an organized effort to professionalize the police. Police reform was part of a much broader political movement known as progressivism between 1900 and 1917. Progressive reformers sought to regulate big business, eliminate child labor, improve social welfare services, reform local government, as well as professionalize the police.[43]

The two most prominent leaders of the police professionalization movement were Richard Sylvester and August Vollmer. Sylvester was superintendent of the District of Columbia police from 1898 to 1915. As president of the International Association of Chiefs of Police (IACP) from 1901 to 1915, he made it the national voice of police reform. Until then, the police had no effective national professional association.[44]

Vollmer was chief of police in Berkeley, California, from 1905 to 1932, where he developed principles of modern police administration. He is most famous for advocating higher education for police officers, hiring college graduates in Berkeley, and organizing the first college-level police science courses at the University of California in 1916. He wrote the 1931 Wickersham Commission *Report on Police*, and trained a number of students who went on to become reform police chiefs.[45]

## The Reform Agenda

The professionalization movement developed an agenda that dominated police reform through the 1960s (see Figure 2–1).[46]

Eliminating politics and hiring qualified leaders went hand in hand. The reformers argued that the police needed chief executives who had proven abilities to manage a large organization. Arthur Woods, a prominent lawyer, served as police commissioner in New York City from 1914 to 1917; Philadelphia hired Marine Corps General Smedley Butler to head its police department from 1911 to 1915.[47]

The reformers sought to define policing as a profession. This meant that the police should be public servants with a professional obligation to serve the entire community on a nonpartisan basis.

To raise personnel standards, departments began to establish minimum recruitment requirements of intelligence, health, and moral character. New York City created the first permanent police training academy in 1895, although it was initially restricted to firearms training. In most cities the process of reform was painfully slow. Some cities did not offer any meaningful training until the 1950s.

Modern management principles called for centralizing command and control within police departments and making efficient use of personnel. Until then, police chiefs had exercised little real control; captains in neighborhood precincts and politicians had the real power. Reformers closed precinct stations and used the new communications technology to control both midmanagement personnel and officers on the street.

The reformers increased the military ethos of police departments, adding parades, close-order drill, and military-style commendations. Until that time, American police departments had in fact been extremely unmilitarylike: They were undisciplined and inefficient.[48]

Reformers also created the first specialized units such as traffic, juvenile, and vice. Previously, police departments had only patrol and detective units. Specialization, meanwhile, increased the size and complexity of the police bureaucracy, complicating the problem of managing departments.

Juvenile units led to a historic innovation: the first female sworn officers. Until then, policing had been an all-male occupation. The Portland (Oregon) police hired the first policewoman, Lola Baldwin, as a juvenile specialist in 1905. Alice Stebbins Wells, appointed to the Los Angeles police department in 1910, organized the International Association of Policewomen in 1915. By 1919 over 60 police departments employed female officers. Policewomen were not assigned to regular patrol duty, usually did not wear uniforms, and did not carry weapons. Most had only limited arrest powers. Policewomen advocates argued that women were specially qualified to work with children and that they should not handle regular police duties.[49]

### The Impact of Professionalization

Police reform progressed very slowly. By 1920 Milwaukee, Cincinnati, and Berkeley had emerged as leaders in the field. Most other departments, however, remained mired in corruption and inefficiency. August Vollmer spent the year 1924 attempting to reform the Los Angeles police, but gave up in despair and returned to Berkeley. Chicago seemed to resist all efforts at reform. In some cities, the police made notable steps forward, only to slide backward a few years later. Philadelphia made considerable strides under a reform mayor and police commissioner between 1911 and 1915, only to have all progress wiped out when the city's political machine regained control.[50]

Despite these failures, the reformers could claim one great success: They firmly established the idea of professionalism as the goal for modern policing, and had defined a specific agenda for reform.

## New Problems in Policing

Professionalization also introduced a number of new problems in policing. The rank-and-file police officer remained a forgotten person. Most reformers did not respect ordinary officers and placed all their hopes on strong administrators. As a result, the rank and file retreated into an isolated and alienated subculture that opposed most reforms.[51]

The most dramatic expression of this development was the 1919 Boston police strike, one of the most famous events in police history. Salaries for Boston police officers had not been raised in nearly 20 years. When their demand for a 20 percent raise was rejected, they voted to form a union. Police Commissioner Edwin U. Curtis suspended the union leaders, and 1,117 officers went out on strike, leaving only 427 on duty. Violence and disorder erupted throughout the city. Governor Calvin Coolidge called out the state militia and won national fame for his comment, "There is no right to strike against the public safety by anybody, anywhere, at any time." The strike quickly collapsed and all the strikers were fired.[52]

Because of the violence in Boston, a national backlash against police unions set in, and other police unions across the country disappeared. Police unionism was dead for the next 20 years, but the problem of an alienated rank and file remained.

Professionalism also created new problems in police administration. As departments grew in size and created new specialized units, they became increasingly complex bureaucracies. The management of police organizations continued to be a major challenge into the 1990s.

## Police and Racial Minorities

Conflict between the police and the African-American community also appeared during the World War I years. Major race riots erupted in East St. Louis, Illinois (1917), and Chicago and other cities in 1919. Investigations of these riots found race discrimination by the police prior to and during the riots. In some cases, officers joined in the rioting themselves. The Chicago riot commission recommended several steps to improve police–community relations, but nothing was done.[53]

Some police departments in northern and western cities hired a few African-American officers, but almost all were assigned to the black community. Southern police departments were rigidly segregated. Many hired no African-American officers at all. Others hired some in a second-class category: They were assigned to the black

---

**POLICE HISTORY ON THE WEB**

The Boston Police Department web site describes the 1919 police strike. Find the web site. What do they say about the strike? How does it compare with the description presented here?

community and not allowed to arrest whites.[54] Conflict between the police and the African-American community remained a serious problem in all parts of the country. It did not receive any serious attention until the riots of the 1960s.

### New Law Enforcement Agencies

Two important new law enforcement agencies appeared in the years before World War I: the state police and the Bureau of Investigation forerunner of the FBI.

Several states created state-level law enforcement agencies in the 19th century, but they remained relatively unimportant agencies. The Texas Rangers were established in 1835. The Pennsylvania State Constabulary, created in 1905, was the first modern state police force, but was not typical of most others. It was a highly centralized, militaristic agency that concentrated on controlling strikes. Business leaders believed that local police and the militia were unreliable during strikes. Organized labor bitterly attacked the constabulary, denouncing its officers as cossacks.[55]

Other states soon created their own agencies. About half were highway patrols, limited to traffic control, and the other half were general law enforcement agencies. Although business interests sought the creation of Pennsylvania-style agencies, in several states organized labor was able to limit their powers or block their creation altogether.[56]

The Bureau of Investigation was established in 1908 by a presidential executive order. Until then, the federal government had no full-time criminal investigation agency. Private detective agencies were sometimes used under contract on an as-needed basis. The new Bureau of Investigation was immediately involved in scandal. Some agents were caught opening the mail of one senator who had opposed creation of the agency. In 1919 and 1920 the bureau conducted a massive roundup of suspected radicals, accompanied by gross violations of due process. More scandals followed in the 1920s.[57]

## THE NEW COMMUNICATIONS TECHNOLOGY

Some of the most important changes in policing were the result of modern communications technology. The patrol car, the two-way radio, and the telephone transformed patrol work, the nature of police–citizen contacts, and police management.[58]

The patrol car first appeared just before World War I, and by the 1920s, it was in widespread use. In certain respects, the police had to keep up with citizens and criminals who were now driving cars. Police chiefs also believed that the patrol car would make possible efficient patrol coverage that would effectively deter crime and allow the police to respond quickly to crimes and other problems. American police departments steadily converted from foot to motor patrol, and by the 1960s only a few major cities still relied primarily on foot patrol.

The patrol car had unintended consequences that created new problems. By removing the officer from the street, it reduced informal contact with law-abiding citizens. Racial minorities increasingly saw the police as an occupying army. This problem remained hidden until the police–community relations crisis of the 1960s.

The two-way radio became widespread in the late 1930s and had two important consequences. First, it completed the communications network and allowed departments to dispatch officers in response to citizen calls. Second, it revolutionized police supervision by allowing the department to maintain continuous contact with patrol officers.

The telephone was invented in 1877, but it did not have a great impact on policing until it was linked with the patrol car and the two-way radio in the mid-20th century. Together, the three pieces of technology completed a communications link between citizens and the police. The telephone allowed citizens to contact the police easily and to request service; the two-way radio enabled the police department to dispatch a patrol officer to the scene; the patrol car, in turn, allowed the patrol officer to reach the scene quickly.

Police departments encouraged people to call, promising an immediate response. Gradually, citizens became socialized into the habit of "calling the cops" to handle even the smallest problems.[59] As a result, citizens developed higher expectations about the quality of life, and the call workload steadily increased. When the rising number of calls overloaded the police, they responded by adding more officers, more patrol cars, and more sophisticated communications systems. More resources, however, only encouraged more calls, and the process repeated itself.

Telephone-generated calls for service altered the nature of police–citizen contacts. Previously, police officers rarely entered private dwellings. Patrolling on foot, they had no way of learning about problems in private areas, and citizens had no way to summon them. The new communications technology made it possible for citizens to invite the police into their homes. The result was a complex and contradictory change in police–citizen contacts. Whereas the patrol car isolated the police from people on the streets, the telephone brought police officers into peoples' living rooms, kitchens, and bedrooms. There, officers became involved in the most intimate domestic problems: husband–wife disputes, alcohol abuse, parent–child conflicts, and other issues.[60]

## NEW DIRECTIONS IN POLICE ADMINISTRATION, 1930–1960

### The Wickersham Commission Report

The 1931 *Report on Lawlessness in Law Enforcement* shocked the country with its conclusion, "the third degree—the inflicting of pain, physical or mental, to extract confessions or statements—is extensively practiced." The report found that police routinely beat suspects, threatened them with worse punishment, and held them illegally for protracted questioning. It cited examples of a suspect who was held by the ankles from a third-story window, and another who was forced to stand in the morgue with his hand on the body of a murder victim. The chief of police in Buffalo, New York, openly declared that he would violate the Constitution if he felt he had to.[61]

The report was one of 14 published by the Wickersham Commission, officially the National Commission on Law Observance and Enforcement, the first national study of the American criminal justice system. It was the first significant attack on police misconduct and set in motion a new era of reform.[62]

## Professionalization Continues

Under the influence of August Vollmer, California police departments took the lead in professionalization from the 1920s through the 1960s. Vollmer's protégés became police chiefs throughout the state, spreading reform agenda of professionalization. The first undergraduate law enforcement program was established at San Jose State College in 1931. California also developed a system of regional training for police officers in the late 1930s.[63]

Vollmer's most important protégé was O. W. Wilson who served as chief of the Wichita, Kansas, police from 1928 to 1935; as dean of the University of California School of Criminology from 1950 to 1960; and as superintendent of the Chicago police from 1960 to 1967.[64] He was the author of two extremely influential textbooks on police management: the International City Management Association's *Municipal Police Administration* and his own *Police Administration* (1950).[65] He emphasized the efficient management of personnel, particularly patrol officers. He led the shift from foot patrol to automobile patrol, and developed a pioneering workload formula for the distribution of patrol officers according to crimes and calls for service. His textbook became the unofficial "bible" of police management and he influenced police administration through the 1960s.

## J. Edgar Hoover and the War on Crime

The most important new figure in American law enforcement in the 1930s was the director of the FBI, J. Edgar Hoover. He was appointed director of the bureau in 1924 after another series of scandals. Capitalizing on public fears about a national crime wave in the 1930s, he increased the size and scope of the bureau's activities and renamed it the Federal Bureau of Investigation. In 1930 he won control of the new Uniform Crime Reports (UCR) system. In 1934 a set of new federal laws gave the FBI increased jurisdiction, including the authority to arrest criminals who crossed state lines in order to avoid prosecution. The following year the FBI opened its National Police Academy, which trained bureau agents and, by invitation, some local police officers.[66]

Hoover was a master at public relations, skillfully manipulating the media to project an image of the FBI agent as the paragon of professionalism: dedicated, honest, trained, and relentlessly efficient.[67] Some of Hoover's reputation was deserved. FBI agents were far better educated and trained than were local police officers. But there was an ugly underside to Hoover's long career (1924–1972) as leader of the bureau. He exaggerated the FBI's role in several famous cases such as that of Pretty Boy Floyd, and manipulated crime data to create an exaggerated impression of the bureau's effectiveness. He concentrated on small-time bank robbers, ignoring organized street crime, white-collar crime, and violations of federal civil rights laws. Even worse, Hoover systematically violated the constitutional rights of citizens, spying on political groups and compiling secret files on elected officials. His misuse of power did not become known until after his death in 1972.[68]

Hoover's leadership of the FBI had a significant impact on local police. His emphasis on education and training set a new standard. He also contributed to the growing emphasis on police work as crime fighting. The introduction of the UCR, the development of the Ten Most Wanted list, and the creation of the FBI crime lab all served to emphasize crime fighting at the expense of other aspects of policing.

## THE POLICE CRISIS OF THE 1960s

In the 1960s the police were at the center of a national crisis over race, crime, and justice.[69] The Supreme Court issued a series of landmark decisions placing constitutional limits on police practices. The 1961 *Mapp v. Ohio* decision held that evidence gathered in an illegal search and seizure could not be used against the defendant. In the even more controversial *Miranda v. Arizona* (1966) decision, the Court held that police officers were required to advise suspects that they had the right to remain silent, that anything they said could be used against them, that they had the right to an attorney, and that, if they could not afford one, a lawyer would be appointed. The *Miranda* warning was designed to ensure the suspect's protection against self-incrimination.

*Mapp*, *Miranda*, and other decisions provoked an enormous political controversy. The police and their supporters claimed that the Court had "handcuffed" them in the fight against crime. Conservative politicians accused the Court of favoring the rights of criminals over the rights of victims and law-abiding citizens.[70]

Meanwhile, the civil rights movement entered a new militant phase in the 1960s, challenging race discrimination in all areas of American life. African-American college students launched sit-ins to protest segregated stores in the South, and civil rights groups challenged job and housing discrimination in northern states. Civil rights groups also attacked race discrimination and physical brutality by the police.[71] The white police officer in the black ghetto became a symbol of white power and authority. Studies of deadly force found that police officers shot and killed African-American citizens about eight times as often as white citizens. As a result of employment discrimination, meanwhile, African-Americans were seriously underrepresented as police officers.[72]

Tensions between the police and the black community exploded in a nationwide wave of riots between 1964 and 1968. Almost all were sparked by an incident involving the police. The 1964 New York City riot began after a white off-duty officer shot and killed a black teenager. The 1965 riot in the Watts district of Los Angeles was sparked by a simple traffic stop. The Kerner Commission counted over 200 disorders in 1967 alone.[73]

Police departments responded to the crisis by establishing police–community relations (PCR) units. PCR programs included speaking to community groups and schools, "ride-along" programs that allowed citizens to view police work from the perspective of the police officer, and neighborhood storefront offices to facilitate communication with citizens. These programs, however, had little impact on day-to-day police work and, therefore, did little to improve police–community relations.[74]

Civil rights leaders demanded the hiring of more African-American officers and the creation of citizen review boards to investigate citizen complaints of excessive force. Although the 1964 Civil Rights Act outlawed race discrimination in employment, minority employment made little progress until the 1980s. The demand for citizen review was also unsuccessful. The Philadelphia Police Advisory Board (PAB), created in 1958, was abolished in 1967 under pressure from the police union. The police union in New York City succeeded in abolishing a citizen-dominated Civilian Complaint Review Board (CCRB) in 1966.[75] By the end of the 1960s, even though the riots had stopped, relations between the police and minority communities remained tense. The steady criticisms from the African-American community were a major force for change over the following thirty years.

### The Police in the National Spotlight

As a result of rising public concern about crimes, riots, and racial conflicts, a series of national commissions examined the police and made recommendations for change. President Lyndon Johnson appointed the President's Commission on Law Enforcement and Administration of Justice (known as the President's Crime Commission) in 1965. The commission's report, *The Challenge of Crime in a Free Society* (1967) endorsed most of the traditional agenda of professionalization: higher recruitment standards, more training, and better management and supervision. The commission sponsored pioneering research, including Albert Reiss and Donald Black's observation of patrol officers at work, and made important recommendations for the control of police discretion.[76] The first two chapters of the commission's *Task Force Report: The Police*, included a thoughtful analysis of the complexity of the police role and the fact that only a relatively small part of police work was devoted to criminal law enforcement.[77]

The National Advisory Commission on Civil Disorders, popularly known as the Kerner Commission, was created after the riots of 1967 to study the national crisis in race relations. Its report found "deep hostility between police and ghetto communities as a primary cause of the disorders." It recommended that routine police operations be changed "to ensure proper individual conduct and to eliminate abrasive practices," that more African-American police officers be hired, and that police departments improve their procedures for handling citizen complaints.[78]

The Kerner Commission raised serious questions about the traditional assumptions of police professionalization. It noted that "many of the serious disturbances took place in cities whose police are among the best led, best organized, best trained, and most professional in the country."[79] The patrol car removed the officer from the street and alienated the police from ordinary citizens, and aggressive crime-fighting tactics, such as frequent stops and frisks, were a particular source of tension.

The Los Angeles Police Department (LAPD) illustrated the commission's point. The LAPD was widely regarded as the most professional department in the country. Since 1950 Chief William Parker had eliminated corruption and installed high personnel standards. Aggressive anticrime tactics, however, aggravated conflict with minority communities. Chief Parker tolerated no criticism and he dismissed complaints about excessive force voiced by the National Association for the Advancement of Colored People (NAACP) and the American Civil Liberties Union (ACLU) as supporting the criminal element.[80]

In 1973 the American Bar Association (ABA) published its *Standards Relating to the Urban Police Function*. The standards reflected a growing body of research on the police and a new understanding of the complex role that police departments play. The emerging view recognized that police officers were primarily peacekeepers rather than crime fighters: They spent most of their time maintaining order rather than fighting crime. The ABA standards also emphasized the need to control the exercise of discretion by police officers.[81]

These reports were accompanied by an explosion of research on the police. Much of this research was funded by the Law Enforcement Assistance Administration (LEAA) (1968–1976), and later the National Institute of Justice (NIJ).

The American Bar Foundation (ABF) had conducted the first field observations of police work in 1956 and 1957, finding that police officers exercised broad discretion and that most police work involved noncriminal activity.[82] Reiss and Black's field studies for the Crime Commission provided more precise quantitative data on these phenomena.[83]

The Crime Commission raised questions about the effectiveness of patrol, which led to the Kansas City Preventive Patrol Experiment, one of the most important pieces of police research ever conducted (1972–1973). The experiment tested the effect of different levels of patrol, and found that increased patrol did not reduce crime and had no significant effect on public awareness about police presence. At the same time, reduced patrol did not lead to an increase in crime or in public fear of crime. Challenging the basic assumptions about the effect of patrol on crime, the experiment had a profound effect on the thinking about the police.[84]

Research also questioned the value of rapid police response. Faster response time did not lead to more arrests. Few calls involved crimes in progress and most crime victims did not call the police immediately.[85] The Rand Corporation study of criminal investigation, meanwhile, shattered traditional myths about the detective. Follow-up investigations are very unproductive: Most crimes are solved through information obtained by the first officer on the scene and most detective work is boring, routine paperwork.[86]

There was also much research on police officers' attitudes and behavior. William Westley identified a distinct police subculture, characterized by hostility toward the public, group solidarity, and secrecy.[87] Jerome Skolnick found a distinct working environment in policing, dominated by danger and exercise of authority. The pressure to achieve results in the form of arrests and convictions, moreover, encouraged officers to violate legal procedures.[88] Most studies indicated that police officer attitudes were shaped by the nature of police work, including the culture of the organization, and not their individual background characteristics.

The rapidly accumulating body of research had a significant effect on reform efforts. Much of the important new research shattered traditional assumptions about policing (e.g., the deterrent effect of patrol, the value of quick response time). The Kerner Commission suggested that many aspects of professionalism have adverse consequences for police–community relations. According to historian Robert Fogelson, police reform was "at a standstill" by the early 1970s.[89] Reform efforts were eventually revitalized in the 1980s with the emergence of community policing and problem-oriented policing.

## NEW DEVELOPMENTS IN POLICING

The crisis of the 1960s stimulated a burst of police reform. Some of these efforts represented a continuation of the traditional reform agenda; others reflected very different ideas about policing.[90]

In 1970 the Ford Foundation established the Police Foundation, with a grant of $30 million. Over the next 20 years The Police Foundation sponsored some of the most important police research, including the Kansas City Preventive Patrol Experiment. Later, the Police Executive Research Forum (PERF), a professional association of big-city police managers, emerged as the leader of innovation in policing.

### The Changing Police Officer

The profile of the American police officer changed significantly between the 1960s and the 1990s. The employment of racial and ethnic minority officers increased slowly but steadily. Underrepresentation of black officers on big-city police departments was one of the major complaints raised by civil rights groups. The Kerner Commission found that in 1967 African Americans represented 34 percent of the population of Cleveland but only 7 percent of the police officers; in Oakland, they were 31 percent of the population and 4 percent of the officers.[91] By 1993 African-American officers were a majority in Detroit, Washington, and Atlanta. In Miami, Hispanic officers comprised 47.7 percent of the police force in 1993, and blacks made up another 17.4 percent.[92] African Americans served as police chiefs in New York City, Los Angeles, Atlanta, Chicago, Houston, and many other cities.

Traditional barriers to the employment of women in policing crumbled under the impact of the 1964 Civil Rights Act, which barred discrimination on the basis of sex, and the women's movement. By the mid-1990s, the percentage of female officers in most big city departments was about 13 percent.[93] Female officers were assigned to routine patrol duty for the first time and departments eliminated barriers to the recruitment of women. Evaluations of female officers on patrol in Washington, DC, and New York City, however, found their performance to be as effective as that of comparable groups of male officers.[94]

Police departments began to recruit college students. Between 1968 and 1976, the federal Law Enforcement Education Program (LEEP) provided nearly $200 million in financial assistance to students in college criminal justice programs. Although only 20 percent of all sworn officers had any college education in 1960, the figure had risen to 65 percent by 1988.[95]

The length of preservice training increased from an average of about 300 hours in the 1960s to over 1,000 hours in many departments by the 1990s. The more professional departments added a field training component to the traditional academy training. Police academy curricula added units on race relations, domestic violence, and ethics. New York and California had introduced mandatory training for all police officers in 1959 and, by the 1970s, every state had a similar requirement. Previously, many small police and sheriff's departments offered no preservice training whatsoever.[96]

### Supervision and the Control of Discretion

As a result of Supreme Court decisions on police practices, minority community protests about misconduct, and a rising tide of lawsuits, police departments instituted procedures to control on-the-street police behavior.[97] This mainly involved written policies covering search and seizure, interrogations, and other aspects of police work. Particularly important were the policies on the use of deadly force, handling of domestic violence, and high-speed pursuits. These policies were collected in the standard operating procedure (SOP), which became the basic tool of police management. They were part of a general movement to control the exercise of discretion in the criminal justice system.[98]

The control of deadly force was one of the most important reforms. Research indicated that police shot eight African Americans for every white citizen. The disparity was especially great with respect to unarmed citizens. Many of the 1960s riots were sparked by a shooting incident. Most police departments at that time had either no policy on deadly force or relied on state statutes that permitted the shooting of fleeing felons. In the early 1970s, they began to adopt more restrictive "defense of life" policies. Pioneering research by James J. Fyfe found that the New York City Police Department's new policy (1972) reduced firearms discharges by 30 percent.[99] As other departments adopted similar policies, the number of citizens shot and killed by the police nationwide dropped by 50 percent between 1970 and 1984. At the same time, the ratio of blacks to whites shot and killed fell by 50 percent.[100]

Rising public concern about domestic violence led to a revolution in police policy in that area as well. Women's groups sued the police in New York City, Oakland, and other cities for failing to arrest men who had committed domestic assault. These suits produced departmental policies prescribing mandatory arrest. Soon other departments across the country adopted similar policies. This trend received a strong boost when a Police Foundation study found that arrest deterred future violence more effectively than either mediation or separation. Although subsequent studies failed to confirm this effect, mandatory arrest policies remained popular.[101]

The cost of law suits against the police led to the creation of the Commission on Accreditation for Law Enforcement Agencies in 1979. It published its first set of standards in 1983 and, by 1997, 368 law enforcement agencies had been accredited.[102] Although accreditation was entirely voluntary, it represented an important step forward in terms of professional self-regulation.

### Police Unions

Police unions, which had been denied the right to exist in 1919 and again in the 1940s, spread rapidly in the 1960s and, by the 1970s, they had established themselves as a powerful force in American policing. Police officers were angry and alienated over Supreme Court rulings, criticisms by civil rights groups, poor salaries and benefits, and arbitrary disciplinary practices by police chiefs.[103]

Unions had a dramatic impact on police administration. They won significant improvements in salaries and benefits for officers, along with grievance procedures that protected the rights of officers in disciplinary hearings. They also produced a revolution in police management. Police chiefs were no longer all-powerful, and now had to negotiate with unions over many management issues. Many reformers were alarmed about the growth of police unions. Unions tended to resist innovations and were particularly hostile to attempts to improve police–community relations.

### Citizen Review of Complaints

Although they had enormous power in many aspects of police administration, police unions steadily lost in one important area: citizen review of complaints against the police. Citizen review was one of the principal goals of civil rights groups, which argued that minority citizens were the victims of systematic police abuse and that police departments did not investigate complaints or discipline officers. Although the citizen review boards had been abolished in New York and Philadelphia in the 1960s, the concept revived in the 1970s. By the 1990s there were citizen review procedures in almost all the big cities.[104] The idea that citizen input into the complaints process was an important mechanism of accountability was, in fact, an international phenomenon. Citizen review procedures were universal in England, Canada, Australia, and New Zealand, and growing in other countries as well.[105]

### Community Policing

The most important new development in policing in the 1980s and 1990s was the advent of community policing. Community policing was a philosophy of policing that embraced many different kinds of programs. The basic idea of community policing was that police departments should work closely with neighborhood residents, develop programs tailored for specific problems, and give rank-and-file officers more decision-making freedom. Instead of crime fighters, officers should function as problem-solvers, planners, and community organizers.[106]

Some of the components of community policing had been tried in the early 1970s under the heading of "team policing." The team policing idea, however, had died a dramatic death and was soon abandoned.[107] Community policing was based on a more solid empirical foundation regarding what the police can and cannot accomplish. In the seminal article, "Broken Windows," James Q. Wilson and George L. Kelling summed up the recent research on policing: that patrol had only limited deterrent effect on crime, that faster response times did not increase arrests and that the capacity of detectives to solve crimes was limited. This research suggested two important points: that the police could not fight crime by themselves, but were very dependent upon citizens, and that the police could reduce fear by concentrating on less serious quality-of-life problems.[108]

Police chiefs, politicians, and community leaders quickly embraced the idea of community policing, and programs spread across the country in the 1980s.

Many programs incorporated the closely related concept of problem-oriented policing (POP). The originator of POP, Herman Goldstein, argued that instead of treating crime and disorder as general categories, the police should identify and focus on specific problems: chronic alcoholics in the neighborhood; abandoned buildings that served as drug houses, and so on.[109]

In the first POP experiment, officers in Newport News, Virginia, attacked crime in a deteriorated housing project by helping the residents organize to improve conditions in the project itself. This included pressuring both government agencies and private companies to fulfill their responsibilities regarding building conditions and sanitation.[110]

In New York City's Community Patrol Officer Program experiment, CPOP officers did not answer routine 911 calls; instead, they were expected to develop innovative strategies to deal with neighborhood problems.[111] New York City's approach later evolved into zero-tolerance policing, which involved aggressive enforcement of laws against minor crimes: public urination, graffiti, and so on. Serious crime in New York City dropped significantly in the mid-1990s. George Kelling argued that the attack on minor offenses was directly responsible. In many cases, he argued, a person arrested for a minor crime was found to be carrying an illegal weapon.[112]

Advocates of community policing hailed it as a new era in policing. As early as 1988, Kelling argued that "a quiet revolution is reshaping American policing."[113] By the late 1990s, it was still too early to assess the impact of community policing. Many programs were traditional anticrime, antidrug efforts. In some departments there was little more than rhetoric. Serious crime, meanwhile, fell nationwide in the mid-1990s, and could not necessarily be attributed to any specific police program such as New York City's zero-tolerance policing.

Whatever the impact of community policing, by the late 1990s, the American police were in the midst of an extraordinary period of innovation. Police chiefs across the country were open to experimentation and evaluation. David Bayley argues that "the last decade of the twentieth century may be the most creative period in policing since the modern police officer was put onto the streets of London in 1829.[114]

### CONCLUSION: THE LESSONS OF THE PAST

As the 21st century approaches, we are aware of the innumerable changes in American policing. Viewed from the perspective of 300 years, the major change was the creation of the modern police: a large, specialized bureaucratic agency devoted to crime control and order maintenance. From the perspective of 100 years, American police departments changed from inefficient and corrupt political enterprises to enterprises with a nonpartisan professional mission.

From the perspective of the last 30 years one can see vast improvements in personnel standards and systems of accountability, including the values of due process and equal protection. The research revolution has produced an impressive body of knowledge about policing. There is a new candor about police discretion and about the limits of the police's ability to control crime. And, as David Bayley argues, the police are remarkably open to innovation and experimentation. [115]

The legacy of the past continues to weigh heavily on the police, however. Problems of abuse of authority—excessive physical force, corruption—continue to plague many departments. Conflict between the police and racial and ethnic minority communities is a problem in nearly every city. The introduction of women and racial and ethnic minority officers led to tension and often open conflict among the rank and file in many departments.[116] And despite the many community policing experiments, routine police work in most cities has not changed that much in 30 years: officers patrol in cars and answer their 911 calls. In a comprehensive review of recent developments in policing, Stephen Mastrofski concludes, "the patrol officers of today can be expected to do their job by and large as they did a decade ago and as they will do a decade hence."[117]

History offers many lessons about the American police. It dramatizes the fact that policing is always changing. Some of those changes are the result of planned innovation; others are the result of external social changes. At the same time, history illustrates the extent to which many aspects of policing, including some serious problems, endure.

## NOTES

**1** Stephen D. Mastrofski, "The Prospects of Change in Police Patrol: A Decade in Review," *American Journal of Police* 9, no. 3 (1990): 1–79.

**2** Samuel Walker, *A Critical History of Police Reform* (Lexington, Mass.: Lexington Books, 1977).

**3** Samuel Walker, *Popular Justice: A History of American Criminal Justice*, 2d ed. (New York: Oxford University Press, 1998), chap. 1.

**4** David H. Bayley, *Police for the Future* (New York: Oxford University Press, 1994), p. 126.

**5** T. A. Critchley, *A History of Police in England and Wales*, 2d ed. (Montclair, N.J.: Patterson Smith, 1972).

**6** Bureau of Justice Statistics, *Local Police Departments, 1993* (Washington: Government Printing Office, 1996).

**7** Allen Steinberg, *The Transformation of Criminal Justice, Philadelphia, 1800–1880* (Chapel Hill: University of North Carolina, 1989).

**8** Critchley, *A History of Police in England and Wales*, chap. 2.

**9** David Bayley, *Patterns of Policing: A Comparative International Analysis* (New Brunswick, N.J.: Rutgers University Press, 1985), p. 23.

**10** Allan Silver, "The Demand for Order in Civil Society: A Review of Some Themes in the History of Urban Crime, Police, and Riot," in *The Police: Six Sociological Essays*, David J. Bordua (New York: Wiley, 1967), pp. 12–13.

**11** Walker, *Popular Justice*, chap. 1.

**12** Julian P. Boyd, "The Sheriff in Colonial North Carolina," *North Carolina Historical Review* 5 (1928): 151–181.

**13** Roger Lane, *Policing the City* (New York: Atheneum, 1971), chap 1.

**14** Ibid., pp. 3–38.

**15** Robert F. Wintersmith, *Police and the Black Community* (Lexington, Mass.: Lexington Books, 1974), pp. 17–21.

**16** Douglas Greenberg, *Crime and Law Enforcement in the Colony of New York, 1691–1776* (Ithaca, NY: Cornell University Press, 1976).

**17** Richard Hofstadter and Michael V. Wallace, eds. *American Violence: A Documentary History* (New York: Vintage Books, 1971).

**18** Walker, *Popular Justice*, chap. 1.

**19** Richard Maxwell Brown, *Strain of Violence: Historical Studies of American Violence and Vigilantism* (New York: Oxford University Press, 1975), pp. 95–179.

**20** Lane, *Policing the City*, chap. 3.

**21** Quoted in Brown, *Strain of Violence*, p. 3.

**22** Hofstadter and Wallace, eds., *American Violence*.

**23** James F. Richardson, *The New York Police: Colonial Times to 1900* (New York: Oxford University Press, 1970); Steinberg, *The Transformation of Criminal Justice*, pp. 119–149.

**24** Lane, *Policing the City*, p. 37.

**25** Wilbur R. Miller, *Cops and Bobbies: Police Authority in New York and London, 1830–1870* (Chicago: University of Chicago Press, 1977).

**26** Walker, *A Critical History of Police Reform*; pp. 3–31 Robert Fogelson, *Big City Police* (Cambridge: Harvard University Press, 1977) pp. 13–39.

**27** Jay Stuart Berman, *Police Administration and Progressive Reform: Theodore Roosevelt as Police Commissioner of New York* (New York: Greenwood Press, 197), p. 71.

**28** Walker, *A Critical History of Police Reform*, pp. 71–72.

**29** W. Marvin Dulaney, *Black Police in America* (Bloomington: Indiana University Press, 1996), chap. 3.

**30** Jonathan Rubenstein, *City Police* (New York: Ballantine Books, 1974), pp. 15–22.

**31** Eric H. Monkkonen, *Police in Urban America, 1860–1920* (Cambridge: Cambridge University Press, 1981), pp. 86–109.

**32** Walker, *A Critical History of Police Reform*, pp. 14–19.

**33** Miller, *Cops and Bobbies*.

**34** Mark Haller, "Historical Roots of Police Behavior: Chicago, 1890–1925," *Law and Society Review* 10 (Winter 1976): 303–324.

**35** Berman, *Police Administration and Progressive Reform*, p. 51.

**36** Ibid.

**37** Richardson, *The New York Police*, pp. 82–108.

**38** Walker, *A Critical History of Police Reform*, pp. 40–43.

**39** Berman, *Police Administration and Progressive Reform*.

**40** Roger Lane, *Violent Death in the City* (Cambridge: Harvard University Press, 1979) pp. 119–123; Walker, *Popular Justice*, pp. 66–69.

**41** Sidney L. Harring, *Policing a Class Society: The Experience of American Cities, 1865–1915* (New Brunswick, N.J.: Rutgers University Press, 1983).

**42** Walker, *A Critical History of Police Reform*, pp. 28–31.

**43** Ibid.

**44** IACP, *Proceedings* (New York: Arno Press, 1971).

**45** Gene E. Carte and Elaine H. Carte, *Police Reform in the United States: The Era of August Vollmer* (Berkeley: University of California Press, 1975).

**46** Walker, *A Critical History of Police Reform*, pp. 53–56, 167–174.

**47** Ibid., pp. 61–66.

**48** Ibid., pp. 63, 66–67.

**49** Dorothy Moses Schulz, *From Social Worker to Crimefighter: Women in United States Municipal Policing* (Westport, Conn.: Praeger, 1995), pp. 21–43.

**50** Walker, *A Critical History of Police Reform*, pp. 61–66.

**51** Ibid, pp. 110–120.

**52** Francis Russell, *A City in Terror—1919—The Boston Police Strike* (New York: Viking Press, 1975).

**53** Chicago Commission on Race Relations, *The Negro in Chicago* (Chicago: University of Chicago Press, 1922).

**54** Dulaney, *Black Police in America*.

**55** Katherine Mayo, *Justice to All: The Story of The Pennsylvania State Police* (New York: Putnam, 1917).

**56** H. Kenneth Bechtel, *State Police in the United States: A Socio-Historical Analysis* (Westport, Conn.: Greenwood, 1995).

**57** Gentry, *J. Edgar Hoover: The Man and The Secrets* (New York: Norton, 1991)

**58** Samuel Walker, "Broken Windows and Fractured History: The Use and Misuse of History in Recent Police Patrol Analysis," *Justice Quarterly* 1 (March 1984): 77–90.

**59** Egon Bittner, *The Functions of the Police in Modern Society* (Rockville, Md.: NIMH, 1970), p. 39.

**60** Walker, "Broken Windows and Fractured History."

**61** Ibid.

**62** National Commission on Law Observance and Enforcement, *Report on Lawlessness in Law Enforcement* (Washington: Government Printing Office, 1931).

**63** Carte and Carte, *Police Reform in the United States.*

**64** William J. Bopp, *O. W.: O. W. Wilson and the Search for a Police Profession* (Port Washington, N.Y.: Kennikat Press, 1977).

**65** O. W. Wilson, *Police Administration* (New York: McGraw-Hill, 1950). International City Management Association, *Municipal Police Administration*, 4th ed. (Chicago: ICMA, 1954)

**66** Curt Gentry, *J. Edgar Hoover: The Man and the Secrets*

**67** Richard Gid Powers, *G-Men: Hoover's FBI in American Popular Culture* (Carbondale: Southern Illinois University Press, 1983).

**68** Athan G. Theoharis and John Stuart Cox, *The Boss: J. Edgar Hoover and the Great American Inquisition* (Philadelphia: Temple University Press, 1988).

**69** Walker, *Popular Justice*, chap. 6.

**70** Fred P. Graham, *The Self-Inflicted Wound* (New York: Macmillan, 1970).

**71** Paul Chevigny, *Police Power* (New York: Vintage Books, 1969).

**72** National Advisory Commission on Civil Disorders, *Report* (New York: Bantam Books, 1968), pp. 315–316, 321–322.

**73** Ibid.

**74** U.S. Department of Justice, *Improving Police/Community Relations* (Washington: Government Printing Office, 1973).

**75** Monrad G. Paulson et al., "Securing Police Compliance with Constitutional Limitations: The Exclusionary Rule and Other Devices," in *Law and Order Reconsidered*, National Commission on the Causes and Prevention of Violence (New York: Bantam Books, 1970), chap. 17.

**76** President's Commission on Law Enforcement and Administration of Justice, *The Challenge of Crime in a Free Society* (Washington: Government Printing Office, 1967).

**77** President's Commission on Law Enforcement and Administration of Justice, *Task Force Report: The Police* (Washington: Government Printing Office, 1967).

**78** National Advisory Commission on Civil Disorders, *Report*, p. 301.

**79** Ibid.

**80** O. W. Wilson, ed., *Parker on Police* (Springfield, Ill.: Charles C. Thomas, 1957).

**81** American Bar Association, *Standards Relating to the Urban Police Function*, 2d ed. (Boston: Little, Brown, 1980), p. 1–99.

**82** Samuel Walker, "Origins of the Contemporary Criminal Justice Paradigm: The American Bar Foundation Survey, 1953–1969," *Justice Quarterly* 9 (March 1992): 47–76.

**83** Albert Reiss, *The Police and the Public* (New Haven: Yale University Press, 1971).

**84** George L. Kelling et al., *The Kansas City Preventive Patrol Experiment* (Washington: The Police Foundation, 1974).

**85** U.S. Department of Justice, *Response Time Analysis* (Washington: Government Printing Office, 1978).

**86** Peter Greenwood, *The Criminal Investigation Process* (Santa Monica, Calif.: Rand, 1975).

**87** William A. Westley, *Violence and the Police* (Cambridge: MIT Press, 1970).

**88** Jerome Skolnick, *Justice without Trial: Law Enforcement in a Democratic Society*, 3d ed. (New York: Macmillan, 1994).

**89** Robert M. Fogelson, *Big City Police* (Cambridge: Harvard University Press, 1977), pp. 269–295.

**90** Samuel Walker, "Between Two Worlds: The President's Crime Commission and the Police, 1967–1992," in *The 1967 President's Crime Commission Report: Its Impact 25 Years Later*, John A. Conley, ed. (Cincinnati: Anderson Publishing, 1994), pp. 21–35.

**91** National Advisory Commission on Civil Disorders, *Report*, pp. 321–322.

**92** Samuel Walker and K. B. Turner, *A Decade of Modest Progress* (Omaha: University of Nebraska at Omaha, 1992); Bureau of Justice Statistics, *Law Enforcement Management and Administrative Statistics, 1993* (Washington: Government Printing Office, 1995). Dulaney, *Black Police in America*.

**93** Susan E. Martin, *Women on the Move: The Status of Women in Policing* (Washington: The Police Foundation, 1990). Walker and Turner, *A Decade of Modest Progress*. Schulz, *From Social Worker to Crimefighter*.

**94** Peter B. Bloch and Deborah Anderson, *Policewomen on Patrol: Final Report* (Washington: The Police Foundation, 1974).

**95** David L. Carter, Allen Sapp, and Darrel Stephens, *The State of Police Education* (Washington: PERF, 1989).

**96** International Association of Directors of Law Enforcement Standards and Training, *Sourcebook of Standards and Training Information* (Charlotte: University of North Carolina at Charlotte, 1993); Bureau of Justice Statistics, *Law Enforcement Management and Administrative Statistics, 1993*.

**97** Samuel Walker, "Historical Roots of the Legal Control of Police Behavior, " in *Police Innovation and the Rule of Law*, David Weisburd and Craig Uchida, eds. (New York: Springer, 1991), pp. 32–55.

**98** Samuel Walker, *Taming the System: The Control of Discretion in Criminal Justice, 1950–1990* (New York: Oxford University Press, 1993).

**99** James J. Fyfe, "Administrative Interventions on Police Shooting Discretion: An Empirical Analysis," *Journal of Criminal Justice* 7 (Winter 1979): 309–323.

**100** William A. Geller and Michael Scott, *Deadly Force: What We Know* (Washington: Police Executive Research Forum, 1992).

**101** Lawrence W. Sherman, *Policing Domestic Violence* (New York: The Free Press, 1992).

**102** Commission Accreditation For Law Enforcement, *Standards for Law Enforcement Agencies*, 3d ed. (Fairfax, VA: CALEA, 1994).

**103** Hervey A. Juris and Peter Feuille, *Police Unions* (Lexington, Mass.: Lexington Books, 1973).

**104** Samuel Walker and Betsy Wright, *Citizen Review of the Police, 1994: A National Survey* (Washington: PERF, 1995).

**105** Andrew Goldsmith, *Complaints against the Police: The Trend to External Review* (Oxford, England: Clarendon Press, 1991).

**106** Jack R. Greene and Stephen D. Mastrofski, eds., *Community Policing: Rhetoric or Reality* (New York: Praeger, 1991).

**107** Lawrence W. Sherman, *Team Policing: Seven Case Studies* (Washington: The Police Foundation, 1973; Samuel Walker, "Does Anyone Remember Team Policing? Lessons of the Team Policing Experiment for Community Policing," *American Journal of Police* 12, no. 1 (1993): 33–55.

**108** James Q. Wilson and George L. Kelling, "Broken Windows: The Police and Neighborhood Safety," *Atlantic Monthly* 249 (March 1982): 29–38.

**109** Herman Goldstein, "Improving Policing: A Problem–Oriented Approach," *Crime and Delinquency* 25 (April 1979): 236–258.

**110** John E. Eck and William Spelman, *Problem-Solving: Problem-Oriented Policing in Newport News* (Washington: PERF, 1987)

**111** Jerome E. McElroy, Colleen A. Cosgrove, and Susan Saad, *Community Policing: CPOP in New York* (Newbury Park, Calif.: Sage, 1992).

**112** George L. Kelling and Catherine M. Coles, *Fixing Broken Windows* (New York: Free Press, 1996). William Bratton and Peter Knobler, *Turnaround* (New York: Random House, 1998).

**113** George L. Kelling, "Police and Communities: The Quiet Revolution," *Perspectives in Policing* (Washington: Government Printing Office, 1988).

**114** David H. Bayley, *Police for the Future* (New York: Oxford University Press, 1994), p. 101.

**115** Ibid.

**116** Robin N. Haarr, "Patterns of Interaction in a Police Patrol Bureau: Race and Gender Barriers to Integration," *Justice Quarterly*, 14 (March 1997): 53–85.

**117** Stephen D. Mastrofski, "The Prospects of Change in Police Patrol: A Decade in Review," *American Journal of Police* 9, no. 3 (1990): 62.

# CHAPTER 3

# THE CONTEMPORARY LAW ENFORCEMENT INDUSTRY

## OVERVIEW OF LAW ENFORCEMENT

### Basic Features of American Law Enforcement

Law enforcement in the United States is a large and extremely complex enterprise. There are over 18,000 federal, state, and local agencies, along with a private security industry that employs over a million additional people.

Several basic features characterize the law enforcement industry. Most important is the tradition of local political control. The primary responsibility for police protection rests with local governments: cities and counties. This tradition was inherited from England during the colonial period (see Chapter 2).

As a result, American policing is highly fragmented.[1] There is no formal, centralized system for coordinating or regulating all the different agencies. There are some mechanisms for federal and state regulation of local police. They are discussed later in this chapter.

Fragmentation produces tremendous variety. Police services are provided by four different levels of government: city, county, state, and federal. Agencies at each level have very different roles and responsibilities. Within each category, moreover, there is tremendous variety. The six largest police departments—New York City, Chicago, Los Angeles, Houston, Philadelphia, and Detroit—are very different from the 6,309 police departments with fewer than 25 officers.[2]

As a result of this variety, it is very difficult to generalize about American policing. All police departments have some characteristics in common, but generalizations about the *typical* police department are extremely risky. Writing about the county sheriff, David N. Falcone and L. Edward Wells reject the common assumption that "policing is policing," and argue that the sheriff "represents an historically different mode of policing that needs to be distinguished more clearly from municipal policing."[3]

### An Industry Perspective

Because of its fragmentation and variety, it is useful to take an industry perspective on American law enforcement. This approach provides a comprehensive picture of all the different producers of police services in a particular area.[4]

---

**SIDEBAR 3–1**

BASIC SOURCES ON LAW ENFORCEMENT AGENCIES

The most comprehensive source of data on American law enforcement agencies is the report from the Bureau of Justice Statistics (BJS), *Law Enforcement Management and Administrative Statistics.* The most recent report is for 1993. BJS intends to conduct new surveys every two or three years. Look for the latest report.

Additional data can be found in the FBI's *Uniform Crime Reports* published annually.

Many law enforcement agencies now maintain their own web sites which provide information about organizational structure and current programs.

---

The industry approach also provides a consumer's perspective on policing. On a typical day, the average citizen receives police services from several different agencies. Consider the case of Mr. and Mrs. Smith. Their suburban neighborhood is patrolled by the small local police department. Mrs. Smith works downtown where she is served by the big-city police department. Mr. Smith is a sales representative and drives through small towns and areas patrolled by the county sheriff. The office building where Mrs. Smith works hires private security guards. On his way home, Mr. Smith drives on the interstate highway which is patrolled by the state patrol. Meanwhile, the Federal Bureau of Investigation (FBI), the Drug Enforcement Agency (DEA), and other federal agencies are at work investigating various violations of federal law.

Figure 3–1 indicates the various components of the law enforcement industry.

### An International Perspective

A quick look at law enforcement in other countries provides a useful perspective on the decentralization and fragmentation of American law enforcement.

England, with a population one-fourth the size of the United States has 43 police departments: 41 provincial departments and 2 police forces in London. This is half the number of law enforcement agencies in the state of Nebraska (total of 93). All 43 agencies

**FIGURE 3–1**
COMPONENTS OF THE AMERICAN LAW ENFORCEMENT INDUSTRY

---

**Government Agencies**
*Local*
  Municipal police
  County police
  County sheriffs
*State*
  State police
  Bureaus of criminal investigation
*Federal*
  Federal law enforcement agencies
  Military law enforcement
*Special district police*
  Public schools
  Transit police
  College and university police
*Native-American tribal police*

**Private Security**
  Private security firms
  Security personnel

---

are administered by the home secretary, who is one of the top officials in the national government (and in some respects the equivalent of the attorney general in the United States). Each provincial department also answers to a local police commission. The home secretary has the power to issue administrative regulations on personnel and police operations. Additionally, each of the 43 police departments receives 51 percent of its annual budget from the home secretary's officer, giving it the power to enforce regulations.[5]

The Japanese police system also balances central coordination with local control. The National Police Agency is responsible for coordinating the operations of the 47 prefectural police. Each prefecture is officially independent, but the National Police Agency can recommend operational standards and, as in England, provides a significant part of each local agency's budget.[6]

## A DEFINITION OF TERMS

### What Is a Law Enforcement Agency?

What do we mean when we talk about a police or law enforcement agency? The question is not as simple as it might seem. Many different kinds of government agencies have some responsibility for enforcing the law and/or providing protection: state game and parks departments, federal agencies such as the U.S. Supreme Court, police, and some college campus police.

This book focuses only on *general service* law enforcement agencies: those that are regularly engaged in (1) preventing crime, (2) investigating crimes and apprehending criminals, (3) maintaining order, and (4) providing other miscellaneous services.

This definition excludes many government regulatory agencies whose personnel often have law enforcement powers. It excludes investigatory and prosecutorial agencies, such as state bureaus of criminal investigation, coroner's offices, and constables. It also excludes correctional agencies even though in many states their officers are legally peace officers with arrest powers.

### Who Is a Police Officer?

The term *police officer* is often used interchangeably with *peace officer*. There is an important distinction, however. All police officers are peace officers, but all peace officers are not police officers. In some states, corrections officials are defined as peace officers, but we do not regard them as police officers. The legal status of peace officer is defined by statute. Iowa law, for example, designates eight categories of peace officer, the last coming under the catchall phrase "all other persons so designated." California law gives peace officer status to more than 30 different occupations.

Peace officer status grants certain powers and provides certain legal protections that ordinary citizens do not have. Under the English common law standard, all citizens have the power to make a "citizen's arrest." Private citizens can also shoot to kill under certain limited circumstances. Sworn peace officers, however, have broader power in taking these actions and have somewhat greater protection from liability when they are acting "in good faith" in carrying out an official duty.

## SIZE AND SCOPE OF THE LAW ENFORCEMENT INDUSTRY

### The Number of Law Enforcement Agencies

There are over 18,000 law enforcement agencies in the United States. This includes 12,361 local police, 3,084 sheriff's departments, 49 state police agencies, 1,626 special district police agencies, and 19 federal agencies that employ 500 or more sworn officers (Table 3–1).[7]

**The Myth of 40,000 Agencies**   For many years there was great controversy over exactly how many law enforcement agencies exist in the United States. In 1967 the President's Crime Commission incorrectly reported that there were 40,000 agencies, repeating an unconfirmed figure that had been used for years.[8] The correct figure is about 18,000 agencies.

The typical police department is very small. As Table 3–2 indicates, half (51.6 percent) have nine or fewer sworn officers. The 76 largest departments, which represent less than 1 percent of the departments, employ 39 percent of all sworn officers.

### The Number of Law Enforcement Personnel

In 1993 there were 622,913 full-time sworn law enforcement officers employed by local and state law enforcement agencies (Table 3–1). In addition there were 68,825 federal law enforcement officers authorized to carry firearms and make arrests (this figure, however, does not include military law enforcement personnel).[9] The number of state and local officers has grown since 1993. The 1994 Violent Crime Control Act provides federal funds to hire 100,000 new officers. By 1997 about 70,000 of those officers had been hired.[10]

**TABLE 3–1**
EMPLOYMENT BY STATE AND LOCAL LAW ENFORCEMENT AGENCIES
IN THE UNITED STATES, 1993

| Type of Agency | Number of agencies | Number of employees | | | | | |
| --- | --- | --- | --- | --- | --- | --- | --- |
| | | Full-time | | | Part-time | | |
| | | Total | Sworn | Civilian | Total | Sworn | Civilian |
| Total | 17,120 | 828,435 | 622,913 | 205,522 | 87,875 | 42,890 | 44,985 |
| Local police | 12,361 | 474,072 | 373,554 | 100,518 | 58,146 | 28,186 | 29,960 |
| Sheriff | 3,084 | 224,236 | 155,815 | 68,421 | 19,660 | 11,048 | 8,612 |
| State police | 49 | 76,972 | 51,874 | 25,098 | 845 | 228 | 617 |
| Special police | 1,626 | 53,156 | 41,670 | 11,485 | 9,224 | 3,428 | 5,796 |

*Note:* Consolidated police-sheriff agencies are included under the local police category.
The special police category includes both state-level and local-level agencies.
Data are for the pay period that included June 30, 1993.
*Source:* Bureau of Justice Statistics, *Local Police Departments, 1993* (Washington, DC: Government Printing Office, 1995), p.1.

**TABLE 3–2**
LOCAL POLICE DEPARTMENTS, BY NUMBER OF SWORN PERSONNEL, 1993

| Number of sworn personnel* | Agencies | | Full-time sworn personnel | |
|---|---|---|---|---|
| | Number | Percent | Number | Percent |
| Total | 12,361 | 100 | 373,554 | 100 |
| 1,000 or more | 38 | 0.3 | 118,460 | 31.7 |
| 500–999 | 38 | 0.3 | 27,351 | 7.3 |
| 250–499 | 86 | 0.7 | 29,344 | 7.9 |
| 100–249 | 326 | 2.6 | 46,983 | 12.6 |
| 50–99 | 692 | 5.6 | 45,779 | 12.3 |
| 25–49 | 1,443 | 11.7 | 45,160 | 12.1 |
| 10–24 | 3,361 | 27.2 | 40,913 | 11.0 |
| 5–9 | 2,940 | 23.8 | 13,906 | 3.7 |
| 2–4 | 2,587 | 20.9 | 5,065 | 1.4 |
| 1 | 851 | 6.9 | 594 | 0.2 |

*Note:* Detail may not add to total because of rounding.
*Includes both full-time and part-time employees.

### Understanding Law Enforcement Personnel Data

There is often much confusion about law enforcement personnel data. The important question is, How much police protection does a community receive? The *total number of employees* includes clerical staff and civilian specialists in computers, criminalistics, and so on. The *number of sworn officers* refers to those employees who are legally recognized as police officers, with full arrest power and so on.

It is also important to distinguish between an agency's authorized strength and the number of sworn officers *currently employed*. Because of retirements, resignations, and terminations, most departments are below their authorized strength. The annual average attrition rate is about 5 percent.[11] Hiring is often delayed as a way of allowing the city or county to cope with a budget shortfall.[12]

Thus, if you want to know the level of police protection in Cleveland, for example, you need to determine the number of full-time sworn officers currently employed.

### Civilianization

Civilianization is the process of replacing sworn officers with nonsworn personnel for certain positions. In 1993, 24.7 percent of all local police department employees were civilians. This represents an increase from 15.2 percent in 1970 and 20 percent in 1980. Nonsworn personnel have been increasingly used as dispatchers, research and planning specialists, crime data analysts, and computer technicians.[13]

There are several reasons for utilizing civilians in police work. First, they free sworn officers for critical police work that requires a trained and experienced officer. Second, they possess needed expertise in such areas as computers or data analysis. Third, in many cases they are less expensive than sworn officers, thereby representing a cost saving.[14] Following the views of many experts, Milner used the percentage of civilian employees as one of eight indices of professionalization in his study of four Wisconsin police departments.[15]

### The Police/Population Ratio

The standard measure for the level of police protection in a community is the police/population ratio, expressed as the number of sworn officers per thousand population. In 1993 the national average was 2.1 sworn officers per thousand. The ratio for large cities with populations of one million or more was 2.6. Small cities (population 50,000–99,999) had the lowest ratio (1.7 per 1,000).[16]

There is tremendous variation in the police/population ratios among big cities. Washington, DC, has a ratio of 7.0/1,000, compared with 3.8 in Detroit, and 1.7 in San Diego.[17] There is no clear relationship between the police/population ratio and the crime rate. In many respects, instead of higher levels of police protection producing lower crime rates, higher crime rates lead to the employment of more police.[18] The relationship of the police population ratio to the crime rate is discussed in detail in Chapter 4.

### The Cost of Police Protection

Law enforcement is an extremely expensive enterprise. In 1993, government agencies spent a total of $44 billion on police services. This represented about 44 percent of all criminal justice system expenditures. These figures do not, however, include the cost of private security. The cost of police protection increased 172.5 percent between 1980 and 1992. Expenditures for corrections increased more than twice as fast (355.9 percent) in the same period, mainly as a result of the soaring prison population.[19]

Law enforcement is a labor-intensive industry. Personnel costs, including salaries and fringe benefits, consume about 85 to 90 percent of an agency's budget. For this reason, the efficiency of a police department depends heavily on how well it manages its personnel and what percentage of officers it places in patrol and investigative units (see Chapter 4).

### MUNICIPAL POLICE

Municipal or city police are the most important component of American law enforcement. In 1993 they represented 72 percent of all law enforcement agencies and employed 57 percent of all sworn officers.[20]

Even more important, municipal police play a more complex role than any other type of law enforcement agency. All agencies are heavily influenced by their external environments.[21] Cities, and big cities in particular, represent the most complex environments, particularly in terms of the diversity of the population. City police departments have the heaviest responsibility for dealing with serious crime, which is disproportionately concentrated in the cities. They are also responsible for difficult order maintenance problems and are asked to provide a wide range of emergency services.[22]

Among all municipal police departments, a few very large departments play a disproportionately important role. A 1991 Police Foundation report on the big six police departments—New York City, Los Angeles, Chicago, Houston, Philadelphia, Detroit—found that they are responsible for 7.5 percent of the U.S. population but face 23 percent of all violent crime in the country, including 34 percent of all robberies.[23] Although these six represent a tiny fraction of all departments, they employ almost 13 percent of all sworn officers. The New York City Police Department towers over all others, with 38,000 sworn officers in 1997. Chicago is second with 12,000 officers.

The big departments dominate public thinking about the police. Events in New York City or Los Angeles—the Rodney King case, for example—are reported by the national news media. Moreover, a disproportionate amount of the research on policing has been conducted in New York City, Chicago, Los Angeles, Philadelphia, Boston, and Washington. Much less is known about medium-sized police departments, and almost no research has been done on small departments, even though they are more representative of policing in America.

The typical municipal police department is very small. Slightly more than half (51 percent) employ fewer than 10 sworn officers. Small town and rural police operate in a very different context than big-city police. There is less serious crime than in urban areas. The majority of calls for police service involve noncriminal events and minor disturbances.[24] In one study, traffic problems accounted for 25 percent of all calls; public disturbances accounted for 19 percent; family disturbances represented 18 percent; and stray dogs another 11 percent. (The remaining 27 percent were miscellaneous calls.)[25]

**County Police**    A few areas are served by county police departments. They are essentially municipal police that operate on a countywide basis, but do not have any of the non-law enforcement roles of the county sheriff (see below). Only about 1 percent of all local departments are county police. The largest are the Nassau County police (2,700 sworn officers) and the Suffolk County police (2,400 sworn).[26]

## THE COUNTY SHERIFF

There are 3,084 sheriff's departments in the United States.[27] The county sheriff's office is unique among American law enforcement agencies, in terms of both its legal status and its role.[28]

The legal status of the sheriff is unique because in 37 states it is a constitutional office whose responsibilities are defined in the state constitution. Also, sheriffs are elected in all but two states. (In Rhode Island they are appointed by the governor; in Hawaii they are appointed by the chief justice of the state supreme court.) As elected officials, sheriffs are directly involved in partisan politics in ways that municipal police chiefs are not. Historically, in rural areas the sheriff was the most powerful politician in the county.[29]

## The Role of the Sheriff

Sheriffs have a unique role because they serve all three components of the criminal justice system: law enforcement, courts, and corrections. As Table 3–3 indicates, almost all sheriff's departments perform the basic law enforcement functions of receiving calls for service, patrolling, and investigating crimes. Almost all serve the courts by process serving (subpoenas, etc.) and providing security for the courts. In many urban areas, sheriffs spend more time on civil court duties than on criminal law enforcement.

Only 79 percent of all sheriff's departments still maintain the county jail. In most big cities the jail is operated by a separate department of corrections.

Lee Brown identified four different models of sheriff's departments according to their responsibilities. (1) Full-service model sheriffs departments carry out law enforcement, judicial, and correctional duties. (2) Law enforcement model agencies carry out only law enforcement duties, with other responsibilities assumed by separate agencies. (3) Civil–judicial model agencies handle only court-related duties (e.g., counties in Connecticut and Rhode Island). (4) Correctional-judicial model agencies (e.g., San Francisco County) handle all responsibilities except law enforcement.[30]

The distribution of sheriff's departments resembles that of the municipal police. There are a few very large departments, and many small ones. The largest is the Los Angeles County Sheriff's Department, which had 7,629 sworn officers in 1993. About 31 percent of all sheriff's departments, however, have fewer than 10 sworn officers.[31]

## OTHER LOCAL AGENCIES

The American law enforcement picture is complicated by the existence of other local agencies that have some law enforcement responsibilities.

**The Constable**    Like the sheriff, the constable is an office whose roots can be traced back to colonial America (see Chapter 1). Urbanization and the consequent growth of city departments have stripped the constable's office of most of its functions. The Advisory Commission on Intergovernmental Relations found it to be "of minor importance" and recommended its abolition.[32]

**TABLE 3–3**
RESPONSIBILITIES OF SHERIFF'S DEPARTMENTS, 1993

| Function | Percent of agencies |
|---|---|
| Routine patrol | 88 |
| Receiving calls for service | 91 |
| Crime investigation | 92 |
| Process serving | 97 |
| Court security | 93 |
| Jail operations | 79 |
| Enforcing traffic laws | 77 |
| Accident investigation | 69 |

*Source:* Adapted from Bureau of Justice Statistics, *Sheriff's Departments, 1993* (Washington, DC: Government Printing Office, 1996), p. iv.

**The Coroner**   The office of the coroner, or medical examiner, is often considered a law enforcement agency because it has the responsibility to investigate crimes. A 1980 Department of Justice survey found a total of 1,683 coroners or medical examiners.[33]

**Special District Police**   Special district police agencies serve particular government agencies. The Los Angeles School District, for example, has its own police force. Some urban transit systems maintain separate law enforcement agencies.[34] The Metropolitan Transit Police Force in the Washington, DC, subway system overlaps three different political jurisdictions: the District of Columbia, Virginia, and Maryland.[35] The New York City Transit Police were merged with the New York City Police Department several years ago, and the Los Angeles police have acquired responsibility for policing the city's buses and subways.

**Campus Police**   College and university campus police are an important example of special district police.[36] About three-fourths of the campus security forces at colleges and universities with 2,500 or more students are state-certified law enforcement agencies. Their officers have general arrest powers, are certified by the state, and participate in the FBI's Uniform Crime Reports (UCR) system. In 1995 they employed about 11,000 full-time sworn officers. The other colleges and universities use private security or their own nonsworn security officers.[37]

## NATIVE-AMERICAN TRIBAL POLICE

A unique aspect of American criminal justice is that many Native-American tribes maintain their own separate criminal justice systems, including tribal police departments, on their reservations. Native-American tribes are separate nations, which signed

---

**SIDEBAR 3–2**

GETTING TO KNOW YOUR CAMPUS POLICE

**1** Is your campus police agency a certified law enforcement agency?

**2** If so, what state-mandated training do they receive? How many hours of training? What is the content of the curriculum? Who provides the training?

**3** If it is not, what are the recruitment standards? What kinds of training do officers receive? Who provides the training?

**4** If your campus police agency is a certified law enforcement agency, and does it file the required UCR report?

**5** If not, does it file an annual crime report anyway?

**6** Are your campus police armed? What kinds of training in firearms use do they receive? What retraining or recertification are they required to receive?

**7** Does your campus police agency have a written deadly force policy? What does that policy say? (See Chapter 11 on deadly force policies.)

---

treaties with the United States government and which retain a significant degree of legal autonomy. In a number of important respects, tribes and reservations are not subject to federal or state law.[38]

There are over 500 Native-American tribes, which include about 1.9 million enrolled members. The exact number of tribal police departments is not known. Tribal affairs have historically been the responsibility of the Bureau of Indian Affairs (BIA) which is located in the U.S. Department of the Interior. The BIA has maintained its own police force. The number of tribal police is growing, mainly as a result of the 1994 Tribal Self-Government Act. In 1995 the U.S. Department of Justice established the Office of Tribal Justice to coordinate relations between tribal governments and the various federal agencies with respect to criminal justice issues.[39]

## STATE LAW ENFORCEMENT AGENCIES

State law enforcement agencies fall into three categories: state police, highway patrols, and state investigative agencies. This book will focus on the first two, because they are regarded as general service law enforcement agencies.[40]

State police are defined as agencies "having statewide police powers for both traffic regulation and criminal investigations." Highway patrols are defined as agencies having "statewide authority to enforce traffic regulations and arrest non-traffic violators under their jurisdiction. . . ."[41]

There are 49 general service state law enforcement agencies in the United States; Hawaii is the only state without one. These agencies are divided about equally between state police and highway patrol. Several states have more than one law enforcement agency. California, for example, maintains both the California Highway Patrol and the California Division of Law Enforcement. Ohio has both the Ohio Highway Patrol and the Ohio Bureau of Criminal Identification and Investigation. The roles and missions of state law enforcement agencies are defined by state law and, hence, vary widely from state to state.

There is considerable variation in the administrative structure of state law enforcement agencies. One report found that "almost every possibility" exists. Several states have an umbrella agency containing a number of different departments responsible for various services. The New Jersey Department of Public Safety includes eight divisions: Division of Law, State Police, Division of Motor Vehicles, Division of Alcoholic Beverage Control, Division of Criminal Justice, Division of Consumer Affairs, Police Training Commission, and State Athletic Commissioner.

### Roles and Responsibilities

State police and highway patrol provide a variety of different law enforcement services. In terms of patrol, state police have concurrent or shared responsibilities with local police agencies. In about half the states, the state police or highway patrol agency has the primary responsibility for enforcing traffic laws on the main highways.[42]

State laws vary regarding responsibility for criminal investigation. In some states, the state police have general responsibility; in others, the investigative powers are limited.

About half of all state agencies provide crime lab services (ballistics, drug testing) for local police departments. Finally, 77.6 percent of state police agencies operate a training academy. In some states, they are responsible for training recruits from local police departments.[43]

## FEDERAL LAW ENFORCEMENT AGENCIES

The federal component of the law enforcement industry is relatively small, but more complex than is generally recognized. In 1996 there were an estimated 74,500 full-time federal law enforcement employees. This figure includes all personnel "authorized to carry firearms and make arrests." It does not include military police, however.[44]

There is no agreement about the exact size of federal law enforcement activities. The confusion is due to the fact that many federal agencies have enforcement or regulatory powers. Most are not general service agencies, as defined above, and do not provide the basic services of protection and criminal investigation.

Seventeen federal law enforcement agencies employ 500 or more sworn officers. The Immigration and Naturalization service is the largest, with about 12,000 officers in 1996. The Federal Bureau of Prisons and the F.B.I. are the next largest with about 11,000 officers each. The DEA employs about 3,000 officers. The complexity and variety of federal law enforcement is indicated by the fact that the largest agencies include the U.S. Fish and Wildlife Service (869 officers) and the U.S. Forest Service (619 officers).[45]

### Roles and Responsibilities

The role of each federal agency is specified by federal statute. Federal agencies have far less complex roles than those of municipal agencies. They do not have the ambiguous and difficult order maintenance responsibilities, do not maintain 911 emergency telephone services, and are not asked to handle vague disturbance calls.

The role of the FBI has historically been shaped by administrative and political factors. Under J. Edgar Hoover (1924-1972), the FBI concentrated its efforts on investigating alleged "subversives" and apprehending bank robbers and stolen cars. Critics charged that the FBI ignored white-collar crime, organized crime, and violations of the civil rights of minorities. After Hoover's death it was discovered that, under his direction, the FBI had committed many violations of citizens' constitutional rights: It was guilty of spying on individuals and groups because of their political beliefs, conducting illegal wiretaps, and even burglarizing the offices of the groups it was spying on.[46]

Since Hoover died, subsequent FBI directors have reoriented the bureau's mission, putting more emphasis on white-collar crime, organized crime, and political corruption. The bureau has been more responsive to the general law enforcement policies of the current presidential administration.[47]

## THE PRIVATE SECURITY INDUSTRY

Private security is an important part of American law enforcement. Its exact size is difficult to determine because it involves many small, private agencies, part-time employees, and security personnel that are employed by private businesses. A 1991

Justice Department survey estimated that 1.5 million people are employed in private security. This figure includes the following jobs: proprietary (in-house) security, guard and patrol services, alarm services, private investigators, armored car services, the manufacturers of security equipment, locksmiths, and consultants and engineers. About 1.1 million people are employed strictly in guard and patrol services.[48]

The size of the private security industry raises a number of important issues. The first is the quality of private security personnel. Requirements for employment are minimal and, in many cases, training is nonexistent. One survey found that the typical guard receives between four to six hours of training.[49] Private security is often a last resort for people unable to find other jobs. Several states have adopted minimum recruitment and training standards and guidelines for private security personnel. Most state laws, however, cover only firearms training and certification. There has been a movement toward enacting laws to require training and certification.

Second, there are problems related to cooperation between public and private police. The Philadelphia Center City District, established in 1990, represents a unique collaboration between the municipal police and private security to improve the quality of life in the downtown business district of the city.[50]

Third, there are equity problems. Wealthy neighborhoods are able to purchase additional protection, whereas poor neighborhoods receive less protection because financially strapped city governments are unable to hire more police.

Finally, there are issues of civil liberties. Supreme Court decisions such as *Miranda* apply to public police. A Justice Department report, however, points out that private security officers are not bound by these decisions, and that many employers do not provide their security officers with adequate training in complex legal issues.[51]

## THE FRAGMENTATION ISSUE

In 1967 the President's Crime Commission concluded that "a fundamental problem confronting law enforcement today is that of fragmented crime repression efforts resulting from the large number of uncoordinated local governments and law enforcement agencies."[52]

The commission published a map of the Detroit metropolitan area indicating the 85 agencies in the area. As Figure 3–2 indicates, almost half of these agencies had 20 or fewer officers ("men" in the now outdated language of the times).

The first problem, according to the critics, is a lack of coordination between agencies in the same geographic area. Criminals do not respect political boundaries. In a large metropolitan area, a burglar may commit crimes in several different communities, each with its own police force. Auto-theft rings are often multistate operations. Detectives in one police department may have information that would help solve a series of crimes in a neighboring jurisdiction. In many instances, agencies compete rather than cooperate with one another.

Second, fragmentation of responsibility can also lead to crime displacement, especially with respect to vice crimes. One community may adopt a policy of strict enforcement of laws against gambling or prostitution. This often has the effect of driving vice activities to a neighboring jurisdiction where different community standards exist.

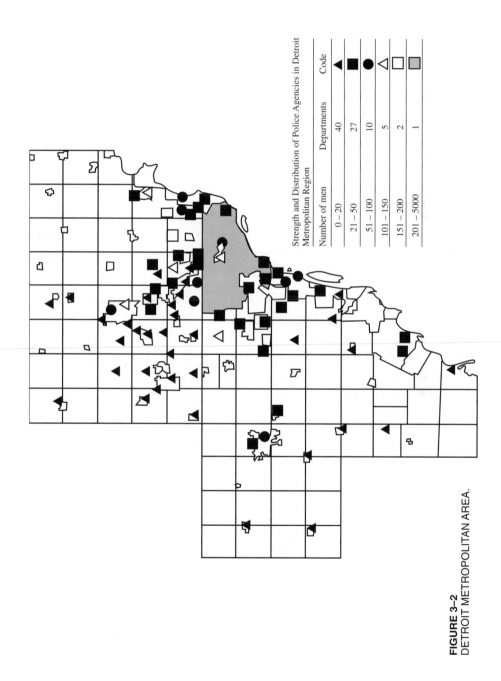

Strength and Distribution of Police Agencies in Detroit Metropolitan Region

| Number of men | Departments | Code |
|---------------|-------------|------|
| 0 – 20 | 40 | ◀ |
| 21 – 50 | 27 | ■ |
| 51 – 100 | 10 | ● |
| 101 – 150 | 5 | ◁ |
| 151 – 200 | 2 | ▢ |
| 201 – 5000 | 1 | ▨ |

**FIGURE 3–2**
DETROIT METROPOLITAN AREA.

Third, many experts believe that there is a serious problem of duplication of services, with the resulting increase in costs. A city police department and the local sheriff's department may operate their own 911 telephone systems and their own training academies. Several agencies in the same area may operate their own crime laboratories.

Fourth, fragmentation leads to inconsistent standards. Law enforcement agencies in the same area may have very different recruitment standards, training programs, and salary scales.

In countries with a single national police force, uniform standards are established at the national level. In England, which has a tradition of local control of the police, minimum national standards are achieved through a process of inspection and financial incentives. Each of the 45 local police constabularies is inspected annually by the home office.

### Alternatives to Fragmentation

The fragmentation problem is not easily solved. The independence of local governments is deeply rooted in American history. The principle of local control, not just of police but of schools and other government services, is deeply rooted in American political culture. There has always been a very strong fear of a national police force and suspicion of federal control of schools and police. The major remedies for fragmentation include the following.

**Consolidation**   Some experts argue that small agencies should be consolidated into larger ones.[53] The National Advisory Commission on Criminal Justice Standards and Goals recommended the consolidation of all agencies with 10 or fewer sworn officers (or more than half the current total).[54] In a few urban areas, the city police and the sheriff's department have been merged. The Charlotte, North Carolina, and the Mecklenburg County Sheriff's Department, for example, were merged in the early 1990s. Some cities, meanwhile, have combined police and fire departments into a single agency.[55]

Consolidation of police and sheriff's departments has made little progress, however. Both are large bureaucracies that do not want to give up their autonomy. Also, there are

---

**SIDEBAR 3–3**

EXERCISE: STUDYING THE FRAGMENTATION PROBLEM IN YOUR AREA

1 Prepare a map and accompanying table indicating the number of law enforcement agencies in your metropolitan area, the names of these agencies, and the number of sworn officers in each.
2 Research the nature of any contract or collaborative arrangements between these agencies (e.g., shared communications systems, jail services, etc.)

practical problems related to merging different entrance requirements, salary schedules, and pension systems.

**Contracting**    A second alternative to fragmentation is for small agencies to contract with larger agencies for specific services. About half of all cities and counties contract with other governmental units for various services. These contracts cover everything from sewage disposal to tax assessment and water supply. The most common criminal justice services include jails and detention facilities and police-fire communications systems.[56] In many cases, the county sheriff maintains the 911 service for small towns in the area. In other cases, small towns contract with the sheriff for all police services. The Los Angeles County Sheriff, for example, contracts with about 40 separate towns. Because of consolidation, the number of police departments has been declining. Nearly a thousand disappeared in the 1970s.[57]

### The Fragmentation Problem Reconsidered

Some experts believe the fragmentation problem may not be as serious as others have argued. The Police Services Study (PSS) undertook the first systematic research on the issue in the 1970s, examining the activities of 1,827 law enforcement agencies in 80 medium-sized metropolitan areas. Contrary to the traditional image of fragmentation, the study found that "informal interagency assistance is common" and "strict duplication of services is almost nonexistent in the production of direct police services."[58]

With respect to patrol, for example, informal arrangements involving coordination, sharing, or alternating responsibility were common. No areas were left completely unpatrolled and no areas were being patrolled by two or more agencies. With respect to auxiliary services, small police departments routinely had access to crime laboratories, training academies, communications systems, and other services provided by larger agencies.

Even more important, the PSS concluded that small police departments were not necessarily less efficient than large departments. Small departments put a higher percentage of their officers on the street, performing direct police services. Larger departments did not necessarily achieve any advantages of scale.[59] Larger agencies had more complex bureaucratic structures, with the result that a smaller percentage of officers are available for direct police services. Gary Cordner found that among Maryland agencies the complexity of the community social structure, not the size of the agency, was most important in determining the effectiveness of criminal investigation: the less complex the community, the more effective the police.[60]

Finally, the emphasis on decentralized policing under community policing suggests that small local law enforcement agencies might be preferable to large consolidated agencies.[61]

### MINIMUM STANDARDS: AMERICAN STYLE

Unlike most other countries, the United States does not have a national police system. There is no federal agency responsible for supervising local agencies or ensuring minimum standards. In England each local department receives half its budget from the national government and undergoes a regular inspection as part of the process.[62] Nonetheless, some minimum standards for law enforcement agencies in the United States are required by federal and state governments. The process for developing and enforcing these standards, however, is not systematic.

### The Role of the Federal Government

The most important set of national standards are the decisions of the U.S. Supreme Court related to police procedures. Decisions such as *Mapp v. Ohio*, *Miranda v. Arizona*, and *Tennessee v. Garner* set minimum national standards based on provisions of the U.S. Constitution. Beginning in the 1960s, these and other Supreme Court decisions were a major instrument of reform, forcing departments to significantly improve personnel standards and management and supervision.[63]

Relying on the Supreme Court to define minimum standards for police has serious limitations, however. First, most aspects of policing do not raise issues of constitutional law—for example, the length of police academy training or the content of that training. Second, enforcing Supreme Court decisions is extremely difficult. A police department may systematically violate the *Miranda* requirement; it is enforced only when someone is convicted and then appeals that conviction on the basis of the *Miranda* decision.[64]

Congress has passed a number of laws that directly apply to state and local law enforcement agencies. Most important is the 1964 Civil Rights Act which prohibits discrimination on the basis of race, color, national origin, religion, or sex. Local and state agencies are forbidden to discriminate in recruitment, promotion, or assignment of officers.[65] The law, however, does not cover many police personnel issues. It does not, for example, establish minimum standards for recruitment or training. No federal law specifies a minimum level of education for police recruits. Nor does any law require a minimum police/population ratio or set standards for patrol operations.

The U.S. Department of Justice also uses grants to encourage changes in policing. The 1994 Violent Crime Control Act provides funds for 100,000 officers. The program is administered through the Office of Community-Oriented Police Services (OCOPS) and money is granted only if the local agency develops a plan for community policing.[66]

### The Role of State Governments

State governments also set minimum standards for police in a number of areas. State supreme courts rule on issues under their state constitutions. State codes of criminal procedure also define what police must do and what they may not do.

The most important role of state governments has been to require the licensing or certification of all sworn officers. In particular, this includes mandatory preservice training. New York and California were pioneers in this area in 1959, and by the 1970s every other state had some kind of certification requirement. Prior to this time, it was not uncommon in small departments for officers to have no preservice training whatsoever.[67]

In a further development of this approach, some states have adopted procedures for delicensing or decertifying police officers. In Florida, for example, when an officer's license is revoked by the state, that person is not eligible to be employed by any other law enforcement agency in the state.[68] In most states, however, it is possible for an officer to be fired by one police department and then to be hired by another.

### Accreditation

A final approach to establishing minimum national standards in policing is through accreditation.[69] Accreditation is a process of professional self-regulation, similar to those that exist in medicine, law, education, and other occupations. The Commission on Accreditation for Law Enforcement Agencies (CALEA) was established in 1979. The third edition of its *Standards for Law Enforcement Agencies* includes 103 separate standards. Some standards are mandatory; while others are only recommended.[70]

The major weakness with accreditation is that it is a voluntary process. Lack of accreditation imposes no penalty on a police department. By comparison, a nonaccredited educational institution is not eligible for certain federal funds, and graduates from nonaccredited institutions find that their credits are not accepted by other schools.[71]

The process of becoming accredited is expensive, in terms of both the formal CALEA fees and the staff time required to meet the various standards.[72] By late 1997, CALEA had accredited 447 agencies, less than 3 percent of the total.

Critics also question the impact of accreditation on police work. Mastrofski suggests that accreditation standards "add[s] to the proliferation of rule in already rule-suffused bureaucracies, without appreciably affecting patterns of police behavior."[73] James J. Fyfe points out that the CALEA standards relate to formal administrative factors, such as having a written policy on a subject, without specifying a "standard of care," in the sense of what police officers should do in specific situations.[74]

In short, American law enforcement agencies must meet *some* minimum standards. These standards cover only a limited range of issues and there is no system for developing and implementing a comprehensive set of standards.

### CONCLUSION

Law enforcement is an extremely complex activity in the United States. The delivery of police services is fragmented among thousands of city, county, state, special district, federal, and private security agencies. There are tremendous differences in the size, role, and activities of these different agencies. Consequently, it is extremely difficult to generalize about the police in America.

### NOTES

1  Elinor Ostrom, Roger Parks, and Gordon P. Whitaker, *Patterns of Metropolitan Policing* (Cambridge Mass.: Ballinger, 1978).
2  Anthony Pate and Edwin E. Hamilton, *The Big Six* (Washington: The Police Foundation, 1991).

3  David N. Falcone and L. Edward Wells, "The County Sheriff as a Distinctive Policing Modality," *American Journal of Police* 14, no. 3/4 (1995): 123–124.
4  Ostrom, Parks, and Whitaker, *Patterns of Metropolitan Policing*.
5  Richard J. Terrill, *World Criminal Justice Systems: A Survey*, 3d ed. (Cincinnati: Anderson, 1997), pp. 12–13.
6  Ibid., pp. 246–248.
7  Bureau of Justice Statistics, *Local Police Departments, 1993* (Washington: Government Printing Office, 1996); Bureau of Justice Statistics, *Federal Law Enforcement Officers, 1996* (Washington: Government Printing Office, 1997).
8  President's Commission on Law Enforcement and Administration of Justice, *The Challenge of Crime in a Free Society* (Washington: Government Printing Office, 1967), p. 91.
9  Bureau of Justice Statistics, *Federal Law Enforcement Officers, 1993*.
10  U.S. Department of Justice, *COPS Office Report* (Washington: Government Printing Office, 1997).
11  President's Commission on Law Enforcement and Administration of Justice, *Task Force Report: The Police* (Washington: Government Printing Office, 1967), p. 9.
12  James J. Fyfe, "Police Personnel Practices, 1986," *Municipal Yearbook, 1987* (Washington, D.C.: ICMA, 1987), p. 17, table 3–2.
13  Bruce L. Heininger and Janine Urbanek, "Civilianization of the American Police: 1970–1980," *Journal of Police Science and Administration* 11 (1983) 200–205; Bureau of Justice Statistics, *Law Enforcement Management and Administrative Statistics, 1993* (Washington: Government Printing Office, 1995).
14  Alfred I. Schwartz, Alease M. Vaughn, John D. Waller, and Joseph S. Wholey, *Employing Civilians for Police Work* (Washington: Urban Institute, 1975).
15  Neal A. Milner, *The Court and Local Law Enforcement* (Beverly Hills, CA: Sage, 1971), pp. 250–251.
16  Bureau of Justice Statistics, *Local Police Departments, 1993*, p. 3.
17  Bureau of Justice Statistics, *Law Enforcement Management and Administrative Statistics, 1993*.
18  Thomas B. Marvell and Carlisle E. Moody, "Specification Problems, Police Levels, and Crime Rates," *Criminology* 34 (November 1996): 609–646.
19  Bureau of Justice Statistics, *Sourcebook of Criminal Justice Statistics—1995* (Washington: Government Printing Office, 1996), p. 3.
20  Bureau of Justice Statistics, *Local Police Departments, 1993*.
21  John P. Crank and Robert Langworthy, "An Institutional Perspective on Policing," *Journal of Criminal Law and Criminology* 83, no. 2 (1992): 341–346.
22  Herman Goldstein, *Policing a Free Society* (Cambridge, Mass.: Ballinger, 1977), pp. 21–44.
23  Anthony Pate and Edwin E. Hamilton, *The Big Six: Policing America's Largest Cities* (Washington: The Police Foundation, 1991).
24  Ralph A. Weisheit, David N. Falcone, and L. Edward Wells, *Crime and Policing in Rural and Small-Town America: An Overview of the Issues* (Washington: Government Printing Office, 1995).
25  John F. Galliher et. al., "Small-Town Police: Troubles, Tasks, and Publics," *Journal of Police Science and Administration* 3 (March 1975): 19–28.
26  Bureau of Justice Statistics, *Law Enforcement Management and Administrative Statistics, 1993*, p. vii.
27  Bureau of Justice Statistics, *Sheriffs' Departments, 1993* (Washington: Government Printing Office, 1996).
28  Falcone and Wells, "The County Sheriff as a Distinctive Policing Modality."

29  National Sheriffs' Association, *County Law Enforcement: Assessment of Capabilities and Needs* (Washington: National Sheriffs' Association, 1976).

30  Lee P. Brown, "The Role of the Sheriff," in *The Future of Policing*, ed. Alvin W. Cohn (Beverly Hills, CA: Sage, 1978), pp. 227–228.

31  Bureau of Justice Statistics, *Sheriffs' Departments, 1993.*

32  U.S. Advisory Commission on Intergovernmental Relations, *State and Local Relations in the Criminal Justice System* (Washington: Government Printing Office, 1971), p. 28.

33  U.S. Department of Justice, *Justice Agencies in the United States: Summary Report, 1980* (Washington: Government Printing Office, 1980).

34  U.S. Department of Justice, *Policing Urban Mass Transit Systems* (Washington: Government Printing Office, 1979).

35  Martin Hannon, "The Metro Transit Police Force: America's First Tri-State, Multi-Jurisdictional Police Force, *FBI Law Enforcement Bulletin* 47 (November 1978): 16–22.

36  John J. Sloan, "The Modern Campus Police: An Analysis of Their Evolution, Structure, and Function," *American Journal of Police* 11, no. 2 (1992): 85–104.

37  Bureau of Justice Statistics, *Campus Law Enforcement Agencies, 1995* (Washington: Government Printing Office, 1996).

38  Eileen Luna, "The Growth and Development of Tribal Police: Challenges and Issues for Tribal Sovereignty," *Journal of Contemporary Criminal Justice*, 14 (February 1998): 75–86.

39  Executive Committee for Indian Country Law Enforcement Improvements, *Final Report To The Attorney General* (Washington, DC: Government Printing Office, 1997).

40  Donald A. Torres, *Handbook of State Police, Highway Patrols, and Investigative Agencies* (New York: Greenwood Press, 1987).

41  Ibid., p. 12.

42  Department of Justice, *Profile of State and Local Law Enforcement Agencies, 1987* (Washington: Government Printing Office, 1989).

43  Ibid.

44  Bureau of Justice Statistics, *Federal Law Enforcement Officers, 1996.*

45  Ibid.

46  Curt Gentry, *J. Edgar Hoover: The Man and the Secrets* (New York: Norton, 1991).

47  Tony Poveda, *Lawlessness and Reform: The FBI in Transition* (Pacific Grove, CA: Brooks/Cole, 1990).

48  William C. Cunningham, John J. Strauchs, and Clifford W. Van Meter, *Private Security: Patterns and Trends* (Washington: Government Printing Office, 1991).

49  These 1976 data are cited in Ibid., p. 3.

50  Jack R. Greene, Thomas M. Seamon, and Paul R. Levy, "Merging Public and Private Security for Collective Benefit: Philadelphia's Center City District," *American Journal of Police* 14, no.2 (1995): 3–20.

51  Marcia Chaiken and Jan Chaiken, *Public Policing—Privately Provided* (Washington: Government Printing Office, 1987).

52  President's Commission on Law Enforcement and Administration of Justice, *Task Force Report: The Police* (Washington: Government Printing Office, 1967), p. 68.

53  Terry W. Koepsell and Charles M. Girard, *Small Police Agency Consolidation: Suggested Approaches* (Washington: Government Printing Office, 1979).

54  National Advisory Commission or Criminal Justice Standards and Goals, *Police* (Washington: Government Printing Office, 1973), pp. 73–76.

55  International City Management Association, *Public Safety Departments: Combining the Police ad Fire Functions* (Washington: ICMA, July 1976).

**56**   International City Management Association, "Intergovernmental Service Arrangements and the Transfer of Functions," *Baseline Data Report* 16 (June 1984).

**57**   U.S. Department of Justice, *Justice Agencies in the United States: Summary Report, 1980.*

**58**   Ostrom, Parks, and Whitaker, *Patterns of Metropolitan Policing.*

**59**   Ibid., pp. xxi, 101.

**60**   Gary W. Cordner, "Police Agency Size and Investigative Effectiveness," *Journal of Criminal Justice* 17, no. 1 (1989): 153.

**61**   Weisheit, Falcone, and Wells, *Crime and Policing in Rural and Small-Town America,* pp. 69–73.

**62**   Terrill, *World Criminal Justice Systems,* pp. 9–25.

**63**   Samuel Walker, "Historical Roots of the Legal Control of Police Behavior," in *Police Innovation and Control of the Police,* eds. David Weisburd and Craig Uchida (New York: Springer, 1993), pp. 32–55.

**64**   Anthony Amsterdam, "Perspectives on the Fourth Amendment," *Minnesota Law Review* 58 (1974): 428.

**65**   Susan E. Martin, *On the Move: The Status of Women in Policing* (Washington: The Police Foundation, 1990), pp. 11–24.

**66**   Department of Justice, *COPS Office Report.*

**67**   International Association of Directors of Law Enforcement Standards and Training, *Sourcebook of Standards and Training Information* (Charlotte: University of North Carolina at Charlotte, 1993).

**68**   Roger Goldman and Stephen Puro, "Decertification of Police: An Alternative to Traditional Remedies for Police Misconduct," *Hastings Constitutional Law Quarterly* 15 (Fall 1987): 45–80.

**69**   Jack Pearson, "National Accreditation: A Valuable Management Tool," in ed. James J. Fyfe *Police Management Today: Issues and Case Studies,* (Washington: ICMA, 1985), pp. 45–48.

**70**   Commission on Accreditation For Law Enforcement Agencies, *Standards for Law Enforcement Agencies,* 3d ed. (Fairfax VA: CALEA, 1994).

**71**   Stephen D. Mastrofski, "Police Agency Accreditation: The Prospects of Reform," *American Journal of Police.* 6, no. 2 (1986) 45–81.

**72**   W. E. Eastman, "National Accreditation: A Costly, Unneeded Make-Work Scheme," in *Police Mangement Today,* ed., Fyfe  pp. 49–54.

**73**   Stephen D. Mastrofski, "The Prospects of Change in Police Patrol: A Decade in Review," *American Journal of Police* 9, no. 2 (1990): 25.

**74**   James J. Fyfe, comments, *ASC Annual Meeting.*

# PART TWO

# POLICE WORK

# PATROL: THE BACKBONE OF POLICING

Patrol is the backbone of policing, the central element of police operations. This chapter examines the nature of patrol work in contemporary American policing: how patrol is organized and delivered, the nature of citizen calls for service, the effectiveness of patrol in deterring crime, and programs designed to improve patrol services.

## THE CENTRAL ROLE OF PATROL

First, the majority of police officers are assigned to patrol and in that capacity deliver the bulk of police services to the public. The marked patrol car and the uniformed patrol officer are the visible symbols of the police in the eyes of the public.

Second, patrol officers are also the most important decision makers in policing, if not the entire criminal justice system. James Q. Wilson points out that police departments are unique in that discretion increases as one moves down the organizational hierarchy.[1] In deciding whether or not to make an arrest, or how to handle a domestic disturbance, patrol officers are the real policymakers in policing, and the gatekeepers of the criminal justice system.

Third, experience on patrol is a formative aspect of a police officer's career. In virtually all American police departments, assignments are based on seniority. Consequently, new officers start out on patrol duty, usually on the evening shift and in the highest-crime neighborhoods. This street experience is an important part of the police officer subculture. It forges a bond of common experience among officers.

Despite its central role in policing, patrol duty is generally considered the least desirable assignment, and career advancement usually means promotion or assignment to something more desirable, especially detective work. The National Advisory Commission on Criminal Justice Standards and Goals comments, "the patrolman is usually the lowest-paid, least-consulted, most taken-for-granted member of the force. His duty is looked on as routine and boring.[2] Many experts argue that enhancing the status of patrol duty and improving the morale of patrol officers are two of the most critical problems facing the police today.

## THE FUNCTIONS OF PATROL

Since the time of Sir Robert Peel, the father of the London police, visible patrol over fixed beats has been the core of the police mission. Patrol has three main functions: (1) to deter crime, (2) to enhance feelings of public safety, and (3) to make officers available for service.

O. W. Wilson, for decades the leading expert on police management, explained that patrol is designed to create "an impression of omnipresence" which will eliminate "the actual opportunity (or the belief that the opportunity exists) for successful misconduct."[3] The effectiveness of traditional patrol in deterring crime is examined in detail below.

The second function of patrol is to maintain feelings of public safety. The visible presence of patrol officers is designed to assure law-abiding citizens that they are being protected against crime. Most people believe that patrol deters crime. When asked to suggest improvements in policing, most citizens call for more police and/or more patrol in their neighborhoods.[4]

The third function of patrol, being available for service, is accomplished by dispersing patrol officers throughout the community. Albert Reiss observes that "no other professional operates in a comparable setting."[5] The clients of other professions—doctors, lawyers, and dentists—must go to the professionals' offices. The police may be the last profession to make house calls. As government officials who make important decisions affecting peoples' lives, and who work on the street, the police have been characterized as "street-level bureaucrats."[6]

## THE ORGANIZATION AND DELIVERY OF PATROL

A number of organizational factors affect the delivery of patrol services to the public. Except in the very small departments, patrol services are housed in a separate division of the police organization, often referred to as the uniform field bureau. In many departments this also includes the traffic enforcement unit. Typically, between 60 and 80 percent of all sworn officers are assigned to patrol duty.[7]

The Commission on Accreditation states that the rational allocation of personnel according to workload needs "is one of the primary means of improving the agency's efficiency and effectiveness."[8] The actual amount of patrol services delivered to the public on any given day is affected by the following factors: (1) the total number of sworn officers currently on duty, (2) the percentage of officers allocated to patrol, (3) the distribution of patrol officers by shift and area, (4) the use of automobile patrol versus foot patrol, and (5) the use of one-officer versus two-officer patrol units.

### Number of Sworn Officers

The traditional measure of the level of police protection in a community is the police/population ratio. The national average is 2.2 officers per 1,000 population; for cities with populations of 250,000 or more, the figure is 2.9 per 1,000.[9] As Table 4–1 indicates, there are enormous variations among cities in police/population ratios.

**TABLE 4–1**
POLICE/POPULATION RATIOS, SELECTED MAJOR CITIES, 1993

| City | Sworn officers per 1,000 citizens |
|------|-----------------------------------|
| District of Columbia | 7.0 |
| Newark, NJ | 4.0 |
| Detroit, MI | 3.8 |
| New York, NY | 3.8 |
| Philadelphia, PA | 3.8 |
| Houston, TX | 2.8 |
| Dallas, TX | 2.8 |
| Los Angeles, CA | 2.2 |
| San Diego, CA | 1.7 |
| San Jose, CA | 1.6 |

*Source*: Bureau of Justice Statistics, *Law Enforcement Management and Administrative Statistics, 1993* (Washington, DC Government Printing Office, 1995), pp. 1–11.

The police/population ratio has little relationship to the crime rate or even to calls for service. Cities with more police per population do not necessarily have lower crime rates. More often, the reverse is true: Cities with high crime rates often have more police officers, as high crime rates produce public demand for more police.[10] Washington, DC, with the highest police/population ratio, does not have a correspondingly low crime rate.

### Allocation and Distribution of Officers to Patrol

The police/population ratio does not indicate how successful a department is in placing officers on patrol. Some departments do a very inefficient job of placing patrol officers on the street in the right areas at the right times of day. In well-managed departments, patrol officers are distributed by shift and geographic area according to a workload formula based on calls for service and reported crimes.[11]

The patrol workload varies according to the time of day. Most serious crimes occur at night, as do the majority of disturbances (family disputes, bar fights, and so on). Figure 4–1 indicates the distribution of 911 calls for service in the Omaha, Nebraska, Police Department by time of day, and the distribution of officers by shift.[12]

Not all police departments allocate and distribute their officers in a rational manner. A 1987 investigation of the Philadelphia police found that "the same number of officers are on the street at all times—during the early morning when there is practically no activity, and on weekend evenings, when the calls for service are heaviest."[13] A 1981 survey of police practices by the Police Executive Research Forum (PERF) found irrational patrol distribution in a number of departments.[14]

Some departments utilize a fourth patrol shift, beginning in the late afternoon and ending in the early morning (e.g., 6:00 P.M. to 2:00 A.M.).[15] This provides additional officers on the evening shift, when the number of calls is highest, and avoids overstaffing in the early morning hours when the number of calls is at its lowest (see Figure 4–1).

The patrol workload also varies by location. Crime and disorder are not evenly distributed throughout the community. Crime is more prevalent in poorer neighborhoods, and low-income people are the heaviest users of police services for order maintenance and community assistance. The National Crime Victimization Survey reports that the household burglary rate for the poorest households (income of $7,500 or less) was 78.7 per 1,000, compared with 40 per 1,000 for households with incomes over $50,000.[16] Low-income people are also the heaviest users of police services for noncrime events such as medical emergencies and other types of situations requiring assistance.

---

**SIDEBAR 4–1**

THE POLICE/POPULATION RATIO IN YOUR COMMUNITY

Check the police/population ratio in your community. How does it compare with cities or towns of comparable size? How does it compare with the ratio for neighboring cities, or comparable cities in your region?

---

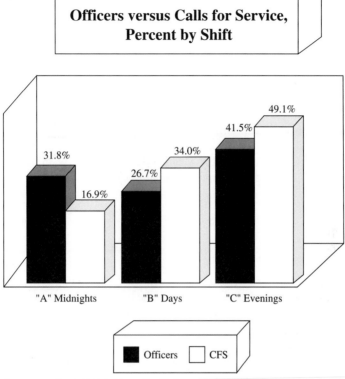

**FIGURE 4–1**
DISTRIBUTION OF 911 CALLS, OMAHA, NEBRASKA

Consequently, police departments utilizing a rational workload formula will assign more patrol officers to low-income neighborhoods. And because racial and ethnic minorities are disproportionately low-income groups, more police are generally assigned to minority neighborhoods as well. The controversy over whether the police provide too much or too little police protection to minority and low-income neighborhoods is examined in detail in Chapter 9.[17]

Many departments fail to redraw beat boundaries regularly in order to adjust for social change. Neighborhoods grow or decline in population. Some deteriorate economically and as a neighborhood shifts from middle income to low income, crime and calls for service generally increase. Some cities expand geographically, incorporating outlying suburban areas. A 1987 report on the Philadelphia police found that the department had not redrawn its boundaries in 16 years. Partly as a result, officers in the Thirty-fifth District handled an average of 494 calls, whereas officers in the Fifth District handled only 225. The disparity in workload was even greater in terms of serious crime: Officers in the Thirty-fifth District handled an average of 38 major offenses per year compared with only 8 for officers in the Fifth District.[18]

---

**POLICE PATROL ON THE WEB**
Many police departments describe their patrol operations on their web sites: maps of patrol districts, crime statistics, and so forth. How useful is this information? Check out the web sites of some police departments. What can you learn that is interesting or useful?

---

**Hot Spots**   Recent research has identified certain hot spots that receive a dispropor-tionate number of calls for police service. A study of calls for service to the Minneapolis Police Department found that only 5 percent of the addresses in the city accounted for 64 percent of all calls. Meanwhile, 60 percent of the addresses never called the police for any reason. Routine police work is heavily skewed: A relatively small number of citizens in a community are extremely high consumers of police services.[21]

### Assignment to Shifts and Areas

Police departments use a variety of different methods for assigning officers to particular shifts and patrol areas. Some assign officers on the basis of a strict seniority system and permit bidding for new assignments every six months or annually. Some departments rotate officers through different shifts every month, or on an even shorter time frame.[19]

A PERF report concludes that frequent changes in shift "is deleterious to the physical and psychological health of the individual and to the well-being of the organization."[20] Problems include loss of sleep, cardiovascular and other health problems, on-the-job accidents, disrupted family lives, and low morale. The report recommends steady shift assignments, based primarily on seniority, with some managerial discretion in assignment based on performance and workload needs.

### Types of Patrol

**Automobile Patrol**   Most police patrol in the United States today is done by auto-mobile: 87 percent of all municipal police patrol units according to the 1993 Law Enforcement Management and Administrative Statistics (LEMAS) report. Foot patrol and motorcycle patrol account for only 5 percent each.[22]

Automobile patrol provides more efficient coverage than foot patrol. A patrol car can cover more area, pass each point more often, return to particular spots in an unpre-dictable manner if necessary, and respond quickly to calls for service. The efficiency of the patrol car in this regard is the reason why police departments converted from foot patrol to car patrol between the 1920s and the 1950s (see Chapter 2).

The automobile, however, removes officers from the street and reduces informal contact with law-abiding citizens. As a result, some people, especially racial minorities, see the police as an occupying army. As early as 1950, William A. Westley noted that "in contrast to the man on the beat, the man in the car is isolated from the community."[23] In

1967 the President's Crime Commission observed: "The most significant weaknesses in American motor patrol operations today is the general lack of contact with citizens except when an officer has responded to a call. Forced to stay near the car's radio, awaiting an assignment, most patrol officers have few opportunities to develop closer relationships with persons living in the district."[24]

**Foot Patrol**   In response to the police-community relations crisis of the 1960s, many police departments experimented with restoring foot patrol in selected neighborhoods. Because a patrol officer on foot can cover only a very limited area, foot patrol is extremely expensive. The gains in police-community relations are offset by the relative inefficiency in patrol coverage.

Foot patrol has been incorporated into some community policing programs (see Chapter 7). Foot patrol remains the exception rather than the rule in policing. According to the 1993 LEMAS data, foot patrol represents only 5 percent of all patrol units.[25] The impact of foot patrol on crime and public attitudes is discussed below.

**One-Officer versus Two-Officer Cars**   Most patrol units involve single police officers. Two one-officer cars can patrol twice as much area and be available for twice as many calls as one two-officer car. In municipal police departments, 89 percent of all patrols involve one-officer units. There are a number of notable exceptions: 99 percent of all patrol units in Buffalo, New York, are two-officer units.[26]

Some rank-and-file officers favor two-officer cars, believing that they are safer. A Police Foundation study of patrol staffing in San Diego, however, found that officers in one-officer units were assaulted less often and were less involved in resisting arrest incidents than those in two-officer units. The one-officer patrol units, moreover, made more arrests and wrote more crime reports than two-officer units. Police officer concern about safety appears to be exaggerated. In 56.5 percent of the incidents where backup officers were dispatched in San Diego, it was later determined that they were not needed. Meanwhile, only 2.8 percent of the incidents were underdispatched, in the sense that the officers responding to the call had to request backup after they had arrived at the scene.[27]

### Staffing Patrol Beats

Staffing a single patrol beat around the clock, seven days a week, requires almost five (4.8) police officers.[28] The three regularly assigned officers must be supplemented because of normal days off, vacations, illnesses, and injuries.

In practice, police departments have a difficult time maintaining full patrol staffing. Retirements, resignations, vacations, and illnesses create frequent shortages. The Newark Foot Patrol experiment found that an average of 19 percent of all beat assignments were not covered during the year. Coverage ranged from a low of 64 percent to a high of 91 percent.[29] In Philadelphia only 47 percent of patrol sectors (190 out of 450) were fully staffed on a randomly selected Saturday night.[30]

### Styles of Patrol

The actual amount of police work undertaken depends on the work style of the officer. Some officers initiate more activity than others. Officer-initiated actions include stopping, questioning, and frisking suspicious citizens; making informal contacts with law-abiding citizens; stopping vehicles for possible violations; writing traffic tickets; checking suspicious events; and making arrests. Patrol officers generally initiate very little contact with citizens. Reiss found that only 14 percent of all citizen contacts were officer initiated.[31]

In citizen-initiated calls for service, some officers take a more active role in handling the situation than others. Bayley and Garofalo found that some officers were likely to simply observe the situation and leave, whereas others took control over the situation, asked probing questions, and had citizens explain themselves.[32] According to National Crime Victimization Survey (NCVS) data, police officers only "looked around" in 20 percent of all reported property crimes, and took a report in only about half of all property crimes.[33]

Muir argues that the style of policing reflects the attitudes of different officers toward law enforcement.[34] Cox and Frank, however, argue that individual officers vary their style depending upon the type of situation and the type of neighborhood where the incident occurs.[35]

### Organizational Styles

Patrol officer activity is also affected by different departmental styles of policing. James Q. Wilson identified three distinct organizational styles. The watchman style emphasizes peacekeeping, without aggressive law enforcement and few controls over rank-and-file officers. The legalistic style emphasizes aggressive crime fighting and attempts to control officer behavior through a rule-bound by-the-book administrative approach. The service style emphasizes responsiveness to community expectations, and is generally found in suburban police departments where there is relatively little crime.[36]

Some departments attempt to influence the work activity of patrol officers through quotas for traffic tickets, arrests, or field interrogations. Most experts, however, believe that numerical quotas are not related to the quality of police work.[37]

### Type of Supervision

The style of supervision also affects the amount of work performed by patrol officers. The basic unit of police patrol consists of a sergeant and a crew of patrol officers. Crews average between 6 and 12 officers. The span of control principle holds that a supervisor can effectively manage only a limited number of people.[38] The optimum crew size must strike a balance between the higher cost of small crews (requiring many sergeants) and the danger of loss of discipline if crews are too large.

Like patrol officers themselves, sergeants can be more or less active. Active sergeants have more contact with the officers under their command and are more likely to communicate specific instructions or patrol objectives.[39]

**TABLE 4–2**
DEPLOYMENT OF PATROL OFFICERS IN TWO HYPOTHETICAL CITIES

|  | City A | City B |
|---|---|---|
| Population | 500,000 | 500,000 |
| Sworn officers | 900 | 600 |
| Percentage of officers assigned to patrol | 50% | 70% |
| Officers assigned to patrol | <u>450</u> | <u>420</u> |
| Percentage of patrol officers assigned to 4 P.M.–12 A.M. shift | 33% | 50% |
| Patrol officers, 4 P.M.–12 A.M. shift | 148 | 210 |
| One-officer patrols | 20 | 190 |
| Two-officer patrols | 64 | 10 |
| Total patrols, 4 P.M.–12 A.M. | 84 | 200 |

### Summary

Table 4–2 illustrates the impact of administrative factors on the delivery of patrol services. City A has a police/population ratio 50 percent larger than City B (which means that it is paying 50 percent more in taxes for police). And yet, through more efficient management, City B provides its citizens with more patrol units during the busy and high-crime evening shift.

## CALLS FOR POLICE SERVICE

Police patrol work is dominated by modern communications technology: the telephone, the two-way radio, and the patrol car. Contemporary 911-driven police work is (1) citizen dominated, (2) reactive, and (3) incident based. Reiss found that 81 percent of all contacts between police officers and citizens originated with a telephone call; another 14 percent were officer initiated (on view), and 5 percent were the result of a citizen contacting a police officer in the field.[40] (Other evidence, however, suggests that police officers have a higher level of non 911-generated contacts with citizens. In Portland, Oregon, for example, one-third of all contacts are officer initiated in the field.)[41] Critics call this system "dial a cop," and argue that the 911 system runs the police department, preventing any rational planning and proactive police response to problems.[42]

### The Communications Center

The communications center is the nerve center of the modern police department. It receives calls from citizens and dispatches police cars to the scene of the incident. Communications center personnel make a series of critical decisions, exercising great discretion and, as a result, play a major role in shaping police work.[43] Antunes and Scott argue that the operator is "the key decision maker in the police bureaucracy."[44] Figure 4-2 offers a schematic diagram of a police communications center.

---

**SIDEBAR 4–2**

INSIDE THE COMMUNICATIONS CENTER

"My impressions of the communications center remain vivid and powerful. It was a smelly, smoky, poorly lit room reeling under the glare of harsh flickering flourescent lights. Windowless, stuffy, with restricted exit and entry, few amenities. Nervous anxiety and worry was the prevalent tone. . . . I have rarely endured such an unpleasant field work experience.

Peter K. Manning, *Symbolic Communication: Signifying Calls and the Police Response* (Cambridge: MIT Press, 1988), p. xiii.

---

In most large police departments today, the communications system is staffed by civilians rather than sworn officers. In many departments they are not employed by the police department itself. Some states have only recently considered legislation to require training and licensing of communications center personnel.[45]

The 911 emergency number was introduced by the American Telephone and Telegraph (AT&T) Company in 1968. By 1993 over 90 percent of all local police departments in cities with populations over 50,000 participated in a 911 system. Because of their convenience, and because police departments advertise the number, 911 systems have contributed to the great increase in calls for service. Some departments experienced increases of over 50 percent in the first 12 months after the 911 system was installed.[46]

## Processing Calls for Service

The operators, dispatchers, and patrol officers are "information brokers" who process citizen calls and translate them into official bureaucratic responses.[47] The operator obtains information from the caller and then makes a decision about the appropriate response. If he or she decides that the call requires a police response, the call is communicated to the dispatcher.

Peter K. Manning provides the most vivid and detailed description of 911 communications center operators at work (see Sidebar 4-2). He describes one call reporting an alleged kidnapping. The operator has available four different kidnapping-related codes, but "there are no rules given to determine selection among these options." The operators have a 300- page procedure manual, but it "is virtually never used" because it is too large and there is no room for it on the operators' consoles.[48]

All incoming calls for service do not result in the dispatch of a police officer. In the Police Services Study (PSS), only 50 percent of the 28,052 incoming calls resulted in a dispatch (the figure was 53 percent in Manning's study). In 17 percent of the cases, the caller was referred to another agency; the operator took information from the citizen in 16 percent of the calls and gave information to the citizen in 9 percent. In the remaining 14 percent of the calls, the citizen was told that the police could not handle the call, or the call was transferred, or some other response was given.[49]

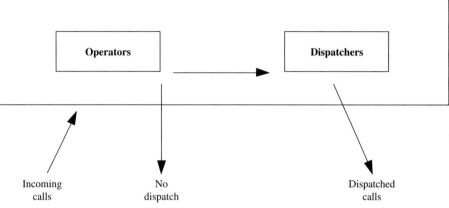

**FIGURE 4–2**
911 COMMUNICATIONS CENTER.

Obtaining the necessary information from the citizen caller is often difficult. Callers frequently provide vague, incomplete, or inaccurate information. Many are confused or frightened. Some are intoxicated or mentally disturbed. A situation that a caller describes as a "disturbance" could range from a party with only loud noise to an armed or mentally disordered person. The information is often incorrect. Bayley and Garofalo, for example, found that a weapon was actually present in only 25 percent of the reported "weapon present" calls.[50]

Gilsinan observed 911 operators in a large midwestern city handle 265 calls over one 24-hour period. He found that operators interpret incoming information from callers and translate it into a category that fits an established bureaucratic response. Operators interact with callers in a problem-solving process, especially asking for more details, to reach the final determination.[51]

The dispatcher must also make important decisions. Manning found that dispatchers can ignore the formal coded classification they receive about a call and "act as if the event has another priority informally," including adding his or her own comments when communicating to patrol officers.[52] The most important is deciding whether the situation is an emergency and requires an expedited response. Reiss found that 18 percent of dispatches received an urgent response.[53]

The dispatcher must also decide which patrol unit to dispatch. The unit assigned to a particular beat is often not available: either "out of service" handling another call, or not on duty at all that day. Consequently, officers are routinely assigned to calls outside their beat.[54]

Manning points out that patrol officers also interpret the information they receive. They frequently "unfound" citizen reported crimes. In most departments, patrol officers are not required to provide detailed records of how they handle calls. Reports are often limited to "service rendered" or "no police action required."[55]

Because the information processed through the communications system is often incomplete and inaccurate, patrol officers respond to calls in the context of great uncertainty. They are dependent upon the information as (1) given by the caller, (2) interpreted by the operator, (3) communicated to the dispatcher, (4) communicated to the patrol officer, and (5) interpreted by the patrol officer.

## THE SERVICE CALL WORKLOAD

Only between 20 percent and 30 percent of all calls for service involve criminal law enforcement. Most calls involve order maintenance or service incidents. Table 4-3 presents the PSS data on calls for service to 24 police departments in three metropolitan areas. Other studies of 911 calls have found a similar distribution of calls. In Minneapolis (1985-1986), about 30 percent of all calls were crime related (1.9 percent crimes against persons, 28.4 percent property crimes), 32.5 percent involved conflict management, and 13.2 were service calls.[56]

The 911 call data in Table 4-3 provide a picture of routine police patrol work. Several basic points stand out. First, as already noted, criminal law enforcement represents a minority of all calls for service (29.1%). For this reason, experts characterize policing as primarily peacekeeping rather than crime-fighting (see Chapter 1).

Second, the vast majority of crime-related calls involve property crimes. Only 3 percent of all calls involve a violent crime. Thus, the media image of policing that emphasizes the crime-fighting role, with a particular emphasis on violent crime and dangerous criminals, is a distortion of routine police work.

Third, all calls classified as crime related do not necessarily involve an actual criminal incident. In the category of suspicious circumstances, the caller may believe that a crime has been committed, but there may not be sufficient evidence to support that belief. Reiss found that citizens defined 58 percent of all incidents as criminal matters but responding police officers recorded only 17 percent as crime related. Reiss argues that "many citizens have only a vague understanding of the difference between civil, private, and criminal matters."[57]

Fourth, most police work involves order maintenance, or conflict management, and service. For this reason, policing is best characterized as peace-keeping (see Chapter 1). Cumming, Cumming, and Edell characterize the police officer as "a philosopher, guide, and friend."[58]

Fifth, many situations are ambiguous and require the exercise of discretion by the police. The best response to a reported dispute or nuisance is not clear. Officers need to use judgment based on the particular circumstances of each situation. Police discretion is examined in detail in Chapter 8.

Sixth, many of the order maintenance and service calls involve family problems that occur in private homes. The 911 system allows people to invite the police into their homes, which the police would normally not have a legal right to enter.[59] As a result, the police encounter, firsthand, the most intimate human problems: family disputes, mental illness, alcoholism, and so on.

**TABLE 4–3**
CRIME AND NONCRIME INCIDENTS AND THEIR DISTRIBUTION
IN POLICE SERVICES STUDY

|  | Percentage of all encounters* |
|---|---|
| Crime incidents | |
| *Violent crimes.* Murder, robbery, assault, kidnapping, rape, child abuse | 3.0 |
| *Nonviolent crimes.* Theft, selling or receiving stolen goods, breaking and entering, burglary, vandalism, arson, fraud, leaving the scene, false report, nonsupport | 15.0 |
| *Morals crimes.* Drug violations , gambling, prostitution, obscene behavior, pornography | 1.3 |
| *Suspicious circumstances.* Reports or observations of prowlers, gunshots, screams, suspicious persons or conditions | 9.8 |
| Total | 29.1 |
| Noncrime incidents | |
| *Traffic (regulation and enforcement).* Violation of traffic laws, traffic-flow problem, accidents, abandoned vehicles | 24.1 |
| *Disputes.* Fights, arguments, disturbances involving interpersonal conflict | 8.6 |
| *Nuisances.* Annoyance, harassment, noise disturbance, trespassing, minor juvenile problem, ordinance violation | 10.7 |
| *Dependent persons.* Drunks, missing persons, juvenile runaway, mentally disordered, other person unable to care for self | 3.4 |
| *Medical.* Injured accident victims, suicide and attempts, deaths, others needing medical attention | 1.9 |
| *Information request.* Road directions, referral, police or government procedures, miscellaneous requests where no additional police action mentioned | 4.0 |
| *Information offer.* Return property, missing or stolen property, false alarm report, complaint or compliment about police, general information provision | 2.8 |
| *General assistance.* Animal problem, lost or damaged property, utility problem, fire or other disaster, assist motorist, lockouts, companionship, irrational or crank call, house check, escort, transportation | 9.2 |
| *Miscellaneous.* Internal legal procedures, assistance request, officer wants to give information, officer wants information, officer assists, courier | 4.4 |
| *Gone on arrival.* Dispatched calls where parties to the problem are not at the scene | 1.8 |
| Total | 70.9 |

*Source*: Stephen Mastrofski, "The Police and Noncrime Services," in G. Whitaker and C. Phillips, eds., *Evaluating the Performance of Criminal Justice Agencies* (Beverly Hills, CA: Sage, 1983), p. 40.

Seventh, calls for service do not come from a representative sample of the community. Some people are very heavy users of police services; others rarely, if ever, call the police. Low-income people are the heaviest users of police services.[60] A analysis of 911 calls in Minneapolis found that 5 percent of the addresses accounted for 64 percent of all calls, while 60 percent of the addresses in the city never called the police.[61]

## ASPECTS OF PATROL WORK

### Response Time

Police departments traditionally put great emphasis on fast response to calls for service under the assumption that this would (1) increase the probability of an arrest and (2) increase public satisfaction. Under traditional policing (i.e., before community policing), professionalism was defined in large part by the fastest possible response to all for service calls.

Several studies have found that response time has little effect on clearance rates.[62] The total amount of time between the commission of a crime and the moment a police officer arrives on the scene includes separate parts:

**1** Discovery time, or the interval between the commission of the crime and its discovery,

**2** Reporting time, or the interval between discovery and when the citizen calls the police,

**3** Processing time, or the interval between the call and the dispatch of a patrol car,

**4** Travel time, or the length of time it takes patrol officers to reach the scene.

A Police Foundation study found that processing time took an average of 2 minutes and 50 seconds, while travel time averaged 5 minutes and 34 seconds.[63] Cordner, Greene, and Bynum found similar times in a study of calls to the Pontiac, Michigan, Police Department.[64]

Items 1, 2, and 3 of the total response time are beyond the control of the police. A PERF study found that 75 percent of all reported crimes are discovery or cold crimes, and only 25 percent are involvement crimes (e.g., a confrontation between the victim and the offender). Most burglaries, for example, are not discovered until hours after they occurred. Cordner, Greene, and Bynum found that the discovery delay, the interval between the time the crime occurred or was discovered and reported, was measured in hours for property crimes and about 30 minutes for personal crimes of violence. The police travel time (item 4) is usually irrelevant in terms of catching the offender on the premises.[65]

In involvement crimes, the PERF study found that victims took an average of between four and five and one-half minutes to call the police. Of these involvement crimes, 13 percent were reported while the crime was in progress and 14 percent were reported within the first minute after it was committed. Victim delay in calling the police undermines any potential gain by a faster police travel time. The study concluded that between 80 percent and 90 percent of serious crimes were reported to the police "too slowly for a response-related arrest to be made, even if the police response time was zero."[66]

Citizens delay calling the police for many reasons. In some cases they want to verify that a crime has actually occurred. In others, they wait to regain their composure or call a friend or family member. In a small number of cases a telephone is not available (e.g., a street robbery). Some people may not know the police phone number; or the caller may have trouble communicating the problem to the police, because of his or her emotional state, or because he or she does not speak English.

Satisfaction with police service is affected by response time. Furstenburg and Wellford found that citizens who had to wait more than 15 minutes for the police to arrive were significantly less satisfied than those who obtained a faster response. For both black and white citizens, satisfaction dropped steadily as response time increased from 5 to more than 15 minutes.[67] Satisfaction is a function of citizen expectations, which can be controlled by the police. Citizens are often dissatisfied because they believe they will receive a quick response but then do not get it. The PSS data indicate that callers were informed of how long they would have to wait for a police unit in only 1 percent of all calls.[68] Experiments with differential response to calls (see pp. 81) found that citizens were satisfied if they were informed that the police would not be there immediately.[69]

### Officer Use of Patrol Time

One of the crucial aspects of patrol work is how officers use their time. Because personnel costs consume 80 to 90 percent of a police department's budget, getting the maximum productivity out of patrol officers is crucial to establishing efficient, cost-effective policing.

The patrol officers' time is divided between committed time, devoted to handling calls (often referred to as out of service), and uncommitted (or in-service) time, when an officer is available for dispatch to a call. Patrol officers spend about 40 percent of each shift handling calls. This average, however, masks tremendous variations among cities, neighborhoods, and shifts. Even in the same city, some beats are very active, with high rates of calls for service, whereas others have little activity.[70]

A St. Louis study found that patrol officers spent about an hour and a half (96 minutes) out of every eight-hour shift handling calls for service. This represented 20 percent of their time. Patrol officers in Wilmington, Delaware, spent 40 percent of their time handling calls (174 minutes out of each eight-hour shift). In San Diego, patrol officers in the Central Division spent an average of four and one-half hours (270 minutes) per shift, compared with only two hours (120 minutes) for officers in the North Division.[71]

Richard Larson estimates that the average call takes about 30 minutes, including 10 minutes of travel time and 20 minutes for handling the call itself.[72] This average also masks great variations. Some calls can be handled quickly; others require more time. Officers have great discretion over how much time to spend on a particular call. One officer might choose to spend a great deal of time at a domestic disturbance, offering counsel to the individuals; another officer might handle the same call very quickly, with only a brusque warning.

Uncommitted time is devoted to a number of different activities. In the Kansas City patrol study, uncommitted time was almost equally divided between patrol, non-police-related activity (eating, personal business), stationary police-related activities (report writing), and residual time (traveling to and from police stations, etc.)[73]

In certain respects, there is no practical difference between some of the categories of uncommitted time. When a citizen sees a patrol car driving down the street it makes no difference if the officer is delivering a report to headquarters, on his or her way to a lunch break, or is engaged in routine patrol. The patrol car's visible presence is the same no matter what.

Arrests have a major impact on patrol officers' use of time. An arrest can take one and one-half to two hours to process. Many arrests require at least two officers, depending on a department's standard operating procedures.[74] Each arrest removes the patrol officer from the street, thereby reducing the amount of time available for preventive patrol and for responding to calls.

### Evasion of Duty

Despite the fact that the two-way radio allows direct communication with patrol officers, officers are still able to avoid work. The easiest way is to delay reporting the completion of a call. A dispatcher assumes that an officer is still busy with a call (committed) until the officer reports that the call has been completed. Officers can create free time for themselves by simply delaying that call.[75]

### High-Speed Pursuits

High-speed pursuits are a major issue in policing. Pursuits are fairly common and pose serious risks to police officers, the persons being pursued, and other citizens. A pursuit is defined as any situation where a police officer attempts to make an arrest and the suspect knowingly increases his or her speed to avoid apprehension.[76]

Alpert and Dunham's study of pursuits by Metro-Dade, Florida, officers found that 33 percent resulted in accidents and 17 percent resulted in injury. Slightly less than 1 percent resulted in the death of the suspect.[77] Other studies have put the accident rate as high as 44 percent and as low as 18 percent. The injury rate ranges from a high of 24 percent to a low of 5 percent of all pursuits.[78] The exact number of pursuits in a department is not always known. Data on pursuits are derived from official reports completed by officers. Yet many pursuits are very short in duration. About 23 percent of the recorded pursuits in Metro-Dade lasted three minutes or less. There is reason to suspect that officers do not record many extremely short pursuits.

Until recently, patrol officers had complete discretion about whether or not to initiate a pursuit. Most police departments today, however, have written policies governing pursuits. These policies fall into three general categories. *Restrictive* policies limit discretion by specifying the conditions under which pursuits may or may not be initiated. *Discouraging* policies advise officers against pursuit in certain situations but are not as rigid as restrictive policies. Finally, *discretionary* policies give officers broad discretion about whether to engage in pursuits.[79]

The Metro-Dade policy prohibits pursuits in cases involving traffic offenses, misdemeanors, and nonviolent felonies where the identity of the violator is known.[80] Many experts argue that the potential risk of a pursuit is not justified in the case of minor offenses. The Metro-Dade policy also advises officers not to pursue when weather or road conditions increase the risk of an accident, or where many pedestrians are present.

## THE EFFECTIVENESS OF PATROL

Since the time of Robert Peel, the basic assumption of policing has been that a visible police presence deters crime. The related assumption is that increasing the number of officers on patrol will increase the deterrent effect. Until the early 1970s, however, there were no scientific experiments testing these assumptions.

. Initial experiments conducted in the 1950s and 1960s did not meet contemporary standards of scientific research. In Operation 25, the New York City Police Department doubled the number of patrol officers in the Twenty-fifth Precinct for four months during 1954. The department claimed that the increased patrol reduced muggings (street robberies) by 90 percent over the same period a year before, and that auto thefts declined by two-thirds.[81]

The Operation 25 experiment was deeply flawed, however. It was not independently evaluated, raising the possibility that department officials manipulated the Uniform Crime Reports (UCR) figures on reported crime to achieve the desired results. The research design did not control for the possible displacement of crime to other areas, or for other variables that might have affected criminal activity.

In another New York City experiment in 1965, the city more than doubled the number of police officers on the subways (from 1,200 to 3,100) between 8:00 P.M. and 4:00 A.M. After a short-term decline, crime began to increase rapidly. By 1970 there were six times as many subway robberies as in 1965, before the additional police were deployed. Moreover, it was later discovered that the transit police deliberately manipulated the crime reports to lower the number of reported crimes during the experimental period.[82]

### The Kansas City Preventive Patrol Experiment

The Kansas City Preventive Patrol Experiment (1972-1973) was a landmark event in American policing. It was the first experiment testing the effectiveness of patrol that met minimum standards of scientific research. The Police Foundation, a private and independent organization, funded the experiment, provided the expertise in research design, and ensured that the evaluation was independent and objective.[83]

The research design involved 15 of the 24 beats in the South Patrol Division (9 were eliminated as unrepresentative of the area). They were matched in terms of crime, calls for service, income, and composition of the population, and assigned one of three levels of patrol:

**1** Reactive beats received "no regular preventive patrol." Police vehicles assigned these beats entered them only in response to calls for service. Noncommitted time was spent patrolling other beats.

**2** Proactive beats received two or three times the normal level of patrol.

**3** Control beats were assigned the normal level of patrol (one car per beat).

The experiment measured the impact of different levels of patrol on (1) criminal activity, (2) community perceptions and attitudes, and (3) police officer behavior and police department practices. Criminal activity was measured through official UCR data on reported crimes and arrests, and through a victimization survey. This was one of the first important applications of the relatively new victimization survey technique. The victimization survey was also used to measure community perceptions and attitudes in terms of fear of crime, protective measures used by citizens, protective measures used by businesses, and attitudes toward the police. Data were also gathered on police response time, arrest practices, police officer use of time, and officer attitudes. No previous police experiment had investigated such a wide range of issues, used such a variety of data sources, or relied on data independent of official departmental records.

The experiment began in July 1972, but was suspended within a month when it was discovered that the experimental conditions were not being maintained. After being reorganized, it was resumed in October 1972 and ran for 12 months.

**Findings and Implications**   The experiment found that variations in the level of patrol had no significant effect on either criminal activity or citizen feelings of safety. The victimization survey found no statistically significant differences in crime in any of the 69 comparisons made among reactive, control, and proactive beats. It also found that citizen fear of crime was not significantly affected by changes in the level of patrol, and citizen attitudes toward police were not significantly affected by the level of patrol.

The Kansas City experiment challenged traditional assumptions about routine patrol. More patrol did not reduce crime, lower levels of patrol did not lead to an increase in crime, and citizens did not notice the different levels of police patrol. Because there was never any area that had absolutely no police presence, the experiment did not prove that routine patrol has no effect on crime. Patrol cars entered the reactive beats in response to calls, and marked police cars from other units also entered these areas.

There are several reasons why different levels of patrol had no impact on either crime or public perceptions. Sherman and Weisburd point out that patrol is spread so thin under normal conditions (the patrol "dosage" level) that doubling it is not likely to have much of any impact.[84] A separate analysis of data from both Kansas City and San Diego concludes that patrol is spread so thin that, for example, any increases in "perceived patrol visibility" resulting from a shift from two-officer to one-officer patrols are "likely [to] occur only on paper."[85]

Many crimes, moreover, are not likely to be deterred by patrol because they occur indoors and are often impulsive acts. NCVS data indicate that 33.7 percent of all sexual assaults occur at home and another 21.3 percent occur at, in, or near someone else's house. More assaults occur inside a home, restaurant, or commercial building than occur on the street.[86] About 60 percent of all murders, are between people who know each other. These offenders do not rationally calculate the risk of arrest and punishment and, in particular, do not assess the level of police patrol in the area. In short, the traditional approach to police patrol has grossly exaggerated the extent to which many crimes are suppressible, or capable of being deterred by patrol.[87]

People did not perceive the different levels of patrol coverage in Kansas City in part because of the "phantom effect," or what criminologists call residual deterrence.[88] People believe the police are present even when there is no patrol because they have seen the police at some other time or place (e.g., the day before or in another area). The original perception carries over, with the same effect as if the police were actually there.

It should be noted that people are not familiar with the boundaries of police beats and do not know that there is no patrol in a certain area.

Critics found a number of flaws in the Kansas City experiment. Larson points out that police vehicles from other specialized units (which were not part of the experiment) operated in the reactive beats, thus adding to a visible police presence. Officers in the reactive beats engaged in more self-initiated activities (such as vehicle stops) and used their sirens and lights more often in responding to calls. There was also a higher incidence of two or more cars responding to a call for service in those beats. All of these actions may have created the perception of a greater police presence than actually existed.[89]

One of the most important implications of the data was that officers' uncommitted time (about 60 percent of their time on duty) might be used more effectively. Anthony Pate argues that, because reduced patrol levels do not result in increased crime, "patrol can be removed, at least temporarily, without incurring negative consequences" and officers can be redeployed to other areas for specific purposes.[90] The implications of this observation are discussed below.

### The Newark Foot Patrol Experiment

The Kansas City experiment led to the Newark Foot Patrol Experiment (1978-1979), which tested the effect of foot patrol on crime and public perceptions. The design of the experiment was similar to the Kansas City experiment. Some beats received additional foot patrol, others received less foot patrol, and others served as control beats. The experiment tested the effect of different levels of foot patrol on crime, arrest rates, and community attitudes.[91]

The Newark Foot Patrol Experiment found that additional foot patrol did not reduce serious crime: "Generally, crime levels. . . are not affected by foot patrol for residents or commercial respondents at a significant level." Different levels of foot patrol did, however, have a significant effect on citizen attitudes. Citizens were "acutely aware" of the different levels of foot patrol, and residents in beats with added foot patrol consistently saw "crime problems diminishing in their neighborhoods more than in neighborhoods."[92]

Reduced fear of crime, moreover, was associated with more positive attitudes toward the police, including other police activities unrelated to foot patrol. At the same time, foot patrol officers reported more positive attitudes about citizens, believing them to be more supportive of the police. Foot patrol officers ranked "helping the public" as the second most important part of the job, whereas motor patrol officers ranked it fifth. The data suggest that the positive benefits of foot patrol on attitudes is a two-way street.

### Summary

The Kansas City and Newark patrol experiments were major watersheds in thinking about the police. The findings indicated that although some police presence probably had some deterrent effect (remember, they never tested having no patrol whatsoever), simply adding more patrol does not reduce crime. By questioning the traditional assumptions about patrol, the experiments encouraged some creative new thinking. The finding that foot patrol reduced fear was encouraging. Also, as some observers pointed out, the experiments tested only the amount of patrol and did not examine what patrol officers actually did while on duty. This new thinking directly contributed to the new idea of community policing (See Chapter 7).[93]

## IMPROVING PATROL

The traditional approach to improving patrol accepted the old assumptions that patrol deterred crime and that the police should respond to all calls for service as quickly as possible. To this end, police departments, following the management principles of O. W. Wilson, attempted to maximize the efficient use of patrol officers: converting from foot patrol to automobile patrol, using one-officer rather than two-officer cars, distributing patrol cars throughout the community on the basis of a workload formula, and improving the communications system to reduce response time.[94] Police executives also sought more sworn officers, more patrol cars, and more sophisticated communications equipment.

Recent innovations, however, are built upon the research on patrol and operate on different assumptions about what patrol can accomplish and what is important in policing.

### Differential Response to Calls

Some police departments have attempted to manage the calls for service workload more effectively. They have rejected the old assumption that the police should respond as quickly as possible to every call. The new approach involves screening incoming 911 calls and providing different responses to different kinds of calls. This approach is based on the assumption that each and every call for service does not require immediate response by a sworn police officer.

Differential response programs classify calls according to their seriousness. Calls receive (1) an immediate response by a sworn officer; (2) a delayed response by a sworn officer; or (3) no police response, with reports taken over the telephone, by mail, or by having the person come to a police station in person. Implementing differential response requires written guidelines and careful training for communications center personnel.[95]

An evaluation of differential response experiments found them successful. In Greensboro, North Carolina, only about half (53.6 percent) of all calls received an immediate dispatch of a police officer, 19.5 percent received no dispatched officer at all (most were cold larcenies where a report was taken over the telephone), and another 26.9 percent received a delayed response.[96]

Both police officers and citizens were satisfied with differential response. Greensboro citizens expressed satisfaction with 90 percent of the alternative responses, except for walk-in reports. In the case of delayed police response, citizen satisfaction was directly related to "whether the caller was informed that a delay might occur."[97] This finding confirmed earlier research suggesting that citizen expectations are not a fixed entity but are dependent on what the police tell people to expect.[98]

The evaluation of differential response experiments also found that it improved the overall quality of the call-for-service system. The new procedures (1) increased the amount of information received from callers; (2) provided callers with a better sense of what kind of response to expect; and (3) gave patrol officers more detailed information about calls.[99]

Robert Worden's study of differential response in Lansing, Michigan, found that it was both efficient and equitable. Cold crimes and other low-priority calls received a delayed response, with a median response time of 16 minutes. Over 90 percent of the citizens were satisfied with this service. Other calls were handled by taking reports over the telephone (almost all were larceny and vandalism incidents). Over 90 percent of the citizens were satisfied with this service. Differential response was equitable in the sense that whites and racial and ethnic minorities were just as likely to be satisfied (although there was some variation in the degree of their satisfaction).[100]

A number of departments have established telephone reporting units (TRUs). Many of these units are staffed by officers on light duty because of injury. The TRUs handle anywhere from 10 to 20 percent of all calls on some shifts, and up to 35 percent of all crime reports. Almost half of all reported crimes are larcenies and almost all of those are cold crimes in which the patrol officer would do nothing more than take a report. One department found that TRUs operators took reports much more efficiently than regular patrol officers. [101]

Another innovation is the addition of a separate 311 telephone number for nonemergency calls. In early 1997, at the request of the Office of Community-Oriented Police Services (OCOPS), the Federal Communications Commission reserved the 311 number for national nonemergency use. The Baltimore, Maryland, police department launched a 311 pilot project, staffing the 311 lines with sworn officers currently on limited duty (because of injuries or other reasons). In the initial six months, the 311 number reduced the total of incoming 911 calls by 20 to 25 percent and increased the efficiency of the emergency number.[102]

The differential response, TRU, and 311 innovations suggest that police departments are not necessarily trapped by an unmanageable call for service workload. That workload was, in fact, something the police themselves created, by adopting the technology that made it possible and promising quick response to all calls. These recent innovations suggest that police departments can effectively resocialize the public about what to expect from the police.

## Police Aides or Cadets

An alternative method of handling low-priority calls is to use nonsworn personnel. Not all police tasks involve the need for a sworn police officer. The President's Crime Commission recommended the creation of a community service officer (CSO) to handle many of these routine assignments, thus freeing sworn officers for more critical tasks.[103] This approach is similar to the way other professions operate: delegating routine tasks to subprofessionals in training (e.g., lawyers use law clerks, college professors use graduate assistants).

In an experiment in Worcester, Massachusetts, police service aides (PSAs) handled 24.7 percent of all calls and assisted in another 8.2 percent. These were nonemergency calls that did not require the presence of a sworn police officer. Citizens expressed satisfaction with the services they received from the PSAs, and did not object to not having a sworn officer respond.[104]

The Seattle CSO program was established in 1971 and by 1993 employed 17 CSOs who were supervised by a sworn sergeant and a sworn lieutenant. CSOs are specially trained in social services and work primarily with street people. CSOs patrol the downtown area on foot and refer homeless people to agencies providing shelter, food, clothing, and alcohol or drug abuse treatment.[105]

Despite the potential for utilizing aides or police cadets, the idea has not been widely adopted. The major obstacle appears to be opposition from police unions, which fear loss of sworn police officer positions.

### Directed Patrol and "Hot Spots"

Directed patrol is a program that provides patrol officers with specific duties to perform during a specified time period during which they are freed from normal 911 dispatches. Traditional patrol gives officers only a general mandate to patrol their beats and to respond to calls for service. A directed patrol program might, for example, involve instruction to look for specific persons or types of crimes, or to patrol certain areas intensively.[106]

Cordner's evaluation of directed patrol in Pontiac, Michigan, found mixed results. There was some evidence that aggressive anticrime activities under the program may have reduced or displaced some kinds of criminal activity. The exact nature of this effect was difficult to determine conclusively, however. Cordner argues, however, that the evidence does lend support to the view that what police officers actually do is more important than the number of officers on patrol.[107]

A more recent version of directed patrol focuses on hot spots, or those areas that receive a very high volume of calls for service. An experiment in Minneapolis used a crackdown-back-off technique in which patrol officers intensively patrolled hot spots for short periods of time. The underlying assumption was that the impact of a short-term police presence would carry over because of residual deterrence.[108]

### Beyond Traditional Patrol

There have been a number of experiments and innovations in police patrol in the last 25 years. Overall, however, the extent of change has been fairly limited. Reviewing developments in police patrol in the 1980s, Stephen Mastrofski concludes that the net effect was "changes in patrol practice of only modest increments in the short run."[109] Traditional preventive patrol and calls for service remain the central aspect of American police departments. The most important innovations in policing look beyond traditional patrol. Advocates of community policing and problem-oriented policing argue that 911-driven policing is reactive and limited to isolated incidents. They argue that the police should be more proactive and, working closely with community residents, should focus on underlying problems. Community policing and problem-oriented policing are covered in detail in Chapter 7.


## CONCLUSION

Patrol is the backbone of policing. Despite many recent innovations in community policing, most police work involves patrol officers who patrol their assigned beats and respond to citizen calls for service. The patrol workload is dominated by calls for service and primarily involves noncriminal incidents. Thus police work is best described as peacekeeping rather than crimefighting. The evidence suggests that increased levels of patrol do not deter crime more effectively than lower levels of patrol. Innovations in patrol emphasize making more efficient use of patrol personnel and reducing the high volume of calls for service.


## NOTES

 1  James Q. Wilson, *Varieties of Police Behavior* (New York: Atheneum, 1973), p. 7.
 2  National Advisory Commission on Criminal Justice Standards and Goals, *Police* (Washington: Government Printing Office, 1973), p. 189.
 3  O. W. Wilson and Roy C. McLaren, *Police Administration*, 4th ed. (New York: McGraw-Hill, 1977), p. 320.
 4  U.S. Department of Justice, *The Police and Public Opinion* (Washington: Government Printing Office, 1977), pp. 39–40.
 5  Albert Reiss, The Police and the Public (New Haven: Yale University Press, 1971), p. 3.
 6  Michael Lipsky, *Street-Level Bureaucracy* (New York: Russell Sage, 1980).
 7  Bureau of Justice Statistics, *Law Enforcement Management and Administrative Statistics, 1993* (Washington: Government Printing Office, 1995), p. ix.
 8  Commission on Accreditation For Law Enforcement Agencies, *Standards for Law Enforcement Agencies*, 3d ed. (Fairfax, Va.: 1994), p. 16–2.
 9  Federal Bureau of Investigation, *Crime in the United States, 1995* (Washington: Government Printing Office, 1996), pp. 290–291.
10  Thomas B. Marvell and Carlisle E. Moody, "Specification Problems, Police Levels, and Crime Rates," *Criminology* 34 (November 1996): 609–646.
11  The original work load formula was developed by O. W. Wilson in 1941. [O. W. Wilson, *Distribution of Police Patrol Force* (Chicago: Public Administration Service, 1941).] Excerpts are found in Wilson and McLaren, *Police Administration*, pp. 633–655, appendix J.
12  Police Executive Research Forum, *Organizational Evaluation of the Omaha Police Division* (Washington: PERF, 1992, p. 226.
13  Philadelphia Police Study Task Force, *Philadelphia and Its Police* (Philadelphia: the City, 1987), p. 49.
14  Police Executive Research Forum, *Survey of Police Operational and Administrative Practices–1981* (Washington: PERF, 1981, pp. 383–387.)
15  Police Executive Research Forum, *Survey of Police Operational and Administrative Practices–1981*, pp. 428–432.
16  Bureau of Justice Statistics, *Criminal Victimization in the United States, 1994* (Washington: Government Printing Office, 1997), pp. 19, 23.

**17** Samuel Walker, Cassia Spohn, and Miriam DeLone, *The Color of Justice* (Belmont, Calif.: Wadsworth, 1996), chap. 4.

**18** Philadelphia Police Study Task Force, *Philadelphia and Its Police*, pp. 48–49.

**19** James L. O'Neill and Michael A. Cushing, *The Impact of Shift Work on Police Officers* (Washington: Police Executive Research Forum, 1991), app. C.

**20** Ibid., p. 66.

**21** Lawrence W. Sherman, Patrick R. Gartin, and Michael E. Buerger, "Hot Spots of Predatory Crime: Routine Activities and the Criminology of Place," *Criminology* 27, no. 2 (1989): 27–55.

**22** Bureau of Justice Statistics, *Law Enforcement Management and Administrative Statistics, 1993*, table C.

**23** William A. Westley, *Violence and the Police* (Cambridge: MIT Press, 1970), p. 35.

**24** President's Commission on Law Enforcement and Administration of Justice, *Task Force Report: The Police* (Washington: Government Printing Office, 1967), p. 54.

**25** Bureau of Justice Statistics, *Law Enforcement Management and Administrative Statistics, 1993*, p. ix.

**26** Ibid., table 11a.

**27** John E. Boydstun, Michael E. Sherry, and Nicholas P. Moelter, *Police Staffing in San Diego: One- or Two-Officer Units* (Washington: The Police Foundation, 1977).

**28** Wilson and McLaren, *Police Administration*, p. 663.

**29** The Police Foundation, *The Newark Foot Patrol Experiment* (Washington: The Police Foundation, 1981), p. 36.

**30** Philadelphia Police Study Task Force, *Philadelphia and Its Police*, p. 48.

**31** Reiss, *The Police and the Public*, p. 11.

**32** David H. Bayley and James Garofalo, "The Management of Violence by Police Patrol Officers," *Criminology* 27 (February 1989):1–25.

**33** Bureau of Justice Statistics, *Criminal Victimization in the United States, 1994*, p. 100.

**34** William Muir, *Police: Streetcorner Politicians* (Chicago: University of Chicago Press, 1977).

**35** Stephen M. Cox and James Frank, "The Influence of Neighborhood Context and Method of Entry on Individual Styles of Policing," *American Journal of Police* II No. 2 (1992): 1–22.

**36** Wilson, *Varieties of Police Behavior*.

**37** Bureau of Justice Statistics, *Performance Measures for the Criminal Justice System* (Washington: Government Printing Office, 1993), pp. 109–140.

**38** Wilson and McLaren, *Police Administration*, p. 83.

**39** John van Maanen, "The Boss: First-Line Supervision in an American Police Agency," *Control in the Police Organization,* in M. Punch, ed. (Cambridge: MIT Press, 1983), pp. 275–317.

**40** Reiss, *The Police and the Public*, p. 11.

**41** City of Portland, *Service Efforts and Accomplishments 1995–96* (Portland, OR: Office of the City Auditor, 1996), p. 15.

**42** Malcolm K. Sparrow, Mark H. Moore, David M. Kennedy, *Beyond 911: A New Era for Policing* (New York: Basic Books, 1990).

**43** Peter K. Manning, *Symbolic Communication: Signifying Calls and the Police Response* (Cambridge: MIT Press, 1988).

**44** George Antunes and Eric J. Scott, "Calling the Cops: Police Telephone Operators and Citizen Calls for Service," *Journal of Criminal Justice* 9 no. 2 (1981): 167.

**45** "Licensing May Loom for 91 Dispatchers in Pa.," *Law Enforcement News*, May 15, 1995, p. 1.

**46** Kent W. Colton, Margaret L. Brandeau, and James M. Tien, *A National Assessment of Police Command, Control, and Communications Systems* (Washington: Government Printing Office, 1983); Bureau of Justice Statistics, *Local Police Departments, 1993* (Washington: Government Printing Office, 1996), p. 11.

**47** Peter K. Manning, "Information Technologies and the Police," in *Modern Policing*, eds., Michael Tonry and Norval Morris, (Chicago: University of Chicago Press, 1992), pp. 349–398.

**48** Manning, *Symbolic Communication*, p. 145.

**49** Eric J. Scott, *Calls for Service: Citizen Demand and Initial Police Response* (Washington: Government Printing Office, 1981), pp. 28–30.

**50** Bayley and Garofalo, *"The Management of Violence,"* p. 7.

**51** James F. Gilsinan, "They Is Clowning Tough: 911 and the Social Construction of Reality," *Criminology* 27 (May 1989): 329–344.

**52** Manning, *Symbolic Communication*, p. 168.

**53** Reiss, *The Police and The Public*, p.6.

**54** Ibid., p. 99.

**55** Manning, "Information Technologies and the Police," p. 371.

**56** Sherman, Gartin, Buerger, "Hot Spots of Predatory Crime."

**57** Reiss, *The Police and the Public*, p. 73.

**58** Elaine Cumming, Ian Cumming, and Laura Edell, "Policeman as Philosopher, Guide, and Friend," *Social Problems* 12 Winter (1965): 276–286.

**59** Aruthur L. Stinchcombe, "Institutions of Privacy in the Determination of Police Administrative Practice," *American Journal of Sociology* 69 (September 1963): 150–160.

**60** Reiss, *The Police and the Public*, p. 63.

**61** Sherman, Gartin, and Buerger, "Hot Spots of Predatory Crime."

**62** William Spelman and Dale K. Brown, *Calling the Police: Citizen Reporting of Serious Crime* (Washington: Government Printing Office, 1984).

**63** Kansas City Police Department, *Response Time Analysis: Executive Summary* (Washington: Government Printing Office, 1978), p. 6.

**64** Gary W. Cordner, Jack R. Greene, and Tim S. Bynum, "The Sooner the Better: Some Effects of Police Response Time," in *Police at Work*, ed. Richard R. Bennett (Beverly Hills: Sage, 1983), pp. 145–164.

**65** Cordner, Greene, and Bynum, "The Sooner the Better."

**66** Spelman and Brown, *Calling the Police*, p. 74.

**67** Frank F. Furstenburg, Jr., and Charles F. Wllford, "Callling the Police: The Evaluation of Police Service," *Law and Society Review 7* (Spring 1973): 393–406.

**68** Antunes and Scott, "Calling the Cops," pp. 175–176.

**69** J. Thomas McEwen, Edward F. Connors, III, and Marica Cohen, *Evaluation of the Differential Police Response Field Test* (Washington: Government Printing Office, 1986).

**70** These studies are summarized in Gordon P. Whitaker et al., *Basic Issues in Police Performance* (Washington: Government Printing Office, 1982), pp. 40–43.

**71** Ibid, pp. 62–63.

**72** Richard C. Larson, "What Happened to Patrol Operations in Kansas City? A Review of the Kansas City Preventive Patrol Experiment," *Journal of Criminal Justice* 3, no. 4 (1975): 273.

**73** George L. Kelling et al., *The Kansas City Preventive Patrol Experiment: A Summary Report* (Washington: The Police Foundation, 1974).

**74** Herman Goldstein, *The Drinking Driver in Madison: Project on the Development of a Problem-Oriented Approach to the Improvement of Policing*, Vol. 2 (Madison: University of Wisconsin Law School, 1982), pp. 67–68.

75 Jonathan Rubenstein, *City Police* (New York: Ballantine, 1974), pp. 117–119.

76 National Institute of Justice, *Restrictive Policies for High-Speed Police Pursuits* (Washington: Government Printing Office, 1989), p. 1.

77 Geoffrey P. Alpert and Roger D. Dunham, *Police Pursuit Driving: Controlling Responses to Emergency Situations* (New York: Greenwood Press, 1990), p. 37.

78 L. Edward Wells and David N. Falcone, "Organizational Variables in Vehicle Pursuits by Police: The Impact of Policy on Practice," *Criminal Justice Policy Review*, 6, no. 4 (1992): 317.

79 Ibid., pp. 324–325.

80 Alpert and Dunham, *Police Pursuit Driving*, p. 80.

81 This and other experiments are summarized in Jan M. Chaiken, "What Is Known about Deterrent Effects of Police Activities?" in *Preventing Crime*, ed. James A. Cramer (Beverly Hills, Sage, 1978), pp. 109–136.

82 Ibid.

83 Kelling et al., *The Kansas City Preventive Patrol Experiment*.

84 Lawrence W. Sherman and David Weisburd, "General Deterrent Effects of Police Patrol in Crime 'Hot Spots': A Randomized Controlled Trial," *Justice Quarterly* 12 (December 1995): 627–628.

85 Edward H. Kaplan, "Evaluating the Effectiveness of One-Officer versus Two-Officer Patrol Units," *Journal of Criminal Justice* 7 (Winter 1979): 339.

86 Bureau of Justice Statistics, *Criminal Victimization in the United States, 1994* (Washington: Government Printing Office, 1997), p. 59.

87 Wesley G. Skogan and George E. Antunes, "Information, Apprehension, and Deterrence: Exploring the Limits of Police Productivity," *Journal of Crimial Justice* 7 (Fall 1979): 229.

88 Lawrence W. Sherman, "Police Crackdowns: Initial and Residual Deterrence," in *Crime and Justice: A Review of Research,* eds. Michael Tonry and Norval Morris, (Chicago: University of Chicago Press, 1990), pp. 1–48.

89 Larson, "What Happened to Patrol Operations in Kansas City?"

90 Anthony M. Pate, "Experimenting with Foot Patrol: The Newark Experience," in *Community Crime Prevention: Does it* Work? ed., Dennis P. Rosenbaum (Beverly Hills: Sage, 1986), p. 155.

91 The Police Foundation, *The Newark Foot Patrol Experiment*; Pate, "Experimenting with Foot Patrol."

92 The Police Foundation, *The Newark Foot Patrol Experiment*, pp. 4–5.

93 James Q. Wilson and George L. Kelling, "Broken Windows: The Police and Neighborhood Safety," *Atlantic Monthly* 249 (March 1982): 29–38.

94 Wilson and McLaren, *Police Administration*, pp. 633–645.

95 McEwen, Connors, and Cohen, *Evaluation of the Differential Police Response Field Test*.

96 Ibid.

97 Ibid.

98 Scott, *Calls for Service*, p. 97.

99 McEwen, Connors, and Cohen, *Evaluation of the Differential Police Response Field Test*, p. 8.

100 Robert E. Worden, "Toward Equity and Efficiency in Law Enforcement: Differential Police Response," *American Journal of Police* 12, no. 1 (1993): 1–32.

**101** Margaret J. Levine and J. Thomas McEwen, *Patrol Deployment* (Washington: Government Printing Office, 1985), pp. 40–41.

**102** U.S. Department of Justice, *COPS Office Report* (Washington: Government Printing Office, 1997), pp. 49–50; Michael Janofsky, "Baltimore Cites Success with Alternative to 911," *New York Times,* October 2, 1997, p. A7.

**103** President's Commission on Law Enforcement and Administration of Justice, *The Challenge of Crime in a Free Society* (Washington: Government Printing Office, 1967), pp. 108–109.

**104** James M. Tien and Richard C. Larson, "Police Service Aides: Paraprofessionals for Police," *Journal of Criminal Justice* 6 (Summer 1978): 117–131.

**105** Martha R. Plotkin and Ortwin A. 'Tony' Narr, *The Police Response to the Homeless: A Status Report* (Washington: Police Executive Research Forum, 1993), pp. 116–117, app. C, 85–90.

**106** U.S. Department of Justice, *Improving Patrol Productivity* (Washington: Government Printing Office, 1977) chap. 4.

**107** Gary W. Cordner, "The Effects of Directed Patrol: A Natural Quasi-Experiment in Pontiac," in *Contemporary Issues in Law Enforcement* ed., James J. Fyfe, (Beverly Hills: Sage, 1981), pp. 37–58.

**108** Sherman and Weisburd, "General Deterrent Effects of Police Patrol in Crime 'Hot Spots', pp. 625–648.

**109** Stephen D. Mastrofski, "The Prospects of Change in Police Patrol: A Decade in Review," *American Journal of Police*, 9, no. 3 (1990):66.

# CHAPTER 5

# PEACEKEEPING AND ORDER MAINTENANCE

Most police work involves peacekeeping and order maintenance, rather than crime fighting. People call the police for an infinite range of problems: arguments, fights, and domestic disputes; medical emergencies, including deaths, suicides, and injuries; assistance for dependent persons, including drunks, missing persons, and juvenile runaways; public nuisances, such as noise, trespassing, and suspicious persons. Table 4–3 in the previous chapter (pp. 81) provides the PSS data on the frequency of these various calls for service. Many order maintenance situations involve what are referred to as "special populations": the mentally ill, public inebriates, and the homeless.[1]

This chapter examines the peacekeeping and order maintenance activities of the police. It gives special attention to several specific situations that frequently arise, and looks at the different police responses to them.

## THE POLICE ROLE

Order maintenance calls raise important questions about the police role. As we discussed in Chapter 1, some people view the police as crime fighters, and think the non-crime calls are unimportant. Many police officers adopt this view and regard order maintenance calls as "garbage," "social work," or "bullshit."[2] This conflict between what the police actually do and what they value produces role conflict.

Some people, meanwhile, believe that noncrime calls are important but primarily because they contribute to effective crime fighting. Stephen Mastrofski identifies four different ways that noncrime calls for service can help improve police effectiveness in dealing with crime: (1) The "crime prophylactic" model holds that police intervention can defuse potentially violent situations and prevent them from escalating into criminal violence. (2) The "police knowledge" model holds that noncrime calls give officers a broader exposure to the community with the result that they have more knowledge that will help them solve crimes. (3) The "social work model" holds that the latent coercive power of the police can help steer potential law breakers into law-abiding behavior. (4) The "community cooperation" model holds that effective response to noncrime calls can help the police establish greater credibility with the public.[3]

---

**SIDEBAR 5–1**

POLICE POLICY TOWARD COMPLEX PROBLEMS

In his book on domestic violence, Lawrence W. Sherman advises that the problem "should be approached with the premise that new information will continue to appear, and that police policy should remain flexible enough to adapt to it."

His advice applies to every aspect of policing. All the issues the police deal with are complex. There are no easy answers. We should continually seek new information and be willing to reexamine our assumptions and the policies we support.

*Source:* Lawrence W. Sherman, *Policing Domestic Violence* (New York: Free Press, 1992), p. 252.

---

All of these models, however, assume that crime fighting is the central part of the police role and that noncrime calls are subordinate to them. Most experts on policing today, however, argue that order maintenance is at least as important as crime fighting, if not more important.[4] They believe that it is a legitimate role for the police to resolve problems that people believe exist. An orderly and peaceful society is a better society. If the police did not respond to these problems, either someone else would have to or the problems would continue unattended. Problem-oriented policing and community policing (see Chapter 7) are based on the idea that the police should focus on quality of life problems, not all of which are crime related.[5]

## CALLING THE POLICE

### Public Expectations

In a classic analysis, Egon Bittner describes police work in terms of situations involving "something-that-ought-not-to-be-happening-and-about-which-someone-had-better-do-something-now!"[6] In short, a citizen believes that there is a problem and wants something done about it. The modern police communications technology encouraged this expectation by creating the possibility that someone could respond to problems (see Chapter 2). The police encouraged people to call and, over time, people were socialized into the habit of "calling the cops."[7]

Citizens have different reasons for calling the police in noncrime situations. John C. Meyer identifies four specific expectations.[8]

**1 Maintaining a Social Boundary**. People often want the police to remove someone they believe does not belong there. The victim of domestic violence, for example, may call the police to remove the assailant. Homeowners may want the police to disperse a group of teenagers from in front of their homes.

In many of these situations, no actual crime has occurred: It is no crime to assemble peacefully on the street. In response, police officers often ask, suggest, or order people to leave. To a great extent, people comply with such requests even when they are not legally required to.

**2 Relieving Unpleasant Situations**. In many situations, someone calls the police because of noise, an argument, a family problem, or a dispute with neighbors. The role of the police is to restore order and keep the peace.

**3 Counterpunching**. In some disputes, someone calls the police about another person as a way of diverting attention away from his or her own behavior.

**4 Obtaining an Emergency Service**. People frequently call the police for emergency services: missing children, medical crises, suicide attempts, being locked out of their cars or homes, and so on.

### Police Response

Police officers exercise great discretion in handling noncrime incidents. Typically, they handle situations informally and take no official action (e.g., arrest). Informal responses

**TABLE 5–1**
SPECIFIC ACTIONS TAKEN DURING CONTACT STAGE BY ESOs AND CSOs—
311 NONTRAFFIC ENCOUNTERS

| Action | ESOs | | CSOs | |
|---|---|---|---|---|
| | % | # | % | # |
| Observed, stood by, took notes | 4.4 | 20 | 14.6 | 26 |
| Sought identity, relationships of parties | 15.4 | 70 | 19.1 | 34 |
| Questioned to elicit nature of problem | 30.8 | 140 | 30.9 | 55 |
| Asked citizens to "explain themselves" | 16.0 | 73 | 7.3 | 13 |
| Stated problem as police saw it | 3.5 | 16 | 3.4 | 6 |
| Verbally tried to defuse, "cool out" situation | 11.0 | 50 | 4.5 | 8 |
| Verbally restrained citizens (gave controlling orders) | 5.9 | 27 | 2.8 | 5 |
| Physically restrained citizens | 2.2 | 10 | 0.6 | 1 |
| Threatened physical force | 1.1 | 5 | 2.2 | 4 |
| Separated disputants in a nonphysical manner | 2.9 | 13 | 4.5 | 8 |
| Physically separated disputants | 1.1 | 5 | 0.0 | 0 |
| Requested dispersal of citizens | 1.1 | 5 | 0.6 | 1 |
| Ordered dispersal of citizens | 0.7 | 3 | 2.8 | 5 |
| Other | 3.9 | 18 | 6.8 | 11 |
| Total | 100.0 | 455 | 100.0 | 177 |

Note: Up to five actions were coded for each officer.

include a wide variety of verbal and nonverbal tactics. In their observation of New York City police officers, Bayley and Garofalo identified 20 different tactics that officers use in handling situations. Table 5–1 compares the activities of the experimental group officers (ESOs) and the control group officers (CSOs).[9]

Some officers are more active than others. Bayley and Garofalo found that the passive officers were more likely to observe and take notes. The more active officers took control of the situation by asking questions, giving advice or information, or warning the persons involved. Some officers accepted the complainant's definition of the situation, whereas others rejected it.

Citizens generally comply with specific police requests. Mastrofski, Snipes, and Supina found that citizens comply with police requests in 78 percent of all encounters. These incidents include requests to leave other people alone, to calm down and cease creating a disorder, to stop illegal behavior, and other miscellaneous requests. Compliance varies with the nature of the situation, the behavior of the officer, and the condition of the citizen. The more serious the situation, the less likely citizens are to comply. They are also less likely to comply with officers who approach the situation with a high degree of authoritativeness and/or who are disrespectful. Citizens are also more likely to comply in situations that occur in public rather than private places.[10]

## POLICING DOMESTIC DISPUTES

Domestic disputes are an important order maintenance situation. Domestic incidents represented 4.5 percent of all calls in the PSS data (see Table 4–3), and 5.3 percent of all calls to the Baltimore County Police between 1984 and 1986.[11] Police response to domestic incidents has been a matter of great controversy over the past 25 years. A revolution in public attitudes about domestic violence has led to new laws and policies, including increased criminal penalties, the development of treatment programs for batterers, and changes in police department policies.[12]

### Defining Our Terms

There is much confusion about police response to domestic incidents in part because many people fail to distinguish between disputes and violent incidents. The police handle many situations that are labeled *disturbances*. These include bar fights, arguments between neighbors, and many other kinds of problems. A *domestic* disturbance is one involving two or more people engaged in an intimate relationship. This includes married or divorced couples, live-in lovers, or people who are on a first date. It includes problems between adults and their children, or adults and their elderly parents. It also includes same-sex relationships. Only some of these—an estimated 30 percent—involve actual or threatened *violence*. The violence is usually an assault. Depending on the degree of seriousness, it is either a felony or a misdemeanor. About two-thirds of all domestic assaults are misdemeanors and one-third are felonies.[13]

Donald Black studied 317 disputes involving "two or more people who were related in some way" and where there was some request that the police "exercise their authority." Thirty-one percent involved a physical fight, injury to someone, or the threat of injury. Another 30 percent involved noise or some other disturbance; 14 percent entailed a dispute over property, and 12 percent concerned a request that someone leave the premises.[14]

### The Prevalence of Domestic Violence

Richard J. Gelles and Murray A. Straus, the two leading experts on the subject, conducted national surveys in 1975 and 1985, using an eight-point scale that distinguishes between severe and less serious forms of violence (Figure 5–1). They found that 11.3 percent of all wives experienced some form of domestic violence and 3 percent experienced severe violence in 1985 (compared with 3.8 percent in 1975).[15] An earlier survey of married women in Kentucky, found that 10 percent of all married women in the state had been victims of domestic violence per year and that 20 percent had suffered some domestic violence at some point in their marriage.[16]

### The Husband-Beating Controversy

The domestic violence issue is generally defined in terms of male violence against females. Yet, Gelles and Straus found that 4.4 percent of the husbands had experienced violence at the hands of their wives in 1985 (a rate somewhat higher than the 3.0 percent rate of male-to-female violence). When their colleague Suzanne K. Steinmetz first published these findings, an enormous controversy erupted. Some critics accused her of distracting attention from male-on-female violence.[17] Several explanations have been offered to explain husband beating. Much of it is self-defense or retaliatory. Female

**FIGURE 5–1**
HUSBAND-TO-WIFE VIOLENCE, 1975 AND 1985.

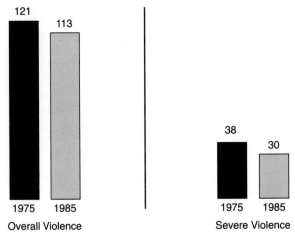

HUSBAND–TO–WIFE VIOLENCE Rates per 1,000 wives
1975 AND 1985.

*Source:* Adapted from Richard J. Gelles and Murray A. Straus, *Intimate Violence: The Causes and Consequences of Abuse in the American Family* (New York: Touchstone Books, 1988), p 176.

violence against men is probably even more highly unreported than male-on-female violence. According to Gelles and Straus, "Men are least likely to call a friend, neighbor, or the police."[18]

The National Crime Victimization Survey (NCVS) data, however, present a somewhat different picture of male versus female victimization. The rate of family violence directed against females (2.7 per 1,000) was more than 10 times that of violence against men (0.2 per 1,000).[19]

The phenomenon of husband beating has important implications for the police. In many domestic disturbance calls, the police arrive to find that both people have committed (or are alleged to have committed) some violent act. The officers face the challenge of determining exactly what happened and assessing responsibility. The Iowa mandatory arrest law directs the police to arrest the "primary aggressor."[20]

### Calling the Police

Most domestic violence victims do not call the police. Gelles and Straus's surveys found that female victims called the police in only 2.5 percent of all incidents and 14.4 percent of all severe incidents.[21] The Kentucky survey found that victims of spousal abuse called the police in only 9 percent of all incidents, and 17 percent of the severe violent incidents.[22] Official police data, then, offer a very unrepresentative picture of domestic violence.

The reporting of domestic violence varies by the status of the victim. Low-income people call the police most frequently. In an Omaha domestic violence study, 50 percent of the victims and 31 percent of the suspects were unemployed at the time of the police call. Only 7.4 percent of all calls to the police came from the western half of the city which includes the middle- and upper-middle-class residential neighborhoods.[23] The Kentucky survey found that working women were three times more likely to call the police than nonworking women (21 percent versus 8 percent). Nonwhite women in Kentucky were twice as likely to call the police as white women (18 percent versus 8 percent).[24]

Middle-class women are more likely to turn to private sources of help: a friend, a family member, a religious counselor, or a social worker. They are also more likely to be embarrassed about calling the police and worried about what neighbors or friends might think. The Kentucky Commission on the Status of Women concluded that "the poor become part of the official police record; the middle class conceals its family violence from public and official view."[25] Finally, the middle-income woman is more likely to be economically dependent upon her spouse (especially if she is a housewife and he is the sole source of income). The low-income woman is more likely to have relatively more economic equality to her husband or male friend.[26]

There are several reasons why victims of domestic violence do not call the police. According to an NCVS report, *Family Violence*, 59 percent of victims did not report the incident to the police because they regarded it as a private matter. Meanwhile, 13 percent did not call because they feared reprisal, 8 percent thought nothing could be done, and another 8 percent thought the police would not want to be bothered.[27]

Domestic violence is concentrated in certain families, and nonexistent in most families. Consequently, repeat calls to the same address are a common occurrence. An Ann Arbor study found that 36 percent of all the domestic disturbance calls in a six-month period involved repeat calls. Six residences had four calls, six had five calls, and three had six calls in that period.[28] In the Omaha study, 65 percent of the suspects had previously been arrested for some offense; 11 percent had been arrested for a past offense against the victim, and 3 percent had been arrested for an offense against the victim in the previous six months.[29] Gelles and Straus found that the average female victim was battered three times a year.[30]

A Police Foundation study in the 1970s found that the police had previously responded at least once to calls from addresses in 85 percent of domestic homicide cases in Kansas City. In 50 percent of those murders, the police had made five or more previous calls. The Police Foundation study suggested that it might be possible to predict, and thus prevent, many of these homicides if the police handled the earlier calls differently.[31] Lawrence Sherman investigated this issue with a more rigorous methodology in Milwaukee and found that it was impossible to predict homicides on the basis of prior domestic disturbance calls.[32]

## Danger to Police?

There is considerable controversy over the extent to which domestic disturbance calls pose a danger to police officers. Some data indicate that domestic calls are the most dangerous situations; other data indicate that they rank third or lower. Joel Garner and Elizabeth Clemmer's analysis of FBI data on officers killed or assaulted in the line of duty found that domestic disturbance calls ranked very low in terms of officers killed. Robbery and burglary incidents were consistently the most dangerous kinds of incidents. There was mixed evidence with respect to assaults on officers.[33] Uchida, Brooks and Kopers analyzed assault and injury rates relative to the frequency of domestic disturbance calls. They found that "domestics present a high risk of danger to police," ranking them first in one analysis and third (out of 20) in another.[34]

Domestic disturbances are more often frustrating than dangerous. The police are frequently able to resolve the immediate dispute, but they cannot do anything about the underlying cause—unemployment, alcohol or drug abuse, or psychological trouble. Black found that some officers deliberately drove slowly to a domestic disturbance, hoping the dispute would resolve itself before they arrived.[35]

### Police Response to Domestic Disturbances

Police officers exercise great discretion in handling domestic disturbances. The alternative responses include (1) arrest, (2) mediation, (3) separation of the parties, (4) referral to a social service agency, or (5) no action at all.

Arrest is not the most common response. As Mastrofski, Snipes, and Supina's study of police encounters (including all types of situations) found, police officers often ask a person to cease illegal behavior rather than make an arrest.[36] Studies have found arrest rates ranging from a high of about 40 percent of all incidents to a low of about 12 percent. (Some studies, however, have not distinguished between violent incidents and disturbances, where no law has been broken and arrest is not an option). The Kentucky domestic violence study found arrests in 41 percent of all violent incidents, but Donald Black's earlier study found arrests in only 25 percent of all violent felonies and 20 percent of all violent misdemeanors.[37]

Mediation includes a variety of different kinds of verbal responses. These include talking sympathetically; talking in an unsympathetic or hostile manner; asking the complainant what action she or he wants, ordering the parties to be quiet; threatening arrest.

Officers often separate the parties to a dispute by asking one of them to leave the premises. If a person is the legal resident of the house or apartment, the police have no legal right to force him or her to leave. Again, to a great extent, people comply with police requests that they leave. In the Omaha domestic violence study, virtually all people left the premises when asked; moreover, couples remained apart an average of three days (70 hours), and 87 percent of the victims reported that the police intervention helped resolve the problem they were having.[38]

Police officers may also refer one or more of the parties to the dispute to social services: marriage counseling, alcohol or drug treatment, or legal aid (for those contemplating separation, divorce, and other legal matters). Many departments provide officers with a list of social agencies. One study, however, found that officers choose this alternative in only 4 percent of all incidents. A police officer has no legal power to compel someone to seek professional help. A study of referrals in Ann Arbor found that only 1 percent of those referred actually contacted the social agency. An experiment designed to increase contacts through follow-up telephone calls succeeded in increasing the rate to only 7 percent of all those referred.[39]

A police officer can also take no action whatsoever. Donald Black found that in about 5 percent of the cases (13 out of 317) the police left the scene almost immediately after listening to one or more of the parties involved.[40]

### Factors Influencing the Arrest Decision

Several studies have explored the factors that influence police officer decisions to arrest in domestic violence situations. Generally, the decision is influenced by the same factors that influence arrest in all situations: the seriousness of the crime, the victim's preference for arrest, the relationship between the victim and the suspect (with arrest less likely the closer the relationship), and whether the suspect is disrespectful toward the police.[41] Studies by Berk and Loeske and also by Worden and Pollitz found that the probability of arrest in domestic violence situations increased if the woman was willing to sign an arrest warrant, if there was evidence that the man had been drinking, and where there was an allegation of violence against the woman.[42]

Several factors have traditionally discouraged officers from making arrests. First, some officers regard domestic violence as a private matter. Some hold to the sexist belief that a husband has a right to beat his wife. Second, many officers have learned from experience that domestic violence arrests are often dismissed because the victim refuses to pursue the case. A Police Foundation survey of officers found that the tendency of victims to drop charges was the second most frequently cited reason for not making arrests.[43]

Third, in the past police departments officially discouraged arrest for domestic violence. The International Association of Chiefs of Police (IACP) training materials in the 1960s advised that arrest should be a "last resort" in domestic disputes.[44] One of the most famous reforms of the 1960s, Morton Bard's Family Crisis Intervention (FCI) project, trained officers in alternatives to arrest.[45]

Fourth, an arrest is work. It requires that the officer perform many tasks (taking the suspect into custody, writing reports), some of which are potentially dangerous. An arrest also raises the visibility of the officer's work bringing it to the attention of other officials who might find it improper. If an officer does not make an arrest, on the other hand, the situation remains hidden from others. As is true in other occupations, police officers often try to reduce their workloads.[46] Moreover, police departments have traditionally not valued domestic violence arrests, placing a higher value on arrests for murder, rape, robbery, or narcotics.

### A Revolution in Policy: Mandatory Arrest

A revolution in public attitudes toward domestic violence began in the 1970s. The women's movement identified spousal abuse as a major problem and demanded protection for victimized women. In two important lawsuits, women's groups in New York City and Oakland sued the local police departments, charging that they had denied women equal protection of the law by failing to arrest persons who had committed

**FIGURE 5–2**

SUMMARY POLICY STATEMENT ON DOMESTIC VIOLENCE BY THE OAKLAND POLICE

---

OFFICE OF CHIEF OF POLICE
OAKLAND POLICE DEPARTMENT

SPECIAL ORDER NO. 3853

November 1, 1979

*Domestic Violence*

1. It is the policy of the Oakland Police Department to treat complaints of domestic violence as alleged criminal conduct. For the purposes of this order, "domestic violence" refers to offensive or harmful physical conduct of one spouse or cohabitant, or former spouse or cohabitant, towards the other.
2. The Police Department will not employ an arrest avoidance policy in response to incidents of alleged domestic violence. Although officers shall exercise discretion and shall utilize less punitive options when appropriate (e.g., citation, dispute mediation, referral, citizen's arrest), arrest shall be presumed to be the most appropriate response in domestic violence cases which involve an alleged felony, physical violence committed in the presence of an officer, repeated incidents, or violation of a restraining order.
3. Departmental policy and procedures regarding domestic violence cases are set forth in detail in Training Bulletin III–J, DOMESTIC VIOLENCE AND DOMESTIC DISPUTES.

---

domestic assaults. The suits led to new department policies on police handling of domestic violence.[47] In *Bruno v. Codd* (1978) the New York City police agreed to adopt a written policy mandating arrest in cases of felonious assault. The *Scott v. Hart* (1979) suit against the Oakland police resulted in a similar policy (Figure 5–2).[48]

Mandatory arrest policies represent one of the first attempts to control officer arrest discretion. The strategy of using written policies is called administrative rule making and has also been used to control officer discretion in the use of deadly force, high–speed pursuits, and other areas of policing.[49] The control of police discretion is covered in detail in Chapter 8.

### The Impact of Arrest on Domestic Violence

Many people believe that arrest deters future domestic violence. The Minneapolis Domestic Violence Experiment (1981–1982) sought to determine the relative deterrent effect of arrest, mediation, and separation in misdemeanor domestic violence incidents. Cases were randomly assigned to one of the three treatments. Each officer carried a color-coded pad of report forms and handled each case according to the approach indicated by the top form. Investigators measured repeat violence over the next six months through follow-up interviews with victims and police department records of calls to the same address.[50]

The Minneapolis study found that arrest produced lower rates of repeat violence than separation or mediation. Rearrest occurred in 10 percent of the arrest cases, compared with 19 percent of the mediation incidents and 24 percent of the separation incidents. The experiment received considerable national attention and had a major impact on public policy. Between 1984 and 1986 the percentage of big-city police departments with "arrest preferred" policies increased from 10 percent to 46 percent.[51] By 1993, 95 percent of all municipal police departments had written policies on domestic disputes (although not necessarily a mandatory arrest policy) and 53 percent had special domestic violence units.[52]

Critics have raised a number of serious questions about the Minneapolis experiment. Some police officers violated the integrity of the experiment by failing to handle the cases as directed, thereby undermining the random assignment of cases. A very small percentage of the participating officers produced the majority of the arrests. They were also more likely to follow the rules of the experiment. When only their cases were examined, the deterrent effect disappeared.[53] There was also a great deal of attrition among the subjects. Only 62 percent of the victims (205 out of 330) could be located for an initial interview, and only 49 percent completed all 12 of the interviews.

Some critics argue that Sherman, the director of the experiment had "prematurely and unduly publicized" the results. It is unwise, they argue, to recommend major changes in public policy on the basis of only one study that had not yet been replicated.[54] The lack of replication is a general problem in police research. Many of the most important experiments, such as the Kansas City Preventive Patrol Experiment (see Chapter 4), have not been replicated at all. It is dangerous to base public policy on one or even a small number of experiments.[55]

Replications of the Minneapolis experiment in other cities, in fact, failed to find a consistent deterrent effects of arrest. In Omaha, there were no significant differences among the effects of arrest, mediation, and separation. Mixed results were also found in the Charlotte, Miami, Colorado Springs, and Milwaukee experiments.[56]

Some of the findings of the Milwaukee experiment were particularly disturbing. Arrest appeared to *escalate* violence among unemployed persons compared with employed, and among unmarried persons compared with married. These data clearly indicate that arrest—at least for domestic violence—has different effects on different kinds of people.[57]

### Impact of Mandatory Arrest Laws and Policies

The full impact of mandatory arrest laws and policies is still not known. One important question is whether officers actually carry out mandatory arrest policies. Data on arrest trends suggest, but do not necessarily prove, that they do. Between 1971 and 1994 arrests for aggravated assault increased 140 percent. During the same time period, arrests for rape increased 33.6 percent, robbery 8.2 percent, while arrests for burglary declined by 24 percent. Arrests for misdemeanor assault, meanwhile, also increased at a far higher rate than for other Part II crimes.[58]

Some commentators have warned that mandatory arrest may discourage calls by women who want only that police calm the immediate situation. Eve Buzawa argues

---

SIDEBAR 5–2

STUDYING YOUR LOCAL POLICE

Do the major law enforcement agencies in your area have written domestic violence policies? Obtain copies of those policies and compare them. Are they *mandatory* arrest or arrest *preferred* policies? How much discretion do they leave to the officer? Do any of the agencies have special domestic violence units or programs? What do these programs involve?

---

that a mandatory arrest policy may deter women victims from calling the police in the first place—because many victims simply want the police to help with the immediate crisis but do not necessarily want an arrest.[59] Also, mandatory arrest is likely to have a disproportionate impact on lower-class men, and poor African-American men in particular.[60] On the other hand, the traditional no-arrest approach had a negative effect primarily on poor, African-American women, by denying them equal protection of the law.

## Other Laws and Policies

In addition to mandatory arrest policies, many departments have added special training for their officers in how to handle family violence situations. Surveys of victims, however, have failed to find greater satisfaction among those victims served by specially trained officers compared with officers who have not received special training.[61]

At the same time, many states have revised their laws on domestic violence. By 1992, 14 states and the District of Columbia mandated arrest for domestic violence. Iowa law directs the officer to identify and arrest the primary aggressor. Eight states require that law enforcement agencies develop written policies on the handling of domestic violence. Several states expanded the arrest power, allowing them to arrest in the case of misdemeanor assaults that did not occur in their presence.[62] Traditionally, police did not have power to arrest in these situations. Eighteen states mandate police officers to make an arrest for violation of a protection order. Traditionally, police did not have the power to arrest in these situations, with the result that many women's advocates regarded protection orders as worthless pieces of paper.[63]

## The Future of Domestic Violence Policy

The future of police policy toward domestic disturbances and domestic violence is not clear. Mandatory arrest policies remain extremely popular, but the full impact of these policies is uncertain. In a comprehensive review of domestic violence policies, Jeffrey Fagan concludes that there is "weak or inconsistent evidence" on the deterrent effect of arrest, prosecution, protection orders, and batterer treatment.[64] Lawrence W. Sherman, who directed the original Minneapolis experiment, no longer supports mandatory arrest in all situations.[65]

**SIDEBAR 5–3**

DOMESTIC VIOLENCE BY POLICE

A 1996 federal law (known as the Lautenberg Amendment) prohibits anyone with a conviction for domestic violence from owning a firearm. The law has serious implications for both the police and the military because possession and possible use of a weapon is an essential part of the job. As of 1998, police departments were wrestling with how to respond to this law.

The law presents several questions for consideration:

1 Is the law good social policy? Is it appropriate to deny firearms to people with a record of domestic violence?
2 Is it fair, or even constitutional, for a law to be applied retroactively?
3 Should a person with any kind of criminal conviction be employed as a police officer?

## POLICING THE HOMELESS

### The Homeless Problem: Old and New

Homeless people represent another order maintenance problem for the police. Because of changes in the nature of homelessness, it is important to distinguish between old and new homeless problems.

**The Old Homeless Problem**   The classic study of police response to the old homeless problem is Egon Bittner's article on policing skid row.[66] Skid row is the name given to that part of the city where the homeless congregate. It is usually located in a warehouse or industrial area near the central business district. The old homeless population consisted primarily of adult males who were unemployed, often had chronic alcohol abuse problems, and had fallen through society's safety nets: They were not eligible for unemployment insurance or welfare benefits and had no family support. They survived through temporary work, panhandling, scavenging, and selling blood. The skid row area contains various private and public agencies that serve the homeless: soup kitchens, shelters, cheap hotels, liquor stores, temporary employment agencies, and blood plasma centers.

Bittner characterized the traditional police response to the homeless as an example of peacekeeping. He found that police officers develop "an immensely detailed factual knowledge" about the area and a have a good feel for its normal routine. Officers have two principal objectives in policing skid row. The first is maintaining the boundaries: keeping homeless people in the skid row area. Business owners in other areas often complain when the homeless engage in aggressive panhandling, and expect the police to remove them. Homeless people almost always comply, even though not legally required to do so.

The second objective is keeping the peace, which means intervening when a homeless person's behavior exceeds certain informally established limits. This includes extremely loud and disruptive behavior, overly aggressive panhandling, or anything else that offends other nonhomeless people. Urinating in public or sleeping in doorways not only violates these rules, but also is a crime in most jurisdictions and tends to cause the police to respond by arresting the offenders.

Even when homeless people are arrested, the purpose is rarely to convict and punish them, but to control the immediate situation. Officers sometimes arrest people for their own protection: chronic alcoholics who are in danger of death through exposure to bad weather and helpless people who are easy prey for muggers.

Bittner found that police officer attitudes toward the homeless are complex. On the one hand, many officers take a tolerant and even parental attitude, regarding them as children who cannot care for themselves. On the other hand, many officers view the homeless with contempt, seeing them as weak and morally flawed people.

**The New Homeless Problem**   The homeless problem increased significantly in the 1980s. There has been much controversy over the actual number of homeless people. In the best study of the subject, Christopher Jencks estimated the total at about 400,000 people in 1988 (far less than the numbers used by some homeless advocates, but more than some government estimates).[67] The new homeless population includes more families than in the past, including more women and children. Some observers also believe there are more mentally ill persons among the homeless than in the past because of changes in mental health services.

Skid row in Los Angeles in the 1990s included a designated "sleeping zone," an area of 50 square blocks where the homeless are allowed to sleep on the streets. A newspaper account found on one night a 69-year-old grandmother and a 32-year-old woman, pregnant with twins, struggling to get into their cardboard boxes for the night. An estimated 12,000 people live in the neighborhood, most in single-room occupancy hotels, although no one knows exactly how many homeless people sleep on the streets.[68]

The new homeless problem created new challenges for the police. Homeless people established semipermanent camps in public parks, resisted transport to homeless shelters, and slept in bus stations and subways in some cities. Advocates for the homeless have filed law suits challenging either police actions and local ordinances designed to restrict the homeless. Some, but not all, of these suits have been successful.[69]

Members of the new homeless population are more likely to commit predatory crime. In the past, the homeless were more likely to be victims than offenders. The Santa Monica, California, Police Department reported that the homeless accounted for 27 percent of all calls for service in 1990 and a steadily increasing percentage of arrests: from 25 percent of all burglary arrests in 1985 to 53 percent in 1990; from 19 percent to 49 percent of all robbery arrests from 1985 to 1990.[70]

The Police Executive Research Forum (PERF) surveyed police departments in 1991 to determine how they were responding to the new homeless problem. About 40 percent reported that they did not keep records on contacts with the homeless, and half provided their officers no special training for dealing with the homeless.

Over 90 percent of the departments reported that homeless people were regarded as a public nuisance. The most frequent reasons for contact between the police and homeless people were calls from citizens, observations by officers, and calls from the business community. Over 88 percent reported that the homeless had alcohol abuse problems, 65 percent reported that the homeless appeared to be mentally disabled, but only 47 percent reported that the homeless were regularly involved in property crime.[71]

The Seattle Police Department uses community service officers (CSOs) to handle many of homeless-related situations. A CSO street team refers the homeless to shelters, alcohol and drug abuse treatment programs, and financial assistance services. During extreme cold weather CSO's distribute clothes and sleeping bags that have been donated, and patrol alleys looking for people who are in danger of death through exposure.[72]

### Police and the Chronic Alcoholic

Many homeless people suffer from chronic alcohol abuse problems. In the past, the police responded by arresting them on charges of public intoxication, vagrancy, or for violating some other ordinance. Police departments conducted occasional "sweep" arrests, picking up all vagrants and chronic alcoholics to clean up the streets. In some instances, the police escorted men to the city limits and ordered them not to return. In St. Louis the police dumped men on the banks of the Mississippi River, calling the area "detox east."[73] Such practices have been severely limited, as many states have decriminalized public intoxication, and advocates for the poor have challenged illegal police practices.

In the 1960s many experts argued that arrest of chronic alcoholics is inappropriate. First, it overloads the criminal justice system and diverts police time and resources from more serious crimes. Second, it fails to deal effectively with the underlying social and medical problems of the chronic alcoholic.[74] Following a recommendation by the President's Crime Commission, many states decriminalized public intoxication and a number of cities developed detoxification centers as alternatives to criminal prosecution.[75] St. Louis established a pioneering detoxification center in 1966. Police officers could offer persons arrested for public intoxication the alternative of either entering the seven-day treatment program or being prosecuted through the courts. In effect, the program was a form of diversion.

Detoxification programs introduce new problems, however. First, where states have decriminalized public intoxication it is not clear that the police have the authority to compel someone to enter a treatment program. Second, detoxification programs are expensive. The St. Louis program actually increased total expenditures: It saved $64,000 in court costs, but had a budget of $200,000, resulting in a net increase in total costs of $140,000 per year.[76] Third, there is no clear evidence that short-term treatment programs solve the underlying problems of chronic alcoholics. Fourth, many officers do not regard public drunkenness as an important part of their role and, consequently, use their discretion to ignore drunken individuals.

Changes in the law and public attitudes about drunkenness have produced changes in police arrest activity. In 1960 American police arrested 1.2 million people for drunkenness, representing 38 percent of all arrests. By 1994 there were only 713,000 drunkenness arrests, representing only 9 percent of all arrests.[77] Arrests also declined because police chose to concentrate their efforts on more serious crimes.

## POLICING THE MENTALLY ILL

Mentally ill persons represent another important order maintenance problem for the police. The police usually become involved because someone defines the situation as a problem and there is no other solution available. The exact frequency of mental illness incidents is difficult to determine precisely because of different definitions of mental illness. In the PSS data set, only 55 of the 26,418 calls for service (or 0.2 percent) were classified as involving "mentally disordered" persons.[78] Another study of 1,072 police–citizen encounters (not including traffic stops) found that 7.3 percent were related to mental disorder. In this study, a person was defined as mentally disordered if he or she exhibited one or more of the following behavior patterns: "confusion/ disorientation, withdrawal/ unresponsivity, paranoia, inappropriate or bizarre speech and/or behavior, and self-destructive behavior."[79] Police officers encounter much behavior that is strange or unconventional, but not all of it involves mental disorder, in a strict sense of the term.

### Police Response to the Mentally Ill

Police officers exercise great discretion in handling the mentally ill. The basic options include (1) hospitalization, (2) arrest, and (3) informal disposition. In one study of police encounters with 85 mentally disordered persons, 11.8 percent were hospitalized, 16.5 percent were arrested, and 71.8 percent were handled informally.[80]

Several institutional and legal factors limit the police response. First, the law limits the ability of the police to commit someone to a mental health facility involuntarily. A person can be committed only if he or she is a danger to himself or to others. The paperwork required to meet this standard discourages officers from trying to commit people except in the most extreme cases.[81]

Second, mental health services are highly fragmented, consisting of a variety of hospitals, homeless shelters, and detoxification facilities. Most have their own admission criteria and refuse to accept people the police bring to them. In some instances, police officers go from one agency to another looking for one that will accept the mentally disordered person.

Arrest of the mentally ill is also infrequent. Arrest is used when a person's behavior is too bizarre to ignore, but the person is not sufficiently mentally ill to be accepted by a hospital. The factors influencing the decision to arrest include (1) the seriousness of the person's apparent illness, (2) the presence of another person who is greatly offended

---

**SIDEBAR 5–4**

INVOLUNTARY CIVIL COMMITMENT IN YOUR STATE

What is the law on involuntary civil commitment of an allegedly mentally ill person in your state? What standard does a police officer have to meet in order to commit someone? Is there a secure mental health facility in your community to hold a seriously mentally ill person?

---

by the individual's behavior and is willing to sign a formal complaint, (3) refusal by a medical facility to accept the person, and (4) the officer's belief that the individual would continue to be a problem.[82]

The vast majority of the mentally ill are handled informally. These people fall into three general categories: neighborhood characters, troublemakers, and quiet, unobtrusive "mentals." Neighborhood characters are well known to the police and others in the community and are often referred to by nicknames such as "Crazy Harry" and "Mailbox Molly." Police officers know from previous contact that they are not dangerous. Informal methods for dealing with them include "cooling them out," which generally means talking with them to make certain they are not dangerous in order to calm them down and reduce their more bizarre behavior. Troublemakers include people the police regard as too difficult to handle through formal means. Though their behavior might warrant arrest or hospitalization, the police decide that it would not be worth the effort. The unobtrusive "mentals" include people who have obvious signs of mental disturbance but whose behavior does not offend anyone to a serious degree.[83]

An important question is, How accurate are police officers in identifying seriously mentally ill persons? A report by PERF found that police recruits receive an average of only 4.3 hours of training in mental health problems.[84] Yet a study of Toronto police officers found that their judgments about people correlated with those individuals' prior record of violence and were generally consistent with the clinical diagnoses by mental health professionals.[85]

### Old Problems/New Programs

A report by PERF cited three model programs for handling the mentally ill. In Madison, Wisconsin, officers receive over 20 hours of training on mental health problems. Officers faced with difficult cases are able to confer with a 24-hour emergency mental health center run by the county. The Galveston County (Texas) Sheriff's Department dispatches six specially trained officers to all known mental health calls. The Birmingham (Alabama) Police Department sends social workers with police officers to the scene of mental health calls.[86]

A U.S. Department of Justice report, meanwhile, emphasizes the importance of police departments establishing networks with social service agencies. The Los Angeles Police Department, for example, has a written agreement with the Los Angeles County Department of Mental Health to maintain a 24-hour unit available to police officers for consultation on difficult cases. The police department created a special mental health evaluation unit, staffed by trained officers who screen all mental health cases.[87]

### POLICING PEOPLE WITH DISABILITIES

The 1990 Americans With Disabilities Act (ADA) prohibits discrimination against persons with disabilities. This covers people with a broad range of physical and mental impairments. The ADA imposes major responsibilities on the police, because they routinely encounter disabled persons in calls for service and because disabled persons often have special needs: as crime victims, as citizens in need of emergency assistance, and because other people sometimes regard them as problems. Under the law, the police may not discriminate against handicapped people, and may not arrest them or order them to leave an area simply because another person does not like them.

The Chicago Police Department adopted a comprehensive human rights policy that included a specific policy related to persons with disabilities in 1992. The department committed itself to making "reasonable modifications in procedures. . .when a Department facility is not accessible due to physical barriers. . ." The policy also included special provisions related to handling the arrest of persons in wheelchairs. The department also provides the services of a sign language or oral interpreter for persons with hearing or speech impairments.[88]

## POLICING PEOPLE WITH AIDS

In the 1980s Acquired Immune Deficiency Syndrome (AIDS) presented the police with a new set of problems. Because police officers often handle people with AIDS (PWAs), there is some risk of infection. Infected bodily fluids can be transmitted through biting, scratching, or spitting, or through throwing infected blood, urine, or feces at an officer. AIDS cannot be transmitted through casual physical contact such as touching, however.[89]

Police officers may not refuse to handle incidents involving people with AIDS. Failure to perform a required task, such as an arrest, represents dereliction of duty as well as discrimination against a class of people. Some departments have disciplined officers who refused to perform assigned duties because of fear of AIDS.

A U.S. Department of Justice report recommended that all law enforcement agencies provide AIDS-related education and training for their officers, and develop formal policies for the handling of HIV-positive individuals in routine encounters, arrest situations, and police lock-ups.[90] A study of sheriffs' deputies in Durham, North Carolina, found that officers who had better knowledge about AIDS and its transmission were also less fearful of contracting the disease themselves.[91]

## POLICING JUVENILES

Juveniles represent a special set of problems for the police. First, the police have a high level of contact with people under the age of 18. Young people are more likely than are adults to be out on the street where they are observed by the police. "Hanging out" on the corner or "cruising" in cars often produces citizen conflict over the proper use of public spaces.

Second, young people are consistently less likely to express favorable attitudes toward the police than older people. In a 1995 survey, 72 percent of people between the ages of 18 and 29 expressed favorable attitudes with respect to the fairness of the police, compared with 90 percent for people in the 40 to 49-year-old age group.[92]

Third, juveniles represent a significant aspect of the crime problem in the United States: 16 percent of all arrests, 29 percent of all Index crime arrests, and 33 percent of

---

**POLICE ON THE WEB**

Some police departments describe their gang unit or other antigang programs on their web sites. Check out the sites for several police departments. Do they describe their gang units? Can you learn anything useful about these units?

---

all property crime arrests. Juveniles are involved in three crimes at a particularly high rate: 49 percent of all arson arrests, 45 percent of all vandalism arrests, and 44 percent of all motor vehicle arrests.[93] Even more serious, homicides by juveniles soared between the mid-1980s and the early 1990s, while homicides by adults were declining.[94] Moreover, there was a sharp increase in firearms-related homicides by juveniles. Part of the murder and firearms problem is due to the increase in organized gang activity by juveniles.

### Controversy over the Police Role

There is significant controversy over the proper police role toward juveniles. Some people favor a strict law enforcement role, emphasizing the arrest of offenders. Others prefer a crime prevention role, arguing that the police should emphasize helping young people who are at risk with advice, counseling, and alternatives to arrest.[95] The International Association of Chiefs of Police (IACP) recommends a middle-of-the-road approach: "Most police departments operate juvenile programs that combine the law enforcement and delinquency prevention roles, and the police should work with the juvenile court to determine a role that is most suitable for the community."[96]

Uncertain or conflicting department policies regarding juveniles often cause role conflict for police officers on the street. One report on police–juvenile operations pointed out that "crime prevention can be viewed as 'social work,' a role which police often see as taking time away from what they consider to be their primary role—the apprehension of criminals."[97]

Police response to juveniles is complicated by conflicting police responsibilities (see Chapter 1). The case of kids hanging out on the streets illustrates the problem. On the one hand the police are expected to maintain order. To this end, a number of cities have passed curfews for juveniles and/or "gang loitering" ordinances. At the same time, however, the police have a responsibility to respect the rights of citizens. Young people have a First Amendment right to assemble in public.

Because of increased public fear of crime and violent juvenile crime in particular, police departments have given greater emphasis to the law enforcement role in recent years. With the exception of programs such as the Drug Abuse Resistance Education D.A.R.E. program (see the following page), traditional crime prevention programs have been deemphasized.

### Specialized Juvenile Units

Police contacts with juveniles are divided between two units within the department: patrol and specialized juvenile units. Patrol officers have the most contact with juveniles as part of their normal patrol duty. They regularly see and have contact with groups of kids hanging out on the street corners, people they suspect to be gang members, and so on.

Most large police departments have special juvenile units. They are often referred to by such names as the juvenile division, the youth division, or the crime prevention bureau. In 1993, 88 percent of all municipal police departments had a special juvenile unit; another 76 percent had a special gang unit. Most departments also had special child abuse and missing children units. The D.A.R.E. program, where police officers provide drug education in the schools, is extremely popular. Law Enforcement Management and Administrative Statistic's (LEMAS) data indicate that 95 percent of all police departments have a special unit for drug education in the schools.[98]

The responsibilities of traditional juvenile units include (1) investigating reports of juvenile crime, (2) arresting delinquents, (3) preparing cases for court, and (4) appearing in court. Juvenile units tend to be small and, according to one study, are declining in significance. Bittner, however, found that police juvenile units occupied low status in most police departments and officers regarded most juvenile-related incidents as trivial.[99]

### On-the-Street Encounters

Black and Reiss found that 72 percent of all encounters between police and juveniles were initiated by a telephone call. Officers appear to initiate contacts with juveniles at a slightly higher rate (28 percent of all contacts) than with adults.[100] This is due to the fact that young people are more likely to be out on the street than adults, and that the police are more likely to regard juveniles as criminal suspects.

On-the-street encounters between juveniles and the police often involve conflicts over lifestyles. Werthman and Piliavin found that juvenile gang members regarded the street corner as a private place for their own recreation. They created "transparent walls" between themselves and other people on the street. Anyone who violated this space was guilty of trespass, even though that person had a legal right to use the public space.[101] Similar conflicts over the use of public space occur with middle-class juveniles. Cruising or hanging out is a popular pastime that many adults regard as obnoxious.

As is the case with all other police activities, officers exercise great discretion in dealing with juveniles on the street (see Chapter 8). The alternative police responses include the following.[102]

**1** Taking no official action. This is the most common outcome. As is the case with domestic disputes and allegedly mentally disturbed people, the police dispose of situations informally, mainly just by talking with people. Talking may involve advising, warning, mediating disputes, or simply listening. In many instances no arrest is made even though there are sufficient legal grounds to make an arrest.

**2** Taking a juvenile into custody but releasing him or her to a parent or guardian. An estimated 30 percent of all juveniles taken into custody are released in this fashion.[103]

**3** Taking the juvenile into custody and releasing him or her to another law enforcement or social service agency. About 3 percent of all juveniles taken into custody are released in this fashion.[104]

**4** Arresting the juvenile and referring him or her to juvenile court. About two-thirds of all juveniles are referred to juvenile court. Some (about 7 percent of the total) are referred to criminal court for prosecution as adults.[105]

Arrest discretion involving juveniles is influenced by the same situational factors that affect encounters with adults. These factors include the seriousness of the offense, the preference of the victim or complaining party, the relationship between complainant and suspect, and the demeanor of the suspect.[106]

### The Issue of Race Discrimination

The police arrest proportionately far more African-American juveniles than white. Several factors account for this disparity. First, police departments generally assign more patrol officers to minority neighborhoods than white neighborhoods (see Chapter 4) and, consequently, observe minority youths more frequently.[107]

Second, minority youths are stopped and questioned at a higher rate than white youths. The San Diego Field Interrogation study found that minorities were stopped for questioning at rates disproportionate to their presence in particular neighborhoods.[108]

Third, the racial disparity in arrests is associated with other factors that influence arrest decisions. Black and Reiss found that the higher arrest rate was explained in large part by greater African-American involvement in serious crime. When the seriousness of the suspected offense was controlled, blacks and whites were arrested at similar rates.[109] Lundman, meanwhile, found that black adults are more likely to ask the police to arrest the suspect than are white adults. Because most complainant–suspect situations are intraracial, black juveniles are arrested at a higher rate.[110] Smith, Visher, and Davidson, in a study of arrests involving persons of all ages, found that police are slightly more likely to arrest when the victim is white than African American. Other studies have also suggested that the police are more likely to arrest a juvenile when an adult is the complaining party.[111]

The demeanor of the suspect also influences police arrest decisions. In separate studies, Black and Reiss and also Piliavin and Briar found that African-American juveniles expressed hostility toward the police more often than did whites, and as a consequence were arrested at higher rates. Piliavin and Briar described the phenomenon as the "self-fulfilling consequences of the original set of police attitudes and behavior toward black youth." The police expect black juveniles to engage in more law breaking, stop and question them at a higher rate, and as a consequence create the perception of harassment and generate more hostile reactions.[112] (David Klinger, however, has raised new questions about the role of demeanor in arrests, arguing that these earlier studies did not control for hostile behavior that occurred after the arrest and which therefore could not have influenced the arrest itself.)[113]

### Police Diversion Programs

In the 1960s diversion emerged as a popular alternative for arrested juveniles. Diversion is a formal program designed to suspend prosecution and remove the suspect from the criminal justice system. The police traditionally diverted many juveniles from the criminal justice system by simply not arresting them. The new diversion that emerged in the 1960s involved formal programs with different forms of treatment.[114]

Diversion rests on several assumptions. First, labeling theorists believe that arrest and prosecution may label the individual and amplify criminal behavior. Second, many experts believe that arrest and prosecution of juveniles for minor offenses overloads the criminal justice system. Finally, many people argue that criminal prosecution is not an appropriate response to a youth's real problems (e.g., family disorganization, drug abuse, lack of education or motivation).

Police diversion programs were endorsed by the President's Crime Commission and were very popular in the 1970s.[115] A survey of California police departments in the mid-1970s estimated that between 150 and 200 police diversion programs were in operation. The survey found that nearly two-thirds of all juvenile offenders were diverted out of the criminal justice system. Nearly half (45.8 percent) were counseled and released; 8.1 percent were referred to community agencies; 8.6 percent were referred to other juvenile justice agencies; 30 percent were referred to juvenile court (another 7.5 percent were handled in some "other" manner).[116]

Evaluations of police diversion programs have questioned their effectiveness.[117] Programs have not achieved their goals of keeping juveniles out of the system. One major problem is the "net widening" phenomenon. Instead of diverting people out of the system, diversion programs tend to bring more juveniles under some form of social control. Diversion also involves its own form of labeling because the person is under some form of sanction. Finally, the decision to divert creates important due process and equal protection considerations.[118]

### Crime Prevention Programs

Police crime prevention efforts have traditionally involved programs designed to steer juveniles away from criminal activity through education, counseling, or role modeling. The basic idea is for the police to present themselves as friends and helpers rather than as law enforcers.

Some current crime prevention programs are part of community policing. The Spokane Police Department, for example, ran a COPY Kids program in 1992. About 300 youths, both male and female, with a median age of 13, spent a week in the program. Police officers and volunteers conducted drug education and other information programs, led the kids in neighborhood clean-up and graffiti eradication, and supervised recreation programs. The officers wore plain clothes at the beginning of the week, but wore their uniforms at the end when they believed they had established rapport with the kids. The purpose of the program was to establish positive relations between the police and at-risk juveniles, to provide information on specific topics such as drugs, and to reinforce the idea that hard work and productivity are rewarded. Follow-up interviews with the kids, the staff, and parents found positive results. The evaluation did not, however, survey either drug use or involvement in crime before and after the program.[119]

The most popular current crime prevention program is D.A.R.E. Created in 1983 by the Los Angeles Police Department (LAPD), D.A.R.E. is an in-school education program consisting of 17 one-hour classes taught by sworn officers. D.A.R.E. is extremely popular with parents and school officials. By 1997 the program was operating in an estimated 70 percent of all school districts, at an annual cost of about $750 million.[120]

Despite its enormous popularity, evaluations have questioned the impact of the D.A.R.E. program on students exposed to it. Although students' attitudes often become more opposed to drugs, there is no evidence that the program reduces actual drug use.[121]

The popularity of the D.A.R.E. program inspired creation of the G.R.E.A.T. (Gang Resistance Education and Training) program. A similar format—in-school education by sworn police officers—is designed to prevent involvement in gangs.[122]

## CONCLUSION

Order maintenance and peacekeeping is an important part of policing for the simple reason that most calls for service fall in this category. How the police respond to these calls raises the basic issues about the police role that we discussed in Chapter 1. How do we think about the police? What do we want them to do?

Traditionally, police officers regarded order maintenance calls as garbage and social work, placing a higher value on crime fighting. Most experts today, however, argue that maintaining order and keeping the peace is a central aspect of policing. Problem-oriented policing and community policing place a high value on dealing with noncrime problems. Many order maintenance situations, moreover, involve special populations: the homeless, the mentally ill, the chronic alcoholic. If we think of the police in terms proposed by Herman Goldstein, as a general service agency providing a wide range of services to the public, it becomes important for police departments to develop special programs and procedures to improve the handling of these problem situations.[123]

## NOTES

1  Peter E. Finn and Monique Sullivan, *Police Response to Special Populations* (Washington: Government Printing Office, 1988).

2  Albert Reiss, *The Police and The Public* (New Haven: Yale University Press, 1971).

3  Stephen Mastrofski, "The Police and Noncrime Services," in G. Whitaker and C. Phillips, eds., *Evaluating the Performance of Criminal Justice Agencies* (Beverly Hills: Sage, 1983), pp. 44–47.

4  Herman Goldstein, *Policing a Free Society* (Cambridge, Mass.: Ballinger, 1977), pp. 21–44.

5  Herman Goldstein, *Problem-Oriented Policing* (New York: McGraw-Hill, 1990).

6  Egon Bittner, "Florence Nightingale in Pursuit of Willie Sutton: A Theory of the Police," in ed., Herbert Jacob *The Potential for Reform of Criminal Justice,* (Beverly Hills: Sage, 1974), pp. 1–25.

7  Samuel Walker, *Popular Justice: A History of American Criminal Justice*, 2d ed. (New York: Oxford University Press, 1998), pp. 165–167.

**8** John C. Meyer, "Patterns of Reporting Noncriminal Incidents to the Police," *Criminology* 12 (May 1974): 70–83.

**9** David H. Bayley and James Garofalo, "The Management of Violence by Police Patrol Officers," *Criminology* 27 (February 1989): 1–25.

**10** Stephen D. Mastrofski, Jeffrey B. Snipes, and Anne E. Supina, "Compliance on Demand: The Public's Response to Specific Requests," *Journal of Research in Crime and Delinquency* 33 (August 1996): 269–305.

**11** Eric J. Scott, *Calls for Service: Citizen Demand and Initial Police Response* (Washington: Government Printing Office, 1981); Craig D. Uchida, Laure Brooks, Christopher S. Kopers, "Danger to Police During Domestic Encounters: Assaults on Baltimore County Police, 1984–1986," *Criminal Justice Policy Review* 2 (No. 2, 1987): 357–371.

**12** Jeffrey Fagan, *The Criminalization of Domestic Violence: Promises and Limits* (Washington: Government Printing Office, 1996); Lawrence W. Sherman, *Policing Domestic Violence: Experiments and Dilemmas* (New York: Free Press, 1992).

**13** Donald Black, "Dispute Settlement by the Police," in *The Manners and Customs of the Police* (New York: Academic Press, 1980), pp. 109–192.

**14** Ibid., p. 112.

**15** Richard J. Gelles and Murray A. Straus, *Intimate Violence: The Causes and Consequences of Abuse in the American Family* (New York: Touchstone Books, 1988).

**16** Mark A. Schulman, *A Survey of Spousal Violence against Women in Kentucky* (Washington: Government Printing Office, 1979).

**17** Suzanne K. Steinmetz, "The Battered Husband Syndrome," *Victimology* 2, no. 3/4 (1978): 499–509.

**18** Gelles and Straus, *Intimate Violence*, p. 150.

**19** Bureau of Justice Statistics, *Family Violence* (Washington: Government Printing Office, 1984).

**20** Code of Iowa (1997), vol. 2, sec. 236.11.

**21** Gelles and Straus, *Intimate Violence*, p. 258.

**22** Schulman, *A Survey of Spousal Violence*, p. 15.

**23** Franklyn W. Dunford, David Huizinga, Delbert S. Elliott, "The Role of Arrest in Domestic Assault: The Omaha Police Experiment," *Criminology* 28 (May 1990): 183–206. Some of these data appear in the unpublished technical report. Franklyn W. Dunford, "The Omaha Domestic Violence Police Experiment," (Boulder, CO: University of Colorado, 1989).

**24** Schulman, *A Survey of Spousal Violence*, p. 38.

**25** Ibid.

**26** Black, "Dispute Settlement by the Police," pp. 125–126.

**27** Bureau of Justice Statistics, *Family Violence*, table 4.

**28** Wayne Hanewicz et al., "Improving the Linkages Between Domestic Violence Referral Agencies and the Police," *Journal of Criminal Justice* 10, no. 6, (1982): 493–503.

**29** Dunford, Huizinga, and Elliott, "The Role of Arrest in Domestic Assault," pp. 193–194.

**30** Gelles and Straus, *Intimate Violence*, p. 104.

**31** The Police Foundation, *Domestic Violence and the Police* (Washington: The Police Foundation, 1977).

**32** Sherman, *Policing Domestic Violence*, pp. 231–238.

**33** Joel Garner and Elizabeth Clemmer, *Danger to Police in Domestic Disturbances—A New Look* (Washington: Government Printing Office, 1986).

**34** Uchida, Brooks, and Kopers, "Danger to Police During Domestic Encounters," p. 367.

**35** Black, "Dispute Settlement by the Police," p. 146.

**36** Mastrofski, Snipes, and Supina, "Compliance on Demand."

**37** Schulman, *A Survey of Spousal Violence*, p. 38; Black, "Dispute Settlement by Police," p. 181.

**38** Dunford, Huizinga, and Elliott, "The Role of Arrest in Domestic Assault."

**39** Hanewicz et al., "Improving the Linkages between Domestic Violence Referral Agencies and the Police."

**40** Black, "Dispute Settlement by the Police," p. 129.

**41** Black, "The Social Organization of Arrest," in Black, *The Manners and Customs of the Police*, pp. 85–108.

**42** Sara Fenstermaker Berk and Donileen R. Loeske, "'Handling' Family Violence: Situational Determinants of Police Arrest in Domestic Disturbances," *Law and Society Review* 15 (1980–1981): 317–346; Robert E. Worden and Alissa A. Pollitz, "Police Arrest in Domestic Disturbances: Another Look," in *Understanding Police Agency Performance*, ed. Gordon P. Whitaker (Washington: Government Printing Office, 1984), pp. 77–92.

**43** Nancy Loving, *Responding to Spouse Abuse and Wife Beating: A Guide for Police* (Washington: Police Executive Research Forum, 1980), p. 42.

**44** International Association of Chiefs of Police, *Training Key #16*, "Handling Disturbance Calls" (Gaithersburg: IACP, 1977).

**45** Morton Bard, *Training Police as Specialists in Family Crisis Intervention* (Washington: Government Printing Office, 1970).

**46** Albert Reiss, *The Police and the Public* (New Haven: Yale University Press, 1971), p. 14.

**47** Loving, *Responding to Spouse Abuse and Wife Beating*, pp. 36–38. Laurie Woods, "Litigation on Behalf of Battered Women," *Women's Rights Law Reporter* 5 (Fall 1978): 7–34.

**48** Loving, *Responding to Spouse Abuse and Wife Beating*, pp. 163–168.

**49** Samuel Walker, *Taming the System: The Control of Discretion in Criminal Justice, 1950–1990* (New York: Oxford University Press, 1993).

**50** Lawrence W. Sherman and Richard A. Berk, "The Specific Deterrent Effect of Arrest for Domestic Assault," *American Sociological Review* 49, no. 2 (1984): 261–272; Sherman, *Policing Domestic Violence*, pp. 75–91.

**51** Sherman, *Policing Domestic Violence*, p. 110.

**52** Bureau of Justice Statistics, *Law Enforcement Management and Administrative Statistics, 1993* (Washington: Government Printing Office, 1995), p. xiv.

**53** Patrick R. Gartin, "Examining Differential Officer Effects in the Minneapolis Domestic Violence Experiment," *American Journal of Police* 14, no. 3/4 (1995): 93–110.

**54** Richard E. Lempert, "From the Editor," *Law and Society Review* 18, no. 4 (1984): 505–513; Lawrence W. Sherman and Ellen G. Cohn, "The Impact of Research on Legal Policy: The Minneapolis Domestic Violence Experiment," *Law and Society Review* 23, no. 1 (1989): 117–144; Richard Lempert, "Humility as a Virtue: On the Publicization of Policy-Relevant Research," *Law and Society Review* 23, no. 1 (1989): 145–161; Sherman, *Policing Domestic Violence*, pp. 92–124.

**55** Lawrence W. Sherman et al., *Preventing Crime* (College Park: University of Maryland, 1997), chap. 8.

**56** Sherman, *Policing Domestic Violence*, pp. 125–153.

**57** Ibid, pp. 154–187.

**58** Bureau of Justice Statistics, *Sourcebook of Criminal Justice Statistics, 1995*, (Washington, DC: Government Printing Office, 1996), p. 403.

**59** Eve Buzawa, "Police Officer Response to Domestic Violence Legislation in Michigan," *Journal of Police Science and Administration* 10, no. 4 (1982): 415–424.

**60** Susan L. Miller, "Unintended Side Effects of Pro-Arrest Policies and Their Race and Class Implications for Battered Women: A Cautionary Note," *Criminal Justice Policy Review 3*, no. 3, (1989): 299–317.

**61** National Institute of Justice, *Evaluation of Family Violence Training Programs* (Washington: Government Printing Office, 1995).

**62** Joan Zorza, "The Criminal Law of Misdemeanor Domestic Violence, 1970–1990," *Journal of Criminal Law and Criminology* 83 (Spring 1992): 240–279.

**63** Barbara J. Hart, *State Codes on Domestic Violence* (Reno: National Council of Juvenile and Family Court Judges, 1992); Eve S. Buzawa and Carl G. Buzawa, *Domestic Violence*: *The Criminal Justice Response* (Newbury Park, Calif.: Sage, 1990), pp. 110–135.

**64** Fagan, *The Criminalization of Domestic Violence*, p. 1.

**65** Sherman, *Policing Domestic Violence*, p. 253.

**66** Egon Bittner, "The Police on Skid Row: A Study in Peacekeeping," *American Sociological Review* 32 (October 1967): 694–715.

**67** Christopher Jencks, *The Homeless* (Cambridge: Harvard University Press, 1994).

**68** "Redevelopment Plans May Hem In Skid Row," *New York Times* (October 23, 1997), p. 1.

**69** George L. Kelling and Catherine M. Coles, *Fixing Broken Windows* (New York: Free Press, 1996).

**70** Barney Melekian, "Police and the Homeless," *FBI Law Enforcement Bulletin* (November 1990).

**71** Martha R. Plotkin and Ortwin A. Narr, *The Police Response to the Homeless: A Status Report* (Washington: Police Executive Research Forum, 1993).

**72** Martha R. Plotkin and Ortwin A. Narr, *The Police Response to the Homeless: A Status Report* (Washington: Police Executive Research Forum, 1993), app. C–85 to C–116.

**73** David E. Aaronson, C. Thomas Dienes, and Michael C. Musheno, *Public Policy and Police Discretion* (New York: Clark Boardman, 1984), pp. 311–314.

**74** President's Commission on Law Enforcement and Administration of Justice, *Task Force Report: Drunkenness* (Washington: Government Printing Office, 1967).

**75** Raymond T. Nimmer, *Two Million Unnecessary Arrests* (Chicago: American Bar Foundation, 1971).

**76** Ibid., p. 96.

**77** David E. Aaronson, C. Thomas Dienes, and Michael C. Musheno, *Public Policy and Police Discretion* (New York: Clark Boardman, 1984), pp. 311–314.

**78** Scott, *Calls for Service*, pp. 28–30.

**79** Linda Teplin, *Keeping the Peace*: *Parameters of Police Discretion in Relation to the Mentally Disordered* (Washington: Government Printing Office, 1986).

**80** Ibid.

**81** Ibid.

**82** Ibid.

**83** Ibid.

**84** Police Executive Research Forum, *Special Care*: *Improving Police Response to the Mentally Disabled* (Washington: PERF, 1988).

**85** Robert J. Menzies, "Psychiatrists in Blue: Police Apprehension of Mental Disorder and Dangerousness," *Criminology*, 25 (August 1987): 429–453. Henry J. Steadman et al., "Psychiatric Evaluations of Police Referrals in a General Hospital Emergency Room," *International Journal of Law and Psychiatry* 8, no. 1 (1986):39–47.

**86** Police Executive Research Forum, *Special Care*.

**87** Peter E. Finn and Monique Sullivan, *Police Response to Special Populations* (Washington: Government Printing Office, 1988).

**88** Chicago Police Department, General Order #92–1 (July 3, 1992).

**89** Theodore M. Hammett, *AIDS and the Law Enforcement Officer: Concerns and Policy Responses* (Washington: Government Printing Office, 1987).

**90** Ibid.

**91** Douglas L. Yearwood, "Law Enforcement and AIDS: Knowledge, Attitudes, and Fears in the Workplace," *American Journal of Police* 11, no. 2 (1992): 65–83.

**92** W. S. Wilson Huang and Michael S. Vaughn, "Support and Confidence: Public Attitudes Toward the Police," in *Americans View Crime and Justice: A National Public Opinion Survey*, eds. Timothy J. Flanagan and Dennis R. Longmire (Newbury Park, Calif.: Sage, 1996), p. 40.

**93** Office of Juvenile Justice and Delinquency Prevention, *Juvenile Offenders and Victims: A National Report* (Washington: Government Printing Office, 1995).

**94** James Alan Fox, *Trends in Juvenile Violence* (Washington: Government Printing Office, 1996).

**95** National Institute for Juvenile Justice and Delinquency Prevention, *Police–Juvenile Operations: A Comparative Analysis of Standards and Practices*, vol. 2 (Washington: Government Printing Office, n.d.), pp. 3–10.

**96** R. Kobetz and B. Borsage, *Juvenile Justice Administration* (Gaithersburg: International Association of Chiefs of Police, 1973), p. 112.

**97** National Institute for Juvenile Justice and Delinquency Prevention, *Police–Juvenile Operations*, vol. 2, p. 3.

**98** Bureau of Justice Statistics, *Law Enforcement Management and Administrative Statistics, 1993* (Washington: Government Printing Office, 1995), p. xiv.

**99** Egon Bittner, "Policing Juveniles: The Social Context of Common Practice," in *Pursuing Justice for the Child*, eds. M. K. Rosenheim, (Chicago: University of Chicago Press, 1976), p. 80.

**100** Donald Black and Albert Reiss, "Police Control of Juveniles," *American Sociological Review*, 35 (February 1970): 63–77.

**101** Carl Werthman and Irving Piliavin, "Gang Members and the Police," in *The Police: Six Sociological Essays,* ed. David J. Bordua (New York: Wiley, 1968), pp. 58–59.

**102** Adapted from National Institute for Juvenile Justice and Delinquency Prevention, *Police–Juvenile Operations*, vol. 2, p. 57.

**103** Office of Juvenile Justice and Delinquency Prevention, *Juvenile Offenders and Victims*, p. 121.

**104** Ibid.

**105** Ibid.

**106** Black and Reiss, *"Police Control of Juveniles."*

**107** Samuel Walker, Cassia Spohn, and Miriam DeLone, *The Color of Justice* (Belmont, Calif.: Wadsworth, 1996), chap. 4.

**108** John E. Boydstun, *San Diego Field Interrogation: Final Report* (Washington: The Police Foundation, 1975).

**109** Black and Reiss, *"Police Control of Juveniles."*

**110** Richard J. Lundman, "Police Control of Juveniles: A Replication," *Journal of Research in Crime and Delinquency*, 15 (January 1978): 74–91.

**111** Douglas A. Smith, Christy A. Visher, and Laura A. Davidson, "Equity and Discretionary Justice: The Influence of Arrest on Police Arrest Decisions," *Journal of Criminal Law and Criminology* 75 (Spring 1984): 234–249.

**112** Carl Werthman and Irving Piliavin, "Gang Members and the Police," in David J. Bordua, ed., *The Police: Six Sociological Essays* (New York: John Wiley, 1968), pp. 58–59.

113 David Klinger, "Demeanor or Crime?: Why 'Hostile' Citizens Are More Likely to Be Arrested," *Criminology* 32, no. 3, (1994): 475–493.

114 Raymond T. Nimmer, *Diversion* (Chicago: American Bar Foundation, 1974), pp. 11–18.

115 President's Commission on Law Enforcement and Administration of Justice, *The Challenge of Crime in a Free Society* (Washington: Government Printing Office, 1967), p. 82.

116 Malcolm W. Klein and Kathie S. Teilman, *Pivotal Ingredients of Police Juvenile Diversion Programs* (Washington: Government Printing Office, 1976).

117 Mark Ezell, "Juvenile Diversion: The Ongoing Search for Alternatives," in *Juvenile Justice and Public Policy*, ed. Ira M. Schwartz (New York: Lexington Books, 1992), pp. 45–58.

118 Thomas G. Blomberg, "Widening the Net: An Anomaly in the Evaluation of Diversion Programs," in *Handbook of Criminal Justice Evaluation*, eds. M. W. Klein and K. S. Teilman (Beverly Hills: Sage, 1980), pp. 572–592.

119 Quint C. Thurman, Andrew Giacomazzi, and Phil Bogen, "Cops, Kids, and Community Policing—An Assessment of a Community Policing Demonstration," *Crime and Delinquency* 39 (October 1993): 554–564.

120 Bureau of Justice Assistance, *An Introduction to DARE*, 2d ed. (Washington: Government Printing Office, 1991).

121 Susan T. Emmett, Nancy Tobler, Christopher Ringwalt, and Robert L. Flewelling, "How Effective Is Drug Abuse Resistance Education? A Meta-Analysis of Project DARE Outcome Evaluations," *American Journal of Public Health* 84 (September 1994): 1394–1401.

122 Finn-Aage Esbensen and D. Wayne Osgood, *National Evaluation of G.R.E.A.T.* (Washington: Government Printing Office, 1997).

123 Herman Goldstein, *Policing A Free Society* (Cambridge, Mass.: Ballinger, 1977).

# CHAPTER 6

# THE POLICE AND CRIME

Crime control is one of the major responsibilities of the police. This involves several specific activities: preventing crime, responding to criminal incidents, conducting criminal investigations, and arresting offenders.

This chapter examines the crime control activities of the police. It describes what the police do, and gives special attention to the popular myths that surround the subject of the police and crime.

## THE POLICE AND CRIME

People usually think about the subject of the police and crime in terms of patrol and arrests. The subject is actually far more complex, involving a number of different assumptions, strategies, and programs.

### Crime Control Strategies

Lawrence W. Sherman provides the most systematic classification of the different crime control strategies used by the police, or are potentially available to them.[1]

**Proactive versus Reactive**   Some police anticrime strategies are proactive, in the sense that are initiated by the police themselves. This reflects the police department's own sense of priorities. Most drug enforcement, for example, is proactive. Other strategies are reactive, in the sense that they occur in response to a citizen request for service. Citizen calls to report crimes involve a reactive police response.

**General versus Specific**   Some police activities are general in the sense that they are directed at the community at large and not at any particular crime. Routine preventive patrol is the most important general crime control strategy. Specific crime control activities, on the other hand, are directed at particular crimes, places, offenders, or victims.

**Particular Crimes**   Routine patrol and the 911 system are general service activities that respond to any and all types of crime. Other programs are directed at particular crimes. These include drunk–driving crackdowns, drug or gang crackdowns, sting operations, or stakeouts designed to catch robbers.

**Specific Places**   Routine patrol serves the community at large with no particular geographic focus. "Hot spots" programs, on the other hand, are directed at specific places that are believed to be the centers of high levels of criminal activity.

**Specific Offenders**   Some anticrime activities are directed at particular offenders. The best examples are the repeat offender programs that target people suspected of currently committing high rates of serious crime.

**Specific Victims**   Some anticrime programs are directed at victims rather than offenders. The most important of these are the domestic violence programs and policies adopted by many police departments. Mandatory arrest policies, for example, are designed to protect victims of domestic assault against future violence.

## Crime Control Assumptions

**Police and Citizens**   Many people see the police, and the entire criminal justice system, as society's primary mechanism for controlling crime. As part of the professionalization movement, the police emphasized their crime-fighting role, and staked out crime as their professional domain.[2] Many experts today believe that this definition of professionalism isolated the police and cut them off from the public. To correct this problem, advocates of community policing emphasize the development of close working relationships with neighborhood residents.[3] This approach is based on the assumption that citizens are coproducers of police services, including crime–fighting activities.[4]

**Police and Other Social Institutions**   A 1997 report on crime prevention programs by the University of Maryland places police activities in the context of other social institutions. The report argues that the traditional distinction between law enforcement and crime prevention is not valid. Law enforcement tactics such as arrest are designed to prevent crime, either through deterrence or incapacitation. Thus it is appropriate to place all programs and institutions on a single crime prevention continuum.[5]

The Maryland report identified seven institutions that play a role in preventing crime. They include communities, families, schools, labor markets, places (in the sense of specific locales), the police, and other criminal justice programs. This innovative approach makes two important points about crime prevention. First, it indicates that the police are only one of several institutions with some impact on crime, and cannot be expected to bear the primary responsibility. Second, the report emphasizes the interdependence of the different institutions. Thus effective school–based crime prevention programs depend on strong families, which in turn depend on healthy communities and good labor markets. Just as school programs are dependent upon this larger social network, so are the effectiveness of police crime control programs.[6]

## Measuring Effectiveness

Measuring the effectiveness of police crime control programs requires both meaningful definitions of what is to be measured and valid and reliable data on outcomes. As is discussed below, there are serious problems with the traditional measures of police effectiveness. Moreover, the move toward community policing involves different assumptions about what the police do and, consequently requires different measures of effectiveness.[7]

**Summary**   The different police activities covered in this chapter can be classified according to strategy, the underlying assumptions, and performance measures.

## PREVENTING CRIME

The primary crime prevention activity of the police is routine patrol. As Chapter 4 explained, the visible presence of police officers in the community is designed to deter individuals from committing crime.

Patrol has only a limited deterrent effect on crime, however. The Kansas City Preventive Patrol Experiment (1972–1973) found that increased levels of patrol officers do not reduce crime. Conversely, reducing the level of patrol does not lead to an increase in criminal activity.[8] Similarly, the Newark Foot Patrol Experiment found that increased levels of foot patrol do not reduce crime.[9]

The Kansas City and Newark experiments did not prove that patrol has *no* effect on crime. A certain amount of patrol does have *some* deterrent effect. The experiments proved only that adding more patrol does not reduce crime any further. Some new problem–oriented policing strategies that focus on specific crimes and places, however, may be more effective in reducing crime. These issues are discussed in greater detail in Chapter 4.

Traditionally, many police departments maintained formal crime prevention programs. In their classic text on police administration, O. W. Wilson and Roy C. McLaren described these programs as including "security improvement, target hardening, and public education to prevent vulnerability to crime."[10] In these programs, crime prevention officers, for example, meet with community groups to explain door locks and alarm systems, marking of valuable property, as well as behavior that can increase personal safety. Some of these programs are housed in police–community relations (PCR) units (see Chapter 9).[11]

Police crime prevention strategies have undergone a revolution since the early 1980s. Instead of a peripheral activity, separated from the basic functions of patrol and criminal investigation, crime prevention is now seen as a central police activity.[12] Crime prevention is a basic element of community policing and many problem–oriented policing programs.[13] The basic principle of community policing is that the police need to establish a better partnership with neighborhood residents. The underlying assumption is that citizens are coproducers of police services. This view of policing rejects the professional model of policing, which holds that the police and only the police have primary responsibility for crime control.[14]

Community–based crime prevention programs include efforts to build neighborhood organizations, improve the physical appearance of the neighborhood, eradicate centers of drug activity, reduce truancy, and so on. In these programs, police officers act as planners, problem solvers, community organizers, and information exchange brokers. Their role is not to fight crime in the traditional manner (e.g., patrol, arrests), but to help citizens mobilize resources to prevent crime.[15]

Because community policing and problem–oriented policing crime prevention programs are so varied and are such an important part of contemporary policing they are covered in detail in Chapter 7.

## APPREHENDING CRIMINALS

The second major crime–fighting responsibility of the police is to apprehend criminals once a crime has been committed. This process involves a complex set of social and

---

**SIDEBAR 6–1**

WHAT IF ALL CRIMES WERE REPORTED?

What would happen if victims reported all crimes to the police. Would it result in more arrests and fewer crimes? Probably not. First, the police workload would increase enormously. There would be many more calls for service and about 200 percent more reported crimes. Patrol officers and detectives would be swamped. Second, most of these additional crimes would be the less serious crimes. The National Crime Victimization Survey (NCVS) data indicate that victims report the more serious crimes at a relatively high rate. Third, there is no reason to assume that there would be that many more arrests. As we will learn below (pp. 137–138) the police are able to solve crimes when there is a good lead at the outset. There is no reason to assume that they would solve many of the additional burglaries and larcenies where there are no good leads.

In short, are we better off because citizens use their discretion not to report most crimes?

---

organizational factors. The police must first learn that a crime has been committed, officially record it as a crime, and then attempt to identify and arrest a suspect.

### Citizen Reporting of Crime

Police learn about crimes through (1) citizen reports, (2) police officer on–view observations, and (3) police–initiated investigations. The first two are reactive responses; the third is a proactive response.

Most of the crimes that come to the attention of the police are the result of citizen reports. Reporting a crime is one of the most important discretionary decisions in the criminal process. In this sense, citizens are the real gatekeepers of the criminal justice system. Patrol officers rarely discover crimes in progress. Albert Reiss found that Chicago patrol officers spent only 0.1 percent of their total patrol time handling on–view criminal incidents.[16]

Victims, however, do not report most crimes to the police. According to the National Crime Victimization Survey (NCVS), victims report only 36 percent of all personal and household crimes.[17] The nonreporting of crime has important implications for the police, in view of the fact that they cannot be held responsible for solving crimes they know nothing about.

The reporting of crime varies according to the type of crime and situational factors related to individual crimes (Table 6–1). Generally, citizens are more likely to report serious crimes than minor crimes, violent crimes rather than property crimes, crimes where there is personal injury rather than those without injury, crimes involving a high dollar loss more than those with little loss, and so on. African Americans report crimes at a slightly higher rate than whites. Men and women report crimes at about the same rate. Except for teenagers, who report crimes at a significantly lower rate, age does not influence the reporting of crime. People at different income levels also report crimes at roughly the same rate.[18]

**TABLE 6–1**
REPORTING OF CRIME, 1994

| | Percent reported to police |
|---|---|
| **All Crimes** | 36 |
| **Violent crime** | 42 |
| Simple assault | 36 |
| Aggravated assault | 52 |
| Robbery | 55 |
| Rape/Sexual assault | 32 |
| **Personal theft*** | 33 |
| **Property crime** | 34 |
| Property thefts | 27 |
| Household burglary | 50 |
| Motor vehicle theft | 78 |

*Includes pocket picking and purse snatching.
*Source:* Bureau of Justice Statistics, *Criminal Victimization in the United States, 1994* (Washington, DC: Government Printing Office, 1997), p. v.

Victims do not report crimes primarily because they do not think the crime is that important. The second most important reason is that victims do not think anything can be done about it. Victims regard certain crimes as private or personal matters. Perception of the police also affects the decision not to report a crime. In 1994 according to the National Crime Victimization Survey (NCVS), 4.3 percent of those not reporting a victimization indicated that they thought the police were "inefficient, ineffective, or biased."[19]

### Reporting and Unfounding Crimes

After a citizen reports a crime, the police must make an official record of it in order to enter it in the Uniform Crime Reports (UCR) system. Police officers often do not complete a crime report, however. This is called "unfounding" a crime. Donald Black found that police completed official crime reports in 64 percent of all crimes where no suspect was present, even though the complainant alleged a crime had occurred.[20] In 1994, meanwhile, crime victims told the NCVS that the police made reports in only 39.3 percent of all violent crimes and 48.9 percent of all property crimes.[21]

There is no penalty—in the law, in Federal Bureau of Investigation (FBI) regulations, or in police department policy—for a police officer who does not complete a crime report. This is an area of unregulated police discretion.

A police officer's decision to complete a crime report is affected by the same factors that influence arrest decisions. Black found that the police were more likely to record the more serious crimes, crimes where the complainant clearly expressed a preference for a crime report, crimes committed by strangers, and crimes where the complainant was deferential to the officer.[22]

There are several reasons why a police officer might unfound a crime. First, citizens do not always understand the criminal law and may believe that something is a crime when in fact it is not. Reiss found that 58 percent of all citizen calls to the Chicago Police Department were defined as a crime by the citizens calling, but that the police recorded only 17 percent of all calls as crime related.[23]

Second, there may be insufficient evidence to convince the officer that a crime was committed. A citizen may report an attempted break–in, but the officer finds no physical evidence to support the allegation. The resident may have heard a storm door banging in the wind. These examples represent the proper exercise of discretion.

Third, officers may also abuse their discretion in unfounding crimes. A police officer may unfound a report of attempted rape because of bias against the victim. LaFree found that police made no arrests in suspected rape incidents when they perceived non-conforming behavior on the part of the victim: drinking or hitchhiking, being in a bar without a male escort, involved in sex outside of marriage, or voluntarily entering the suspect's house or car.[24]

On a few occasions, police departments have been caught systematically unfounding crimes to lower the crime rate. In the early 1970s the news media caught the Washington, D.C., police systematically lowering the value of stolen property to take the crimes out of the Index crime category. (At the time, the UCR system recorded larceny/thefts only when the value of the property was $50 or more.)[25]

Crime reports can also be altered later. A crime can be either unfounded completely or changed to a lesser criminal offense. Thus, a rape can be changed to an assault, or a robbery to a larceny or an assault. If the change is based on new information about the crime, it is legitimate. If it is done simply to lower the crime rate, however, it is illegitimate. Recording a crime in a lower category can alter public perception of community safety. The news media and the public tend to focus their attention on a few "high fear" crimes: murder, robbery, rape, and burglary. Recording a robbery as a larceny makes the community appear safer than it really is.

## CRIMINAL INVESTIGATION

Once a crime has come to the attention of the police, and it has been officially recorded, and no suspect has been immediately arrested, the criminal investigation process begins.

### Myths about Detective Work

Criminal investigation, or detective work, is surrounded by myths. Movies and television police shows usually portray detective work as exciting and dangerous work. Individual detectives are presented as heroic characters, possessing either great personal courage or extraordinary skill. The media often foster the idea that a good detective "can solve any crime," if he or she is only given the freedom and enough time to do it.[26]

There is no empirical basis for any of these myths. Moreover, they have several harmful effects on the public and the police. First, they create unreasonable public expectations about the ability of the police to control crime. This results in public dissatisfaction when the police fail to solve a crime. Second, the glamorous image of detective work leads many officers to regard it as *real* police work and devalue routine patrol work.[27] Some detectives, in fact, imitate the behavior they see in the movies. Herman Goldstein observes that "many of the techniques employed by detectives today are more heavily influenced by a desire to imitate stereotypes than by a rational plan for solving crimes."[28]

### The Organization of Detective Work

Criminal investigation is located in a separate unit of the department (except in very small departments). Nationally, only about 12 percent of all sworn officers are assigned to detective units.[29] Large departments have specialized units devoted to particular types of crime (e.g., homicides, crimes against property, etc.). Medium–sized departments usually have a separate but unspecialized unit in which detectives handle all types of crime. Very small departments often have no specialized detective unit.

Assignment as a detective is generally considered a high-status assignment by most police officers. In most departments it is a discretionary assignment, and one of the greatest rewards that a police chief has to hand out. In some departments, on the other hand, it is a separate rank, with a higher pay than patrol officers, and must be obtained through a competitive examination.

Detective work appeals to officers for several reasons. It offers greater opportunity to control one's work and to exercise initiative. Patrol work, by contrast, is largely reactive, in response to citizen calls. Detectives have considerable discretion over which cases to work on, how much time to spend on each case, and how to investigate it. Working in civilian clothes enhances the sense of individuality and frees detectives from stereotyped reactions from citizens based on the uniform.

Criminal investigation also offers a clearly defined measure of success: arrest of the suspect. The quality of work can be measured in terms of the number of arrests, the importance of a particular arrest (for example, an arrest related to a highly publicized crime), and the percentage of arrests resulting in conviction.[30] Patrol work, by contrast, involves mainly order maintenance and peacekeeping activities (see Chapter 4), for which there have never been any real performance measures.[31]

Not all detective assignments are the same, however. William B. Sanders points out, "The status of an individual detective is linked to the kinds of crimes he investigates."[32] Homicide traditionally occupies the highest status, followed by robbery and sexual assault. Investigating the more serious crimes carries greater moral significance because of the harm involved. Homicide units also have the smallest workload and the highest clearance rate. Property crime units (burglary and larceny), on the other hand, rank lowest in terms of moral significance, have the highest workloads and the lowest clearance rates.

Vice units (narcotics, gambling, prostitution) are a special case. Because they involve victimless crimes, they require proactive police work, asking officers to exercise initiative. Undercover work also requires special skill, involves the greatest dangers, and poses the greatest moral hazards. Traditionally, the worst police corruption has been found in vice units (see Chapter 10).[33] For these reasons, some police officers do not seek assignment in vice units (see p. 143–145).[34]

## THE INVESTIGATION PROCESS

The process of investigating a crime consists of two basic stages: the preliminary investigation and the follow–up investigation.

### The Preliminary Investigation

The preliminary investigation consists of five basic steps: (1) identifying and arresting any suspects, (2) providing aid to any victims in need of medical attention, (3) securing the crime scene to prevent loss of evidence, (4) collecting all relevant physical evidence, and (5) preparing a preliminary report.[35]

In practice, patrol officers rather than detectives make about 80 percent of all arrests.[36] The explanation for this is simple. Most arrests occur because a suspect is on the scene or immediately identifiable and nearby. For those crimes where the suspect is not immediately arrested and there is no good information about him or her, arrests are relatively rare. Patrol officers, in short, handle the easy arrests, whereas detectives are assigned those that are inherently difficult to solve.

### Arrest Discretion

Police officers exercise great discretion in making arrests. Black found that officers make arrests in only about half the situations where there is sufficient legal basis for an arrest.[37] Mastrofski, Snipes, and Supina found that in a number of situations officers simply ask the person to stop the illegal behavior. In over 80 percent of these situations the person complies with the officer's request.[38]

The decision to arrest is influenced by a number of situational factors. Generally, the probability of arrest rises when the evidence is relatively strong, the crime is serious in nature, the victim requests an arrest, the victim and suspect are strangers rather than acquaintances, and the suspect is hostile or disrespectful toward the officer.[39] Smith, Visher, and Davidson also found that arrest is more likely in lower-income neighborhoods, regardless of the race of the suspect.[40] Arrest discretion with respect to domestic violence situations and juveniles is discussed in more detail in Chapter 5.

### Follow–Up Investigations

A case is assigned to the detective bureau for follow–up investigation after an arrest has been made or if there has been no arrest. The Police Executive Research Forum (PERF) study divided follow–up investigations into three categories of activities: routine, secondary, and tertiary activities.[41]

Routine activities include interviewing victims and checking the crime scene. These steps are taken in about 90 percent of all burglaries and robberies. Secondary activities include canvassing for witnesses, interviewing other people, interviewing witnesses,

---

SIDEBAR 6–2

POLICE, DISCRETION, AND CRIME

Police response to crime is affected by a number of discretionary decisions. They include (1) the citizen's decision to report a crime, (2) a police officer's decision to officially record the crime, (3) the officer's decision to arrest the suspect, or (4) the decision of detectives to investigate the case. The issue of discretion is covered in more detail in Chapter 8.

---

discussing the case with supervisors, and collecting physical evidence. Tertiary activities include discussing the case with patrol officers, interviewing suspects, discussing the case with other detectives, checking department records, checking the National Crime Information Center (NCIC) computer files, checking other records, interviewing informants, and conducting stakeouts.

### The Reality of Detective Work

Contrary to popular belief, detective work is neither glamorous nor exciting. The Rand Corporation conducted the first detailed evaluation of detective units in the early 1970s, surveying 153 police departments by mail and interviewing officials in 29 departments. The study found detective work to be superficial, routine, and nonproductive. Many crimes receive only "superficial" attention, and some are not investigated at all. Only 30 percent of all residential burglaries and 18 percent of all larcenies were worked on by detectives, for example. Moreover, most investigative work involves "reviewing reports, documenting files, and attempting to locate and interview victims."[42] Most cases receive one day or less of investigative work, and most of that work involves paperwork: transferring information from one set of reports to another.

A PERF study of burglary and robbery investigations, meanwhile, found that about 25 percent of all burglary cases received slightly less than two hours of investigative work, and only 11.9 percent were investigated for three days or more (at an average of about one hour per day). Only 24.8 percent of the robberies, meanwhile, were investigated for two days or more.[43] Harold Pepinsky argues that "most detectives spend the bulk of their time at their desks, going through papers and using the telephone."[44]

### Case Screening

In practice, detectives routinely screen cases, deciding how much effort to put into different cases. Screening decisions are based primarily on the seriousness of the crime and the existence of evidence that is likely to lead to an arrest. The PERF study found that a detective's caseload actually consists of three components. The *nominal* caseload includes all cases assigned to that officer. The *workable* caseload includes those cases "that have sufficient leads and therefore are worth attempting to solve." Finally, the *actual* caseload includes those cases "actually worked by detectives."[45]

**TABLE 6–2**
CRIMES CLEARED BY ARREST, 1995

| | |
|---|---|
| All Index crimes | 21.2% |
| Murder | 64.8 |
| Rape | 51.1 |
| Robbery | 24.7 |
| Aggravated assault | 55.7 |
| Burglary | 13.4 |
| Larceny | 19.6 |
| Auto theft | 14.1 |

*Source:* Federal Bureau of Investigation, *Crime in the United States, 1995* (Washington, DC: Government Printing Office, 1996), pp. 199, 200.

## MEASURING THE EFFECTIVENESS OF CRIMINAL INVESTIGATION

### The Clearance Rate

The traditional measure of success in criminal investigation is the clearance rate.[46] The FBI defines a crime as cleared when the police have "identified the offender, have sufficient evidence to charge him, and actually take him into custody, or in exceptional instances, when some element beyond police control precludes taking the offender into custody."[47]

Nationally, 21 percent of all reported Index crimes are cleared. Table 6–2 indicates national clearance rates for the eight UCR Index crimes for 1995.

The clearance rate is not a reliable performance measure for several reasons.[48] First, it is based on reported crimes, and because only 36 percent of all crimes are reported, the *true* clearance rate is much lower than the *official* rate. Only 50 percent of all burglaries are reported and, therefore, the police actually clear only 7 percent of all burglaries, rather than 13 percent.

Second, despite the UCR guidelines, police departments do not use the same criteria for clearing crimes. The PERF study, for example, found that in one city, only 58 percent of the burglary cases recorded as cleared were actually cleared by an arrest.[49] Thus, official clearance rates do not provide meaningful comparisons of the relative effectiveness of different police departments.

Third, the data can be manipulated to produce an artificially higher official clearance rate.[50] If officials unfound a large number of crimes, for example, this will lower the denominator and produce a higher percentage of crimes cleared. Alternatively, officials can attribute additional crimes to a suspect in custody and record them as cleared. This also raises the official clearance rate. In some instances, attributing additional crimes to a suspect is legitimate. There may be some evidence that the suspect did commit these other crimes, but not enough to present to the prosecutor. In this situation, there is no reason to look for another suspect. The procedure can also be abused, however. Detectives may clear additional crimes even though there is no evidence to connect them with a suspect.

---

**CRIME DATA ON THE WEB**

Check out recent clearance rate data on the web. Check the most recent FBI UCR data. Have national clearance rates changed for any crimes? Check out the web sites for some local police departments. Do they provide their clearance rates? If so, how do different departments compare with the national clearance rates for particular crimes?

---

Clearance rate data, along with the entire UCR system, are not audited by outsiders. A Police Foundation study, for example, found wide variation in the quality of arrest data,[51] and there is good reason for assuming that similar variations exist with respect to official clearance rate data.

### Defining an Arrest

Official data on arrests are also extremely problematic. The event referred to as an arrest has four different dimensions: legal, behavioral, subjective, and official.[52]

*Legally*, an individual is under arrest or in custody when deprived of his or her liberty by legal authority. A police officer must have the intent to arrest, must communicate that intent to the person, and must actually take the person into custody.[53] Many people are detained on the street and then released. Others are taken to the police station and later released. During the time they are in the custody of the police and not free to leave, they are legally under arrest.[54]

*Behaviorally*, taking a suspect into custody can involve a number of different actions by the police officer: a stop (in which the officer tells the individual not to leave), a verbal statement that the person is "under arrest," or simply physically restraining a person.

*Subjectively*, persons are under arrest whenever they believe they are not free to go. A police officer may regard an encounter as only a stop, but the individual may believe that he or she is under arrest.

*Officially*, an arrest occurs only when the police make an official arrest report of it. Arrest record-keeping practices vary greatly from department to department, however, and may even vary within individual departments. Departments do not make arrest reports at the same stage in the process of detaining and taking someone into custody. A Police Foundation study found that only 16 percent of police departments always record an arrest whenever any restraint has been imposed on the suspect; only 11 percent always record an arrest whenever a suspect is brought to the station house. All departments make a record whenever the suspect is booked.[55]

The result is that in many departments, a lot of people are legally arrested (in custody on the street or at the station house) but no official record is made of these arrests. The lack of standard procedures makes it difficult, if not impossible, to use arrest data to compare departments. A police department that records all arrests at an early stage, for example, will appear to be working harder and engaging in more aggressive crime fighting than one that only records arrests at the booking stage. In fact, however, the two

**FIGURE 6–1**
CRIMES CLEARED BY THE LOS ANGELES POLICE.

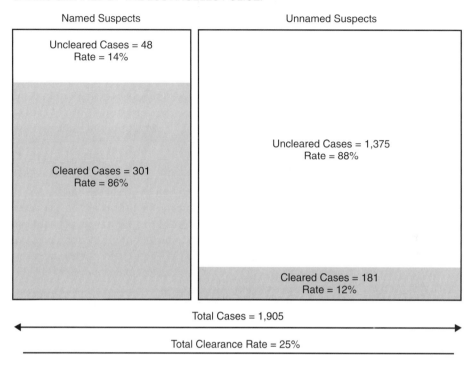

Total Cases = 1,905

Total Clearance Rate = 25%

departments might be taking people into custody at exactly the same rate. The official data are not a reliable indicator of their real levels of activity.

Law enforcement agencies compile arrest statistics for different purposes and different audiences. One officer said, "We keep one set of statistics for the City Council and another for the BCS (the California Bureau of Criminal Statistics) and the FBI."[56] As already mentioned, despite UCR guidelines, police arrest data are not independently audited.

## SUCCESS AND FAILURE IN SOLVING CRIMES

The police solve only 21 percent of all Part I felonies each year. As Table 6–2 indicates, they are far more successful in solving some crimes than others. The single most important factor is whether the police immediately obtain the name or description of a suspect. The data in Figure 6–1 represent a sample of 1,905 crimes investigated by the Los Angeles Police Department. The LAPD cleared 86.2 percent of the 349 crimes in which a suspect was named, but only 11.6 percent of those in which a suspect was not named.[57]

Reiss and Bordua argue that most cleared crimes "solve themselves in the sense that the violator is 'known' to the complainant or to the police at the time the crime initially comes to the attention of the police."[58] Clearance rates are highest for violent crimes because they involve direct contact between offenders and victims. Few property crimes involve the same kind of direct contact, and consequently have low clearance rates. Robbery is a violent crime, but usually committed by a stranger, resulting in low rates of identification and low clearance rates.

Detective screening of cases (see p. 140) is based primarily on whether or not there is a good lead at the outset. Sanders found, "Robberies, rapes, and assaults were typified as having leads, since the victim serves as a witness."[59] Burglaries and thefts, on the other hand, were routinely considered not to have leads.

The presence or absence of a good lead is a *structural* factor, in the sense that it is related to the nature of the crime and independent of police effort. Studies of criminal investigation have found that changes in police effort—more detectives, more or different levels of training, different management practices—have little effect on clearance rates. The Rand study of criminal investigation concluded that clearance rates are not higher where there are more detectives or where they put more effort into cases, or where they receive more training.[60] Even though detectives complain about being overworked, and do in fact have very heavy caseloads, the lack of resources is not the primary factor that keeps clearance rates low.

Subsequent research by Eck, and also Brandl and Frank, reached more optimistic conclusions than the Rand study about the effect of police effort. They argue that investigative effort does make a difference. Their analyses involve a "triage" model that categorizes cases according to the strength of the evidence: weak, moderate, or strong. Brandl and Frank found that the probability of arrest in moderate evidence burglary and robbery cases increased as a result of more investigative effort.[61]

### Eyewitness Identification

Although victim and witness identification of suspects is extremely important in solving crimes, eyewitness identifications are also very problematic. The victim is often traumatized by the crime, frequently has only an incomplete description of the suspect, may exaggerate certain features (such as height or weight), or may resort to stereotyping in the sense of being unable to distinguish the individual features of a member of a certain racial or ethnic group. Psychologist Elizabeth Loftus, the leading expert on the subject, warns that despite the importance of eyewitness identifications, they are "not always reliable," for all the problems associated with human perception and memory.[62]

### Criminalistics

Technical specialists from the crime lab may be used in some investigations. Large departments maintain their own criminalistics specialists; the smaller departments utilize the services of either a neighboring large department or a state police agency. Virtually all police departments, including the smallest, have technical services available to them through cooperative arrangements with other agencies.[63]

Despite the great publicity they receive, fingerprints are rarely an important factor in solving crimes. A major part of the problem is that it is difficult to obtain useful prints. New York City police are able to obtain a usable print in only 10 percent of all burglaries. Even when prints were obtained, only 3 percent led to an arrest. In 1985 this meant only 300 arrests in 126,028 burglaries.[64] Joan Petersilia found that fingerprints were equally unproductive in the six California police departments she studied. In Long Beach, for example, fingerprint technicians were requested in only 58 percent of all criminal cases. They successfully obtained prints in only half the cases (or 29.4 percent of all cases), and a suspect was identified by fingerprints in only 1.5 percent of the total cases.[65]

## Officer Productivity

There are significant differences in the productivity of detectives, as measured in terms of the number of arrests. Some make far more arrests than others. Productivity depends on a number of factors. Detectives assigned to high–solvability crimes such as robberies will have more chances to make arrests than those assigned to low–solvability crimes such as burglaries. Nonetheless, it is also clear that, given the same assignment, some officers work harder and make more arrests than others. Riccio and Heaphy found that the number of arrests for Index crimes ranged from a low of 2.18 to a high of 12.06 per officer.[66]

More important than the total number of arrests is the *quality* of arrests—that is, whether the arrests lead to prosecution and conviction for a felony. The Institute of Law and Society found that in one department 15 percent of the officers made over half the arrests that resulted in a conviction.[67]

## The Problem of Case Attrition

Only about half of all felony arrests result in conviction of the suspect.[68] These data raise serious questions about whether the attrition is the result of poor police work or some other factor. In Petersilia's analysis of California arrests, 11 percent of persons arrested were released by the police; 15 percent were declined for prosecution by prosecutors; and 18 percent of the cases resulted in dismissal or acquittal.[69] The total attrition rate was 44 percent. (And this analysis did not take into account persons who were legally arrested by the police but for whom no arrest report was made.)

Petersilia, Abrahamse, and Wilson attempted to identify those aspects of police work that were associated with high case attrition rates. They found that department practices explained little of the variation among the 25 departments studied. These practices included a case–screening process, a modus operandi(MO) file, a known offender file, a special victim/witness program, and other elements. Departments that used arrest statistics as a performance measure actually had lower clearance rates than departments that did not. The report did find that attrition rates were somewhat lower in cities that spent more money per arrest, a figure that seemed to indicate a connection between clearance rates and the availability of greater resources.[70]

An INSLAW study found that detectives expressed little interest in the performance measures associated with low attrition rates. None of the detectives interviewed knew what percentage of their cases were rejected by prosecutors. No supervisor reported evaluating detectives on the basis of the percentage of cases that resulted in convictions. None of the detectives expressed interest in feedback from prosecutors about the quality of their work.[71]

## IMPROVING CRIMINAL INVESTIGATIONS

Several proposals have been made for improving criminal investigations. The most important is a PERF–Stanford Research Institute (SRI) recommendation for formal case-screening systems to determine which cases should receive the most investigative effort. Instead of the traditional method of relying on detectives' hunches and intuitions about which cases are likely to be solved, the PERF–SRI model involves a point system based on factors (e.g., eyewitness identification) that contribute to success in clearing crimes.[72]

A second approach involves developing closer working relationships between patrol officers and detectives. Traditionally, officers in these two units have competed with one another instead of cooperating. Officers jealously guard information and sources in the hope of reaping the reward of an important arrest.[73]

The Rochester, New York, Police Department experimented with a team policing approach to investigations. Each team consisted of 30 patrol officers and 6 detectives. The team was responsible for the full range of police services in a given geographic area on a 24–hour basis. A four–month evaluation of the experiment in 1973 indicated that the team approach was three times more effective than the traditional approach in securing arrests for robbery and 50 percent more effective for burglary arrests. The report concluded that "a police department can improve its arrest and clearance rates by assigning detectives to work as part of police teams," rather than having them work independently in a centralized criminal investigation unit.[74]

A third approach focuses on increasing police–citizen cooperation. Citing the importance of victim or witness information about suspects in clearing crimes, Skogan and Antunes argue that citizens should be viewed as coproducers of information.[75] Community policing and problem–oriented policing programs (see Chapter 7) are based on this concept.

The Fear Reduction Experiment in Houston included a victim recontact program. Police officers recontacted crime victims by telephone to ask if they needed any assistance. The officers were prepared to offer advice on filing insurance claims and to answer any questions about the progress of the investigation or prosecution. The objective of the program was to provide the "information, recognition, advice, support, protection, and reassurance" that victims appeared to be seeking.[76] Contrary to expectations, however, the recontact program did not achieve its goals—and the most notable impact ran counter to the program's goals. Victims who were recontacted did not have more positive attitudes toward the police and were not less worried about crime.

Hispanic and Asian crime victims who were recontacted were more fearful of crime and less satisfied with their neighborhood than other victims. They were slightly more positive in their evaluation of the police, but not to a significant degree. Language appeared to be a factor. Victims whose command of English was rated fair or poor were among those more fearful of crime (although this did not entirely explain the effect). The evaluators hypothesized that these people may not have understood why the recontact person was calling them. The experiment dramatized "the importance of sensitivity to cultural differences in the implementation of police programs."[77]

### Targeting Career Criminals

In the 1980s several police departments experimented with programs to target career criminals, defined as people believed to be currently committing a high rate of offenses. This idea was based on the Wolfgang birth cohort study which estimated that a very small number of people (6 percent of any group of young men) commit an extremely high percentage of all serious crime.[78] Arresting, convicting, and imprisoning these career criminals, it was argued, would yield tremendous payoff in terms of crime reduction.[79]

Repeat offender programs consist of three different types: (1) targeting suspected high-rate offenders for surveillance and arrest, (2) special warrant services for suspected high-rate offenders who have outstanding warrants or are wanted for probation or parole violations, (3) case–enhancement programs to provide prosecutors with full information about the criminal histories of high–rate offenders.[80]

The Repeat Offender Program (ROP) in Washington, D.C., involved a team of 88 officers (later reduced to 60) assigned to locate and arrest persons believed to be committing five or more Index crimes per week. The suspects were selected on the basis of information provided by other police department units. Suspects remained on the list for 72 hours. Officers in the ROP team sought to locate the suspect through information in existing criminal records, supplemented by information available from the Department of Motor Vehicles, the phone company, and other sources. Many of the targeted individuals were already being sought on outstanding arrest warrants.[81]

An evaluation of ROP by the Police Foundation compared 212 suspects assigned to the ROP unit with a group of 212 comparable suspects. The arrest activity of ROP unit officers was also compared with the activity of a control group of officers. The evaluation found that ROP "increased the likelihood of arrest of targeted repeat offenders." Half the suspects in the experimental group (106 out of 212) were arrested by ROP officers (another 17 were arrested by other officers), compared with only 4 percent (8 out of 212) in the control group.

Other data, however, raised some questions about the efficiency of the program. ROP officers made fewer arrests than comparison officers (although most of the additional arrests by the comparison officers were for nonserious crimes). The ROP program cost $60,000 in direct expenses, and took officers away from other police responsibilities, raising serious questions about the cost–effectiveness of the program.[82]

## TRAFFIC ENFORCEMENT

Traffic enforcement produces perhaps the broadest range of contact between the police and the public. Although citizen–initiated calls for service are heavily skewed toward a relatively small segment of any community, virtually all adult citizens drive cars, and minor violations of traffic laws are common. Traffic stops are the source of low–level but significant friction between the police and the public. Citizens resent being stopped, asked to produce identification, and ticketed. For their part—because of citizen resentment—police officers generally find traffic enforcement a distasteful task.[83] Traffic stops are also one of the most dangerous police tasks, in terms of officers killed or injured on duty, because some stops involve armed and dangerous criminals.[84]

All patrol officers are responsible for traffic law enforcement, but departments with more than 200 sworn officers generally maintain a separate traffic unit. An average of about 7 percent of all officers are allocated to these units.[85]

The enforcement of traffic law violations varies widely from department to department. John Gardiner found that Dallas police officers wrote 20 times as many tickets as officers in Boston, even though both cities were approximately the same size at the time of the study.[86] James Q. Wilson found similar variations in traffic law enforcement in his study of police organizations.[87]

The level of traffic enforcement is generally the result of formal or informal department policies. In some instances, community pressure dictates vigorous enforcement. In others, it is the decision of the top police administrator. Some departments have formal or informal quotas on traffic tickets for officers.[88]

Police departments occasionally engage in highly publicized traffic enforcement crackdowns. There is mixed evidence about whether such efforts effectively reduce traffic accidents or other crimes. A Dayton, Ohio, traffic enforcement experiment involved intensified enforcement on one high-traffic street over a six-month period. Officers were instructed to write many traffic tickets, and to make frequent and highly visible traffic stops. This particular street was compared with another street where no crackdown occurred. An evaluation found that the crackdown had no significant impact on crime, arrests, or traffic accidents.[89]

There are three possible reasons why the crackdown had no effect. First, it is possible that increased enforcement simply has no deterrent effect. Second, it is possible that the increased level of enforcement was too small to make any difference. [The same issue arose with respect to the Kansas City patrol experiment (see Chapter 4)]. Third, it is possible that some effect occurred but that the methods used in the evaluation lacked sufficient statistical power to detect it.[90]

## Drunk–Driving Crackdowns

In the 1980s, public concern led to a national crusade against drunk driving. Most states increased the penalties for drunk driving, federal regulations forced states to raise the legal drinking age to 21,[91] and local police departments intensified enforcement efforts. Drunk-driving crackdowns included such tactics as random stops of drivers and roadblocks to stop all drivers. The goals were to apprehend actual drunk drivers and deter potential drunk drivers.

There is considerable debate over whether enforcement crackdowns reduce drunk driving. Evaluations of crackdowns in England and Scandinavia found short–term reductions in traffic fatalities followed by a return to previous levels.[92] Several factors appear to contribute to this phenomenon. The publicity surrounding a tough enforcement effort may cause changes in peoples' behavior: people drink less, or ask someone else to drive them home, or have a friend who stops them from driving. As the publicity surrounding the crackdown wears off, however, people return to their previous behavior patterns and drunk–driving fatalities increase.

The actual risk of arrest for drunk driving is extremely low. The probability of a police officer spotting a drunk driver is limited by several factors. First, a very small percentage of all drivers are drunk: an estimated 5 percent of all drivers on an average evening, with a higher percentage on weekends. Second, there are relatively few police officers on duty at any given moment relative to the number of cars on the road. Third, not all drivers who are in fact drunk exhibit impaired driving.[93]

Each arrest, meanwhile, sharply reduces the probability of catching other drunk drivers. An arrest is an extremely time–consuming event, involving one or more officers for anywhere from one to four hours. For the duration, each officer is out of service, unable to make further arrests or to deter drunk driving through patrol. Finally, crackdowns are difficult to sustain. Police officers, like drinkers, slip back into their normal routines and reduce their levels of arrest activity.

The rate of alcohol–related traffic fatalities (based on the number of licensed vehicles and drivers) has declined steadily since the 1920s. Experts believe that several factors have contributed to this trend: safer cars, better roads and traffic safety measures, seat belts, air bags, and most recently the increase in the legal drinking age. The tough antidrunk driving enforcement programs have made, at best, some contribution to this trend, but they are only one part of a larger social control effort.[94]

## POLICING VICE

Crimes of vice—involving prostitution, gambling, and narcotics—present special enforcement problems because they are "victimless crimes," with no complaining party.[95] First, the police must initiate investigations on their own. Wiretaps, informants, undercover work, and other covert investigative techniques raise a number of difficult legal and moral questions. Second, victimless crimes involve behavior that many people regard as legitimate, or at least a private matter. The result is conflicting public attitudes about how vigorously the laws should be enforced. Enforcement, consequently, is often selective, inconsistent, and arbitrary.[96]

Giacopassi and Sparger found that, as a result of conflicting social attitudes, vice unit officers experience cognitive dissonance. The theory of cognitive dissonance holds that when people experience things that are not consistent with their values and beliefs they will attempt to make them consistent. Vice officers develop three strategies for resolving cognitive dissonance. First, because vice work often requires officers to do things that are not approved by their religious value systems, such as watching topless dancing, some officers avoid such assignments. A second strategy is depersonalization, in the sense of not thinking of the people engaged in vice activities as human beings (i.e., thinking of them as "trash"). Finally, officers cope by telling themselves that they are just doing a job that they are legally required to do.[97]

## Prostitution

Prostitution takes two different forms, each presenting the police with a different law enforcement problem.[98] Streetwalkers represent the lower end of the social and economic scale of prostitution. Prostitutes themselves are generally low–income people, and this is often a last–resort source of employment for them.[99] Because they solicit on the streets, they are highly visible to both the police and the general public. Streetwalkers also include male prostitutes soliciting male customers.[100] In many cities, a low level of streetwalking is tolerated by the police. It is usually confined to certain parts of the central business district where it is not seen by most of the public. For the patrol officer, streetwalking is essentially an order maintenance problem similar to the policing of skid row (see Chapter 5). The primary police objectives are (1) to keep streetwalking confined to a limited area (maintain the boundaries) and (2) to prevent related disorders from breaking out (keep the peace).[101]

Prostitution is often accompanied by ancillary crimes: more serious offenses that result from prostitution. Customers may be robbed, or prostitutes may be assaulted by their pimps or managers.

Periodically, streetwalking increases to the point where it becomes more visible to the public. The resulting public outcry leads to a police crackdown: sweep arrests of all prostitutes. Like crackdowns related to other crimes, they have a short–term impact after which things return to normal.

Call girls represent the upper end of the economic scale of prostitution. They cater to a more affluent customer and generally make their arrangements over the telephone. Because they are not on the street, their activities are not visible to either the public or the police. Prostitution of this sort may, however, come to public attention if prostitutes are working out of a motel or apartment complex in a way that causes other people to notice, take offense, and complain.

When prostitutes are arrested, conviction and punishment is not always the primary goal. Many arrests are designed to control streetwalking, either by confining it to a certain area or deterring it altogether. Convictions are usually for misdemeanors, with a sentence of, at most, several hundred dollars in fines and a few weeks or months in the county jail. The prostitutes themselves regard this as a routine business expense. In some instances, police attack prostitution by citing the pimps for numerous traffic violations.[102]

Prostitution arrests pose a number of legal problems for the police. The most difficult is the issue of entrapment, which occurs if the police officer initiates the idea of payment for sex. Also, equal protection problems are raised by the traditional police practice of arresting only the prostitute (usually female) and ignoring the customer (usually male), even though both are guilty of violating the law against commercialized sex. Finally the informal practice of confining streetwalking to a certain area of a city involves an illegal form of selective enforcement: enforcing the law in some areas but not others.[103]

## Gambling

The status of gambling in the United States has changed dramatically in the last 25 years. Many states have established lotteries, a number have legalized casino gambling, and many Native American tribes operate casinos on reservations.

Despite the spread of opportunities for legal gambling, much illegal gambling continues to exist. Nonetheless gambling represents a difficult problem in law enforcement because it is a victimless crime and an activity that many Americans regard as a legitimate form of recreation.[104] Illegal gambling has traditionally been the major source of revenue for organized crime and a factor in police corruption.[105]

Gambling enforcement often involves covert investigative techniques. Detectives must initiate investigations proactively, often using informants, undercover officers, or wiretaps. Similar tactics are often necessary for drug enforcement. All three tactics involve difficult legal questions. They are discussed in a separate section below.[106]

## DRUG ENFORCEMENT

By the end of the 1980s, drugs represented the most serious problem facing the police, the criminal justice system, and American society as a whole. An epidemic of crack cocaine usage fostered the growth of organized gangs that virtually took over entire neighborhoods in Los Angeles, New York, Washington, D.C., and other cities. Competition for control of the drug market produced a dramatic increase in homicides.[107]

### Drug Enforcement Strategies

Local police employ two basic strategies to combat illegal drug trafficking and use. The traditional supply reduction strategy includes four different tactics. The first is the simple buy–and–bust strategy: undercover officers purchase drugs and then arrest the dealers. A second and related strategy is the attempt to disrupt the drug syndicate by "trading up": arresting low–level dealers and offering them leniency in return for information about higher–level dealers.[108] A third strategy involves penetrating the drug syndicate through long–term undercover work. The fourth is the drug crackdown, an intensive enforcement effort concentrated in a specific area over a limited period of time.[109]

The demand reduction strategy involves attempting to reduce the demand for drugs on the part of potential users. This includes drug education programs such as D.A.R.E.

The traditional supply reduction strategies have never proven to be effective. Illegal drug use continues to remain at high levels, and in the poorest neighborhoods drug trafficking is often open and rampant. Several reasons explain this failure.

First, there is no persuasive evidence that the threat of arrest, per se, deters drug use or sale (or deters any other form of criminal activity, for that matter). Second, through what is known as the "replacement effect," new drug dealers quickly replace those who are arrested. Particularly in poor neighborhoods where legitimate career opportunities are limited, the incapacitation of dealers does not affect the behavior of other new potential dealers. Third, the strategy of arresting low–level dealers and trading up to get key individuals in drug trafficking organizations has never proven to be effective in disrupting these organizations.[110]

An important question is, Why do police continue to engage in these activities despite their apparent ineffectiveness? Peter K. Manning argues that drug arrests are made for their "dramaturgical effect": They generate publicity and create the appearance of doing something about the drug problem.[111] As Crank and Langworthy argue, police organizations exist in a larger social and political environment and need to create at least the impression that they are handling the problems that are within their professional domain.[112]

## Drug Crackdowns

Drug crackdowns deserve special attention.[113] One highly publicized effort was Operation Pressure Point (OPP) in New York City in the early 1980s. OPP was directed toward an open drug marketplace on the city's lower east side, where all kinds of drugs were readily available. Under OPP, 240 additional police officers were assigned to the area for the sole purpose of disrupting the drug trade. They swept through the area, dispersing crowds, writing traffic tickets, conducting drug searches, and making arrests. Later, narcotics officers conducted covert surveillance operations and buy–and–bust operations.[114]

In the first month, OPP officers made over 2,000 arrests, an average of 67 per day. Officers also engaged in deliberate harassment: stopping and questioning people in known drug areas and often telling them to move on. Much of the harassment was directed at suspected buyers rather than at sellers, in an effort to dry up the drug market. The U.S. attorney agreed to process many drug cases in federal court, where sentences were more severe. The police department, meanwhile, waived the desk appearance ticket (DAT) policy, which normally allows a person charged with a misdemeanor to be released immediately. Thus, all OPP drug offenders were subjected to full arrest, booking, and arraignment.[115]

Evaluations of OPP failed to prove conclusively that OPP effectively reduced drug trafficking. There was some reduction in the level of open drug dealing in the target area. Dealers adapted by using "lookouts" and "steerers" to warn off police and to direct buyers to sellers. The evaluation did not, however, attempt to measure the displacement of drug dealing to other neighborhoods. In fact, the drug problem in New York City as a whole worsened in the years after OPP with the arrival of crack. Analysis of the outcome of arrests failed to indicate any significant increase in the level of punishment meted out or any meaningful deterrent effect. There are also serious questions about cost–effectiveness, given the number of officers involved. The hidden costs, meanwhile, included the program's encouragement of harassment tactics by officers.[116]

Evaluations of crackdowns in other cities have produced mixed findings: in some cases there was a short–term reduction in crime; in others there was no positive effect.[117]

Kinlock argues that evaluations of drug crackdowns must be regarded with caution because of inadequate measures. Drug crackdowns often have several goals, including reducing crime, drug, and gang activity, improving the quality of neighborhood life, improving the health and well–being of drug users, preventing drug experimentation by children, and maintaining the integrity of criminal justice institutions. Most evaluations have not developed measures for these goals. Even with respect to crime, most evaluations have used data on officially reported crime, which are known to be problematic. Kinlock argues in favor of a problem–oriented data collection approach that is related to the full range of goals and effects of drug crackdowns.[118]

**FIGURE 6–2**
AFRICAN AMERICANS AND DRUG POSSESSION.

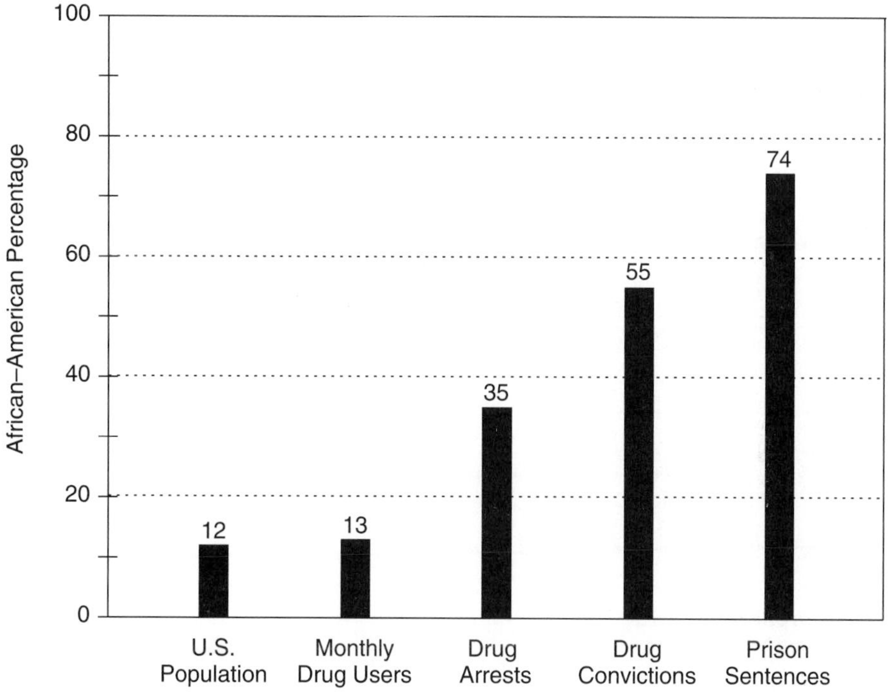

*Source:* Marc Mauer and Tracy Huling. *Young Black Americans and the Criminal Justice System: Five Years Later* (Washington, DC: The Sentencing Project, 1995), p. 12.

## Minorities and the War on Drugs

There is a significant disparity in the arrest of racial and ethnic minorities for drug offenses. The National Household Survey has found that African Americans are only somewhat more likely than whites to be using illegal drugs in any given month.[119] Yet as Figure 6–2 indicates, African Americans, in relation to their numbers in the population as a whole, are significantly more likely to be arrested for drug offenses. Jerome Miller argues that the entire criminal justice system's policy toward young African-American men represents a "search and destroy" mission.[120]

Many critics argue that the racial disparity in drug arrests is the result of department policies that deliberately target minority neighborhoods. As Castellano and Uchida point out, "Drug arrests are largely police–initiated (proactive) rather than citizen–initiated (reactive)." As a result, "local drug arrest rates and patterns are largely dependent upon the arrest policies and enforcement priorities in police departments."[121] That is to say, it is not the result of discriminatory decisions by individual officers on the street, but of policy decisions made by commanders (see Chapter 7).

## Demand Reduction: The D.A.R.E. Program

The most popular demand reduction strategy is the drug education program known as D.A.R.E. (Drug Abuse Resistance Education). D.A.R.E. originated with the Los Angeles Police Department (LAPD) in cooperation with the Los Angeles public schools in 1983. The program consists of 17 one–hour classroom sessions conducted by a sworn police officer. The content of the program involves both information about illegal drugs and their consequences and training in social skills to help resist illegal drug use.[122]

The D.A.R.E. program is extremely popular. By 1997 it was operating in an estimated 70 percent of all public school systems at an annual cost of $750 million per year. Several factors explain the program's popularity. First, it addresses parent concern about juvenile drug abuse. Second, there is a widespread belief that education is an effective approach. Third, both police and public school officials want to appear to be doing something about the drug problem.

Evaluations of D.A.R.E., however, have not found any significant reduction in actual drug use as a result of the program. Moreover, evaluations have generally been limited to one–year follow–up periods, and serious questions remain about the long–term effect of the program as students exposed to it reach late teenage years when rates of illegal drug use normally increase.[123]

## New Approaches to Drug Enforcement

A number of new approaches to drug enforcement are incorporated into community policing or problem–oriented policing programs.

One example is the Oakland SMART (Specialized Multi–Agency Response Team) program. Under SMART, the Oakland police worked closely with other city agencies and emphasized non–law enforcement strategies. These included attacking drug houses through vigorous enforcement of city building codes, by using a state nuisance law, and educating landlords on how to identify drug dealers. An evaluation of SMART found that it not only reduced signs of illegal behavior in the target sites, but also did not displace crime or disorder to the surrounding areas and, in fact, produced a diffusion of reduced crime and disorder to the immediately surrounding areas.[124]

## TARGETING GUNS AND GUN CRIMES

### The Kansas City Gun Experiment

The Kansas City Gun Experiment was designed to reduce gun–related crimes by removing guns from the streets. The experiment represented a combination of both problem–oriented policing, by focusing on a particular problem, and hot spots, by concentrating on particular areas of high criminal activity.[125]

The experiment targeted a high–crime precinct in Kansas City where the murder rate in 1991 was 177 per 100,000, compared with a national rate of about 10 per 100,000. For a period of 29 weeks in 1992 and 1993 an extra pair of two–officer patrol cars patrolled the area for six hours a night between the hours of 7 P.M. and 1 A.M. The officers were directed to stop vehicles with people they believed to be carrying illegal handguns. The officers were directed to make only legally justified stops (e.g., traffic law violations) and then make legally justified searches for weapons (e.g., search incident to an arrest). The underlying assumption was that this program would reduce crime both by removing guns from the streets and by sending a deterrent message about aggressive enforcement in the area.

During the course of the experiment, the special unit officers seized 29 guns; another 47 guns were seized in the target beat by other officers. Gun crimes fell by 49 percent in the target beat, compared with a 4 percent increase in a control beat. Changes in gun crimes in other beats across the city were mixed. There was no evidence either of displacement of gun crimes or the diffusion of benefits. The experiment suggested the potential positive effect of hot spots oriented anticrime programs. A replication of the gun experiment in Indianapolis, however, was surrounded by controversy over the data on guns seized.[126]

## SPECIAL INVESTIGATIVE TECHNIQUES

### Undercover Police Work

Undercover police work presents a number of special problems for the police.[127] First, it involves deliberate deception by the officer: lying about who he or she is. The danger is that officers become socialized into the habit of lying and may be tempted to lie in other contexts as well, such as when testifying under oath.

Second, an officer working undercover associates with criminals and attempts to become their friends. This socialization can erode the values and standards of policing. Ties to peer officers and family are weakened. Some officers have "gone native," embraced the criminal subculture, and become criminals themselves.

Third, undercover officers are often subject to less direct supervision than other officers. This is particularly true of deep undercover operations where the officer must spend weeks or months attempting to penetrate a criminal enterprise. The Knapp Commission found that detectives in the New York City Special Investigative Unit (SIU), for example, did not see their supervisors for weeks, and this contributed to the corruption that developed.[128]

Traditionally, police departments have had few, if any, meaningful controls over undercover work. Officers learned how to work undercover through informal training by veteran officers.[129]

To prevent possible abuses, police departments have instituted formal controls over undercover work. The Commission on Accreditation requires law enforcement agencies to have "written procedures for conducting vice, drug, and organized crime surveillance, undercover, decoy, and raid operations. . . ." These procedures should cover such activities as "supplying officers with false identity, disguises, and necessary credentials," "designating a single person as supervisor and coordinator," and "providing close supervision."[130] The city of Seattle, meanwhile, passed an ordinance limiting police investigations into political, religious, and private sexual activity. The ordinance included restrictions on the use of undercover officers in these areas.[131]

## Informants

Informants are an important source of information about criminal activity. They are especially useful in victimless crimes and other covert criminal activity. Informants have special knowledge because they are often criminals themselves or are associated with criminals. Developing a group of informants is part of the art of police work. Jonathan Rubinstein observes that "vice information is a commodity, and the patrolman learns that he must buy it on a restricted market."[132]

The use of informants creates a number of potential problems. First, the police are involved in an exchange relationship with someone who is usually a known criminal offender. The police must give something in order to obtain the information they want. The most valuable commodity is a promise of leniency: an agreement not to arrest, or to recommend leniency to the prosecutor or judge. With respect to not arresting an offender, there are serious moral questions about the police knowingly overlooking criminal activity. Critics argue that the relationship compromises the integrity of the police and sets the stage for corruption. New York City police officers in the 1970s provided their informants with drugs, thereby turning the officers into drug dealers.[133] The information provided by informants may be questionable. Informants may invent information simply to please their handlers, or provide information only against their enemies. Jerome Skolnick found that in "Westville" narcotics detectives allowed their informants to steal, and burglary detectives allowed their informants to engage in drug dealing.[134] The danger, as Gary Marx points out, is that the informer begins "to control the sworn agent rather than the reverse."[135]

To control the potential problems involved in the use of informants, the CALEA (Commission on Accreditation for Law Enforcement Agencies) accreditation standards require that police departments maintain a set of "policies and procedures" covering the master file of informants, the "security of the informant file," "criteria for paying informants," and other "precautions to be taken with informants."[136] A joint Bureau of Justice Assistance–Police Executive Research Forum report recommended, "All understandings with a criminal informant should be put in the form of a written agreement."[137]

## CONCLUSION

Crime control is one of the major responsibilities of the police. Crime–related programs involve a number of different strategies and assumptions. There is mixed evidence about the effectiveness of these strategies in reducing crime, however. Patrol has only limited deterrent effect on crime. The police clear or solve only about 21 percent of all crimes that come to their attention. They are able to solve a high percentage of those crimes where a suspect is immediately known. Many experts today argue that the most promising programs are crime prevention efforts embodied in community policing and problem–oriented policing programs.

## NOTES

1 Lawrence W. Sherman, "Attacking Crime: Police and Crime Control," in *Modern Policing,* eds., Michael Tonry and Norval Morris, (Chicago: University of Chicago Press, 1992), pp. 159–230.

**2** Peter Manning, *Police Work* (Cambridge: MIT Press, 1977).

**3** George L. Kelling and Mark H. Moore, "From Political Reform to Community: The Evolving Strategy of Policing," in eds., Jack R. Greene and Stephen D. Mastrofski *Community Policing: Rhetoric or Reality*, (New York: Praeger, 1991), pp. 3–25.

**4** Wesley G. Skogan and George E. Antunes, "Information, Apprehension, and Deterrence: Exploring the Limits of Police Productivity," *Journal of Criminal Justice* 7 (Fall 1979): 232.

**5** Lawrence W. Sherman et al., *Preventing Crime* (Washington: Government Printing Office, 1997).

**6** Ibid.

**7** Geoffrey Alpert and Mark H. Moore, "Measuring Police Performance in the New Paradigm of Policing," in Bureau of Justice Statistics, *Performance Measures for the Criminal Justice System* (Washington: Government Printing Office, 1993), pp. 109–140.

**8** George L. Kelling et al., *The Kansas City Preventive Patrol Experiment* (Washington: The Police Foundation, 1974).

**9** The Police Foundation, *The Newark Foot Patrol Experiment* (Washington: The Police Foundation, 1981).

**10** O. W. Wilson and Roy C. McLaren, *Police Administration*, 4th ed. (New York: McGraw–Hill, 1977), p. 410.

**11** Fred A. Klyman and Joanna Kruckenberg, "A National Survey of Police–Community Relations Units," *Journal of Police Science and Administration* 7 (March 1979): 72–79.

**12** David Bayley, *Police for the Future* (New York: Oxford University Press, 1994).

**13** Dennis P. Rosenbaum, Eusevio "Ike" Hernandez, and Sylvester Daughtry, Jr., "Crime Prevention, Fear Reduction, and the Community," in ed., William A. Geller, *Local Government Police Management*, 3d ed., (Washington: International City Management Association, 1991), pp. 96–130.

**14** Kelling and Moore, "From Political Reform to Community: The Evolving Strategy of Policing."

**15** Jerome E. McElroy, Colleen A. Cosgrove, and Susan Sadd, *Community Policing: The CPOP in New York City* (Newbury Park, Calif.: Sage, 1993), pp. 9–11.

**16** Albert Reiss, *The Police and the Public* (New Haven: Yale University Press, 1971), p. 95.

**17** Bureau of Justice Statistics, *Criminal Victimization in the United States, 1994* (Washington: Government Printing Office, 1997), p. v.

**18** Ibid.

**19** Ibid., pp. 94–95.

**20** Donald Black, "Production of Crime Rates," in *The Manners and Customs of the Police* (New York: Academic Press, 1980), p. 69.

**21** Bureau of Justice Statistics, *Criminal Victimization in the United States, 1994*, pp. 100–101.

**22** Black, "Production of Crime Rates."

**23** Reiss, *The Police and the Public*, p. 73.

**24** Gary LaFree, *Rape and Criminal Justice* (Belmont, Calif.: Wadsworth, 1989), pp. 73, 76.

**25** David Seidman and Michael Couzens, "Getting the Crime Rate Down: Political Pressure and Crime Reporting," *Law and Society Review* 8 (Spring 1974): 457–493.

**26** Herman Goldstein, *Policing a Free Society* (Cambridge, Mass.: Ballinger, 1977), pp. 55–57.

**27** William A. Westley, *Violence and the Police* (Cambridge: MIT Press, 1970), p. 36.

**28** Goldstein, *Policing a Free Society*, p. 55.

**29** Police Executive Research Forum, *Survey of Police Operational and Administrative Practices, 1981* (Washington: PERF, 1981), pp. 22–23.

**30** William B. Sanders, *Detective Work* (New York: Free Press, 1977), pp. 39–47.

**31** Alpert and Moore, "Measuring Police Performance in the New Paradigm of Policing."

**32** Sanders, *Detective Work*, p. 43.

**33** Westley, *Violence and the Police*, pp. 36–42.

**34** David J. Giacapassi and Jerry R. Sparger, "Cognitive Dissonance in Vice Enforcement," *American Journal of Police*, X (No. 2, 1991): 39–51.

**35** John E. Eck, *Solving Crimes: The Investigation of Burglary and Robbery* (Washington: Police Executive Research Forum, 1983), pp. 69–93.

**36** Reiss, *The Police and the Public*, p. 104.

**37** Black, "The Social Organization of Arrest," in *The Manners and Customs of the Police*, pp. 85–108.

**38** Stephen Mastrofski, Jeffrey B. Snipes, and Anne E. Supina, "Compliance on Demand: The Public's Response to Specific Police Requests," J*ournal of Research in Crime and Delinquency* 33 (August 1996): 269–305.

**39** Black, "The Social Organization of Arrest."

**40** Douglas A. Smith, Christy A. Visher, and Laura A. Davidson, "Equity and Discretionary Justice: The Influence of Race on Police Arrest Decisions," *Journal of Criminal Law and Criminology* 75 (Spring 1984): 234–249.

**41** Eck, *Solving Crimes*, pp. 124–127.

**42** Peter W. Greenwood et al., *The Criminal Investigation Process*, Vol. 1, *Summary and Policy Implications* (Santa Monica: Rand, 1975), p. 35.

**43** Eck, *Solving Crimes*, pp. 106–110.

**44** Harold E. Pepinsky, "Police Decision Making," in *Decision Making in the Criminal Justice System* in ed., Don Gottfredson (Washington: Government Printing Office, 1975), p. 27.

**45** Eck, *Solving Crimes*, p. 250.

**46** Alpert and Moore, "Measuring Police Performance in the New Paradigm of Policing."

**47** Federal Bureau of Investigation, *Crime in the United States, 1995* (Washington: Government Printing Office, 1996)

**48** Greenwood et al., *The Criminal Investigation Process*, p. 32.

**49** Eck, Solving Crimes, p. 203.

**50** Black, "Production of Crime Rates."

**51** Lawrence W. Sherman and Barry D. Glick, *The Quality of Police Arrest Statistics* (Washington: The Police Foundation, 1984).

**52** Edna Erez, "On the 'Dark Figure' of Arrest," *Journal of Police Science and Administration* 12 (December 1984): 431–440.

**53** Steven H. Gifis, *Law Dictionary*, 2d ed. (New York: Barron's 1984), pp. 28–29.

**54** Floyd Feeney, *Arrests without Conviction* (Washington: Government Printing Office, 1983).

**55** Sherman and Glick, *The Quality of Police Arrest Statistics*.

**56** Malcolm W. Klein, Susan Labrin Rosensweig, and Ronald Bates, "The Ambiguous Juvenile Arrest," *Criminology* 13 (May 1975): 82.

**57** President's Commission on Law Enforcement and Administration of Justice, *Task Force Report: The Police* (Washington: Government Printing Office, 1967), p. 8.

**58** Albert Reiss and David J. Bordua, "Environment and Organization: A Perspective on the Police," in *The Police: Six Sociological Essays*, ed., D. J. Bordua (New York: Wiley, 1967), p. 43.

**59** William B. Sanders, *Detective Work: A Study of Criminal Investigations* (New York: Free Press, 1977), p. 96.

**60** Greenwood et al., *The Criminal Investigation Process*, p. vi.

**61** Eck, *Solving Crimes*. Steven G. Brandl and James Frank, "The Relationship between Evidence, Detective Effort, and the Disposition of Burglary and Robbery Investigations," *American Journal of Police* 13, no. 3 (1994): 149–169.

**62** Elizabeth Loftus, *Eyewitness Testimony* (Cambridge: Harvard University Press, 1979), p. 7.

**63** Elinor Ostrom et al., *Patterns of Metropolitan Policing* (Cambridge, Mass.: Ballinger, 1977), chap. 7.

**64** *New York Times*, August 17, 1986, p. 1.

**65** Joan Petersilia, "Processing Latent Fingerprints—What Are the Payoffs? "*Journal of Police Science and Administration* 6 (June 1978): 157–167.

**66** Lucius J. Riccio and John F. Heaphy, "Apprehension Productivity of Police in Large U.S. Cities," *Journal of Criminal Justice* 5 (Winter 1977): 271-278.

**67** Brian Forst, *Arrest Convictability as a Measure of Police Performance* (Washington: Government Printing Office, 1982).

**68** Bureau of Justice Statistics, *The Prosecution of Felony Arrests, 1986* (Washington: Government Printing Office, 1989).

**69** Joan Petersilia, *Racial Disparities in the Criminal Justice System* (Santa Monica: Rand, 1983), p. 21.

**70** Joan Petersilia, Allan Abrahamse, and James Q. Wilson, *Police Performance and Case Attrition* (Santa Monica: Rand, 1987).

**71** Brian Forst, Judith Lucianovic, and Sarah J. Cox, *What Happens after Arrest?* (Washington: Institute For Law and Social Research, 1977).

**72** Eck, *Solving Crimes*, pp. 278-282.

**73** Jonathan Rubenstein, *City Police* (New York: Ballantine Books, 1974), pp. 121-122.

**74** Peter B. Bloch and James Bell, *Managing Investigations: The Rochester System* (Washington: The Police Foundation, 1976).

**75** Wesley G. Skogan and George E. Antunes, "Information, Apprehension, and Deterrence: Exploring the Limits of Police Productivity," *Journal of Criminal Justice* 7 (Fall 1979): 232.

**76** Wesley G. Skogan and Mary Ann Wycoff , "Some Unexpected Effects of a Police Service for Victims," *Crime and Delinquency* 33 (October 1987): 490–501.

**77** Ibid.

**78** Marvin E. Wolfgang, Robert Figlio, and Thorsten Sellin, *Delinquency in a Birth Cohort* (Chicago: University of Chicago Press, 1972).

**79** William Spelman, *Repeat Offender Programs for Law Enforcement* (Washington: Police Executive Research Forum, 1990).

**80** Ibid, pp. 25–26.

**81** Susan E. Martin and Lawrence W. Sherman, *Catching Career Criminals: The Washington, DC, Repeat Offender Project* (Washington: The Police Foundation, 1986).

**82** Ibid.

**83** Westley, *Violence and the Police*, p. 57.

**84** Federal Bureau of Investigation, *Law Enforcement Officers Killed and Assaulted, 1994* (Washington: Government Printing Office, 1995).

**85** Police Executive Research Forum, *Survey of Police Operational and Administrative Practices, 1981*, p. 22.

**86** John A. Gardiner, *Traffic and the Police: Variations in Law Enforcement Policy* (Cambridge: Harvard University Press, 1969).

**87** James Q. Wilson, *Varieties of Police Behavior* (New York: Atheneum, 1973), pp. 95–99.

**88** Ibid.

**89** Alexander Weiss and Sally Freels, "The Effects of Aggressive Policing: The Dayton Traffic Enforcement Experiment," *American Journal of Police* 15, no. 3 (1996): 45–64.

**90** Ibid.

**91** James B. Jacobs, *Drunk Driving: An American Dilemma* (Chicago: University of Chicago Press, 1989); H. Laurence Ross, *Confronting Drunk Driving: Social Policy for Saving Lives* (New Haven: Yale University Press, 1992).

**92** Ross, *Confonting Drunk Driving*.

**93** Ross, *Confronting Drunk Driving*. Jacobs, *Drunk Driving*.

**94** Ibid.

**95** Robert F. Meier and Gilbert Geis, *Victimless Crime?* (Los Angeles: Roxbury, 1997).

**96** Wayne R. LaFave, *Arrest* (Boston: Little, Brown, 1965).

**97** David J. Giacopassi and Jerry R. Sparger, "Cognitive Dissonance in Vice Enforcement," *American Journal of Police* 10, no. 2 (1991): 39–51.

**98** Jerome Skolnick, *Justice without Trial*, 3d ed. (New York: Macmillan, 1994), pp. 94–104.

**99** Diana Lewis, *The Prostitute and Her Clients* (Springfield, Ill.: Charles C. Thomas, 1985).

**100** Cudore L. Shell, *Young Men in the Street* (Westport, Conn.: Praeger, 1994); Robert P. McNamara, *The Times Square Hustler* (Westport, Praeger, 1994).

**101** Egon Bittner, "The Police on Skid Row: A Study of Peacekeeping," in *Aspects of Police Work* (Boston: Northeastern University Press, 1990), pp. 30–62.

**102** LaFave, "Arrest to Control the Prostitute," in *Arrest*, pp. 450–464.

**103** Ibid.

**104** Department of Justice, *Gambling Law Enforcement in Major American Cities* (Washington: Government Printing Office, 1978).

**105** President's Commission on Law Enforcement and Administration of Justice, *The Challenge of Crime in a Free Society* (Washington: Government Printing Office, 1967), pp. 187–210.

**106** LaFave, *Arrest*, pp. 471–482.

**107** Elliot Currie, *Reckoning: Drugs, the Cities, and the American Future* (New York: Hill and Wang, 1993).

**108** Mark H. Moore, *Buy and Bust* (Lexington, Mass.: Lexington Books, 1977).

**109** Lawrence W. Sherman, "Police Crackdowns: Initial and Residual Deterrence," *Crime and Justice: A Review of Research*, Vol. 12, eds., Michael Tonry and Norval Morris, (Chicago: University of Chicago Press, 1990), pp. 1–48.

**110** Currie, *Reckoning*; Arnold S. Trebach, *The Great Drug War* (New York: Macmillan, 1987).

**111** Peter K. Manning, *The Narcs' Game* (Cambridge: MIT Press, 1978).

**112** John P. Crank and Robert Langworthy, "An Institutional Perspective of Policing," *Journal of Criminal Law and Criminology*, 83 no. 2, (1992): 338–363.

**113** Sherman, "Police Crackdowns."

**114** Lynn Zimmer, "Proactive Policing Against Street–Level Drug Trafficking," *American Journal of Police* 9, (1990, no 1) :43–74.

**115** Ibid.

**116** Ibid.

**117** Sherman, "Police Crackdowns." Lawrence W. Sherman et al., *Preventing Crime* (College Park: University of Maryland, 1997), chap. 8.

**118** Timothy W. Kinlock, "Problem–Oriented Data Collection: Toward Improved Evaluations of Police Drug Crackdowns," *American Journal of Police* 13, no. 3 (1994): 59–94.

**119** Department of Health and Human Services, *National Household Survey on Drug Abuse: Main Findings 1995* (Washington, DC: Government Printing Office, 1997).

**120** Jerome G. Miller, *Search and Destroy: African–American Males in the Criminal Justice System* (New York: Cambridge University Press, 1996).

**121** Thomas C. Castellano and Craig G. Uchida, "Local Drug Enforcement, Prosecutors and Case Attrition: Theoretical Perspectives for the Drug War," *American Journal of Police* 9, no. 1, (1990): 147.

**122** Bureau of Justice Assistance, *An Introduction to DARE*, 2d ed. (Washington: Government Printing Office, 1991).

**123** Susan T. Emmett et al., "How Effective Is Drug Abuse Resistance Education?: A Meta–Analysis of Project DARE Outcome Evaluations," *American Journal of Public Health* 84 (September 1994): 1394–1401.

**124** Lorraine Green, "Cleaning Up Drug Hot Spots in Oakland: The Displacement and Diffusion Effects," *Justice Quarterly* 12 (December 1995): 737–754.

**125** Lawrence W. Sherman, James W. Shaw, and Dennis P. Rogan, *The Kansas City Gun Experiment* (Washington: Government Printing Office, 1995).

**126** "Indy Gun-Interdiction Drive Proves an Inviting Target," *Law Enforcement News* (July 20, 1995), p. 1.

**127** Gary T. Marx, *Undercover: Police Surveillance in America* (Berkeley: University of California Press, 1988).

**128** Knapp Commission, *Report on Police Corruption* (New York: Braziller, 1973).

**129** Marx, *Undercover*, pp. 188–190.

**130** Commission on Accreditation for Law Enforcement Agencies, *Standards for Law Enforcement Agencies*, 3d ed. (Fairfax: CALEA, 1994), Standard 43.1.6.

**131** Samuel Walker, "The Politics of Police Accountability: The Seattle Police Spying Ordinance as a Case Study," in *The Politics of Crime and Criminal Justice*, eds. E. S. Fairchild and V. Webb, (Beverly Hills: Sage, 1985), pp. 144–157.

**132** Jonathan Rubenstein, *City Police* (New York: Ballantine, 1973), p. 381.

**133** Robert Daley, *Prince of the City* (Boston: Houghton Mifflin, 1978).

**134** Skolnick, *Justice without Trial*, p. 129.

**135** Marx, *Undercover*, p. 152.

**136** Commission on Accreditation for Law Enforcement Agencies, *Standards for Law Enforcement Agencies*, 3d ed., Standard 42.2.9.

**137** Bureau of Justice Assistance and Police Executive Research Forum, *Informants and Undercover Investigations* (Washington: Government Printing Office, 1990), p. 16. .

# CHAPTER 7

# POLICING COMMUNITIES

Some experts believe a "quiet revolution" is under way in American policing.[1] This involves a concept called community policing, which its advocates believe represents a new philosophy of policing.[2] This chapter examines both community policing and the concept of problem-oriented policing, which shares many of the same features.[3]

## THE ROOTS OF COMMUNITY POLICING

Both community policing and problem-oriented policing originated in the late 1970s and early 1980s as a result of a series of crises in policing. First, the police–community relations crisis of the 1960s had created a crisis of legitimacy. Local police departments were isolated from and alienated from important segments of the community, particularly racial and ethnic minority populations.[4]

Second, research had undermined the assumptions of traditional police management and police reform. The Kansas City patrol experiment found that there were limits to the ability of traditional police patrol to deter crime (Chapter 4). Studies of the criminal investigation process raised doubts about the ability of the police to significantly increase the number of arrests (Chapter 5). Faster response time is not likely to increase the likelihood of arrests. In short, the traditional reforms of more police, more patrol, more detectives, and faster response time were seen as not likely to improve policing. At the same time, the traditional police goal of providing an immediate response to all citizen calls for service, regardless of the nature of the call, burdened the police with an enormous workload (Chapter 4).

Third, experts recognized that the police role is extremely complex, involving many different tasks and responsibilities (Chapter 1), and that the traditional police activities of patrol and investigation were not adequate for dealing with specific problems.

Fourth, experts began to recognize the importance of citizens as coproducers of police services.[5] The police depend on citizens to report crime and to request help in dealing with disorder. The decision to arrest is heavily influenced by the expressed preference for arrest on the part of a citizen. Successful prosecution of offenders depends heavily on the cooperation of victims and witnesses. Even more important, informal social control at the neighborhood level was increasingly recognized as the key to limiting crime and disorder. In short, there was growing recognition that the police cannot control crime by themselves.

## PROBLEM–ORIENTED POLICING

Herman Goldstein pioneered in proposing a new approach to the police role in 1979 with his concept of problem-oriented policing.[6] Goldstein had played a pivotal role in recognizing the complexity of the police role through his work with the American Bar Foundation Survey of Criminal Justice in the 1950s.[7] He then helped draft the American Bar Association (ABA) standards which emphasized the many different responsibilities of the police.[8] In his 1977 book, *Policing a Free Society*, Goldstein argues that we should think of the police as a government agency providing a wide range of miscellaneous services.[9]

The central idea in Goldstein's initial article on problem-oriented policing is that the police had traditionally defined their roles in terms of vague and general categories: crime, order maintenance, and service. In practice, however, each of these general categories includes many different kinds of problems. The category of crime, for example, includes murder, burglary, and drunk driving, each of which is a very different kind of social event. The category of disorder includes domestic disputes, mental health problems, public drunkenness, and many other problems. Goldstein argues that the police should take these categories and break them down into discrete problems and then develop specific responses to each one—in short, problem-oriented policing.[10]

Goldstein also points out that the traditional measures of police effectiveness are not useful. Not only are the data in the official Uniform Crime Reports (UCR) system extremely problematic, but the UCR system collapses all crimes into one global category. A problem-oriented approach requires specific measures of effectiveness for specific problems.[11]

Along with a growing number of experts, Goldstein argues that the police are the prisoners of their communications system. The 911 system forces them into a reactive role: devoting most of their resources to responding to calls for service.[12] This reactive role means that the police think in terms of isolated incidents (calls). Goldstein argues that this prevents any serious planning with respect to underlying problems.

Figure 7–1 illustrates the difference between traditional, 911-driven, incident-based policing and problem-oriented policing. Under the traditional approach, each incident is handled as an isolated event. Police officers are concerned only with responding to each and every incident. Problem-oriented policing, on the other hand, emphasizes the analysis of incidents to identify underlying problems, and to develop appropriate solutions.

## "BROKEN WINDOWS"

The second important development was a 1982 article entitled "Broken Windows" by James Q. Wilson and George L. Kelling.[13] "Broken Windows" summarizes the research on the limits of police crime-fighting ability and argues that the police should instead focus on disorder problems affecting the quality of neighborhood life. In particular, they should address those problems that create fear of crime and lead to neighborhood decay.

The image of broken windows symbolizes the relationship between disorder, neighborhood decay, and crime. A broken window, Wilson and Kelling argue, is a sign that nobody cares about the appearance of the property. Left unrepaired, it encourages other neighborhood residents to neglect their property. This sets in motion a downward spiral of deterioration. Houses become dilapidated; homeowners move out; homes are converted to rental properties; houses are converted from single-family to multifamily dwellings; some houses are abandoned; as the income level of the neighborhood declines, neighborhood stores close and property values decline. Gradually, crime in the neighborhood increases.[14]

These initial signs of disorder include drunks hanging out on the street, or groups of teenagers on street corners. Such events create fear for personal safety in the minds of law-abiding residents in the neighborhood. Out of fear, they stay at home and withdraw

**FIGURE 7–1**
TRADITIONAL VERSUS PROBLEM–ORIENTED POLICING

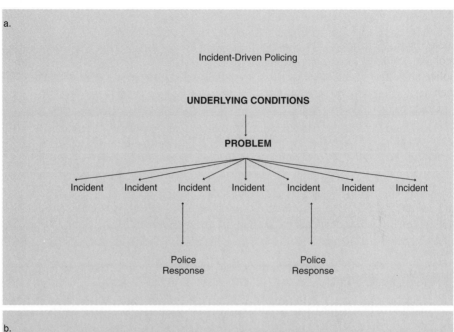

a.

Incident-Driven Policing

**UNDERLYING CONDITIONS**

**PROBLEM**

Incident   Incident   Incident   Incident   Incident   Incident   Incident

Police
Response

Police
Response

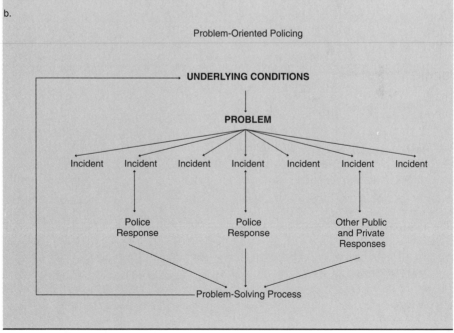

b.

Problem-Oriented Policing

**UNDERLYING CONDITIONS**

**PROBLEM**

Incident   Incident   Incident   Incident   Incident   Incident   Incident

Police
Response

Police
Response

Other Public
and Private
Responses

Problem-Solving Process

*Source:* Eck and Spelman, *Problem Solving*, Fig. 1, p. 4

from active participation in the neighborhood. In extreme cases they move out of the neighborhood altogether. The withdrawal of law-abiding citizens undermines the fabric of neighborhood life. The disorderly elements gain control of many public areas, such as street corners and parks, and the process of deterioration accelerates. The ultimate end of this process is serious predatory crime—burglary and robbery.

Wilson and Kelling maintain that traditional policing focuses on the end result of this process: serious crime. Yet the evidence indicates that the police officer's ability to fight crime is very limited. They argue that the police should intervene at the beginning of the process of neighborhood deterioration—at the first signs of neglect and disorder.

The Newark Foot Patrol Experiment provided some empirical foundation for the broken windows idea. The experiment found that additional foot patrol did not reduce crime but that it did increase feelings of safety. Moreover, citizens generalized these positive feelings to the police department—not just the foot patrol officers but the department as a whole.[15] This finding led Wilson and Kelling to speculate that, although the police might not be able to reduce crime, perhaps they could reduce fear of crime. And if people were less fearful they might not withdraw and the process of neighborhood deterioration might not begin.

## TYPES OF DISORDER

Wilson and Kelling emphasize the importance of disorder rather than serious crime in shaping the quality of neighborhood life. Disorder is an extremely broad category. Wesley Skogan has distinguished two major subcategories: (1) human and (2) physical. Human disorder includes:[16]

- **Public Drinking**. In a survey of 40 different neighborhoods, Skogan found public drinking to be the most common form of disorder.
- **Corner Gangs**. A few kids hanging out on the corner are a relatively minor disturbance, but organized and armed gangs pose a serious problem to the neighborhood.
- **Street Harassment**. Women and the elderly are the most frequent targets of harassment, which involves offensive comments or gestures.
- **Drugs**. Street sale and use of drugs also ranked high in Skogan's neighborhood survey. The level of drug sales ranges from isolated incidents to open drug "supermarkets."
- **Noisy Neighbors**. Noise problems range from households with chronic disturbances to simple conflicts between neighbors over proper conduct in public and private places. "Stoop sitting" is part of the lifestyle of some groups, but not others.
- **Commercial Sex**. The most visible form of commercial sex is streetwalking prostitution.

Physical disorder, meanwhile, includes:

- **Vandalism**. The act of vandalism is a crime, but unrepaired damage to buildings or graffiti on public places is a sign of neglect and decay.

- **Dilapidation and Abandonment**. Unrepaired or abandoned dwellings are a sign of lack of concern about the neighborhood. Abandoned buildings often become the site of drug trafficking or residences for homeless people.
- **Rubbish**. Uncollected trash, abandoned automobiles, and trash-filled vacant lots all lead to physical decay.

The key element of Goldstein's concept of problem-oriented policing is that each of these problems should be identified and responded to as a separate problem.

## INITIAL EXPERIMENTS

The ideas of Goldstein, Wilson, and Kelling sparked widespread interest in new approaches to policing. The U.S. Department of Justice sponsored the *Perspectives on Policing* seminars at the Harvard University Kennedy School of Government, which refined and publicized the concept of community policing.[17] In the 1980s, several police departments moved quickly to launch experiments in community policing and problem-oriented policing.

### Fear Reduction in Houston and Newark

The Fear Reduction Experiment in Houston and Newark was a direct outgrowth of the Newark Foot Patrol Experiment—an attempt to identify different ways that the police could reduce fear of crime. The Houston program included storefront community police stations, victim recontact, community newsletters, citizen contact patrol, and a community-organizing response team of police officers.[18]

- The community stations were staffed by a combination of patrol officers, civilian community service officers, and a civilian office manager. Officers assigned to the station were available to citizens who walked in with questions. The officers also organized community meetings, met with school officials about truancy, offered a blood pressure testing program, fingerprinted children at the request of concerned parents, and conducted a ride-along program. Eventually, the community station officers patrolled a neighborhood park to control rowdy youths who had taken it over and created fear among parents with small children.[19]
- The citizen contact patrol program required officers to initiate informal contacts with citizens and businesspeople. Officers were instructed to introduce themselves and say they were simply attempting to get acquainted and learn about any problems in the neighborhood.
- The community-organizing response team (CORT) involved efforts by police officers to organize neighborhood crime reduction programs.
- In the victim recontact program, officers telephoned recent crime victims to express their sympathy and offer further assistance. If the victim asked for more information about the investigation or prosecution, the officers could supply it. The program was designed to overcome the persistent complaints by crime victims that they are forgotten by the criminal justice system and, in particular, are never informed about the status of the police investigation.

- The community newsletters provided information about crime in the neighborhood and possible steps that people could take to reduce the risk of crime.

An evaluation of the Houston Fear Reduction Experiment found mixed results. Neighborhood residents who were aware of the community stations were less fearful of crime in the neighborhood and felt that crime and disorder problems in the area had declined. One significant finding, however, was that white residents visited or called the community station more often than blacks (12 percent versus 2 percent); homeowners did so more often than renters (26 percent versus 12 percent); older people used the station more often than younger people; and middle-income people used it more than low-income people (under $15,000 per year) (24 percent versus 9 percent).[20]

The newsletters had no effect on fear of crime in the neighborhood. The victim recontact program also had no effect on reducing fear of crime. In fact, victims with poor English skills (primarily Hispanic) expressed more fear of crime. Investigators hypothesized that such victims were confused and fearful about the nature of the telephone call.

The findings of the Houston evaluation were confirmed and amplified by a comprehensive review of all crime prevention programs by the University of Maryland and presented in *Preventing Crime*. This review found that programs are generally more successful among people and in communities that need them least (middle-class, homeowners, neighborhoods with relatively little crime, families with relatively minor problems), and less successful among people and in neighborhoods and schools that have the most severe problems.[21]

### Problem–Oriented Policing in Newport News

The first significant problem-oriented policing experiment occurred in Newport News, Virginia. For several years the police had faced a problem of a high rate of burglaries in the New Briarfield apartment complex. Increased police presence in the area reduced reported burglaries by 60 percent, but when the officers were transferred to other areas, the burglary rate increased again. By 1984 the apartment complex was generating more calls for service than any other residential area in the city. At this point, the police department decided to abandon traditional methods and to experiment with problem-oriented policing.[22]

The project utilized the SARA process for problem solving: scanning, analysis, response, assessment (Figure 7–2).

The scanning phase began with an analysis of crime patterns in the area and an opinion survey of apartment residents. The survey helped reveal the extent to which the physical deterioration in the buildings contributed to burglaries. The police department task force assigned to New Briarfield responded with tactics that addressed the physical condition of the buildings. The police also organized a meeting of the various government agencies that had some responsibility for the housing project. Figure 7–3 lists the public agencies contacted. The purpose of the meeting was to develop a coordinated strategy to improve conditions in the complex. A police officer assigned to the project helped organize a tenants' group, which put pressure on city officials to make improve-

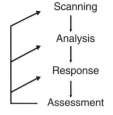

Scanning

Analysis

Response

Assessment

**FIGURE 7–2**
A PROBLEM-SOLVING PROCESS
   *Source:* John E. Eck and William Spelman, *Problem-Solving: Problem-Oriented Policing in Newport News* (Washington: Police Executive Research Forum, 1987), table 9, p. 70.

ments in the apartments before demolition began. Ultimately, however, a decision was made to demolish the apartments and relocate the residents.

Official statistics did indicate a drop in reported crime because of problem-oriented policing. More important, the activities of the officers represented a new role for the police in problem-oriented and community policing, such as surveying public opinion to identify neighborhood problems. By initiating the meetings about the apartment complex, police officers were acting as community organizers and brokers of government services.

## PRINCIPLES OF COMMUNITY POLICING

By the 1990s, community policing and problem-oriented policing had, together, become a national movement. Many, if not most police departments claimed to be engaged in one or the other. Community policing received a major boost with the 1994 Violent Crime Control Act which provided over $8 billion to hire 100,000 additional police officers. The program was administered by the Office of Community Oriented Police Services (COPS), which required that departments develop a community policing plan in order to receive federal funds for additional police officers.[23] The Community Policing Consortium, meanwhile, provided training and technical assistance to departments engaged in community policing. The Police Executive Research Forum (PERF) and the San Diego Police Department host an annual Problem-Oriented Policing Conference to further discussions of problem-oriented policing. The conference confers the Herman Goldstein Award to the police departments with the most innovative examples of problem solving.

As the community policing movement developed, a set of basic principles for community emerged. These principles include:

- Deemphasize responding to calls for service.
- Deemphasize crime fighting.
- Concentrate on neighborhood-level disorder.
- Develop closer ties with citizens as coproducers of police services.
- Develop closer ties with other government agencies that have responsibilities for community problems.
- Redefine the police role in terms of problem solving and community organizing.

**FIGURE 7–3**
PUBLIC AGENCIES CONTACTED FOR INFORMATION ON THE NEW BRIARFIELD
BURGLARY PROBLEM.

---

**Newport News city agencies**
  Office of Business Licenses—business license records
  Clerk of Courts—deed records
  Department of Codes Compliance—building safety information
  Fire Department—fire and arson data
  Planning Department—land use and census data
  Department of Public Works—street cleaning and sanitation information
  Redevelopment and Housing Authority—data on housing subsidy programs
  Tax Assessor's Office—property values and tax payments

**State agencies**
  Virginia Corporation Commission—corporate records
  California Corporation Commission—corporate records

**Federal agencies**
  Federal Bureau of Investigation (local office)—fraud investigation issues
  Internal Revenue Service—ownership patterns
  Department of Housing and Urban Development (Washington, D.C., central office)—housing
  standards and loan default data
  Office of Management and Budget—multifamily housing problems and HUD assistance
  programs

---

*Source:* John E. Eck and William Spelman, *Problems-Solving: Problem-Oriented Policing in Newport News*
(Washington: Police Executive Research Forum, 1987), table 9, p. 70.

## COMMUNITY POLICING EXPERIMENTS: CAPS IN CHICAGO

Chicago Alternative Policing Strategy (CAPS) represents one of the most ambitious
community policing efforts in the nation. With over 12,000 sworn officers, the Chicago
Police Department is the second largest in the country. An ongoing evaluation by
Wesley Skogan and other scholars provides valuable insights into both the possibilities
and the problems of implementing a new policing philosophy in a big-city department.[24]

### The CAPS Plan

CAPS began with extensive planning, involving a number of experts from outside the
police department. After much discussion and revision, CAPS was designed around six
basic points:

**1** Involvement of the entire police department and the entire city. Some community
policing programs, by contrast, involve specialized units separate from the basic operations of the department and/or particular neighborhoods.

**2** Permanent beat assignments for officers. To enhance officer knowledge of and
involvement in neighborhood problems, officers would be given permanent beat assignments. This idea was originally tried with team policing in the early 1970s (see
p. 173–174).

**3** A serious commitment to training. If community policing truly represents a different philosophy, it is necessary to train officers regarding the new expectations about their jobs.

**4** Significant community involvement. One of the basic principles of community policing is that it involves a high level of citizen input and partnership with the police.

**5** A close link between policing and the delivery of other city services. As was the case with the initial problem-oriented policing experiment in Newport News, CAPS was intended to address neighborhood problems by helping citizens mobilize other city agencies to improve the delivery of services.

**6** Emphasis on crime analysis. A heavy emphasis was placed on geographic analysis of crime patterns, using sophisticated computer analysis, to identify problems.

CAPS leaders assumed at the outset that the program would take between three to five years to implement. Although CAPS was implemented citywide, five districts were selected as prototype districts and subject to extensive evaluation. These districts had a combined population of about 500,000 people, or about the size of many big cities.

### Obstacles to Change

Implementation of CAPS encountered a number of major obstacles. The first was the problem of resources. Strong public opposition killed a proposed tax increase to fund additional officers. Consultants, however, identified 1,600 officers in the department who could be reassigned to provide more efficient police services. Finally, the city obtained federal and state grants to hire more officers and support CAPS.

A second and related problem was strong public opposition to the planned closing of precinct station houses. Although designed as an efficiency measure, many residents believed that they were losing "their" police presence and the proposal was killed.

A third and major problem involved getting the rank-and-file officers committed to CAPS. Unlike some other community policing programs, CAPS did not rely on volunteers. Police officers often resist change. Surveys of Chicago officers, however, found significant differences in attitudes within the rank-and-file. Generally, older officers, racial and ethnic minority officers, and female officers were more open to change than younger, white, male officers. A majority of all officers were extremely pessimistic at the outset, believing that community policing would blur the lines of authority between police and citizens, and put unreasonable demands on the police to solve all community problems.

The attitudes of the rank and file were related to another serious problem: supervision and performance evaluations. Because CAPS represented a new philosophy and a new role for the police, it required new forms of supervision and performance evaluation. Rank-and-file officers understandably asked what they were expected to do under CAPS and how they would be evaluated. This proved to be a major controversy, however, and was not immediately resolved.

Another major problem was the 911 system. The traditional approach to calls for service would pull officers away from problem-solving activities and dispatch officers outside their beats (thereby violating the beat integrity principle of the program). CAPS

CAPS ON THE WEB

The Chicago Police Department maintains a web site with information about CAPS. Check out the site. What can you learn about the program? Are there any new developments since this book was written?

attempted to address this extremely difficult problem in several ways. First, it capped the number of times officers could be dispatched out of their beats. Second, it created special rapid-response teams to handle critical incidents. Third, it attempted to limit the number of calls by developing new dispatching priorities.[25]

### CAPS in Action

The heart of CAPS is citizen interaction with the police. This is attempted through a regular series of beat meetings, where citizens and beat officers meet to discuss neighborhood problems and possible solutions.

As Skogan and Hartnett point out in their evaluation of CAPS' initial phase, "Making beat meetings work was hard."[26] Officers thought meetings took time away from "real" police work. The typical meeting involved about 22 citizens and 5 officers, and took about an hour and a half. The agenda for each meeting was "just frank talk."[27] Attendance tended to be higher in African-American neighborhoods, primarily because of concern about crime.

Figure 7–4 indicates the problems identified at beat meetings in five districts evaluated by Skogan and Hartnett. Drug dealing was clearly the problem of greatest concern. Other crime-related issues were also frequently mentioned. Many of the problems fell in the disorder category: youth problems, loud music, and so on. Significantly, police disregard for citizens was the fourth most frequently mentioned problem, indicating that CAPS faced a significant problem in public distrust.

Observations of beat meetings found that the goal of police-citizen partnerships was not met. Police officers generally dominated meetings and controlled the agenda. The goals were met at a higher rate in some neighborhoods (Rogers Park) than in others (Morgan Park).

Getting other city agencies involved in problem solving was a major problem. An evaluation of community policing in eight cities, for example, had found that this effort failed in seven of them.[28] In Chicago, a special Mayor's Office of Inquiry and Information (MOII) was responsible to seeing that other agencies cooperated with CAPS. The key instrument was a one-page service request form, which indicated a problem and the agency responsible for it. Specific requests involved replacement of missing street signs, closing or demolition of abandoned buildings, removal of graffiti, and towing of abandoned vehicles. These involved the physical decay category of disorder.

CAPS produced a number of different problem-solving activities. Under Operation Beat Feet, 60 residents in Rogers Park marched through part of the neighborhood at

**FIGURE 7–4**
TOP PROBLEMS AT BEAT MEETINGS.

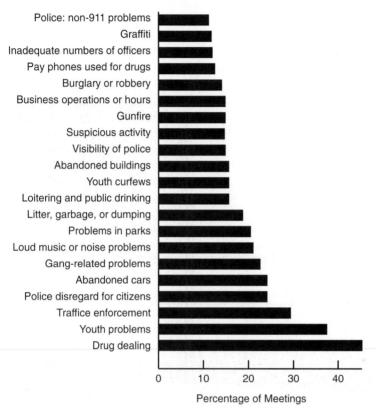

*Source:* Wesley G. Skogan and Susan M. Hartnett, *Community Policing: Chicago Style* (New York: Oxford University Press, p. 121, fig. 5–1).

night in a form of "positive loitering" to deter potential criminals. Members of the Englewood community also conducted a march against drugs. Rogers Park residents initiated court action against the owner of a building that was the center of criminal activity. Morgan Park developed a Beatlink program that allowed business owners to contact patrol officers directly through beepers.

## Evaluation of CAPS

A wide-ranging evaluation of the first years of CAPS found mixed results. Telephone surveys found a relatively high level of awareness of the program, but that awareness did not increase as time went on. Citizens in most evaluation districts also reported seeing police officers more often than before. In most of the evaluation districts there was also an increase in the visibility of informal contacts between police and citizens.

There were also significant increases in public perceptions that the police were responding to their concerns and dealing with crime, along with reduced fear of crime. Especially important, over 80 percent of the respondents indicated that police stopping too many people and being too tough was not a problem in their area. Consistent with previous surveys, African Americans (13 percent) were far more likely than whites (3 percent) to say that police use of excessive force was a problem.

In the end, CAPS met some but not all of its goals. Most important, officers did change the way they went about their jobs, spending more time on problem solving. There were significant perceived changes in the quality of life in the prototype districts: less crime, less fear, fewer gangs, and a greater sense of police responsiveness. The police department did not, however, succeed in fully implementing its crime-mapping program. There were also problems in achieving the desired level of citizen involvement.

The major achievement in Chicago is that some small but notable changes were accomplished in a citywide reorientation of policing. Most community policing projects in other cities have been small pilot projects, focusing on limited areas or problems, and usually involving volunteers. The CAPS experience suggested that a reorientation of a major police department is possible.

The one major failure of CAPS was the inability to include the Hispanic community. Hispanic residents of Chicago were least aware of and least involved in CAPS. This is partially consistent with other community-oriented projects (see Fear Reduction in Houston and Newark, p. 162), which are generally more effective with whites and home owners than racial and ethnic minorities and renters.

## EIGHT INOP PROGRAMS

The wide variety of community policing programs is indicated by the Innovative Neighborhood Oriented Policing (INOP) projects funded by the Bureau of Justice Assistance (BJA).[29]

- The Tempe, Arizona, Beat 16 project involved a team of volunteer officers assigned to answer calls for service only in Beat 16 and to engage in problem solving.
- The Norfolk, Virginia, PACE program was citywide and almost entirely enforcement oriented and involved undercover operations and saturation patrol in target areas, particularly public housing areas.
- The New York City program involved a large police van parked near a public school, with the immediate area designated a drug-free zone.
- The Hayward, California, INOP program also involved a police van that served as a substation.
- The Portland, Oregon, INOP program focused on a public housing project, while the police department was also attempting a citywide conversion to community policing. The INOP program included high visibility patrol, a special neighborhood response team, partnerships with other public and private agencies, and organizing and empowerment of the public housing residents.
- Prince George's County programs involved police offices in problem-ridden apartment complexes, a youth explorer program, a "knock and talk" program to

establish contact between officers and citizens, and the use of civil court procedures to reduce nuisances.

• Houston's Operation Siege was entirely an enforcement effort directed at two target areas. Activities included saturation patrol, zero-tolerance enforcement, target hardening, and neighborhood cleanups.

• Louisville, Kentucky, focused on voluntary participation by 66 officers in the Fourth District, with special training in problem solving.

The eight INOP programs indicate the tremendous variety that has always existed in community policing programs. Some were very traditional crime-fighting programs, whereas others involved community organizing and networking with other agencies. Some were citywide; others focused on very limited geographic areas. Some, like the New York City van were very unimaginative. Some called for citizen involvement; others did not. The title of a book by Jack Greene and Stephen Mastrofski asks the rhetorical question, *Community Policing: Rhetoric or Reality.*[30] The point of their question is important: Some community policing programs do represent a substantively innovative approach to policing, others are nothing more than rhetoric.

The impact of the INOP projects varied widely. With respect to perceived drug trafficking, respondents in some areas believed that it was reduced, others saw no impact, and still others believed that it had been displaced to other areas. With respect to drug-related crime, respondents in some areas thought the program had been very effective, whereas others saw either no effect or mixed results. Respondents in three areas believed that fear of crime had been reduced, and others saw no reduction or mixed results. Most INOP respondents perceived an improvement in police-community relations. Community organization and involvement were very high in several sites, but were almost nonexistent in New York City.[31]

## OTHER PROGRAMS

### COPE in Baltimore County

The Baltimore County police began a citizen-oriented police enforcement (COPE) project in 1982. COPE involved a 15-member team assigned to each of the three patrol regions. Officers were assigned motorcycles and subcompact cars to distinguish them from regular patrol officers. Their primary mission was to reduce fear of crime, but there was no rigidly defined program of activity.[32]

Initially COPE officers engaged in intensive patrolling of their areas. Citizen contact with police was increased through door-to-door surveys asking residents about their fear of crime. The data from these surveys were then used to plan other programs. At the suggestion of Herman Goldstein, who was brought in as a consultant, surveys focused on specific neighborhood problems.

The COPE program claimed accomplishments in several neighborhoods. In the Belmont area, the surveys identified a "tree house" in a vacant lot that was the center of open alcohol and drug use by teenagers and the cause of considerable fear among neighborhood residents. COPE officers located the property owner and obtained his permission to have the county roads department remove the tree. In the Garden Village

---

**RESEARCHING YOUR COMMUNITY**

Are the law enforcement agencies in your community doing community policing or problem–oriented policing? Research the activities of your local agencies. For each agency consider the following questions: (1) What label is used to describe the program (COP, POP)? (2) What is the content of the program (community meetings, intensive drug enforcement, coordinated activities with noncriminal justice programs)? (3) Is the program departmentwide or operated by a special unit? (4) Has it been evaluated and, if so, what were the results of that evaluation? (5) Did the agency receive funds for additional officers from the COPS office? (6) What did the agency do with those officers?

---

neighborhood, an area with 342 federally subsidized townhouses, COPE officers got the county roads department to improve the lighting in streets and alleyways. They also helped organize an apartment residents association, and helped prepare a grant proposal for the construction of a community park.

COPE illustrated community policing principles. Officers adopted new roles: they conducted neighborhood surveys, organized and brokered government services, and helped to write grant proposals. Area residents noticed the increased police presence as a result of COPE and became slightly more satisfied with the police. There was also some decrease in the fear of crime. These decreases were greatest during the later stages of the program, after it adopted a more specific problem-oriented approach.

### SMART in Oakland

The SMART (Specialized Multi-Agency Response Team) in Oakland[33] incorporated the concept of "hot spots": particular locations with high levels of reported crime, disorder, and/or high rates of calls for service.[34] The Oakland program concentrated on drug hot spots, particularly houses or apartment buildings where there were believed to be high rates of drug activity. The most important element of the program involved site visits by representatives of many different government agencies: housing code enforcement, fire department, utilities, and so on (see the section on Newport News, pp. 162–163). Special emphasis was placed on aggressive enforcement of housing code violations to force land-lords to fix up their properties (see "Broken Windows", p. 158). The California Health and Safety Code makes it a violation to maintain a dwelling where controlled substances are manufactured, sold, or used. In addition, there was a landlord training program to help apartment owners screen tenants and keep out potential drug dealers.

Lorraine Green's evaluation of SMART found reductions in crime and disorder in most of the properties targeted by the program. Moreover, crime and disorder were not displaced to the surrounding areas and, in fact, there appeared to be a "diffusion" of the benefits to those areas. In short, targeting specific hot spots led to a general improvement in the quality of life in the immediately surrounding area.

SMART, in short, combined many of the basic elements of problem-oriented policing: identifying specific problems (in this case problem locations), coordinating the

---

**SIDEBAR 7–1**

SAN DIEGO: CIVIL REMEDIES AS A PROBLEM–SOLVING TOOL

One of Herman Goldstein's main arguments is that the police should look beyond the criminal justice system for tools and resources to deal with problems of crime and disorder. The Oakland SMART program, for example, used aggressive housing code enforcement to attack drug hot spots.

The San Diego Police Department attacked the problem of street prostitution through restraining orders. One neighborhood was particularly affected by streetwalkers who would flag down cars and solicit pedestrians. This activity degraded the quality of life for neighborhood residents and harmed local businesses by scaring away customers. Instead of the traditional approach of arresting the prostitutes, which rarely eliminates the problem, the San Diego police obtained restraining orders against individually named prostitutes, barring them from loitering and flagging down motorists. Violation of the restraining order would result in a five-day jail term and a $1,000 fine. The restraining order approach appeared to work, as prostitutes disappeared from the area.

*Sources:* Office of Community Oriented Policing Services, *COPS Office Report* (Washington: Government Printing Office, 1997), p. 32. Peter Finn and Maria O'Brien Hylton, *Using Civil Remedies for Criminal Behavior* (Washington: Government Printing Office, 1994).

---

efforts of many different government agencies, and relying on measures outside the criminal justice system.

## NEW YORK CITY: FROM CPOP TO ZERO TOLERANCE

New York City launched its Community Patrol Officer Program (CPOP) in 1984. The ultimate fate of the program, however, illustrated the potential threat to community policing from changing political circumstances.[35]

CPOP officers in each precinct were freed from responsibility for answering calls for service, which were handled by regular patrol officers assigned to the neighborhoods. They were expected to identify neighborhood problems and develop short-term and long-term strategies for solving them. Each CPOP officer maintained a "beat book" in which he or she was expected to identify the major problems in the area and list strategies to deal with them. This device forced rank-and-file officers to think about problems and solutions—to act as planners.[36]

An early evaluation of CPOP pilot beats was cautiously optimistic about its success. As planners, CPOP officers identified quality-of-life problems that were normally not considered the responsibility of the police. CPOP officers, for example, helped neighborhood residents clear up abandoned lots that had become safety hazards. Although trash-filled lots and unsafe playgrounds are not crime problems in the traditional sense, they were perceived by residents as threats to their safety and the quality of their neighborhoods. Many of the strategies developed by CPOP officers fell into a traditional law enforcement mode, however. Officers gave a great deal of emphasis to the drug problem, and many of their tactics were traditional, such as aggressive arrests of drug dealers. This represented a tendency to value crime fighting, which had high status within the police department, rather than the newer and still less-valued aspects of the police role. As community organizers, CPOP officers were relatively successful in mobilizing existing organizations to work on problems, but not in creating community groups.

Initially, CPOP was an experimental program limited to a few experimental precincts. In 1990, however, as a result of public fear of crime, the mayor and the police commissioner expanded CPOP citywide. Many thought that this rapid expansion was unwise. In 1993, however, the newly elected mayor Rudolph Giuliani announced that he thought community policing was too "soft" and ordered a return to the "basics". Under his new police commissioner, William Bratton, the department adopted zero-tolerance policing. This ended the CPOP program in New York City.[37]

### Zero–Tolerance Policing

Zero-tolerance policing in New York City involves aggressive law enforcement, but not entirely in the traditional manner. Adopting the broken windows theory, it focuses on relatively minor crimes: urinating in public, fare beating (not paying the fare on the subway by jumping the turnstiles), aggressive panhandling on the subway, subway graffiti, and cracking down on squeegeeing (kids who wash the windows of cars stopped at traffic lights).[38] Many of these efforts are concentrated in the New York City subways. Dennis J. Kenney's research found that serious crime on the subways is too infrequent to measure, but the conditions in the subway stations and on the trains are very unpleasant and create considerable fear of crime.[39]

Zero-tolerance policing is based on the theory that attacking minor offenses helps reduce major offenses in two ways. Specifically, kids arrested for fare beating were often found to be in possession of illegal weapons. Arrest for the minor offense led either to prosecution on more serious charges and/or removal of an illegal weapon from the streets. More generally, zero tolerance communicates a general message that law breaking will not be tolerated.

Serious crime fell dramatically in New York City in the mid-1990s. Murders reached their lowest level in 30 years. There is much controversy over whether zero-tolerance policing deserves credit for this accomplishment. William Bratton, the police commissioner who instituted the policy, and criminologist George Kelling claim that zero tolerance is directly responsible.[40] Former New York City mayor, David Dinkins, and former police commissioner, Lee P. Brown, claim that the community policing program (CPOP) they initiated in the 1980s set in motion the reduction in crime. A number of criminologists, meanwhile, point out that serious crime also declined in other cities, and that the reduction in New York City is part of a general trend. Serious crime fell in Washington, D.C., for example, where the police department was marked by scandals and inefficiency. It also fell in Los Angeles where officers were making fewer arrests in the aftermath of the 1991 Rodney King incident.[41]

**COMMUNITY POLICING AND PROBLEM–ORIENTED POLICING ON THE WEB**

Many police agencies describe their community policing and problem–oriented policing programs on the web. Check out the web sites for several departments. What can you learn? Do they describe their programs in detail that is useful to you?

Zero-tolerance policing is also heavily criticized for encouraging officers to be overly aggressive. Critics cite an increase in citizen complaints against New York City police officers in the 1990s. And in 1997 the department was hit with a major scandal involving the grotesque physical abuse of Abner Louima, a Haitian immigrant.[42]

The verdict is still out on the impact of zero-tolerance policing. The abrupt termination of the CPOP program and the shift to zero-tolerance policing illustrates how vulnerable community policing can be to changing political circumstances.

## PERSPECTIVES ON COMMUNITY POLICING

To clarify what community policing and problem-oriented policing *are*, it is useful to understand what they are *not*. Comparisons with team policing and police-community relations programs are particularly instructive.

### Team Policing

Team policing was a popular police reform effort in the late 1960s and early 1970s. It was based on many of the same assumptions as community policing and included many of the same program elements: decentralization, community input, and so forth. Yet, team policing failed, and is almost completely forgotten today. It is instructive to explore what went wrong with team policing, and how community policing and problem-oriented policing differ.[43]

The goals of team policing included developing a neighborhood focus, making police operations relevant to particular neighborhood problems, and increasing interaction with citizens. To achieve this, it attempted to decentralize decision making in the police organization and give rank-and-file officers greater decision-making responsibility. A team of officers would be assigned to a particular neighborhood on a semipermanent basis and was responsible for all police services in that area. It was believed that this approach would improve police-community relations, enhance police officer morale, and facilitate change within the police organization.[44]

### Team Policing in Operation

One major team policing experiment was Community Sector (COMSEC) policing in Cincinnati (1971–1976).[45] An evaluation found mixed results. On the positive side, fewer people in the experimental area believed that their neighborhood was very unsafe, and satisfaction with police services, already high, remained high. On the negative side, police officer attitudes toward the community did not change and in some cases worsened. Despite 40 hours of human relations training, the majority of police officers assigned to the experimental low-income neighborhood still believed that poverty was proof of a lack of character. Also, the officers' assessment of community problems did not become closer to citizens' assessment; even worse, after 30 months officers in the experimental district thought that citizens were less cooperative (in reporting crimes, helping to identify suspects, and other areas) than before the experiment began. In summary, COMSEC illustrated the difficulties in improving police-community relations.

### The Failure of Team Policing

The team policing movement collapsed very suddenly in the 1970s and was completely abandoned. It failed for several reasons. First, most of the experiments were poorly planned and hastily implemented. As a result, officers assigned to the experiments did not have a good understanding of what they were supposed to do. Many middle-management officers felt threatened because decentralization undermined their authority and, as a result, some officers sabotaged the experiments.[46]

Second, team policing areas were not well integrated into the main operations of the police department. One part of the police department had a neighborhood focus; the rest had a citywide orientation. The problem was especially acute with respect to the 911 communications system, which continued to operate on a citywide basis in terms of citizen calls for service.[47]

Finally, and perhaps most important, the advocates of team policing did not develop a different view of police work. The program emphasized organizational restructuring but not a different style or philosophy of policing. Thus, team policing officers engaged in the traditional forms of police work: responding to calls for service, deterring crime through patrol, and apprehending criminals. Although team policing was supposed to include greater contact with citizens and citizen input into police policy making, there were no clear guidelines about how this should take place or how policing might be different as a result.

The team policing experience offers several lessons for community policing and problem-oriented policing. The first is the need for careful planning. As the CAPS program in Chicago indicates, this planning needs to include reorientation of police officers toward the new approach.[48] Second, there is a need for clear guidelines regarding what officers are supposed to do. Third, the experience illustrated the difficulty in changing a large organization where traditions and habits are deeply ingrained. Fourth, developing and maintaining a process for meaningful citizen input is extremely difficult. Fifth, it is extremely difficult to maintain the continuity of an innovative program and to continually reassess goals and strategies.[49]

### Police–Community Relations

Some elements of community policing resemble some of the goals of traditional police–community relations (PCR) programs (see Chapter 9 for a full discussion of these programs). The two concepts are very different in important respects, however.

Police–community relations programs were designed as add-ons, with little direct connection to patrol or other elements of traditional policing. The principal focus of PCR programs was to improve relations with the public and with racial and ethnic minorities in particular. Most were created in the 1960s in response to the urban riots.[50]

Officers assigned to PCR units spent most of their time in public speaking activities, talking to civic groups and in schools.[51] Other programs such as ride-alongs and store-front offices were designed to increase citizen understanding of police work. Critics argued that PCR programs were not central to police operations. They considered PCR essentially *public relations* rather than a change in basic police operations.

## COMMUNITY POLICING: PROBLEMS AND PROSPECTS

Although community policing is an important development, many unanswered questions about it remain.[52] Some advocates maintain that the era of community policing has already arrived.[53] Critics argue, however, that it is premature to claim that community policing either dominates contemporary policing or has proved to be a long-term success. There are a number of key questions about community policing and problem-oriented policing that need to be addressed.

### Rhetoric or Reality?

The basic question, according to Greene and Mastrofski, is whether the concept is "rhetoric or reality."[54] Do particular community policing programs represent something genuinely new or simply new rhetoric to describe traditional policing.[55] Many of the team policing programs in the early 1970s were little more than rhetoric, with little change in actual police operations. This explains why team policing disappeared as quickly as it did.[56] Hunter and Barker warn that for many people community policing "seeks to be all things to all people," with little meaningful content. At the same time, some police executives use the rhetoric of community policing as a way of appearing to be progressive and innovative without actually abandoning traditional policing.[57]

The evaluations of the INOP programs (see pp. 168–169) suggest that some so-called community policing programs are little more than rhetoric or very conventional law enforcement programs.[58] Nonetheless, it is also clear that the Chicago CAPS program does represent a genuinely new approach to policing.[59]

### Too Rapid Expansion

Closely related to the problem of rhetoric rather than substantive programming is the danger of too rapid expansion. Because of its great popularity, some cities have adopted community policing without careful planning. This was one of the major reasons for the failure of team policing in the 1970s. The Chicago CAPS program illustrates the problems of reorienting police officers, securing compliance with other city agencies, and ensuring genuine community participation.[60]

## A Legitimate Police Role?

One key issue in the community policing debate involves the question of the proper police role. Should police officers function as community organizers, and work on housing problems and cleaning up vacant lots? Is this the proper role for a police officer with arrest power? Or should police officers spend their time and energy on serious crime?

There is no right or wrong answer to this question. It is a matter of policy choice. A community may define the police role in those terms if it wishes to do so. Another community may prefer the more traditional police role. The fact that the police role has been defined one way for many years does not mean that it cannot be defined in a different way. Change is not impossible. As historians of the police point out, the crime-attack role that dominates today is not as traditional as many people think. In fact, it developed only over the last 50 years (see Chapter 2).

## A Political Police?

David Bayley warns that one aspect of changing the police role is the danger of involving the police in politics. One of the basic principles of Anglo-American law is the idea of clearly defined limits on all government power, and on the police in particular. Bayley refers to this as the "minimalist" tradition of policing.[61] These limits are embodied in the Bill of Rights. Community policing, however, expands the police role and erodes the traditional limits. Bayley refers to this as "maximilist" policing. Should police officers, for example, be going door to door, calling on law-abiding citizens when those people have not called the police? If the police organize community groups, there is the danger that they will turn into political advocacy groups that will lobby for candidates or issues the police support.[62]

## Changing the Police Culture

A more practical question is whether it is possible to change the police culture as community policing requires. Many, perhaps most police officers are strongly committed to the traditional police role. Changing to community policing would involve reorienting those officers. In a contribution to the *Perspectives on Policing* series, Malcolm Sparrow points out that "for the police," community policing "is an entirely different way of life." He warns that a police chief faces the task of changing "the fundamental culture of the organization." Sparrow notes that the peer group subculture in police departments is particularly strong and resistant to change (see Chapter 13). Changing this subculture, he warns, will take time and will inevitably be accompanied by turmoil.[63]

The initial experiments in community policing provided a hopeful outlook on this problem. In Baltimore, COPE officers "started out more satisfied with their jobs than were control group officers, and remained more satisfied." They developed more positive attitudes toward the community as the program progressed. Their attitudes toward the police role also changed, and they became more positive about the community policing style.[64] Officers assigned to the New York City CPOP program had a favorable reaction to it, believing that it gave them more responsibility and opportunity to exercise

---

**SIDEBAR 7–2**

PERSONNEL EVALUATION UNDER COMMUNITY POLICING

Because community policing and problem-oriented policing represent a different role for the police, new systems of personnel evaluation are required. Reprinted below is the patrol officer's monthly work sheet developed for the Houston Police Department's neighborhood-oriented policing (NOP) program (see Figure 7–5).

*Source:* Mary Ann Wycoff and Timothy N. Oettmeier, *Evaluating Patrol Officer Performance under Community Policing* (Washington: Government Printing Office, 1994), pp. 22–23.

---

initiative. On the other hand, however, there was conflict between them and regular patrol officers who felt that the CPOP officers had an easier job and were not doing "real" police work.[65]

The conflict between Community policing officers and regular patrol officers raises an important implementation issue. Herman Goldstein warns that although there are many arguments for beginning a Community policing program with a special unit, "separate units with different orientations are simply not workable in the long run."[66] Being separate and isolated from mainstream police operations was one of the problems encountered by the special police–community relations units that many departments created in the 1960s (see Chapter 9).[67]

## Community Coproduction

One of the basic assumptions of community policing is that it will increase the involvement of citizens in the coproduction of police services. Earlier research found that the police are heavily reliant on citizens for virtually all important police services: the reporting of crime, cooperation as victims and witnesses, and so on.[68] Community policing is designed to break down the barriers between police and citizens, increase citizen involvement, and thereby improve police effectiveness.

A study by Frank, Brandl, Worden, and Bynum challenges this assumption about community policing. They used a two-wave panel survey of citizens in four areas of a midwestern city, focusing on narcotics enforcement. Residents were surveyed about both private behaviors (whether they reported drugs, crack, illegal activity, or suspicious activity to the police) and collective behavior (whether they attended a community or black club meeting, reported drug or other illegal activity to the police, or participated in other neighborhood activities). They found that citizens' attitudes toward the police had little impact on their likelihood of engaging in coproductive activities. Citizen perception of their neighborhoods had the greatest impact on their activities. When people think neighborhood problems are getting bad, they are more likely to take some kind of action. But they are also likely to cease that action when they see the situation getting better. Particularly important, people are likely to act when they believe they have a

# HOUSTON POLICE DEPARTMENT

## Patrol Officer's **Monthly** Worksheet

**EMPLOYEE INFORMATION**

NAME: _____
　　　　　　 *Last*　　　　　　　　　　　　 *First*　　　　　　　　　　　　　 *MI*

EMPLY. NO. _____   SHIFT: _____   DIST/BEAT: _____   NEIGHBORHOOD: _____

　　　　　　　　　　 DATE: _____

### SECTION 1: Objective Setting/Reporting

**OBJECTIVE #1**　　　 ☐ NEIGHBORHOOD　 ☐ BEAT　 ☐ DISTRICT

PROGRESS/STATUS:　 ☐ COMPLETED　　 ☐ ON-GOING　 ☐ MODIFIED　 ☐ DEFERRED　 ☐ CANCELLED

**OBJECTIVE #2**　　　 ☐ NEIGHBORHOOD　 ☐ BEAT　 ☐ DISTRICT

PROGRESS/STATUS:　 ☐ COMPLETED　　 ☐ ON-GOING　 ☐ MODIFIED　 ☐ DEFERRED　 ☐ CANCELLED

**OBJECTIVE #3**　　　 ☐ NEIGHBORHOOD　 ☐ BEAT　 ☐ DISTRICT

PROGRESS/STATUS:　 ☐ COMPLETED　　 ☐ ON-GOING　 ☐ MODIFIED　 ☐ DEFERRED　 ☐ CANCELLED

**FIGURE 7–5**

| **OBJECTIVE #4** | ☐ NEIGHBORHOOD | ☐ BEAT | ☐ DISTRICT |
|---|---|---|---|

**PROGRESS/STATUS:**  ☐ COMPLETED   ☐ ON-GOING   ☐ MODIFIED   ☐ DEFERRED   ☐ CANCELLED

## SECTION II–Community Contacts

RESIDENTIAL/CIVIC ASSOCIATION:

1. Name: _____
   Phone No. _____
2. Name: _____
   Phone No. _____
3. Name: _____
   Phone No. _____
4. Name: _____
   Phone No. _____
5. Name: _____
   Phone No. _____

BUSINESS/OTHER ORGANIZATIONS:

1. Name: _____
   Phone No. _____
2. Name: _____
   Phone No. _____
3. Name: _____
   Phone No. _____
4. Name: _____
   Phone No. _____
5. Name: _____
   Phone No. _____

## SECTION III—Special Project Assignment

## SECTION IV—Officer Comments / Suggestions

stake in the future of the community. These findings raise serious questions about the ability of the police to obtain greater citizen cooperation and involvement merely as a result of improving attitudes toward the police department.[69]

### Decentralization and Accountability

One of the basic principles of community policing and problem-oriented policing is decentralized decision making: giving rank-and-file officers more authority to decide what problems to work on and how to use their time. Decentralization, however, creates the problem of potential loss of control over police behavior, resulting in abuse of authority. As Herman Goldstein puts it, "How free should community officers be to select alternatives for solving problems?"[70]

Most of the gains in controlling police misconduct, including corruption (Chapter 10) and use of force (Chapter 11) have been achieved through centralized command and control. One major device has been administrative rule making: providing officers with written rules about what kinds of conduct are not permitted (Chapter 8).

The Cincinnati team policing experiment wrestled with the tension between the desire for flexibility and creativity and the need for centralized control, but did not successfully resolve it. An evaluation of the New York City CPOP program found that the traditional methods of supervising patrol officers was inappropriate for community policing. These methods are bureaucratic in nature, asking officers to account for the use of their time and their contacts with the public, and designed primarily to control misbehavior. In New York City there was special concern that giving officers too much leeway would lead to corruption—a recurring problem in the department. The CPOP program required that sergeants play more of a leader-guide role than a strictly disciplinarian role. Sergeants had to assist officers engage in problem solving, represent the CPOP unit to the rest of the department (where there was some hostility), and also represent it to the community.[71]

George L. Kelling and James K. Stewart warn of the dangers inherent in encouraging police officers to be responsive to community residents. A majority of the residents may demand things that are illegal or improper. Kelling and Stewart point out that "a neighborhood anti-crime group that consists exclusively of homeowning whites in a racially mixed neighborhood" may only increase the level of racial conflict in the area.[72] Critics of community policing point to the "kick ass" policing style described in Wilson and Kelling's "Broken Windows." In that article, a Chicago police officer explains how the police remove gang members from a public housing project: "We kick ass." Wilson and Kelling note that this approach is not consistent "with any conception of due process and fair treatment."[73] The issue here is the tension between community demands for order and the requirements of due process and equal protection.

### Conflicting Community Interests

Problem solving and working with the community sound wonderful in theory, but Michael Buerger's study of the Minneapolis RECAP program found that, in some instances, community interests conflict with the objectives of an innovative police program. One program targeted shoplifting at convenience stores. It turned out, however, that corporate officials were more worried about potential lawsuits from customers than shoplifting, which they tended to regard as a normal business expense. Some store owners, meanwhile, were afraid that a strong police presence would alienate and scare off their good customers. A proposal to exclude juveniles from stores after curfews conflicted with a larger corporate program to provide safe havens to children. The police also tried to discourage landlords from renting to suspected drug dealers. But many landlords preferred some drug dealers because they paid their rent on time, in cash, and generally tried to avoid attracting attention. In short, conflicting interests—especially financial interests—of some community residents can obstruct creative programs to solve community problems.[74]

### Policing Where "Community" Has Collapsed

One major question surrounding community policing is whether it is a realistic strategy for the poorest and most crime-ravaged neighborhoods. Community organizing assumes that there is a viable "community" to help organize. The worst neighborhoods of many big cities—what some commentators call the "underclass"—are so devastated by unemployment, crime, and all the related social problems that no meaningful community remains. Most of the natural community leaders have left: those with stable employment, with families, and with a commitment to their neighborhood. In the absence of positive influences, gangs often become a focal point for young peoples' lives.

In their contribution to the *Perspectives on Policing* series, Hubert Williams and Patrick V. Murphy warn, "community-oriented approaches that are effective in most neighborhoods work less well, or not at all, in areas inhabited by low-income blacks and other minority groups."[75] Their point was confirmed by the University of Maryland report, *Preventing Crime*. Sherman and his colleagues found that programs directed at families, schools, and communities tend to be most effective where they are needed least. They are least effective in the families, schools, and communities that need the most help. The Maryland report made a very significant contribution to our understanding of crime prevention by emphasizing the interrelationships among families, schools, neighborhoods, and economic opportunities (what it called "labor markets").[76]

At the same time, communities in the traditional sense often do not exist in newer and rapidly expanding cities. The Houston Fear Reduction Program found that the city had an "almost nonexistent neighborhood life."[77]

Another problem is that community-organizing efforts may help organize only the middle class. The fear reduction experiment in Houston and the community-organizing programs in Chicago and Minneapolis encountered the same phenomenon: They were more successful among middle-income people, home owners, and whites than among the really poor, renters, and racial minorities.[78] Successful community organizing among white home owners may be motivated by racism: their fear of blacks and Hispanics moving into the neighborhood. If this is the case, police-sponsored community-organizing activities may heighten racial conflict. A review of community-organizing efforts, in fact, reached the disturbing conclusion that the strongest

---

SIDEBAR 7–3

TEN WAYS TO UNDERMINE COMMUNITY POLICING

In a paper for the Police Executive Research Forum, John Eck lists 10 ways to undermine community policing:

1 Oversell it (promise more than can possibly be achieved).
2 Don't be specific (don't explain what you mean by cooperation, problem solving, etc.).
3 Create a special unit (which tends to create divisions among officers).
4 Create a soft image (e.g, that you are not concerned about crime).
5 Leave the impression that community policing is only for minority neighborhoods (and ignores the rest of the community).
6 Divorce community policing officers from "regular" police work (see 3, above).
7 Obfuscate means and ends (in particular, make the means seem more important than the ends: reduced disorder, less fear).
8 Present community members with problems and plans (e.g., don't let them become really involved).
9 Never try to understand why problems occur (e.g., demand quick action, without an adequate knowledge base or planning).
10 Never publicize a success.

*Source:* John E. Eck, "Helpful Hints for the Tradition–Bound Chief," *Fresh Perspectives* (Washington: Police Executive Research Forum, 1992).

---

community organizations it could identify "arose in response to impending or actual racial change." It would be tragic if community-policing efforts assisted resistance to equal housing opportunity.[79]

## SUMMARY: A NEW ERA IN POLICING?

Kelling argues that community policing represents a new era in policing. There is no doubt that it represents a new *idea* and a new philosophy of policing, but there are serious questions about whether the new era has in fact arrived. For many police officials, "community policing" and "problem solving" are simply buzzwords that mask traditional policing.[80]

There is mixed evidence on the extent to which these new ideas about policing represent real change. Zhao and Thurman surveyed 228 municipal police departments (population 25,000 or more) and found that their organizational priorities had not changed significantly. Crime control received the highest priority and service the lowest. They conclude that the "revolution" in policing was a lot "quieter" than Kelling had suggested.[81] Maguire and his colleagues, meanwhile, surveyed almost 6,000 small police departments (population 50,000 or less) regarding 31 specific community policing activities and found a very mixed picture. Half (52 percent) either engaged in or were planning community policing. Although most had partnerships with civic groups, schools, and other government agencies, relatively few had citizen advisory groups. More important, Maguire and his colleagues warn that a response on a mail survey does not necessarily mean that a police department has fully adopted the new philosophy of policing represented by community policing.[82]

Nonetheless, despite these limitations, it is clear that the ideas of community policing and problem-oriented policing have inspired a remarkable level of innovation in American policing. Bayley concludes that "the last decade of the twentieth century may be the most creative period in policing since the modern police officer was put onto the streets of London in 1829."[83]

As a final note, Goldstein and Skolnick, and also Bayley, point out that we should not be too quick to argue that the innovations under community policing and problem-oriented policing have not *proven* effective. Most of the activities labeled "traditional" policing have also been ineffective. As we have already learned, patrol (Chapter 4), criminal investigation (Chapter 5), and other activities are rarely subjected to rigorous evaluations; even fewer evaluations have proven effective.[84]

## NOTES

1 George L. Kelling, "Police and Communities: The Quiet Revolution," no. 1 of *Perspectives on Policing* (Washington: Government Printing Office, 1988).

2 Jack R. Greene and Stephen D. Mastrofski, eds., *Community Policing: Rhetoric or Reality* (New York: Praeger, 1988).

3 Herman Goldstein, *Problem–Oriented Policing* (New York: McGraw–Hill, 1990).

4 George L. Kelling and Mark H. Moore, "The Evolving Strategy of Policing," no. 4 of *Perspectives on Policing* (Washington: Government Printing Office, 1988), p. 8; John P. Crank, "Watchman and Community: Myth and Institutionalization in Policing," *Law and Society Review* 28, no. 2 (1994):325–351.

5 Wesley G. Skogan and George E. Antunes, "Information, Apprehension, and Deterrence: Exploring the Limits of Police Productivity," *Journal of Criminal Justice* 7 (Fall 1979): 232; James Frank, Steven G. Brandl, Robert E. Worden, and Timothy S. Bynum, "Citizen Involvement in the Coproduction of Police Outputs," *Journal of Crime and Justice* 19, no. 2 (1996): 1–30.

6 Herman Goldstein, "Improving Policing: A Problem–Oriented Approach," *Crime and Delinquency* 25 (1979): 236–258; Goldstein, *Problem–Oriented Policing*.

7 Samuel Walker, "Origins of the Contemporary Criminal Justice Paradigm: The American Bar Foundation Survey, 1953–1969," *Justice Quarterly* 9 (March 1992): 47–76.

8 American Bar Association, Standard 1–2.2 in *Standards Relating to the Urban Police Function*, 2d ed. (Boston: Little, Brown, 1980) pp. 1–31 to 1–32.

9 Herman Goldstein, *Policing a Free Society* (Cambridge, Mass.: Ballinger, 1977).

10 Goldstein, "Improving Policing."

11 See the discussion in Geoffrey Alpert and Mark H. Moore, "Measuring Police Performance in the New Paradigm of Policing," in U.S. Department of Justice, *Performance Measures for the Criminal Justice System* (Washington: Government Printing Office, 1993), pp. 109–140.

12 Malcolm K. Sparrow, Mark H. Moore, and David M. Kennedy, *Beyond 911* (New York: Basic Books, 1990).

13 James Q. Wilson and George L. Kelling, "Broken Windows: The Police and Neighborhood Safety," *Atlantic Monthly* 249 (March 1982): 29–38.

**14** Wesley G. Skogan, *Disorder and Decline: Crime and the Spiral of Decay in American Neighborhoods* (New York: Free Press, 1990), pp. 21–50.

**15** The Police Foundation, *The Newark Foot Patrol Experiment* (Washington: The Police Foundation, 1981).

**16** Skogan, *Disorder and Decline.*

**17** *Perspectives on Policing,* 13 vols. (Washington: Government Printing Office, 1988–1990).

**18** Anthony M. Pate et al., *Reducing Fear of Crime in Houston and Newark: A Summary Report* (Washington: The Police Foundation, 1986); Lee P. Brown and Mary Ann Wycoff, "Policing Houston: Reducing Fear and Improving Service," *Crime and Delinquency* 33 (January 1986): 71–89.

**19** Wesley G. Skogan and Mary Ann Wycoff, "Storefront Police Offices: The Houston Field Test," in ed., D. Rosenbaum *Community Crime Prevention: Does it work?* Beverly Hills: Sage, 1986), pp. 179–199.

**20** Brown and Wycoff, "Policing Houston."

**21** Lawrence W. Sherman et al., *Preventing Crime* (Washington: Government Printing Office, 1997).

**22** John E. Eck and William Spelman, *Problem–Solving: Problem–Oriented Policing in Newport News* (Washington: Police Executive Research Forum, 1987).

**23** U.S. Office of Community Oriented Policing Services, *COPS Office Report* (Washington: Government Printing Office, 1997).

**24** Wesley G. Skogan and Susan M. Hartnett, *Community Policing: Chicago Style* (New York: Oxford University Press, 1997).

**25** Ibid., pp. 67–68.

**26** Ibid., p. 113.

**27** Ibid., p. 114.

**28** Susan Sadd and Randolph Grinc, "Innovative Neighborhood Policing: An Evaluation of Community Policing Programs in Eight Cities," in *The Challenge of Community Policing: Testing the Promises,* ed., Dennis P. Rosenbaum (Newbury Park, Calif.: Sage, 1994), pp. 27–52.

**29** Ibid.

**30** Greene and Mastrofski, eds., *Community Policing: Rhetoric or Reality.*

**31** Ibid.

**32** Gary W. Cordner, "A Problem–Oriented Approach to Community–Oriented Policing," in *Community Policing: Rhetoric or Reality,* eds., Greene and Mastrofski, pp. 135–152.

**33** Lorraine Green, "Cleaning Up Drug Hot Spots in Oakland, California: The Displacement and Diffusion Effects," *Justice Quarterly* 12 (December 1995): 737–754.

**34** Lawrence W. Sherman, Patrick R. Gartin, and Michael Buerger, "Hot Spots of Predatory Crime: Routine Activity and the Criminology of Place," *Criminology* 27 No. 1, (1989): 27–55.

**35** Jerome E. McElroy, Colleen A. Cosgrove, Susan Sadd, *Community Policing: The CPOP in New York* (Newbury Park, Calif.: Sage, 1993).

**36** Ibid.; Anthony M. Pate and Penny Shtull, "Community Policing Grows in Brooklyn: An Inside View of the New York City Police Department's Model Precinct," *Crime and Delinquency* 40 (July 1994): 401–402.

**37** George L. Kelling and Catherine M. Coles, *Fixing Broken Windows* (New York: Free Press, 1996), pp. 144–146; William Bratton and Peter Knoblach, *Turning Point,* (New York: Random House, 1998).

**38** Kelling and Coles, *Fixing Broken Windows.*

**39** Dennis J. Kenney, *Crime, Fear, and the New York Subways* (New York: Praeger, 1988).

**40** Bratton and Knoblach, *Turnaround.*

**41** Kelling and Coles, *Fixing Broken Windows*; Samuel Walker, *Sense and Nonsense about Crime*, 4th ed. (Belmont, Calif.: Wadsworth, 1998), pp. 273–279.

**42** *The New York Civil Liberties Union, Third Anniversary Overview of the CCRB* (New York: New York Civil Liberties Union, 1996).

**43** Samuel Walker, "Does Anyone Remember Team Policing? Lessons of the Team Policing Experience for Community Policing," *American Journal of Police* 12, No. 1 (1993): 33–55.

**44** Lawrence W. Sherman et al., *Team Policing: Seven Case Studies* (Washington: The Police Foundation, 1973); U. S. Department of Justice, *Neighborhood Team Policing* (Washington: Government Printing Office, 1977).

**45** Alfred I. Schwartz and Sumner N. Clarren, *The Cincinnati Team Policing Experiment* (Washington: The Police Foundation, 1977).

**46** Sherman et al., *Team Policing*.

**47** Ibid.

**48** Skogan and Hartnett, *Community Policing, Chicago Style*.

**49** These issues are addressed in excellent detail in ibid.

**50** U.S. Department of Justice, *Improving Police/Community Relations* (Washington: Government Printing Office, 1973).

**51** Fred A. Klyman and Joanna Kruckenberg, "A National Survey of Police–Community Relations Units," *Journal of Police Science and Administration* 7 (March 1979): 72–79.

**52** David Bayley, "Community Policing: A Report from the Devil's Advocate," in *Community Policing: Rhetoric or Reality*, eds., Greene and Mastrofski, pp. 225–237.

**53** George L. Kelling and Mark H. Moore, "The Evolving Strategy of Policing," no. 4 of *Perspective on Policing* (Washington: Government Printing Office, 1988).

**54** Greene and Mastrofski, eds., *Community Policing: Rhetoric or Reality*.

**55** Ibid.

**56** Walker, "Does Anyone Remember Team Policing?"

**57** Ronald D. Hunter and Thomas Barker, "BS and buzzwords: The New Police Operational Style," *American Journal of Police* 12, no. 3 (1993): 157–158.

**58** Rosenbaum, ed., *The Challenge of Community Policing*.

**59** Skogan and Hartnett, *Community Policing, Chicago Style*.

**60** Ibid.

**61** David H. Bayley, *Police for the Future* (New York; Oxford University Press, 1994), pp. 126–128.

**62** Bayley, "Community Policing: A Report form the Devil's Advocate."

**63** Malcolm K. Sparrow, "Implementing Community Policing," no. 9 of *Perspectives on Policing* (Washington: Government Printing Office, 1988), p. 2.

**64** Cordner, "A Problem–Oriented Approach to Community-Oriented Policing."

**65** Pate and Shtull, "Community Policing Grows in Brooklyn," pp. 407, 410.

**66** Herman Goldstein, "Toward Community–Oriented Policing: Potential, Basic Requirements, and Threshold Questions," *Crime and Delinquency* 33 (January 1987): 12.

**67** U.S. Department of Justice, *Improving Police/Community Relations* (Washington: Government Printing Office, 1973).

**68** Skogan and Antunes, "Information, Apprehension, and Deterrence."

**69** Frank, Brandl, Worden, and Bynum, "Citizen Involvement in the Coproduction of Police Outputs."

**70** Goldstein, "Toward Community–Oriented Policing," p. 21.

**71** McElroy, Cosgrove, and Sadd, *Community Policing: The CPOP in New York*, pp. 84–127.

**72** George L. Kelling and James K. Stewart, "Neighborhoods and Police: The Maintenance of Civil Authority," no. 10 of *Perspectives on Policing* (Washington: Government Printing Office, 1989), p. 4.

**73** Wilson and Kelling, "Broken Windows."

**74** Michael E. Buerger, "The Problems of Problem–Solving: Resistance, Interdependencies, and Conflicting Interests," *American Journal of Police* 13, no. 3 (1994): 1–36.

**75** Hubert Williams and Patrick V. Murphy, "The Evolving Strategy of Police: A Minority View," no. 13 of *Perspectives on Policing* (Washington: Government Printing Office, 1990), p. 12.

**76** University of Maryland, *Preventing Crime*.

**77** Skogan, *Disorder and Decline*, p. 95.

**78** Ibid., p. 148.

**79** Wesley G. Skogan, "Fear of Crime and Neighborhood Change," in *Communities and Crime*, eds. Albert Reiss and Michael Tonry (Chicago: University of Chicago Press, 1986), p. 222.

**80** Hunter and Barker, "BS and Buzzwords."

**81** Jihong Zhao and Quint Thurman, "Community Policing: Where Are We Now?" *Crime and Delinquency* 43 (July 1997): 345–357.

**82** Edward R. Maguire, Joseph B. Kuhns, Craig D. Uchida, and Stephen M. Cox, "Patterns of Community Policing in Nonurban American." *Journal of Research in Crime and Delinquency* 34 (August 1997): 368–394.

**83** Bayley, *Police for the Future*, p. 101.

**84** Goldstein, "Toward Community–Oriented Policing," p. 27; Jerome H. Skolnick and David H. Bayley, *The New Blue Line* (New York: Free Press, 1986), p. 229.

# PART THREE

# POLICE PROBLEMS

# CHAPTER 8

# POLICE DISCRETION

## EXAMPLES OF DISCRETION

Police officers routinely make critical decisions involving the life and liberty of citizens. These decisions call for discretion, or judgment, on the part of the officer. Previous chapters have already covered many examples of police discretion. They include:

- **Felony Arrests.** Donald Black found that only 58 percent of people suspected of felonies were arrested.[1]
- **Mental Health Commitments.** Linda Teplin reported that only 11.8 percent of persons judged mentally disordered were referred to a medical facility.[2]
- **Traffic Tickets.** John Gardiner found that Dallas police officers wrote traffic tickets at a rate 20 times higher than that of Boston police.[3]
- **Juvenile Court Referrals.** Nathan Goldman found that in one city 8.6 percent of arrested juveniles were referred to juvenile court, compared with 71.2 percent in another city.[4]
- **Deadly Force.** The decision to use deadly force is the ultimate life and death decision made by police officers.[5]

This chapter examines the phenomenon of police discretion. It gives special attention to the underlying reasons for discretion, how discretion is used, the problems that result, and the impact of different strategies for controlling it.

## A DEFINITION OF DISCRETION

Discretion may be defined as an official action, by a criminal justice official, based on that individual's judgment about the best course of action.[6]

The power to exercise discretion is not unlimited. Most important, it is limited by the law and administrative policy. Judges, for example, have broad discretion to sentence convicted offenders. If a judge goes beyond the limits prescribed by law (as in sentencing someone to a longer prison term than permitted by statute), it is an illegal abuse of discretion. A police officer, by the same token, may not shoot and kill a person for no reason.

Most controversies over discretion involve not questions of legality but whether the decision was wise. A judge, for example, sentences an offender to probation. The judge has legal authority to give that sentence but it may not be the appropriate sentence given the offender's crime and prior record. By the same token, most controversies over police discretion involve questions of whether the decision was proper. A police officer stops and questions a young man on the street. The officer has the legal right to make stops, but in this instance questions arise as to whether the officer had any reason to question this person (e.g., some suspicious behavior) and possibly singled out this person because he is African American or Hispanic.

## ASPECTS OF POLICE DISCRETION

### Low–level Decision Making

One of the special features of policing is that the lowest-ranking employees—patrol officers—exercise the greatest amount of discretion. James Q. Wilson comments that, in policing, "discretion increases as one moves down the organizational hierarchy."[7] Thus, patrol officers have been described as street-level bureaucrats who make the most important decisions regarding agency policy.[8] Attempts to control those low-level decisions are complicated by the fact that officers generally work alone or in pairs, away from the direct observation of their supervisors.[9] Some experts question whether the decisions of police officers on the street can effectively be controlled. Michael K. Brown argues that control efforts simply create new problems, as officers try to mediate between rigid departmental rules and the immediate situations they face on the street.[10] Samuel Walker, on the other hand, argues that police discretion can be effectively controlled by clearly written policies.[11]

### Police Discretion and the Criminal Justice System

Police officers are the most important decision makers in the criminal justice system. They are the "gatekeepers" who determine most of the workload of the system when they decide whether or not to make an arrest. At the same time, police discretion is affected by the decisions of other officials. Goldman, for example, found that police referrals to juvenile court were affected by officers' attitudes toward the court and their assessment of what would happen to a case.[12]

Discretion is not confined to the police. It pervades the criminal justice system. Wayne LaFave argues, "it is helpful to look at the total criminal justice system as a series of interrelated discretionary choices."[13] The administration of justice is essentially the sum total of a series of discretionary decisions, from arrest through prosecution, trial, sentencing, and parole release. Controlling discretion is essential to establishing consistent criminal justice policy and ensuring fair and equal treatment of all citizens.[14]

### Problems with Discretion

Experts generally agree that discretion itself is not necessarily a problem, and in fact often serves useful functions.[15] The real problem is *uncontrolled* discretion, which can produce the following undesirable results:

• **Denial of Due Process.** In his study of police discretion in Chicago, Davis found that much police activity is illegal. He found officers deliberately harassing suspected drug dealers, prostitutes, and pimps, often using illegal tactics not involving arrests.[16] Skolnick comments, "police work constitutes the most secluded part of an already secluded system of criminal justice and therefore offers the greatest opportunity for arbitrary behavior."[17]

• **Denial of Equal Protection of the Law.** The Fourteenth Amendment guarantees equal protection of the law to all citizens. Discretionary decisions that result in unequal treatment violate this principle. Studies of police use of deadly force in the 1960s and 1970s suggested that the police had two trigger fingers: one for whites and one for African Americans.[18]

• **Poor Police–Community Relations.** Uncontrolled discretion in arrests, stops, and frisks, and use of deadly force that result in discriminatory treatment of racial and ethnic minorities create serious police–community relations problems.[19]

• **Poor Personnel Management.** Effective supervision requires clear performance standards. Officers need to be provided clear guidelines regarding how they are to handle different situations. If there are no guidelines and discretion is completely unregulated, it is impossible to fairly evaluate their performance.[20]

• **Poor Planning and Policy Development.** To implement a law enforcement policy (e.g., community policing), it is necessary that officers on the street make decisions consistent with the policy. If their discretion is not guided there is no guarantee that the policy will be carried out.

Most experts agree that discretion itself is not bad, and have rejected the idea of trying to abolish it. The best approach is to try to control it and prevent its abuse.[21]

## DECISION POINTS AND DECISION MAKERS

Police discretion is not limited to one decision point. Officers at different ranks make discretionary decisions covering a wide range of actions.[22] As James Q. Wilson observes, police organizations are unique in that discretion increases as one moves down the organization.[23]

The following is a list of some of the major discretionary decisions made by officers in different assignments.[24]

### Patrol Tactics Decisions

Discretionary decisions by patrol officers include:

- To stop, question, or frisk a suspect.
- To write a crime report.
- To make an arrest.
- To use physical or deadly force.
- To patrol an area more intensively than normal.
- To conduct a high-speed pursuit.

### Order Maintenance Decisions

Decisions by patrol officers in order maintenance situations (Chapter 5) include:

- To mediate a domestic dispute.
- To suggest that one party to a dispute leave the premises.
- To refer a person to a social service agency (e.g., alcohol abuse treatment).
- To commit a mentally disturbed person to a mental health facility.

### Investigative Decisions

Decisions by detectives related to criminal investigations (Chapter 6) include:

- To drop a case and not investigate it further.
- To seek a warrant for a search.

- To conduct a stakeout.
- To seek authorization for a wire tap.

## Law Enforcement Priorities

Police managers make discretionary decisions about law enforcement priorities. These include:

- To give high priority to traffic law violations.
- To ignore minor drug offenses such as possession of small amounts of marijuana.
- To crack down on prostitution.
- To give social gambling low priority.

## Police Role

Decisions by police managers about the basic police role include:

- To adopt community policing.
- To adopt problem-oriented policing.
- To adopt zero-tolerance policing.

## SOURCES OF POLICE DISCRETION

Several factors account for the existence of police discretion by rank-and-file officers on the street.

### The Nature of the Criminal Law

The criminal law is one of the basic sources of police discretion. First, definitions of crimes are inherently vague. The police officer on the street has to determine whether an assault has occurred, and whether it was a simple or aggravated assault. LaFave argues, "no legislature has succeeded in formulating a substantive criminal code which clearly encompasses all conduct intended to be made criminal and which clearly excludes all other conduct."[25]

Second, criminal law in the United States reflects conflicting public expectations about what behavior should be illegal. The law criminalizes much behavior that some people regard as acceptable forms of recreation: gambling, drinking, certain forms of sexual behavior. Officers are often caught between these conflicting expectations and use their discretion about the best course of action.[26]

Third, the criminal law is often used to deal with social and medical problems such as homelessness or chronic alcohol abuse.[27] Police officers on the street have to use their discretion about whether arrest or referral to a social service program is the appropriate response to the situation.

## The Work Environment of Policing

The work environment of policing contributes to the exercise of discretion. Patrol officers generally work alone or in pairs.[28] In many critical situations there is no direct supervision. Also, the majority of police-citizen encounters occur in private places, with no other observers present—observers who might be able to testify about the officer's behavior.[29] For this reason, policing has been described as low-visibility work.[30] The most important decisions are hidden from public view. As a result, police officers have tremendous opportunity to choose whatever course of action they prefer. This work environment creates the opportunity for abusing discretion.

## Limited Police Resources

Limited resources encourage officers to exercise discretion.[31] Because of the broad scope of the criminal law, there is far more illegal behavior than the police could possibly handle. Full enforcement of the law is not possible. An arrest is a time-consuming event. Arresting, transporting, and booking a suspect may take between one and four hours. Some arrests may involve more than one officer.

As a result, police officers make decisions about how best to use their time and energy. They often decide not to make an arrest even though they have sufficient legal grounds to do so.[32] Detectives screen cases and choose not to spend time investigating some cases (Chapter 6). Detectives decide that some cases cannot be solved and consequently devote very little time to them. Other cases receive considerable attention.

Some experts argue that the decision not to enforce the law is the major positive aspect of police discretion. Because their decisions are hidden from public view, officers are able to make reasonable judgments about the relative importance of different offenses. According to Davis, "The common sense of the officers very often prevails over the legislative excesses in criminal legislation."[33] Police decisions not to enforce the law help the criminal justice system cope with its workload.

## FACTORS INFLUENCING DISCRETIONARY DECISIONS

Police discretion in general is a product of the factors discussed above. Particular decisions are influenced by additional factors. The important factors can be divided into four categories: situational factors, the immediate work environment, official department policy, and characteristics associated with individual officers.

## Situational Factors

Police discretion is influenced by the circumstances of each situation. Studies of the decision to arrest, for example, have found that it is affected by the following situational factors.

- **Seriousness of the Crime.** The more serious the crime, the more likely the officer is to make an arrest. Black found that officers made arrests in 58 percent of suspected felonies but only 44 percent of suspected misdemeanors. He concluded, "The probability of arrest is higher in legally serious crime situations than those of a relatively minor nature."[34]

The seriousness of the situation also affects the handling of mental illness incidents. The more serious the disorder, or the more likely it is to offend other people, the higher the probability of arrest or commitment to a medical facility.[35]

• **Strength of the Evidence.** The police are more likely to arrest in situations where the evidence of the crime is strong. In crimes against persons, and in many property crimes, the primary evidence is the testimony of a victim or witness. When that kind of evidence or testimony does not exist, arrest is much less likely.[36]

• **Preference of the Victim.** A number of studies have found that an arrest is more likely when the victim or complaining party asks for an arrest. Conversely, police are unlikely to arrest when the victim clearly indicates that he or she does not want an arrest. Black found that "arrest practices sharply reflect the preferences of citizen complainant."[37]

• **Relationship between Victim and Suspect.** Arrests are more likely when the victim and offender are strangers, and are least likely when the two parties are married. Police officers traditionally regarded these incidents as private matters.[38] There has been much controversy and some litigation over the failure of the police to arrest in domestic violence situations involving married couples (Chapter 5). Recent mandatory arrest policies are designed to ensure arrest in all felonious assault cases regardless of the relationship of the two parties.

• **Demeanor of the Suspect.** Black and others found that the demeanor of the suspect is a very important factor in arrest decisions: "The probability of arrest increases when a suspect is disrespectful toward the police."[39] Along the same lines, Reiss found that the police used physical force most often against people who were disrespectful.[40] Worden, meanwhile, found that police are more likely to use force, including both reasonable and unjustified force, against citizens who are antagonistic or who actively resist the police.[41]

Klinger, however, has challenged the early research on the relationship between demeanor and arrest. He argues that in many instances the disrespect occurred after the arrest and, therefore, was a consequence and not a cause of the arrest.[42]

• **Characteristics of the Victim.** Some decisions are based on characteristics of the victim. Decisions reflect a moral judgment about the victim by the police officer. LaFree found substantial evidence that police officers discounted the allegations of rape victims whose lifestyles were nonconformist.[43]

There is also some evidence that arrest decisions are based on race. Smith, Visher, and Davidson found that police officers were more responsive to white victims who complained about black suspects, particularly in property crimes.[44] Donald Black, meanwhile, did not find any direct evidence of race discrimination in arrests, but did find some indication that black officers were more responsive to complaints by black victims and, thus, more likely to arrest in those situations.[45]

Visher found some evidence that the gender of the suspect influences arrest decisions, although this depends on the perceived behavior of the woman. Women who conform to traditional gender role stereotypes are more likely to be treated more leniently than men who are suspected of the same offense. Women who violate gender role expectations, however, do not receive preferential treatment.[46]

The major contribution of the research on the situational factors that influence the arrest decision is the recognition that police discretion is patterned and somewhat predictable. That is to say, it is erroneous to think of discretion as being completely random or arbitrary.[47]

### The Immediate Work Environment

The immediate work environment also influences police discretion. Fyfe found that officers working in high-crime neighborhoods fired their weapons more than twice as often as officers working in low-crime areas.[48] Higher-crime areas have more incidents (especially robberies) in which an officer is likely to confront an armed criminal and use deadly force in response.

Smith, Visher, and Davidson, meanwhile, found that police officers were more likely to make arrests in low-income neighborhoods than in higher-income areas (with the result that poor whites and poor blacks were both more likely to be arrested than those in higher-income areas).[49] Arrests for vagrancy are rare on skid row, but more common when a homeless person wanders into the central business district.[50]

### Department Policy

Official department policies have a powerful influence over police discretion. Fyfe found that a restrictive shooting policy adopted by the New York City Police Department in 1972 reduced firearms discharges 30 percent over the next three and a half years.[51] Shootings of fleeing felons in Memphis disappeared following the adoption of a restrictive shooting policy.[52] Restrictive policies on high-speed pursuits reduce the number of pursuits. Alpert found that pursuits in the Miami-Dade police department declined 82 percent after the introduction of a restrictive policy. In Omaha, meanwhile, pursuits increased 600 percent after a permissive policy was reintroduced.[53] Mandatory arrest policies on domestic violence have contributed to a relative increase in arrests for aggravated assaults since the 1970s.[54]

The impact of written department policies on police discretion is discussed in more detail below in the section on the control of discretion, and in Chapter 11.

### Characteristics of the Individual Officer

The characteristics of individual officers do not appear to have a major influence over police behavior. The behavior of white, African-American, and Hispanic officers is remarkably similar. Fyfe found that, when assignment and location are controlled, officers fire their weapons at the same rate, regardless of race and ethnicity.[55] Reiss found that black officers are slightly more likely to use physical force than white officers, but that all officers are more likely to use force against members of their own race.[56] In San Jose and New York City, the distribution of citizen complaints by race and ethnicity matches the racial and ethnic composition of those departments. Whites represent 75 percent of the officers in New York City and they account for about 75 percent of all complaints.[57]

Studies comparing male and female officers have found similar patterns of behavior in most but not all situations. Male and female officers in New York City used the various control techniques—arrest, orders, reasoning, display of weapon, and so on—at similar rates.[58] Alissa Worden found that although sex discrimination exists with respect to the employment of women, female officers do not differ significantly from male officers with respect to their attitudes toward the job, citizens, and their departments.[59] Female officers in San Jose and New York City, however, receive citizen complaints at half the expected rate, given their presence in these departments.[60]

Studies have failed to identify any significant differences in the behavior of officers with different levels of education.[61] Officers with college educations do not act differently than officers with only a high school diploma. One study, however, found that officers with more education are less likely to receive citizen complaints than officers with less education.[62]

## THE CONTROL OF DISCRETION

### The Need for Control

Virtually all experts agree on the need to control police discretion. Over 30 years ago, Herman Goldstein wrote, "there is a demonstrated need for control," given the documented history of police abuse of authority.[63] The President's Crime Commission recommended, "Police departments should develop and enunciate policies that give police personnel specific guidance for the common situations requiring exercise of police discretion.[64] The American Bar Association standards for police include a similar recommendation (Figure 8–1).[65]

Davis and Goldstein argue that the first step toward controlling police discretion is candor: admitting that it exists, that it can create problems, and that control is necessary.[66] Historically, the police denied that they exercise discretion, claiming, instead, that they fully enforce all laws. The so-called myth of full enforcement exists for several reasons.[67] First, the police want to maintain a public image of authority. Admitting that they sometimes do not enforce the law would undermine their authority in encounters

**FIGURE 8–1**

STANDARD 1–4.3   ADMINISTRATIVE RULE MAKING

Police discretion can best be structured and controlled through the process of administrative rule making by police agencies. Police administrators should, therefore, give the highest priority to the formulation of administrative rules governing the exercise of discretion, particularly in the areas of selective enforcement, investigative techniques, and enforcement methods.

with citizens. It would give suspects a basis for challenging an arrest, with comments like "Why me?" and "You don't arrest everyone."

Second, if the police admit that they do not arrest everyone it would raise serious questions about equal protection of the law.

Third, to admit that the police exercise discretion in enforcing certain laws would raise questions about all police policies and how departments determine what their enforcement policies are.

Fourth, most states have legislation that requires the police to enforce all laws fully. Some states have criminal penalties for police and other officials who do not enforce the law. For this reason, some legal scholars have questioned whether police discretion is legal.[68]

Finally, denying that discretion exists enables supervisors to allow officers under their command to exercise personal judgment. It frees supervisors from the burdens of closely reviewing officer behavior, developing standards for conduct, and disciplining officers who violate policy. Moreover, commanders can justify this neglect on the ground that they trust the professional judgment of officers on the street. Uviller's study of New York City officers found that supervisors approve of the exercise of discretion far more than the officers under their command believe.[69]

Leading experts on the subject of police discretion argue that the myth of full enforcement creates a number of serious problems (as discussed above). Most important, it represents a denial of the basic reality of police work. It also makes it impossible for the police to deal effectively with problems related to due process or equal protection. In addition, it makes meaningful planning very difficult. Planning involves decisions about the use of scarce departmental resources; it requires a realistic understanding of what decisions are currently being made and how those decisions might be changed. Finally, denying that discretion exists puts the police in a defensive position when controversies arise. When critics make accusations about police performance, the police fall into the habit of denying that anything is wrong.[70]

### Bureaucracy and the Control of Discretion

To a certain extent, police discretion is controlled by the bureaucratic setting of the criminal justice system. An arrest, for example, raises the "visibility" of a police officer's behavior. The arrest is reviewed by a supervisor, a prosecutor, defense attorney, and one or more judges. A competent defense attorney will challenge improper or illegal behavior, and may succeed in persuading the judge to dismiss the case. In short, a police officer is not totally free to act out his or her prejudices. Reiss, for example, found that about 75 percent of the officers in his field study made verbal expressions of racial prejudice in the presence of the observers. Yet his observation of arrests did not find a pattern of race discrimination.[71] In short, police officer attitudes do not automatically translate into behavior. Bureaucratic procedures, involving routine review by other persons, constrains officers' behavior. (This issue is discussed in more detail in Chapter 13).

At the same time, however, the police bureaucracy can cover up abuses of discretion. Supervisors, especially sergeants who are responsible for officers on the street, are caught between conflicting pressures. On the one hand, they are charged with the responsibility of enforcing departmental rules. On the other hand, they need the cooperation of the officers under their command, and cannot afford to become rigid rule enforcers or be perceived by their officers as always out to "get them." Thus, they are under pressure to overlook and excuse certain behavior.[72]

## Strategies for Controlling Discretion

There are three basic strategies for controlling discretion: abolishing it, enhancing the professional judgment of police officers, and regulating it through written policies.

### Abolishing Discretion

In one of the first studies of police discretion, Joseph Goldstein concluded that it was illegal and should be abolished.[73] He and others have argued that the police do not have the legal authority to nullify the criminal law by not arresting a criminal offender.

Virtually all other experts have rejected the idea of abolishing discretion. They argue that discretion is both inevitable and, in some instances, desirable. Davis argues that discretion allows police officers to make sensible decisions about what offenses are really serious. He argues, "the common sense of the police officers very often prevails over the legislative excesses in the criminal legislation. That is the police accomplishment."[74]

The debate over abolishing police discretion parallels similar debates over the control of discretion in other parts of the criminal justice system.[75] The National Advisory Commission on Criminal Justice Standards and Goals, for example, recommended abolishing plea bargaining.[76] Despite some attempts to do so, most experts argue that plea bargaining serves some useful purposes and cannot be completely abolished in any event. Instead, it has been regulated by administrative rules issued by prosecutors.[77] Along the same lines, mandatory sentencing systems represent an attempt to abolish the discretion of sentencing judges. Research on sentencing reform indicates that mandatory sentencing provisions are often evaded. Experts on sentencing reform argue in favor of controlling (but not eliminating) discretion by narrowing the range of sentences available to judges.[78]

### Enhancing Professional Judgment

A second means of controlling discretion is to enhance the professional judgment of police officers. This emulates the professional model employed by the professions of medicine, law, and education. In these occupations, practitioners are granted broad discretion to make judgments about how to handle specific incidents. Control is exercised through the process of screening, training, and socialization. Admission standards to medical schools, for example, are very high; medical school training is long and rigorous; and the training process serves to socialize prospective doctors into high standards of professionalism. Once a doctor is licensed, however, there is little direct supervision of day-to-day practice.[79]

Many critics argue that the traditional professional model does not and cannot apply to policing. First, recruitment standards are low compared to law and medicine. Preservice training is very short (six months even in the best departments) compared with these other professions (three years for law school). Second, the peer culture of policing has often tolerated and even covered up improper behavior.[80] Third, policing has been described as a craft rather than a profession; that is to say, it involves a set of skills that are learned through practice. There is no body of specialized professional knowledge equivalent to the body of knowledge that the tax lawyer or the heart specialist possesses. Police officers are generalists rather than specialists. For all these reasons, James Q. Wilson argues, "The police are not in any of these senses professionals."[81] Consequently, the traditional professional model of controlling discretion is not applicable.

Brown points out that the traditional professional model involves freedom from external controls.[82] On the one hand, Americans are not willing to allow the police to be completely free from political control (see Chapter 11). On the other hand, the traditional autonomy of the traditional professions is eroding, particularly in medicine. Thus, this approach to the control of discretion is not relevant for law enforcement and increasingly irrelevant for medicine.

### Written Policies

The method of control that has evolved is through the use of written policies that guide the police officer's exercise of discretion. This approach is called administrative rule making. Because it is currently the dominant approach in American police management, it is discussed at length below.

### ADMINISTRATIVE RULE MAKING

Administrative rule making seeks to control police discretion through written departmental rules. These rules are intended to guide discretion, rather than eliminate it. Rules typically indicate what an officer may not do and identify areas where an officer may use discretionary judgment. The Commission on Accreditation for Law Enforcement Agencies (CALEA) accreditation *Standards for Law Enforcement Agencies* is almost entirely based on the principle of administrative rule making. Virtually every standard involves a requirement that the agency have a written directive on that particular subject. For example, Standard 1.2.2 requires that "A written directive governs procedures for assuring compliance with all applicable constitutional requirements."[83]

### Examples of Administrative Rule making

• **Deadly Force.** The defense-of-life standard for the use of deadly force clearly spells out when deadly force may be used (threat to the life of the officer or another person) and when it may not be used (toward an unarmed fleeing felon).[84] Many department policies also include specific prohibitions on the use of warning shots, shots to wound, or shots at moving vehicles.

- **Domestic Violence.** Mandatory arrest policies related to domestic violence instruct police officers that they may not exercise their discretion and must make an arrest when a felonious assault has occurred.
- **High-Speed Pursuits.** Department policies on high-speed pursuits instruct officers to consider road conditions, the presence of pedestrians, and other potential risks before initiating a pursuit.[85]

### Principles of Administrative Rule Making

Kenneth Culp Davis, a leading authority on administrative law, describes the principles of administrative rule making in terms of a strategy to fill the gap between law and practice.[86] Laws are written in very broad language. The criminal law, for example, describes categories of criminal behavior in general terms ("threat to do serious bodily harm"). In practice, someone has to use his or her discretion to apply these general definitions to a specific situation. Administrative rule making is designed to fill in the gap by providing additional detail on how to handle specific situations.

The specific objectives of administrative rule making, according to Davis, are to confine, structure, and check discretion.[87]

- **Confining Discretion.** Rules confine discretion by "fixing the boundaries." The defense-of-life standard on the use of deadly force, for example, fixes the boundaries by clearly indicating situations where an officer may not shoot. A mandatory arrest policy on domestic violence fixes the boundaries by instructing officers that an arrest is required if there is a felonious assault.
- **Structuring Discretion.** Discretion is structured, according to Davis, when there is a rational system for developing policies. Such a system calls for open policy statements and open rules. This approach is designed to eliminate the secrecy surrounding discretion. With respect to policing, it informs the public about what official policy is. It also offers an opportunity to object to an existing policy. Both Davis and Herman Goldstein argue that a system of open rule making would create an atmosphere of openness that would have a positive effect on police-community relations.[88]
- **Checking Discretion.** Discretion is checked when decisions are reviewed by another person. The use of deadly force is checked by the requirement that officers fill out reports after each firearms discharge and by having those reports automatically reviewed by supervisors. New York City policy on deadly force specifies such a report-and-review mechanism.[89] It puts officers on notice that their decisions will be set in writing and examined by other people, including the chief of police.

The Omaha Police Department, to cite one example, requires officers to complete a Chief's Report whenever they are involved in any one of nine different situations (Figure 8–2). Each report is reviewed to determine if further investigation is needed. If so, the incident is referred to the Internal Affairs Unit.[90]

### The Advantages of Written Rules

Written rules offer obvious advantages. They provide directions for officers on how to handle critical incidents. Because they are in writing, there can be no dispute about

**FIGURE 8–2**

CHIEF'S REPORT

**Policy:**

It shall be the policy of the Omaha Police Department that for certain police-related incidents not part of the basic crime report system, a CHIEF'S REPORT PO 214 shall be made in addition to any defense, incident, or administrative reports.

**Procedure:**

The following list includes incidents that shall be reported on a Chief's Report:

**A** Discharge of Firearms.
**B** Vehicle Chase (Pursuit).
**C** Damage to Property by Police Officer (other than police equipment).
**D** Resisting Arrest.
**E** Use of Mace/Baton.
**F** Information or Complaints (from sworn and civilian employees).
**G** Lateral Vascular Neck Restraint
**H** Injured on Duty (I.O.D.).
**I** Searches of Private Residences.

*Source:* Omaha Police Department, *Standard Operations Procedure Manual,* Ch. 3, p. 3.

official policy. Policy directives are circulated to all sworn officers, are collected in a standard operating procedure (SOP) manual, and promote consistency of performance. This, in turn, helps ensure equal protection of the law. Written policies provide the basis for effective supervision. Officers can be rewarded for following policy and can be disciplined for violations.[91]

One of the main arguments in favor of administrative rule making is that it is likely to be more effective in controlling police behavior than other means. Police officers are more likely to respect and follow rules developed by the police department itself than rules imposed externally. A number of observers argue that externally imposed rules, such as the exclusionary rule and other requirements imposed by the Supreme Court, are less likely to be effective because police officers see them as externally imposed. Goldstein observes, "External controls are likely to be effective only if they induce a desire and willingness on the part of police admininstrators and their supervisors to elicit conformity from their subordinates".[92]

### The Impact of Administrative Rule Making

There is persuasive evidence that administrative rule making has produced some significant improvements in policing.

• Fyfe examined the impact of the restrictive policy on deadly force adopted by the New York City police department in 1972. Analyzing firearms discharges between 1971 and 1975, he found that the weekly mean number of discharges declined by about one-third (29.1 percent). The most significant reduction occurred in the category of shootings to "prevent or terminate crime." These incidents are usually the most controversial, because there is no imminent threat to the life of the officer or other citizens. Fyfe also found that the reduction in the use of deadly force was not accompanied by an increased number of police officer injuries or deaths.[93]

• Alpert found a significant reduction in high speed pursuits in the Miami Police Department after it adopted a more restrictive pursuit policy, and a dramatic rise in pursuits in Omaha after it adopted a more permissive policy.[94]

## The Limits of Administrative Rule Making

Administrative rule making also has some significant limitations. First, it is impossible to write a rule that covers every possible situation. In this respect, a police department rule is similar to the criminal law: The language is inevitably vague, and someone still has to exercise discretion in interpreting it. The reply to this criticism is that although a rule inevitably leaves some room for discretion, it narrows the range of situations in which the officer has to make a decision. Virtually all police rules on deadly force, for example, prohibit shooting at unarmed fleeing felons or firing warning shots.

Second, formal rules may only encourage evasion and lying. Some observers have argued that the exclusionary rule encourages police officers to lie about how they obtain evidence. With respect to narcotics, observers cited the "dropsy" phenomenon: Officers lied, claiming that the suspect dropped the narcotics on the ground (thus making the seizure legal).[95] Fyfe found that in New York City the number of reported "accidental" firearms discharges increased after the restrictive shooting policy was implemented, suggesting that officers were using this category to cover improper shootings. But accidents as a percentage of all shootings increased from 3.6 percent to 9 percent of all discharges, suggesting that if this did represent an attempt to evade policy it was still rather limited.[96]

Compliance with written rules governing discretion is enhanced by the requirement that officers file reports after each incident and by having those reports automatically reviewed by supervisors. Virtually all policies on deadly force in effect in American police departments today have this report-and-review requirement. The CALEA accreditation standards require that a police officer file a written report whenever he or she "discharges a firearm," causes "injury or death of another person," uses "lethal or less-than-lethal weapons," or "applies physical force as defined by the agency."[97]

Another factor influencing compliance is the immediate work setting. Firearms discharges are, by definition, highly public events: They occur in public areas and are accompanied by a loud noise and the presence of at least one citizen, along with other potential witnesses. All these factors put pressure on the officer to comply with the reporting requirement. There is always the chance that a citizen might report the incident and/or contradict the officer's report. High-speed pursuits are public events in the same way. Domestic violence incidents, however, are very private events. They occur indoors, usually with no witnesses other than the immediate parties. Thus it is easier for the officer to ignore both the policy and the reporting requirement.[98]

In *Working the Street*, Michael K. Brown argues that written rules may only make the situation worse, creating more uncertainty for the police officer rather than less. He observes, "simply enveloping policemen in a maze of institutional controls without grappling with the grimy realities of police work does not necessarily promote account-ability and may only exacerbate matters."[99] Harold Pepinsky agrees, citing the example of the *Miranda* decision. He argues that the decision created more uncertainty: When is the suspect "in custody"? What is an "interrogation"? This serves to increase dis-cretion.[100] If written rules are too complex, officers will not be able to remember the details and, in practice, will be likely to ignore the rules altogether.

Advocates of written rules reply that a police officer's job is easier when clear, written guidelines are provided on how to handle critical incidents. Although some inci-dents still leave room for discretion, the range of situations is greatly limited. Davis sees this as the major contribution of confining discretion.[101]

Finally, the existence of many rules creates a negative atmosphere in the department. Police organizations have been characterized as punishment-centered bureaucracies. They have many ways to punish an officer for doing the wrong thing and few ways of rewarding officers for performing well. Officers learn that the safest course of action is to do as little as possible, to avoid making a mistake.[102] In the absence of tangible rewards for good behavior, the development of rules only adds to the restrictions on police productivity.

### Codifying Rules: The Standard Operating Procedure Manual

Written rules and policies are collected and codified in department standard operation procedure (SOP) manuals. The SOP manual is the central tool of modern police man-agement. The typical SOP manual in a big-city department is several hundred pages long.

SOP manuals have certain limits. First, they have traditionally overemphasized rela-tively trivial issues (such as proper uniforms) and ignored critical issues in the use of law enforcement power (such as arrest and deadly force). Brown found that 89 percent of the sergeants and watch commanders in two Los Angeles Police Department precincts and two small police departments in the Los Angeles area agreed with the statement, "It is important for field supervisors to enforce departmental rules regarding dress, hair length, tardiness, etc."[103]

In recent years most departments have adopted written policies on deadly force, pur-suits, and other important matters. Yet many important issues remain uncovered. Many departments still do not have policies on the use of informants or on arrest discretion in situations other than domestic violence.

A second problem is the "crisis management" process by which manuals develop. New policies are typically adopted in response to an immediate crisis: a law suit, a com-munity protest. Peter Manning quotes a British police sergeant as saying that his department's procedures manual represented "140 years of screw-ups. Every time some-thing goes wrong, they make a rule about it."[104] The result of crisis management is that SOP manuals are generally unsystematic. Some areas of police discretion are covered, but many are not. Manuals are often not revised for many years and, as a result, important subjects are not reviewed or updated.

## Making Rule Making More Systematic

Leading experts on police discretion have urged the police to engage in systematic rule making. Davis and Goldstein argue that a systematic approach allows the police to anticipate problems before they become crises and represents a professional approach to planning. Despite these recommendations, police departments have not engaged in systematic planning. Davis points out that the "research and planning" units in most police departments are usually occupied with trivial matters.[105]

Several attempts have been made to encourage systematic rule making. The CALEA accreditation *Standards for Law Enforcement Agencies* require departments to have a system of written directives governing police policy.[106] Accreditation, however, is a voluntary system and by 1997 fewer than 400 agencies had been accredited. In 1987 the International Association of Chiefs of Police (IACP) established the National Law Enforcement Policy Center, which began publishing model policies on specific discretionary decision points.[107] The Police Executive Research Forum (PERF) also adopts model policies on various aspects of police work. Finally, a number of citizen review agencies engage in policy review, recommending new policies in areas that have generated citizen complaints.[108]

Wayne Schmidt proposes that, to make administrative rule making systematic, each state create an administrative council on law enforcement. This council would have the authority to develop policies for all local police departments in the state.[109] Samuel Walker recommends that states enact laws requiring police departments to develop rules on a specific set of critical decision points.[110] To a certain extent, this approach already exists for some decisions. Police use of deadly force, for example, is covered by state statute. The 1985 Supreme Court decision in *Tennessee v. Garner* ruled as unconstitutional state laws embodying the "fleeing felon" standard. Some states have enacted laws governing police pursuits. Walker's proposal would require that police adopt rules on a broader range of police decision points.

## Rule Making and Community Policing

Administrative rule making represents a traditional centralized, bureaucratic approach to controlling official behavior: written rules are promulgated by the chief executive and enforced in a consistent fashion against all employees. One of the basic principles of community policing (Chapter 7) is the decentralization of decision-making authority within police departments. Rank-and-file officers are to be given more freedom (that is, discretion) to identify community problems and engage in problem solving.

The question is whether there is a basic incompatibility between the need for consistency, which is achieved through centralized administrative rule making, and the decentralized flexibility and creativity needed for community policing. This tension appeared in some of the team policing experiments of the 1970s and was never fully resolved.[111] Mastrofski, Worden, and Snipes examined the impact of community policing on arrest decisions in Richmond, Virginia. They found some differences among officers based on their attitudes toward community policing. Officers who were more favorable toward community policing were somewhat less likely to make arrests and were somewhat less influenced by strictly legal factors. Nonetheless, the pro-community policing officers were not any more likely to make arrests based on extralegal factors such as race. In short, community policing in this particular setting did not unleash improper use of discretion in arrests.[112]

The Richmond study was confined to the question of arrest, however. It did not investigate the question of whether decentralized decision making under community policing or problem-oriented policing leads to the abuse of discretion in non-arrest-related crime prevention or problem-solving programs.

## CONCLUSION

Discretion is a pervasive part of policing. Officers routinely make critical decisions affecting the life and liberty of citizens. Uncontrolled discretion results in serious problems, including denial of due process and equal protection of the law.

Discretion can be controlled through formal written policies adopted by police departments. Written policies do not completely eliminate discretion; they guide it by providing directions on what the officer should or should not do in certain situations. There is evidence that written policies have reduced the number of persons shot and killed by police. Some controversy remains, however, over whether written policies can effectively control all discretionary decisions.

The control of discretion is only one aspect of the larger problem of achieving accountability of the police. This issue is examined in detail in Chapter 11.

## NOTES

1  Donald Black, "The Social Organization of Arrest," in *The Manners and Customs of the Police* (New York: Academic Press, 1980), p. 90.
2  Linda Teplin, *Keeping the Peace: Parameters of Police Discretion in Relation to the Mentally Disordered* (Washington: Government Printing Office, 1986).
3  John A. Gardiner, *Traffic and the Police: Variations in Law Enforcement Policy* (Cambridge: Harvard University Press, 1969).
4  Nathan Goldman, *The Differential Selection of Juvenile Offenders for Court Appearance* (New York: National Council on Crime and Delinquency, 1963).
5  William A. Geller and Michael Scott, *Deadly Force: What We Know* (Washington: Police Executive Research Forum, 1992).
6  Kenneth Culp Davis, *Discretionary Justice: A Preliminary Inquiry* (Urbana, Ill.: University of Illinois, 1971), p. 4.
7  James Q. Wilson, *Varieties of Police Behavior* (New York: Atheneum, 1973), p. 21.
8  Michael Lipsky, *Street-Level Bureaucracy* (New York: Russell Sage Foundation, 1968).
9  Herman Goldstein, "Administrative Problems in Controlling the Exercise of Police Authority," *Journal of Criminal Law, Criminology, and Police Science* 58, no. 2 (1967): 165.
10  Michael K. Brown, *Working the Street: Police Discretion and the Dilemmas of Control* (New York: Russell Sage Foundation, 1981), pp. 291, 294, 303.
11  Samuel Walker, *Taming the System: The Control of Discretion in Criminal Justice, 1950–1990* (New York: Oxford University Press, 1993).
12  Goldman, *The Differential Selection of Juvenile Offenders.*
13  Wayne R. LaFave, *Arrest* (Boston: Little, Brown, 1965), p. 9.
14  Walker, *Taming the System.*

**15** Kenneth C. Davis, *Police Discretion* (St. Paul: West, 1975); Walker, *Taming the System.*

**16** Davis, *Police Discretion*

**17** Jerome H. Skolnick, *Justice without Trail*, 3d ed. (New York: Macmillan, 1994), p. 13.

**18** James J. Fyfe, "Reducing the Use of Deadly Force: the New York Experience," in U.S. Department of Justice, *Police Use of Deadly Force* (Washington: Government Printing Office, 1978), p. 29.

**19** Samuel Walker, Cassia Spohn, and Miriam DeLone, *The Color of Justice* (Belmont, Calif.: Wadsworth, 1996).

**20** Frank J. Landy *Performance Appraisal in Police Departments* (Washington: The Police Foundation, 1977; Timothy N. Oettmeier and Mary Ann Wycoff, *Personnel Performance Evaluations in the Community Policing Context* (Washington: Police Executive Research Forum, 1997).

**21** Walker, *Taming the System*; Davis, *Police Discretion.*

**22** Albert J. Reiss, Jr., "Consequences of Compliance and Deterrence Models of Law Enforcement for the Exercise of Discretion," *Law and Contemporary Problems* 47 (Autumn 1984):88–89.

**23** Wilson, *Varieties of Police Behavior*, p. 7.

**24** Herman Goldstein, *Policing a Free Society* (Cambridge, Mass.: Ballinger, 1977), pp. 94–101.

**25** LaFave, *Arrest*, pp. 70, 84–87.

**26** Ibid., pp. 83–101.

**27** Raymond T. Nimmer, *Two Million Unnecessary Arrests* (Chicago: American Bar Foundation, 1971).

**28** Albert Reiss, *The Police and the Public* (New Haven: Yale University Press, 1971).

**29** Goldstein, "Administrative Problems in Controlling the Exercise of Police Authority," p. 165.

**30** Joseph Goldstein, "Police Discretion Not to Invoke the Criminal Process: Low Visibility Decisions in the Administration of Justice," *Yale Law Journal* 69, no. 4 (1960): 543–588.

**31** LaFave, *Arrest*, pp. 102–104.

**32** Black, "The Social Organization of Arrest."

**33** Davis, *Police Discretion*, pp. 62–66.

**34** Black, "The Social Organization of Arrest."

**35** Teplin, *Keeping the Peace.*

**36** Black, "The Social Organization of Arrest."

**37** Black, "The Social Organization of Arrest," p. 101.

**38** Ibid., p. 104.

**39** Ibid., pp. 107–108.

**40** Albert Reiss, "Police Brutality—Answers to Key Questions," *Transaction* 5 (July–August, 1968): 10–19.

**41** Robert E. Worden, "The 'Causes' of Police Brutality: Theory and Evidence on Police Use of Force," in *And Justice for All* eds. W. A. Geller and H. Toch (Washington: Police Executive Research Forum, 1995), pp. 31–60.

**42** David A. Klinger, "Demeanor of Crime? Why 'Hostile' Citizens Are More Likely to Be Arrested," *Criminology* 32, no. 3 (1994): 475–493.

**43** Gary LaFree, *Rape and Criminal Justice* (Belmont, Calif.: Wadsworth, 1989), p. 76.

**44** Douglas A. Smith, Christy A. Visher, and Laura A. Davidson, "Equity and Discretionary Justice: The Influence of Race on Police Arrest Decisions," *Journal of Criminal Law and Criminology* 75 (Spring 1984): 234–249.

**45** Black, "The Social Organization of Arrest," pp. 107–108.

**46** Christy A. Visher, "Gender, Police Arrest Decisions, and Notions of Chivalry," *Criminology* 21 (February 1983): 5–28.

**47** M. P. Baumgartner, "The Myth of Discretion," in *The Uses of Discretion*, ed., Keith Hawkins (Oxford, England: Clarendon Press, 1992), pp. 129–162.

**48** James J. Fyfe, "Who Shoots?: A Look at Officer Race and Police Shooting," *Journal of Police Science and Administration* 9 (December 1981): 367–382.

**49** Smith, Visher, and Davidson, "Equity and Discretionary Justice."

**50** Egon Bittner, "The Police on Skid Row: A Study in Peacekeeping," *American Sociological Review* 32 (October 1967): 694–715.

**51** James J. Fyfe, "Administrative Interventions on Police Shooting Discretion: An Empirical Examination," *Journal of Criminal Justice* 7 (Winter 1979): 309–323.

**52** Jerry R. Sparger and David J. Giacopassi, "Memphis Revisited: A Reexamination of Police Shootings after the Garner Decision," *Justice Quarterly* 9 (June 1992): 211–225.

**53** Geoffrey P. Alpert, *Police Pursuit: Policies and Training* (Washington: Government Printing Office, 1997).

**54** Lawrence W. Sherman, *Policing Domestic Violence* (New York: Free Press, 1992), pp. 109–111.

**55** James J. Fyfe, "Who Shoots? A Look at Officer Race and Police Shooting," *Journal of Police Science and Administration* 9 (December 1981): 367–382.

**56** Reiss, "Police Brutality—Answers to Key Questions."

**57** San Jose, *Report of the Independent Police Auditor*; New York City, Civilian Complaint Review Board, *Annual Report*.

**58** Joyce Sichel et al., *Women on Patrol: A Pilot Study of Police Performance in New York City* (Washington: Government Printing Office, 1978).

**59** Alissa Pollitz Worden, "The Attitudes of Women and Men in Policing: Testing Conventional and Contemporary Wisdom," *Criminology* 31, no. 2 (1993): 203–241.

**60** San Jose, *Report of the Independent Police Auditor*; New York City, Civilian Complaint Review Board, *Annual Report*.

**61** Lawrence W. Sherman, *The Quality of Police Education* (San Francisco: Jossey-Bass, 1978), pp. 238–239.

**62** Victor E. Kappeler, David Carter, and Allen Sapp, "Police Officer Higher Education, Citizen Complaints and Departmental Rule Violations," *American Journal of Police* 11, no. 2 (1992): 37–54.

**63** Goldstein, "Administrative Problems in Controlling the Exercise of Police Authority," p. 161.

**64** President's Commission on Law Enforcement and Administration of Justice, *The Challenge of Crime in a Free Society* (Washington: Government Printing Office, 1967), p. 104.

**65** American Bar Association, Standard 1–4.3 in *Standards Relating to the Urban Function*, 2d ed. (Boston: Little, Brown, 1980), p. 1–103.

**66** Herman Goldstein, *Policing a Free Society* (Cambridge, Mass.: Ballinger, 1977), pp. 93–130; Davis, *Police Discretion*, pp. 70–78.

**67** Davis, *Police Discretion*, pp. 52–78.

**68** Davis, *Police Discretion*, pp. 52–78; Ronald Allen, "The Police and Substantive Rule-making: Reconciling Principle and Expediency," *University of Pennsylvania Law Review* 125 (Spring 1976): 62–118.

**69** Richard Uviller, "The Unworthy Victim: Police Discretion in the Credibility Call," *Law and Contemporary Problems* 47 (Autumn 1984): 28.

**70** Davis, *Police Discretion*, pp. 70–78. Goldstein, "Police Discretion, Not to Invoke the Criminal Process," pp. 146–147.

**71** Reiss, *The Police and the Public*, p. 147.

**72** Brown, *Working the Street*, pp. 96–131.

**73** Goldstein, "Police Discretion Not to Invoke the Criminal Process."

**74** Davis, *Police Discretion*, p. 62.

**75** Walker, *Taming the System*.

**76** National Advisory Commission on Criminal Justice Standards and Goals, *Courts* (Washington: Government Printing Office, 1973), p. 46.

**77** William F. McDonald, *Plea Bargaining: Critical Issues and Common Practices* (Washington: Government Printing Office, 1985).

**78** Walker, *Taming the System*, pp. 112–144.

**79** Wilbert E. Moore, *The Professions: Roles and Rules* (New York: Russell Sage Foundation, 1970).

**80** William A. Westley, *Violence and the Police* (Cambridge, Mass.: MIT Press, 1970).

**81** Wilson, *Varieties of Police Behavior*, p. 30; see the discussion, pp. 29–31.

**82** Brown, *Working the Street*, p. 40.

**83** Commission on Accreditation for Law Enforcement Agencies, Standard 1.2.2 in *Standards for Law Enforcement Agencies*, 3d ed. (Fairfax: CALEA, 1994), p. 1–1.

**84** Fyfe, "Administrative Interventions."

**85** Geoffrey P. Alpert and Roger D. Dunham, *Police Pursuit Driving: Controlling Responses to Emergency Situations* (New York: Greenwood, 1990).

**86** Davis, *Discretionary Justice*.

**87** Ibid.

**88** Davis, *Police Discretion*; Goldstein, *Policing a Free Society*, pp. 119–120.

**89** Fyfe, "Administrative Interventions."

**90** Omaha Police Division, "Chief's Report," *Standard Operating Procedure Manual*, December 1992.

**91** Walker, *Taming the System*, pp. 21–53.

**92** Goldstein, "Administrative Problems in Controlling the Exercise of Police Authority," pp. 161–162.

**93** Fyfe, "Administrative Interventions."

**94** Alpert, *Police Pursuit Driving*.

**95** Dallin H. Oaks, "Studying the Exclusionary Rule in Search and Seizure," *University of Chicago Law Review* 37 (1970): 665–757.

**96** Fyfe, "Administrative Interventions."

**97** Commission on Accreditation for Law Enforcement Agencies Standard 1.3.6 in *Standards for Law Enforcement Agencies*.

**98** Walker, *Taming the System*.

**99** Brown, *Working the Street*.

**100** Harold E. Pepinsky, "Better Living through Police Discretion," *Law and Contemporary Problems* 47 (Autumn 1984): 249–267.

**101** Davis, *Discretionary Justice*, pp. 52–96.

**102** John Van Maanen, "Police Socialization: A Longitudinal Examination of Job Attitudes in an Urban Police Department," *Administrative Science Quarterly* 20 (June 1975): 223–224.

**103** Brown, *Working the Street*, p. 105.

**104** Peter K. Manning, *Police Work* (Cambridge: MIT Press, 1977), p. 165.

**105** Davis, *Police Discretion*, pp. 32–33 Goldstein, *Policing a Free Society*, pp. 116–126.

**106** Commission on Accreditation for Law Enforcement Agencies, *Standards for Law Enforcement Agencies*, chap. 1.

**107** National Law Enforcement Policy Center, Policy Review (Washington: International Association of Chiefs of Police, 1987).

108 Samuel Walker and Betsy Wright Kreisel, "Varieties of Citizen Review: The Implications of Organizational Features of Complaint Review Procedures for Accountability of the Police," American Journal of Police, 15, no. 3 (1996): 65–88.

109 Wayne Schmidt, "A Proposal for a Statewide Law Enforcement Administrative Law Council," Journal of Police Science and Administration 2 (no. 2, 1974): 330–338.

110 Samuel Walker, "Controlling the Cops: A Legislative Approach to Police Rulemaking," University of Detroit Law Review 63 (Spring 1986): 361–391.

111 Alfred I. Schwartz and Sumner N. Clarren, The Cincinnati Team Policing Experiment: A Summary Report (Washington: The Police Foundation, 1977); Samuel Walker, "Does Anyone Remember Team Policing? Lessons of the Team Policing Experience for Community Policing," American Journal of Police 12, no. 1 (1993): 33–55.

112 Stephen D. Mastrofski, Robert E. Worden, and Jeffrey B. Snipes, "Law Enforcement in a Time of Community Policing," Criminology 33 (November 1995): 539–563.

# CHAPTER 9

# POLICE–COMMUNITY RELATIONS

Conflict between the police and racial minority communities is one of the most serious problems in American policing. The 1991 Rodney King incident dramatized the seriousness of the problem. A bystander videotaped a group of Los Angeles police officers beating Rodney King, an African American who had been stopped for a traffic violation. Four of the officers were later prosecuted for assault. When they were acquitted of criminal charges in state court in April 1992 (three officers were later convicted on federal charges), riots erupted in Los Angeles and other cities. The Los Angeles riot resulted in 58 deaths, 2,500 injuries, 16,000 arrests, and an estimated $1 billion in property damage.[1]

For many people, the King incident—the original beating, the first trial, the riots, and the second trial—symbolizes the larger problem of police–community relations in America: police use of excessive force against minorities, the failure of the justice system to deal with police misconduct, and the general distrust of the justice system by minorities.[2] In a public opinion survey after the riots, 80 percent of African Americans in Los Angeles agreed or strongly agreed with the statement that "blacks usually don't get fair treatment in the courts and criminal justice system."[3]

This chapter examines the police–community relations (PCR) problem. It reviews the history of the problem, public attitudes toward the police, the different aspects of policing that affect racial and ethnic minorities, and programs designed to solve the problem.

## A DEFINITION OF POLICE–COMMUNITY RELATIONS

Police–community relations (PCR) refers primarily to *relations between the police and racial and ethnic minority communities*. The police have never had the same kinds of conflicts with the white majority community as they have with minorities.

The PCR problem is one aspect of the larger problem of racial inequality in America. The National Academy of Sciences concluded that "black crime and the position of blacks within the nation's system of criminal justice administration are related to past and present social opportunities and disadvantages and can be best understood through consideration of blacks' overall social status."[4] Political scientist Andrew Hacker argues that the United States is divided into *Two Nations: Black and White, Separate, Hostile, Unequal.*[5]

Discrimination and disparities based on race and ethnicity are found in all parts of the criminal justice system.[6] African Americans are caught up in the criminal justice system out of all proportion to their presence in society. They represent only 12 percent of the population, but 31 percent of all persons arrested and 49 percent of all persons in prison.[7] Walker, Spohn, and DeLone conclude that "the criminal justice system is characterized by obvious disparities based on race and ethnicity."[8] Jerome Miller believes the problem is even more serious, arguing that the criminal justice system has been conducting a "search and destroy" mission against African-American males.[9]

The PCR problem has a long history. Serious urban racial violence erupted during three separate periods: World War I (1917–1919), World War II (1943), and the 1960s (1964–1968). Almost all of the 1960s riots were sparked by an incident involving the police.[10] After the riots of the 1964–1968 period, many observers felt that police–

community relations improved in the 1970s.[11] Yet, the Rodney King incident and other highly publicized incidents of brutality in other cities suggested that the problem had worsened by the 1990s.

Although race and ethnicity represent the primary aspect of the PCR problem, problems also exist with respect to other communities. Studies have found patterns of police disrespect and excessive use of force directed toward homosexuals, for example.[12] Also, there are problems with respect to the police and women: inadequate response to crimes against women, moral condemnation of some victims, employment discrimination, and other problems.[13]

## RACE AND ETHNICITY IN AMERICA

Although the most serious PCR problems have historically involved the African-American community, similar problems also exist with respect to other racial and ethnic groups. There is coflict between the police and the Hispanic-American community.[14] Hispanic Americans actually consist of several different nationality groups: people whose countries of origin include Mexico, Cuba, Haiti, and other Central American and Latin American countries and the commonwealth of Puerto Rico. Problems also exist between the police and Native Americans, both in urban areas and in communities near Indian reservations.[15] Similar problems exist in cities with large Asian-American communities, which include recent immigrants from a variety of different countries: Vietnam, Laos, Cambodia, and others.

Because of immigration and other demographic factors, the face of America is changing significantly. In Los Angeles, for example, the Hispanic population increased from 19.2 percent of the total in 1980 to 25.8 percent in 1990. The composition of the Asian-American population changed significantly since the 1970s, with the addition of many people from Vietnam, Cambodia, Thailand, and other countries.[16]

The changing demographic face of America creates new challenges for all social institutions, including the police. A report, *Policing a Multicultural Community* by the Police Executive Research Forum concludes, "Preventing, mitigating and negotiating intergroup conflict in the community must become an integral part of police practice. . . . To remain effective, indeed to increase effectiveness, police must become skilled intercultural craftspeople."[17]

### Definitions of Race and Ethnicity

The subject of race has traditionally referred to the major biological divisions of the people of the world. The traditional categories are Caucasian, Negroid, and Mongoloid. Anthropologists today, however, do not believe that differences in skin color, hair texture, and body proportions represent fundamental differences among people. There are substantial differences in physical features among people *within* each traditional racial category. Ethnicity, meanwhile, refers to cultural differences, such as language, religion, family patterns, and foodways. A person in the United States may be ethnically Hispanic, for example, but white, black, or Native American in terms of race.[18] In the

**FIGURE 9–1**

OFFICIAL GOVERNMENT CATEGORIES OF RACE AND ETHNICITY

Office of Management and Budget Directive No. 15, Race and Ethnic Standards for Federal
Statistics and Administrative Reporting (as Adopted on May 12, 1977)

This Directive provides standard classifications for recordkeeping, collection, and presentation of
data on race and ethnicity in Federal program administrative reporting and statistical activities.
These classifications should not be interpreted as being scientific or anthropological in nature, nor
should they be viewed as determinants of eligibility for participation in any Federal Program. They
have been developed in response to needs expressed by both the executive branch and the
Congress to provide for the collection and use of compatible, nonduplicated, exchangeable racial
and ethnic data by Federal agencies.

1 Definitions
  The basic racial and ethnic categories for Federal statistics and program administrative
  reporting are defined as follows:
  a *American Indian or Alaskan Native.* A person having origins in any of the original peoples of
    North America and who maintains cultural identification through tribal cultural identification
    through tribal affiliations or community recognition.
  b *Asian or Pacific Islander.* A person having origins in any of the original peoples of the Far
    East, Southeast Asia, the Indian subcontinent, or the Pacific Islands. This area includes, for
    example, China, India, Japan, Korea, the Philippine Islands, and Samoa.
  c *Black.* A person having origins in any of the black racial groups of Africa.
  d *Hispanic.* A person of Mexican, Puerto Rican, Cuban, Central or South American, or other
    Spanish culture or origin, regardless of race.
  e *White.* A person having origins in any of the original peoples of Europe, North Africa, or the
    Middle East.

U.S. Census, individuals self-identify their race and ethnicity. Figure 9–1 presents the
official racial and ethnic categories used by the United States government.

### Discrimination and Disparity

The PCR problem involves allegations of discrimination against minorities.
Discrimination is defined as the *differential treatment* based on some extralegal category
such as race or gender. If an employer refuses to hire members of a certain religion, for
example, that represents discrimination. Disparity, on the other hand, refers to *different
outcomes that are not caused by differential treatment*. Most college students, for
example, are in their 20s. This is not the result of discrimination, but because of the
normal life course: younger people have not completed high school, and middle-aged
people have either finished college or do not plan to attend.

There are different forms of discrimination. Figure 9–2 represents the discrimination–disparity continuum developed by Walker, Spohn, and DeLone.

**FIGURE 9–2**
DISCRIMINATION–DISPARITY CONTINUUM

| Systematic Discrimination | Institutionalized Discrimination | Contextual Discrimination | Individual Acts of Discrimination | Pure Justice |
| --- | --- | --- | --- | --- |

**Definitions**

*Systematic discrimination.* Discrimination at all stages of the criminal justice system, at all times, and in all places.

*Institutionalized discrimination.* Racial and ethnic disparities in outcomes that are the result of the application of racially neutral factors such as prior criminal record, employment status, demeanor, etc.

*Contextual discrimination.* Discrimination found in particular contexts or circumstances (e.g., certain regions, particular crimes, special victim–offender relationships).

*Individual acts of discrimination.* Discrimination that results from the acts of particular individuals but is not characteristic of entire agencies or the criminal justice system as a whole.

*Pure justice.* No racial or ethnic discrimination al all.

Source: Samuel Walker, Cassia Spoahn, and Miriam DeLone, *The Color of Justice* (Belmont, CA: Wadsworth, 1996), p. 16.

## PUBLIC OPINION AND THE POLICE

Public opinion polls examining attitudes toward the police are a useful starting point for analyzing police–community relations. Many national and local opinion surveys have been conducted since the 1960s. Tuch and Weitzer found that national attitudes are remarkably stable over time, although local incidents, such as a police shooting or beating, can have short-term effects on local attitudes.[19] Table 9–1 presents the findings of a 1996 survey of public confidence in the police. Almost 90 percent of all Americans report having a great deal or some confidence in the police. Only 11 percent have very little or no confidence.[20]

### Racial and Ethnic Differences

There are significant differences in the attitudes of different racial and ethnic groups toward the police. Table 9–1 indicates that 22 percent of African Americans have very little or no confidence in the police, compared with only 9 percent of whites. Other polls that have treated Hispanics as a separate group have found that their attitudes fall somewhere between those of whites and African Americans. Similar responses have been obtained in local public opinion surveys. A 1986 survey in Philadelphia found that 83 percent of white residents gave the police a good or excellent rating, compared with 53 percent of African Americans and 59 percent of Hispanics.[21]

The racial differences in attitudes toward the police have been remarkably stable over time. The President's Crime Commission reported in 1967 that 16 percent of non-whites rated the police as poor, compared with 7 percent of whites.[22] A 1975 National Crime Survey (NCS) study found that 9 percent of whites rated the police as poor compared

**TABLE 9–1**
REPORTED CONFIDENCE IN THE POLICE
BY DEMOGRAPHIC CHARACTERISTICS, UNITED STATES, 1996

Question: "I am going to read you a list of institutions in American society. Please tell me how much confidence you, yourself, have in each one—a great deal, quite a lot, some, or very little: the police?"

|  | Great Deal/quite a lot | Some | Very little | None[a] |
|---|---|---|---|---|
| National | 60% | 28% | 11% | 1% |
| Sex |  |  |  |  |
| Male | 57 | 28 | 14 | 1 |
| Female | 63 | 29 | 8 | 1 |
| Race |  |  |  |  |
| White | 65 | 26 | 9 | (b) |
| Nonwhite[c] | 34 | 42 | 20 | 3 |
| Black | 31 | 43 | 22 | 4 |
| Age |  |  |  |  |
| 18 to 29 years | 51 | 27 | 20 | 1 |
| 30 to 49 years | 61 | 30 | 8 | 1 |
| 50 to 64 years | 59 | 32 | 9 | 0 |
| 50 years and older | 66 | 27 | 7 | (b) |
| 65 years and older | 73 | 21 | 5 | 1 |

*Source:* Bureau of Justice Statistics, *Sourcebook of Criminal Justice Statistics 1995* (Washington, DC: Government Printing Office, 1996), p.133.

with 19 percent of blacks. In that survey 84 percent of whites and 74 percent of blacks rated the police as good or average.[23]

It is important to note that a majority of African Americans and Hispanics have a favorable attitudes toward the police. In Table 9–1, a combined total of 74 percent of African Americans have either a great deal or some confidence in the police.

At the same time, there are differences within racial and ethnic communities. In a study of five different neighborhoods in Miami, however, Dunham and Alpert found that attitudes about the police role varied according to social class as well as by race and ethnicity. Thus, middle-class and lower-class African Americans did not share identical attitudes.[24]

### Attitudes about Police Use of Force

The gap between white and minority group attitudes widens when people are asked specifically about police use of force. Huang and Vaughn found that 60 percent of whites had a favorable attitude toward the police with respect to the use of force, compared with only 33 percent of blacks and 42 percent of Hispanics.[25] In 1996 71 percent of whites but only 45 percent of African Americans indicated that they could imagine "any situations" where they would approve a police officer striking an adult male.[26] In a survey of Cincinnati residents, 46.6 percent of African Americans indicated they have been personally hassled by the police, compared with only 9.6 percent of whites. Hassled was defined as being "stopped or watched closely by a police officer, even when you had done nothing wrong." Additionally, 66 percent of African Americans reported that someone they knew had been hassled, compared with only 12.5 percent of whites.[27]

### Other Demographic Variables

Age ranks second to race and ethnicity as a factor in public attitudes toward the police. Young people consistently express more dissatisfaction with the police than older people and, as Table 9–1 indicates, very favorable attitudes steadily increase with age.[28]

Poor people generally rate the police less favorably than do middle- or upper-income people. People with more education consistently rate the police more favorably. Gender has little effect on attitudes toward the police. Most surveys have found little significant difference in the attitudes of men and women toward the police. Crime victims rate police performance less favorably than nonvictims. In the NCS survey, 16 percent of crime victims but only 10 percent of the nonvictims rated the police as "poor."[29]

### Intercity Variations

Attitudes toward the police vary from city to city. The 1975 NCS survey found that the police in Cleveland and Newark had much lower ratings than the police in Baltimore and Denver. Significantly, white and African-American attitudes are closely linked. Both whites and African Americans in Cleveland gave the police lower ratings than the national average, whereas both groups in Baltimore rated them higher than the national average.[30] These data suggest that in any particular community the attitudes of whites and African Americans are influenced by the same factors: the reputation of the police department and personal experience with the police.

### The Impact of Controversial Events

Public attitudes are affected by controversial events, particularly incidents that create negative publicity about the police. Tuch and Weitzer found that the 1991 Rodney King beating had a dramatic, although short-term, effect on attitudes toward the Los Angeles Police Department. Prior to the incident about 70 percent of whites consistently indicated that they approved of the way the LAPD did its job. From March 1991 through May 1992, responses fell into the 40 percent range. By 1993, however, responses of whites had returned to the 70 percent range. The percentage of African Americans indicating that they approved of the LAPD fell even more dramatically (to only 14 percent in late March 1991). Approval ratings of African Americans returned to previous levels but at a slower rate than for whites.[31]

## The Detroit Exception

The major exception to the general pattern of attitudes toward the police by race is found in a survey of Detroit residents. Contrary to all prior research, more African Americans (71.8 percent) indicated they were very satisfied or somewhat satisfied with the police than whites (52.8 percent). The survey's directors concluded that these responses are a result of the fact that the political establishment in the city of Detroit is dominated by African Americans (including an African American mayor since 1973) and that a majority of the police force is African American. Thus, African Americans are more likely than whites to identify positively with the symbolic sources of power, particularly the police.[32]

## The Police and the Larger Society

The attitudes toward the police do not necessarily reflect personal experience with a local police department. Albrecht and Green argue that attitudes toward the police reflect a broader set of attitudes toward society, government, and the criminal justice system. People who express the greatest dissatisfaction with the police also have the most negative attitudes toward courts and judges. They are more alienated from society and participate less in politics than people with more favorable attitudes toward the police.[33]

Public attitudes about the police reflect the symbolic role of the police as the agents of authority who represent the coercive power of the state. The badge, baton, and gun are the visible reminders of the police officer's power to use force, which Bittner argues is the defining aspect of the police role.[34] Blumberg argues that the police are a "social lightning rod" for public attitudes about other social and political issues.[35] Niederhoffer called the police officer a "'Rorschach' in uniform"—someone onto whom people project their fears and fantasies.[36] Thus, people who are the victims of general patterns of discrimination, or who feel powerless or alienated from society, are likely to have more negative attitudes toward the police than people who feel integrated into the mainstream of society.

## Comparisons with Other Occupations

The police compare very favorably with other occupations in terms of public perception. A 1996 survey found that they ranked seventh out of 26 occupations in terms of perceived honesty and ethical standards (see Table 9–2). Almost half (49 percent) rated the police very high or high, compared with only 17 percent for both newspaper reporters and lawyers. Additionally, public estimates of police honesty have been rising. The percentage of people rating the police very high and high rose from 37 percent in 1977 to 49 percent in 1996.[37]

**Summary**    The available data allow us to draw several conclusions about public attitudes toward the police: (1) The vast majority of Americans have a positive attitude toward the police; (2) racial and ethnic minorities consistently rate the police less favorably than whites; (3) minorities, nonetheless, still give the police a generally

**TABLE 9–2**
RESPONDENTS' RATINGS OF THE HONESTY AND ETHICAL STANDARDS OF VARIOUS OCCUPATIONS
(By type of occupation, United States, 1996)

Question. "Please tell me how you would rate the honesty and ethical standards of people in these different fields—very high, high, average, low , or very low?"

| Occupation | Very high | High | Average | Low | Very low | No opinion |
|---|---|---|---|---|---|---|
| Druggists, pharmacists | 14% | 50% | 30% | 3% | 1% | 2% |
| Clergy | 18 | 38 | 30 | 7 | 2 | 5 |
| College teachers | 11 | 44 | 33 | 4 | 1 | 7 |
| Medical doctors | 11 | 44 | 35 | 7 | 2 | 1 |
| Dentists | 8 | 45 | 38 | 5 | 2 | 2 |
| Engineers | 9 | 39 | 41 | 2 | 1 | 8 |
| Police | 10 | 39 | 38 | 8 | 3 | 2 |
| Bankers | 3 | 23 | 59 | 9 | 3 | 3 |
| Funeral directors | 6 | 29 | 46 | 10 | 3 | 6 |
| Journalists | 3 | 20 | 50 | 19 | 4 | 4 |
| TV reporters, commentators | 4 | 19 | 49 | 19 | 7 | 2 |
| Newspaper reporters | 2 | 15 | 48 | 24 | 7 | 4 |
| Building contractors | 3 | 20 | 49 | 18 | 4 | 6 |
| Senators | 2 | 13 | 48 | 26 | 8 | 3 |
| Lawyers | 3 | 14 | 39 | 27 | 14 | 3 |
| Business executives | 2 | 15 | 58 | 17 | 3 | 5 |
| Congress members | 2 | 12 | 45 | 28 | 10 | 3 |
| Local officeholders | 2 | 17 | 57 | 16 | 4 | 4 |
| Labor union leaders | 3 | 13 | 39 | 29 | 9 | 7 |
| Real estate agents | 2 | 13 | 56 | 20 | 5 | 4 |
| Stockbrokers | 2 | 13 | 58 | 14 | 2 | 11 |
| State officeholders | 2 | 11 | 54 | 23 | 6 | 4 |
| Insurance salespeople | 1 | 10 | 49 | 29 | 8 | 3 |
| Advertising practitioners | 1 | 10 | 46 | 28 | 9 | 6 |
| Car salespeople | 2 | 6 | 29 | 42 | 18 | 3 |
| Public opinion pollsters | 4 | 20 | 54 | 12 | 4 | 6 |

*Source:* George Gallup, Jr., *The Gallup Poll* (Princeton, NJ: The Gallup Poll, Jan. 2, 1997), p. 2. Reprinted by permission

favorable rating; (4) young people rate the police less favorably than older people; (5) poor people, less educated people, and crime victims tend to rate the police lower than other Americans.

## POLICE PERCEPTIONS OF CITIZENS

Police officers generally do not have an accurate perception of public attitudes toward them. James Q. Wilson argues that police officers "probably exaggerate the extent of citizen hostility."[38] In his pioneering work on the police subculture, William A. Westley found that 73 percent of the officers thought that the public was "against the police, or hates the police." Only 12 percent felt that the public "likes the police."[39] Jerome

Skolnick also found that suspicion of and hostility toward the public were among the key ingredients of the police officer's "working personality."[40]

In the 1960s a study sponsored by the Kerner Commission found that 31 percent of police officers in 13 large cities believed that most African Americans "regard the police as enemies," and 31 percent thought that most African Americans were "on their side." The study concluded that white police officers were more likely "to project their own prejudices and fears upon blacks, ascribing to them a level of hostility that more adequately reflects the hostility of the perceiver."[41] Bayley and Mendelsohn's study of police–community relations in Denver is the only one to find that police officers had a "rosier" view of public attitudes toward the police than actually existed.[42]

### Sources of Police Attitudes

Police officer misperception of public attitudes is the result of several factors. Most important is the pattern of *selective contact* between police and public. Officers do not have regular contact with a cross section of the community. An analysis of police emergency (911) calls in Minneapolis found that 5 percent of the addresses in the city generated 64 percent of all the calls.[43] A Bureau of Justice Services survey estimated that in 1996 only 20 percent of all Americans had face-to-face encounters with police officers.[44] Low-income people and racial minorities, moreover, have a disproportionate level of contact with the police. Police departments deploy more patrol officers in their neighborhoods because of higher crime levels and they are more likely than other Americans to call the police. Finally, the police have relatively more contact with low-income young males who use public places as their recreation spots.[45]

In addition to selective contact, police officer attitudes are shaped by the phenomenon of *selective perception*. Most contacts between citizens and the police are civil; only between 2 percent and 5 percent involve hostility or conflict.[46] Like most people, however, police officers, are more likely to remember unpleasant or traumatic incidents than routine uneventful ones.[47] Observations of police work by Piliavin and Briar and also by Black found that young African-American men were more likely than young white men to express hostility to the police.[48] Consequently, officers tend to stereotype young African-American males in terms of what Skolnick called the "symbolic assailant" and a potential source of conflict.[49]

### SOURCES OF POLICE–COMMUNITY RELATIONS PROBLEMS

The public opinion poll data raise a number of important questions. How do we explain the apparent contradiction between the generally favorably ratings given the police by racial and ethnic minority communities and the persistence of conflict between the police and these groups? Is it simply because the media exaggerate a small number of bad incidents? Or are there systematic problems affecting racial and ethnic minorities?

One way to answer these questions is to examine specific police activities as they affect minority communities and specific segments of those communities. These include (1) law enforcement policy; (2) police officer field practices, (3) administrative practices, (4) employment practices.

## LAW ENFORCEMENT POLICY

Some criticisms of the police by racial and ethnic minorities involve matters of basic law enforcement policy. This includes policy decisions by the department as a whole rather than decisions by individual officers.

### Inadequate Police Protection

Some minority community leaders accuse the police of providing inadequate protection. Their argument is that the police do not provide a sufficient number of patrol officers for their neighborhoods, given the level of crime. In a 1975 survey African Americans expressed greater interest in more police protection than in better quality of police service.[50]

Historically, African Americans have been the victims of underenforcement of the law. During the period of institutionalized segregation in the South, the criminal justice system was used to maintain white supremacy. Gunnar Myrdal's classic study of race relations in America found that the police disregarded many crimes in the African-American community.[51] LaFave found a pattern of nonenforcement of the law in African-American communities in northern cities in the 1950s.[52] The result was four different systems of justice, depending on the racial components of the offender/victim relationship.[53] The four systems were:

1 Crimes by whites against whites were handled as "normal" crimes.
2 Crimes by whites against African Americans were rarely prosecuted, if at all.
3 Crimes by African Americans against whites received the harshest response.
4 Crimes by African Americans against African Americans were often ignored.

Failure to enforce the law in minority neighborhoods has often involved crimes of vice. Historically, gambling, after-hours drinking, prostitution, and narcotics trafficking have been allowed to exist in low-income and racial minority neighborhoods. A 1986 survey of attitudes in Philadelphia found that 65 percent of Hispanic residents believed that the police underenforced gambling laws, compared with 55 percent of African-American and 46 percent of white Philadelphians.[54]

Tolerating vice crimes harms low-income and racial minority communities in several ways. First, it breeds disrespect for the law and the police. The toleration of vice crimes is often accompanied by corruption. The Knapp Commission investigation of police corruption in New York City found that the monthly vice payoffs to police in the predominantly African-American areas of Harlem averaged $1,500, compared with $300 in predominantly white downtown precincts.[55] A 1966 survey found that 10 times as many nonwhites as whites believed the police were "almost all corrupt."[56]

Second, underenforcement of the law exposes law-abiding citizens in minority communities to criminal activity. Prostitution and drug dealing are often accompanied by secondary crimes such as shootings and robberies. These crimes expose individuals and their families to personal risk and lower the quality of life in the neighborhood. Exposure to criminal activity, meanwhile, increases the risk that juveniles will engage in crime themselves.

The question of whether racial and ethnic minority neighborhoods receive an adequate level of police protection is extremely complex. Generally, police departments assign more patrol officers to low-income and racial minority neighborhoods than to other parts of the community because of higher rates of reported crimes and more calls for service (see Chapter 4). Thus, the police are a more visible presence than in other neighborhoods. Bayley and Mendelsohn argue, "The police seem to play a role in the life of minority people out of all proportion to the role they play in the lives of the dominant white majority."[57]

One attempt to measure the adequacy of police protection in African-American neighborhoods resulted from a Washington, D.C., lawsuit where African-American residents alleged insufficient police protection *(Burner v. Washington, D.C.)*. Peter Bloch compared two areas, one about 90 percent African American and another about 90 percent white. He measured the level of police protection in terms of calls per officer, police per 100 reported robberies, and officers per 100 Index crimes. He concluded that "police units are distributed equally and that both neighborhoods were receiving levels of police service equal to their apparent needs."[58]

It is possible, however, that in some poorly managed police departments patrol officers are not distributed according to the recommended workload formula, with the result that white, middle-class, and relatively low-crime neighborhoods receive more patrol than is reasonable. A 1981 Police Executive Research Forum (PERF) survey of administrative practices found a number of departments that were not allocating patrol officers in a rational manner by time of day.[59]

**A Contradiction?**    The allegation that the police fail to provide adequate police protection contradicts the more commonly heard complaint about overpolicing: too many stops and frisks, too many arrests, and so on. (These issues are discussed in detail in the section on police field practices.) This apparent contradiction can be explained by the diversity *within* racial and ethnic minority communities. Complaints about police harassment generally come from young males who have a high level of contact with the

---

**SIDEBAR 9–1**

AN INTERNATIONAL PERSPECTIVE: POLICE–COMMUNITY RELATIONS IN ENGLAND

Conflict between the police and racial and ethnic minority communities is not confined to the United States. Similar problems exist in England. Serious riots erupted in London and other cities in April 1981 as a result of incidents involving the police. The Scarman Report on the disorders concluded that the police "were partly to blame for the breakdown in community relations," in part because of "instances of harassment and racial prejudice among junior officers"and a "failure to adjust policies and methods to meet the needs of policing a multiracial society."

*Source:* Lawrence W. Sherman, "After the Riots: Police and Minorities in the United States, 1970–1980," in *Ethnic Pluralism and Public Policy,* eds. Nathan Glazer and Ken Young, (Lexington, MA: Lexington Books, 1983), pp. 232–233. Lord Scarman, *The Scarman Report* (London: Penguin Books, 1982), pp. 118–119.

---

police. Most members of racial minority communities, however, are law-abiding adults with jobs and families. Like their white counterparts, they want more not less police protection.[60] Dunham and Alpert found differences in public attitudes about such issues as police responsibility for crime control *within* different racial and ethnic groups on the basis of social class. They concluded that the police "need to approach crime control in each of these areas in a different manner."[61]

## POLICE FIELD PRACTICES

Police field practices are the greatest source of tensions between the police and racial minorities. This category includes actions by individual police officers such as use of deadly force, physical force, stops and frisks, verbal abuse, and slow response to calls for service.

### Deadly Force

The use of deadly force has been the source of the major conflict between minorities and the police. James Fyfe concluded that "blacks and Hispanics are everywhere overrepresented among those on the other side of police guns."[62] In the 1960s and 1970s, the ratio of African Americans to whites shot and killed by the police was as high as 6 to 1 or even 8 to 1. Gerald Robin found that between 1950 and 1960, Chicago police shot and killed African Americans at a rate of 16.1 per 100,000, compared with 2.1 whites per 100,000 (for a ratio of 7.4 to 1).[63] The disparity between whites and African Americans, moreover, has been greatest among unarmed people—the category usually defined as "fleeing felon." Between 1969 and 1974 Memphis police officers shot and killed 13 African Americans but 1 white person in this category.[64]

Police department policies on the use of deadly force have changed significantly in the past 25 years. Since the early 1970s the permissive fleeing felon rule, which allowed the police to shoot, for example, an unarmed burglary suspect, has been replaced by the more restrictive defense-of-life rule. The U.S. Supreme Court, meanwhile, ruled the fleeing-felon standard unconstitutional in the 1985 *Tennessee v. Garner* decision.[65]

Fyfe found that adoption of the defense-of-life standard by the New York City police in 1972 reduced the average number of shots fired by 30 percent. The greatest reduction occurred in fleeing-felon situations.[66] In Memphis, a restrictive shooting policy eliminated all shootings in the unarmed and nonassaultive category, greatly reducing the racial disparity in the process.[67] Sherman and Cohn's survey of shooting trends in the 50 largest cities found that the total number of persons shot and killed per year was cut in half between 1970 and 1984. Meanwhile, the ratio of African Americans to whites shot and killed fell from about 6 to 1 to 3 to 1.[68] The data suggest that permissive shooting policies permit racially prejudiced attitudes to affect shootings, whereas restrictive policies, by controlling discretion, curb the impact of prejudice.[69]

The important question is whether the current disparity between African Americans and whites shot and killed represents *systematic* discrimination as defined by Walker, Spohn, and DeLone (Figure 9-2,), or whether it is *contextual* discrimination (e.g., certain departments), or *individual* discrimination (e.g., particular officers). Some analysts argue that the proper standard involves the number of persons in each racial and ethnic group who are at risk of a shooting incident. "At risk" may be defined in terms of involvement in serious crime. Geller and Karales examined shootings by Chicago police between 1974 and 1978. They found that African Americans were shot and killed six times as often as whites in terms of their presence in the total population. When they controlled for participation in violent crimes, however, the disparity disappeared. Whites were shot and killed at a rate of 5.6 per 1,000 arrests for forcible felonies, compared with 4.5 blacks shot per 1,000 arrests for the same category of crime.[70]

### Use of Physical Force

Civil rights leaders argue that racial and ethnic minorities are the frequent victims of police brutality, defined as the use of excessive physical force by the police. The videotape of the 1991 Rodney King beating provided dramatic evidence of one incident.[71] Police officers assigned to a high crime, predominantly African-American neighborhood in St. Louis, meanwhile, expressed a strong desire to use "kick ass" methods against suspected criminals (but apparently were constrained from doing so by department policies and fear of possible negative consequences).[72]

The issue of excessive force is particularly complex. Police officers are authorized by law to use force in certain situations. The relevant question is, When is the use of force excessive? Excessive or unjustified force is defined as *more force than is necessary to accomplish a lawful police purpose.* Lawful police purposes include making an arrest, protecting oneself or another from attack, or bringing a potentially dangerous situation under control. A police officer is not justified in using force in response to mere disrespect, for example. Applying this definition to specific situations is often difficult, however. Whether or not force was necessary is frequently a matter of opinion. It involves conflicting perceptions of whether a person was resisting arrest, or whether he or she posed a threat to the safety of the officer.[73]

**FIGURE 9–3**
PHOENIX POLICE DEPARTMENT CONTINUUM OF FORCE CATEGORIES

| Police | Suspects |
|---|---|
| 0. No force | 0. No resistance |
| 1. Police presence | 1. Psychological intimidation |
| 2. Verbal commands | 2. Verbal noncompliance |
| 3. Control and restraint (handcuffs) | 3. Passive resistance |
| 4. Chemical agents | 4. Defensive resistance |
| 5. Tactics and weapons* | 5. Active aggression |
| 6. Firearms /deadly force | 6. Firearms/deadly force |

*Includes all physical tactics and weapons used, except chemical agents and firearms.
*Source:* Joel Garner, John Buchanan, Tom Schade, and John Hepburn, *Understanding the Use of Force By and Against the Police* (Washington, DC: National Institute of Justice, 1996), p. 5.

Many police departments have adopted a use of force continuum, indicating the different levels of force (Figure 9–3). Officers are trained to use the appropriate level of force for each particular situation.

Police use of force—including both justified and unjustified force—is a statistically infrequent event. It is estimated that police officers use some kind of force in only about 1 percent of all encounters with citizens. The rate is higher, between 4 and 6 percent, in encounters with criminal suspects. About two-thirds of all uses of force are justified; about one-third are unjustified. Thus, police use excessive force in about one-third of 1 percent (0.3 percent) of all encounters with citizens.[74] A 1996 Bureau of Justice Statistics (BJS) survey found that 1 percent of all people who had face-to-face contact with a police officer that year experienced the use of force or a warning that force might be used. This represented a total of 500,000 people during the year.[75]

Police use of force is associated with certain situational factors. Worden's analysis of Police Services Study (PSS) data on force incidents found that most of the citizens involved were men, about two-thirds of those were young men, and a disproportionate number were African American. Police officers were most likely to use force in situations involving violent crime, and against male suspects who were African American, drunk, and antagonistic to the police. Physical resistance to a police officer significantly increased the likelihood of use of force. Even when a citizen's demeanor was controlled for, police officers were more likely to use both reasonable and unreasonable force. Worden concluded that "the use of force *is* affected by race as well as by gender."[76]

In an earlier study, Reiss found that white and African-American officers were about equally likely to use force, and were most likely to use force against members of their own race.[77] Official complaint data from San Jose and New York City indicate that officers of different racial and ethnic backgrounds receive complaints at rates equal to their presence on the police force.[78]

**Examining the 1 Percent Rate**    Some people regard the 1 percent estimate of the use of force as extremely low, and believe that the real incidence is much higher. The 1 percent figure acquires a different meaning when examined more closely. The BJS estimate of 500,000 force incidents per year translates into 1,369 per day. If we accept the estimate that one-third involve excessive or unjustified use of force, the result is about 456 excessive force incidents every day of the year. If we further assume that most of these incidents occur in the cities, the result is a large number of annual incidents in every city. Moreover, most incidents involve young males, and disproportionately involve racial and ethnic minority males. Thus, as Reiss points out, use of force incidents accumulate over time with the result that "a sizeable minority of citizens experience police misconduct at one time or another."[79] Young racial and ethnic minority males will have a very strong perception of police harassment.

## Arrests

African Americans are arrested more often than whites relative to their numbers in the population. In 1995 they represented 31 percent of all arrests, and 40 percent of all Part I felony arrests, despite the fact that they constitute only 12 percent of the U.S.

---

**SIDEBAR 9–2**

HOW MUCH POLICE USE OF FORCE IN YOUR COMMUNITY?

Estimate the prevalence of police use of force and excessive force in your community. Use the annual total of 911 calls as a crude estimate of the number of contacts between police officers and citizens. Calculate 1 percent of that figure as the number of use-of-force incidents. One-third of that figure yields an estimate of the number of excessive force incidents per year. Compare this figure with the number of citizen complaints filed with the department.

---

population. Arrest is an extremely common experience for young African-American men in the inner city. Tillman estimated that 65.5 percent of all African-American males are arrested before the age of 30, compared with 33.9 percent of white males. Meanwhile, 29.6 percent of all African-American females are arrested before the age of 30 compared with only 10.1 percent of white females.[80]

Donald Black's study of arrest found that police decisions to arrest are influenced by a number of situational factors. These include (1) the strength of the evidence, (2) the seriousness of the crime, (3) the preference of the victim, (4) the relationship between victim and suspect, (5) the demeanor of the suspect.[81] Race was not a direct factor in arrest decisions. African Americans were more likely to be disrespectful of the police, however, and arrested for that reason.

Although the evidence is not strong, it appears that the characteristics of crime victims have some impact on the racial pattern of arrests. African Americans who call the police request arrests more often than whites and, because most crimes are *intra-racial* (with victim or complainant the same race as the suspect), this results in more arrests of African Americans.[82] Lundman and his colleagues also found that "the preference of black citizens explained the higher arrest rate for black juveniles.[83] At the same time, the Police Services Study data indicate that the police are more likely to comply with the wishes of white victims when they seek the arrest of African-American suspects than in other situations, particularly in property crimes.[84]

The effect of the demeanor on arrests is extremely complex. Black found that African Americans were more likely to be antagonistic to the police, and more likely to be arrested for that reason.[85] Piliavin and Briar found a similar pattern among juveniles.[86] David Klinger, however, argues that these earlier studies did not control for when the antagonistic demeanor occurred. He concludes that much of it occurs after the arrest and in those instances, therefore, is a consequence and not a cause of arrest.[87]

There have been no studies, however, to determine the extent to which the demeanor of suspects is provoked by police officers. Bayley and Mastrofski and Parks argue that police officers approach encounters with citizens with a "script" representing their preliminary perception on the situation.[88] Thus, an officer may approach an encounter with an expectation of conflict and, as a consequence, provoke a hostile response through informal cues or unconscious behavior. To the extent that officers stereotype young

African-American males as potential suspects,[89] they may provoke high rates of antagonistic behavior that, in turn, results in higher rates of arrest.

Several studies have found that African Americans are arrested on the basis of less stringent legal criteria than whites. Hepburn found that arrests of blacks were more likely to be declined for prosecution than arrests of whites, suggesting that many arrests were based on relatively weak evidence.[90] A Rand study of the criminal process in California found that African Americans were more likely to have arrest charges dropped by the police or prosecutor. Although these data might suggest greater leniency at the prosecution stage, they could also mean that African Americans were more likely to be arrested on weaker evidence.[91]

One of the greatest racial disparities in arrest involves drug offenses. About 37 percent of all drug arrests in 1995 involved African Americans, even though the National Household Survey of Drug Use estimates that African Americans are only slightly more likely to use illegal drugs than whites.[92] The National Criminal Justice Commission argues that the racial disparity in arrests is a result of police department policies: "*police enforcement of new drug laws . . . focus almost exclusively on low-level dealers in minority neighborhoods.*"[93]

### Stops and Frisks

Racial minorities often accuse the police of singling them out for harassment by stopping, questioning, and frisking them without justification. The President's Crime Commission found that field interrogations were a major cause of tensions between the police and minority communities.[94] A 1990 report by the Massachusetts attorney general concluded that the Boston police "engaged in improper, and unconstitutional, conduct. . . with respect to stops and searches of minority individuals."[95] The San Diego field interrogation study found that 66 percent of the people stopped for questioning were African-American and Mexican-American men, despite the fact that they represented only 30 percent of the population in the areas studied. All the people stopped were male and almost two-thirds were juveniles.[96] A Cincinnati survey found that 46.6 percent of African Americans reported being hassled by the police, compared with only 9.6 percent of whites.[97]

Field interrogations pose a serious conflict over police goals. On the one hand, many police officers regard them as legitimate and effective crime fighting tactics. In their view, stopping, questioning, and frisking suspects produces arrests for crimes and communicates a deterrent message to other potential law breakers. On the other hand, however, overly aggressive tactics are often perceived as harassment, particularly by young African Americans.

The problem with aggressive anticrime tactics is racial stereotyping of possible suspects. As Skolnick points out, police officers are not only trained to be suspicious but develop a visual "shorthand" for suspects, based on visual cues. Inevitably, this involves a certain amount of stereotyping by gender, age, and race. Skolnick concludes that "a disposition to stereotype is an integral part of the policeman's world."[98] In some instances this is reinforced by department policy. The Christopher Commission concluded that the aggressive war-on-crime style of the Los Angeles Police Department "in some cases seems to become an attack on [minority] communities at large. The communities, and all within them, become painted with the brush of latent criminality."[99]

On the other hand, however, the San Diego Field Interrogation Study interviewed people who had been stopped and questioned about their perception of police activity and found that "the majority of all citizens who were subjects of field investigation contacts felt that the contact was justified and properly conducted."[100]

## Verbal Abuse and Racial and Ethnic Slurs

Verbal abuse, particularly racial and ethnic slurs, are also a source of tension between the police and minority communities. The Christopher Commission found transcripts of offensive racist terminology in Los Angeles police officer communications with dispatchers.[101] Reiss found that 75 percent of all police officers in his study were heard using offensive racial terms (in conversation with other officers and not to citizens). In that study, officers "openly ridiculed and belittled" citizens in only 5 percent of all encounters.[102]

Most departments have official policies forbidding the use of offensive language toward citizens. See, for example, the policy of the Chicago Police Department on Human Rights presented in Sidebar 9–3.

## Traffic Citations

Minorities often allege that they are singled out for traffic stops. This phenomenon has been labeled "driving while black." An ACLU law suit against the Maryland State Police cited evidence that 73 percent of the drivers stopped were African American even though they represented only 17 percent of all drivers. The department's Criminal Interdiction Team tried to justify concentrating on African-American drivers because of suspected drug trafficking. Yet, 70 percent of the searches in these incidents produced no evidence of drugs.[103] Chambliss spent more than 100 hours riding with the Rapid Deployment Unit (RDU) of the Washington, D.C. Metropolitan Police Department.

---

SIDEBAR 9–3

CHICAGO POLICE DEPARTMENT HUMAN RIGHTS AND RESOURCES POLICY

Members [of the Chicago Police Department] will not exhibit any bias or prejudice against any individual or group because of race, color, gender, age, religion, disability, national origin, ancestry, sexual orientation, marital status, parental status, military discharge status or source of income. Members will not direct any derogatory terms toward any person in any manner.

*Source:* Chicago Police Department, General Order 92–1, "Human Rights and Human Resources," July 4, 1992.

---

Created in response to the riots of the 1960s, the RDU consists of three two-officer cars engaged on aggressive anticrime tactics. Chambliss found that "It . . . became common-place for the RDU officers to stop any car with young black men in it."[104]

In one experiment, a professor at California State College (Los Angeles) found that students with Black Panther Party bumper stickers on their cars received a suspiciously high number of traffic tickets in a short period of time. At the time of the experiment (1969–1970), the Black Panther Party was a militant political organization that had been involved in a number of confrontations with the police. In the experiment, 15 students (5 white, 5 black, 5 Hispanic) with no moving violations on their driving records voluntarily placed Black Panther Party bumper stickers on their cars. Within 17 days the group had received 33 citations; the fund to pay their fines was exhausted and the experiment terminated. The experiment suggested that, during a period of tension in police–community relations, the police singled out cars believed to be driven by politically militant blacks for harassment.[105]

## Delay in Responding to Calls

Several studies of police work found that patrol officers often deliberately delayed responding to calls for service, especially in the case of family disturbances.[106] Furstenburg and Wellford's interviews with citizens in Baltimore who had called the police found that black citizens perceived greater delay than did whites. A higher percentage of whites reported the police responding in less than 5 minutes; nearly twice as many blacks as whites reported that the police took more than 15 minutes to respond.[107] A recent study of a high crime, predominantly African-American neighborhood in St. Louis found that "most complaints about policing . . . centered around poor police response." This included delayed response time and complete failure to respond to a 911 call.[108]

## Summary

In conclusion, there is considerable evidence that racial and minority citizens, especially young African-American males, are subject to differential treatment by police officers because of their race. These incidents, moreover, accumulate over time and create the perception of systematic police harassment.

## ADMINISTRATIVE PRACTICES

Certain police administrative practices generate distrust among racial and ethnic minority community members. The most serious problem is the belief that police departments fail to investigate citizen complaints and to discipline officers who are guilty of misconduct. The 1978 U.S. Civil Rights Commission report on Memphis found that "the single most aggravating factor . . . is the failure of the existing internal and external mechanisms which purportedly exist to prevent and combat" police misconduct. The commission cited the case of two officers who shot and killed a 16-year-old boy fleeing from the scene of a burglary. The officers were temporarily suspended for two days and then reinstated. Later, two other officers were fired for killing a dog.[109]

In the first national study of police use of force, Pate and Fridell found that for the municipal police departments surveyed African Americans represented 21.4 percent of the population but 42.3 percent of all complaints filed against the police. Additionally, these city police departments were more likely to sustain complaints filed by whites than by African Americans.[110]

Hispanic Americans, on the other hand, are less likely to file complaints against the police than African Americans.[111] A study of citizen perceptions of the complaint process in Omaha found that Spanish-speaking Hispanic residents were extremely fearful of the police and the possible consequences of filing a complaint. Much of this fear was the result of concern about being arrested for not having proper immigration documents.[112]

Because of distrust of police complaint procedures, civil rights leaders have demanded the creation of external or citizen review procedures. Citizen review is discussed in detail in Chapter 11, along with other mechanisms of police accountability.

## POLICE EMPLOYMENT PRACTICES

Discrimination in employment by police departments is another important cause of PCR tensions. Racial and ethnic minority officers are underrepresented in most police departments. Underrepresentation exists when the percentage of a minority group as sworn officers does not equal the percentage of that group in the local community served by that department. Virtually every national commission that has studied the police over the past 30 years has recommended that police departments hire more minority officers: the President's Crime Commission (1967), the Kerner Commission (1968), the National Advisory Commission on Criminal Justice Standards and Goals (1973), and the American Bar Association (1980).[113] Most police experts argue that the police should represent the communities they serve. The Commission on Accreditation for Law Enforcement Agencies (CALEA) accreditation standards recommend that each law enforcement "agency has minority group and female employees in the sworn law enforcement ranks in approximate proportion to the makeup of the agency's law enforcement service community."[114] Alpert, Smith, and Watters argue, "Police agencies must mirror the communities that they serve."[115]

In 1968 the Kerner Commission concluded that the underrepresentation of African Americans in big-city police departments was a contributing factor to the riots of the 1960s. At that time, African Americans represented 34 percent of the population in Cleveland but only 7 percent of the sworn officers in the Cleveland police department. In Detroit, meanwhile, African Americans were 39 percent of the population but only 5 percent of the sworn officers.[116]

The 1964 Civil Rights Act outlawed employment discrimination on the basis of race, color, or national origins. Amendments to the law in 1972 strengthened the enforcement powers of the federal Equal Employment Opportunity Commission (EEOC) with respect to employment practices by public agencies. At the same time, Executive Order #11246 requires all organizations receiving federal funds to develop affirmative action plans.

The employment of African Americans and Hispanics in municipal police departments has increased significantly since the early 1970s. The percentage of all sworn officers who were African American rose from an estimated 6.5 percent in 1973 to about 10 percent 1993. Hispanics represented about 7 percent of all sworn officers in municipal departments in 1993.[117]

Certain cities have made particularly significant progress in minority employment in 1993. African Americans represented 53.3 percent of all sworn officers in the Detroit Police Department and 67.8 percent of the Washington, D.C. Metropolitan Police Department. Hispanic officers represented 61.1 percent of the El Paso police and 36.3 percent of the San Antonio police in 1993. New York City, on the other hand, made almost no progress in the employment of African-American officers between the mid-1980s and the mid-1990s, despite a massive hiring program.[118] A report on the Los Angeles Police Department five years after the Rodney King incident found that, in terms of total sworn officers, the LAPD had a good record with respect to African Americans (14 percent of the population; 13 percent of all officers) but lagged with respect to Hispanic Americans (40 percent of the population vs. 28 percent of the officers).[119]

By 1992, 38 percent of the police departments in the 50 largest cities had achieved the ideal of representing their local communities in terms of African-American officers. Only 20 percent had reached the ideal level with respect to Hispanic officers. And only 5 of the 50 departments had reached the ideal level for both racial and ethnic groups.[120]

Ethnic and racial minorities are even more seriously underrepresented in supervisory positions. By 1996 the Los Angeles Police Department had made some progress in the promotion of African-American officers to higher ranks but much less progress with respect to Hispanic officers.[121]

Discrimination also exists with respect to assignment. In the past, police departments deliberately assigned incompetent officers to racial minority neighborhoods. The President's Crime Commission reported in 1967 that Philadelphia officers known as "goof-offs" were assigned to the ghetto areas of the city as a form of punishment.[122] Albert Reiss commented that "slum police precinct stations, not unlike slum schools, collect the rejects' of the system."[123]

There are no data on whether this practice continues today. In most departments, however, union contracts require assignments to be made on the basis of seniority, thereby limiting the opportunity of the department to engage in blatant race discrimination in assignments. A report on the Los Angeles Police Department, however, found that minorities were underrepresented in recognized "coveted positions—ones that are generally perceived as more desirable, attractive, and prestigious or that provide career-enhancing promotional opportunities."[124]

## Increasing Minority Employment in Policing

As a strategy for improving police–community relations, increased employment of racial and ethnic police officers has three separate objectives.[125] First, it is intended to end unlawful employment discrimination. Among police leaders there is little dispute about the goal of having police forces represent the communities they serve. There is, however, considerable dispute over affirmative action as the proper *means* to that end.[126]

Second, many civil rights leaders argue that increased employment of minority officers will improve the quality of police services. This argument is based on the assumption that minority officers will be better able to relate to minority citizens, and will not engage in discriminatory behavior.

There is little evidence, however, that police officer behavior is affected by the race or ethnicity of the officer. Fyfe found that white and black officers assigned to comparable precincts used deadly force at the same rate.[127] Reiss found that white and black officers used excessive physical force at about the same rate (9.8 per 100 black officers, compared with 8.7 per 100 white officers).[128] No study has found a clear pattern of differences in arrest activity by the race or ethnicity of the officer. Citizen complaint data from San Jose and New York City indicate that officers receive complaints in proportion to their presence in those departments.[129] One study, however, found that African American officers were more likely to be knowledgeable about African American neighborhoods and more aware of local citizen organizations than were white officers.[130]

Third, some observers argue that adding minority officers will alter the police subculture and, through peer pressure, affect the attitudes and behavior of other officers. There is some evidence to support this argument. In Los Angeles and other cities, African-American officer groups have spoken out against brutality, challenging the view of the predominantly white police union.[131] The National Black Police Officers Association (NBPOA) published a pamphlet on how to stop police brutality, encouraging officers to report misconduct by fellow officers.[132]

Fourth, the presence of more minority-group officers may improve the perception of the department in the community. A survey of Chicago residents found a small but significant number of people who thought that the police department had improved in recent years as a result of having more minority officers. Significantly, no white respondents believed that the department had gotten worse because of increased minority employment.[133] Finally, a recent survey of attitudes in Detroit found it to be the only city where African Americans expressed more positive attitudes toward the police than whites. The authors suggest that this may be the result of greater African-American representation in both city government as a whole and the police department in particular.[134]


## IMPROVING POLICE–COMMUNITY RELATIONS

Police departments have adopted several specific programs for improving police–community relations. The two most important are (1) creating special police–community relations units, and (2) providing officers with training in race relations and human relations.


### Special Police–Community Relations Units

In response to the urban riots of the 1960s most big-city police departments created special police–community relations (PCR) units which operated programs designed to improve relations with minority communities. PCR units spent most of their time speaking in schools and to community groups.[135] About half also operated "ride-along" programs that allowed citizens to spend a few hours riding in a patrol car.[136] Ride-along police cars were generally driven by a PCR unit officer. They followed patrol cars to calls for service but, in the interests of safety and privacy, did not allow citizens to observe actual encounters too closely.

Some departments also created neighborhood storefront offices, staffed by PCR unit officers, in an effort to overcome the isolation of the police and provide a more convenient access for community residents.[137] Police headquarters buildings are often forbidding places for many citizens and can be difficult to reach. The Detroit Police Department established 52 "ministations" throughout the city beginning in 1975. Each precinct had at least three, and some had four. Crime prevention officers (CPOs) assigned to the ministations did not engage in regular patrol and did not answer calls for service. Their activities included organizing teenage summer employment programs, encouraging trash pickup in neglected areas, and maintaining a volunteer escort service for the elderly.[138] The Houston Fear Reduction Experiment (Chapter 7) also included neighborhood offices.[139]

Critics questioned the effectiveness of PCR units. The President's Crime Commission found that minorities regarded most PCR programs as "public relations puff," and a "deliberate" con game."[140] Most police officers did not regard PCR units as an essential part of police operations. A Justice Department report found that PCR units "tended to be marginal to the operations of the police department," with little or no relationship to patrol or criminal investigation activities.[141] Using 1968 public opinion data, Decker, Smith, and Uhlman found that in cities with special PCR units public attitudes toward the police were only slightly more positive than in those cities where no PCR unit existed. The existence of a program had no effect on the attitudes of whites, but did have a positive effect among those respondents who expressed the least trust in government.[142]

Ride-along programs, meanwhile, tend to attract only those people who already have a favorable attitude toward the police and, consequently, do not reach those people who have serious complaints about the police. Many departments have abandoned their ride-along programs because of budget constraints. Some have been replaced by Citizen–Police Academies which attempt to provide interested citizens with a more comprehensive understanding of policing.[143]

Special PCR programs encounter the same problems as community policing programs (Chapter 7). Generally, they tend to be more successful with those groups of people who already have favorable attitudes toward the police: whites, homeowners, and older people. In the Houston fear reduction program, as well as many other experiments, innovations designed to improve relations with the public were less successful with racial minorities than whites.[144]

### Race Relations and Human Relations Training

Police training programs have improved dramatically over the past 30 years. The average length of preservice training has more than doubled, and most police academies have either added or greatly expanded coverage of race relations and human relations. In 1952 police academy training programs devoted an average of 4 hours to human relations; by 1982 the average was 25.3 hours.[145]

No research has established a direct connection between race relations training and either improved police officer behavior or improved public attitudes, however. A study of a police–community relations program in San Francisco found a significant change in police officer attitudes as a result of structured meetings with community residents. Officers reported more positive attitudes toward African-American residents and perceived less community hostility toward them as a result of the training sessions. There was no evaluation of police officer behavior, however.[146] The Los Angeles Police Department (LAPD) instituted a program of cultural awareness training after the 1991 Rodney King incident. Five years later, however, only 2,700 of the more than 9,000 officers had undergone the training program.[147]

A number of experts question the value of classroom training. A review of cultural diversity training programs for police found that the content of these programs had not changed much since the 1960s, that they tended to perpetuate negative stereotypes of racial minorities, and that they focused on individual officers and ignored problems related to the organization as a whole.[148] Alpert, Smith, and Watters argue that "mere classroom training" on issues of race relations "is insufficient." They stress the importance of on-the-street police behavior, and recommend that both new recruits and veteran officers "experiment with methods of communicating with members of racial and cultural groups other than their own."[149] A Detroit crime-victims training program found that recruits' attitudes toward citizens changed dramatically after only four months on the job, suggesting that street experience is a far more powerful influence over officer attitudes than classroom training.[150]

**Summary**    Lawrence W. Sherman points out that the period following the riots of the 1960s was a time of tremendous change in American policing. Many of those changes were directed toward improving police–community relations; others were part of a general move toward professionalization. These changes included the development of PCR units, race relations training, the recruitment of more minority officers, tougher discipline, and more controls over police discretion. It is not possible, however, to say that any one of these changes, by itself, improved police–community relations. The combined effect of these and other changes, however, has had some positive effect.[151]

## NEW APPROACHES TO IMPROVING POLICE–COMMUNITY RELATIONS

Community policing represents a different approach to improving police–community relations in several respects. First, as Alpert, Smith, and Watters point out, it represents a comprehensive philosophy of policing. It may better address on-the-street police behavior than most of the traditional PCR programs that emerged after the riots of the 1960s and were essentially "add-ons" to basic police operations.[152] Second, community policing is directed toward the community as a whole, and not just racial and ethnic minority communities. A survey of large police departments found that over 87 percent claimed that community policing had led to improved relations with minority communities.[153] These claims have not been independently confirmed, however.

## CONCLUSION

Conflict between the police and racial and ethnic communities remains a serious problem in American policing. This problem persists despite general improvements in policing. There is evidence of racial discrimination in police field practices, such as the use of force, in the handling of citizen complaints about police behavior, and in police employment practices. Many of these problems are the responsibility of the police themselves. At the same time, conflict between the police and minorities is a product of the larger structure of racism and racial discrimination in American society.

## NOTES

1 James H. Johnson, Jr., and Walter C. Farrell, Jr., "The Fire This Time: The Genesis of the Los Angeles Rebellion of 1992," in *Race, Poverty, and American Cities*, eds., John Charles Boger and Judith Welch Wagner, (Chapel Hill: University of North Carolina Press 1996), p. 166.

2 Jerome H. Skolnick and James J. Fyfe, *Above the Law: Police and the Excessive Use of Force* (New York: Free Press, 1993).

3 Lawrence Bobo, "Public Opinion Before and After a Spring of Discontent, in "*The Los Angeles Riots: Lessons for the Urban Future*, ed., Mark Baldassare, (Boulder: Westview, 1994), p. 111.

4 National Research Council, *A Common Destiny: Blacks and American Society* (Washington: National Academy Press, 1989), p. 453.

5 Andrew Hacker, *Two Nations: Black and White, Separate, Hostile, Unequal* (New York: Scribner's 1992).

6 Samuel Walker, Cassia Spohn, and Miriam DeLone, *The Color of Justice: Race, Ethnicity, and Crime in America* (Belmont, Wadsworth, 1996).

7 Bureau of Justice Statistics, *Sourcebook of Criminal Justice Statistics,* 1996 (Washington: Government Printing Office, 1997), pp. 384, 524.

8 Walker, Spohn, and DeLone, *The Color of Justice*, p. 229.

9 Jerome G. Miller, *Search and Destroy: African-American Males in the Criminal Justice System* (New York: Cambridge University Press, 1996).

10 National Advisory Commission on Civil Disorders (Kerner Commission), *Report* (New York: Bantam Books, 1968).

11 Lawrence W. Sherman, "After the Riots: Police and Minorities in the United States, 1970–1980," in *Ethnic Pluralism and Public Policy,* eds. Nathan Glazer and Ken Young, (Lexington, Mass.: Lexington Books, 1983), pp. 212–235.

12 Gregory M. Herek and Kevin T. Berrill, eds., *Hate Crimes: Confronting Violence against Lesbians ad Gay Men* (Newbury Park, Calif.: Sage, 1992), p. 32.

13 Susan E. Martin and Nancy C. Jurik, *Doing Justice, Doing Gender* (Thousand Oaks, Calif.: Sage, 1996).

14 Leo M. Romero and Luis G. Stelzner, "Hispanics and the Criminal Justice System," in *Hispanics in the United States: A New Social Agenda*, eds. Pastora San Jaun Cafferty and William C. McCready (New Brunswick, N.J.: Transaction Books, 1985), pp. 215–233.

15 Marianne O. Nielsen and Robert A. Silverman, eds., *Native Americans, Crime, and Justice* (Boulder: Westview, 1996).

16 Henry I. DeGeneste and John P. Sullivan, *Policing a Multicultural Community* (Washington: Police Executive Research Forum, 1997).

17 Ibid., p. 20.

**18** Definitions of race and ethnicity are discussed in Walker, Spohn, and DeLone, *The Color of Justice*, pp. 5–15.

**19** Steven A. Tuch and Ronald Weitzer, "Racial Differences in Attitudes Toward the Police," *Public Opinion Quarterly* 61 (1997): 642–663.

**20** W. S. Wilson Huang and Michael S. Vaughn, "Support and Confidence: Public Attitudes toward the Police," in *Americans View Crime and Justice: A National Public Opinion Survey*, eds. T. J. Flanagan and D. R. Longmire, (Newbury Park, Calif.: Sage, 1996), pp. 31–45.

**21** Philadelphia Police Study Task Force, *Philadelphia and Its Police: Toward a New Partnership* (Philadelphia: City of Philadelphia, 1987), p. 164.

**22** President's Commission on Law Enforcement and Administration of Justice, *The Challenge of Crime in a Free Society* (Washington: Government Printing Office, 1967), p. 99.

**23** U. S. Department of Justice, *Public Opinion About Crime* (Washington: Government Printing Office, 1977), p. 86.

**24** Roger G. Dunham annd Geoffrey P. Alpert, "Neighborhood Differences in Attitudes toward Policing: Evidence for a Mixed-Strategy Model of Policing in a Multi-Ethnic Setting," *Journal of Criminal Law and Criminology* 79, no. 2 (1988): 504–523.

**25** Huang and Vaughn, "Support and Confidence," pp. 40–41.

**26** U. S. Department of Justice, *Sourcebook of Criminal Justice Statistics, 1996* (Washington: Government Printing Office, 1997), pp. 130–131.

**27** Sandra Lee Browning, Francis T. Cullen, Liqun Cao, Renee Kopache, and Thomas J. Stevenson, "Race and Getting Hassled by the Police: A Research Note," *Police Studies*, 17, no. 1 (1994)): 1–11.

**28** Huang and Vaughn, "Support and Confidence," pp. 40–41.

**29** U. S. Department of Justice, *Public Opinion about Crime*, p. 86.

**30** Ibid.

**31** Tuch and Weitzer, "Racial Differences in Attitudes Toward the Police," pp. 647–649.

**32** James Frank, Steven G. Brandl, Francis T. Cullen, and Amy Stichman, "Reassessing the Impact of Race on Citizens' Attitudes Toward the Police: A Research Note," *Justice Quarterly* 13 (June 1996): 321–334.

**33** Stan L. Albrecht and Miles Green, "Attitudes Toward the Police and the Larger Attitude Complex," *Criminology* 15 (May 1977): 67–86.

**34** Egon Bittner, *The Functions of the Police in Urban Society* (Rockville: NIMH, 1970), pp. 36–47.

**35** Abraham Blumberg, *Criminal Justice*, 2d ed. (New York: New Viewpoints, 1979), p. 58.

**36** Arthur Niederhoffer, *Behind the Shield: The Police in Urban Society* (Garden City, N.Y.: Anchor books, 1967), p. 1.

**37** U. S. Department of Justice, *Sourcebook of Criminal Justice Statistics*, 1996, p. 125

**38** James Q. Wilson, *Varieties of Police Behavior* (New York: Atheneum, 1973), p. 28.

**39** William A. Westley, *Violence and the Police* (Cambridge: MIT Press, 1970), p. 93.

**40** Jerome H. Skolnick, *Justice without Trial*, 3d ed. (New York: Macmillan, 1994), pp. 41–68.

**41** W. Eugene Groves and Peter H. Rossi, "Police Perceptions of a Hostile Ghetto: Realism or Projection?" in *Police in Urban Society*, ed. Harlan H. Hahn (Beverly Hills: Sage, 1971), pp. 175–191.

**42** David H. Bayley and Harold Mendelsohn, *Minorities and the Police* (New York: Free Press, 1969), p. 40.

**43** Lawrence W. Sherman, Patrick R. Gartin, and Michael E. Buerger, "Hot Spots of Predatory Crime: Routine Activities and the Criminology of Place," *Criminology* 27 (No. 1, 1989): 27–55.

**44** Bureau of Justice Statistics, *Police Use of Force: Collection of National Data*, (Washington: Government Printing Office, 1997), p. 6.

**45** Albert Reiss, *The Police and the Public* (New Haven: Yale University Press, 1971), p. 63.

**46** Ibid., pp. 50–54; Robert Worden, "The 'Causes' of Police Brutality: Theory and Evidence on Police Use of Force," in *And Justice for All*, eds. W.A. Geller and H. Toch (Washington, Police Executive Research Forum, 1995), p. 44.

**47** John A. Groeger, *Memory and Remembering: Everyday Memory in Context* (New York: Addison-Wesley, 1997), pp. 189–196.

**48** Irving Piliavin and Scott Briar, "Police Encounters with Juveniles," *American Journal of Sociology* 70 (September 1964): 206–214; Donald Black, "The Social Organization of Arrest," in *The Manners and Customs of the Police* (New York: Academic Press, 1980), pp. 85–108.

**49** Skolnick, *Justice without Trial*, pp. 44–47.

**50** U. S. Department of Justice, *Public Opinion about Crime*, p. 164.

**51** Gunnar Myrdal, *An American Dilemma: The Negro Problem and Modern Democracy* (New York: Harper and Brothers, 1944); pp. 536–546 Samuel Walker, " 'A Strange Atmosphere of Consistent Illegality': Myrdal on 'The Police and Other Public Contacts,' " in *An American Dilemma Revisited* ed., O. Clayton, (New York: Russell Sage, Foundation 1996), pp. 226–246.

**52** Wayne R. LaFave, *Arrest* (Boston: Little, Brown, 1965), pp. 110–114.

**53** Guy B. Johnson, "The Negro and Crime," *Annals of the American Academy of Political and Social Science* 217 (September 1941): 93–104.

**54** Philadelphia Police Study Task Force, *Philadelphia and Its Police*, p. 169.

**55** The Knapp Commission, *Report on Police Corruption* (New York: Braziller, 1973), p. 75.

**56** President's Commission on Law Enforcement and Administration of Justice , *The Challenge of Crime in a Free Society* (Washington: Government Printing Office, 1967), p. 99.

**57** David H. Bayley and Harold Mendelsohn, *Minorities and the Police (*New York: Free Press, 1969), p. 109.

**58** Peter B. Bloch, *Equality of Distribution of Police Services—A Case Study of Washington, D.C.* (Washington: Urban Institute, 1974).

**59** Police Executive Research Forum, *Survey of Police Operational and Administrative Practices, 1981* (Washington: PERF, 1981), pp. 606–610.

**60** U. S. Department of Justice, *The Police and Public Opinion* (Washington: Government Printing Office, 1977), pp. 39, 40.

**61** Dunham and Alpert, *"Neighborhood Differences in Attitudes toward Policing,"* pp. 504–523.

**62** James J. Fyfe, "Reducing the Use of Deadly Force: The New York Experience," in U. S. Department of Justice, *Police Use of Deadly Force* (Washington: Government Printing Office, 1978), p. 29.

**63** Gerald Robin, "Justifiable Homicide by Police Officers," *Journal of Criminal Law, Criminology, and Police Science*, 54 (Fall 1963): 225–231.

**64** James J. Fyfe, "Blind Justice: Police Shootings in Memphis," *Journal of Criminal Law and Criminology* 73, no. 2 (1982): 707–722.

**65** *Tennesse v. Garner*, 471 U.S. 1 (1985); William A. Geller and Michael S. Scott, *Deadly Force: What We Know* (Washington: Police Executive Research Forum, 1992)

**66** James J. Fyfe, "Administrative Interventions on Police Shooting Discretion: An Empirical Assessment," *Journal of Criminal Justice* 7 (Winter 1979): 309–323.

**67** Jerry R. Sparger and David J. Giacopassi, "Memphis Revisited: A Reexamination of Police Shootings after the Garner Decision," *Justice Quarterly* 9 (June 1992): 211–225.

**68** Lawrence W. Sherman and Ellen G. Cohn, *Citizens Killed by Big City Police* (Washington: Crime Control Institute, 1986); Geller and Scott, *Deadly Force: What We know*, pp. 147–156.

**69** Samuel Walker, *Taming the System: The Control of Discretion in Criminal Justice, 1950–1990* (New York: Oxford University Press, 1994), pp. 21–53.

**70** William A. Geller and Kevin J. Karales, *Split Second Decisions* (Chicago: Chicago Law Enforcement Study Group, 1981), p. 119.

**71** Skolnick and Fyfe, *Above the Law*.

**72** Carolyn M. Ward, "Policing in the Hyde Park Neighborhood, St. Louis: Racial Bias, Political Pressure, and Community Policing," *Crime, Law, and Social Change* 26 (No.1 1997): 171.

**73** Carl B. Klockars, "A Theory of Excessive Force and Its Control," in *And Justice for All*, eds., Geller and Toch, pp. 11–29.

**74** Kenneth Adams, "Measuring the Prevalence of Police Abuse of Force,: in *And Justice for All*, eds., Geller and Toch, pp. 61–97; Albert Reiss, *The Police and the Public* (New Haven: Yale University Press, 1971), p. 142.

**75** Bureau of Justice Statistics, *Police Use of Force*.

**76** Worden, "The 'Causes' of Police Brutality: in *And Justice for All*, eds., Geller and Toch, p. 52.

**77** Albert Reiss, "Police Brutality—Answers to Key Questions," *Transaction* 5 (July–August 1968): 10–19.

**78** San Jose, Independent Police Auditor, *First Quarterly Report*; New York City, Civilian Complaint Review Board, *Annual Report, 1993*.

**79** Reiss, *The Police and the Public*, p. 151.

**80** Robert Tillman, "The Size of the 'Criminal Population': The Prevalence and Incidence of Adult Arrest," *Criminology* 25 (August 1987): 561–579.

**81** Donald Black, "The Social Organization of Arrest," in *The Manners and Customs of the Police* (New York: Academic Press, 1980), p. 85–108.

**82** Robert Friedrich, "Racial Prejudice and Police Treatment of Blacks," in *Evaluating Alternative Law Enforcement Policies*, eds., R. Baker and F. Meyer (Lexington, Mass.: Lexington Books, 1979), pp. 160–161.

**83** Richard Lundman et al., "Police Control of Juveniles: A Replication," *Journal of Research in Crime and Delinquency* 15 (January 1978): 74–91.

**84** Douglas A. Smith, Christy A. Visher, and Laura A. Davidson, "Equity and Discretionary Justice: The Influence of Race on Police Discretion," *Journal of Criminal Law and Criminology* 75 (Spring 1984): 234–249.

**85** Black, "The Social Organization of Arrest," pp. 95–100.

**86** Irving Piliavin and Scott Briar, "Police Encounters with Juveniles," *American Journal of Sociology* 70 (September 1964): 206–214.

**87** David A. Klinger, "Demeanor or Crime? Why 'Hostile' Citizens Are More Likely to Be Arrested," *Criminology* 32 (No. 3, 1994): 475–493.

**88** David H. Bayley, "The Tactical Choices of Police Patrol Officers," *Journal of Criminal Justice* 14 (No. 1, 1986): 329–348; Stephen Mastrofski and Roger B. Parks, "Improving Observational Studies of Police," *Criminolgy*, 28, no. 3 (1990) 475–496.

**89** Skolnick, *Justice without Trial*, pp. 44–47.

**90** John R. Hepburn, "Race and the Decision to Arrest: An Analysis of Warrants Issued," *Journal of Research in Crime and Delinquency* 15 (1978): 54–73.

**91** Joan Petersilia, *Racial Disparities in the Criminal Justice System* (Santa Monica: Rand, 1983), pp. 20–33.

**92** Bureau of Justice Statistics, *Sourcebook of Criminal Justice Statistics*, 1996, p. 382.

**93** Steven R. Donziger, ed., *The Real War on Crime: the Report of The National Criminal Justice Commission* (New York: Harper, 1996), p. 115.

**94** President's Commission on Law Enforcement and Administration of Justice, *Task Force Report: The Police* (Washington: Government Printing Office, 1967), pp. 183–186.

**95** *Report of the Attorney General's Civil Rights Division on Boston Police Department Practices* (Boston: Attorney General's Office, 1990), p. 60.

**96** John H. Boydstun, *San Diego Field Interrogation: Final Report* (Washington: The Police Foundation, 1975), p. 61.

**97** Browning et. al., "Race and Getting Hassled by the Police: A Research Note."

**98** Skolnick, *The Police and the Urban Ghetto*, (Chicago: American Bar Foundation, 1968).

**99** Christopher Commission, *Report of the Independent Commission on the Los Angeles Police Department* (Los Angeles: The Commission, 1991), p. 74.

**100** Boydstun, *San Diego Field Interrogation Study*, p. 55.

**101** Christopher Commission, *Report of the Independent Commission on the Los Angeles Police Department*, pp. 71–74.

**102** Reiss, *The Police and the Public*, p. 142.

**103** David A. Harris, "Driving While Black," *Journal of Criminal Law and Criminology*, 87 Winter 1997, pp. 544–582.

**104** William J. Chambliss, "Policing the Ghetto Underclass: The Politics of Law and Law Enforcement," *Social Problems* 41 (May 1994): 179.

**105** F. K. Heussenstamm, "Bumper Stickers, and the Cops," *Transaction* 8 (February 1971): 32–33.

**106** Black, *Manners and Customs of the Police*, p. 117; Richard J. Lundman, "Domestic Police–Citizen Encounters," *Journal of Police Science and Administration* 2 (March 1974): 25.

**107** Frank Furstenburg and Charles Wellford, "Calling the Police: The Evaluation of Police Service," *Law and Society Review* 7 (Spring 1973): 402.

**108** Ward, "Policing in the Hyde Park Neighborhood, St. Louis,", p. 169.

**109** U.S. Civil Rights Commission, Tennessee Advisory Committee, *Civic Crisis–Civic Challenge: Police Community Relations in Memphis* (Washington: Government Printing Office, 1978), pp. 1, 88.

**110** Anthony M. Pate and Lorie A. Fridell, *Police Use of Force*, Vol. 1 (Washington: The Police Foundation, 1993), p. 95.

**111** Ibid.

**112** Samuel Walker, "Citizen Perceptions of Police Misconduct and the Complaint Process," *Criminal Justice Review,* 22 (Forthcoming).

**113** Walker, Spohn, and DeLone, *The Color of Justice*, pp. 108–114.

**114** Commission on Accreditation for Law Enforcement Agencies, Standard 31.2.1 in *Standards for Law Enforcement Agencies*, 3d ed. (Fairfax: CALEA, 1994).

**115** Geoffrey P. Alpert, William C. Smith, and Daniel Watters, "Implications of the Rodney King Beating," *Criminal Law Bulletin* 28 (September–October 1992): 477.

**116** National Advisory Commission on Civil Disorders, (Kerner Commission) *Report* (New York: Bantam Books, 1968), chap. 11.

**117** Bureau of Justice Statistics, *Law Enforcement Management and Administrative Statistics*, 1993 (Washington: Government Printing Office, 1995), p. ix.

**118** Samuel Walker and K. B. Turner, A *Decade of Modest Progress* (Omaha: University of Nebraska, 1992).

**119** Merrick J. Bobb, *Five Years Later: A Report to the Los Angeles Police Commission* (Los Angeles: Police Commission, 1996), p. 21.

**120** Walker and Turner, *A Decade of Modest Progress*.

**121** Ibid.

**122** President's Commission on Law Enforcement and Administration of Justice, *Task Force Report: The Police*, p. 165.

**123** Reiss, *The Police and the Public*, p. 168.

**124** Bobb, *Five Years Later*, pp. 23–24.

**125** National Advisory Commission on Civil Disorders, *Report*, p. 315.

**126** Samuel Walker, "Declaration," Filed in Coalition For Economic Equality v. Wilson, 110 F. 3d 1431 (9th Cir.).

**127** James J. Fyfe, "Who Shoots: A Look at Officer Race and Police Shooting," *Journal of Police Science and Administration* 9, No. 4 (1981): 367–382.

**128** Reiss, "Police Brutality—Answers to Key Questons."

**129** San Jose, Independent Police Auditor, *Report*, 1994; New York, Civilian Complaint Review Board, *Annual Report*, 1993).

**130** Stephen Mastrofski, "Police Knowledge of the Patrol Beat as a Performance Measure," in *Understanding Police Agency Performance*, ed., Gordon Whitaker (Washington: Government Printing Office, 1984), pp. 68–70.

**131** "Black Officers Take On the LAPD and Protective League: An Interview with Sgt. Leonard Ross," *Policing by Consent*, October 1995, 8–9.

**132** National Black Police Officers Association, *Police Brutality: How to Stop the Violence* (Washington: NBPOA, nd).

**133** Samuel Walker and Vincent J. Webb, "Public Perceptions of Racial and Minority Employment" Paper American Society of Criminolgy. Annual Meeting, 1997.

**134** Frank, Brandl, Cullen, and Stichman, "Reassessing the Impact of Race on Citizens' Attitudes toward the Police."

**135** Fred A. Klyman and Joanna Kruckenberg, "A National Survey of Police–Community Relations Units," *Journal of Police Science and Administration* 7 (March 1979): 74.

**136** Charles E. Reasons and Bernard A. Wirth, "Police–Community Relations Units: A National Survey," *Journal of Social Issues* 31 (Winter 1975): 27–34.

**137** Ibid.

**138** Jerome Skolnick and David Bayley, *The New Blue Line: Police Innovation in Six American Cities* (New York: Free Press, 1986), pp. 54–70.

**139** Lee P. Brown and Mary Ann Wycoff, "Policing Houston: Reducing Fear and Improving Service," *Crime and Delinquency* 33 (January 1986): 71–89.

**140** President's Commission on Law Enforcement and Administration of Justice, *Field Studies*, 4, Vol. 1, (Washington, Government Printing Office, 1967), p. 58.

**141** U.S. Department of Justice, *Improving Police/Community Relations* (Washington: Government Printing Office, 1973), pp. 3–4.

**142** Scott H. Decker, Russell L. Smith, and Thomas M. Uhlman, "Does Anything Work? An Evaluation of Police Innovations," in *Evaluating Alternative Law Enforcement Policies*, eds. Baker and Meyer pp. 43–54.

**143** Ellen G. Cohn, "The Citizen Police Academy: A Recipe for Improving Police–Community Relations," *Journal of Criminal Justice* 24, no. 3 (1996): 265–271.

**144** Brown and Wycoff, "Policing Houston"; Lawrence W. Sherman et al., *Preventing Crime* (College Park: University of Maryland, 1997), pp. 8–25 to 8–27.

**145** Thomas M. Frost and Magnus J. Seng, "Police Entry Level Curriculum: A Thirty-Year Perspective," *Journal of Police Science and Administration* 12 (September 1984):27.

**146** Terry Eisenberg, *Police–Community Action* (New York: Praeger, 1973).

**147** Bobb, *Five Years Later*, p. 27.

**148** Jerome L. Blakemore, David Barlow, and Deborah L. Padgett, "From the Classroom to the Community: Introducing Process in Police Diversity Training," *Police Studies*, 18, no. 1, (1995): 71–83.

**149** Alpert, Smith, and Watters, "Implications of the Rodney King Beating," p. 477.

**150** Arthur J. Lurigio, Jr., and Dennis P. Rosenbaum, "The Travails of the Detroit Police–Victims Experiment: Assumptions and Important Lessons," *American Journal of Police* 11, no. 3 (1992): 22–23.

**151** Sherman, "After the Riots."

**152** Alpert, Smith, and Watters, "Implications of the Rodney King Beating," p. 477.

**153** Robert Trojanowica and Cynthia J. Lent, eds., *Community Policing: A Survey of Police Departments in the United States* (Washington: National Center for Community Policing, 1994).

# CHAPTER 10

# POLICE CORRUPTION

"For as long as there have been police," Lawrence Sherman observes, "there has been police corruption."[1] Corruption is one of the oldest and most persistent problems in American policing. Historians have found evidence of bribery in the earliest years of colonial America (Chapter 2). Although a number of police departments have successfully reduced corruption in recent years, it persists as a major problem in some departments today. The Mollen Commission found serious corruption in the New York City Police Department in the 1990s. Officer Michael Dowd was on the payroll of drug dealers, earning up to $4,000 in some weeks.[2] Many experts believe that the spread of drugs in the 1980s and 1990s significantly increased the temptations for police officers to become corrupt.[3] In 1991 Detroit Police Chief William Hart was sentenced to 10 years in prison for embezzling $2.6 million from a drug enforcement fund.[4]

This chapter examines the nature of police corruption, the factors that cause it, and strategies for controlling it.

## A DEFINITION OF POLICE CORRUPTION

Herman Goldstein defines police corruption as "acts involving the misuse of authority by a police officer in a manner designed to produce personal gain for himself or for others."[5] The two key elements are (1) misuse of authority and (2) personal gain.

Corruption is only one form of misconduct or deviant behavior by police officers. Barker and Carter's typology of police deviance distinguishes between occupational deviance and abuse of authority. Occupational deviance includes criminal and noncriminal behavior "committed during the course of normal work activities or committed under the guise of the police officer's authority." This includes improper behavior that is not illegal, such as sleeping on the job. Abuse of authority includes an action by a police officer "that tends to injure, insult, trespass upon human dignity . . . and/or violate an inherent legal right" of a citizen.[6] An illegal arrest or use of excessive force is wrong but does not involve any personal gain. Some illegal activity by a police officer, however, is not occupational deviance. A criminal assault on a friend or family member by an off-duty police officer is a private act. Finally, some actions are unwise but not necessarily illegal. Some police departments, for example, do not allow their officers to receive free meals at restaurants. Taking a free meal is a violation of department policy, but not a crime.

Figure 10–1 represents an excerpt from the personnel standards of the Omaha Police Department indicating behavior that is prohibited.

## THE COSTS OF POLICE CORRUPTION

Corruption imposes high costs on the police, the criminal justice system, and society. First, a corrupt act by a police officer is a criminal act. Criminal activity by a police officer undermines the basic integrity of law enforcement.

Second, corruption usually protects other criminal activity. Much corruption involves bribes to protect illegal gambling or narcotics trafficking. Historically, corruption protected gambling syndicates that were the major source of income for organized crime.

**FIGURE 10–1**

PERSONNEL STANDARDS, OMAHA POLICE DIVISION

---

CHAPTER 1: SECTION 18

**Receiving or accepting any fee, reward or gift, of any kind for services rendered, or pretending to be rendered:**

No officer or employee of the Police Department shall expect or accept extra compensation in any form from any person, outside the Police Department, for services rendered as part of his official duties, unless same is approved by the Chief of Police.

No officer or employee shall solicit or accept any form of compensation or gift for the performance of, or failure to perform, an act or service which is part of his official duties. This includes, but is not limited to, accepting or soliciting free or reduced rate meals at restaurants/food establishments, or free or reduced admission into theaters/sporting events.

Any person offering anything of value to an officer or employee as an incentive to influence the action of said employee, shall be brought immediately before a Command Officer for investigation of attempted bribery.

The assurance that any law enforcement officer or employee can carry out his lawfully assigned duties in a fair and impartial manner is based completely on the premise that he is not under obligation to anyone.

*Source:* Omaha Police Department, *Standard Operating Procedure Manual*, p.77.

---

The Mollen Commission found that corrupt New York City police officers were protecting major drug dealers in the city.[7]

Third, police corruption undermines the effectiveness of the criminal justice system. The New York City Commission to Combat Police Corruption argues that "the honesty and integrity of police officers is . . . critical to the workings of the criminal justice system."[8] Officers routinely testify in court, and if they have a reputation for dishonesty their credibility in criminal cases is damaged. In Philadelphia, hundreds of drug convictions have been threatened because of revelations that police officers framed individuals by planting drugs on them and then lying about it.[9]

Fourth, corruption undermines the professionalism of a police department. Effective discipline becomes impossible if supervisors are corrupt and threatened with exposure by officers under their command. Corruption encourages police lying, as officers protect one another. Lying to protect oneself or other officers can then spread to other areas of policing, such as covering up excessive use of force.[10]

Fifth, as former *New York Times* reporter David Burnham argues, corruption is "a secret tax totalling millions of dollars a year" on individual citizens of New York City.[11] In some instances, it is a direct tax, as when corrupt police extract bribes from businesses.

Sixth, corruption undermines public confidence in the police. The belief that a department is corrupt undermines respect for officers and public support for the department as a whole. This has a special impact on police–community relations (see Chapter 9). Illegal vice activities have generally been relegated to low-income and racial-minority neighborhoods. The President's Crime Commission found that minorities are 10 times more likely than whites to believe that police officers are "almost all corrupt."[12]

The Mollen Commission's report on police corruption in New York City addressed the racial, ethnic, and social class aspects as police corruption only indirectly. It noted that the worst examples of corruption and brutality existed "particularly in crime-ridden, drug-infested precincts, often with large minority populations."[13] It did not, however, specifically discuss the point that the officers in these areas probably felt free to engage in rampant corruption and brutality because they perceived the residents to be politically powerless.

On the positive side, public opinion polls consistently indicate that the police rank relatively high compared with other occupations in terms of perceived honesty and integrity. In a 1997 Gallup Poll, for example, the police ranked seventh out of 26 occupations, just ahead of bankers and much higher than lawyers (see Chapter 9, Table 9–2).[14]

The percentage of white Americans rating the honesty and ethical standards of the police as "high" or "very high" rose somewhat between the late 1970s and the early 1990s, but then declined slightly. The ratings by nonwhites remained consistently lower than that of whites, rising and falling over the same period.[15]

## TYPES OF CORRUPTION

Corruption takes many different forms. Some are far more serious than others. For some activities, such as receiving free meals, there is debate over whether they should be defined as corruption. Different corrupt acts have different causes and call for different control strategies.[16]

### Gratuities

The most common form of police corruption involves gratuities: free meals, free dry cleaning, or discounts on other purchases. Some departments prohibit gratuities, whereas others do not. A 1982 survey found that only half of all police departments had written policies mentioning free meals—and not all of those policies clearly prohibited the practice.[17]

Gratuities involve mixed motives on the part of businesspeople. In some cases they represent a sincere effort to thank police officers for doing a dangerous job to protect the community. In other cases, they reflect self-interest: the belief that the presence of police cars near their stores will deter robbers and burglars, or the expectation that the police will return the favor by providing extra patrol coverage in the area.

People who believe that the police should never be allowed to receive gratuities argue that they open the door to more serious forms of corruption.[18] Gratuities encourage officers to believe they are entitled to special privileges and may lead them to demand such privileges. The Knapp Commission, which investigated New York City corruption in the early 1970s, made a distinction between "grass eaters," who passively accept what is offered to them, and "meat eaters," who aggressively demand favors.[19]

**TABLE 10–1**
SURVEY STATEMENTS, QUESTIONS, AND RESPONSES

| Statements | Strongly agree | Agree | Disagree | Strongly disagree |
|---|---|---|---|---|
| It is appropriate for a police officer to accept an occasional free coffee, nonalcoholic drink, or discounted meal when on duty. | 51 (5%) | 549 (59%) | 265 (28%) | 69 (8%) |
| It is appropriate for a police officer to accept free meals in restaurants when off duty. | 10 (1%) | 201 (22%) | 589 (64%) | 122 (13%) |
| It is appropriate for a police officer to accept repairs at no cost to privately owned vehicles. | 1 (0%) | 70 (8%) | 668 (71%) | 191 (21%) |
| It is appropriate for a police officer to show special consideration toward someone who has given him/her one of these favors in the past. | 4 (0%) | 79 (8%) | 608 (66%) | 246 (26%) |

| Questions | Yes | No |
|---|---|---|
| If you ran a small business such as a coffee shop, restaurant, movie theater, or automotive repair shop, would you offer police officers free gifts or discounts on items like coffee, meals, movie tickets, or vehicle repairs? | 334 (37%) | 558 (63%) |
| If you offered these gifts or discounts, and they were accepted, would you expect special consideration by the police in return, such as extra patrol or a warning on a traffic stop instead of a citation? | 242 (26%) | 689 (74%) |

| | Prohibited by the department | Left to the officer's discretion |
|---|---|---|
| Do you think gratuities and favors to police officers should be prohibited by the department or left to the discretion of the officer? | 569 (64%) | 319 (36%) |

*Source:* Mark Jones, "Police Officer Gratuities and Public Opinion," *Police Forum*, 4 (October 1997):9.

A survey of North Carolina residents found very mixed opinions about police accepting gratuities (Table 10–1). Only 36 percent did not believe it was appropriate for a police officer to accept an occasional free coffee, nonalcoholic drink, or discounted meal when on duty. At the same time, however, only 23 percent thought accepting a meal when off duty was appropriate.[20]

## Bribes

Accepting bribes not to enforce the law is a far more serious form of corruption. Some bribes are isolated acts, such as when an officer takes money not to write a traffic ticket. Other bribes are more systematic, particularly regular payoffs to protect a gambling operation. Historically, the most serious police corruption has involved regular payoffs to protect an ongoing illegal activity—gambling, prostitution, after-hours drinking, or narcotics. In New York City, regular payoffs were referred to as "the pad." Police officers "on the pad" in the early 1970s received between $300 and $1,500 a month to protect illegal gambling activities. A Philadelphia bar owner who served drinks after hours paid a total of $800 a month to members of six different units in the Philadelphia Police Department.[21]

Corrupt officers can also be bribed to sell information about criminal investigations, either before or after arrests are made. A tip about an investigation may help gamblers or drug dealers avoid arrest. In the 1950s New York City police officers reportedly took bribes to remove people's cards from the "known gambler" file.[22] Robert Daley reported in 1978 that New York City detectives regularly sold information to defense attorneys about pending cases. Officers took money in exchange for altering their testimony, "forgetting" important points on the witness stand, destroying evidence, or revealing important points about the prosecution's case.[23] A person engaged in a civil lawsuit against someone else may bribe a police officer for damaging information about that person contained in police files. In the past, before bail reform, police officers frequently took kickbacks for referring arrested persons to certain bail bondsmen or defense attorneys.

Some bribes protect illegal activities; others support legitimate businesses. David Burnham found that New York City building contractors regularly paid the police $50 a week to avoid being ticketed for such violations as double parking, blocking streets and sidewalks.[24]

## Theft and Burglary

Theft or burglary by officers on duty is a particularly serious form of corruption. One example involves officers taking money from people arrested for drunkenness. The victim often has a hard time remembering how much money he or she actually had, much less convincing anyone that the officer stole any money. Another example involves officers who steal property, money, or drugs from the police department's property room. In a series of famous scandals in the late 1950s and early 1960s, police officers in Chicago, Denver, and Omaha participated in burglary rings. Some officers patrolled the area to cover for the others who actually committed the burglaries.[25]

Narcotics arrests offer special temptations for theft. Officers making a drug raid usually find large amounts of both money and drugs. As described in *The Prince of the City*, New York City detectives in the late 1960s regularly skimmed off money and drugs, often using the drugs to supply their informants.[26] Twenty years later, the Mollen Commission found that corrupt officers stole drugs, money, and guns from drug dealers. One officer took $32,000 in money and goods in one theft. In some instances, officers arranged for phoney 911 calls that allowed them to enter business premises and steal goods.[27]

## Internal Corruption

In very corrupt departments, promotions or favored assignments must be purchased with bribes. During the 19th century, payment for promotion was so systematic in the New York City Police Department that there was a printed schedule of the "price list" for each rank.[28] The Knapp Commission found a "widespread" pattern of police officers bribing other officers "to gain favorable assignments." It was rumored that a bribe of between $500 to $2,000 could gain assignment as a detective.[29]

## Corruption and Brutality

The Mollen Commission argues that a new form of corruption emerged in the 1980s and 1990s, characterized by a convergence of corruption and brutality. Officers brutally beat drug dealers, stole their drugs and money, and then sold the drugs to other dealers or other officers. Not all corruption involved brutality, and not all brutality in the department was associated with corruption. Nonetheless, the two were closely related. Particularly disturbing was the extent to which officers testified that brutality was their "rite of initiation" into other forms of misconduct: "Once the line was crossed without consequences, it was easier to abuse their authority in other ways, including corruption."[30]

## LEVELS OF CORRUPTION

The level of corruption varies from department to department. In some, corrupt acts involve only an occasional deviant officer. In others, the corruption is systemic through the department. Sherman argues that the relevant question is, "Why are there different kinds and extents of police corruption in different communities, and in the same communities at different points in their history?"[31]

Measuring the level of corruption is extremely difficult. By definition, it is a covert crime. Normally, there is no victim to complain, because the person who offers a bribe is also guilty of a crime. Consequently, no reliable data exist on the extent of police corruption. The available data consist of the revelations of corruption scandals, and the reports of investigations that usually follow major scandals. The exposure of corruption, however, is contingent on a variety of often arbitrary factors (e.g., an especially aggressive news reporter), and the resulting information cannot be regarded as systematic evidence of the problem.[32]

Sherman identified different levels of corruption, using a three-part typology based on "the pervasiveness of corruption, its organization, and the sources of bribes."[33]

• **Type I: Rotten Apples and Rotten Pockets.** The least serious form of corruption exists when it involves only a few police officers acting on their own. The "rotten apple" theory describes a situation where only a few officers are independently engaged in corrupt acts. A "rotten pocket" exists when several corrupt officers cooperate with one another. An example of a rotten pocket is a group of narcotics officers stealing money or drugs during a narcotics raid. The Mollen Commission found corruption centered in crews. In the Thirtieth Precinct, for example, groups of three to five officers worked semi-independently, protecting and assisting each other.[34]

• **Type II:  Pervasive Unorganized Corruption.** Corruption reaches a higher degree of intensity when it has "a majority of personnel who are corrupt, but who have little relationship to each other."[35] Many officers may be taking bribes for not issuing traffic tickets, but the officers are not actively cooperating with one another. Here the corruption is pervasive, but unorganized.

• **Type III:  Pervasive Organized Corruption.** The most serious form of corruption exists at an organized level that penetrates the higher levels of the department. An example is a systematic payoff to protect illegal activities, with the payoff shared among all members of a unit and their supervisors. In his study of one West Coast city, William Chambliss describes how one restaurant owner had to pay $200 a month to the beat officers (the sum was divided up equally among them) and $250 a month to the higher-ranking officers (also divided among several officers). Failure to pay meant that the owner faced frequent citations for building code violations.[36] The Knapp Commission found that in New York City a newly assigned plainclothes detective was not entitled to a share of the payoffs for about two months until he was checked out for reliability. The earnings lost by this delay were made up in the form of two months' "severance pay" when the officer left the division.[37]

## THEORIES OF POLICE CORRUPTION

Theories of police corruption fall into four different categories, depending on whether they focus on the individual officer, the social structure, the nature of police work, or the police organization.

### Individual Officer Explanations

The most popular explanation of police corruption is the so-called rotten-apple theory. It is appealing because it emphasizes the moral failings of one or more individuals, provides convenient scapegoats, and avoids dealing with more difficult issues. It also points in the direction of a simple remedy.

Police officials prefer the rotten apple theory because it allows them to blame a few individuals without having to investigate larger problems in the department. The department can appear to solve the problem by firing the guilty officers. The rotten apple theory also appeals to private citizens, because they can understand personal guilt more easily than complex legal or organizational issues. Further, the theory allows citizens to avoid considering the extent to which police corruption may be rooted in their own preferences for gambling or other illegal activities.

Most experts, however, believe that the rotten apple theory fails to adequately explain most police corruption. It does not account for the long history of corruption or its pervasiveness in certain departments. How could so many "bad" people be concentrated in one organization? Also, it does not explain why some honest people become corrupt. Studies of police recruitment indicate that most people attracted to policing are not morally inferior; they are rather average people, attracted to policing for the same reasons that people choose other careers.[38] Finally, the rotten apple theory does not explain why some police departments have long histories of corruption and others are relatively free of corruption. The Knapp Commission concluded that "the rotten-apple doctrine has in many ways been a basic obstacle to meaningful reform."[39]

### Social Structural Explanations

Most experts explain police corruption in terms of the American social structure. In their view, closely related aspects of the criminal law, cultural conflict, and politics encourage and sustain corruption.[40]

**The Criminal Law.** The criminal law is a major cause of much police corruption. State and federal laws prohibit or seek to regulate many activities that people regard as legitimate recreation or matters of private choice. These include gambling, alcohol and drug consumption, and various sexual practices. The basic problem is a conflict of cultures and lifestyles. Some people believe these activities are immoral and harmful; others believe they are acceptable and not harmful.[41]

Prohibition in the 1920s is an excellent example of the extent to which an industry will arise to provide products or services that have been outlawed. The providers of illegal goods and services have a self-interest in maintaining their enterprises. The profits from these nontaxed enterprises provide sufficient revenue to corrupt the administration of justice—to bribe police, prosecutors, and judges as needed. Police corruption, then, is a routine business expense—an "insurance policy" designed to guarantee continuation of the enterprise. In 1967 the President's Crime Commission estimated that organized crime elements received gross revenues of $50 billion per year from gambling activities. Profits were estimated to be in the range of $6 to $7 billion.[42]

Criminal syndicates have sufficient financial resources to support candidates for political office who, in turn, may use their power to influence the administration of justice including, for example, blocking investigation of certain criminal activities. In 1935, V. O. Key noted a change in the nature of police corruption as the delivery of vice services became more centralized and criminal syndicates took on the characteristics of legitimate big business enterprises.[43]

The law also includes many regulatory ordinances that contribute to police corruption. Laws prohibiting double parking, for example, are designed to facilitate the smooth flow of traffic, but some business owners are afraid the tough enforcement will deny them some customers. There have been payoffs to the police to ignore certain traffic law violations, particularly in cities with congested central business districts.

The example of regulatory ordinances illustrates an important distinction among different types of corruption. Some forms of corruption involve the use of deviant means to further deviant goals. An example is bribery to protect illegal gambling. Other forms of corruption involve deviant means to achieve legitimate goals. An example is a bribe to sustain a profitable business.

William Chambliss emphasizes the intimate connection between the law, the political structure, the police, and criminal activity. "Organized crime," he argues, "becomes not something that exists outside law and government but is instead a creation of them." Chambliss adds that "the people who run the organizations which supply the vices in American cities are members of the business, political, and law enforcement communities—not simply members of a criminal society."[44]

**Cultural Conflict.**  The criminal law is a reflection of the cultural diversity of American society. Different groups have used the law to prohibit behavior that offends their values. Other groups, however, regard the same behavior as legitimate. McMullen argues that conflict over the goals of the legal system is a basic precondition for corruption: "A high level of corruption is the result of a wide divergence among the attitudes, aims, and methods of the government of a country and those of the society in which they operate."[45]

**Local Political Culture.**  The level of corruption in a police department is heavily influenced by the local political culture. Sherman argues that there will be less corruption in "communities with a more public-regarding ethos." Some communities develop traditions of efficient and honest public service; others develop self-serving, or "private-regarding," traditions that encourage corruption.[46] Police corruption persists in New York City and New Orleans because corruption pervades other parts of government. But police corruption has been largely eliminated in other cities where the local political culture emphasizes good government.

The police are not necessarily the passive objects of political influence. In *Scandal and Reform*, Sherman cites the example of Oakland, California, where a reform-minded police chief successfully resisted political influence and succeeded in reducing corruption in the police department and other parts of local government.[47]

The impact of local political culture on policing was first identified by James Q. Wilson in *Varieties of Police Behavior*.[48] Although an important factor, the concept of political culture has not been clearly defined or investigated. It is not clear why some cities and counties have a different political culture, or exactly how it affects law enforcement.

### The Nature of Police Work

Barker argues that the "occupational setting" of police work "provides the police officer with more than ample opportunity for a wide range of deviant activities."[49] Three aspects of police work contribute to police corruption. First, police work exposes officers to many opportunities to be corrupt. The police enforce the law and, inevitably, some people seek to avoid arrest by offering a bribe. Thus, officers face constant temptations from people seeking to corrupt them. Organized crime syndicates, in particular, have enormous financial resources at their disposal. This helps explain why corruption has generally been worst among vice officers. The increase in drug activity in the 1980s, particularly with the advent of crack cocaine, exposed officers to greater temptations than in the past.

Second, policing is low-visibility work.[50] Officers generally work alone or in pairs, with no direct supervision. The risk of being caught is often very low. Detectives work with even less direct supervision than patrol officers. Thus they face the greatest temptations and have the lowest risk of being caught.

Third, the impact of police work on officer attitudes also contributes indirectly to corruption. Herman Goldstein argues that "the average officer—especially in large cities—sees the worst side of humanity. He is exposed to a steady diet of wrongdoing. He becomes intimately familiar with the ways people prey on one another." As a result, officers easily develop a cynical attitude toward people. Constant exposure to wrongdoing can lead to the belief that "everyone does it."[51]

### The Police Subculture

The occupational subculture of policing is a major factor in both creating police corruption, by initiating officers into corrupt activities, and sustaining it, by covering up corrupt activities by other officers.

In his classic study of the police subculture, Westley found that officers were willing to lie to cover up an illegal act by another officer.[52] In a survey of officers in a medium-sized department in the 1970s, Barker found that less than half (44 percent) would "always" report another officer for receiving financial kickbacks, 19 percent would "rarely" report it, and 12 percent would never report it.[53] The Mollen Commission found a very strong "code of silence" in the New York City Police Department. The commission asked one officer, "Were you ever afraid that one of your fellow officers might turn you in?" The officer replied, "Never. . . . Because it was the Blue Wall of Silence. Cops don't tell on cops."[54]

### The Police Organization

Some departments have more corruption than others, and some have succeeded in reducing it. The most important organizational variable is leadership: the quality of management and supervision. Corruption flourishes in departments that tolerate it. Assuming that temptations or "invitations" to corruption are prevalent in all communities, individual officers are more likely to succumb if they believe they won't be caught. In departments where either rotten pockets or pervasive situations of corruption exist, officers are likely to be socialized into corrupt acts by other officers.[55]

The effect of different management styles is illustrated by the examples of departments that successfully reduced or eliminated corruption. William Parker quickly cleaned up a corrupt Los Angeles Police Department after becoming chief in 1950. His management style was extremely authoritarian, but it included no tolerance of corruption. Even his worst critics conceded that the Los Angeles police were honest. During the same period, Chief Wyman Vernon significantly reduced corruption in the Oakland Police Department. Patrick V. Murphy, commissioner of the New York City Police Department (1970–1973), reduced corruption through new anticorruption management policies.[56]

A second organizational variable is the current level of corruption in a department. Peer group pressure is one of the most important factors in both sustaining corruption and turning honest officers into corrupt ones.[57] Peer pressure is particularly strong among police officers. The police subculture puts a high value on loyalty and group solidarity. Officers defend one another in the face of criticism because they expect their colleagues to come to their aid as well. This kind of group solidarity, however, tends to foster lying.[58] In a corrupt department, the new and honest officer encounters strong pressure to participate in corrupt activities. He or she may be ostracized by other officers for refusing to do so.

In departments with little or no corruption, peer pressure works in the opposite direction. Veteran officers teach new recruits that certain things "aren't done here" and this informal pressure helps maintain standards of integrity.

## BECOMING CORRUPT

### The Moral Careers of Individual Officers

With very few exceptions, police officers are honest at the outset of their careers. (The exceptions are those individuals who have prior histories of criminal activity and who are not rejected during recruitment.) The Mollen Commission found that "most corrupt officers start off as honest and idealistic." In fact, "some of the most notoriously corrupt cops in the [New York City] Department were ideal recruits on paper."[59] Officers who do become corrupt typically go through a process involving a series of stages that move from lesser to greater tolerance and/or involvement in corrupt activities. Sherman describes this process as the "moral career" of an officer.[60]

The moral career of a corrupt officer begins with relatively minor gratuities. The officer begins to regard free meals as a normal part of the job. Peer pressure is extremely important in this first stage. The new officer is introduced to corrupt acts by veteran officers. Sherman writes that the "moral experience about accepting these perks usually occurs in the recruit's first days on duty, and the peer pressure to accept them is great."[61] The Mollen Commission found that in New York City the unpunished use of excessive force initiated many officers into patterns of misconduct, including corruption.[62]

At the same time, the officer is under pressure from citizens offering bribes. There are many stories of free meals being forced on police officers even though they are willing to pay.

The second and third stages of becoming corrupt, according to Sherman, involve regulatory offenses: an officer accepts a free drink from a bar owner and allows the bar to remain open after the legal closing hour, or the officer takes a bribe from a driver who has exceeded the speed limit. Peer pressure is important if the officer knows that other officers routinely do the same thing. At this point, the individual officer is still passively accepting such offers.

At some point, the officer becoming corrupt changes from one who only passively accepts gratuities (the "grass eater") into one who aggressively solicits bribes (the "meat eater").[63] Corrupt acts begin to involve more serious violation of the law, become more systematic, and involve larger amounts of money; the officer begins to initiate corrupt acts. The fourth, fifth, and sixth stages in Sherman's hypothetical model involve regular payoffs for the protection of gambling, prostitution, and narcotics trafficking. Sherman points out that "accepting narcotics graft . . . is the most difficult moral experience of all." Officers must adjust their self-image to accept the fact that they are actively assisting the sale and distribution of what they know to be an illegal and destructive drug. At this point the moral career of the officer is complete. The officer has reached the final point of not just accepting, but actively furthering, illegal and harmful activities.

### Corrupting Organizations

Entire organizations become corrupt as they move through similar stages from less serious to more serious corruption. The "moral career" of a department can be viewed as moving through the various stages identified by Sherman. Initially, corruption involves isolated individuals or a few isolated groups. When virtually all officers are engaged in corrupt acts, the second and third stages have been reached. The final stages involve "pervasive organized corruption," in which virtually all officers are engaged in systematic arrangements with criminal elements. A police department becomes progressively corrupt because corruption is not actively combated by the department's leadership.

### CONTROLLING CORRUPTION

Controlling police corruption is extremely difficult. The history of the police indicates that many apparently successful reform efforts have been only temporary. Herman Goldstein observes that "the history of reform provides many illustrations of elaborate attempts to eliminate dishonesty followed by rapid reversion to prior practices."[64] In

---

**SIDEBAR 10–1**

INVESTIGATIONS OF POLICE CORRUPTION, NEW YORK CITY

- 1985—Lexow Commission
- 1913—Curran Commission
- 1932—Seabury Commission
- 1954—Gross Commission
- 1973—Knapp Commission
- 1994—Mollen Commission

*Source:* Frank Anechiarico and James B. Jacobs, *The Pursuit of Absolute Integrity* (Chicago: University of Chicago Press, 1996), p. 157.

---

New York City, for example, there have been corruption scandals followed by special investigations every 20 years since the 1890s (see Sidebar 10–1). Each investigation made recommendations for reform, and yet corruption continued to flourish.

At the same time, however, there are examples of police departments that have successfully reduced or eliminated corruption: Los Angeles and Oakland in the 1950s. Sherman calls the reform of the Oakland Police Department during that period "one of the most lasting of any American police agency."[65]

The control of corruption involves two different tasks. The first is to prevent it from occurring in the first instance. The second is to reduce and eliminate it once it exists. There are two basic approaches to the control of corruption. One involves *internal* approaches, including activities undertaken by a police department itself. The other involves *external* approaches, including agencies outside the department.

## INTERNAL CORRUPTION CONTROL STRATEGIES

There are several components of an effective internal corruption control program.

### The Attitude of the Chief

Experts agree that successful control of corruption begins with the attitude of the chief administrator. The head of the department must make it clear that corruption will not be tolerated. The Mollen Commission argued that "commitment to integrity cannot be just an abstract value. It must be reflected not only in the words, but in the deeds, of the Police Commissioner, the Department's top commanders, and the field supervisors who shape the attitudes of the rank and file."[66] The known examples of successful corruption control all involved strong action by chiefs: William Parker in Los Angeles, Wyman Vernon in Oakland, Clarence Kelley in Kansas City, and Patrick Murphy in New York City.

A police chief faces certain risks in taking a strong public stand against corruption. Open discussion of the subject is an admission of existing or possible wrongdoing. The

---

**SIDEBAR 10–2**

LAW ENFORCEMENT CODE OF ETHICS EXERPT

> I recognize the badge of my office as a symbol of public faith, and I accept it as a public trust to be held so long as I am true to the ethics of police service. I will never engage in acts of corruption or bribery, nor will I condone such acts by other police officers. I will cooperate with all legally authorized agencies and their representatives in the pursuit of justice.

*Source:* O.W. Wilson and Roy C. McLaren, *Police Administration*, 4th ed. (New York: McGraw-Hill, 1977), p.8

Mollen Commission found that anticorruption mechanisms in New York City failed, in part, because department officials did not want any bad publicity. As a result, allegations of corruption were not investigated.[67]

### Rules and Regulations

The second step in a corruption control process involves clearly defining what actions will not be tolerated. One way to draw the line clearly is to develop written policies that specify forbidden acts. The use of written policies, or what is known as administrative rule making, is also used to control police discretion (see Chapter 8) and to achieve police accountability (Chapter 11). Carter and Barker argue that administrative rules on corruption serve six basic purposes. They (1) "inform officers of expected standards of behavior," (2) inform the community about those standards, (3) establish the basis for consistency in police operations, (4) "provide grounds for discipline and counseling of errant officers," (5) "provide standards for officer supervision," and (6) "give direction for officer training."[68] The personnel standards of the Omaha Police Division, indicating prohibited activity, are presented in Figure 10–1.

There is much disagreement over where to draw the line on some issues.[69] Not all law enforcement officials believe that it is necessary or possible to prohibit free meals or other discounts, for example. A Police Foundation survey of Oregon State Police officers found that 62 percent did not think it was proper for officers to accept discounts even if they were offered to other customers, and 20 percent thought it was acceptable.[70]

Other leaders, however, argue that the line must be drawn prohibiting all gratuities. Patrick V. Murphy told his officers, "Except for your paycheck there is no such thing as a clean buck."[71] William Parker in Los Angeles and O. W. Wilson in Chicago believed that even a free cup of coffee compromised the integrity of the police. The argument against all gratuities is premised on the belief that this one small step creates a climate in which successively larger steps become possible. Other experts, however, argue that anticorruption efforts should focus on serious acts of corruption.

A 1982 survey found an inconsistent pattern among departments with respect to written policies. Only half (49 percent) of the departments surveyed had policies that even mentioned free meals. Only 52 percent had policies that mentioned accepting money from lawyers ("kickbacks") for referring clients to them. A total of 61 percent had policies mentioning shaking down criminals for money, and 74 percent had policies that covered accepting money from traffic law violators.[72]

### Managing Anticorruption Investigations

The effective control of corruption requires meaningful investigation of suspected corruption by the department itself. Typically, this is the responsibility of the internal affairs unit (IAU) or Office of Professional Standards (OPS) (see Figure 10–2).

A successful anticorruption effort requires several elements. First, as already noted, it needs the strong backing of the chief executive. The International Association of Chiefs of Police (IACP) recommends that the unit commander "should report directly to or have regular access to the chief," because that person is ultimately responsible for

**FIGURE 10–2**

INTERNAL AFFAIRS UNIT, ST. PETERSBURG POLICE DEPARTMENT

**IV** Internal Affairs Unit Procedures
  **A.** Purpose of the Internal Affairs Unit
    **1.** To conduct complete investigations and to make fair and impartial evaluations of complaints which are made against employees of the department in the following instances:
      **a.** Upon receipt of an allegation or complaint of misconduct against the department or its employees.
      **b.** Any matter as directed by the Chief of Police.
    **2.** To make randam inspections to ensure proper conduct and integrity in the following areas:
      **a.** Property and evidence
      **b.** Cellular phones
      **c.** Bail bond procedures
      **d.** Wrecker service
  **B.** Organizing and Staffing
    **1.** The Internal Affairs Unit shall report directly to the Major of Staff Inspections, who shall report directly to the Chief of Police. The unit will be staffed by such personnel and assigned to such duty hours as directed by the Major of Staff Inspections and approved by the Chief of Police.
    **2.** The Chief of Police will be familiar with the basis for each formal complaint investigated by the Internal Affairs Unit and may become personally involved in an investigation when its severity so warrants, or when, in his judgement, it is appropriate to do so.

*Source:* St. Petersburg Police Department, *Annual Report 1994* (St. Petersburg, FL: City of St. Petersburg, 1994), p. 3.

discipline.[73] The Mollen Commission, however, found that in New York City command officers sent strong messages to investigators that they should not aggressively pursue certain reports of corruption. The most notorious officer in that scandal, Michael Dowd, was in fact arrested on drug charges by suburban Suffolk County police, and not by New York City police.[74]

Second, an IAU needs a sufficient number of personnel to handle the investigative workload. Patrick V. Murphy increased the size of the Internal Affairs Division (IAD) in the New York City Police Department, bringing the ratio of investigators to officers from 1 to 533 line officers, to 1 to 64. Sherman found investigator-to-officer ratios of 1 to 110 and 1 to 216 in two other departments he studied.[75] Murphy also decentralized anticorruption by creating a network of field internal affairs units (FIAUs). Twenty years later, however, the Mollen Commission found that IAD investigated few corruption allegations, and that most cases were delegated to the FIAUs, which were then too overloaded to conduct effective investigations.[76] The problem was not necessarily the structure of the anticorruption effort but the lack of administrative commitment to make it work effectively.

There is disagreement over whether anticorruption efforts should be centralized or decentralized within the department. Most police departments have centralized the management of investigations, with the commander of the IAU reporting directly to the chief. Patrick V. Murphy took a different approach in New York City in the early 1970s, creating a decentralized structure of FIAUs.[77]

Staffing IAUs is a problem in many departments. Police officers generally do not like IAUs, regarding internal affairs officers as "snitches," and do not want the assignment themselves. Interviews with current and former internal affairs officers in one southwestern metropolitan area found many examples of the stigma attached to internal affairs assignments. One officer was told by a friend, "You're crazy, what the hell do you want to work there for?" Another was told "I thought you were better than that."[78]

From the perspective of many officers, internal affairs violates the norms of group solidarity. Also, many officers regard internal affairs investigations as more intrusive than criminal investigations. Under the *Garrity* ruling, an officer can be disciplined and even dismissed for refusing to answer questions by internal affairs (although anything the officer discloses cannot then be used against him in a criminal prosecution). Finally, many officers believe that internal affairs is biased and out to "get" certain officers.[79]

In some departments, because of union contracts, the chief has no choice over who is assigned to the IAU. Common sense suggests that someone who does not want the assignment, or who may have a problematic performance record, is not likely to be an aggressive anticorruption investigator. In other departments the chief has full control over assignment to the IAU, and it is a preferred assignment that is considered a key to promotion.

### Investigative Tactics

The major obstacle facing anticorruption investigations is the same one that all detectives face: obtaining credible evidence. Corruption is a victimless crime with no complaining party. Investigators usually have to initiate investigations on their own. In corrupt departments, the major problem has always been the "blue curtain," the refusal of officers to testify against corrupt officers. Even honest officers are reluctant to inform on their colleagues.

Successful investigations have often relied on a few corrupt officers who decided to cooperate with investigators. In the New York City scandal of the 1970s, officers David Durk, Frank Serpico, and Robert Leuci provided the most important evidence for investigators. These officers did so, however, only at a tremendous personal cost: ostracism within the department and even potential threats against their lives. Robert Daley's book *The Prince of the City* portrays the great personal agony of Detective Leuci as he gradually provided information about officers who were close to him.[80]

Because of the problem of obtaining good information, some departments have resorted to questionable tactics. The New York Civil Liberties Union (NYCLU) criticized the Knapp Commission investigation for using techniques that violated the rights

## FIGURE 10–3

NEW ORLEANS POLICE DEPARTMENT PUBLIC INTEGRITY DIVISION, INTEGRITY TESTS

The Public Integrity Division (PID) implemented a process to ensure that employees of the New Orleans Police Department abide by the rules and procedures established to provide the highest level of protection to the citizens and visitors of New Orleans. The Integrity Test program is a process by which investigators observe employees performing routine law enforcement duties. Two types of tests are utilized: *Directed*, where the test is focused on a specific individual or unit; and *random*, which is not directed toward a specific individual or unit.

Scenarios are set up mimicking situations common to everyday law enforcement duties and officers are summoned to the scene to conduct an investigation. The officer(s) under observation are unaware that they are being tested. Scenarios such as staged auto accidents, found personal property, and information on search warrants have been used.

**Integrity test results, January through June 1997**

- Number of tests conducted:            15
- Number of individual employees tested: 15
- Number of employees passed:           14
- Number of employees failed:            1
- *Attempts:                             2

*Attempts are scenarios enacted, but officers were unable to respond to the scene before the operatives secured from the location.
*Source:* New Orleans Police Department, Public Integrity Division, *Report, 1977* (New Orleans: City of New Orleans, 1997), np.

of police officers: the use of unreliable informers; possible entrapment through the use of undercover officers; and unauthorized electronic eavesdropping. The NYCLU concluded that the Knapp Commission's tactics were a civil liberties "disaster."[81]

### Cracking the "Blue Curtain"

The so-called blue curtain of silence—the refusal of officers to testify against other officers—is one of the major factors protecting police corruption. In Los Angeles and New York City new initiatives have been developed to catch and punish officers who give false testimony. In Los Angeles, the inspector general for the Los Angeles Police Commission launched a new effort in 1997 to identify officers who give "false and misleading testimony" in investigations.[82] The Commission to Combat Police Corruption, established in the wake of the Mollen Commission investigation, reviewed the police department's handling of perjury cases and concluded that "the penalties imposed for lying are insufficient." It recommended that officers be automatically terminated for lying unless there were special circumstances.[83]

### Proactive Integrity Tests

In response to a series of corruption scandals the New Orleans Police Department created a new Public Integrity Division in the mid-1990s. The division began conducting integrity tests of police officers to identify corruption. Figure 10–3 represents excerpts of a report by the division on the conduct of integrity tests.

### Effective Supervision

Standards of integrity also require effective supervision of routine officer behavior. Herman Goldstein comments that "corruption thrives best in poorly run organizations where lines of authority are vague and supervision is minimal."[84] If officers learn from experience that their day-to-day behavior is not being monitored, or that they are not being disciplined for minor neglect of duty, they will conclude that corrupt acts will not be caught. Historically, departments with reputations for pervasive corruption have also had reputations for general inefficiency. The Mollen Commission, however, found that officer Michael Dowd, who eventually was on the payroll of drug dealers, received excellent performance evaluations. One evaluation said that he "has excellent street knowledge . . . is empathetic to the community . . . [and has] good career potential."[85]

Both the IACP and the Justice Department's Police Integrity conference recommend early warning (EW) systems to identify officers with chronic problems. EW systems are designed not just to punish officers, but to "address, and hopefully resolve, problems early in their development."[86]

### Rewarding the Good Officers

Experts on police corruption argue that corruption flourishes because police departments fail to reward the honest officers. As Herman Goldstein points out: "Many competent officers have found that to have reported corruption even once had the effect of permanently impairing their careers."[87] The Mollen Commission argued, "Reforms must focus on making honest officers feel responsible for keeping their fellow officers honest, and ridding themselves of corrupt ones." Unfortunately, it found that honest officers "were often discouraged from doing so." Officers were told not to report corruption, and when they did report corrupt officers the information was ignored.[88]

### Personnel Recruitment

Effective screening of recruits is an important element in controlling corruption. Unfortunately, however, it is not always possible to spot potentially corrupt officers at this stage. The Mollen Commission found that some of the most corrupt officers were ideal recruits in terms of their backgrounds.[89]

The Miami, Florida, and Washington, D.C., police departments have both had major corruption scandals as a result of hiring officers with crime- and drug-related histories. The problem, however, was that both departments were under political pressure to hire more officers to fight crime and did not conduct the normal background checks.[90] The Miami Police Department was ordered to hire 200 new officers, with 80 percent being minority residents of the city. By 1988 more than one-third of the group had been fired, and 12 members of the so-called River Cops had been convicted of crimes including drug dealing and murder.[91]

Background investigations of job applicants are regarded as essential parts of an effective anticorruption effort. Experience indicates that persons with prior arrest records (even without convictions) and particularly people with prior involvement with drugs are extremely high risk in terms of becoming corrupt if employed as police officers.

There is considerable disagreement among police departments over whether applicants should be automatically eliminated on the basis of any prior criminal activity and/or drug involvement. Virtually all agencies refuse to hire anyone with a felony conviction. Only half, however, automatically reject someone with a misdemeanor conviction. About a third reject applicants with a misdemeanor arrest but no conviction.[92]

With respect to drugs, the IACP argues that the ideal standard should be "no prior drug abuse of any kind."[93] However, given the extent of drug usage in contemporary society, maintaining an absolute standard would screen out a very large percentage of applicants. Generally, most departments are willing to hire individuals with some prior drug history, making distinctions between experimentation, use, and abuse. Most departments are willing to accept individuals with some minor usage or experimentation, but not recent and/or heavy use.

Many departments have initiated drug-testing programs to identify both applicants and currently employed officers who are involved with drugs. A 1986 report found that 73 percent of all departments gave drug-screening tests to applicants; 21 percent indicated that they were considering mandatory drug testing for all employees. Of those departments that had some kind of drug-testing program, several tested officers currently in or seeking transfer to "sensitive" assignments (internal affairs, vice, or narcotics units). Officers found to be using drugs were not necessarily dismissed automatically. Many departments indicated that they preferred to offer counseling to the officers.[94]

## EXTERNAL CORRUPTION CONTROL APPROACHES

Once corruption exists in a department, it is extremely difficult to eliminate. Often, the internal mechanisms of control have broken down or, in the case of pervasive corruption, are inadequate to the task. In those situations, external corruption control strategies may be necessary.

### Special Investigations

Because of the difficulties in investigating corruption, special investigating commissions have sometimes been used. The Knapp Commission investigated the New York City police in the early 1970s and the Mollen Commission conducted another investigation in the 1990s.

Special commissions have the advantage of being independent of the police department. On the other hand, outsiders often lack intimate knowledge of the inner, day-to-day workings of the department. Also, external investigations arouse the hostility of the rank and file, aggravating the existing tendency of the police to close ranks and refuse to cooperate.

## Criminal Prosecution

Because police corruption involves violations of criminal law, prosecution under federal or state law is one potential remedy. Criminal offenses include specific corruption-related offenses, theft, possession and sale of narcotics, and perjury. Prosecution on federal charges offer certain advantages over prosecution on state charges. The U.S. attorney's office usually has fewer ties with local criminal justice officials who also may be implicated in corrupt activities.[95]

Criminal prosecution of alleged corruption is in many respects easier than prosecution of excessive force complaints. It is usually easier to prove that, for example, an officer received a bribe and had criminal intent to receive it, than that an officer had criminal intent in beating someone. Nonetheless, there are reasons to question the effectiveness of criminal prosecution, by itself, as a long-term remedy for police corruption. In almost all investigations of corruption in the New York City Police Department officers have been prosecuted and convicted. And yet corruption persists. The lesson appears to be that criminal prosecution can remove individual officers but cannot eliminate the factors that cause corruption.

## Mobilizing Public Opinion

Many experts argue that police corruption flourishes in certain departments because of a local political culture that tolerates it. Controlling corruption, therefore, requires mobilizing public opinion. The media play a major role in shaping public opinion about corruption. The media often expose the existence of corruption and set in motion the reform process. *New York Times* reporter David Burnham, for example, was instrumental in exposing corruption in the New York City Police Department in the 1970s. His front-page article on corruption on April 25, 1970, led to the Knapp Commission investigation.[96] It is worth noting that the *Times* took up the issue only after both the mayor and high ranking officials in the police department had refused to follow up on the allegations brought to them by officers Frank Serpico and David Durk.

Relying on the media has certain limitations, however. Media-generated scandals tend to be short lived. Both the media and the public have very short attention spans, and they quickly turn to other crises. The media also tend to cover the most dramatic aspects of a scandal, usually focusing on individuals who become scapegoats. The underlying causes of corruption are complex and do not offer a dramatic newsworthy event. Finally, scandals tend to produce dramatic responses, such as the removal or transfer of certain officers, that do not necessarily address the underlying problem. Departments often reassign personnel in response to a scandal. Kornblum found that mass transfers in New York City affected honest officers as well as corrupt ones and failed to address the underlying causes of corruption.[97]

## Altering the External Environment

Sherman argues that police departments are not completely at the mercy of the external political environment. He cites Oakland in the 1950s where a reform-minded police chief influenced that environment by threatening to arrest politicians who were involved in gambling and other illegal activities. The threat helped reduce corruption both in the police department and in the city as a whole. The result was a new political environment that was less supportive of corruption.[98]

### The Limits of Anticorruption Efforts

In a provocative book, Frank Anechiarico and James B. Jacobs argue that anticorruption efforts have not only been ineffective but also made government itself ineffective. In their view, rules and regulations designed to prevent corruption limit the capacity of government agencies to be creative and flexible in carrying out their basic missions.[99]

The Anechiarico–Jacobs argument is a provocative one. As they point out, corruption persists in the New York City Police Department despite special investigations every 20 years since the 1890s. Nonetheless, their argument is almost entirely New York specific. Other cities do not have the same level of corruption as New York, and police departments in other cities have successfully reduced corruption.[100]

### The Future of Police Integrity

In 1996 the U.S. Department of Justice sponsored a national symposium on Police Integrity. This first-ever conference focused on the full spectrum of integrity-related issues: corruption, citizen complaints, and both individual and organizational ethics. The symposium resulted in a national plan for research, training, and demonstration projects related to police integrity.[101]

### CONCLUSION

Police corruption remains one of the most serious problems in policing. It not only has a long history, but the current drug problem threatens to make it even worse. Controlling corruption is extremely difficult. Corruption is not simply the result of a few bad apples, but is deeply rooted in the nature of American society and criminal law. Despite these problems, there are some hopeful signs. A few departments have succeeded in reducing or eliminating corruption through effective control techniques.

### NOTES

1 Lawrence W. Sherman, ed., *Police Corruption: A Sociological Perspective* (Garden City, N.Y.: Anchor Books, 1974), p. 1.

2 Mollen Commission to Investigate Allegations of Police Corruption, [Mollen Commission], *Commission Report* (New York: The Mollen Commission, 1994).

3 International Association of Chiefs of Police, *Building Integrity and Reducing Drug Corruption in Police Departments* (Washington: Government Printing Office, 1989).

4 Victor E. Kappeler, Richard D. Sluder, and Geoffrey P. Alpert, *Forces of Deviance: Understanding the Dark Side of Policing* (Prospect Heights, Ill.: Waveland, 1994), P. 23.

5 Herman Goldstein, *Police Corruption: A Perspective on Its Nature and Control* (Washington: The Police Foundation, 1975), p. 3.

6 Thomas Barker and David L. Carter, "A Typology of Police Deviance," in *Police Deviance*, 2d ed., eds. T. Baker and D. L. Carter (Cincinnati: Anderson, 1991), pp. 3–12.

7 Mollen Commission, *Commission Report*.

8 New York City Commission to Combat Police Corruption, *The New York City Police Department's Disciplinary System* (New York: City of New York, 1996), p. 10.

9 "Philadelphia Shaken by Criminal Police Officers," The *New York Times*, August 28, 1995, p. 1.

10 William A. Westley, *Violence and the Police* (Cambridge: MIT Press, 1970), pp. 109–152.

11 David Burnham, "How Police Corruption Is Built into the System —And a Few Ideas for What to Do about It," in *Police Corruption*, ed. Sherman, p. 305.

12 President's Commission on Law Enforcement and Administration of Justice, *The Challenge of Crime in a Free Society* (Washington: Government Printing Office, 1967), p. 99.

13 Mollen Commission, *Commission Report*, p. 45.

14 U.S. Department of Justice, *Sourcebook of Criminal Justice Statistics, 1996* (Washington: Government Printing Office, 1997), p. 125.

15 Goldstein, *Police Corruption*, pp. 16–22.

16 Tom Barker and Robert O. Wells, "Police Administrators' Attitudes toward the Definition and Control of Police Deviance," *Law Enforcement Bulletin*, March 1982, p.11.

17 Richard Kania, "Should We Tell the Police to Say 'Yes' to Gratuities?" *Criminal Justice Ethics* 7, no. 2 (1982): 37–49.

18 Knapp Commission, *Report on Police Corruption* (New York: George Braziller, 1973), p. 4.

19 Mark Jones, "Police Gratuities and Public Opinion," *Police Forum*, October 1997, pp. 6–11.

20 Steven A. Tuch and Ronald Weitzer, "Racial Differences in Attitudes toward the Police," *Public Opinion Quarterly* 61 (Winter 1997): 642–663.

21 Knapp Commission, *Report on Police Corruption*, p. 1.

22 Allan Kornblum, *The Moral Hazards: Police Strategies for Honesty and Ethical Behavior* (Lexington, Mass.: Lexington Books, 1976), p. 54.

23 Robert Daley, *Prince of the City* (Boston: Houghton Mifflin, 1978).

24 David Burnham, "How Police Corruption Is Built into the System," p. 305.

25 Ralph Lee Smith, *The Tarnished Badge* (New York: Thomas Crowell, 1965).

26 Daley, *The Prince of the City*.

27 Mollen Commission, *Commission Report*, pp. 22–31.

28 Jay Stuart Berman, *Police Administration and Progressive Reform: Theodore Roosevelt as Police Commissioner of New York* (New York: Greenwood Press, 1987).

29 Knapp Commission, *Report on Police Corruption*, pp. 3, 167–168.

30 Mollen Commission, *Commission Report*, p. 47.

31 Sherman, ed., *Police Corruption*, p. 3.

32 See the attempt to resolve this problem in Lawrence W. Sherman, *Scandal and Reform* (Berkeley: University of California Press, 1978).

33 Sherman, ed., *Police Corruption*, p. 7.

34 Mollen Commission, *Commission Report*, p. 17.

35 Sherman, ed., *Police Corruption*, p. 9.

36 William Chambliss, "The Police and Organized Vice in a Western City," in *Police Corruption*, ed. Sherman, pp. 153–170.

37 Knapp Commission, *Report on Police Corruption*, p. 74.

38 David H. Bayley and Harold Mendelsohn, *Minorities and the Police* (New York: Free Press, 1969), pp. 1–33.

39 Knapp Commission, *Report on Police Corruption*, p. 7.

40 Goldstein, *Police Corruption*, pp. 32–38.

41  Robert F. Meier and Gilbert Geis, *Victimless Crime?* (Los Angeles: Roxbury, 1997).

42  President's Commission on Law Enforcement and Administration of Justice, *Task Force Report: Organized Crime* (Washington: Government Printing Office, 1967).

43  V. O. Key, "Police Graft," *American Journal of Sociology*, 40 (March 1935): 624–636.

44  Chambliss, "The Police and Organized Vice," p. 154.

45  M. McMullen, "A Theory of Corruption," *Sociological Review* 9 (June 1961): 184–185.

46  Sherman, ed., *Police Corruption*, pp. 16–17.

47  Sherman, *Scandal and Reform*. pp.141–143

48  James Q. Wilson, *Varieties of Police Behavior* (New York: Atheneum, 1973), pp. 233–271.

49  Thomas Barker, "Peer Group Support for Police Occupational Deviance," *Criminology* 15 (November 1977): 353–366.

50  Joseph Goldstein, "Police Discretion Not to Invoke the Criminal Process: Low-Visibility Decisions in the Administration of Justice," *Yale Law Journal* 69, no. 4 (1960): 543–588.

51  Goldstein, *Police Corruption*, p. 25.

52  Westley, *Violence and the Police*.

53  Barker, "Peer Group Support for Police Occupational Deviance."

54  Mollen Commission, *Commission Report*, p. 53.

55  Ibid., pp. 28–30.

56  Sherman, *Scandal and Reform*, pp.146-183.

57  Ellwyn R. Stoddard, "The 'Informal Code' of Police Deviancy: A Group Approach to 'Blue-Coat Crime'," *Journal of Criminal Law, Criminology, and Police Science* 59, no. 2 (1968): 201–222.

58  Westley, *Violence and the Police*.

59  Mollen Commission, *Commission Report*, pp. 5, 20.

60  Lawrence W. Sherman, "Becoming Bent: Moral Careers of Corrupt Policemen," in *Police Corruption*, ed. Sherman, pp. 191–208.

61  Ibid., p. 199.

62  Mollen Commission, *Commission Report*, p. 47.

63  Knapp Commission, *Report on Police Corruption*, p. 4.

64  Goldstein, *Police Corruption*, p. 37.

65  Sherman, *Scandal and Reform*, p. xxxiv.

66  Mollen Commission, *Commission Report*, p. 112.

67  Ibid., pp. 70–109.

68  David L. Carter and Thomas Barker, "Administrative Guidance and Control of Police Officer Behavior: Policies, Procedures, and Rules," in *Police Deviance*, 2d. ed., eds., Barker and Carter, pp. 22–23.

69  Kania, "Should We Tell the Police to Say 'Yes' to Gratuities?", 37.

70  Karen Amendola, *Assessing Law Enforcement Ethics: A Summary Report Based on the Study Conducted with the Oregon Department of State Police* (Washington: The Police Foundation, 1996), p. 12.

71  Goldstein, *Police Corruption*, p. 29.

72  *Law Enforcement Bulletin*, March (1982) p. 11.

73  International Association of Chiefs of Police, *Building Integrity*, P. 68.

74  Mollen Commission, *Commission Report*, p. 91.

75  Lawrence W. Sherman, *Controlling Police Corruption*, (Washington, DC: Government Printing Office, 1978) p. 10.

76  Mollen Commission, *Commission Report*, pp. 85–90.

77  Sherman, *Controlling Police Corruption*, p. 8.

78 Aogan Mulcahy, " 'Headhunter' or 'Real Cop': Identity in the World of Internal Affairs Officers," *Journal of Contemporary Ethnography* 24 (April 1995): 99–130.

79 Ibid. *Garrity v New Jersey*, 385 U.S. 493 (1967).

80 Daley, *Prince of the City.*

81 New York Civil Liberties Union, *Civil Liberties in New York* (New York: NYCLU, 1972), pp. 4–8.

82 Inspector General, *First Annual Report* (Los Angeles: Los Angeles Police Commission, 1997).

83 New York Commission to Combat Police Corruption, *The New York City Police Department's Disciplinary System: How the Department Disciplines Members Who Make False Statements*, pp. 32, 39.

84 Goldstein, *Police Corruption*, p. 42.

85 Mollen Commission, *Commission Report*, p. 81.

86 U.S. Department of Justice, *Police Integrity: Public Service with Honor* (Washington: Government Printing Office, 1997), p. 55.

87 Goldstein, *Police Corruption*, pp. 50–51.

88 Mollen Commission, *Commission Report*, p. 5.

89 Mollen Commission, *Commission Report*, p. 20.

90 "D.C. Police Force Still Paying for Two-Year Hiring Spree," *Washington Post,* August 28, 1994, p. 1.

91 Edwin J. Dellatre, *Character and Cops: Ethics in Policing*, 3d ed. (Washington: American Enterprise Institute, 1996), pp. 8–9.

92 Terry Eisenberg et al., *Police Personnel Practices* (Washington: The Police Foundation, 1973), p. 23.

93 International Association of Chiefs of Police, *Building Integrity* , p. 26.

94 J. Thomas McEwen, Barbara Manili, and Edward Connors, *Employee Drug-Testing Policies in Police Departments* (Washington: Government Printing Office, 1986).

95 Herbert Biegel, "The Investigation and Prosecution of Police Corruption," *Journal of Criminal Law and Criminology*, 65 (June 1974): 135–156.

96 David Burnham, *The Role of the Media in Controlling Corruption* (New York: John Jay College, 1977).

97 Kornblum, *The Moral Hazards*, pp. 58–59.

98 Sherman, *Scandal and Reform*, pp. 140–145.

99 Frank Anechiarico and James B. Jacobs, *The Pursuit of Absolute Integrity* (Chicago: University of Chicago Press, 1996).

100 Samuel Walker, "Author Meets Critics," Comments, American Society of Criminology, Annual Meeting, 1997.

101 U.S. Department of Justice, *Police Integrity.*

# 11

## ACCOUNTABILITY OF THE POLICE

## POLICE ACCOUNTABILITY IN A DEMOCRATIC SOCIETY

A basic principle of a democratic society is that all government agencies, including the police, are accountable to the public. Accountability is defined as having to answer for your conduct.[1] Accountability distinguishes democratic from totalitarian societies. In totalitarian regimes, the police do not have to answer to either the public or the law. They are "lawless" in the sense that they can do whatever they want. As the title of Herman Goldstein's book indicates, the challenge for America is policing a *free* society.[2]

This chapter examines the issue of police accountability. Specifically, it covers the questions of what the police should be accountable for and how accountability should be achieved.

## BASIC ISSUES IN POLICE ACCOUNTABILITY

Police accountability is an extremely complex subject, involving two basic questions. The first question affects substantive issues: *What* should the police be held accountable for? The second question involves procedural issues: What *procedures* are necessary for holding the police accountable?

With respect to the substantive issues, the police should be accountable both for *what* they do and *how* they do it.[3] David Bayley categorizes these issues in terms of effectiveness, efficiency, and rectitude.[4] What police do includes the basic law enforcement responsibilities of law enforcement, order maintenance, and service (see Chapter 1). The police should be held accountable for preventing crime, apprehending criminals, reducing public fear of crime, maintaining order, and providing miscellaneous services to the public. These responsibilities can be measured in terms of whether the police perform them in an effective and an efficient manner. Effectiveness involves the question of whether, in fact, they accomplish their tasks (e.g., Do the police control crime?). Efficiency involves the question of whether they accomplish them in a cost–effective manner (e.g., How many police officers does it take to control crime?).

At the same time, the police are responsible for how they perform their duties. Bayley refers to these as rectitude issues, including: obeying the law, respecting the constitutional rights of citizens, and treating citizens in a respectful and equal manner.

As noted in Chapter 1, the police have many different responsibilities (see Chapter 1, Table 1–1),[5] and that they often conflict. As Skolnick notes in *Justice without Trial*, certain law enforcement tactics can violate standards of due process and the rights of citizens.[6] and can damage police–community relations (see Chapter 9). One of the major challenges of accountability, therefore, is to maintain effectiveness in one area without doing harm in another area.

With respect to the procedural question of how to achieve police accountability, many different officials, agencies, and groups have some control or influence over the police. Government agencies can be classified according to their locus in one of the three branches of government: legislative, judicial, and executive. Other groups play important roles in controlling the police. The most important include the news media, public interest groups (e.g., the NAACP, ACLU), and police unions.[7]

## A Historical Perspective on Accountability

Meaningful accountability of the police is a relatively recent development. Through most of their history, the American police were not accountable at all (see Chapter 2). The 19th century was a time of rampant corruption and inefficiency. Individual officers evaded duty, abused citizens, and were rarely disciplined for improper conduct.[8]

Political influence was the major culprit in creating and sustaining these problems. Politicians were primarily interested in graft, protection of illegal enterprises, and jobs for their friends. Mayors and city council members took no interest in standards of on-the-street police behavior. At the same time, the courts imposed few standards on police behavior. The Supreme Court took a "hands off" attitude toward all components of the criminal justice system. This did not change until the late 1950s and the 1960s, when the Court began to rule on questions of search and seizure, interrogations, and other details of police work. Finally, there were no standards of professionalism among police chiefs in the 19th century. There were no textbooks on police administration, and chiefs were selected on the basis of their political connections rather than on any qualifications.[9]

## SUBSTANTIVE ACCOUNTABILITY ISSUES

### Traditional Issues

Traditionally, the police role has been defined primarily in terms of crime fighting (see Chapter 1). Although police perform many other tasks, public attention focuses on crime control. Consequently, most of the measures of police performance are crime related. The traditional measures include the crime rate, the number of arrests, the clearance rate, and response times.[10] As discussed in Chapter 6, these data are not reliable measures of police performance.

The official Uniform Crime Reports (UCR) crime rate is limited to eight Index crimes and provides no data on several major categories of crime, including white-collar crime, organized crime, and narcotics offenses. For the eight Index crimes, the UCR includes only reported crimes, omitting two-thirds of all crimes that are not reported.[11] Police officers unfound, or refuse to record, an unknown number of crimes reported by citizens.[12] Also, an unknown number of crimes are lost through inefficiency. Because of extreme variations in department practices about recording crimes and maintaining records, the UCR is not a reliable performance measure for comparing different departments.

Official arrest data are unreliable because, as Sherman and Glick found, there are wide variations in police department practices.[13] Some departments complete an official arrest report only when a suspect is booked. Others complete an arrest report whenever a suspect is detained and questioned. Because report practices are not comparable, arrest data are not reliable for comparing the performance of different departments.

The clearance rate, or the percentage of reported crimes solved or cleared by an arrest, is also unreliable as a performance measure. The data are not independently audited, and there are many opportunities for manipulating the data to produce high clearance rates. Officers can unfound reported crimes or improperly count certain crimes as cleared.

Even if the data are reliable, most experts consider the traditional crime-related measures inappropriate for two reasons. First, crime represents only one part of the police role.[14] The traditional approach includes no measures of non-crime-related police activities. A second and more fundamental problem with using the crime rate as a performance measure is that, as many criminologists argue, crime is a product of social factors that are beyond the control of the police. It is not legitimate to hold someone responsible for something he or she cannot control.

Traditionally, there have been no valid or reliable indicators of the *quality* of police services.[15] There are serious limitations with official data on citizen complaints. There are wide variations in complaint rates among police departments and over time. Experts argue that these variations reflect administrative features of complaint procedures rather than the quality of police work. Complaint procedures that are perceived as more open and independent generate more citizen complaints, with the result that doing a better job of receiving complaints tends to make a department look worse.[16]

Complaint data represent only alleged bad behavior by police officers. There have been no measures of good police performance. Other data, such as law suits filed against the police and damage awards paid to plaintiffs, are not reliable measures because they represent only a tiny fraction of all work done by the police.[17]

## New Measures

Advocates of community policing argue that new measures are necessary to correspond to the new role of the police. One of the principal goals of community policing is to improve the quality of life in neighborhoods. Quality of life can be measured in several ways. Citizen surveys, using the standard victimization technique, can assess fear of crime and disorder.[18] Measuring actual disorder is difficult, however, because disorder is a vague concept and perceptions of disorder are highly subjective.

The quality of police services can also be measured through regular citizen surveys. The City Auditor's office in Portland, Oregon, for example, regularly surveys citizens about their perceptions of the quality of the police department. As a measure of the effectiveness of community policing, for example, the survey asks whether people can name the officer assigned to their neighborhood.[19] Another approach is to communicate with citizens who have had contact with the police and ask them to evaluate the responding police officer's performance. The citizen feedback form developed for community policing in the Houston Police Department is in Figure 11–1.[20]

## THE POLITICAL PROCESS AS A MECHANISM
## OF ACCOUNTABILITY

Citizens control the police and other government agencies through the political process.[21] The most direct control is exercised through the executive and legislative branches of government. Elected mayors, appointed city managers, and city council members are authorized to control municipal police departments in various ways.

# HOUSTON POLICE DEPARTMENT

## Calls for Service - Citizen Feedback

**OFFICER INFORMATION**

NAME: _____
                *Last*                         *First*                *MI*

SHIFT: _____ DIST/BEAT: _____ NEIGHBORHOOD: _____

DATE OF CALL: _____ LOCATION OF CALL: _____

### SECTION I - Assessment Criteria

1) He/she was courteous/polite to me.     ☐ AGREE     ☐ DISAGREE

2) He/she was knowledgeable in addressing my problem.     ☐ AGREE     ☐ DISAGREE

3) He/she offered advice on how to address my problems.     ☐ AGREE     ☐ DISAGREE

4) He/she demonstrates concern while attempting to address my problem.     ☐ AGREE     ☐ DISAGREE

5) He/she handled the call in a professional manner.     ☐ AGREE     ☐ DISAGREE

### SECTION II - General Comments

COMPLAINANT'S NAME: _____ SUPERVISOR'S NAME: _____
                                                              *(Employee No.)*

DATE COMPLETED: _____ DATE RECEIVED: _____

**FIGURE 11–1**

---

**SIDEBAR 11–1**

POLITICS AND THE POLICE

In 1993 Rudolph Giuliani was elected mayor of New York City. He ended the police department's community policing program (CPOP) and announced that the police would go "back to basics." He appointed Police Commissioner William Bratton, who adopted zero-tolerance policing. Giuliani and Bratton got into a feud, however, over who should receive credit for the drop in crime in New York City. Mayor Giuliani eventually forced the resignation of Commissioner Bratton.[22]

Did Mayor Giuliani's actions represent a legitimate exercise of control over police department policy, or political interference in policing?

---

Sheriffs are elected directly, and their departments are also governed by county boards of commissioners or supervisors. Governors and state legislators control state law enforcement agencies. Finally the president and the Congress are responsible for federal law enforcement agencies.

The executive branch is responsible for the details of administration. A police chief is responsible for directing and managing police operations, including the supervision of personnel.

The judicial branch of government serves as a check and balance on the legislative branch, ensuring compliance with the law.

A few cities have special commissions to govern their police departments. In the 19th century this approach was very common (see Chapter 2).[23] Only a few survive today, however. The Los Angeles Police Commission, for example, consists of five members, appointed by the mayor, and has full responsibility for running the Los Angeles Police Department.[24] Detroit and San Francisco also have police commissions.[25]

### The Dilemma of Democracy

The basic principles of democratic self-government pose serious dilemmas for police accountability. On the one hand, the people have a basic right to control government agencies through their elected officials. On the other hand, as the history of the police indicates, politics has been associated with the worst aspects of policing: corruption and inefficiency. The basic dilemma is that police professionalism requires a certain amount of independence from direct political interference. Too much independence, however, results in isolation of the police and alienation from the community. The challenge of accountability is to strike a proper balance between political control and professional independence. As a report on the Los Angeles Police Commission concludes, "The challenge is to include public opinion in a sound decision-making process, without being consumed by political byplay inherent in such a process."[26]

**SIDEBAR 11–2**

WHAT ROLE FOR THE LOS ANGELES POLICE COMMISSION?

A Police Foundation report on the Los Angeles Police Commission highlighted the problem of defining the proper role for the commission.

With whose interest at heart should they act? Was the Commission to be a reflection of the mayor, who had the power to appoint [Commission members], a reflection of the citizenry at large, or a reflection of the commissioners' consciences and constituencies? And finally, how was the commission supposed to relate to the department it ostensibly headed?

*Source:* C. A. Novak, *The Years of Controversy: The Los Angeles Police Commission, 1991–1993* (Washington: The Police Foundation, 1995), p. 15.

## Community Control

A radical form of controlling the police through the political process is known as community control. Under this concept, a municipal police department would be divided into separate agencies according to neighborhood, each with its own board of commissioners. A proposal for community control of the police was placed on the ballot in Berkeley, California, in 1971. It called for dividing the city into five districts with independent police forces: two in the African-American communities, one in the student/campus area, and two in the white, middle-class residential neighborhoods. Each police force would be governed by an elected council of 15 members that would choose a police commissioner and develop general policies. Berkeley voters rejected the proposal by a margin of 2 to 1, with both the white and African-American neighborhoods voting against it.[27]

Although community control has never been adopted, the concept illustrates a number of fundamental issues related to accountability. First, as a practical matter, drawing clear-cut community boundaries is probably impossible. Urban neighborhoods are not homogeneous. Even though we commonly refer to the African-American community and the white community, the boundaries between these areas are not clear and are constantly changing.[28]

Second, the Berkeley community control proposal incorrectly assumes that there is a consensus of opinion among people of the same race. Dunham and Alpert found different points of view about police policy *within* racial and ethnic groups as well as *between* groups.[29] African Americans or Hispanics of different social classes or age do not necessarily feel the same way about the police. Some African Americans complain about police harassment, but many others want more police protection, not less.[30]

Third, having separate police departments divided along racial lines creates potential equal protection problems. The residents of one community, for example, may want the police to keep "other" kinds of people out of the neighborhood. This may encourage racial discrimination or unconstitutional "rousting" of people by the police. The

Cincinnati Team Policing Experiment in the 1970s encountered the problem of the tension between decentralized authority and the need for consistent standards enforced through centralized administration.[31] As Chapter 8 pointed out, effective control of police discretion, and the reduction of improper conduct, has been accomplished through administrative rule making, in the form of centralized written policies.[32]

Fourth, as the history of the police in the 19th century illustrates (see Chapter 2), direct political control can contribute to corruption and other misuse of the police for political purposes.[33]

## THE SUPREME COURT AS A MECHANISM OF ACCOUNTABILITY

The judicial branch of government is an indirect part of the political process. Although federal judges are appointed by the president and confirmed by the Senate, thereby ensuring some political control, judicial independence insulates them from direct political influence once they are appointed. Courts at all levels of government play some role in holding the police accountable. At bail settings, preliminary hearings, and trials, local court judges rule on the admissibility of evidence and other issues that impact on police work.[34]

The most important court with respect to police accountability is the U.S. Supreme Court. In the 1960s the Supreme Court issued a series of rulings that imposed new standards for police conduct. The most controversial case was *Mapp v. Ohio* (1961). The Court ruled that the evidence used against Dolree Mapp had been obtained illegally, violating her Fourth Amendment right to protection against "unreasonable searches and seizures." The Court imposed the exclusionary rule, which holds that "all evidence obtained by searches and seizures in violation of the Constitution is, by that same authority, inadmissible in a state court." The Court had previously applied the exclusionary rule to federal criminal proceedings in 1914 (*Weeks v. United States*), and a number of state supreme courts had applied it to state proceedings, including California in 1955 (*People v. Cahan*).[35]

The significant aspect of *Mapp* was that the Supreme Court applied the exclusionary rule to state and local police through the Fourteenth Amendment, which holds that no state may deprive one of its citizens due process of law. Thus, the Court set national standards for all police agencies, and assumed the role of policing local police.[36]

Another controversial case was *Miranda v. Arizona* (1966).[37] The Court ruled that to guarantee the Fifth Amendment right to protection against self-incrimination, the police must advise a suspect of his or her rights. The resulting *Miranda* warning includes the right to remain silent, the right to have an attorney, and the right to have a court-appointed attorney if the suspect cannot afford one. After reviewing police investigation manuals, the Court found that the police used techniques that were coercive and likely to induce people to waive their protection against self-incrimination. It concluded that the atmosphere inside the police station is inherently coercive. Chief Justice Earl Warren ruled that "when an individual is taken into custody or otherwise deprived of his freedom by the authorities in any significant way and is subjected to questioning, the privilege against self-incrimination is jeopardized." The *Miranda* decision incorporated

**FIGURE 11–2**

TEXT OF THE FOURTEENTH AMENDMENT, U.S. CONSTITUTION

---

**Amendment XIV [1868]**

Section 1. All persons born or naturalized in the United States, and subject to the jurisdiction thereof, are citizens of the United States and of the State wherein they reside. No State shall make or enforce any law which shall abridge the privileges or immunities of citizens of the United States; nor shall any State deprive any person of life, liberty, or property, without due process of law; nor deny to any perosn within its jurisdiction the equal protection of the laws.

---

both the Fifth Amendment protection against self-incrimination and the Sixth Amendment right to an attorney with the due process clause of the Fourteenth Amendment, (see Figure 11–2).

## Impact of the Supreme Court Decisions

The Supreme Court decisions on police practices touched off a major political and legal controversy. The police argued that they were being "handcuffed" in their effort to control crime.[38] This argument stimulated much research on the impact of Supreme Court decisions on the police.

Studies have found that the exclusionary rule does not limit the crime-fighting capacity of the police.[39] The rule is largely confined to drug, gambling, and weapons cases, which often raise issues of how the police obtained evidence. The rule has little impact on murder, robbery, rape, or burglary cases. Reviewing criminal cases in Boston, Sheldon Krantz and colleagues found, "Very few motions to suppress evidence are raised, and very few of these are granted."[40] Motions to suppress evidence were raised in only 48 of 512 district court cases (or 9.4 percent), and only 10 of those 48 motions were granted. Thus, the defendant was successful in only 20.8 percent of the motions and 1.9 percent of all cases. A General Accounting Office (GAO) study found that defense attorneys filed motions to suppress evidence in only 11 percent of 2,804 cases. Less than 20 percent of those motions were successful, producing an overall success rate of 2.2 percent.[41]

Paul Cassell and Bret S. Hayman estimated that *Miranda* results in a net loss of convictions in 3.8 percent of all criminal cases. Although critics of the decision, their data do not support their contention that *Miranda* seriously undermines effective law enforcement. In fact, 84 percent of the suspects in the study voluntarily waived their *Miranda* rights.[42] Richard Leo observed interrogations in one West Coast police department (and observed videotapes of interrogations in others) and found that 78 percent of the suspects waived their *Miranda* rights and talked to the police. He also found that in 30 percent of the cases the police lied to the suspect by falsely claiming that they had a confession from a partner or some other incriminating evidence.[43] In short, the specific intent of *Miranda* is widely undermined by both police and suspects.

Milner studied four Wisconsin police departments and found considerable variation in the impact of the *Miranda* decision. Officers in the most professional of the four departments he studied were less hostile to the decision than in the other three less professional departments. The officers in all four departments indicated a high degree of knowledge of the *Miranda* requirements and all indicated that changes had been made as a result of the decision. These changes include use of new methods to gather evidence and improved education and training. The majority of officers in all departments indicated that their jobs had been changed by the *Miranda* requirements.[44]

Supporters of the Supreme Court's decisions on the police argue that they had three positive effects. First, the Court defined basic principles of due process. Second, decisions such as *Mapp* and *Miranda* created penalties for police misconduct (excluding the evidence or the confession). This served as a basic mechanism of accountability. Third, the decisions stimulated police reform, including improvements in recruitment, training, and supervision.[45]

Orfield's interviews with Chicago narcotics officers found several positive effects of the exclusionary rule. The *Mapp* decision led to better training of officers, including closer supervision of warrants by prosecutors. Detectives were also more likely to use warrants than to conduct impulsive warrantless searches. Many officers indicated that the exclusionary rule was a good thing that helped maintain high standards of professionalism.[46]

The Supreme Court decisions also increased public awareness about the details of police procedures. This knowledge, and the consequent tendency to demand one's rights, serves as a constraint on the police, preventing many abuses. Increased awareness of individual rights has also led to higher public expectations about police performance. The Court decisions defined an ideal against which actual performance is measured. By raising public expectations, the decisions generated pressure for continued police reform.

At the same time, there are significant limitations on the role of the Court as a mechanism of accountability. First, the Court cannot supervise day-to-day police operations. It cannot ensure that individual police officers are in fact complying with its decisions.[47] An individual has a remedy only if he or she is arrested and convicted. Second, most police work does not involve an arrest and, therefore, never comes before a court.[48] Third, the police may or may not be informed about current court decisions. Wasby found that small-town police in Massachusetts and Illinois did not receive information of Court decisions in a systematic fashion in the 1970s.[49] Fourth, some critics argue that Court-imposed rules only encourage evasion or lying by police officers. Finally, the exercise of rights may become an empty formality, with little real meaning. Cassell, Hayman, and Leo, for example, found that most suspects waive their right to silence and agree to be interrogated by the police.

## LEGAL REMEDIES FOR POLICE MISCONDUCT

There are a number of other possible legal remedies for police misconduct.[50]

## Civil Damages

A person who believes that he or she has been abused by the police may sue for civil damages under state or federal law. An 1871 federal law (now 42 U.S.C. 1983) provides that a person can sue for damages if he or she has been deprived of any rights by an official acting "under color of law" (that is, in an official capacity). Lawsuits under this law are often referred to as "1983 actions."[51]

The number of successful damage suits against the police has risen dramatically in recent years. The total damages paid by the city of Los Angeles for police-related cases increased from $7,000 in 1965 to $1.5 million in 1975 and $8 million in 1990.[52] The City of Albuquerque paid an average of between $1 and $2 million a year in police-related damage suits in the mid-1990s, despite having a department of only about 900 sworn officers.[53]

The primary purpose of a damage suit is to compensate the victim or victims of police misconduct for the harm done. Lawsuits, however, are expensive, time consuming, difficult to win, and offer a potential remedy only in cases of extreme harm. The potential damage awards in cases of minor misconduct do not make litigation worthwhile. A report on civil litigation related to police misconduct found that, even among those cases where the plaintiff won, the average award was only 10 percent of the initial claim. The median award, in fact, was only $8,000.[54]

Some research suggests that the strategy of suing police departments to achieve general reforms is not successful. Edward Littlejohn's study of police misconduct litigation in Detroit through the 1970s found that suits produced few reforms.[55] A study of 149 police misconduct suits filed in Connecticut between 1970 and 1977 found that they had little apparent effect on the police. The plaintiffs rarely won, because juries tended to be sympathetic to the police, and neither the individual officers nor the department directly bore the financial cost of losing.[56]

Other evidence, however, suggests that in some cases damage suits can result in broader reforms in the police department. A class action suit against the Pittsburgh Police Department, initiated by the American Civil Liberties Union (ACLU) and settled by the U.S. Department of Justice in 1997, resulted in a number of court-ordered reforms. The Pittsburgh Police Department was ordered to develop a completely new personnel records system, to monitor citizen complaints closely, to develop an "early warning" system to identify officers with multiple complaints, along with other changes. The U.S. district court also appointed a monitor to ensure compliance with the order. A similar Justice Department suit against the Steubenville, Ohio, Police Department resulted in a court order similar to the one in Pittsburgh. Under the 1994 Violent Crime Control Act the Justice Department is authorized to bring suits against police departments where there is a "pattern or practice" of violations of citizens' rights.

McCoy argues that rising damage awards involving police abuse provoked a insurance crisis in many cities by the late 1970s and forced them to take steps to curb misconduct.[57] Some cities established risk management offices, responsible for handling all suits against the city. The special counsel to the Los Angeles Sheriffs' Department was hired for the specific purpose of reducing tort claims against the department.[58] In

Portland, Oregon, for example, the risk management office works closely with the police department to provide feedback to the police department about problems that need to be corrected. In Albuquerque, however, the risk management office took no active role in providing feedback to the police department.[59] McCoy argues that city attorneys need to provide feedback to the police department not just in the few cases where large damages are awarded, but in all cases that are filed.[60] The director of the Institute for Liability Management argues that an effective risk management program must include training for all officers, ensuring that officers have copies of department policies, regular training for supervisors, an atmosphere of accountability in the department, constant monitoring of changes in relevant laws, and good legal advice.[61]

### Injunctions

In the case of police practices that systematically violate citizen rights, civil rights groups have sought court injunctions against the police to stop the alleged practice.[62] If, for example, police officers are systematically stopping, questioning, and frisking all African-American males in a community—without regard for individualized sus-picion—members of that group can seek an injunction ordering the practice stopped. For the most part, however, injunctions have not been an effective remedy for police misconduct.[63] In an important case involving the Philadelphia police department (*Rizzo v. Goode*, 1976), the U.S. Supreme Court held that the plaintiffs had failed to prove that the police chief and other city officials were directly responsible for the alleged police misconduct and that the plaintiffs themselves were likely to be the targets of this mis-conduct in the future.[64]

### Criminal Prosecution

Police officers can also be prosecuted for criminal law violations. Prosecution has been used in cases of extreme police corruption (see Chapter 10).

Successful criminal prosecution of a police officer is extremely difficult, however. Except for corruption allegations, it is difficult for prosecutors to prove that the accused officer had criminal intent. This is extremely difficult to prove in cases of police use of force. The officer can always claim that his or her actions were legitimate exercises of police powers under the circumstances. (In such cases, it is important to distinguish between *improper* police action, which can be subject to internal departmental disci-pline, and *illegal* action, where the prosecution must prove criminal intent.)[65] The suc-cessful conviction on federal charges of three Los Angeles police officers involved in the Rodney King beating was a rare exception.[66] Also, local prosecutors work closely with police departments and, therefore, are reluctant to file criminal charges against these departments' officers.

Finally, criminal prosecution *by itself* appears to have limited deterrent effect in departments where other effective controls do not exist. A number of New York City police officers were prosecuted and convicted in the scandals of the 1970s and 1980s, and yet the Mollen Commission found serious criminal law violations in the 1990s.

## INTERNAL MECHANISMS OF POLICE ACCOUNTABILITY

Primary responsibility for holding police officers accountable for their behavior lies with the police department itself.[67] Herman Goldstein argues, "The nature of the police function is such that primary dependence for the control of police conduct must continue to be placed upon internal systems of control."[68] This function is carried out in two different ways. The first and most important involves the routine supervision of officer behavior by higher ranking officers. The second involves the investigation of alleged misconduct. These investigations are carried out by the internal affairs unit (IAU) or the office of professional standards. The responsibilities of IAU include (1) receiving and investigating citizen complaints, and (2) proactively monitoring officer behavior and investigating possible misconduct. (The role of IAU with regard to corruption is examined in Chapter 10.)

Most police experts argue that internal mechanisms of accountability are more likely to be effective than external mechanisms. Department officials have direct, day-to-day contact with police work, and are better able to obtain the facts about particular situations. Police officers, meanwhile, are more likely to understand and respect rules and regulations that are developed by police departments rather than those imposed by external agencies.[69]

At the same time, there is persuasive evidence that many police departments have failed to carry out their responsibilities for effective internal regulation. As noted in Chapter 9, there is widespread public distrust of the handling of citizen complaints by IAU, particularly on the part of racial and ethnic minorities. As noted in Chapter 10, there is a long history of police corruption, and repeated corruption scandals in some departments.

### Routine Supervision

There have traditionally been a number of serious problems with the routine supervision of officer behavior by police departments. First, in many departments, top officials have failed to communicate to supervisors and rank-and-file officers the importance of maintaining high standards of performance. Goldstein and other experts argue that leadership is the crucial element in any effective internal system of accountability.[70]

Second, police departments have failed to develop adequate performance evaluation systems that specify both proper and improper conduct. Some departments have evaluation systems on paper but fail to implement them effectively. A 1972 report on the Dallas Police Department concluded, "In the past, performance evaluation . . . has been a largely meaningless bi-annual exercise in numerically grading employees with little thought to the true purpose of performance evaluation."[71]

Third, most police department accountability systems are almost entirely negative, oriented toward punishing bad behavior. There are few meaningful rewards for good behavior.[72]

The failure of performance evaluations has been documented by the Christopher Commission and the Mollen Commission. The Christopher Commission identified 44 Los Angeles Police Department (LAPD) officers with extremely high rates of citizen complaints. Yet, many of them received excellent performance evaluations. One officer who had been accused of striking a handcuffed suspect with the butt of a shotgun for no apparent reason was evaluated as having an "easy going manner which he used to his best advantage in the field."[73] The Mollen Commission, meanwhile, found that one of the most corrupt and brutal New York City officers, Michael Dowd, received excellent performance evaluations.[74]

### Internal Affairs Units

Internal affairs units (IAU) or Offices of Professional Standards (OPS) are responsible for investigating alleged misconduct by police officers. Investigations are either reactive, in response to citizen complaints or a report filed by a supervisor, or proactive, in response to information that comes to the attention of the unit.

Standard 52.1.2 of the Commission on Accreditation in Law Enforcement (CALEA) accreditation standards, specifies, "A written directive specifies that the position responsible for the internal affairs functions has the authority to report directly to the agency's chief executive officer."[75] The accompanying commentary explains that "the sensitivity and impact of internal affairs matters on the direction and control of an agency require that the agency's chief executive officer receive all pertinent information directly." The Police Executive Research Forum (PERF) model policy argues that an effective method of reviewing complaints about officer misconduct helps achieve three goals: enhancing community support and confidence in the police department, allowing supervisors to monitor police officer conduct and to ensure compliance with policies and procedures; and clarifying the rights of "citizens and officers alike."[76]

Internal affairs units occupy a difficult position with police departments. Because their responsibility is to investigate other officers, they face hostility from the rank and file. Officers assigned to IAU are often regarded as "snitches" for the chief. A study of IAU in a metropolitan area in the southwest quoted an internal affairs (IA) lieutenant as saying, "It's always been the perception of any internal affairs function . . . that they are a bunch of headhunters, and they're headhunters for the police chief."[77] Officers traditionally do not like to serve in IAU. One officer who requested the assignment said that his friends "thought I was nuts."[78] Because of the reluctance of officers to work in IAUs, many departments assign them against their will.

Internal affairs officers frequently encounter serious obstacles when investigating alleged officer misconduct. Studies of the police subculture (see Chapter 13) have found a strong sense of solidarity among officers. An informal but powerful code of silence, often called the blue curtain, emphasizes protecting fellow officers.[79] The Christopher Commission found that the code of silence was a major factor in protecting abuse of force by Los Angeles police officers.[80] The code of silence among police officers is one of the main reasons why civil rights groups have demanded the creation of external forms of citizen review to investigate complaints against the police (see p. 282–284).

Officers in many departments believe that IA investigations are biased, favoring some officers and targeting others. A PERF report on the Omaha Police Department found that "some employees perceive that regulations are selectively enforced and severity of discipline for infractions is inconsistent."[81] The perception of inconsistent discipline has led some departments to adopt a formal discipline matrix, specifying the punishment for each offense and taking into consideration the officer's disciplinary record.[82] These discipline matrices are designed to control discretion and are similar to the sentencing guidelines used by the criminal courts in many states.

The effectiveness of IAUs depends on several factors. Most important are the attitudes and actions of the chief. Goldstein and virtually all experts on the subject agree that the chief must communicate to all officers that misconduct will not be tolerated, and follow up with meaningful discipline against officers who are in fact found guilty.[83]

To be effective, IAUs also need sufficient resources. This is measured in terms of the number of IA investigators per sworn officer. Following the Knapp Commission investigation of corruption in the New York City Police Department in the 1970s, Police Commissioner Patrick V. Murphy increased the ratio of IA investigators to officers from 1 to 533 to 1 to 64.[84]

Training for IA investigators is an important issue. Many departments provide no special training related to investigating citizen complaints or corruption allegations. The PERF evaluation of the Omaha Police Department found that "no formal training is provided, [and] all training is on the job."[85] Most IA officers had prior experience in criminal investigation, however.

The auditor form of citizen review (see p. 283) is a process for monitoring the performance of IAUs and making recommendations for change. The San Jose independent police auditor, for example, recommended changes in the classification of citizen complaints, and developed specific guidelines for investigating use of force incidents.[86] The San Jose auditor and the Portland Police Internal Investigations Auditing Committee (PIIAC) also monitor the tape recordings of complaint investigations. All interviews with complainants and officers by IA are tape recorded. The auditors in these cities review the tapes for the purpose of identifying bias (either against the complainant or in favor of the officer) or inadequate investigations.[87]

## Early Warning Systems

A new mechanism of accountability is the early warning (EW) system. An EW system monitors complaints against police officers and identifies those officers who receive multiple complaints. These officers are then subject to counseling or training. The U.S. Civil Rights Commission recommended the adoption of EW systems in 1981.[88] A 1997 Justice Department report, *Police Integrity*, made a similar recommendation.[89]

Research has found that in nearly every police department, a small group of officers receive a disproportionate share of all citizen complaints. They are referred to as "problem prone" officers. The Christopher Commission identified 44 problem officers in the Los Angeles Police Department. They averaged 7.6 complaints for excessive force or improper tactics, compared with only 0.6 for all other officers.[90] In Kansas City, 2 percent of the officers were responsible for 50 percent of all citizen complaints.[91]

EW systems vary in several respects. In Minneapolis and San Jose, officers who receive three or more complaints in a 12 month period are identified by the system. Miami, however, uses a broader range of indicators that an officer has repeated performance problems, including departmental reprimands, and firearms discharges.[92] (See

**FIGURE 11–3**

EARLY WARNING SYSTEM, MIAMI POLICE DEPARTMENT

**8.1 Policy.** Quality police service requires sensitivity and self-discipline on the part of those providing such service, often under trying circumstances. Absence of these qualities is most often indicated by instances of inappropriate use of force, or by behavior which has resulted in disciplinary action or complaints from citizens. The Early Warning System is designed to identify and monitor such behavior and bring about corrective action through structured supervisory review, with the officer involved, of his/her course of conduct.

**8.2 Organization.** The Early Warning System is mandated by the Chief of Police and is monitored by the Internal Affairs Section.

Source: Miami Police Department, Departmental Order 2, Chapter 8, "Early Warning System."

Figure 11–3.)The intervention also varies. In Portland, Oregon, officers identified by the EW system receive informal counseling from their immediate supervisors. In San Jose, officers have an informal meeting with the chief of police, the head of internal affairs, and his or her immediate supervisor. In Kansas City, officers attend a strategic communication training class.[93]

## CIVILIAN OVERSIGHT OF THE POLICE

Civil rights groups have demanded external review, or citizen oversight of the police, as an alternative to review of complaints by internal affairs. They allege that police departments fail to investigate citizen complaints or discipline officers guilty of misconduct. Reports by the U.S. Civil Rights Commission have consistently found deep distrust of police internal affairs units among racial and ethnic minorities.[94] A Police Foundation study of police use of force found that African Americans are overrepresented among people filing complaints but are less likely than whites to have their complaints sustained.[95]

The first important citizen review procedures, in New York City and Philadelphia, were abolished in the 1960s as a result of pressure from police unions. In the 1970s, however, citizen review revived, and by 1998 there were over 90 procedures in different cities and counties.[96]

### Forms of Citizen Review

Citizen review is designed to provide an independent review of complaints against the police. The basic principle is that people who are not sworn police officers will have some input into the complaint process. This input takes many different forms, and almost no two citizen review procedures are exactly alike. Walker and Bumphus identify four basic forms of citizen review, according the level of the citizen input.[97]

In Class I systems a separate agency investigates citizen complaints and makes a recommendation about disposition to the police chief. Members of these boards are appointed community representatives. The board employs full-time professional staff to investigate complaints. The Minneapolis Civilian Review Authority (CRA) and the San Francisco Office of Citizen Complaints (OCC) are examples of Class I systems.

In Class II systems, complaints are investigated by internal affairs, but the civilian review agency examines the complaint files and makes recommendations regarding discipline. The Kansas City Office of Citizen Complaints (OCC) is an example of a Class II system.

In Class III systems, the police department is responsible for investigating and disposing of citizen complaints. If a complainant is not satisfied with the result, he or she may appeal to the citizen review procedure. Omaha is an example of a Class III system.

Class IV systems are referred to as auditor systems. The police department retains full responsibility for handling citizen complaints. An independent agency, however, has the authority to audit or monitor the performance of the department's internal affairs unit. The Portland, Oregon, Police Internal Investigations Auditing Committee (PIIAC) and the San Jose Independent Police Auditor are examples of Class IV systems.

### The Role of Citizen Review

The basic mission of citizen review is to provide a fair, independent, and unbiased review of complaints against police officers. Advocates of citizen review argue that complaint procedures perceived as independent instill public confidence in the process and result in more complaints. San Francisco, with an independent office of citizen complaints, for example, receives about five times as many complaints as the Los Angeles Police Department.[98] Two factors explain the low rate of complaints in Los Angeles. First, the Christopher Commission found that the LAPD was often hostile to potential complainants.[99] The practice obviously discouraged potential complainants. Second, the LAPD did not make an official record of all complaints. When the department revised its record-keeping system in 1998, the number of complaints increased dramatically.[100]

The more effective citizen review procedures take a broader view of their role and mission.[101] Some engage in an active program of community outreach. The San Francisco Office of Citizen complaints, for example, has regular meetings with community groups in their neighborhoods, explaining the complaint procedure, and hearing citizen views about police problems.[102]

Some citizen review procedures engage in systematic *policy review*, investigating police problems and recommending changes in policy. The San Francisco OCC, for example, developed a new police department policy for handling crowds and demonstrations.[103] The San Diego County Citizens' Law Enforcement Review Board (CLERB) issued 11 policy recommendations in 1993 alone.[104]

The auditor forms of citizen review monitor the activities of IAU and recommend changes where necessary (see above). The Portland auditor, for example, recommended increasing the number of officers assigned to IA in order to reduce the delay in disposing complaints. The San Jose auditor recommended changes in the way the police department recorded complaints.[105]

## Citizen Review: Pro and Con

Opponents of citizen review argue that (1) it intrudes on the professional independence of the police, (2) people who are not police officers are not qualified to review police operations, (3) it is expensive and unnecessarily duplicates the work of IAs, and (4) that IAUs sustain more complaints against police officers.[106]

Advocates of citizen review, on the other hand, argue that it serves to open up police departments, ending the historic isolation from the public. They cite evidence that the number of citizen complaints is higher in cities with some form of external review, suggesting that it enhances public confidence in the complaint process.[107] Hudson's research on the Philadelphia complaints process found that internal affairs sustained a higher percentage of complaints than the external Police Advisory Board, primarily because it generally handled violations of departmental rules, which are inherently easier to sustain than citizen complaints about use of force.[108]

There have been few evaluations of citizen review procedures. Kerstetter and Rasinski found that public confidence in the complaint process did improve with the existence of a citizen review procedure.[109] A Vera Institute study of the New York City Civilian Complaint Review Board (CCRB) found that both complainants and police officers thought it was biased against them.[110] The New York City CCRB is regularly criticized by the New York Civil Liberties Union, the leading advocate of citizen review.[111] An evaluation of the Independent Counsel in Albuquerque, New Mexico, found that it failed to use all the powers it possessed.[112]

In short, some forms of citizen review appear to be relatively more effective than others. Effectiveness depends on several factors, including the agency's definition of its role, its resources, the quality of its staff, and the degree of political support it receives from the community.

## ACCREDITATION

In 1979 the law enforcement professional associations established a formal accreditation system for agencies. Accreditation is a process of professional self-governance that is used by virtually all professions. In law, medicine, education, and other occupations, members of the professions develop and enforce minimum standards for their agencies and for entry into their professions.[113] An accreditation process also exists for correctional agencies.

The Commission on Accreditation for Law Enforcement Agencies (CALEA) originally included representatives from the International Association of Chiefs of Police (IACP), the National Sheriffs' Association (NSA), the National Organization of Black Law Enforcement Executives (NOBLE), and the Police Executive Research Forum (PERF). CALEA published its first set of standards in *Standards for Law Enforcement*

*Agencies* in 1983, and accredited the first police departments in 1984. By early 1998, over 460 agencies had been accredited.

CALEA establishes minimum standards for all law enforcement agencies. Some standards are mandatory; others are recommended, but optional. Some standards are mandatory for large agencies, but not small ones. The third edition of the *Standards*, published in 1994, includes 436 specific standards. Accredited departments are required, for example, to have a written policy on the use of force and the use of deadly force, a system of written directives for all rules and regulations, an affirmative action plan, a system for handling citizen complaints, and so on.[114]

Advocates of accreditation argue that it is an essential aspect of any occupation that aspires to professional status. Self–governance is preferable to regulation and control by external groups because members of the profession know the field best.[115]

Accreditation has serious limits, however. First, it is a voluntary process. No police department suffers any penalty for not being accredited. This is unlike education, where lack of accreditation means that credentials of students may not be accepted by other institutions, and students may face possible ineligibility for federal education funds. Some critics believe that accreditation standards set minimum conditions only—a floor—but do not define standards of excellence, that is, a ceiling. Some critics fear that the "floors" will become the "ceilings." Finally, some critics argue that the accreditation standards address purely formal aspects of administration, without addressing specific content, or what is called the "standard of care" in the medical field.[116]

Relatively few law enforcement agencies have been accredited to date. Only about 460 had been accredited by 1998, representing less than 3 percent of all law enforcement agencies in the United States. Critics argue that the process is too costly and does not produce the needed improvements.[117]

## BLUE-RIBBON COMMISSIONS

Before the accreditation process was developed, minimum standards for law enforcement agencies were frequently set by special blue-ribbon commissions. Commissions of this sort have played a major role in American police history.[118] The most important were the Wickersham Commission (1931), the President's Commission on Law Enforcement and Administration of Justice (1967), the American Bar Association *Standards for Criminal Justice*, and the National Commission on Criminal Justice Standards and Goals (1973) (see Chapter 2).

Blue-ribbon commissions serve several important functions. First, as national-level efforts, they usually bring together the leading experts in the field. The President's Crime Commission sponsored original research in order to gather new data on important issues. Second, they are usually comprehensive in scope, addressing the full range of police issues, and not just a single problem. Third, by reflecting the best thinking in the field, they serve as a reference point for other reform efforts. Courts frequently cite ABA standards and other sets of recommendations in deciding cases. On the other hand, the reports of blue-ribbon commissions are not mandatory, and can be ignored by local officials if they choose to do so.[119]

## THE NEWS MEDIA

The news media also play a role in holding the police accountable.[120] On a day-to-day basis, the media report on what the police are doing. This informs the public and, hopefully, helps them make intelligent political choices related to policing. The media have also been important in exposing serious police problems. The investigation of corruption in the New York City Police Department by the Knapp Commission in the early 1970s was sparked by front-page articles in the *New York Times* by reporter David Burnham.[121]

At the same time, the news media often contribute to police problems. First, they tend to emphasize sensational stories, especially violent crimes or major police misconduct. They do not provide good coverage of routine police activities because these events are not dramatic. Second, the media present a distorted picture of police work by focusing on crime and ignoring the non-crime-related aspects of police work. Third, the media tend to emphasize the negative aspects of policing. They will give considerable coverage to a questionable shooting by a police officer, for example, but not cover the fact that there are long periods with no shootings. One of the unwritten rules of the news media is that good news is not news.

## PUBLIC INTEREST GROUPS

Public interest groups also play an important role in police accountability. For the most part, they have been involved in attacking police misconduct.

The National Association for the Advancement of Colored People (NAACP) has a long record of fighting police use of excessive force against African Americans.[122] The American Civil Liberties Union (ACLU) was responsible for some of the most important Supreme Court cases involving the police. ACLU briefs were the basis for the Court's decisions in the landmark *Mapp* and *Miranda* cases, for example.[123] The ACLU has been the leading advocate of citizen review of the police in New York City, Los Angeles, and many other cities. At the same time, the ACLU has defended the rights of police officers in cases involving, for example, grooming standards and department investigations of alleged police misconduct. The ACLU published a handbook, *The Rights of Police Officers*, outlining the various constitutional rights of sworn officers.[124]

## A MIXED APPROACH TO POLICE ACCOUNTABILITY

No single mechanism is the key to achieving police accountability. Each of the different mechanisms has its strengths and weaknesses. Internal mechanisms are both strong, because they are internal and the officials involved are close to the situation, and weak, because these same officials are too close to the officers they have to monitor. By the same token, external mechanisms are strong because they are independent of the police, but weak because they are remote from the activities they attempt to monitor.

The current approach represents a mix of internal and external mechanisms. In important respects, this reflects the concept of checks and balances, which is one of the fundamental principles of American democracy. Elected officials have significant control over police departments, but not total control. Police administrators have a great deal of autonomy, but not complete autonomy. The courts have some influence over policing, but only in limited areas. Citizens have some input, but not total control over the police.

Viewed from a historical perspective, there has been a shift in the mix of internal and external forms of accountability. Direct political interference in policing declined as a result of the professionalization movement (see Chapter 2). Some other forms of external accountability—particularly the courts and citizen review—have grown in recent decades. At the same time, some forms of internal accountability have also grown, with the development of better mechanisms for the control of misconduct and the supervision of routine police work.

## CONCLUSION

Holding the police accountable to the public for what they do and how they do it is an essential feature of a democratic society. In the past, few meaningful accountability mechanisms existed. The result was widespread inefficiency, abuse of citizens, and corruption. A variety of accountability mechanisms have developed in recent years, representing a mix of internal and external approaches. New measures of police performance are needed, however, to assess the effectiveness of these new mechanisms in improving the quality of policing.

## NOTES

1 Harold E. Pepinsky, "Better Living through Police Discretion," *Law and Contemporary Problems* 47 (Autumn 1984): 250.
2 Herman Goldstein, *Policing a Free Society* (Cambridge, Mass.: Ballinger, 1977).
3 Geoffrey Alpert and Mark H. Moore, "Measuring Police Performance in the New Paradigm of Policing," in Bureau of Justice Statistics, *Performance Measures for the Criminal Justice System* (Washington: Government Printing Office, 1993), pp. 109–142.
4 David H. Bayley, *Police for the Future* (New York: Oxford University Press, 1994), pp. 79–101.
5 American Bar Association, *Standards Relating to the Urban Police Function*, 2d ed. (Boston: Little, Brown, 1980), pp. I-31 to I-32.
6 Jerome H. Skolnick, *Justice without Trial*, 3d ed. (New York: Macmillan, 1994).
7 William A. Geller, ed., *Police Leadership in America: Crisis and Opportunity* (New York: Praeger, 1985), pp. 99–143.
8 Samuel Walker, *Popular Justice: A History of American Criminal Justice*, 2d ed. (New York: Oxford University Press, 1998), pp. 49–79.
9 Samuel Walker, "Historical Roots of the Legal Control of Police Behavior," in *Police Innovation and the Rule of Law*, eds., David Weisburd and Craig Uchida, (New York: Springer, 1991), pp. 32–55.
10 Alpert and Moore, "Measuring Police Performance."

**11** Bureau of Justice Statistics, *Criminal Victimization in the United States, 1994* (Washington: Government Printing Office, 1997).

**12** Donald Black, "Production of Crime Rates," in *The Manners and Customs of the Police* (New York: Academic Press, 1980), pp. 65–84.

**13** Lawrence W. Sherman and Barry D. Glick, *The Quality of Police Arrest Statistics* (Washington: The Police Foundation, 1984).

**14** Goldstein, *Policing a Free Society*, pp. 21–44.

**15** Alpert and Moore, "Measuring Police Performance."

**16** Samuel Walker and Vic W. Bumphus, "The Effectiveness of Civilian Review: Observations on Recent Trends and New Issues Regarding the Civilian Review of the Police," *American Journal of Police* 11, no. 4 (1992): 1–26.

**17** Kenneth Adams, "Measuring the Prevalance of Police Abuse of Force," in *And Justice for All*, eds., W. A. Geller and Hans Toch, (Washington: Police Executive Research Forum, 1995), pp. 61–97.

**18** Bureau of Justice Assistance, *A Police Guide to Surveying Citizens and Their Environment* (Washington: Government Printing Office, 1993).

**19** Portland, Oregon, Police Internal Investigations Auditing Committee, *Report*, 1997.

**20** Mary Ann Wycoff and Timothy N. Oettmeier, *Evaluating Patrol Officer Performance under Community Policing: The Houston Experience* (Washington: Government Printing Office, 1994), p. 26.

**21** Goldstein, "Directing Police Agencies through the Political Process," in *Policing a Free Society*, pp. 131–156.

**22** William Bratton and Peter Knobler, *Turnaround* (New York: Random House, 1998).

**23** Samuel Walker, *A Critical History of Police Reform* (Lexington, Mass.: Lexington Books, 1977), pp. 25–28.

**24** C. A. Novak, *The Years of Controversy: The Los Angeles Police Commission, 1991–1993* (Washington: The Police Foundation, 1995).

**25** Edward Littlejohn, "The Civilian Police Commission: A Deterrent of Police Misconduct," *University of Detroit Journal of Urban Law* 59 (Fall 1981): 5–62.

**26** Novak, *The Years of Controversy*, p. 9.

**27** Jerome Skolnick, "Neighborhood Police," in *Police in America*, eds. Jerome Skolnick and Thomas Gray, (Boston: Little, Brown, 1975), pp. 288–291.

**28** Albert J. Reiss, *The Police and the Public* (New Haven: Yale University Press, 1971), pp. 207–212.

**29** Roger G. Dunham and Geoffrey P. Alpert, "Neighborhood Differences in Attitudes toward Policing: Evidence for a Mixed-Strategy Model of Policing in a Multi-Ethnic Setting," *Journal of Criminal Law and Criminology* 79, no. 2 (1988): 504–523.

**30** U.S. Department of Justice, *The Police and Public Opinion* (Washington: Government Printing Office, 1977), pp. 39–40.

**31** Alfred I. Schwartz and Summer N. Clarren, *The Cincinnati Team Policing Experiment: A Summary Report* (Washington: The Police Foundation, 1977).

**32** Samuel Walker, *Taming the System: The Control of Discretion in Criminal Justice, 1950–1990* (New York: Oxford University Press, 1994).

**33** Walker, *A Critical History of Police Reform*, pp. 3–31.

**34** Herman Goldstein, "Trial Judges and the Police," *Crime and Delinquency* 14 (January 1968): 14–25.

**35** *Mapp v Ohio*, 367 U.S. 643 (1961). *Weeks v. United States*, 232 U.S. 383 (1914) *People v Cahon*, 282, p. 2d 905 (1955).

**36** Walker, "Historical Roots of the Legal Control of Police Behavior."

**37** *Miranda v. Arizona*, 384 U.S. 436 (1966).

**38** Fred Graham, *The Self-Inflicted Wound* (New York: Macmillan 1970).

**39** Samuel Walker, *Sense and Nonsense about Crime*, 4th ed. (Belmont, Calif.: Wadsworth, 1998), pp. 86–92.

**40** Sheldon Krantz et al., *Police Policymaking* (Lexington, Mass.: Lexington Books, 1979).

**41** Controller General of the United States, *Impact of the Exclusionary Rule on Federal Criminal Prosecutions*, Report #GGD–79–45, April 19, 1979.

**42** Paul G. Cassell and Bret S. Hayman, "Police Interrogation in the 1990s: An Empirical Study of the Effects of *Miranda*," *UCLA Law Review* 43 (February 1996): 860.

**43** Richard A. Leo, "Inside the Interrogation Room, " *Journal of Criminal Law and Crimnology* 86, no. 2 (1996): 266–303.

**44** Neal Milner, *The Court and Local Law Enforcement* (Beverly Hills: Sage, 1971).

**45** Walker, "Historical Roots of the Legal Control of Police Behavior."

**46** Myron W. Orfield, Jr., "the Exclusionary Rule and Deterrence: An Empirical Study of Chicago Narcotics Officers," *University of Chicago Law Review* 54 (Summer 1987): 1016–1055.

**47** Carl McGowan, "Rulemaking and the Police," *Michigan Law Review* 70 (March 1972): 659–694.

**48** Goldstein, "Administrative Problems in Controlling the Exercise of Police Authority," p. 168.

**49** Stephen Wasby, *Small-Town Police and the Supreme Court* (Lexington, Mass.: Lexington Books, 1976).

**50** The best overview is still Monrad G. Paulson et al., "Securing Police Compliance with Constitutional Limitations," in National Commission on the Causes and Prevention of Violence, *Law and Order Reconsidered* (New York: Bantam Books, 1970), chap. 17.

**51** Michael Avery, David Rudovsky, and Karen Blum, *Police Misconduct: Law and Litigation*, 3d ed. (St. Paul: West, 1997).

**52** *New York Times*, March 15, 1991, p. 1.

**53** Samuel Walker and Eileen Luna, *An Evaluation of the Oversight Mechanisms of the Albuquerque Police Department* (Albuquerque: City Council, 1997), pp. 104–113.

**54** Charldean Newell, Janay Pollock, and Jerry Tweedy, "Financial Aspects of Police Liability," *ICMA Baseline Data Report* 24 (March–April 1992): 1–8.

**55** Edward J. Littlejohn, "Civil Liability and the Police Officer: The Need for New Deterrents to Police Misconduct," *University of Detroit Journal of Urban Law* 58 (1981): 365–431.

**56** "Project: Suing the Police in Federal Court," *Yale Law Journal* 88 (Spring 1979): 781–824.

**57** Candace McCoy, "Lawsuits against Police: What Impact Do They Really Have*?*" *Criminal Law Bulletin* 20 (January–February 1984): 53.

**58** Special Counsel, Los Angeles County, *6th Semiannual Report*, 1996, pp. 33–39.

**59** Walker and Luna, *An Evaluation of the Oversight Mechanisms of the Albuquerque Police Department*, pp. 104–113.

**60** McCoy, "Lawsuits against Police."

**61** Cited in Newell, Pollock, and Tweedy, "Financial Aspects of Police Liability," p. 8.

**62** Avery, Rudovsky, and Blum, *Police Misconduct*, chap. 15.

**63** Paulson, et al. "Securing Police Compliance," pp. 402–405.

**64** *Rizzo v. Goode*, 423 U.S. 362 (1976)

**65** Goldstein, "Administrative Problems in Controlling the Exercise of Police Authority," p. 162.

**66** Jerome Skolnick and James J. Fyfe, *Above the Law* (New York: Free Press, 1993).

**67** Goldstein, "Controlling and Reviewing Police–Citizen Contacts," in *Policing a Free Society*, pp. 157–186.

**68** Goldstein, "Administrative Problems in Controlling the Exercise of Police Authority," p. 171.

**69** Ibid.

**70** Goldstein, *Policing a Free Society*, pp. 225–256.

**71** Quoted in Wycoff and Oettmeier, *Evaluating Patrol Officer Performance under Community Policing*, p. 1.

**72** Goldstein, *Policing a Free Society*, p. 168. [Mollen Commission], Commission to Investigate Allegations of Police Corruption, *Commission Report* (New York: The Mollen Commission, 1994), p. 5.

**73** Christopher Commission, *Report of the Independent Commission to Investigate the Los Angeles Police Department* (Los Angeles: The Commission, 1991), p. 43.

**74** Mollen Commission, *Report*, p. 81.

**75** Commission on Accreditation for Law Enforcement Agencies, Standard 52.1.2 in *Standards for Law Enforcement Agencies*, 3d ed., Fairfax, Va.: CALEA, 1994)

**76** Police Executive Research Forum, *Police Agency Handling of Officer Misconduct: A Model Policy Statement* (Washington: PERF, 1981).

**77** Aogan Mulcahy, "'Headhunter' or 'Real Cop'? Identity in the World of Internal Affairs Officers," *Journal of Contemporary Ethnography* 24 (April 1995): 106.

**78** Ibid., p. 108.

**79** William A. Westley, *Violence and the Police* (Cambridge: MIT Press, 1970), pp. 109–152, Lawrence W. Sherman, "The Breakdown of the Police Code of Silence," *Criminal Law Bulletin* 14 (March–April 1978): 149–153.

**80** Christopher Commission, *Report of the Independent Commission*, pp. 168–171.

**81** Police Executive Research Forum, *Organizational Evaluation of the Omaha Police Division* (Omaha: City of Omaha, 1992), p. 72.

**82** Walker and Luna, *An Evaluation of the Oversight Mechanisms of the Albuquerque Police Department*, pp. 71–103.

**83** Herman Goldstein, *Police Corruption* (Washington: The Police Foundation, 1975), pp. 40–41.

**84** Lawrence W. Sherman, *Controlling Police Corruption* (Washington: Government Printing Office, 1978), p. 10.

**85** Police Executive Research Forum, *Organizational Evaluation of the Omaha Police Division*, p. 75.

**86** San Jose Independent Police Auditor, *First Quarterly Report* (San Jose, Calif: City of San Jose, 1994), pp. 8–13.

**87** Interviews, San Jose Independent Police Auditor, 1997; Portland, Oregon, Police Internal Investigations Auditing Committee 1992.

**88** U. S. Civil Rights Commission, *Who Is Guarding the Guardians?* (Washington: Government Printing Office, 1981), p. 159.

**89** U.S. Department of Justice, *Police Integrity* (Washington: Government Printing Office, 1997), p. 55.

**90** Christopher Commission, *Report of the Independent Commission on the Los Angeles Police* (Los Angeles: The Christopher Commission, 1991), pp. 39–48.

**91** "Kansas City Police Go After Their 'Bad boys,'" The *New York Times*, September 10, 1991, p. 1.

**92** Miami Police Department, "Early Warning System," Departmental Order #2, chap. 8.

**93** San Jose Independent Police Auditor, *First Quarterly Report*; Kansas City Police Department, personal communication with author, 1997.

**94** U.S. Civil Rights Commission, *Who Is Guarding the Guardians?*, pp. 50–58.

**95** Anthony M. Pate and Lorie A. Fridell, *Police Use of Force*, vol. 1 (Washington: The Police Foundation, 1993), pp. 95, 103.

**96** Samuel Walker, *Citizen Review of the Police: 1998 Update* (Omaha: University of Nebraska, 1998).

**97** Samuel Walker and Vic W. Bumphus, *Citizen Review of the Police*, 1991 (Omaha: University of Nebraska, 1992).

**98** Anthony M. Pate and Edwin E. Hamilton, *The Big Six* (Washington: The Police Foundation, 1991), p. 144.

**99** Christopher Commission, *Report of the Independent Commission*, pp. 158–9.

**100** Interview, Inspector General for the Los Angeles Police Commission, March, 1998.

**101** Samuel Walker and Betsy Kreisel, "The Varieties of Citizen Review: The Implications of Organizational Features of Complaint Review Procedures for Accountability of the Police," *American Journal of Police* 15, no. 3 (1996): 65–68.

**102** San Francisco, Office of Citizen Complaints, *Annual Report*, 1997 (San Francisco: OCC, 1997).

**103** San Francisco Police Department, General Order 8.03, August 3, 1994.

**104** San Diego County, Citizens' Law Enforcement Review Board, *1993 Annual Report* (San Diego: CLERB, 1994).

**105** Portland, Oregon, Police Internal Investigations Auditing Committee, *Report*, 1997. San Jose Independent Police Auditor, *First Quarterly Report*.

**106** Americans for Effective Law Enforcement, *Police Civilian Review Boards AELE Defense Manual,* Brief 82–3 (San Francisco: AELE, 1982). Douglas Perez, *Common Sense about Police Review* (Philadelphia: Temple University Press, 1994).

**107** Walker and Bumphus, "The Effectiveness of Civilian Review."

**108** James R. Hudson, "Organizational Aspects of Internal and External Review of the Police," *Journal of Criminal Law, Criminology, and Police Science* 63 (September 1972): 427–432.

**109** Wayne A. Kerstetter and Kenneth A. Rasinski, "Opening a Window into Police Internal Affairs: Impact of Procedural Justice Reform on Third-Party Attitudes," *Social Justice Research* 7, no. 2 (1994): 107–127.

**110** Michele Sviridoff and James E. McElroy, *Processing Complaints against Police in New York City* (New York: Vera Institute of Justice, 1989).

**111** New York Civil Liberties Union, *A Third Anniversary Overview of the Civilian Complaint Review Board*, July 5, 1993–July 5, 1996 (New York: NYCLU, 1996).

**112** Walker and Luna, *An Evaluation of the Oversight Mechanisms of the Albuquerque Police Department*, pp. 34–54.

**113** Wilbert E. Moore, *The Professions: Roles and Rules* (New York: Russell Foundation Sage, 1970), pp. 109–130.

**114** Commission on Accreditation for Law Enforcement Agencies, *Standards for Law Enforcement Agencies*

**115** Jack Pearson, "National Accreditation: A Valuable Management Tool," in *Police Management Today*, ed. James J. Fyfe, (Washington: ICMA, 1985), pp. 45–48.

**116** James J. Fyfe, comments to author.

**117** W. E. Eastman, "National Accreditation: A Costly, Unneeded Make-Work Scheme," in *Police Management Today*, ed., Fyfe, pp. 49–54.

**118** Walker, *Popular Justice*, pp. 154–157, 202–208.

**119** Samuel Walker, "Setting the Standards: The Efforts and Impacts of Blue-Ribbon Commissions on the Police," in *Police Leadership in America: Crisis and Opportunity*, ed. W. A. Geller (New York: Praeger, 1985), pp. 354–370.

**120** See the contributions in "The Chief and the Media," Part III, in *Police Leadership in America: Crisis and Opportunity*, ed. W. A. Geller, pp. 99–146.

**121** David Burnham, *The Role of the Media in Controlling Corruption* (New York; John Jay College, 1977).

**122** National Association for the Advancement of Colored People, *Beyond the Rodney King Story: An Investigation of Police Misconduct in Minority Communities* (Boston: Northeastern University Press, 1995).

**123** Samuel Walker, *In Defense of American Liberties: A History of the ACLU* (New York: Oxford University Press, 1990), pp. 246–252.

**124** Gilda Brancato annd Eliot E. Polebaum, *The Rights of Police Officers* (New York; Avon Books, 1981).

# PART FOUR

# OFFICERS AND ORGANIZATIONS

# POLICE OFFICERS I:
# ENTERING POLICE WORK

## THE CHANGING AMERICAN POLICE OFFICER

The profile of the American police officer has changed dramatically over the past 25 years. The typical officer today is better educated, better trained, and more representative of the community he or she serves than ever before. Educational levels have risen; training programs have improved; and there are more African-American, Hispanic, and women police officers (see Figure 12–1).

This chapter approaches policing from the perspective of occupational sociology. It examines policing in terms of the kinds of people who are recruited into police work, how different factors influence that selection process, and what happens to officers once they are hired. It attempts to explain how these different factors influence the attitudes and behavior of police officers on the job.

### A Career Perspective

It is important to look at police personnel from a career perspective, examining officers' progress from recruitment to retirement. Too often discussions of police personnel focus only on recruitment, and on particular requirements such as education. The quality of policing, however, is affected by a series of policies and procedures at each stage of officers' careers. Good policies at one stage can be offset by poor practices at another. A department might, for example, recruit outstanding individuals but then fail to train them adequately. Or it might do an excellent job of recruiting and training but lose the best officers because of poor management practices. Failure to adequately reward officers for good performance may lead to cynicism, burnout, and reduced levels of effort by senior officers.

### Beyond Stereotypes of Cops

The public image of policing is heavily influenced by stereotypes about police officers: who they are, what they believe, and how they act. These stereotypes fall into two categories. On the one side, a negative stereotype views officers as uneducated, untrained, prejudiced, brutal, and corrupt. On the other side, a positive stereotype views them as heroic saints, risking their lives in the face of hostility from the public, the media, and the courts. Arthur Niederhoffer characterized the police officer as "a 'Rorschach' in uniform. . . . To people in trouble the police officer is a savior," but to others he is "a fierce ogre."[1]

Neither stereotype is accurate. As Bayley and Mendelsohn concluded in their study of police–community relations in Denver, the average police officer is a rather average person in terms of values and political beliefs, although a little more conservative than the population as a whole.[2] Studies of the police have found a distinct subculture among officers, with its own set of values and habits. The police subculture is primarily a product of the special working conditions of policing.[3] It is discussed in detail in Chapter 13.

### The Personnel Process: A Shared Responsibility

Personnel decisions in policing are a shared responsibility. Police departments control some of the decisions, but other government agencies, such as the civil service system

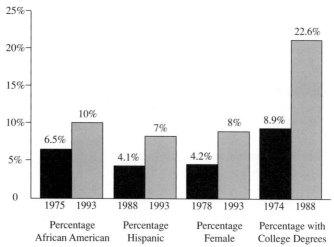

**FIGURE 12–1**
THE CHANGING PROFILE OF THE AMERICAN POLICE OFFICER

or the city personnel department, control other decisions. A police chief, for example, cannot unilaterally change recruitment standards (such as requiring all recruits to have a college degree).

Typically, the civil service agency has the responsibility for (1) developing job descriptions; (2) establishing the minimum standards required for each position; (3) developing tests for each position; (4) announcing job openings; (5) conducting some, but not all, of the tests; and (6) certifying a list of persons to be hired or promoted. Police departments generally (1) advise the civil service agency on job descriptions, requirements, and tests; (2) conduct some of the recruiting; and (3) administer some of the tests.[4] Civil service systems are discussed in more detail in Chapter 14.

## RECRUITMENT

Recruitment is the process of attracting a pool of applicants. It includes three separate elements: (1) the minimum standards established by an agency, (2) the recruitment effort, and (3) the applicant's decision to apply for a position.

### Minimum Qualifications

**Age**  Most law enforcement agencies require that all applicants be at least 21 years old. Younger persons are considered not mature enough for the responsibilities of police work. Some departments have recently raised the minimum age level, on the grounds that many 21–year–olds are not mature enough for the difficult decisions that police work requires.

Most departments used to have maximum age limits for recruits, typically setting 35 as the upper limit. These limits were primarily designed to reduce financial strains on pension systems by officers who would retire after fewer years on the job than younger officers. Federal law banning age discrimination has forced most departments to eliminate these limits, however. In 1994 only 12 percent of all big city departments had a maximum age limit for new officers.[5]

**Height and Weight**   Height and weight requirements have changed dramatically. Thirty years ago, nearly all police departments (85 percent) required officers to be at least 5 foot 8 inches tall.[6] This requirement reflected the old stereotype that police work frequently involved physical confrontations with suspects, and the assumption that officers needed to be physically imposing in order to gain the respect of citizens. As discussed in Chapters 4 and 6, however, police work rarely involves physical confrontations, citizens generally comply with officers' requests, and communication skills and good judgment are considered more important for police work than physical strength.[7]

The old height requirements were challenged in lawsuits arguing that they discriminated against both women and Hispanic applicants. Only a handful of big-city departments still had minimum height requirements by 1994.[8] Departments today require that weight be proportional to height.

**Education**   The vast majority of police departments (86 percent) require only a high school education or the equivalent. Only 1 percent require a four–year college degree and 12 percent require at least some college.[9] Minimum requirements, however, do not reflect actual hiring practices. Many departments select applicants with more than the minimum level of education. The average recruit in the San Diego Police Department in the late 1980s had two years of college, despite the fact that there was no formal college education requirement.[10] Susan Martin found that both male and female recruits in Birmingham and Detroit averaged about two years of college.[11] By 1988, 65.2 percent of all sworn officers had some college education, and 22.6 percent had undergraduate or graduate degrees.[12]

The increase in the educational levels of police officers is due in part to the growth of criminal justice education programs. Between 1968 and 1976 the federal Law Enforcement Education Program (LEEP) provided scholarships and loans to criminal justice personnel enrolled in "law enforcement related" college programs.[13] LEEP and other programs operated by the Law Enforcement Assistance Administration (1968–1976) supported the growth of criminal justice programs at colleges and universities, which now provide a large supply of graduates.

Some people argue that all police officers should have a college degree.[14] In 1967 the President's Crime Commission recommended, "The ultimate aim of all police depart-

---

**POLICE ON THE WEB**

Check out the web sites of some police departments. What minimum standards are required? Are there any departments with notably higher or lower standards than others? Are there any consistent patterns in these differences, by region or size of department?

ments should be that all personnel with general enforcement powers have baccalaureate degrees."[15] According to Worden, advocates of the college education requirement argue that it is likely to contribute to improved policing in three ways. First, higher education will shape the values of students and make them better appreciate the role of the police in a democratic society. Second, it will improve on–the–street performance directly by giving them the resources to make better judgments. Third, education itself may not have any direct effect, but the requirement will select out people who differ in better ways from those who do not go to college.[16] Others point out that police officers need to be able to deal with the complex and constantly changing laws of criminal procedure, and that the police need to raise their requirements to keep pace with rising levels of education in society. Between 1960 and 1996 the percentage of adults completing high school doubled, from 41 to 82 percent, and the percentage graduating from college tripled, from 7.7 to 23.6 percent.[17] Finally, community policing and problem–oriented policing place new responsibilities on rank-and-file officers, asking them to be planners and problem–solvers. Many experts argue that college-educated officers are better prepared to perform these tasks.[18]

The college degree requirement is opposed primarily because it limits the pool of applicants. In particular, it has a disparate impact on racial minorities who have been the victims of inferior schooling. Also, there is no conclusive evidence that officers with college degrees perform more effectively than those without degrees.[19] In 1985, however, federal courts upheld a requirement by the Dallas Police Department that recruits have at least 45 hours of college education with a minimum average of C.[20] A 1991 Police Executive Research Forum (PERF) discussion paper concluded, "There appears to be an adequate pool of both minority and majority college–educated men and women interested in police employment" to justify a college requirement.[21]

Some evidence, however, suggests that officers with relatively more education are more likely to become dissatisfied with their jobs than officers with less education, primarily because of a lack of rewards and opportunities for career advancement. Dantzker suggested that college-educated officers may become "more easily frustrated with how the police system actually works, and with how their police agencies failed to accept and utilize their knowledge and skills."[22] In some departments where the average educational levels are low, officers with more education are informally punished by being denied certain career opportunities.[23]

Many police departments have pay incentive programs to encourage their officers to continue their education. The PERF study of police education found that 62 percent of all departments had a program of tuition assistance or reimbursement, and 53.7 percent offered incentive pay to officers with a college education. Nearly half (42.6 percent) allowed officers to adjust their assignments in order to pursue an education.[24]

**Criminal Record**   There is much controversy over whether anyone with a criminal record should be eligible for police employment. Some experts argue that a criminal record of any sort should automatically disqualify an applicant, on the grounds that it indicates a lack of ethical standards. Others argue in favor of a variable standard, depending on the nature of the offense (felony or misdemeanor; adult or juvenile), the number of offenses, and how recently the last offense was committed.

A U.S. Department of Justice survey found that 95 percent of all departments refuse to hire anyone with an adult felony conviction, and 75 percent reject those with a juvenile felony conviction. Only 30 percent, however, reject applicants with either an adult or a juvenile misdemeanor conviction. Twenty percent reject those with an adult felony arrest but no conviction, and 25 percent reject those with a juvenile arrest but no conviction.[25]

Drug offenses pose the most difficult problem with respect to recruitment standards. On the one hand, there is evidence that people with any kind of drug involvement history are far more likely to become corrupt. On the other hand, drug use is extremely prevalent. According to the National Household Survey, 31.1 percent of all Americans reported "ever" having used marijuana. Among persons 18 to 25 (the age of potential police recruits) the figure was 41 percent.[26] Rejecting every applicant who has a juvenile drug arrest would severely limit the applicant pool. Some experts suggest that applicants should be considered as long as the drug involvement was limited to "experimentation" rather than heavy use, to "soft" drugs (marijuana) rather than "hard" drugs (heroin), and as long as there had been no use for several years.

**Residency** Only 22 percent of the big-city police departments require their officers to live within the city limits in 1994.[27] Residency requirements are intended to heighten the familiarity of officers with the city and their commitment to the well–being of the community. Opponents of residency requirements argue that it infringes on the freedom of officers to choose where they live. Others argue that where persons choose to live does not predict their behavior as police officers. In New York City, for example, officers who live outside the city receive fewer citizen complaints than officers who live inside the city.[28]

Some departments have programs offering housing subsidies for police officers who agree to live in the neighborhoods where they work. These programs are based on the assumption that officers will take a greater interest in policing neighborhoods if they live there themselves, and that other residents will feel more positively about the police department if they know an officer lives in the area. The U.S. Department of Housing and Urban Development (HUD) program, Officer Next Door, offers federal assistance to such programs.[29]

### The Recruitment Effort

The number and quality of persons in the applicant pool depend in part on the department's recruitment effort. A more active effort is likely to produce a larger applicant pool with more qualified applicants. If a department wishes to increase the representation of certain kinds of people on the force—college educated, African American, Hispanic, female—active recruitment efforts directed toward those groups are necessary.

Historically, police departments did not engage in active, publicized recruitment efforts. This approach gave an advantage to persons with political or family ties to the police department, because they were most likely to hear about hiring opportunities. Open recruitment efforts, including public advertising of opportunities, is required by law today. The U.S. Equal Employment Opportunity Commission recommends that employers "contact media, agencies, organizations, schools, colleges, community groups and others who have special contacts with women and minority groups."[30] The

1994 Academy of Criminal Justice Sciences (ACJS) survey of recruitment, selection, and training standards found that 90 percent of all departments had special recruitment strategies for minorities; slightly more than half (52.5 percent) had special strategies for recruiting women, 37.3 percent actively sought veterans and college graduates, and 20 percent had special programs for recruiting people with prior police experience.[31]

Hochstedler points out that even affirmative action efforts can be relatively "passive" (e.g., merely sending announcements to racial minority groups) rather than "active" (e.g., making personal contact with minority group members).[32] The Cleveland Police Department made a significant improvement in the employment of African-American officers between the 1980s and 1990s in part through an active recruitment effort. This included 14 officers assigned to recruitment, and targeting recruitment efforts toward minority neighborhoods.[33]

### Choosing Law Enforcement as a Career

Surveys of police officers consistently indicate that they choose law enforcement as a career for two main reasons: the nature of police work and the material benefits of the job. The nature of the job includes the opportunity to help people and the perceived excitement or nonroutine aspects of police work. The material benefits of the job include salary, fringe benefits, and job security.

With regard to the nature of police work, officers consistently indicate that they are attracted to the nonroutine aspects of the job, the opportunity to work with people, and the chance to help the community. Contrary to the negative stereotypes about police, recruits appear to be relatively idealistic, perhaps even slightly more than the average person. The Crime Commission study found that 14 percent of officers said that they were attracted by the prospect of working with people or by the variety of the work.[34] Among the female recruits in New York, 14 percent cited "opportunity to help others" and 12 percent said it was "interesting work."[35]

A survey of male and female officers in two midwestern police departments found that they listed the top five reasons for choosing policing as a career in the following rank order: (1) "help people," (2) "job security," (3) "fight crime," (4) "excitement of job," and (5) "prestige of job." There were no significant differences between the male and female officers. Interestingly, the women ranked "excitement of the job" third; the men ranked it fourth.[36]

Significantly, both male and female officers ranked authority and power ninth out of a total of 11 items. Contrary to the negative stereotype about police, officers are not primarily motivated by a desire to enforce the law, or to use force against other people. Only 7 percent of the female officers in Ermer's study of New York policewomen, for example, listed law enforcement orientation as their motivation.[37]

Earlier studies have made similar findings about police officers' motivations. The President's Crime Commission's survey of police officers in Chicago, Boston, and Washington, D.C., in the 1960s found that job security or some other economic factor was the most frequently cited reason for entering police work.[38] Salary was the most frequently cited reason from female officers in New York City in the mid–1970s.[39]

For many applicants, a law enforcement career offers better pay, higher benefits, and greater job security than their parents' occupations. Traditionally, most officers were white males who came from blue-collar backgrounds (70 percent of those in Westley's study of Gary, Indiana, and 69.7 percent in McNamara's study of New York City officers).[40] Bayley and Mendelsohn found that many Denver police officers were upwardly mobile; policing represented an advance over their parents' occupational status, and most had tried other jobs before settling on the police department.[41]

The appeal of jobs with a police department often depends on the state of the economy, and how the pay and benefits of a police job compare with those of other jobs available to the applicant. In the 1960s police salaries did not compare favorably with other occupations, and police departments had great difficulty recruiting and retaining officers.[42] By the mid–1970s police salaries and benefits had improved substantially, and departments were getting large numbers of applicants for each opening.

Police officers enjoy a high degree of job security because of civil service rules and police union contract provisions that prevent arbitrary firings.[43] After the probationary period, officers can be fired only for specific causes, and any officer who is terminated has the right to appeal. Job security is a particularly appealing factor for individuals whose family experience includes periodic unemployment. James Q. Wilson found that security was the primary motivation for 76.2 percent of the Chicago officers who had joined the department during the depression of the 1930s, but for only 48.5 percent of those who joined during the prosperous 1950s.[44]

The economic problems of many cities in the 1970s and 1980s, however, forced some departments to lay off police officers. A 1986 survey found that 5 percent of all departments had been forced to lay off officers, and that 25 percent had postponed filling vacancies.[45] These events are the exception rather than the rule in policing.

Racial minorities and women are motivated by essentially the same factors as white recruits. Nicholas Alex concluded that "the motives of the white policeman for choosing police work seem little different from those of the black policeman."[46] Some studies, however, found that economic factors are a little more important for African Americans than for whites.[47]

Some people are attracted to police work because of a family connection—a parent, sibling, or other relative who is a police officer. In one study, 15 percent of the white recruits listed family as a factor, compared with only 1 percent of African Americans.[48] In Ermer's study, 7 percent of the women cited family influence.[49] Because of past discrimination, African Americans, Hispanics, and women are less likely to have family members who provide role models or encouragement in choosing law enforcement as a career.

Not all police recruits have clearly defined goals when they initially apply for jobs with a police department. Several studies found that individuals "drifted" into police work, often after trying several other jobs.[50]

Most of the studies of officers' motivations for choosing police work are based on surveys of recruits regarding their perceptions and expectations. In some important respects, their expectations are not fulfilled. Persons expecting an exciting job discover that patrol work is often very boring. Others expecting good opportunities for advancement are also disappointed by the limited opportunities in police organizations. Many officers believe that they do not receive enough support from the public. As a result, officer attitudes change significantly after they are on the job. These changes, and the concept of a police subculture, are discussed in detail in Chapter 13.

## People Who Do Not Apply

An important aspect of the recruitment process involves those people who are potentially eligible but choose *not* to apply for jobs. Some potential African-American recruits may not apply because of the negative image of the police in their community. In a survey of high school seniors, Kaminski found that African Americans were significantly less likely than whites to accept a job with the Albany Police Department if it were offered to them.[51] Young African-American men consistently express more negative attitudes toward the police than do any other group.[52] Nicholas Alex found that African-American police officers experience conflict between their identification with their community, on the one hand, and with the police department, on the other.[53]

Many women may not choose to apply for jobs as police officers because policing has traditionally been an all–male occupation and they believe they will encounter hostility on the job. In two separate studies, Susan Martin found that women in fact do encounter resistance and discrimination in police departments. Her 1986 survey found that, although women represent over 40 percent of the adult workforce, they represented only 20 percent of all job applicants in 319 departments surveyed.[54]

## SELECTION

Once a pool of applicants has been recruited, various tests are used to select a group of new officers from it. Virtually all big-city police departments conduct a background check, give written and medical exams, and interview finalists. About 70 percent use a polygraph or lie detector (see Table 12–1).[55]

**TABLE 12–1**
PERCENT OF DEPARTMENTS USING THESE SELECTION PROCEDURES

|  | 1990 (N = 71) | 1994 (N = 59) | Change (N = 58) |
|---|---|---|---|
| Background check | 98.6 | 96.6 | −1.7 |
| Medical exam | 95.9 | 98.3 | 3.4 |
| Written test | 94.3 | 96.6 | 1.7 |
| Police interview | 94.3 | 98.3 | 3.4 |
| Fitness test | 80.3 | 84.7 | 5.2 |
| Psychological interview | 83.1 | 91.5 | 12.0* |
| Intelligence test | 76.1 | 94.5 | 15.5* |
| Polygraph | 69.0 | 69.5 | 3.4 |
| Written references | 57.7 | 71.2 | 17.2* |
| Psychometric tests | 56.4 | 55.9 | −6.9 |
| Drug test | 23.9 | 22.2 | −0.0 |
| Handwriting analysis | 11.2 | 10.2 | −3.4 |
| Practical tests | 7.0 | 28.8 | 22.4* |

*Source:* Robert Langworthy, Thomas Hughes, and Beth Sanders, *Law Enforcement Recruitment, Selection and Training: A Survey of Major Police Departments in the U.S.* (Highland Heights, IL: ACJS, 1995), p. 26.
*$p < .05$

The recruitment and selection process often takes many months and is delayed by various administrative or economic factors. In 1994 the average elapsed time of the recruitment and selection process was 8.1 months in big city departments, an increase from about 6 months in 1990.[56] As a result of delay, many applicants drop out, either finding other jobs or losing interest. Cohen found that delay accounted for a significant degree of attrition among minority applicants in New York City. Nearly 60 percent of black applicants who passed the initial written and physical examinations dropped out before the background investigation phase. This compared with an overall dropout rate of 18 percent.[57]

About one–third of all police departments test job applicants for drug use. Most of the large police departments have some kind of drug-testing program, however. Among departments serving cities with populations between 500,000 and 999,999 people, 70 percent test applicants for drugs and 66 percent have a mandatory program.[58]

## Oral Interviews

Oral interviews of applicant finalists are used by almost all big-city police departments. Interviews typically last about 45 minutes and involve two to three interviewers. On the one hand, interviews are a good opportunity to detect applicant attitudes that might be incompatible with good police work (e.g., arrogance, inability to listen, extreme passivity, racial bias, etc.). The ACJS survey found that interviews explore such areas as common sense, verbal communication skills, motivation, appearance, quick thinking, racism, compassion, sexism, and patience. On the other hand, interviews are time consuming and expensive, and open the door to possible bias on the part of the interviewers. Several strategies have been devised to ensure consistency and eliminate potential bias. The ACJS survey found that almost all departments utilize an identical interview format, about three–quarters have a structured marking sheet, and a similar percentage train their interviewers.[59]

Doerner's study of oral interviews given by the state law enforcement training academy in Florida, however, raises serious questions about the reliability of the ratings of candidates. He found a "persistent inability of this selection technique to isolate suitable candidates" for law enforcement.[60]

## Background Investigations

Background investigation of applicants is perhaps the most important part of the selection process. A thorough investigation can identify factors such as a good work record in previous jobs, the ability to get along with people, and the absence of disciplinary problems that indicate potential success on the job. It can also identify a criminal record, prior involvement with drugs, or behavior problems in school or on jobs that indicate potential problems as a police officer. The ACJS survey found that virtually all big–city departments conduct background investigations. These investigations cover previous employment, possible criminal records, interviews with neighbors, a check of educational attainment, a review of applicants' financial status, and a home visit.[61]

Background investigations can be subjective, however, and open the door to discrimination. In 1972 Anthony Bouza, then deputy chief inspector of the New York City Police Department, argued that character investigations traditionally reflected the "biases of the investigating sergeant." The problem was greatest with respect to African-American and Hispanic applicants, whose character backgrounds were being assessed by white sergeants unfamiliar with the culture and lifestyle of racial minority communities. The NYPD later adopted standardized procedures in an effort to eliminate bias.[62]

Failure to conduct adequate background investigations can lead to serious problems. The Washington, D.C., Police Department experienced a major scandal in the early 1990s when it hired a number of unqualified recruits. The department was directed by Congress to quickly hire an additional 2,000 officers. In its haste, the department abandoned its standard background investigations. A large number of applicants, some of whom had criminal records related to drugs, submitted false references and work histories. Many of these officers became corrupt and involved in drug activity after they were hired.[63] The department, in short, failed to follow long–established selection procedures.

## THE PROBLEM OF SELECTING GOOD POLICE OFFICERS

One of the major problems facing the police experts is the challenge of selecting applicants who will prove to be good police officers.

Some studies have attempted to correlate background characteristics with subsequent performance records. Cohen and Chaiken studied 1,608 New York City police officers hired in 1957. Thirty–three background characteristics were examined, including race, age, IQ, father's occupation, previous occupational history (last job, number of jobs, and so on), military record, marital status, education, and criminal record. The only factor that correlated with good on-the-job performance (as indicated by their official records), however, was the recruit training score.[64] In short, no method has been found for predicting which individuals will become good officers on the basis of background characteristics.

The basic problem is that the various recruitment and selection procedures used by police departments are crude instruments. They screen *out* applicants who are clearly unqualified, but they do not necessarily screen *in* those individuals who will be the best police officers. Many applicants, for example, have two years of college education. Some of them are likely to be excellent police officers, but others are not. At best, written tests screen out the illiterate and very poorly educated. In a cohort of applicants, however, the person who writes the best may not be able to work with people under conditions of stress. Psychological tests screen out only those candidates with serious problems, and do not identify people who have good judgment. A study of Tallahassee, Florida, police recruits found that neither preemployment psychological test scores (the MMPI and CPI tests were used) nor clinical assessments by a psychologist correlated with recruits' performance ratings during field training.[65] Oral interviews may give high ratings to people who are skilled performers in that kind of exercise. The Christopher Commission, reviewing psychological evaluations given to LAPD applicants, concluded, "This initial screening can identify obvious social misfits in the grossest sense, but cannot test for more subtle abnormalities which may make an individual ill–suited to be a police officer, such as poor impulse control and the proclivity toward violence."[66]

Another part of the problem, as Cohen and Chaiken point out, is that there are no objective measures of police performance. Performance evaluations by supervisors are inherently subjective (e.g., works well with people), and may reflect the values and/or biases of the supervisors. Supervisors who value aggressive policing and frequent use of force, for example, will give high ratings to officers who perform in that manner. Performance standards tend to "reflect the internal standards of police departments rather than the requirements of the community being served."[67]

The difficulty of predicting good police performance was noted by the Fifth Circuit Court of Appeals in a suit over the Dallas Police Department's requirement of 45 hours of college credits. The court ruled that the desirable characteristics in a police officer include "individual judgment, ability to intervene in volatile situations (i.e., domestic quarrels), ability to make important decisions, [and] presence and performance as a witness in Court." It concluded that these characteristics "are not easily measured in terms of statistical analyses."[68] None of the recruitment and selection procedures currently used adequately measure judgment or the ability to make decisions under conditions of stress. In his study of the oral interview process in Florida, Doerner concluded, "A holistic scheme for identifying or pinpointing the qualities that make one a suitable police officer still eludes administrators."[69]

Some experts believe that the best predictor of officer performance is actual performance on the job. This can be ascertained in two ways: through their performance during the probationary period (see p. 310) and through careful supervision once on the job. Early warning systems are designed to identify officers who receive high rates of citizen complaints.

## EQUAL EMPLOYMENT OPPORTUNITY

Discrimination on the basis of race, ethnicity, and sex continues to be one of the major controversies in American policing. Discrimination in employment is illegal under federal and state laws.[70] Title VII of the 1964 Civil Rights Act prohibits discrimination on the basis of race, color, religion, sex, or national origin. Title VII provides that it is unlawful for an employer "to fail or refuse to hire or to discharge any individual, or otherwise to discriminate against any individual with respect to his compensation, terms, conditions, or privileges of employment, because of such individual's race, color, religion, sex, or national origin," The 1972 Equal Employment Opportunity Act extended the coverage of the 1964 law to state and local governments, which includes most police and sheriffs' departments, and strengthened the enforcement powers of the federal Equal Employment Opportunity Commission (EEOC) to investigate discrimination complaints.

As Figure 12–2 indicates, federal laws prohibit other forms of employment discrimination. The term "protected class" refers to any category specifically identified by an employment discrimination law (e.g., race, religion).

At the same time, state and local laws also prohibit employment discrimination. Virtually all cover discrimination on the basis of race, religion, age, and national origin. Some state laws cover other categories not covered by federal law. Several states and

**FIGURE 12–2**
FEDERAL EMPLOYMENT DISCRIMINATION LAWS

The ADA is just one of many Federal laws governing employment discrimination. The key Federal provisions are:

- *The Equal Pay Act of 1963*,which extends the prohibition against sex discrimination and requires equal pay for equal work by forbidding pay differentials predicated on gender.
- *The Civil Rights Act of 1964* (Title VII), which prohibits employment discrimination on the basis of race, color, religion, sex, age, or national origin by employers who employ 15 or more persons and are engaged in an industry affecting commerce.
- *The Age Discrimination in Employment Act of 1967*, which prohibits employment discrimination against persons over the age of 40.
- *Rehabilitation Act of 1973*, which prohibits discrimination on the basis of disability by programs receiving Federal funds or by Federal agencies. This law, the precursor to the ADA, was created to help persons with disabilities receive rehabilitation, obtain access to public buildings, and enjoy equal employment opportunity.
- *The Americans with Disabilities Act of 1990 (ADA)*, which makes it illegal to discriminate against qualified individuals with disabilities. The purpose of the law is to provide the estimated 43 million persons with disabilities equal access to employment opportunities; the programs, services, and activities provided by government entities; and public accommodations, such as restaurants, hotels, shopping centers, and businesses, open to the general public.
- *The Civil Rights Act of 1991*, which reverses a series of cases decided by the United States Supreme Court in 1989 that had revised long-standing interpretations (previously favorable to employees) of several Federal employment discrimination laws. The Act reinstates the earlier interpretations. In large part, the Act changes technical court rules that affect employment discrimination litigation. Highlights of the Act include permitting full-jury trials and, in certain cases, allowing for recovery of emotional suffering and punitive damages.
- *The Family and Medical Leave Act of 1993*,which requires employers with 50 or more employees to provide eligible employees with up to 12 weeks of unpaid, job-protected leave for family and medical reasons such as birth, adoption, or foster care of a child or care of a spouse, child, or parent with a serious health condition.
- *The Pregnancy Discrimination Act*, which extends the prohibition against sex discrimination and amends the Civil Rights Act of 1964 to add pregnancy, childbirth, and pregnancy-related medical conditions as protected against employment discrimination.
- *Vietnam Era Veterans Readjustment Assistance Act*, which requires Federal contractors with contracts of $10,000 or more to actively endeavor to hire qualified veterans of any war who have disabilities and, specifically, qualified Vietnam War veterans who may or may not have disabilities.

*Source:* Paula N. Rubin, *Civil Rights and Criminal Justice: Employment Discrimination Overview* (Washington: Government Printing Office, 1995). P. 4.

over 60 cities, for example, prohibit discrimination on the basis of sexual orientation, meaning that employers may not discriminate against homosexuals.

### Job–Related Qualifications

Equal employment opportunity laws and affirmative action programs do not guarantee a job to every person in a protected class. Employers may establish bona fide occupational qualifications (BFOQ) and refuse to hire people who do not possess those quali-

---

**RESEARCHING YOUR COMMUNITY**

What laws does your state have regarding equal employment opportunity? Check the current law. What groups of people are covered as "protected classes"? Does your state specifically prohibit discrimination based on family status? Does it outlaw discrimination based on sexual preference?

Does the city in which you live have laws prohibiting employment discrimination? Do they cover groups not covered by state law?

---

fications. A BFOQ is any requirement that is "reasonably necessary to the normal operation of that particular business."[71]

A few examples illustrate the general parameters of job–related standards. Because driving a patrol car is one of the basic tasks of a police officer, a department can legitimately refuse to hire someone who cannot drive a car because of a certain handicap. On the other hand, the old height requirements are not job related because it has not been demonstrated that people shorter than 5 feet 8 inches cannot effectively perform police work. In *Davis v. City of Dallas*, the Fifth Circuit Court of Appeals ruled that a requirement of 45 hours of college credits was reasonably related to the job of a police officer, on the grounds that officers are expected to exercise judgment in complex and difficult situations.[72]

The 1990 Americans With Disabilities Act (ADA) has added a new element to police employment practices. There are a number of issues that have not been resolved by the courts as to what conditions represent a disability and which disabilities legitimately disqualify a person from employment as a police officer.[73]

### Employment of Racial and Ethnic Minorities

The employment of racial and ethnic minority police officers has increased significantly in recent years. In the mid–1960s, African Americans represented only 3.6 percent of all sworn police officers. The figure rose to 6 percent in 1973, 7.6 percent in 1982, and 11.3 percent by 1993.[74] [The trend data are not strictly comparable because many of the earlier surveys reported data only for the large police departments. The 1993 data are from the Law Enforcement Management and Administration Statistics (LEMAS) survey which samples all law enforcement agencies.] In 1993 Hispanics represented 6.2 percent of all sworn officers, up from an estimated 4.1 percent in 1988. (Earlier surveys did not ask for data on Hispanic employment.)

The aggregate figures on minority employment are somewhat misleading, however. Racial and ethnic minorities are not evenly distributed throughout the United States. African Americans are concentrated in the South and the big cities in the North, Midwest, and West Coast. Hispanic Americans are concentrated in particular cities in the East, South, and Southwest.

A more useful measure of employment practices is the extent to which a police department reflects the composition of the community it serves. Federal courts have used the percentage of minorities in the local adult workforce as the standard in settling

**FIGURE 12–3**

Standard 31.2. The agency has minority group and female employees in the sworn law enforcement ranks in approximate proportion to the makeup of the available work force in the law enforcement agency's service community. . . .

*Source:* Commission on Accreditation for Law Enforcement Agencies, *Standards for Law Enforcement Agencies*, 3d ed. (Fairfax, VA: Commission on Accreditation for Law Enforcement Agencies, 1994), p. 31–2.

employment discrimination suits. The Commission on Accreditation in Law Enforcement Agencies (CALEA) *Standards for Law Enforcement Agencies* recommend that the composition of police departments reflect the composition of the community.

Lewis and Walker each independently developed an equal employment opportunity index to measure the extent to which a police department reflects the community it serves. The EEO Index is computed by dividing the percentage of a particular minority group on the police force by the percentage in the population of the local community. Thus, if a community is 30 percent Hispanic and the police department is 15 percent Hispanic, the EEO Index is.50.[75]

The index is useful for measuring the employment record of individual departments and for measuring change over time; In particular, it takes into account the changing racial and ethnic composition of cities. A police department, for example, might hire more Hispanic officers over a ten year period, but if the Hispanic population of the city also increases, it may still be unrepresentative of the community. In the mid–1960s, African Americans were significantly underrepresented in cities with large minority populations. In 1966 they represented 23 percent of the population of Oakland, California, but only 2.3 percent of the police officers (resulting in an index of .10). African Americans were 30 percent of the population of Detroit in 1966, but only 3.9 percent of the police officers (for an index .13). Similar disparities were found in Chicago, Cleveland, and other cities.[76]

Minority employment increased significantly in most departments beginning in the 1970s. In some departments people of color represented a majority of the officers by 1992. African-American officers represented 53 percent of the Detroit Police Department, which raised its index to .70. In Atlanta, 56 percent of the officers were African American. The Miami Police Department was 42.4 percent Hispanic and 17.4 percent African American.[77] Figure 12–4 presents the EEO Indices for selected police departments in 1992.

## Women in Policing

Prior to the late 1960s, police departments did not hire women on an equal basis with men. They were restricted to a separate job category of *policewoman*, excluded from many assignments, including patrol, and in some departments not eligible for promotion above a certain rank. Official discrimination against women was outlawed by the 1964 Civil Rights Act. Nonetheless, many forms of covert discrimination continue to exist. As a result, women are even more seriously underrepresented in police departments than are racial and

**FIGURE 12–4**
EEO INDICES, SELECTED CITIES, 1992

| City | Population percentage | Sworn officer percentage | EEO Index |
|---|---|---|---|
| African-American officers | | | |
| Cleveland | 46.6 | 26.3 | .56 |
| Detroit | 75.7 | 53.3 | .70 |
| New York City | 28.7 | 11.4 | .40 |
| Los Angeles | 14.0 | 14.1 | 1.00 |
| San Jose | 4.7 | 4.1 | .85 |
| Hispanic officers | | | |
| Denver | 23.0 | 9.1 | .40 |
| Miami | 62.5 | 47.2 | .75 |
| New York City | 24.4 | 13.6 | .56 |
| San Antonio | 55.6 | 36.3 | .65 |
| San Diego | 20.7 | 11.6 | .56 |

*Source:* Samuel Walker and K. B. Turner, *A Decade of Modest Progress* (Omaha: University of Nebraska, 1992).

ethnic minorities. The percentage of all sworn officers who are women increased from 2 percent in 1972 to 4.2 percent in 1978, and 8 percent in 1993. The percentage is generally higher in large police departments, but reaches 20 percent in only a handful of departments. Yet, in 1993, women made up over 40 percent of the adult labor force.[78]

The assignment of women to patrol duty was a major change in American policing. In 1967 only 3.5 percent of all departments assigned female officers to patrol duty; by 1979 the figure was 87 percent.[79]

The entry of women into policing forced police departments to change many traditional practices.[80] One of the first female officers in Cleveland, for example, found that there were no locker rooms or rest rooms for women in neighborhood precinct stations.[81] Departments had to develop policies for pregnant officers. The federal Pregnancy Discrimination Act prohibits employment discrimination on the basis of pregnancy, childbirth, or any pregnancy–related medical condition.

## Employment Discrimination Litigation

Employment discrimination suits under Title VII of the 1964 Civil Rights Act have been a major factor in increasing the number of minorities and women in policing. Successful suits produce a number of different results. First, they can result in direct benefit to the plaintiffs, including financial damages. Second, they often result in a court order eliminating tests or procedures that were discriminatory (e.g., height requirements that discriminated against women and Hispanics). Third, there may be a court–ordered affirmative action plan with specific goals and timetables for future recruiting.

In 1980 the Los Angeles Police Department signed a consent decree with the U.S. Department of Justice awarding $2 million in back pay and agreeing that 45 percent of all new recruits would be African American or Hispanic, and that 20 percent of all new recruits would be women. By 1990 the department had met its target of having 10.9 percent African-American officers, but was still short of its goal on Hispanic officers (20 percent versus 24.6 percent target) and women (12 percent versus 20 percent target).[82]

Increasing the number of racial and ethnic minority officers has three objectives.[83] First, it is designed to end discrimination and ensure compliance with equal employment opportunity laws. Second, some reformers believe that minority officers will be better able to relate to minority citizens, and thereby improve police–community relations. This argument is examined in detail in Chapter 9. Third, many people believe that to have a police department representative of the community it serves will improve public opinion about the department. A survey of Chicago residents found that a significant minority of residents believe that the increase in minority police officers had contributed to the improvement of the department. Significantly, no residents indicated that the increase in minority officers had made the department worse than before.[84]

## THE AFFIRMATIVE ACTION CONTROVERSY

The most controversial issue in police employment is affirmative action. The concept of affirmative action means that an employer must take positive steps (hence, "affirmative action") to remedy past discrimination. Affirmative action originated in 1965, with presidential Executive Order 11246 requiring all federal contractors to develop written affirmative action programs. Today, all private employers and government agencies receiving federal funds are required to have affirmative action plans. The basic premise of affirmative action is that simply ending discrimination (as required by the 1964 Civil Rights Act) does not automatically correct for the legacy of past discrimination. (As a result of several court decisions, however, the future of affirmative action was uncertain by the late 1990s.)

An affirmative action plan consists of several elements. The employer must (1) conduct a census of current employees, (2) identify underutilization or concentration of minorities and women, and (3) develop a recruiting plan to correct any underutilization. The U.S. Equal Employment Opportunity Commission defines underutilization as "having fewer minorities or women in a particular job category than would reasonably be expected by their presence in the relevant labor market."[85] The EEO Index (see above) is a useful tool for identifying underutilization. Concentration is defined as the overrepresentation of minorities or women in the lowest-level job categories.

A 1991 report by the International City Management Association (ICMA) found that 67 percent of all cities and 70 percent of all counties had affirmative action policies. Only about one–fourth, however, used numeric goals as part of their policy.[86]

### The Issue of Quotas

Affirmative action plans generally include goals and timetables for correcting underutilization. An employer establishes a goal of having a certain percentage of female employees by a certain date. Goals and timetables do not necessarily include hiring quotas, however.

Some hiring quota plans are adopted voluntarily by employers. The Detroit Police Department, for example, substantially increased its employment of African-American officers through a voluntary affirmative action plan adopted 1974. In addition to a new recruitment plan, it adopted a policy of promoting one black officer to sergeant for every white officer promoted.[87]

Most affirmative action plans with quotas, however, are court ordered. Employment discrimination suits are frequently settled through a consent decree, with the employer agreeing to a recruitment plan to increase either minorities or women. In 1980, for example, the Omaha Police Department settled a discrimination suit with a consent decree requiring that 40 percent of all new recruits be African Americans until the department's total officer population was 9.5 percent African American. The target was based on the percentage of blacks in the Omaha labor force.[88]

Supporters of affirmative action argue that it is necessary to correct past employment discrimination. Susan Martin found that affirmative action plans succeeded in increasing the number of women in applicant pools. Women represented 20.5 percent of all applicants in those departments with a court–ordered plan, but only 16.7 percent in those with a voluntary plan, and 12.9 percent in those with no plan.[89] In other words, affirmative action worked primarily at the recruitment stage, increasing the number of applicants. Ellen Hochstedler also found that the use of a specific hiring quota was one of the most important correlates of increased minority employment.[90]

Opponents of both affirmative action and quotas argue that they involve reverse discrimination against whites and/or males, in violation of the 1964 Civil Rights Act and the equal protection clause of the Fourteenth Amendment to the U.S. Constitution. White officers, for example, challenged the Detroit one–for–one promotion plan.

The U.S. Supreme Court has issued a confusing and often contradictory series of decisions on affirmative action. In 1987 it upheld the constitutionality of a voluntary affirmative action plan in Santa Clara, California. Quotas for increasing the number of female employees were acceptable as long as the program was executed in the short run and ended as soon as past discrimination was corrected.[91] Since 1987, however, the Supreme Court has become increasingly opposed to any form of preference based on race. The state of California banned all racial preferences through Proposition 209 in 1996, and the ban was upheld by the U.S. Supreme Court.

Opponents of affirmative action also argue that it lowers personnel standards by forcing the employer to hire people with lower qualifications. Law professor John Lott argues that affirmative action lowered police personnel standard, and led to higher crime rates.[92] His study, however, included no data on actual recruitment standards and studied crime trends from 1987 to 1990. Inclusion of crime data from 1992 to 1998 would find that affirmative action lowers the crime rate.[93] There is no conclusive evidence regarding the impact of any personnel standard, including affirmative action, on crime rates.

A PERF study, however, found a steady rise in the levels of education among police officers from the 1960s through the late 1980s, a period that included affirmative action programs. The educational levels of white, African-American, and Hispanic officers in 1988, moreover, were nearly comparable. It found that 62.2 percent of whites had some college credits, compared with 67.5 percent of Hispanics and 63.2 percent of African Americans.[94]

The question of whether affirmative action lowers personnel standards depends on how an affirmative action plan is implemented. If an agency hires people who do not meet the minimum standards, simply to meet a quota, then it is lowering its standards. The intent of affirmative action is to prod employers to recruit more aggressively in order to find qualified employees. The Washington, D.C. Police Department experienced a major corruption scandal in the early 1990s because it failed to conduct the standard background investigations of applicants.[95] If, on the other hand, an agency fails to meet a required quota, the proper course of action is to suspend the hiring process and to conduct a more vigorous recruitment effort in order to increase the size of the qualified applicant pool.

## TRAINING

Over the past 30 years, significant changes have been made in preservice training for police officers. The typical training period is much longer than before, covers more subjects, and is required by state law.

About three–quarters of all big-city police departments operate their own academies (departments in smaller cities tend to use state–run academies).[96] The status of police academies has risen over the years. In the 1950s training occupied "a minor position within the [police] organization." By the 1980s, most big–city academies had been elevated to the level of a division within the organization. Academy staff tend to be much larger, and are provided access to greater classroom and gymnasium space.[97]

The average length of preservice training programs tripled between the 1950s and 1993, increasing from about 300 to over 1,000 hours, including both classroom and field training. In 1993, police departments in cities with populations between 500,000 and 999,999 provided an average of 757 hours of classroom training and 396 hours of field training, for a combined total of about 30 weeks of preservice training.[98]

The police academy experience serves several formal and informal functions. First, it provides formal training. Second, it is a process for weeding out recruits who prove to be unqualified. An average of about 10 percent of all recruits fail the police academy training program according to the ACJS survey.[99] Third, it is a rite of passage that socializes recruits into the police subculture. This subculture includes a strong ethos of identification with the profession, the department, and fellow officers.[100]

The content of police academy curricula has changed significantly, with less emphasis on the purely technical aspects of policing (e.g., effecting an arrest, booking a suspect, firing a weapon) and more on the legal and behavioral aspects. One survey found that in the 1950s, 93 percent of all firearms–related training time involved skill development in shooting; almost no time was devoted to the legal aspects of when an officer could fire a weapon or to the general issue of discretion in shooting.[101] As the law of police work changed in the 1960s, largely as a result of Supreme Court rulings, the amount of preservice training devoted to criminal procedure increased. Subjects such as race relations, human relations, domestic violence, and ethics were also added to curricula.

Police academy instructors vary according to background, expertise, and orientation toward education. In an observational study of three police academies, Berg developed a typology of five different categories of instructors. "Police academics" were sworn police officers who had obtained college credentials and used college–style teaching techniques. "Police careerists" were sworn officers who relied primarily on "war stories" of the lessons of their experience. "Maladaptive generalists" were officers who were not prepared to teach, who offered personal advice, and sometimes contradicted departmental policy. "Legalists" were instructors who confined their teaching to legal issues. Finally, "civilians" were people who were not sworn officers but were specialists in some particular area.[102]

### Field Training

To supplement classroom academy training, most departments also operate field training programs. These involve practical experience in police work under the supervision of an experienced field training officer (FTO). A 1986 survey found that nearly two–thirds (64 percent) of the departments had field training programs. More than half (57 percent) indicated that their programs were directly modeled after the innovative San Jose program created in 1972.[103]

The original San Jose FTO program consisted of 16 weeks of classroom training, followed by 14 weeks of field training. During field training, the recruit is assigned to three different FTOs for four–week periods each, followed by a final two weeks with the original FTO. Each FTO makes daily reports on the recruit's performance, and supervisors complete weekly evaluation reports.[104]

FTO programs also vary in quality. A sex discrimination suit by female officers in one department exposed serious problems with the existing informal post–academy field training program. The officers alleged that the field training officers were biased against them. The suit found that the FTO program had no curriculum, no performance evaluation system based on actual tasks, and no training for the field training officers. The suit resulted in a new and improved FTO program.[105] This particular case illustrated the way in which employment discrimination suits often result in general reforms of police department policies and practices.

### State Training and Certification

One of the most important changes in police training in the past 30 years has been the development of state laws requiring preservice training for all officers. California and New York were the first states to adopt this requirement in 1959. By the early 1980s, every state had some form of mandated training.[106] The impact of state–mandated training has been greatest among small police departments, which cannot afford to operate their own training academies. Historically, these departments put officers on duty with no formal training whatsoever. A 1965 International Association of Chiefs of Police (IACP) survey of 4,000 police departments found that 85 percent of all officers had received no preservice training.[107]

In most states, small departments send their new officers to a state training academy or program certified by the state. Some programs are operated through community colleges. The separate police academies run by the large police departments are similarly certified by the state. The minimum state training requirements are usually lower, in terms of the number of hours of training, than the programs operated by big city police academies.

Officers who complete the training are then certified or licensed as peace officers in the state. A majority (39) of states now have procedures for decertifying officers by revoking their license to work as police officers in the state. Decertification addresses the problem of officers who are fired from one department for misconduct but are then hired by another. If they are decertified, this is not possible. The process does not, however, prevent the fired officer from being hired in another state (assuming the individual meets the requirements, and the hiring department does not check the person's work history).[108]

Florida was one of the first states to adopt a comprehensive decertification process. Between 1976 and 1983 the Florida Criminal Justice Standards and Training Commission took action against 148 officers. It decertified 132, suspended 14, and placed 2 on probation. Most cases involved private or departmental misconduct; only 22 of the 148 involved official misconduct.[109]

### Shortcomings of Current Police Training

Despite the recent improvements, police training programs suffer from a number of limitations. Many programs still do not cover important subjects such as discretion, the use of informants, and ethics. Also, preservice training by itself may not adequately prepare officers for the tasks they face. A one–hour police academy lecture on spousal abuse, for example, may have no effect on how officers handle a domestic violence incident months or years later. A short session on mental illness may not prepare officers to recognize serious mental illness or provide adequate guidance on how to handle mentally ill people.

The Detroit Police Department conducted an experimental training program for recruits on dealing with crime victims. An evaluation found that crime victims did not rate officers who had received the training any better than officers who had not been through the program. (Both groups of officers, in fact, received very high ratings.) Even more serious, all recruits experienced a significant change in attitudes after being out on the street, developing significantly less positive attitudes toward the public.[110] McNamara found a similar shift in attitudes after one year on the street in a study of New York City recruits.[111] These findings lend support to the argument that the working environment of policing—rather than background characteristics or training—is the principal factor in shaping police officer attitudes and behavior.[112] The police subculture is discussed in more detail in Chapter 13.

Because of persistent police–community relations problems (Chapter 9), most departments have introduced race relations, human relations, or cultural diversity training into the curriculum. A review of cultural diversity training programs, however, found that the content has not changed much since the 1960s, that they tend to perpetuate negative stereotypes about racial and ethnic minorities, and focus on the attitudes of individual officers and ignore the policies of the department as a whole.[113] Alpert, Smith, and Watters argue that "mere classroom training" on issues such as race relations "is insufficient." In particular, they recommend experimenting with training officers in communication skills with racial and ethnic groups "other than their own."[114]

## THE PROBATIONARY PERIOD

Upon completing preservice training, a recruit is sworn in and assigned to regular duty. The officer is on probationary status for a period that may range from six months to two years, depending on the department (some departments count the time in training as part of this period). In 1994 the average length was about one year.[115] During the probationary period an officer can be dismissed without cause. After the probationary period is completed, dismissal must be based on cause under rules established by the local civil service regulations and/or police union contract.[116]

About 7 percent of the recruits either resign or are dismissed during this period.[117] Susan Martin found significant differences in how departments used the probationary period, however. In Phoenix, 47 percent of all officers who left the department were on probation at the time. This included 26 percent of all female recruits and 14 percent of all males. In Washington, D.C., however, only 15 percent of those leaving the department were in the probationary phase (representing 5 percent of both males and females).[118] Many experts argue that a longer probationary period permits more time for observing performance and an opportunity to dismiss those whose performance is unsatisfactory. In Philadelphia the 6–month probationary period includes 19 weeks of academy training, leaving only a 7–week period of on–the–street experience. A report found this "insufficient to allow supervisors to determine whether a particular candidate is qualified to be a police officer" and recommended at least a six–month probationary period following completion of academy training.[119]

## CONCLUSION

The profile of the American police officer has changed significantly over the past 25 years. There are now more racial minority, female, and college–educated officers than ever before. Many old personnel practices have been eliminated because they discriminated against particular groups. Meanwhile, the training of officers has improved substantially during the same period. In short, the police recruit of today is a very different kind of person from the recruit of 25 years ago.

## NOTES

1  Arthur Niederhoffer, *Behind the Shield: The Police in Urban Society* (Garden City, N.Y.: Anchor Books, 1967), p. 1.
2  David H. Bayley and Harold Mendelsohn, *Minorities and the Police: Confrontation in America* (New York: Free Press, 1969), pp. 1–33.

**3** Jerome H. Skolnick, *Justice without Trial*, 3d ed. (New York: Macmillan, 1994), pp. 41–68.

**4** George W. Griesinger, Jeffrey S. Slovak, and Joseph J. Molkup, *Civil Service Systems: Their Impact on Police Administration* (Washington: Government Printing Office, 1979).

**5** Robert Langworthy, Thomas Hughes, and Beth Sanders, *Law Enforcement Recruitment, Selection and Training: A Survey of Major Police Departments in the U.S.* (Highland Heights, IL: Academy of Criminal Justice Sciences, 1995), p. 24.

**6** President's Commission on Law Enforcement and Administration of Justice, *Task Force Report: The Police* (Washington: Government Printing Office, 1967), p. 130.

**7** Stephen D. Mastrofski, Jeffrey B. Snipes, and Anne E. Supina, "Compliance on Demand: The Public's Response to Specific Police Requests," *Journal of Research in Crime and Delinquency* 33 (August 1996): 269–305.

**8** Langworthy, Hughes, and Sanders, *Law Enforcement Recruitment, Selection and Training*, p. 24.

**9** Bureau of Justice Statistics, *Local Police Departments, 1993* (Washington: Government Printing Office, 1996), p. 5.

**10** David L. Carter, Allen D. Sapp, and Darrell W. Stephens, *The State of Police Education* (Washington: Police Executive Research Forum, 1989), p. 84.

**11** Susan E. Martin, *On the Move: The Status of Women in Policing* (Washington: The Police Foundation, 1990), p. 78.

**12** Carter, Sapp, and Stephens, *The State of Police Education*, p. 38.

**13** James B. Jacobs and Samuel B. Magdovitz, "At LEEP's End: A Review of the Law Enforcement Education Program," *Journal of Police Science and Administration* 5, no. 1 (1977): 1–17.

**14** Michael Heidingsfield, "Six Reasons to Require College Education for Police Officers," *Subject to Debate* 9 (December 1995): 5–7.

**15** President's Commission on Law Enforcement and Administration of Justice, *The Challenge of Crime in a Free Society* (Washington: Government Printing Office, 1967), p. 109.

**16** Robert E. Worden, "A Badge and a Baccalaureate: Policies, Hypotheses, and Further Evidence,": *Justice Quarterly* 7 (September 1990):566–567.

**17** Bureau of the Census, *Statistical Abstract of the United States, 1997* (Washington: Government Printing Office, 1997), table 243.

**18** Wesley G. Skogan and Susan M. Hartnett, *Community Policing, Chicago Style* (New York: Oxford University Press, 1997), pp. 70–109.

**19** Lawrence W. Sherman, *The Quality of Police Education* (San Francisco: Jossey–Bass, 1978), chap. 7.

**20** David L. Carter, Allen D. Sapp, and Darrel W. Stephens, "Higher Education as a Bona Fide Occupational Qualification (BFOQ) for Police: A Blueprint," *American Journal of Police* 7 (Fall 1988): 1–27; *Davis v. City of Dallas*, 777 F.2d.205 (5th Cir. 1985).

**21** David L. Carter and Allen D. Sapp, *Police Education and Minority Recruitment: The Impact of College Requirement* (Washington: Police Executive Research Forum, 1991), p. 27.

**22** M. L. Dantzker, "Do College Education Requirements for Police Create an Overeducation Problem?" *Subject to Debate* 9 (December 1995): 4.

**23** Lawrence W. Sherman, *The Quality of Police Education* (San Francisco: Jossey–Bass, 1978), pp. 185–188.

**24** Carter, Sapp, and Stephens, *The State of Police Education*, p. 61.

**25** Griesinger et al., *Civil Service Systems*, p. 102.

**26** U.S. Department of Health and Human Services, *National Household Survey on Drug Use: Population Estimates, 1995* (Washington: Government Printing Office, 1996), pp. 23–27.

**27** Langworthy, Hughes, and Sanders, *Law Enforcement Recruitment, Selection and Training*, p. 24.

**28** New York City Civilian Complaint Review Board, *Annual Report, 1993* (New York: CCRB, 1993) p. 28.

**29** "A Place to Call Home," *Law Enforcement News,* July/August 1997, p. 1.

**30** U.S. Equal Employment Opportunity Commission, *Affirmative Action and Equal Employment*, vol. 1 (Washington: Government Printing Office, 1974), p. 23.

**31** Langworthy, Hughes, and Sanders, *Law Enforcement Recruitment, Selection and Training*, p. 23.

**32** Ellen Hochstedler, "Impediments to Hiring Minorities in Public Police Agencies," *Journal of Police Science and Administration* 12 (June 1984):233.

**33** "Gains Despite Downsizing," *Law Enforcement News* (October 31, 1992). P. 1.

**34** President's Commission on Law Enforcement and Administration of Justice, *Studies in Crime and Law Enforcement*, vol. 2, p. 18.

**35** Virginia B. Ermer, "Recruitment of Female Police Officers in New York City," *Journal of Criminal Justice* 6 (Fall 1978): 233–246.

**36** M. Steven Meagher and Nancy Yentes, "Choosing a Career in Policing: A Comparison of Male and Female Perceptions," *Journal of Police Science and Administration* 14, no. 4 (1986):320–327.

**37** Ermer, "Recruitment of Female Police Officers in New York City," pp. 233–246.

**38** President's Commission on Law Enforcement and Administration of Justice, *Field Surveys: III, vol. 2, Studies in Crime and Law Enforcement in Major Metropolitan Areas* (Washington: Government Printing Office, 1967), p. 18.

**39** Ermer, "Recruitment of Female Police Officers in New York City."

**40** William A. Westley, *Violence and the Police* (Cambridge: MIT Press, 1970), p. 205; John H. McNamara, "Uncertainties in Police Work: The Relevance of Police Recruits' Backgrounds and Training," in *The Police: Six Sociological Essays*, ed., David J. Bordua, (New York: Wiley) pp. 163–252.

**41** Bayley and Mendelsohn, *Minorities and the Police*, p. 6.

**42** President's Commission, *Task Force Report: The Police*, pp. 133–136.

**43** Griesinger et al., *Civil Service Systems*.

**44** James Q. Wilson, "Generational and Ethnic Differences among Career Police Officers," *American Journal of Sociology* 69 (March 1964): 522–528.

**45** James J. Fyfe, "Police Personnel Practices, 1986," *Municipal Yearbook 1987* (Washington: International City Management Association, 1987), table 3/2.

**46** Nicholas Alex, *New York Cops Talk Back* (New York: Wiley, 1976), p. 9.

**47** Ermer, "Recruitment of Female Police Officers in New York City."

**48** President's Commission on Law Enforcement and Administration of Justice, *Field Surveys, III* (Washington, DC: Government Printing Office, 1967), Section 2, p. 85.

**49** Ermer, "The Recruitment of Female Police Officers in New York City."

**50** Bayley and Mendelsohn, *Minorities and the Police*, p. 30.

**51** Robert J. Kaminski, "Police Minority Recruitment: Predicting Who Will Say Yes to an Offer for a Job as a Cop," *Journal of Criminal Justice* 21 (no. 2, 1993):395–409.

**52** W. S. Wilson Huang and Michael S. Vaughan, "Support and Confidence: Public Attitudes toward the Police," in *Americans View Crime and Justice: A National Public Opinion Survey*, eds., T. J. Flanagan and D. R. Longmire, (Newbury Park, CA: Sage, 1996), pp. 31–45.

**53** Nicholas Alex, *Black in Blue: A Study of the Negro Policeman* (Englewood Cliffs, NJ: Prentice-Hall, 1969).

**54** Martin, *On the Move*, pp. 26–29.

**55** Langworthy, Hughes, and Sanders, *Law Enforcement Recruitment, Selection and Training*, p. 26.

**56** Ibid., p. 24.

**57** Bernard Cohen, "Minority Retention in the New York City Police Department: A Policy Study," *Criminology* 11 (November 1973): 287–306.

**58** Bureau of Justice Statistics, *Local Police Departments, 1993*, p. 6.

**59** Langworthy, Hughes, and Sanders, *Law Enforcement Recruitment, Selection and Training*, p. 27.

**60** Willaim G. Doerner, "The Utility of the Oral Interview Board in Selecting Police Academy Admissions," *Policing* 20, no. 4 (1997): 784.

**61** Langworthy, Hughes, and Sanders, *Law Enforcement Recruitment, Selection and Training*, p. 29.

**62** Anthony V. Bouza, "The Policeman's Character Investigation: Lowered Standards or Changing Times?" *Journal of Criminal Law, Criminology, and Police Science* 63 (March 1972): 120–124.

**63** "D.C. Police Force Still Paying for Two-Year Hiring Spree," *The Washington Post* (August 28, 1994), p. 1.

**64** Bernard Cohen and Jan M. Chaiken, *Police Background Characteristics and Performance* (Lexington, MA: Lexington Books, 1973), pp. 87, 90–91.

**65** Benjamin S. Wright, William G. Doerner, and John C. Speir, "Pre-employment Psychological Testing as a Predictor of Police Performance during an FTO Program," *American Journal of Police* 9, no. 4 (1990): 65–84.

**66** [Christopher Commission], *Report of the Independent Commission on the Los Angeles Police Department* (Los Angeles: City of Los Angeles, 1991), p. 110.

**67** Cohen and Chaiken, *Police Background Characteristics and Performance*, p. 4.

**68** *Davis v. City of Dallas*, 777 F.2d 205, 216 (Fifth Cir. 1985).

**69** Doerner, "The Utility of the Oral Interview Board in Selecting Police Academy Admissions," p. 784.

**70** Paula N. Rubin, *Civil Rights and Criminal Justice: Employment Discrimination Overview* (Washington: Government Printing Office, 1995).

**71** Rubin, *Civil Rights and Criminal Justice: Employment Discrimination Overview*, p. 102.

**72** *Davis v. City of Dallas*, 777 F.2d 205.

**73** Paula N. Rubin, *The Americans With Disabilities Act and Criminal Justice: An Overview* (Washington: Government Printing Office, 1993).

**74** Bureau of Justice Statistics, *Local Police Departments, 1993*, p. 4.

**75** Samuel Walker, *Employment of Black and Hispanic Police Officers* (Omaha: University of Nebraska at Omaha, 1983). William G. Lewis, "Toward Representative Bureaucracy," *Public Administration Review*, 49 (May–June 1989): 257–267.

**76** President's Commission, *Task Force Report: The Police*, pp. 167–174; [Kerner Commission], *Report of the National Advisory Commission on Civil Disorders* (New York: Bantam Books, 1968), pp. 315–316, 321–322.

**77** Margo Wiliams, "What Happens When the Police Department Goes from White to Black: The Changing Face of the Detroit Police Department," *Crisis* 98 (December 1991): 15–17. Samuel Walker and K. B. Turner, *A Decade of Modest Progress* (Omaha: University of Nebraska, 1992).

**78** Bureau of Justice Statistics, *Local Police Departments, 1993*, p. 4.

**79** Cynthia G. Sulton and Roi D. Townsey, *A Progress Report on Women in Policing* (Washington: The Police Foundation, 1988), p. 25.

**80** Martin, *On the Move*, pp. 11–24.

81 Tamar Husansky and Pat Sparling, *Working Vice: The True Story of Lt. Lucy Duvall— America's First Woman Vice Squad Chief* (New York: Harper Paperbacks, 1993).

82 George Felkenes and Peter Charles Unsinger, *Diversity, Affirmative Action, and Law Enforcement* (Springfield, Ill.: Charles C. Thomas, 1992).

83 Samuel Walker, Cassia Spohn, and Miriam DeLone, *The Color of Justice* (Belmont, CA: Wadsworth, 1996), pp. 108–109.

84 Samuel Walker and Vincent J. Webb, "Public Perceptions of Racial and Minority Employment and Its Perceived Impact on Police Service," (paper presented at the annual meeting of the American Society of Criminology, 1997), San Diego, CA.

85 U.S. Equal Employment Opportunity Commission, *Affirmative Action and Equal Employment*, vol. 1 (Washington: Government Printing Office, 1974), p. 23.

86 Evelina R. Moulder," Affirmative Action in Local Government," *Municipal Yearbook, 1991* (Washington: International City Management Association, 1991), app. 6.

87 Lawrence W. Sherman, "Minority Quotas for Police Promotions (a Comment on *Detroit Police Officers Association v. Young*)," *Criminal Law Bulletin*, 15 (Jan./Feb. 1979):79–84.

88 *Midwest Guardians v. Omaha* (1980).

89 Martin, *On the Move*, p. 39.

90 Hochstedler, "Impediments to Hiring Minorities."

91 *Johnson v. Transportation Agency*, 480 U.S. 616 (1987); Melvin I. Urofsky, *A Conflict of Rights: The Supreme Court and Affirmative Action* (New York: Scribner's, 1991).

92 John Lott, "Does a Helping Hand Put Others at Risk? Affirmative Action, Police Departments, and Crime," *Subject to Debate* 12 (May 1998), p. 1.

93 Samuel Walker, "Reply to Lott," *Subject to Debate* (May 1998), p. 1.

94 Carter, Sapp, and Stephens, *The State of Police Education*, p. 41.

95 "D.C. Police Force Still Paying for Two-Year Hiring Spree," p. 1.

96 Langworthy, Hughes, and Sanders, *Law Enforcement Recruitment, Selection and Training*, p. 32.

97 Thomas M. Frost and Magnus J. Seng, "The Administration of Police Training: A Thirty Year Perspective," *Journal of Police Science and Administration* 12 (March 1984):66–73.

98 Bureau of Justice Statistics, *Local Police Departments, 1993*, p. 5.

99 Langworthy, Hughes, and Sanders, *Law Enforcement Recruitment, Selection and Training*, p. 32.

100 Westley, *Violence and the Police*, pp. 153–159; Richard N. Harris, *Police Academy: An Inside View* (New York: Wiley, 1973).

101 Thomas M. Frost and Magnus J. Seng, "Police Entry-Level Curriculum: A Thirty–year Perspective," *Journal of Police Science and Administration*, 12 (September 1984): p. 254.

102 Bruce L. Berg, "Who Should Teach Police: A Typology and Assessment of Police Academy Instructors," *American Journal of Police* 9, no. 2 (1990): 79–100.

103 Michael S. Campbell, *Field Training for Police Officers: State of the Art* (Washington: Government Printing Office, 1986).

104 Ibid.

105 William G. Doerner and E. Britt Patterson, "The Influence of Race and Gender upon Rookie Evaluations of Their Field Training Officers," *American Journal of Police* 11, no. 2 (1992):23–36.

106 Richard C. Lumb, ed., *Sourcebook of Standards and Training Information in the United States* (Charlotte: University of North Carolina, 1993).

107 President's Commission, *Task Force Report: The Police*, p. 138.

108 Steven Puro, Roger Goldman, and William C. Smith, "Police Decertification: Changing Patterns among the States, 1985–1995," *Policing* 20, no. 3 (1997):481–496.

**109** Roger Goldman and Steven Puro, "Decertification of Police: An Alternative to Traditional Remedies for Police Misconduct," Hastings *Constitutional Law Quarterly* 15 (Fall 1987): 45–80.

**110** Arthur J. Lurigio and Dennis P. Rosenbaum, "The Travails of the Detroit Police-Victims Experiment: Assumptions and Important Lessons," *American Journal of Police* 11, no. 3 (1992):1–34.

**111** McNamara, "Uncertainties in Police Work," 208–223.

**112** Skolnick, *Justice without Trial*, pp. 41–68.

**113** Jerome L. Blakemore, David Barlow, and Deborah L. Padgett, "From the Classroom to the Community: Introducing Process in Police Diversity Training," *Police Studies* 18, no. 1 (1995):71–83.

**114** Geoffrey P. Alpert, William C. Smith, and Daniel Watters, "Implications of the Rodney King Beating," *Criminal Law Bulletin* 28 (September–October 1992): 477.

**115** Langworthy, Hughes, and Sanders, *Law Enforcement Recruitment, Selection and Training*, p. 39.

**116** Griesinger et al., *Civil Service Systems*.

**117** Fyfe, "Police Personnel Practices, 1986."

**118** Martin, *On the Move*, pp. 131–132.

**119** Philadelphia Police Study Task Force, *Philadelphia and Its Police: Toward a New Partnership*, (Philadelphia: City of Philadelphia, 1986), p. 94.

# CHAPTER 13

# POLICE OFFICERS II:
# ON THE JOB

Upon completing the probationary period a police officer enters into a law enforcement career. Many factors influence the course of an individual career. Some officers enjoy promotion and advancement; others do not and remain at the rank of police officer for their entire careers. Some officers leave law enforcement, in some cases by choice but in other cases involuntarily. Officers' attitudes about the job, the profession, and citizens often change over the course of a career.

This chapter examines the experience of being on the job as a police officer. Particular attention is given to those factors that influence the attitudes and behavior of police officers.

## BEGINNING POLICE WORK: REALITY SHOCK

The first weeks and months on the job for a new police officer are often a rude awakening. In his classic study of the police subculture, Westley describes the experience as "reality shock."[1] The new officer quickly encounters the unpleasant aspects of dealing with the public, the criminal justice system, and the department itself.

### Encountering Citizens

Police officer attitudes toward the public change significantly during the first weeks and months on the job. McNamara found that the percentage of officers agreeing with the statement "patrolmen almost never receive the cooperation from the public that is needed to handle police work properly" rose from 35 percent at the beginning of academy training to 50 percent after two years on the job. Meanwhile, at the start of academy training, 31 percent agreed that it was necessary to use force to gain respect in "tough" neighborhoods; two years later 55 percent agreed.[2] A similar change in attitudes toward the public occurred among new Detroit police officers who participated in a special victims' services training program. After four months on the job, officers gave substantially lower ranking to the importance of "listening attentively when victim expresses feelings or emotions."[3]

Changes in officers' attitudes are the result of several different aspects of police work. Officers encounter some hostility from citizens. This is a shock because officers tend to choose law enforcement as a career because they want to work with people and help the community (see Chapter 12). Although citizen hostility is statistically infrequent (about 10 percent of all encounters),[4] officers are likely to remember such experiences. Recalling unpleasant or traumatic experiences is a phenomenon common to all people.[5]

Officers also experience being stereotyped, with citizens reacting to the uniform, the badge, and the gun. As is the case with racial stereotyping, it is an unpleasant experience to have someone react to what you are, rather than to your individual characteristics or behavior. In still other instances, citizens feel discomfort at being around a person with arrest powers. Sometimes citizens will even openly make jokes about breaking the law. To avoid the discomfort of these incidents, police officers tend to socialize primarily with other officers, thereby increasing their isolation from the public.[6]

Police officer attitudes also change because they perform society's "dirty work," handling unpleasant tasks that no one else wants to perform or is able to handle. The police see humanity at its worst.[7] They are the first people to find the murder victim, for example. Officers encounter the victims of serious domestic abuse, child abuse, and rape firsthand. These kinds of situations accumulate over time, affecting their attitudes about people in general. In one study, for example, officers ranked dealing with an abused child as the most stressful kind of situation they encounter.[8]

### Encountering the Criminal Justice System

A second shock involves learning about the criminal justice system. Police officers are insiders in the sense that they have firsthand knowledge about how the system works. They see what happens to arrests, how cases are plea bargained, and how judges work. They observe incompetent prosecutors, defense attorneys, and judges every day. As a result, many become cynical about the ability of the system to do justice. Generally, police officers believe that the courts are too lenient with offenders.[9] In a 1996 study, only 27 percent of police officers in Washington, D.C., expressed trust in the courts, compared with 63 percent who expressed trust in their commanders and 87 percent who indicated trust in their fellow officers.[10] Officers also react negatively to the fact that they are not respected by lawyers, judges, and other actors in the criminal justice system.[11]

### Encountering the Department

New officers' experiences with their own departments are often disillusioning. They discover the politics of the organization, and learn that it does not always act in a rational and efficient manner. They discover that some of their supervisors are incompetent, that promotions are not necessarily based on merit, and that personal favoritism governs some decisions. Many officers quickly conclude that hard work will not be rewarded and that the best approach is to do as little as possible and avoid situations that might create trouble for them.[12]

As in other large organizations, there is conflict between the rank and file and the top command. A study of Washington, D.C., police officers found that 82 percent were satisfied with their jobs, 87 percent expressed trust in their fellow officers, 63 percent trusted their commanders, and only 51 percent expressed trust in the chief of police.[13] Conflict between the rank and file and management is now channeled through police unions and the process of collective bargaining (see Chapter 14).

Finally, as is discussed below (pp. 328–331), many police departments are characterized by internal conflicts along racial, ethnic, and gender lines.

### The Seniority System

New officers are generally assigned to patrol duty, usually in high-crime areas, and on the evening shift. Assignments in most police departments are governed by civil service procedures or union contracts that embody the principle of seniority.[14] Officers with more experience have first priority in requesting assignments. This leaves the least desirable assignments to the new officers.[15]

The seniority principle has both good and bad points. On the positive side, it eliminates favoritism and discrimination. In the 1960s, the President's Crime Commission found that some departments assigned their worst officers to black neighborhoods.[16] On the negative side, it means that the least-experienced officers get the most difficult assignments: patrolling the highest-crime neighborhoods on the busiest shift with the most crime and calls for service. On the other hand, in departments that have significantly improved their personnel standards, the younger officers are likely to be better qualified and better trained for such work than the older officers.

Because many departments have hired significant numbers of racial and ethnic minority and female officers in recent years, these officers tend to be disproportionately represented in the least desirable assignments, such as assignment to high-crime precincts.[17]

## POLICE OFFICER ATTITUDES AND BEHAVIOR

Police officer attitudes, and the relationship between attitudes and behavior, are complex. Public stereotypes about police officers are generally inaccurate. Much of the scholarly research on police officer attitudes has arisen from an attempt to explain bad police officer behavior: the use of force and police–community relations tensions. With the exception of Muir's study, *Streetcorner Politicians*, little attention has been given to understanding good officers and good behavior.[18] It is significant, for example, that the title of William Westley's pioneering study of the police subculture is *Violence and the Police*.[19]

Explanations of attitudes and behavior fall into two general categories. One focuses on the sociological aspects of policing: the special characteristics of police work, the nature of police organizations, and the situational factors associated with police–citizen encounters. The other approach focuses on the background characteristics of individual officers: social and economic status, race, ethnicity, gender, and education. The bulk of the research tends to support the sociological interpretation of police work as an explanation of officer attitudes and behavior.[20]

### The Concept of a Police Subculture

The first study of police officers, William A. Westley's 1950 study of the police in Gary, Indiana, approached the subject from the standpoint of occupational sociology. He sought "to isolate and identify the major social norms governing police conduct, and to describe the way in which they influence police action in specific situations."[21] He found a distinct subculture among police officers that still exists and emphasizes secrecy and violence. Many police officers view the public as the enemy, and believe that they are justified in lying to protect other officers from criticism by citizens. Of the officers interviewed by Westley, 73 percent considered citizens hostile to the police.[22]

Westley argues that police attitudes are a product of selective contact with the public. Officers rarely meet the average person but, instead, meet people with problems who often resent the police presence. Officers also resent the fact that the other professionals they routinely deal with—lawyers, news reporters, social workers, and so on—have negative attitudes about the police.[23]

In the face of perceived public hostility, Westley continues, officers believe they can rely only on their fellow officers in times of crisis. Group solidarity requires secrecy "as a shield against the attacks of the outside world." Secrecy justifies lying. Westley asked officers if they would report a fellow officer who took money from a citizen (a person arrested for drunkenness). A total of 73 percent said they would not. Westley concludes that most officers believe that "illegal action is preferable to breaking the secrecy of the group."[24]

Group solidarity also justifies violence against citizens, according the Westley. Officers are particularly concerned about maintaining respect in encounters with citizens. More than a third of the officers (39 percent) surveyed by Westley thought that they were justified in using force when faced with citizen disrespect. Two-thirds of the officers (66 percent) gave some rationalization for the illegal use of force.[25]

The code of silence, through which officers refuse to testify against other officers, has been a major obstacle to eliminating police misconduct. The Christopher Commission report on Los Angeles police officers states, "It is basically a nonwritten rule that you do not roll over, tell on your partner, your companion."[26] In this respect, the police subculture is an obstacle to the development of police accountability (Chapter 11), the reduction of police use of force, and the improvement of police–community relations (Chapter 9).

Jerome Skolnick developed Westley's concept of a police subculture further in a study of the police in "Westville" (Oakland, California). He argues that police officers develop a working personality shaped by two aspects of the police role: danger and authority. Because the potential for danger is a constant feature of police work, and because danger comes from people, officers become routinely suspicious about people. This suspicion is particularly strong with respect to certain categories of people. Officers develop a "perceptual shorthand" of visual cues associated with criminals and/or dangerous people. This shorthand is a form of stereotyping, applied with particular intensity to males: young men, low-income young men, and low-income racial minority men.[27] This aspect of the police subculture is a major contributor to police-community relations problems (Chapter 9).

Authority further isolates the officer from the public. Bittner argues that the capacity to use force is the defining feature of police.[28] Skolnick argues that "authority . . . becomes a resource to reduce perceived threats."[29] Challenges to their authority, or other disrespectful behavior, increase both the likelihood of arrest and police officer use of force.[30]

Skolnick also found that the norms of police work often conflicted with constitutional standards regarding the rights of suspects. Officers are under pressure to produce to get results, usually in the form of arrests, evidence, confessions, and convictions. The law, however, limits police powers in order to protect the rights of individual citizens. Officers feel pressured to evade or bend the rules: to conduct illegal searches or to obtain confessions through coercion.[31] Herbert Packer defines the tension between the demand for results and the rule of law as a conflict between "crime control" values and "due process" values.[32]

Arthur Niederhoffer, meanwhile, argues that the police subculture is characterized by cynicism and authoritarianism. A former New York City police officer himself, he argues in *Behind the Shield* that police officers are cynical about both the outside world and the inside world of the police department. Cynicism contributes to authoritarianism. Drawing upon earlier research in social psychology, Niederhoffer maintains that the police personality fits the cluster of values associated with authoritarianism: conventional social values, cynicism, aggression, superstition, and a tendency to stereotype, to project personal values onto others (projectivity), and to define the world in terms of good versus bad people.[33]

## Criticisms of the Police Subculture Concept

The initial research by Westley, Skolnick, and Niederhoffer on the police subculture paints a highly negative view of police officers, portraying them as isolated, hostile to the public and to the norms of a democratic society, prejudiced, and opposed to accountability. The major elements of this view have been heavily criticized, however. Reviewing the literature on the concept of a police personality, Joel Lefkowitz concludes that "a significant portion of the relevant literature is primarily mere opinion." Moreover, "almost all of the research studies reviewed are methodologically inadequate to the task of supporting reasonable inferences" about the existence or origins of a police personality. He concludes that the personalities of police officers "do differ in systematic ways from the rest of the population, but differ in an evaluatively neutral sense." In short, police officers are somewhat different, but their personality traits are not pathological.[34]

In their study of Denver police officers, Bayley and Mendelsohn found that "on all personality scales the data show that policemen are absolutely average people." Research on police officers' reasons for choosing law enforcement as a career has consistently found that most seek to help people and to serve the community (Chapter 12). In this respect, officers are rather idealistic, at least at the outset of their careers. The police officers surveyed by Bayley and Mendelsohn, were somewhat more conservative than the population at large (regardless of whether they were Republican or Democratic) but were not authoritarian.[35]

Critics argue that Niederhoffer's concept of police cynicism is impressionistic and not based on systematic research. It was derived, perhaps unconsciously, from popular negative stereotypes about the police. In particular, the early studies did not systematically compare police officers with members of other occupations. Using the same scale employed by Niederhoffer, John McNamara found evidence that police recruits are less authoritarian than the general public and less punitive in their attitudes than community leaders.[36] Regoli and colleagues argue that Niederhoffer's concept of police cynicism is simplistic, and that cynicism is a multidimensional phenomenon, involving relations with the public, organizational functions, police dedication to duty, police social solidarity, and police training and education. He concludes that "it is possible the police can be cynical toward one aspect of the occupation and not others, or toward any combination of aspects simultaneously." Subsequent research failed to establish the concept of cynicism as a generalizable measure of police officer attitudes. Langworthy argues that research on police cynicism is at a dead end.[37]

---

**POLICE OFFICERS ON THE WEB**

Many police officers maintain their own personal web pages. Locate and read some of these pages. What do they talk about? Are there any patterns in terms of the kinds of officers and the subjects they put on their web sites? Do these officers appear to be representative of most officers, in terms of background and attitudes, based on the material in this chapter and Chapter 12?

---

Studies of police cynicism emphasize its negative aspects and fail to take into account its positive features. Detachment and impersonality protect officers from the unpleasant aspects of police work. Officers cannot afford to get emotionally involved in the human suffering they encounter. In this respect, the police play a role similar to that of medical personnel in the emergency room who regularly encounter extremes of human suffering. Muir argues that a certain element of detachment from the immediate situation (which is not the same thing as indifference) is one of the characteristics of a professional attitude on the part of police officers.[38]

## THE CHANGING RANK AND FILE

The original concept of a homogeneous police subculture is ahistorical and fails to account for significant changes in the composition of the rank and file, as well as other changes in policing over the past 30 years.[39] At the time the early research was conducted (1950s through 1960s), police officers were overwhelmingly male and white, with most coming from blue-collar backgrounds with little college education. Changing employment patterns (see Chapter 12) have brought significant numbers of African American, Hispanic, female, and college-educated officers (see Table 13–1). Robin Haarr argues that "the initial concept of a single, unified occupational culture is now being replaced by an alternative conceptualization of diversity, variation, and contrast within the police organization and occupation."[40]

### Gender

Susan Martin found that the introduction of women into the police ranks broke up the traditional solidarity of the group. Women officers, for example, do not share the same outside interests as male officers: hunting, fishing, and cars. Martin also argues that policewomen "alter the rules of the game" of how to act as a police officer. Traditional masculine characteristics of not expressing emotion publicly and of settling disputes physically are no longer appropriate. Expressions of friendship, which are acceptable between two male officers, are problematic between officers of different sexes.[41]

Equally important, Martin found significant differences among the male officers, especially in terms of their attitudes toward women officers. The traditionals are emotionally committed to the image of policing as dangerous physical work, and put an emphasis on aggressive policing. Holding stereotyped views about women's physical

---

**SIDEBAR 13–1**

THE DIVERSE POLICE SUBCULTURE ON THE WEB

Many organizations representing different groups of police officers maintain their own web sites. Check out the web sites for such groups as the National Hispanic Police Association, the International Association of Women Police, the Emerald Society of Boston, the Federation of Lesbian and Gay Police Organizations, and others.

Who do these organizations represent? Do they provide their membership figures? What do they do? What activities do they sponsor? Do they offer any reports or other literature?

---

strength and their role in society, the traditionals have the most difficulty accepting women officers. The moderns, on the other hand, accept policewomen relatively easily. They recognize that police work rarely calls for physical strength, accept the idea that job opportunities should be open to everyone on the basis of individual merit, and are not tied to traditional views of women's roles. The moderates have more complex attitudes. Many accept the idea of policewomen in principle but do not like the idea of women on patrol duty. Others support some policewomen but are highly critical of others. In short, Martin's research suggests that the traditional male police rank and file are more diverse than earlier studies had suggested.[42]

### Race and Ethnicity

The addition of substantial numbers of African-American officers has also affected the police subculture. By the early 1990s, people of color had become a majority of the officers in several police departments: Detroit, Washington, D.C., Miami, San Antonio.[43]

There are notable differences in attitudes between white and African-American officers on some issues. In several cities, African-American officers have spoken out publicly on the issue of police use of force, criticizing their own departments, and in some cases the police union, which is dominated by white officers.[44] The National Black Police Officers Association published a pamphlet on fighting police brutality that urges officers to report misconduct by other officers.[45] These actions represent a significant break in the traditional solidarity of the officer rank and file.

At the same time, there are differences among African-American officers. Alex notes a generational difference between the older and younger officers. The newer officers are more likely to be assertive and willing to express their criticisms of the department than are the older officers.[46] Martin found that African-American female officers are multiple minorities, representing both race and gender, who have a unique and more critical perspective on policing.[47]

There is very little research on Hispanic police officers. In a 1986 study, Carter found that Hispanic officers believed that the department discriminated against Hispanic citizens and that it also discriminated against Hispanic officers in promotions.[48]

**TABLE 13–1**
CHANGES IN THE MIAMI POLICE DEPARTMENT, 1974 TO 1994

Number of Sworn Officers

|      | BF | BM  | HF | HM  | WF | WM  |
|------|----|-----|----|-----|----|-----|
| 1974 | 10 | 72  | 1  | 77  | 26 | 589 |
| 1994 | 90 | 167 | 33 | 497 | 43 | 242 |

Sources: Miami Police Department, Report 1994 (Miami, FL: Miami Police Department, 1994), p. 8.

## Sexual Orientation

A number of police officers are lesbian or gay. In some departments they are open about their sexual orientation, and in some have formed their own organizations. The Gay Officer Action League (GAOL) in New York City began publishing a newsletter in 1982. By 1992 at least 10 police departments openly recruited lesbian and gay officers. Some of these departments are in states where antidiscrimination laws cover sexual orientation. Others are in cities with large lesbian and gay communities, and they have gay and lesbian officers designated as liaisons to these communities.[49]

Lesbian and gay officers represent a clear challenge to the traditional stereotype of policing as a tough, macho, male occupation. In New York City the police union, along with a coalition of 25 religious and social organizations attempted to block the police department's program for recruiting lesbian and gay officers.

## Patterns of Interaction

In a study of one midwestern department Haarr found that, although the number of African-American and female officers had increased, there was limited interaction between members of different groups on a daily basis. Interactions were measured in terms of daily "meets" with other officers, including handling calls together, backing each other up, eating meals together, and gossiping or joking. White male officers largely interacted with other white male officers. Most (75 percent) of the African-American male officers indicated that other male officers (either African American or white) were the officers they interacted with on duty. The three African-American female officers interacted primarily with other African-American officers, either male or female. White female officers were the least likely to identify interactions and friendships with partners or former partners, and to interact with female officers in other units. Finally, at roll call, officers "separated themselves spatially by race and gender as to where they sat and whom they interacted with."[50]

### Intergroup Conflict

Haarr also found a relatively high level of conflict between different groups in the department. White officers believed that they were being discriminated against because promotions and preferred assignments were being given to African-American officers who were less qualified.[51] In a study of a Texas police department, David Carter found that Hispanic officers believed there was discrimination against them on the job. In 1996 in Washington, D.C., 66 percent of the white officers believed that the promotion system favored African Americans, and 49 percent of the African-American officers thought that it favored whites.[52]

Women police officers often experience open hostility from some male officers. This hostility was especially strong for the first women officers assigned to patrol duty in the early 1970s. Martin and Jurik report, "The resistance faced by the first women on patrol was blatant, malicious, widespread, organized, and sometimes life-threatening."[53] With the passage of time, the hostility has become less blatant and more subtle.[54]

These divisions along racial, ethnic, and gender lines are reflected in the fact that in many departments police officers have formed separate organizations. There are separate African-American, Hispanic, and female organizations. In most instances, the official police union reflects the views of the white officers. Frequently the African-American organization brings a law suit alleging race discrimination in employment.

In short, there is no homogeneous police subculture, and the rank and file are marked by strong divisions along racial, ethnic, and gender lines.

### Education

The educational levels of police officers have also been rising steadily. In 1960, 80 percent of all sworn officers had only a high school education. By 1988 the figure had fallen to 34.8 percent. The percentage of officers with a four-year college degree rose from 2.7 percent to 22.6 percent in the same period.[55] In many departments there is a generation gap between the younger, better-educated officers and the veteran officers with less education.

## Cohort Effects

The dominant attitudes of rank-and-file officers also change over time, as new groups of officers enter a department. Whereas experienced officers might react negatively to a dramatic change (e.g., a Supreme Court decision, the introduction of community policing), new cohorts of officers find these circumstances an established fact of life.

Skolnick's finding that established officers are hostile to the Supreme Court and other limitations of their practices arose from research on officers who reacted to the most controversial Supreme Court decisions in the early 1960s.[56] With the passage of time, however, new cohorts of recruits continually enter the ranks of policing. These officers find constitutional requirements regarding search and seizure and interrogations an established fact of life, not something new imposed on them as was the case for officers in the 1960s. A study of narcotics officers in Chicago found a high degree of support for the exclusionary rule. On the whole, officers did not regard it as a barrier to effective police work, and many officers believed that it played an important role in deterring police misconduct.[57]

Along the same lines, Reuss-Ianni found two cultures among police officers in the department she studied. One group identified with the old street cop culture that values street experience and a tough, personalized way of dealing with people on the street. The other group identified with the new bureaucratic style of written rules and formal procedures for dealing with both police work on the street and departmental governance. This latter group is more accepting of, for example, Supreme Court rules on police practices, along with other formal procedures designed to control discretion (Chapter 8) and ensure police accountability (Chapter 11).[58] Milner found a higher degree of support for the *Miranda* decision in the more professionalized departments than in the less professionalized ones.[59] In short, the informal culture of a police organization affects officer attitudes toward certain important subjects.

With the retirement of officers who identify with the old street cop culture, and the recruitment of more officers with higher education, the dominant culture of particular police departments changes significantly over the course of 20 years.

## Summary

In short, the composition of the rank and file of police departments has changed dramatically over the past 30 years. Earlier research suggesting the existence of a set of attitudes based on a homogeneous police subculture failed to take into account this new reality. Female, racial and ethnic minority, lesbian and gay, and college-educated officers bring different backgrounds and experiences to their jobs as police officers. As a result, they have different attitudes on some, but not necessarily all, aspects of policing. The changes in police employment patterns raise many new questions about the police rank and file.

## THE RELATIONSHIP BETWEEN ATTITUDES AND BEHAVIOR

The relationship between police officer attitudes and on-the-job behavior is complex. Common sense suggests a one-to-one relationship: that prejudicial attitudes about race or gender, for example, automatically transfer into discriminatory behavior; or, that support for higher education translates into different behavior on the street. Research on policing, however, suggests that the relationship is extremely complex and that attitudes are mediated by a number of factors.

In his research for the President's Crime Commission, Reiss found that verbal expressions of racial prejudice were common among white officers. Of the 510 white officers studied in Boston and Chicago, 38 percent were deemed highly prejudiced, and 35 percent prejudiced, against African Americans. Three-quarters of the officers expressed some racial prejudice in the presence of field observers.[60] Yet, these attitudes did not translate directly into the observed patterns of discrimination. Analyzing Reiss and Black's data, Friedrich found that the more prejudiced officers were somewhat more likely to make arrests, but the influence was meager. At the same time, the less prejudiced officers were more likely to treat citizens in a neutral manner—that is, neither punitively nor favorably. At the same time, however, white officers with positive racial attitudes were more likely to arrest African-American suspects. Friedrich suggests that this may be the result of their "particularly dim view of black offenders."[61]

Donald Black, meanwhile, found some evidence that African-American officers were more likely to arrest African-American suspects, although the differences were not great. He suggested that this might be a result of their stronger tendency to comply with the expressed preferences of African-American victims, who are more likely to complain about African-American suspects. In the end, all studies of arrest practices have found only a very weak correlation between officer attitudes and performance.[62]

The bureaucratic aspects of the police department and the criminal justice system also limit the influence of officer attitudes on behavior. An arrest is a highly visible action, in the sense that it comes to the attention of other people—sergeant, prosecutor, judge (in many departments, sergeants review all arrests). The values and expectations of these other officials, along with prevailing legal rules, limit the ability of the officer to act solely on the basis of his or her personal prejudices.[63]

## BACKGROUND CHARACTERISTICS AND BEHAVIOR

The background characteristics of individual police officers have also been examined as an explanation of officer attitudes and behavior. One of the assumptions of police reform over the past 30 years has been that different kinds of people will act differently as police officers. Specifically, many people have assumed that racial and ethnic minority officers will be better able to relate to minority citizens; that female officers will be less aggressive (and thus less violent) than male officers; and that college-educated officers will be better able to deal with the complex demands of policing.

### Race and Ethnicity

Civil rights leaders have urged police departments to hire more African-American officers as a way to improve police–community relations. They argue that these officers will have more rapport with the African-American community and will not discriminate in arrests or other police actions (see Chapter 9).[64]

There is some evidence that African-American officers do have different attitudes than white officers on some issues. Alex found strong differences in outlooks and identities between white and African-American officers in New York City.[65] In a survey of 522 police officers assigned to minority-group neighborhoods in 13 large cities, Peter Rossi found that African-American officers had more positive attitudes toward their assigned districts. They were less likely than white officers to rate the assignment as more difficult than other assignments, three times more likely to live in the precinct where they worked, and more likely to have friends there. The African-American officers were also more likely to believe that the residents of the area where they were assigned were honest and industrious.[66]

And as noted above, African-American and white officers have different views on whether there is race discrimination in employment within their departments, including both recruitment and promotion.

There is, however, no strong evidence that the different attitudes of African-American officers translate into different behavior. As noted above, the race of the officer appears to have only a weak influence on arrest rates. Moreover, that relationship is extremely complex. African-American officers tend to arrest African-American suspects slightly more often than white officers. Again, this may reflect the greater responsiveness of African-American officers to the requests of African-American complainants. At most, however, the differences between white and black officers are slight.[67]

Reiss did not find significant differences in the use of force by white and African-American officers.[68] White, African-American, and Hispanic officers receive citizen complaints in proportion to their presence in police departments.[69]

Fyfe found that, after controlling for place of assignment, white and African-American officers fire their weapons at the same rate; that is, the nature of the precinct is the primary variable influencing police shootings. Officers assigned to high-crime precincts in New York City use deadly force more frequently than those assigned to low-crime precincts. Within each type of precinct, white and black officers use deadly force at essentially the same rate. The characteristics of the neighborhood rather than race or personal attitudes influence their behavior.[70]

There are no studies that systematically compare the behavior of Hispanic police officers with white and African-American officers.


### Gender

Some women's rights advocates argue that female officers will be less aggressive than male officers and better able to handle difficult situations verbally.[71] Comparisons of the performance of male and female officers have found only slight differences in their on-the-job behavior.[72] Bloch and Anderson compared 86 new female recruits with 86 new male recruits in Washington, D.C. They concluded that, in general, males and females performed patrol work in a similar manner. Both groups responded to similar types of calls for police service while on patrol and encountered similar proportions of citizens who were dangerous, angry, upset, drunk, or violent. The study found "no reported incidents which cast serious doubt on the ability of women to perform patrol work satisfactorily." Slight differences between men and women were found, but they were not significant. Female officers made slightly fewer arrests and issued fewer traffic citations. On the other hand, female officers were less likely to engage in conduct unbecoming to an officer.[73]

A study of patrol officers in New York City compared 41 male and 41 female officers over a seven-month period between 1975 and 1976. The researchers found that the style of police work used by the female officers was almost indistinguishable from that used by the male officers. Male and female officers used different verbal and nonverbal techniques to control situations at virtually identical rates. Although the female officers were slightly less active than the male officers, "civilians rated the female officers more competent, pleasant, and respectful."[74]

Data on citizen complaints consistently indicate that female officers receive only half as many complaints as male officers. Moreover, virtually all of the so-called problem officers, defined as officers who receive high rates of citizen complaints, are male.[75]

### Education

There is no strong evidence that the officer with a college education behaves differently on the street than the officer with only a high school education.[76] One study, however, did find that college educated officers tend to receive fewer complaints than officers with less education.[77]

### Summary

In short, race, ethnicity, gender, and education appear to have little impact on police officer behavior. One possible explanation for this, however, is that the recruitment, selection, and training process screens out individuals with attitudes that are inconsistent with the dominant values of police officers. It is possible that many people with different attitudes do not even apply for jobs as police officers. Individuals who do not fit in with the majority may be screened out during the selection process or they may quit their jobs early in their careers because they think they do not fit it.

Peer pressure from other officers also exerts a powerful influence. Individuals who begin with slightly different attitudes, and who may behave differently, are socialized into the attitudes and behavior of the group. Thus, new African-American officers are socialized into thinking and acting like the other (predominantly white) officers. Female officers adopt the attitudes and behavior of the dominant male police culture.[78]

### STYLES OF POLICE WORK

Individual police officers perform with different styles. One important distinction is between active and passive officers. Active officers are those who (1) initiate more contacts with citizens (field interrogations, traffic stops, building checks); (2) assert control of situations with citizens; and (3) make more arrests. Passive officers respond only when calls are dispatched and make few arrests.

Most studies of police work have found that officers generally initiate little activity. Most contacts are citizen initiated rather than officer initiated.[79] Studies of arrest productivity have found that many officers make no arrests and that a small number of officers make a very high proportion of all arrests.[80] Van Maanen argues that new officers quickly learn that hard work will not be rewarded and, consequently, try to avoid situations that might create trouble. Officers who work harder than everyone else are disliked as "rate busters."[81]

Bayley and Garofalo's study of New York City police officers identifies specific actions that distinguish active from passive officers in asserting control of situations. Passive officers are more likely simply to observe a situation and take notes. Active officers are more likely to ask probing questions and request that citizens explain themselves.[82]

Differences in work style are the result of both personal temperament and career expectations. James Leo Walsh identifies three distinct career styles. Street cops are attracted to policing by the prospects of a secure work environment (good pay, good job security, and so on). Action seekers are attracted to policing by the potential for exciting work, particularly crime-fighting tasks. Middle-class mobiles are attracted by the professional status of policing and the opportunities for career advancement and upward social mobility. Street cops are likely to be much less aggressive than the other two types. Action seekers initiate activity for the immediate excitement, whereas middle-class mobiles do so for the eventual reward.[83]

Broderick constructed a typology based on how officers deal with the tension between maintaining order and respect for due process of law. Enforcers emphasize order with little respect for due process. Idealists emphasize both social order and due process. Optimists give low priority to social order and high priority to due process. Realists put little emphasis on either due process or social order.[84]

William K. Muir created a typology of police officers on the basis of how they use power. Muir's approach is somewhat unique in the literature because it seeks to identify the qualities that make a *good* police officer. Virtually all the other studies of the police subculture and officer attitudes focus on explaining police misconduct.[85]

The professional police officer, Muir argues, is one who develops two virtues: passion and perspective. The professional officer grasps the nature of human suffering intellectually (passion), but at the same time understands that unjust means cannot be used to deal with this problem (perspective). Officers who respond with passion to human problems but see no limits on their power are enforcers. Reciprocators have perspective but no passion; they are too objective, too detached from the human problems they encounter, and fail to act. Finally, the avoiders have neither passion nor perspective; they do not respond to the problems they face and take no action.[86]

**Do Police Types Exist?**  Although much effort has gone into identifying police *types*, there is some question about whether they exist in reality. Ellen Hochstedler tested five different typologies through secondary analysis of data on 1,134 Dallas police officers in 1973. The data involved confidential questionnaires that explored officers' commitment to crime fighting (e.g., "Much time should be spent on questioning suspicious persons"), service (e.g., "Much time should be spent explaining rights to suspects"), and other aspects of policing. Hochstedler was unable to confirm the existence of the types defined by Broderick, Muir, and others. She concluded that the various qualities (crime fighting, respect for due process) "vary between individuals, between situations, and even with the same individual in similar situations at different times." In short, the "attitudes and behavior of police officers are very difficult phenomena to explain or predict."[87]

## CAREER DEVELOPMENT

Many experts on police administration argue that one of the most serious problems in American policing is a lack of adequate career opportunities. The problems include (1) limited opportunities for promotion, (2) inadequate rewards for good job performance, and (3) lack of opportunities for professional development and personal fulfillment. In a two-wave survey of Detroit police officers, over half in both 1978 (53 percent) and 1988 (54 percent) indicated low satisfaction with the opportunity for career advancement. Few (10 percent in 1978 and 16 percent in 1988) expressed high satisfaction with the advancement opportunities.[88]

### Promotion

Opportunities for promotion are severely limited in American police departments. First, civil service regulations usually require that an officer serve a certain number of years in rank before being eligible to apply for promotion. Time-in-rank requirements range from two to five years.[89]

Second, promotional opportunities occur at irregular intervals. The decision to promote may depend on the city's financial condition rather than on the needs of the police department. Sometimes promotions are postponed for many years as a way of coping with a financial crisis. In 1986 about 25 percent of all departments reported that they had not filled vacancies in the previous three years because of budget cuts.[90]

Third, promotions are based on a formal testing process, involving a written examination and an oral interview. Interviews are generally conducted by the chief of police, a committee of high-ranking officers, and often members of the local civil service agency group.[91] Some departments use the assessment center technique, which attempts to evaluate the ability of the applicant to handle the job being sought.

There is considerable controversy over whether the commonly used tests select the best-qualified persons. Written examinations, for example, test for factual knowledge but may not indicate the applicant's potential for working as a supervisor. Oral interviews may be extremely subjective, and reflect the biases of the interviewers.[92] In an unprofessional department, officers with high standards of integrity and college educations could receive low scores. If the command staff conducting the interviews are all white males, women and racial minorities may be at a disadvantage.[93]

### Salaries and Benefits

The salaries and benefits offered police officers in most departments are generally very attractive.[94] Along with job security, they are one of the main reasons people choose law enforcement as a career (see Chapter 12). Salaries are rigidly structured by civil service

---

**SIDEBAR 13–2**

STUDYING YOUR OWN COMMUNITY

What are the salary schedules for the major law enforcement agencies in your community? How does the major municipal police department compare with the county sheriffs' department? How do starting salaries compare? What are the maximum salaries for the entry-level positions (e.g., police officer, deputy sheriff)?

---

procedures and/or union contracts, however. Pay is tied to an officer's rank. Typically, there are several pay steps at the rank of police officer, which an officer gains through seniority. Other raises result from renegotiation of the entire department's pay scale.

The only way to achieve a significant pay increase is through promotion. Unlike employees in the private sector, a police chief cannot reward an outstanding officer through a bonus or discretionary pay increase. Thus, there are no immediate financial rewards for outstanding performance.

Most departments offer additional pay for certain assignments or qualifications. Seventy percent of all municipal departments offer incentive pay for college education; 25 percent offer hazardous duty pay for certain assignments; and 43 percent provide shift differential pay. Another 30 percent offer various forms of merit pay increases.[95]

The major source of additional pay is overtime. Certain assignments, particularly those that involve frequent court appearances such as criminal investigations and traffic violations, offer the greatest opportunities for overtime.

### Assignment

The principal reward available to a police officer is to be given a preferred assignment. These assignments are generally made at the discretion of the chief, subject to applicable seniority rules. Thus, for example, an officer may bid for assignment as a detective or to the training or gang unit. The choice is at the discretion of the chief. Traditionally, giving preferential assignments to friends and allies was one of the informal ways a chief maintained control over a department. These allies could be counted on to provide information about what was really going on in particular units.[96]

Assignments must be within the officer's rank. A sergeant, for example, cannot be assigned as commander of a unit if that position is designated as a lieutenant's position. The rigidity of these personnel classification systems limits both the career opportunities for individual officers and the management flexibility of the chief executive.[97]

Special assignments play an important role in promotional opportunities. Holding a number of different assignments allows an officer to become known to a wide range of other officers, to establish a reputation for ability, and to learn about different aspects of the department. These reputations and the knowledge gained can lead to more favorable evaluations in promotion interviews.

Racial, ethnic, and gender conflicts within police departments affect personnel assignments, and subsequent opportunities for promotion. Martin found that female officers are less likely to be given certain preferred special assignments.[98]

### Lateral Entry

The opportunity to move to other police departments is extremely limited. Virtually all American police departments start new officers as rookies, discounting any experience with other departments. The officer who moves to another department loses all of his or her seniority. Thus, a sergeant in one department must start all over again at a new department at the rank of police officer. Police pension systems pose another obstacle to officer mobility. Most are local systems that cannot be transferred. Officers who move face the loss of some or all of their previous investment in the pension system. By contrast, college professors are able to participate in a national retirement system (TIAA/CREF), which is portable: The faculty member who changes jobs remains in the same system. The President's Crime Commission recommended developing a national police retirement system that would permit the transfer of personnel without the loss of benefits.[99] A few experiments with portable police pensions have been tried, but they are the exception rather than the rule.[100]

Lateral entry, or moving to another department at the same or higher rank, is very uncommon in American policing. The exception is hiring at the rank of chief. A 1986 survey found no large police departments (cities with populations of 250,000 or more) that allowed lateral entry at lower ranks. Meanwhile, 19 percent of all departments permitted hiring a police chief from "outside," and most of those were in smaller cities (populations of 50,000 or less).[101]

Some experts regard lateral entry as a potential means of enhancing police professionalism. They argue that it would create greater career opportunities for talented and ambitious officers and would allow departments to bring in fresh blood and new ideas.[102] Lateral entry is opposed because officers jealously guard the few promotional opportunities that do arise in a department and resent the idea of outsiders getting these jobs.

### PERFORMANCE EVALUATION

In the course of a career, a police officer's performance will be regularly evaluated by supervisors. The Commission on Accreditation for Law Enforcement Agencies (CALEA) accreditation standards include the following requirement: "A written directive requires that a performance evaluation of each employee be conducted and documented at least annually."[103] There are probably some departments where regular evaluations are not conducted. These departments do not meet the accreditation standards, and would generally be considered unprofessional and poorly managed.

Traditional police performance evaluation systems have been heavily criticized, however. A 1977 Police Foundation report concluded that "the current status of performance appraisal systems is discouragingly low."[104] Changes over the next 20 years resulted in only marginal improvements. A 1997 report by the Community Policing

Consortium concluded, "Most performance evaluations currently used by police agencies do not reflect the work officers do."[105]

Figure 13–1 represents a traditional performance evaluation form (taken from the 1977 Police Foundation report). This document illustrates some of the problems with the evaluation process. First, the definitions are not clear. How is effectiveness measured, for example? Second, because of the halo effect, a person who scores very high on one factor is likely to be rated high on all others. Third, because of the central tendency phenomenon, the ratings of all officers tend to cluster around one numerical level. Finally, there is a tendency to rate everyone highly.[106]

Performance evaluations by supervisors may also reflect racial, ethnic, or gender bias. There is some indication that African-American and Hispanic officers are more likely to be cited for departmental violations. Martin and Jurik argue that traditional performance criteria such as aggressiveness are male oriented and inevitably biased against female officers.[107]

Another serious problem is the fact that official evaluations do not always reflect the actual performance of officers. The Mollen Commission found that officer Michael Dowd, one of the most brutal and corrupt officers in the New York City Police Department, had received outstanding performance evaluations. His 1987 evaluation concluded that he had "excellent street knowledge" and could "easily become a role model for others to emulate."[108] The Christopher Commission found that some of the officers with the highest number of citizen complaints had received excellent performance evaluations.[109]

Even the traditional measure of arrest is not necessarily used systematically in performance evaluations. Some departments evaluate officers on the basis of the number of arrests, and few of those departments keep systematic records on arrest outcomes. Thus, they do not reward officers who make quality arrests (defined as leading to a felony conviction) as opposed to a large number of arrests.[110]

Perhaps the most serious problem is that performance evaluation systems have few if any procedures for identifying and rewarding good behavior in the non-law enforcement situations that comprise the bulk of police work.

Another serious problem with police personnel systems is that they focus on punishing misconduct rather than rewarding good behavior. Police organizations have been characterized as punishment-centered bureaucracies.[111] There are elaborate rules that can be used, often selectively, to catch and punish officers, but few methods for positively rewarding officers.

The CALEA accreditation standards require that evaluations include explanatory comments to justify the rating, and that officers be counseled about the rating, and have an opportunity to sign and make written comments about their ratings. Officers whose performance is deemed unsatisfactory should be advised in writing of that evaluation.[112]

A more positive view of police personnel evaluation emerged from Bayley and Garofalo's study of New York City police officers. Officers in three precincts were asked in confidence to identify three other officers they thought were "particularly skilled at handling conflict situations." The officers receiving the highest scores were then matched with comparison groups in the same precincts. An analysis of 467 police–citizen encounters involving potential violence found that officers rated highly by their peers

**FIGURE 13–1**

METROPOLITAN DADE COUNTY

E M P L O Y E E   P E R F O R M A N C E   R E P O R T

WORK SHEET

| Name   *(Last)* | *(First)* | *(Initial)* | Period Covered | |
|---|---|---|---|---|
| | | | From | To |
| Civil Service Title | | | Civil Service Status | If Prob, Date Ends |
| Department | Division | | Unit | |

CHECK ITEMS

| ☐ Strong ☐ Weak | | | | |
|---|---|---|---|---|

| CHECK ITEMS | INDICATE FACTOR RATING BY "X" | | | |
|---|---|---|---|---|
| ☐ Satisfactory  ☐ Not applicable | UNSATISFACTORY | NEEDS ATTENTION | SATISFACTORY | OUTSTANDING |
| **1. QUANTITY OF WORK**<br>☐ Amount of work performed<br>☐ Completion of work on schedule | Seldom produces enough work or meets deadlines. | Does not always complete on acceptable amount of work. | Consistently completes an acceptable amount of work. | Amount of work produced is consistently outstanding. |
| **2. QUALITY OF WORK**<br>☐ Accuracy<br>☐ Effectiveness<br>☐ Compliance with instructions<br>☐ Use of tools & equipment<br>☐ Neatness of work product<br>☐ Reports & correspondence<br>☐ Thoroughness | Too poor to retain in job without improvement. | Quality below acceptable standards. | Performs assigned duties in a satisfactory manner. | Performs all duties in an outstanding manner. Exceptional accuracy, skill or effectiveness. |
| **3. WORK HABITS**<br>☐ Attendance<br>☐ Observance of working hours<br>☐ Observance of rules<br>☐ Safety practices<br>☐ Personal Appearance | Too poor to retain in job without improvement. | Work habits need improvement. | Work habits satisfactory. | Exceptional work habits. Always observes rules and safe practices. |
| **4. PERSONAL RELATIONS**<br>☐ With fellow employees and supervisors<br>☐ With public | Too poor to retain in job without improvement. | Personal relations need improvement. | Maintains satisfactory work relations with others. | Exceptionally co-operative with public, co-workers and supervisors. |
| **5. SUPERVISORY ABILITY**<br>☐ Planning & assigning<br>☐ Training & instructing<br>☐ Disciplinary control<br>☐ Evaluating performance<br>☐ Delegating<br>☐ Making decisions<br>☐ Fairness & impartiality<br>☐ Unit morale | Poor supervisory ability. Work of unit frequently unsatisfactory. | Supervisory ability inadequate in some respects. Works results of unit below par at times. | Obtains good results from subordinates. Controls unit efficiently. | Outstanding ability to get maximum from unit and available resources. |

(FOR SUPERVISORS ONLY)

RATER'S COMMENTS: *(attach additional sheets if needed)*

| RATER'S RECOMMENDATION (for employees under consideration for a merit raise or permanent status) | I have reviewed this report. It represents the facts to the best of my knowledge. I concur in the recommendation, if any, as to merit raise or permanent status. |
|---|---|
| This is to certify that the overall performance of the subject employee ☐ is  ☐ is not   satisfactory<br>The employee ☐ is  ☐ is not   recommended for<br>☐ a merit raise  ☐ permanent status.<br>This report is based on my observation and knowledge. It represents my best judgment of the employee's performance.<br>RATER ............................... Date ............................... | REVIEWER ...................................... Date ............................<br>In signing this report I do not necessarily agree with the conclusions of the rater. I understand that I may write my comments on the reverse side. I have received a copy of this report.<br>EMPLOYEE'S<br>SIGNATURE ........................................ Date ........................ |

*Source:* Frank J. Landy, *Performance Appraisal in Police Departments* (Washington DC: The Police Foundation, 1977), p. 7.

handled situations differently than the members of the comparison groups. They were more likely to take charge of situations, less likely to simply stand by and observe, more likely to probe with questions and ask citizens to explain themselves, and more likely to verbally defuse situations. They were less likely to threaten the use of physical force, more likely to request people to disperse, and less likely to order people to do so.[113]

Bayley and Garofalo found that peer evaluations corresponded with observed differences in officer behavior. Also important, the officers who were rated more highly by their peers and who performed better on the job also received higher ratings in official departmental evaluations. They received higher ratings in such categories as appearance, community relations skills, impartiality, decision making, ethics, and street knowledge.[114]

Experts on community policing argue that it requires a new approach to police officer performance evaluation. New procedures are necessary to take into account the new role of the police and the different tasks that officers are expected to perform.[115] Figure 13–2 represents portions of an experimental assessment report developed for the Houston Police Department's Neighborhood Oriented Policing Program.

## JOB SATISFACTION AND JOB STRESS

Police officer job satisfaction and job stress are often treated as separate subjects, despite the fact that they are closely related. The same factors cause satisfaction or stress, depending upon whether they are present or absent.

The factors that cause satisfaction or stress fall into five general categories: (1) the nature of police work; (2) organizational factors such as perceived support from leaders, relations with fellow officers, and opportunities for career advancement; (3) relations with the community; (4) relations with the media and the political establishment; and (5) personal or family factors that influence a person's job.[116]

A majority of police officers are generally satisfied with their jobs. In 1996 in Washington, D.C., 82 percent indicated that they were satisfied or very satisfied. A study of Detroit police officers found that in 1988, 61 percent expressed medium satisfaction and 8 percent expressed high satisfaction. This represents lower levels of satisfaction than 10 years earlier, when 53 percent expressed medium and 28 percent expressed high satisfaction with their jobs. About three-quarters (78 percent) said they would choose law enforcement again as a career, but 64 percent also said that the work is stressful. Few of the Detroit officers indicated that they felt low satisfaction in terms of job fulfillment (3 percent in 1978 and 8 percent in 1988), defined in terms of freedom to make decisions and overall feelings of accomplishment.[117]

There is some disagreement over whether policing is more stressful than other demanding occupations. Some studies have reported higher rates of suicide, alcoholism, heart attack, and divorce among police officers than among the general population. A study of suicides in New York City between 1964 and 1973 found a rate of 17.2 per 100,000 among police officers compared with 8.3 for the city as a whole and 11 per 100,000 for males in the city. Niederhoffer found inconsistent evidence on divorce rates. Some studies claimed to find divorce rates as high as 30 percent in some police departments, but it was not clear that the rate for police officers was significantly higher than for the general populations in the areas studied.[118]

# HOUSTON POLICE DEPARTMENT

## Patrol Officer's Bi-Annual
## Assessment Report

| OFFICER INFORMATION | | ACTIVITY PERIOD BASED ON DATE OF ENTRY |
|---|---|---|
| NAME: _____ | | |
| *Last*                    *First*                    *MI* | | |
| EMP. # ____   SHIFT: ____   DIST/BEAT: _____   NEIGH.: _____ | | From:(m/d/y) _____ |
| COMMAND/BUREAU/DIVISION: _____ | | To:(m/d/y) _____ |

### SECTION 1

| WORK ASSIGNMENT | List any changes in work assignment, responsibilities, or work environment which affect an officer's ability to complete assigned tasks. |
|---|---|
| **PROGRESS** | Describe status of and progress made toward attaining objectives set forth in previous monthly assessments. |
| **ACCOMPLISHMENTS** | List successful completion of specific projects, notable actions taken, and any other significant deed(s) initiated by the officer. |
| **SPECIAL RECOGNITION** | List any awards, letters of commendation, or recognition for activities performed by the officer. |

FIGURE 13–2

## SECTION II

**DIRECTIONS:** From the following scale, circle the response which most closely describes the quality of work demonstrated by the officer. Following each response, a written explanation of each choice is necessary. If the performance criterion is not observed by the supervisor or not verified through other means (i.e., survey questionnaires), circle the "Not Observed" (N.O.) response.

| STATEMENTS and EXPLANATIONS | SCALE |
| --- | --- |

| PROFESSIONALISM | Not Observed | Strongly Disagree | Disagree | Average | Agree | Strongly Agree |
| --- | --- | --- | --- | --- | --- | --- |
| 1. Consistently exhibits a professional appearance. | N.O. | 1 | 2 | 3 | 4 | 5 |
| Explanation:_____ | | | | | | |
| 2. Displays adaptability and flexibility. | N.O. | 1 | 2 | 3 | 4 | 5 |
| Explanation:_____ | | | | | | |
| 3. Shows initiative in improving skills. | N.O. | 1 | 2 | 3 | 4 | 5 |
| Explanation:_____ | | | | | | |

| KNOWLEDGE | | | | | | |
| --- | --- | --- | --- | --- | --- | --- |
| 4. Demonstrates working knowledge of laws. | N.O. | 1 | 2 | 3 | 4 | 5 |
| Explanation:_____ | | | | | | |
| 5. Demonstrates working knowledge of General Orders/SOPs. | N.O. | 1 | 2 | 3 | 4 | 5 |
| Explanation:_____ | | | | | | |

| RELATIONSHIPS | | | | | | |
| --- | --- | --- | --- | --- | --- | --- |
| 6. Effectively expresses oneself verbally. | N.O. | 1 | 2 | 3 | 4 | 5 |
| Explanation:_____ | | | | | | |
| 7. Successfully interacts well with other officers. | N.O. | 1 | 2 | 3 | 4 | 5 |
| Explanation:_____ | | | | | | |

**FIGURE 13–2 Continued**

| STATEMENTS and EXPLANATIONS | SCALE |
|---|---|

| **PATROL MANAGEMENT** | Not Observed | Strongly Disagree | Disagree | Average | Agree | Strongly Agree |
|---|---|---|---|---|---|---|
| 8. Efficiently manages uncommitted time.<br><br>Explanation:_____ | N.O. | 1 | 2 | 3 | 4 | 5 |
| 9. Identifies problems and concerns in his/her area.<br><br>Explanation:_____ | N.O. | 1 | 2 | 3 | 4 | 5 |
| 10. Formulates appropriate plan(s) of action.<br><br>Explanation:_____ | N.O. | 1 | 2 | 3 | 4 | 5 |
| 11. Efficiently manages calls for service.<br><br>Explanation:_____ | N.O. | 1 | 2 | 3 | 4 | 5 |
| 12. Maintains self-control in stressful situations.<br><br>Explanation:_____ | N.O. | 1 | 2 | 3 | 4 | 5 |

## SECTION III

**OFFICER COMMENTS** — This section is reserved for officer's comments relative to his/her interpretation of this assessment.

## SECTION IV

This report is based on my observation and knowledge. It represents my best judgement of the officer's performance.

Rated by: _____ Date: _____
(Signature of Immediate Superior Officer)   Title

Received by: _____ Date: _____
(Signature of Higher Superior Officer)   Title

Approved by Department Head: _____ Date: _____

Report Furnished to Civil Service Commission: _____ Date: _____

I certify this report has been discussed with me.
My signature indicates that I   ☐ Agree   ☐ Disagree with this assessment.

Officer's Signature: _____ Date: _____

*Source:* Mary Ann Wycoff and Timothy N. Oettmeier, *Evaluating Patrol Officer Performance Under Community Policing: The Houston Experience* (Washington, DC: U.S. Government Printing Office, 1994), pp. 18–21.

The threat of danger is a basic element of police work that creates stress. Threatening incidents, such as physical assaults in the form of being attacked with a weapon, are statistically infrequent. The number of police officers feloniously killed in the line of duty, in fact, fell by 50 percent between the 1970s and 1990s, and averages less than 70 a year at present.[119] In fact, measured in terms of on-the-job deaths, mining, construction, and farming are considerably more dangerous. The fatality rate in coal mining was 38 per 100,000 employees in 1995, compared with 22 in agriculture and 15 in construction. The rate for law enforcement is about 20 per 100,000, including both accidental and felonious deaths.[120] Nonetheless, as Skolnick argues, the potential threat is a constant factor that affects officers' attitudes toward the public.[121]

Citizen disrespect and challenges to police authority are another source of on-the-job stress. Even though such incidents are statistically infrequent, they loom large in an officer's consciousness. Equally important is the problem of boredom. Routine patrol work often involves long periods of inactivity. Shifting suddenly from inactivity to a high state of readiness is another source of stress. Another major cause of stress in policing involves dealing with extreme human suffering. Officers regularly administer to people who have been killed or seriously injured, or who are in a state of extreme psychological disorder.

The police department itself is a major source of stress. For many officers it is more serious than problems arising from dealing with the public. Officers often feel that command officers do not support them adequately, that incompetent officers are given preferred assignments because of personal friendships, and that the department changes policies in reaction to criticism from the media or politicians. As noted above, racial, ethnic, and gender conflicts exist in many police departments, causing stress among officers. Some police departments rotate shifts on a regular basis. This disrupts a person's family life and has adverse physiological effects, including loss of sleep.[122]

Female police officers experience special gender-related forms of stress. Some stress involves a lack of acceptance by male police officers and the absence of the supportive behavior (e.g., sharing of information, sponsorship for special assignments) that other officers receive. Sexual harassment creates additional stress.[123] Finally, female officers often have greater child care responsibilities than male officers, and take more sick leave in order to meet those needs.

## Coping with Stress

Until recently, few police departments took on the responsibility of helping officers cope with job stress. Either the problem was ignored or the officer with obvious difficulties was quietly assigned to an easier job. For their part, troubled officers either relied on the support of their fellow officers or internalized their problems—a response which often led to alcohol abuse, mental illness, or even suicide.[124]

Today, many police departments maintain programs to help officers cope with the pressures of the job and/or other personal problems. These programs take several different forms. Some use mental health professionals; others rely on peer support. Mental health professionals are employed either on a contract/referral basis, or as full-time staff members of an employee assistance program (EAP). Many EAP programs serve all city or county employees. Many experts regard peer counseling as particularly valuable, because the officer can relate well to the counselor as a fellow police officer. For example, some peer counselors can act as role models who have dealt with alcohol abuse problems.[125]

One of the key issues in employee assistance programs is confidentiality. Officers seek out assistance when they are assured that the information will not be used against them in a disciplinary action. Some EAP programs have been damaged by unauthorized leaks of information, or the belief that such leaks occur.[126] Many officers refuse to seek professional help when they are having problems because of the traditional macho image of police officers as tough individuals who can handle any problem.

## THE RIGHTS OF POLICE OFFICERS

Police officers enjoy the same civil and constitutional rights as other citizens, subject only to certain limitations related to the special circumstances of law enforcement. This was not always the case. In the past, the law held that all public employees, including police officers, gave up certain rights when they began their jobs. Public employment was considered a privilege, and the employee accepted it on the employer's terms. In a famous opinion over 100 years ago, involving an officer who had been fired for discussing politics on the job, Massachusetts judge (and later Supreme Court Justice) Oliver Wendell Holmes declared that the person "may have a constitutional right to talk politics, but he has no constitutional right to be a policeman."[127]

Over the past 20 years this view has been rejected, and police officers, along with other public employees, now enjoy basic constitutional rights of freedom of speech and association, due process of law, and privacy. The U.S. Supreme Court ruled in the 1966 *Garrity* case that "policemen [*sic*], like teachers and lawyers, are not relegated to a watered-down version of constitutional rights."[128] In 1981 the American Civil Liberties Union published a short handbook entitled *The Rights of Police Officers* summarizing these rights.[129]

Under the First Amendment, police officers may not be barred from employment or be disciplined for private political or religious activities. Thus, a police officer has a constitutional right to belong to unpopular political or religious organizations. This right is not absolute, however, and departments may place restrictions on an officer's participation in partisan political activity, such as running for political office. Political or religious activity on the job is not permitted. The right of freedom of speech includes, to a limited extent, the right of an officer to criticize his or her own department publicly. Generally, a department may discipline an officer if the public criticism undermines the department's effectiveness.

Polygraph examinations are an exception to the rights enjoyed by other citizens. The federal Polygraph Protection Act prohibits employers from using lie detectors in recruitment. Law enforcement agencies, however, are exempted, and may administer polygraphs to job applicants.

Officers also enjoy procedural due process protections on the job. They may not be fired or disciplined without adequate cause. Due process in personnel decisions is guaranteed in part by existing civil service regulations, by union contract in some departments, and by a police officers' "bill of rights" in Florida and other states.

## OUTSIDE EMPLOYMENT

A significant number of police officers supplement their incomes with outside employment. Many of those jobs are in private security where the officer wears his or her police uniform. A 1988 U.S. Department of Justice study found that half of all officers in some departments worked off duty but in uniform.[130] In addition, many officers who are frustrated by the lack of career opportunities look for challenges and rewards outside the department.

Outside employment creates a number of potential problems. First, it may diminish an officer's commitment to his or her job with the police department. A study of arrest productivity among New York City police officers found that those officers who held outside jobs made significantly fewer arrests than officers who did not. Apparently, officers were deterred from making arrests out of fear that the resulting court appearances would interfere with their outside work.[131]

Second, off-duty work in uniform creates potential conflicts of interest. An off-duty officer working in a bar, for example, may be caught between the duty to enforce the law and the interests of the bar owner. Finally, outside work in uniform may lower the dignity of the department.[132]

The San Jose Independent Police Auditor exposed another conflict of interest by pointing out that some officers working off duty were hiring their supervisors as employees on those jobs. This practice potentially undermines discipline in the department, as a supervisor might be afraid to discipline an officer under his or her command out of fear of being fired from the off-duty job.[133]

## TURNOVER: LEAVING POLICE WORK

Every year, about 5 percent of all police officers leave their jobs. This attrition rate appears to have been steady since the 1960s. Officers leave police work because of retirement, death, dismissal, voluntary resignation, or layoffs resulting from financial constraints.[134]

Martin found that women leave policing at a slightly higher rate than men, but for reasons other than retirement (6.3 percent annually compared with 4.6 percent). Women are more likely than men to resign voluntarily (4.3 percent versus 3.0 percent) and to be terminated involuntarily (1.2 percent versus 0.6 percent). Women officers experience a more hostile work environment. Women, especially single parents, have greater difficulty combining work with family responsibilities. Inadequate pregnancy leave policies make it difficult or impossible for women to have children and continue to work.[135]

Doerner found significantly higher attrition rates for female officers, both African-American and white, compared with male officers in the Tallahassee Police Department. He suggests that this pattern raises an issue of concern for affirmative action programs, which focus almost exclusively on recruitment and ignore long-term employment patterns.[136]

Relatively little research has been done on the reasons for voluntary resignation. A Memphis study of police officers who resigned found that dissatisfaction with opportunities for promotion and with department policies was more important than inadequate pay and benefits or the feeling that their efforts were not being appreciated. Not all officers who are unhappy choose to resign, however. The Memphis study concludes that "dissatisfaction is a necessary but not a sufficient condition to cause resignation." As is the case with employees in all occupations, the decision is made in the context of many different personal, familial, and economic factors, including perceived career alternatives. The Memphis study identifies several key "turning points" leading to the decision to resign. These include, in order of importance, (1) the feeling that one's career had stagnated (e.g., "I just can't see any future in being a police officer"); (2) a particularly intense experience that brought accumulated frustrations to a head; (3) lack of a sense of fulfillment on the job; (4) family considerations; (5) the conduct of co-workers; (6) particular department policy or policies; and (7) new employment opportunities.[137]

## CONCLUSION

Careers in law enforcement are subject to many different influences. Most popular stereotypes about police officer attitudes and behavior are not supported by the evidence. There is no evidence that a particular type of person is attracted to law enforcement, or that this explains police behavior. The evidence does suggest, however, that certain aspects of police work do exert powerful influences on both attitudes and behavior. At the same time, it is evident that recent changes in police employment patterns have brought new diversity to the rank and file. Racial and ethnic minorities and women bring different expectations to policing. Law enforcement careers are heavily influenced by factors associated with police departments, particularly the opportunities for career advancement. The nature of police organizations is explored in more detail in Chapter 14.

## NOTES

1  William A. Westley, *Violence and the Police* (Cambridge: MIT Press, 1970), pp. 159–160.
2  John H. McNamara, "Uncertainties in Police Work: The Relevance of Police Recruits' Backgrounds and Training," in *The Police: Six Sociological Essays*, ed. David J. Bordua, (New York: Wiley, 1967), pp. 163–252.
3  Arthur J. Luirgio and Dennis P. Rosenbaum, "The Travails of the Detroit Police–Victims Experiment: Assumptions and Important Lessons," *American Journal of Police* 11, no. 3 (1992): 24.
4  Albert Reiss, *The Police and the Public* (New Haven: Yale University Press, 1971), p. 51.
5  John A. Groger, *Memory and Remembering: Everyday Memory in Context* (New York: Longman, 1997), pp. 189–197.
6  John P. Clark, "Isolation of the Police: A Comparison of the British and American Situations," *Journal of Criminal Law, Criminology, and Police Science* 56 (September 1965): 307–319.

**7** Westley, *Violence and the Police*, pp. 18–19.

**8** Stephen B. Perrott and Donald M. Taylor, "Crime Fighting, Law Enforcement and Service Provider Role Orientations in Community-Based Police Officers," *American Journal of Police* 14, no. 3/4 (1995): 182.

**9** Ibid., p. 7.

**10** Richard Seltzer, Sucre Aone, and Gwendolyn Howard, "Police Satisfaction with Their Jobs: Arresting Officers in the District of Columbia," *Police Studies* 19, no. 4 (1996): 33.

**11** Westley, *Violence and the Police*, pp. 76–82.

**12** John Van Maanen, "Police Socialization: A Longitudinal Examination of Job Attitudes in an Urban Police Department, " *Administrative Science Quarterly* 20 (June 1975): 222.

**13** Seltzer, Aone, and Howard, "Police Satisfaction with Their Jobs," p. 33.

**14** George W. Griesinger, Jeffrey S. Slovak, and Joseph J. Molkup, *Civil Service Systems: Their Impact on Police Administration* (Washington: Government Printing Office, 1979).

**15** James L. O'Neill and Michael A. Cushing, *The Impact of Shift Work on Police Officers* (Washington: Police Executive Research Forum, 1991).

**16** President's Commission on Law Enforcement and Administration of Justice, *Task Force Report: The Police* (Washington: Government Printing Office, 1967), p. 165.

**17** James J. Fyfe, "Who Shoots? A Look at Officer Race and Police Shooting," *Journal of Police Science and Administration* 9 (December 1981): 373.

**18** William K. Muir, *Police: Streetcorner Politicians* (Chicago: University of Chicago Press, 1977).

**19** Westley, *Violence and the Police*.

**20** Lawrence W. Sherman, "Causes of Police Behavior: The Current State of Quantitative Research," *Journal of Research in Crime and Delinquency* 17 (January 1980): 69–100.

**21** Westley, *Violence and the Police*, p. 11.

**22** Ibid.

**23** Ibid., pp. 76–82.

**24** Ibid., p. 113.

**25** Ibid, pp. 121–122.

**26** [Christopher Commission], *Report of the Independent Commission to Investigate the Los Angeles Police Department* (Los Angeles: City of Los Angeles, 1991), pp. 168–171.

**27** Jerome H. Skolnick, *Justice without Trial*, 3d ed. (New York: Macmillan, 1994), pp. 44–47.

**28** Egon Bittner, *The Functions of the Police in Modern Society* (Washington: Government Printing Office, 1970), pp. 36–47.

**29** Skolnick, *Justice without Trial*, pp. 65–66.

**30** Donald Black, "The Social Organization of Arrest," in *The Manners and Customs of the Police* (New York: Academic Press, 1980), pp. 85–108; Robert Worden, "The 'Causes' of Police Brutality," in *And Justice for All*, eds. W. A. Geller and H. Toch (Washington: Government Printing Office, 1995), pp. 31–60.

**31** Skolnick, *Justice without Trial*, pp. 1–21, 199–223.

**32** Herbert Packer, *The Limits of the Criminal Sanction* (Stanford, Calif.: Stanford University Press, 1968), chap. 8.

**33** Arthur Niederhoffer, *Behind the Shield* (Garden City, N.Y.: Anchor Books, 1967), pp. 100, 112–113.

**34** Joel Lefkowitz, "Psychological Attributes of Policemen: A Review of Research and Opinion," *Journal of Social Issues* 31, no. 1 (1975):3–26.

**35** David H. Bayley and Harold Mendelsohn, *Minorities and the Police* (New York: Free Press, 1969), pp. 15–18.

**36** McNamara, "Uncertainties in Police Work," p. 195.

**37** Robert H. Langworthy, "Comment—Have We Measured the Concept(s) of Police Cynicism Using Niederhoffer's Cynicism Index?" *Justice Quarterly* 4 (June 1987): 277–280; Robert M. Regoli, John P. Clark, Robert G. Culbertson, and Eric D. Poole, "Rejoinder—Police Cynicism: Theory Development and Reconstruction," *Justice Quarterly* 4 (June 1987): 281–286.

**38** *Police: Streetcorner Politicians*, pp. 82–100.

**39** Samuel Walker, "Racial-Minority and Female Employment in Policing: The Implications of 'Glacial Change'," *Crime and Delinquency* 31 (October 1985): 555–572.

**40** Robin N. Haarr, "Patterns of Interaction in a Police Patrol Bureau: Race and Gender Barriers to Integration," *Justice Quarterly* 14 (March 1997): 53.

**41** Susan Martin, *Breaking and Entering* (Berkeley: University of California Press, 1980), pp. 79–108.

**42** Ibid., pp. 102–107.

**43** Bureau of Justice Statistics, *Law Enforcement Management and Administrative Statistics, 1993* (Washington: Government Printing Office, 1995), pp. 37–47.

**44** "Black Officers Take On the LAPD and Protective League: An Interview with Sgt. Leonard Ross," *Policing by Consent*, October 1995, pp. 8–9.

**45** National Black Police Officers Association, *Police Brutality: How to Stop the Violence* (Washington: NBPOA, nd.).

**46** Nicholas Alex, *Black in Blue* (Englewood Cliffs, NJ: Prentice Hall, 1969).

**47** Susan E. Martin, "'Outsider within' the Station House: The Impact of Race and Gender on Black Women Police," *Social Problems* 41 (August 1994): 398.

**48** David L. Carter, "Hispanic Police Officers' Perceptions of Discrimination," *Police Studies* 9 (Winter 1986): 204–210.

**49** Stephen Leinen, *Gay Cops* (New Brunswick, NJ: Rutgers University Press, 1993).

**50** Haarr, "Patterns of Interaction in a Police Patrol Bureau," p. 65.

**51** Ibid.

**52** Seltzer, Aone, and Howard, "Police Satisfaction with Their Jobs," p. 33.

**53** Susan Ehrlich Martin and Nancy C. Jurik, *Doing Justice, Doing Gender: Women in Law and Criminal Justice Occupations* (Thousand Oaks, CA: Sage, 1996), p. 68.

**54** Susan Ehrlich Martin, *On the Move: The Status of Women in Policing* (Washington: The Police Foundation, 1990), pp. 158–163.

**55** David L. Carter, Allen D. Sapp, and Darrel W. Stephens, *The State of Police Education* (Washington: Police Executive Research Forum, 1989), p. 38.

**56** Skolnick, *Justice without Trial*, pp. 199–223.

**57** Myron Orfield, "The Exclusionary Rule and Deterrence: An Empirical Study of Chicago Narcotics Officers," *University of Chicago Law Review* 54 (Summer 1987): 1016–1055.

**58** Elizabeth Reuss-Ianni, *The Two Cultures of Policing* (New Brunswick, NJ: Transaction Books, 1983).

**59** Neal A. Milner, *The Court and Local Law Enforcement: The Impact of Miranda* (Beverly Hills: Sage, 1971).

**60** Reiss, *The Police and the Public*, p. 147.

**61** Robert Friedrich, "Racial Prejudice and Police Treatment of Blacks." *Evaluating Alternative Law-Enforcement Policies*, eds., Ralph Baker and Fred A. Meyer (Lexington, Mass.: Lexington Books, 1979), pp. 149–167.

**62** Donald Black, *The Manners and Customs of the Police* (New York: Academic Press, 1980), pp. 107–108.

63 Friedrich, "Racial Prejudice and Police Treatment of Blacks," pp. 156–158.

64 President's Commission on Law Enforcement and Administration of Justice, *The Challenge of Crime in a Free Society* (Washington: Government Printing Office, 1967), pp. 101–102.

65 Alex, *Black in Blue*, pp. 85–113.

66 Peter H. Rossi et al., *The Roots of Urban Discontent: Public Policy, Municipal Institutions, and the Ghetto* (New York: Wiley, 1974).

67 Black, *The Manners and Customs of the Police*, pp. 107–108.

68 Albert Reiss, "Police Brutality—Answers to Key Questions," *Transaction* 5 (July–August, 1968): 10–19.

69 New York City, Civilian Complaint Review Board, *Annual Report,* 1997, (New York: City of New York, 1997), pp. 60–61; San Jose, Independent Police Auditor, *Annual Report*, 1996 (San Jose: City of San Jose, 1997), p. 26.

70 Fyfe, "Who Shoots? A Look at Officer Race and Police Shooting," pp. 367–382.

71 Catherine E. Milton, *Women in Policing* (Washington: The Police Foundation, 1972).

72 The various studies are summarized in Martin and Jurik, *Doing Justice, Doing Gender*, chap. 3, 4. For a critique of these studies, however, see Merry Morash and Jack R. Greene, "Evaluating Women on Patrol: A Critique of Contemporary Wisdom," *Evaluation Review* 10 (April 1986): 230–255.

73 Peter B. Bloch and Deborah Anderson, *Policewomen on Patrol: Final Report* (Washington: The Police Foundation, 1974).

74 Joyce L. Sichel, Lucy N. Friedman, Janice C. Quint, and Michael E. Smith, *Women on Patrol: A Pilot Study of Police Performance in New York City* (Washington: Government Printing Office, 1978).

75 New York City, Civilian Complaint Review Board, *Annual Report*, 1997, pp. 62–63.

76 Lawrence W. Sherman, *The Quality of Police Education* (San Francisco: Jossey-Bass, 1978).

77 Victor E. Kappeler, David Carter, and Allen Sapp, "Police Officer Higher Education, Citizen Complaints, and Departmental Rule Violations," *American Journal of Police* 11, no. 2 (1992): 37–54.

78 Sherman, "Causes of Police Behavior."

79 Reiss, *The Police and the Public*, pp. 69–70.

80 Joan Petersilia et al., *Police Performance and Case Attrition* (Santa Monica: Rand, 1987).

81 Van Maanen, "Police Socialization."

82 David H. Bayley and James Garofalo, "The Management of Violence by Police Patrol Officers," *Criminology* 27 (February 1989): 1–25.

83 James Leo Walsh, "Career Styles and Police Behavior," in ed. *Police and Society*, D. Bayley, (Beverly Hills: Sage, 1977), pp. 149–167.

84 J. J. Broderick, *Police in a Time of Change* (Morristown, NJ: General Learning Press, 1977).

85 Muir, *Police: Streetcorner Politicians*.

86 Ibid.

87 Ellen Hochstedler, "Testing Types: A Review and Test of Police Types," *Journal of Criminal Justice* 9, no. 6 (1981): 451–466.

88 Eve Buzawa, Thomas Austin, and James Bannon, "The Role of Selected Sociodemographic and Job-Specific Variables in Predicting Patrol Officer Job Satisfaction: A Reexamination Ten Years Later," *American Journal of Police* xiii (no. 2, 1994): 51–75.

89 Police Executive Research Forum, *Survey of Police Operational and Administrative Practices, 1981* (Washington: PERF, 1981), pp. 378–382.

90 James J. Fyfe, "Police Personnel Practices, 1986," *Municipal Yearbook, 1987* (Washington: International City Management Association, 1987), pp. 16–17.

**91** Police Executive Research Forum, *Survey of Police Operational and Administrative Practices, 1981*, pp. 342–346.

**92** William G. Doerner, "The Utility of the Oral Interview Board in Selecting Police Academy Admissions, *Policing*, 20 (No. 4, 1994): 784.

**93** Martin and Jurik, *Doing Justice, Doing Gender*.

**94** Comparative salary data are available in Bureau of Justice Statistics, *Law Enforcement Management and Administrative Statistics, 1993* (Washington: Government Printing Office, 1995), pp. 85–95.

**95** Ibid., p. x.

**96** Westley, *Violence and the Police*, pp. 28–30.

**97** Dorothy Guyot, "Bending Granite: Attempts to Change the Rank Structure of American Police Departments," *Journal of Police Science and Administration* 7, no. 3 (1979): 253–284.

**98** Martin, *On the Move*, pp. 77–103.

**99** President's Commission on Law Enforcement and Administration of Justice, *The Challenge of Crime in a Free Society* (Washington: Government Printing Office, 1967), p. 111.

**100** Geoffrey N. Calvert, *Portable Police Pennons—Improving Interagency Transfers* (Washington: Government Printing Office, 1971).

**101** Fyfe, "Police Personnel Practices, 1986," p. 20.

**102** Herman Goldstein, *Policing a Free Society* (Cambridge, Mass.: Ballinger, 1977), pp. 241–243.

**103** Commission on Accreditation for Law Enforcement Agencies, Standard 35.1.2 in *Standards for Law Enforcement Agencies*, 3d ed. (Fairfax: CALEA, 1994), p. 35-1.

**104** Frank J. Landy, *Performance Appraisal in Police Departments* (Washington: The Police Foundation, 1977), p. 1.

**105** Timothy N. Oettmeier and Mary Ann Wycoff, *Personnel Performance Evaluations in the Community Policing Context* (Washington: Community Policing Consortium, 1997), p. 5.

**106** Landy, *Performance Appraisal in Police Departments*.

**107** Martin and Jurik, *Doing Justice, Doing Gender*, pp. 86–87.

**108** Mollen Commission, *Commission Report* (New York: City of New York, 1994), p. 81.

**109** Christopher Commission*, Report of the Independent Commission,* (Los Angeles: City of Los Angeles, 1991), pp. 40–48.

**110** Petersilia et al., *Police Performance and Case Attrition*.

**111** John H. McNamara, "Uncertainties in Police Work," ed. pp. 177–178.

**112** Commission on Accreditation for Law Enforcement Agencies, *Standards for Law Enforcement Agencies*, p. 35-2.

**113** Bayley and Garofalo, "The Management of Violence by Police Patrol Officers," pp. 1–25.

**114** Ibid.

**115** Oettmeier and Wycoff, *Personnel Performance Evaluations in the Community Policing Context*.

**116** See the categories used in Jack R. Greene, "Police Officer Job Satisfaction and Community Perceptions: Implications for Community–Oriented Policing," *Journal of Research in Crime and Delinquency* 26 (May 1984): 168–183.

**117** Eve Buzawa, Thomas Austin, James Bannon, "The Role of Selected Sociodemographic and Job-Specific Variables in Predicting Patrol Officer Job Satisfaction: A Reexamination Ten Years Later," *American Journal of Police* 13, no. 2 (1994): 70.

**118** Arthur Niederhoffer, *The Police Family* (Lexington, Mass.: Lexington Books, 1978), pp. 30–40.

**119** Federal Bureau of Investigation*, Law Enforcement Officers Killed and Assaulted* (Washington: Government Printing office, annual).

**120** Ibid.; Bureau of the Census, *Statistical Abstract of the United States, 1997* (Washington: Government Printing Office, 1997), table 686.

**121** Skolnick, *Justice without Trial*, pp. 41–68.

**122** O'Neill and Cushing, *The Impact of Shift Work.*

**123** Martin and Jurik, *Doing Justice, Doing Gender*, p. 95.

**124** Gail A. Goolkasian, *Coping with Police Stress* (Washington: Government Printing Office, 1985), pp. 11–12.

**125** Peter Finn and Julie Esselman Tomz, *Developing a Law Enforcement Stress Program for Officers and Their Families* (Washington: Government Printing Office, 1997), pp.56–70.

**126** Ibid., pp. 79–88.

**127** *McAuliffe v. New Bedford*, 155 Mass. 216, 29 N. E. 51 (1895).

**128** *Garrity v. New Jersey*, 385 U. S. 493 (1966).

**129** Gilda Brancato and Eliot E. Polebaum, *The Rights of Police Officers* (New York: Avon Books, 1981).

**130** Albert J. Reiss, *Private Employment of Public Police* (Washington: Government Printing Office, 1988).

**131** William F. Walsh, "Patrol Officer Arrest Rates: A Study of the Social Organization of Police Work," *Justice Quarterly* 3 (September 1986): 276.

**132** Reiss, *Private Employment of Public Police.*

**133** San Jose, Independent Police Auditor, *Annual Report*, 1995, pp. 2–12.

**134** President's Commission on Law Enforcement and Administration of Justice, *Task Force Report: The Police*, p. 9.

**135** Martin, *On the Move*, pp. 126–137.

**136** William G. Doerner, "Officer Retention Patterns: An Affirmative Action Concern for Police Agencies?" *American Journal of Police* 14, no. 3/4 (1995): 197–210.

**137** Jerry Sparger and David Giacopassi, "Swearing In and Swearing Off: A Comparison of Cops' and Ex-Cops' Attitudes Toward the Workplace," *Police and Law Enforcement*, eds., Daniel B. Kennedy and Robert J. Homat, (New York: Ams, 1987), pp. 35–54.

# 14

# POLICE
# ORGANIZATIONS

Police services are delivered to the public through organizations. The quality of policing depends on how well a department is organized and managed. Some critics argue that the nature of police organizations is a major problem in policing: that the departments are isolated from the public, resist change, and do not make good use of their personnel.

This chapter examines the dominant features of American law enforcement organizations. Some of these features are unique to police organizations; others are common to all large bureaucracies. The chapter identifies the major strengths and weaknesses of the prevailing style of organization, and discusses alternative ways of organizing police work. It also discusses the impact of both civil service and police unions on police organizations.

## THE QUASI-MILITARY STYLE OF POLICE ORGANIZATIONS

American law enforcement agencies are organized along quasi-military lines.[1] That is, they resemble the military in some but not all respects. This style of organization originated with Robert Peel's plan for the London Metropolitan Police in 1829, and was adopted by American police departments (see Chapter 2).

The police resemble the military in the following respects. First, police officers wear uniforms. Second, police departments use military-style rank designations, such as sergeant, lieutenant, and captain. Third, the command structure is hierarchical, with commands flowing from the top. Fourth, the organizational style is authoritarian, with penalties for failing to obey orders. Fifth, police officers carry weapons and have the legal authority to use deadly force, physical force, and to deprive people of their liberty through arrest.

At the same time, however, the police are different from the military in several important respects. First, the police serve a citizen population rather than fight a foreign enemy. Second, they provide services designed to help people, and these services are often requested by individual citizens. Third, they are constrained by laws protecting the rights of citizens. Fourth, they routinely exercise individual discretion (see Chapter 8), whereas military personnel are trained and expected to operate as members of military units.[2]

### Criticisms of the Quasi-Military Style

Many experts believe that the quasi-military style is inappropriate for the police. They argue that, first, the military ethos cultivates an "us versus them" attitude that justifies mistreatment of citizens. Second, it encourages the idea of a "war on crime," that is inappropriate for serving a citizen population.[3] Third, the authoritarian command style is contrary to democratic principles of participation and self-governance. Fourth, the authoritarian style and the rigid rank structure fail to provide sufficient job satisfaction for police officers, creating morale problems. In other occupations, professionalism is based on participation and peer review of performance.[4]

In the 1960s and early 1970s, some critics argued that the police should deemphasize their military image, primarily in order to improve police–community relations. Specifically, they suggested using civilian-style blazers rather than military-style uniforms. A few small police departments experimented with using blazers. The Menlo Park (California) Police Department found that they created no serious problems. The Lakewood (Colorado) police department adopted blazers and did not use the traditional rank designations when the department was first organized in the 1970s. After a few years, however, it returned to the traditional style. Problems arose because the public image of the police is so closely associated with military-style uniforms that it was difficult for one department to depart from the norm.[5]

## POLICE DEPARTMENTS AS ORGANIZATIONS

The quasi-military aspect is only one feature of American police departments. To understand how police departments operate, and how they deliver services to the public, it is necessary to understand them as *organizations*. Many of the problems in policing are related to organizational features. It is important to also understand why these features exist and what positive contributions they make.

### The Dominant Style of American Police Organizations

American police departments are remarkably similar in terms of organizational structure and administrative style. The typical police department is a complex bureaucracy, with a hierarchical structure and an authoritarian management style. The only exceptions to this rule are the very small departments, which have simple organizational structures and more informal management styles. At the same time, all but the very smallest agencies are governed by some form of civil service rules which regulate personnel policies. Finally, most of the large police departments are legally bound by collective bargaining contracts with unions representing rank-and-file officers.

### Police Organizations as Bureaucracies

The modern police department is a bureaucratic organization, as are other large organizations in modern society: private corporations, universities, religious organizations, government agencies, and so on. Police departments share similar characteristics of bureaucracy with these other organizations.[6]

The bureaucratic form of organization exists because it is the most efficient means that has been developed for organizing and directing many different activities in the pursuit of a common goal. This does not mean that the bureaucratic form is completely efficient, but only that no other organizational form has been found that is better able to carry out multiple tasks simultaneously in the pursuit of a common goal.

The modern bureaucracy has the following characteristics:[7]

**1** It is a complex organization performing many different tasks in pursuit of a common goal.

**2** The different tasks are grouped into separate divisions, or "bureaus" (hence the term bureaucracy).

**3** The organizational structure is hierarchical or pyramidal, with a clear division of labor among workers, first-line supervisors, and chief executives.

**4** Responsibility for specific tasks is delegated to lower-ranking employees.

**5** There is a clear chain of command, which indicates who is responsible for each task, and who is responsible for supervising each employee.

**6** There is a clear unity of command, so that each employee answers to one and only one supervisor.

**7** Written rules and regulations are designed to ensure uniformity and consistency.

**8** Information flows up and down through the organization according to the chain of command.

**9** There are formal career paths by which personnel move upward through the organization in an orderly fashion.

### The Problems with Bureaucracy

There are several major criticisms of the bureaucratic form of organization, all of which apply to police organizations.[8] First, bureaucracies are often rigid, inflexible, and unable to adapt to external changes. Thus, for example, many business administration experts argue that American corporations have failed to adapt to changing markets and the new global economy. Police departments have often failed to respond to changes in patterns of crime, and in the composition of the communities they serve.[9]

Second, communication within the organization often breaks down. Important information does not reach the people who need it. As a result, bad decisions are made, or the organization pursues conflicting goals.

Third, bureaucracies tend to become inward looking, self-serving, and isolated from the people they serve. Organizational self-protection and survival take precedence over the basic goals of the organization. Thus businesses are accused of not catering to customer demands, universities are accused of not serving the needs of students, and police departments are accused of being isolated from the public. The problem of isolation is particularly acute with respect to police–community relations, as police departments have been accused of not listening to the concerns of racial and ethnic minority communities (see Chapter 9).

Fourth, bureaucracies are accused of not using the talents of their employees and even stifling creativity.[10] Many observers have found a serious morale problem among rank-and-file police officers, and argue that departments need to provide greater opportunities for personal fulfillment and career advancement.[11]

### Police Organizations as Bureaucracies

Police departments embody the bureaucratic form of organization. The modern police bureaucracy began to emerge in the early 20th century, as a part of the professionalization movement.[12] With the creation of new specialized units (traffic, juvenile, vice, training, and so on), departments became more complex organizations. The new field of police management developed in order to help cope with this new complexity. Experts borrowed modern management principles from business administration and applied them to police administration. The leaders of this movement were August Vollmer,

Bruce Smith, and O. W. Wilson. Wilson's original textbook, *Police Administration*, became the unofficial bible on the subject by the 1950s.[13]

Figure 14–1 represents the 1998 organizational chart of the Milwaukee Police Department. It has been selected at random for this chapter, but it is representative of other big-city police departments and illustrates the main features of the modern police bureaucracy.

First, as is evident, the structure is pyramidal, reflecting the hierarchical management style. Second, the organization performs many different tasks simultaneously: patrol, traffic, criminal investigation, records, training, research and development, and so on. Third, related tasks are grouped together in a logical fashion: patrol is in one bureau and criminal investigation is in another; administrative services are in one bureau, and training is in another.

Fourth, the lines of authority are clear, with responsibility for supervision flowing from the chief down through the organization. It is possible to identify who is responsible for particular tasks. This approach reflects the principle of unity of supervision: Each person reports to one supervisor. Under the principle of span of control, each supervisor is responsible for a limited number of people. In the patrol units, the ideal span of control involves a sergeant supervising between 8 and 12 patrol officers.

The degree of specialization in a police department depends on the size of the community, the nature of its problems, and the size of the department itself.[14] The police department in a medium-sized city with relatively little serious crime does not need a separate homicide unit. The police department in a big city with many murders does need, and can afford to create, a homicide unit. Small and medium-sized departments cannot afford to maintain their own training academies. These tasks can be performed more efficiently for them by a state agency that serves many departments.[15]

What is not evident from the organizational chart is the set of rules governing employee behavior. As Chapters 8 and 11 explained, police departments issue written rules and collect them in a standard operating procedure (SOP) manual or policy manual. The career paths for officers, meanwhile will be indicated in its civil service procedures.

## PROBLEMS WITH POLICE ORGANIZATIONS

Police departments share all the problems characteristic of other bureaucracies. First, they have been accused of failing to respond creatively to changing social conditions they are responsible for. This criticism was particularly prevalent during the police–community relations crisis of the 1960s (see Chapter 9). Second, they have been

---

**POLICE ON THE WEB**

Many police departments have their organizational charts on their web sites. Find the organizational charts for several very large (3,000 sworn officers), large (700+ sworn officers), medium-sized (200–700 sworn), and small (under 100 sworn) departments.

What are the obvious differences? How do they compare in terms of degree of specialization?

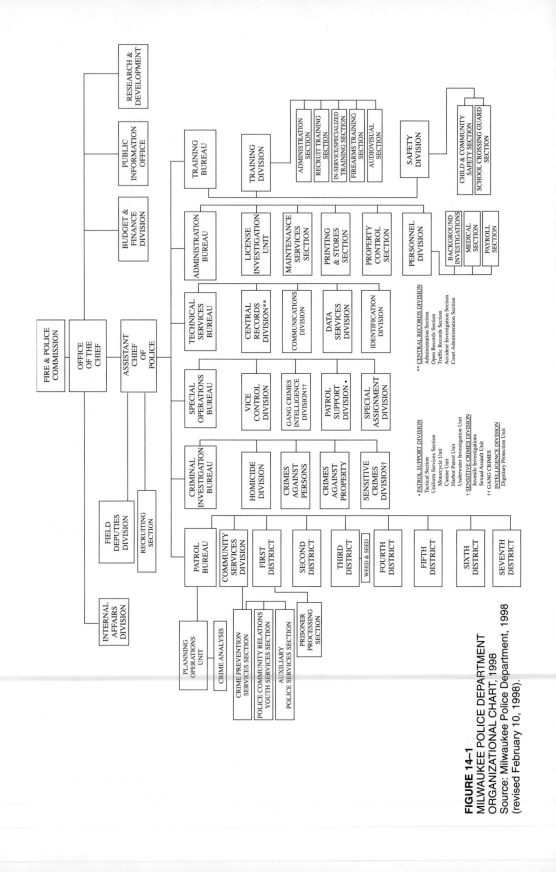

**FIGURE 14–1**
MILWAUKEE POLICE DEPARTMENT
ORGANIZATIONAL CHART, 1998
Source: Milwaukee Police Department, 1998
(revised February 10, 1998).

accused of being closed and unresponsive to the citizens they serve. New developments such as citizen review of complaints against the police are designed to make the police more responsive and accountable to the public (Chapter 11). Third, they have been accused of failing to utilize the talents of rank-and-file police officers, and of failing to offer sufficient opportunities for career advancement.[16]

A fourth criticism is that police organizations in practice are not true bureaucracies but are actually mock bureaucracies. That is to say, they have the appearance of a bureaucracy, and some of the form, but without the actual substance. For example, despite many written rules, police departments do not necessarily control the behavior of their officers on the street making routine decisions. In practice, officers exercise a great deal of discretion (see Chapter 8).

Community policing (Chapter 7) is an attempt to respond to many these criticisms of police organizations.

### The Positive Contributions of Bureaucracy in Policing

Because of the widespread dissatisfaction with the state of police organization and management, the positive contributions of bureaucracy to policing are often overlooked. These contributions are best appreciated from a historical perspective (see Chapter 2).

A comparison of the typical police department in 1900 with the typical big-city department today illustrates the contributions of the modern bureaucracy. The police department of 1900 was very unspecialized, with only patrol and detective units. The development of many specialties—juvenile, traffic, community relations, training, criminalistics—has required the growth of complex organizations that have the capacity to coordinate all these activities.[17]

The control of police discretion and the reduction of misconduct has also been achieved through bureaucratic principles (Chapters 8 and 11). Written rules on the use of deadly force or the response to domestic violence (Chapter 5) represent the technique of administrative rule making. The paperwork involved in this approach is characteristic of bureaucracies.[18]

### Informal Aspects of Police Organizations

The formal aspects of police organizations represent only one part of their actual operations. Every organization has important informal aspects, which are often referred to as office politics.[19] Dorothy Guyot argues that "within police departments, as in any formal organization, there are subdivisions, hierarchies, status groupings, and other formal arrangements. There are also informal relationships, cliques, friendship patterns, and temporary collaborations."[20]

Information does not always flow up and down the organization in the manner prescribed by the organizational chart. Sensitive and potentially embarrassing information is often withheld. Rank-and-file officers cover up each others' mistakes. Sergeants cover up mistakes by officers under their command because it would reflect poorly on their own performance. In some important respects, chief executives do not want to know about certain things. This allows them to publicly deny that such things exist when questioned by the news media or members of the public.

At the same time, however, information does flow to friends in the organization, by means outside of the prescribed channels. Such information is often referred to as gossip. Gossip falls into two general categories: true and false information. Gossip that is false is created and circulated to discredit someone. Gossip that is true is often useful. It may be important to know, for example, that someone is planning to retire or leave the organization.

Important informal relationships in a police department are based on work groups. Officers who work together day in and day out, on patrol or as detectives, tend to develop close personal ties. They see things from the perspective of their units and, when conflicts arise, defend their colleagues, even if they know their colleagues are wrong.

One dysfunctional result of this process is rivalry among different units. Patrol officers often resent the higher status that detectives enjoy, for example. There are also rivalries among patrol officers assigned to different shifts. To a certain extent, the seniority system aggravates these tensions, as the evening shift gets the youngest officers and the day shift has the older officers.

At the same time, there are networks of relationships throughout the organization based on personal friendships. Often these relationships originated in shared experiences as members of the same recruit class or members of the same patrol crew. The folklore of policing includes the belief that some police officers develop closer relationships with their partners than with their spouses. A partner is someone who can understand the unpleasant aspects of policing that an officer would not want to discuss at home.

Friendship patterns become important in the management of a police department. Westley found that a police chief needs both information about what is going on in the organization and people to perform sensitive tasks. As a result the chief relies on "a group of favorites within the department whom he can depend on to handle delicate assignments."[21] A chief maintains this network of friends by handing out rewards in the form of favorable assignments and by punishing real or imagined enemies by giving them low-status assignments.

## BUREAUCRACY AND POLICE PROFESSIONALISM

The bureaucratic aspects of the police organization conflict in many ways with professionalism as understood in other occupations. In law, medicine, education, and other professions, a professional is someone with special expertise, resulting from extensive training and experience, who exercises independent judgment about critical events. The doctor, for example, makes critical decisions about diagnosis and treatment of patients. The professional is not expected to follow a rigid set of rules.[22]

The bureaucratic aspects of policing represent a different approach to the control of behavior. First, the quasi-military nature of police organizations has emphasized hierarchical command and control rather than collegial decision making. Second, police organizations attempt to control police officer behavior through formal, written rules (see Chapter 11).

Because of the history of the American police, police professionalism acquired a special meaning. Professionalism meant the same thing as bureaucratization. Thus, the professional departments were the ones that adopted O. W. Wilson's principles of police administration: specialization, hierarchy, clear lines of authority, written rules and policies, and so on.[23] Professional departments were the ones in which officers did their jobs "by the book," meaning that they followed written departmental rules.[24]

To a certain extent, however, the professional autonomy of the traditional professions is disappearing. Doctors increasingly work in large hospitals or medical facilities. Like other bureaucracies, these organizations impose formal controls over doctors' behavior. Lawyers increasingly work in large law firms that seek to control their behavior by closely monitoring the number of hours billed.

## CHANGING POLICE ORGANIZATIONS

There is much dissatisfaction with the current state of police organizations. There are two schools of thought on how to improve them. The dominant school of thought accepts the basic principles of bureaucratic organization and seeks to apply them more effectively. Advocates of this approach, for example, support greater control of discretion through written rules, as described in Chapter 8.[25] The other school of thought seeks to "de-bureaucratize" police organizations by adopting a different organizational structure.[26]

### The Team Policing Experiment

One of the most important attempts to change the organizational form of American police departments was the team policing experiment in the early 1970s. In 1973 the National Advisory Commission on Criminal Justice Standards and Goals recommended, "Every police agency should examine the team policing concept."[27] By 1974 an estimated 60 departments had adopted team policing, but within a few years all had dropped it. The failure of team policing provides an instructive lesson in the difficulty of making major changes in police organizations.[28]

Team policing, also called neighborhood team policing, involved several basic elements. First, responsibility for basic police services was delegated to teams of officers assigned to particular neighborhoods. Teams were responsible for all police services in the area: patrol, criminal investigation, juvenile work, and so on. Officers would be assigned to teams for extended periods of time. Second, responsibility for decisions about basic police operations was delegated to officers in the neighborhood teams. Third, team members were to make decisions with input from neighborhood residents.[29]

Team policing had several different purposes: overcoming the isolation of police departments and establishing close relations with community residents; helping officers become familiar with and committed to serving the neighborhoods they police; developing police strategies appropriate for each neighborhood; developing a capacity to respond quickly to changing conditions in neighborhoods; overcoming the fragmentation of police services among different units; enhancing the professional development and morale of rank-and-file officers; improving police–community relations.

In practice, team policing experiments had many problems. First, many programs labeled team policing did not contain the basic program elements. A Police Foundation evaluation of seven experiments found that only two included most, but not necessarily all, program elements.[30] Second, most of the experiments suffered from poor planning, and in some cases almost no planning at all.

Third, officers assigned to team policing units were not given clear instructions about what they were expected to do. That is to say, there were no directions about what activities they should engage in during a regular tour of duty, and how that would be different from traditional police work.

Fourth, team policing units were not well integrated into the rest of their departments. In nearly all cases, team policing was limited to only one neighborhood. The 911 communications systems were a major problem. They operate citywide, whereas team policing units were expected to concentrate on particular neighborhoods.

Fifth, in some cases other officers often resented the team policing unit officers because of their special status within the department. Sixth, some of the experiments were sabotaged by middle-management officers who thought that team policing undercut their power by delegating authority to lower-ranking officers.

Seventh, most of the departments that experimented with team policing did not collect systematic data about crime, disorder, and public attitudes that would make it possible to evaluate the success or failure of the experiment. A U.S. Department of Justice evaluation concluded that "none of the Basic Patrol Teams have collected the kinds of evaluative information which would make it possible for us to judge whether or not the program was effective."[31] An evaluation of COMSEC (Community Sector Policing) concluded that "no easy conclusions" could be drawn about COMSEC. Positive accomplishments in some areas were offset by problems in other areas.[32]

Eighth, as an evaluation of the Cincinnati COMSEC program found, the attempt to decentralize decision making under team policing created basic problems related to accountability. Cincinnati officials discovered that, "Although they wanted to be responsive to the community and also to provide their officers with a more satisfying work experience," they "feared that with the promised autonomy and reduction in central control, their officers might become less productive or even corrupt." In short, "autonomy and control were competing issues."[33] Because team policing as a movement collapsed and disappeared so quickly, this problem was never resolved.

The failure of team policing offers a number of lessons for community policing.[34] As is obvious, the two programs have much in common: decentralization, increased officer autonomy, and so forth. The major lesson involves the difficulty of making significant changes in a police organization in a short period of time. Organizations are complex, and police departments have established traditions that are difficult to change.[35] Team policing also suffered from exaggerated expectations that could not be met. The lack of planning. The failure to specify what police officers were expected to do. The problem of making a major change in one part of a department while everyone else continues in the traditional manner.

## Task Forces

An alternative to changing the structure of police organizations is to develop decision-making procedures that operate within the existing formal structure. One example is a force comprised of officers from different ranks. A task force on problem-oriented policing, for example, might include a captain, a lieutenant, two sergeants, and three police officers. This approach allows the police chief to select particular officers from different ranks, based on their talents rather than just their rank.[36]

The task force approach addresses several problems related to the traditional police organizational structure. It recognizes the fact that many officers at the lowest rank are competent to make intelligent decisions about police policy. Involving them offers them greater job satisfaction, prepares them for supervisory responsibilities later in their careers, and increases the likelihood that innovations will be accepted within the organization. The Police Foundation, for example, found that in most of the team policing experiments the officers who were to carry them out did not understand the basic concept because they had been excluded from the planning process.[37]

Task forces were used effectively in creating the Kansas City Preventive Patrol Experiment. In 1971, Chief Clarence Kelley established four planning task forces in the department and instructed them to identify critical problems in their respective areas and to propose solutions. The South Patrol Task Force eventually proposed the experiment to test the deterrent effect of routine patrol—which is perhaps the single most important experiment in the history of American policing.[38]

### Community Policing

Community policing represents another alternative to the traditional form of police organizations (Chapter 7). It keeps the formal structure, but decentralizes decision making, placing greater responsibility on rank-and-file officers at the neighborhood level, and to become more responsive to neighborhood residents.

One of the major issues in community policing is whether particular programs succeed in achieving their goals. The Chicago Alternative Policing Strategy (CAPS) program, for example, achieved success in some respects, but still faced difficult problems in attaining meaningful citizen participation.[39] Because community policing includes many of the program elements of team policing, the failure of this earlier concept in the 1970s raises important questions about the implementation of community policing. The relevant questions include: Are programs launched with adequate planning? Are officers at all ranks adequately informed about the program so that they are committed to it? Are rank-and-file officers given clear direction as to what is expected of them? Given the attempt to decentralize decision making, are there adequate controls in place to ensure consistency and to guard against misconduct?[40]

### Creating Learning Organizations

Since the 1960s, police executives and academic experts have wrestled with the challenge of revitalizing police organizations. Police departments are alleged to be highly resistant to change. Dorothy Guyot defined the problem as equivalent to "bending granite."[41] Many bold experiments have failed. A Police Foundation project designed to overhaul the Dallas, Texas, Police Department ended in failure. And, as already noted, team policing did not succeed.[42]

William A. Geller defines the challenge in terms of creating learning organizations. It is not a matter of working harder, he argues, but of working *smarter*. Also, the challenge is to institutionalize the learning process so that departments develop the capacity to think about their own needs, plan and implement changes, and then learn from the achievements and failures.[43] To a great extent, change in policing has been initiated and then conducted by people and organizations outside the police departments.[44]

There are several obstacles to the development of learning organizations in policing. First, there is much cynicism among rank-and-file police officers. Many have seen innovative programs such as team policing come and go, and consequently believe that the latest innovation is also just another temporary fad. This attitude affects attempts to implement community policing, for example.[45] Another problem is that traditional research and planning units did not have the capacity to do any real research or planning. In many cases the officers assigned to those units did not have either the technical skills or the administrative support for this task.[46]

Geller lists six beliefs that prevent police departments from becoming learning organizations. First, many police officers believe that research is impractical and an "ivory tower" enterprise. Second, they are often reluctant to cooperate with outside researchers. Third, they fear evaluation research because of unfavorable results of previous evaluations. Fourth, many believe that findings from another jurisdiction do not apply to them. The belief, "My city is *different*," is widespread. Fifth, many command officers are afraid that encouraging critical thinking among rank-and-file officers will undermine discipline. Sixth, there is the widespread belief that "*thinking* inhibits *doing*."[47]

Geller describes 13 steps a police department needs to take to become a genuine learning organization. First, it has to establish a research and planning unit with adequate resources and staff who understand research. Second, it needs to develop a process that spans all units in the department (patrol, criminal investigation, and so on). Third, it needs to develop a process for reducing turf battles among units in the department. Fourth, it needs to take a talent inventory of its own employees, to see what skills are available, and perhaps not currently being used. Fifth, it needs to take a similar talent inventory of community groups to see what resources it can draw upon. Sixth, it needs to organize planning around particular problems, in the problem-oriented policing approach (see Chapter 7).

Seventh, departments might try to avoid the problem of "groupthink," where no one challenges the official policy, by designating certain people to serve as devil's advocates and to question official assumptions and policies. Eighth, middle managers can be designated to facilitate critical thinking. Ninth, performance evaluations could assess how well officers engage in critical thinking. Tenth, departments need to develop meaningful procedures for soliciting suggestions from the rank-and-file. Eleventh, procedures need to be developed for convincing officers that research and innovation in other departments have led to real improvements (e.g., increased officer safety). Twelfth, departments need to expand their cooperative efforts with outside organizations. Thirteenth, and last, departments should contract with researchers they trust to serve as research brokers.[48]

It is not clear that police departments will succeed in becoming true learning organizations. There is reason for some optimism, however. David Bayley argues that there is a tremendous amount of creative experimentation occurring in policing, and that the last years of the 20th century may be the most creative period in the history of modern policing.[49]

## Strategic Management of Police Organizations

A new approach to the management of police departments embodies the concept of strategic management. Borrowed from the private sector, the concept of strategic management is based on the principle of choice of purpose. That is, an organization consciously chooses the goals it wants to pursue and then organizes its activities around those goals. Traditionally in policing, as with other governmental agencies, policy is determined by elected officials and managers are responsible for implementing policy. Under strategic management, managers (e.g., police chief executives) play a more active role in determining policy.[50]

The idea of strategic management emerged along with community policing. As Mark Moore and Darrel Stephens explain, strategic management involves (1) questioning the effectiveness of traditional police tactics (routine patrol, fast response time, and so on). It acknowledges that both crime prevention and the reduction of fear are, or at least should be, major police goals, and recognizes that citizens play a major role as coproducers of police services and that police departments need to develop closer working relationships with other organizations in the community. Many community policing and problem-oriented policing projects, such as the Oakland Specialized Multi-Agency Response Team (SMART) program, embody these principles (see Chapter 7).

David Bayley's discussion of options for policing in *Police for the Future* represents the kind of thinking that strategic management incorporates. His point is that police managers have the following choices: dishonest law enforcement, determined crime prevention, honest law enforcement, efficient law enforcement, and stratified crime prevention.[51]

The point is that police organizations have choices about what goals they want to pursue. And as Bayley and also Moore and Stephens explain, different goals have important implications for how police departments deploy their resources, how they manage their personnel, and how they measure the effectiveness of what they do.[52]

## CIVIL SERVICE

Civil service procedures are a major feature of American police organizations. Civil service represents a set of formal and legally binding procedures governing personnel decisions. Civil service is nearly universal. With the exception of some of the very smallest departments, almost every law enforcement agency in the United States operates under some form of civil service.[53] The purpose of civil service is to ensure that personnel decisions are based on objective criteria, and not on favoritism, bias, and political influence.

Civil service systems are established by state law or local ordinance. In 80 percent of the cities ultimate authority over personnel procedures rests with a board or commission consisting of three to five persons. Board members are typically appointed by the mayor or city manager for a specified term. The board sets basic policy and hires a personnel director to administer policy on a day-to-day basis.[54]

Responsibility for personnel policies is shared by the civil service agency and the police department. Civil service agencies are responsible for developing job descriptions and pay scales; developing recruitment procedures; developing and administering recruitment tests; certifying qualified applicants; developing promotional criteria; developing and administering promotional tests; developing disciplinary procedures; and hearing appeals of disciplinary actions. Police departments provide input on job descriptions, participate in recruiting, conduct some of the recruitment tests, and select recruits from certified lists.

Civil service systems reinforce the quasi-military rank structure of police departments. Dorothy Guyot points out that there are two different types of rank systems—rank in job and rank in person—in which an officer carries his or her rank permanently, until promoted (demotions are extremely rare under civil service).[55] An officer holding the rank of sergeant is restricted to those jobs designated for sergeants by civil service job descriptions. Under a rank-in-job system, an employee carries a title and responsibilities while assigned to a particular job; if demoted or reassigned, the employee loses both the title and the responsibilities. Management has considerable flexibility in making personnel decisions.

Civil service creates a number of problems for police organizations. First, it limits the power of police chiefs in making personnel decisions. A chief cannot hire, fire, or promote people at will, nor change existing personnel standards at will (i.e., impose a college education requirement for all new recruits).

Second, it limits the opportunities and incentives for individual officers. Officers cannot earn financial bonuses or receive rapid promotions for exceptional performance.

Third, many critics argue that the provisions for discipline make it extremely difficult for chiefs to terminate bad officers, or even to discipline officers for poor performance.

## POLICE UNIONS

Police unions are another structural feature of police organizations. A police union is an organization legally authorized to represent police officers in collective bargaining with the employer. Under American labor law, employers are required to recognize and negotiate with democratically chosen unions. Police unions are extremely powerful, and union contracts are an important feature of police organizations.

### Aspects of Police Unions

The majority of sworn police officers in the United States today are members of police unions. According to the 1993 LEMAS (Law Enforcement Management and Administrative Statistics) survey, officers are represented by unions in 73 percent of all municipal police departments and 45 percent of all sheriff's departments.[56] Almost all big and medium-sized cities have police unions; the small cities and county departments (10 sworn officers or fewer) do not have them. Although union membership has been declining in the private sector of the economy, it has been growing in the public sector. The police are not the most heavily unionized group of public employees. A higher percentage of firefighters and public school teachers are members of unions.[57]

Unlike other parts of the economy, no single national union represents all police officers. The United Automobile Workers union, for example, represents all employees in the automobile industry; the Teamsters union represents all truck drivers, and so on.

Police unions are fragmented among several different national federations. The major union federations include the Fraternal Order of Police (FOP), and the International Union of Police Associations (IUPA).[58]

Police officers also belong to many other social and fraternal associations. These other organizations, however, do not represent officers in negotiating with their employers. The Fraternal Order of Police (FOP) is the oldest and largest police association, currently representing several hundred thousand officers nationwide. Some, but not all, FOP lodges act also as police unions. Most other associations are based on racial or ethnic groups. African-American officers in many departments belong to chapters of the Guardians. The Latino Police Officers Association is a national group representing Latino and Hispanic officers. In New York City Irish-American officers belong to the Emerald Society, Italian-American officers to the Columbia Association, German-American officers to the Steuben Association.

## Collective Bargaining

Collective bargaining is defined as "the method of determining conditions of employment through bilateral negotiations." The basic principles of collective bargaining are that (1) employees have a legal right to form unions of their own choosing, (2) employers must recognize employee unions, (3) employees have a right to participate in negotiations over working conditions, and (4) employers are required to negotiate with the union's designated representatives. The process is designed to provide a structured framework for settling differences between employers and employees.[59]

In some departments, the union represents all officers except the chief. In others, it represents all officers from the rank of captain on down; deputy chiefs are excluded on the grounds that they are part of management. In some large departments there are separate unions for different ranks: one for police officers, one for sergeants, and so on. In these cases, the chief must negotiate with two and, in some cases, three unions. There may also be a separate union for the civilian employees.

The 1935 National Labor Relations Act defined the scope of collective bargaining as "wages, hours, and other conditions of employment." The scope of conditions of employment is ambiguous, and subject to negotiation. It generally excludes management rights issues, such as the right to recruit, assign, transfer, or promote employees. In some cities, however, the union has won the right to control such issues as patrol staffing.[60]

## Grievance Procedures

One of the most important conditions of work involves disciplinary procedures. Almost all police unions have formal grievance procedures designed to protect officers against unfair discipline. Grievance procedures provide due process for employees.

The typical grievance procedure (see Figure 14–2) requires that an officer has a right to file a formal grievance, be given a written response to it, within a specified period of

**FIGURE 14–2**

ARTICLE 8: GRIEVANCE PROCEDURE

**Step 1** An employee or Union who has a grievance shall present the same, in writing, to the Police Chief, or his designated representative, within ten (10) working days from the date on which the employee or Union became aware of the grievance. The written grievance must set forth the sections and articles of this Agreement upon which the matter of interpretation or application is involved. The Chief, or his designated representative, will respond to the grievant in writing within ten (10) working days from the date on which the written grievance was received.

**Step 2** If satisfactory settlement is not reached under Step 1 hereof, then the aggrieved employee or Union may, within ten (10) working days of receipt of the Chief's response to Step 1 hereof appeal the Chief's decision to the Department Head, or his designated representative, shall have ten (10) working days in which to respond, in writing, to the employee.

**Step 3** In the event the employee or Union is still dissatisfied with the response of the Department Head, or his designated representative, then the employee or Union may, within ten (10) working days from the date of the response given by the Department Head or his designated representative appeal said decision, in writing to the Labor Relations Director, or his designated representative. The Labor Relations Director or his designated representative shall respond to the grievant, in writing, within ten (10) working days from the date on which the grievance appeal was received. An extension on the time period may be granted when mutually agreed to by the Labor Relations Director and the Union.

**Step 4** If satisfactory settlement is not reached under Step 3 hereof, either the aggrieved employee, the Union or the City of Omaha by and through the Labor Relations Director, or his representative shall, within twenty (20) working days from the expiration of the limits as set forth in Step 3 or any extenstion thereof as set forth in Section 3, by written notice to the other party, request arbitration. The City shall furnish the Union with a copy of any such notice sent or received requesting arbitration.

The arbitration proceeding shall be conducted by an arbitrator to be mutually selected by the parties within thrity (30) calendar days after the submission of written demand for arbitration. The UNION shall at its discretion become a party for the purpose of selecting an arbitrator. The UNION and the grievant shall together be considered one party. If the parties are unable to mutually agree as to the selection of an arbitrator within such time limit and either party continues to demand arbitration, the parties shall jointly request  the Federal Mediation and Conciliation Service to provide a list of five (5) arbitrators. Each party shall have the right to strike two (2) names from the list of arbitrators as submitted. The party requesting arbitration shall have the right to stike the frist name and the other party shall then strike one name with the same process being repeated so that the person remaining on the list shall be the arbitrator.

*Source:* Omaha Police Department, "Union Contract," *Standard Operating Procedure Manual*, pp. 12–13.

time, and has the right to appeal an unfavorable decision. In some instances, these procedures are referred to as the police officers' bill of rights (see Figure 14–3).

## Unions and Shared Governance

Collective bargaining represents a form of shared management. Unions give officers a voice in some, but not all, decisions about the operation of the department. The major impact of police unions, therefore, has been to greatly reduce the power of police chiefs. Prior to the late 1960s, chiefs had an almost completely free hand in managing their departments.

The chief, for example, might announce a plan to add a fourth patrol shift. The union might argue that this represents a change in working conditions, because the officers involved will have to work different hours. The chief will reply that his power to create a fourth shift is a management right. The two sides will try to settle this disagreement informally. If they can't, the union may file a grievance under the contract. Contracts normally contain a formal grievance procedure to settle these conflicts.

## Impasse Settlement and Strikes

When the union and the city or county cannot agree on a contract, an impasse exists. In the private sector, the union often goes out on strike, or the employer conducts a lockout of the employees. Police strikes are illegal in many states, and other impasse settlement procedures exist, such as mandatory mediation, fact finding, or arbitration.

Strikes are the most controversial aspect of police unionism. Many people argue that the police have absolutely no right to strike: that it is unprofessional and that it creates a serious danger to the public. Police unions reply that they should have the same right to strike that other unions have. Withholding one's labor is the ultimate weapon that working people have to force the employer to reach an agreement. Most union leaders, however, are opposed to strikes because they are either illegal in that state or because of the negative public reaction.[61]

Instead of actual strikes, police officers occasionally engage in job actions, defined as a deliberate disruption of normally assigned duties. One example is the "blue flu," where many officers do not go to work, claiming they are sick.[62] In some cases, such as in San Francisco in 1975, police officers tried to exert pressure on the city by refusing to write any traffic tickets, or writing massive numbers of tickets.[63] A police strike is a major crisis for the community. Police strikes in Baltimore (1974), San Francisco (1975), and New Orleans (1979) resulted in violence and disorder. In many strikes, some officers remain on duty, feeling a sense of obligation to the community.

Police strikes are actually very rare, and there have been very few since the 1970s. Public school teachers strike far more often than police officers. Even in the private sector, the number of strikes has declined substantially since the 1970s.[64]

## The Impact of Police Unions

Police unions have had a powerful impact on American policing. First, they have produced significant improvements in police officer salaries and benefits. In the mid-1960s

**FIGURE 14–3**

FLORIDA POLICE OFFICERS' BILL OF RIGHTS

---

### 112.532   Law Enforcement Officers' and Correctional Officers' Rights

All law enforcement officers and correctional officers employed by or appointed to a law enforcement agency or a correctional agency shall have the following rights and privileges:

1 **Rights of Law Enforcement Officers and Correctional Officers While Under Investigation.** Whenever a law enforcement officer or correctional officer is under investigation and subject to interrogation by members of his agency for any reason which could lead to disciplinary action, demotion, or dismissal, such interrogation shall be conducted under the following conditions:

   **a** The interrogation shall be conducted at a reasonable hour, preferably at a time when the law enforcement officer or correctional officer is on duty, unless the seriousness of the investigation is of such a degree that immediate action is required.

   **b** The interrogation shall take place either at the office of the command of the investigating officer or at the office of the local precinct, police unit or correctional unit in which the incident allegedly occurred, as designated by the investigating officer or agency.

   **c** The law enforcement officer or correctional officer under investigation shall be informed of the rank, name, and command of the officer in charge of the investigation, the interrogating officer, and all persons present during the interrogation. All questions directed to the officer under interrogation shall be asked by and through one interrogator at any one time.

   **d** The law enforcement officer or correctional officer under investigation shall be informed of the nature of the investigation prior to any interrogation, and he shall be informed of the name of all complainants.

   **e** Interrogating sessions shall be for reasonable periods and shall be timed to allow for such personal necessities and rest periods as are reasonably necessary.

   **f** The law enforcement officer or correctional officer under interrogation shall not be subjected to offensive language or be threatened with transfer, dismissal, or disciplinary action. No promise or reward shall be made as an inducement to answer any questions.

   **g** The formal interrogation of a law enforcement officer or correctional officer, including all recess periods, shall be recorded, and there shall be no unrecorded questions or statements.

   **h** If the law enforcement officer or correctional officer under interrogation is under arrest, or is likely to be placed under arrest as a result of the interrogation, he shall be completely informed of all his rights prior to the commencement of the interrogation.

   **i** At the request of any law enforcement officer or correctional officer under investigation, he shall have the right to be represented by counsel or any other representative of his choice, who shall be present at all times during such interrogation whenever the interrogation relates to the officer's continued fitness for law enforcement or correctional service.

Source: Florida Statutes, Sec. 112.532.

many police departments were having great difficulty recruiting and holding qualified officers. By the late 1980s the picture had changed dramatically. Police departments generally had many applicants for each opening and were able to recruit people with at least some college education. In other words, jobs with the police department were competitive with other jobs that a person with some college education might consider (see Chapter 12).

Second, police unions have radically altered the process of police management, reducing the power of chiefs and introducing a process of shared governance. Third, unions have introduced due process into union discipline procedures, limiting the power of police chiefs to arbitrarily or unfairly discipline officers.

Fourth, critics argue that unions have had an important, and negative, impact on police–community relations. Generally, police unions have represented white police officers in opposition to civil rights leaders and, in some cases, racial minority officers. In Boston, New York, and Cleveland police unions strongly opposed changes proposed by mayors designed to improve police–community relations. In recent years, police unions have often represented white police officers who have sued to block affirmative action plans designed to increase the number of racial minority officers.[65]

Fifth, many critics argue that unions have hindered the development of police professionalism. Historically, reform relied on powerful and often charismatic police chiefs whose power is now limited by unions. Unions in some cities, for example, have opposed the creation of a fourth patrol shift. And many unions fought programs designed to improve police–community relations.[66]

## THE INSTITUTIONAL ENVIRONMENT OF POLICE ORGANIZATIONS

Police organizations are social institutions that operate in relation to their external social and political environment. John Crank and Robert Langworthy argue that understanding the relationship between police organizations and their external environment is important to understanding how police departments function. They point out that the police do not produce a product (as does a factory, for example). Instead, police organizations interact with other institutions and receive their legitimacy from them. In short, how well a department functions depends in large part on how well it meets the expectations of these other institutional actors.[67]

The institutional reality of police organizations is the product of myths and myth building. Much of the behavior of police organizations represents efforts to define their legitimacy in the eyes of other organizations and actors and to respond to challenges to their legitimacy. Traditionally, for example, the police have claimed crime control as their professional domain, and sought to maintain their authority over this domain by creating and maintaining the appearance of effective crime control.[68] The community policing movement represents an attempt to redefine the professional domain of police and their central role in it.

## CONCLUSION

Police organizations are a critical element in policing. They are the instruments through which police services are organized and delivered to the public. Many police problems are associated with the problems of bureaucracy. Past attempts to restructure police departments, such as team policing, have not been successful. More recent attempts, such as community policing and problem-oriented policing, represent efforts to revitalize police organizations by making them more open and responsive to the communities they serve and to changing social conditions.

## NOTES

1 Egon Bittner, *Aspects of Police Work* (Boston: Northeastern University Press, 1990), pp. 136–147.
2 Ibid.
3 Ibid., pp. 132–136.
4 W. E. Moore, *The Professions: Rules and Roles* (New York: Russell Sage Foundation, 1970), pp. 109–130.
5 James H. Tenzel, Lowell Storms, Harvey Sweatwood, "Symbols and Behavior: An Experiment in Altering the Police Role," *Journal of Police Science and Administration* 4 (no. 1, 1976): 21–28.
6 Charles Perrow, *Complex Organizations: A Critical Essay* (Glenview, Ill.: Scott, Foresman, 1972).
7 Ibid.
8 James Q. Wilson, *Bureaucracy* (New York: Basic Books, 1989).
9 Henry I. DeGeneste and John P. Sullivan, *Policing a Multicultural Community* (Washington: Police Executive Research Forum, 1997).
10 Perrow, *Complex Organizations*, pp. 6–7.
11 National Advisory Commission on Criminal Justice Standards and Goals, *Police* (Washington: Government Printing Office, 1973), pp. 195–198.
12 Samuel Walker, *A Critical History of Police Reform* (Lexington, Mass.: Lexington Books, 1977), pp. 33–49.
13 O. W. Wilson and Roy C. McLaren, *Police Administration*, 4th ed. (New York: McGraw-Hill, 1977).
14 Ibid., pp. 77–79.
15 Elinor Ostrom, Roger Parks, and Gordon Whitaker, *Patterns of Metropolitan Policing* (Cambridge, MA: Ballinger, 1978), pp. 243–271.
16 National Advisory Commission, *Police*, pp. 195–198.
17 Walker, *A Critical History of Police Reform*, pp. 53–78.
18 Samuel Walker, "Legal Control of Police Behavior," in *Police Innovation, and Control of the Police* (New York: Springer-Verlaq, 1993), pp. 32–55, eds. D. Weisburd and C. Uchida.
19 William A. Westley, *Violence and the Police* (Cambridge: MIT Press, 1970), pp. 15–47.
20 Dorothy Guyot, "Police Departments under Social Science Scrutiny," *Journal of Criminal Justice* 5 (Summer 1977): 109.
21 Westley, *Violence and the Police*, p. 23.
22 Moore, *The Professions: Rules and Roles*, pp. 87–108.
23 Walker, *A Critical History of Police Reform*, pp. 167–174.
24 James Q. Wilson, *Varieties of Police Behavior* (New York: Atheneum, 1973).

**25** Samuel Walker, *Taming the System: The Control of Discretion in Criminal Justice, 1950–1970* (New York: Oxford, 1994).

**26** John E. Angell, "Toward an Alternative to the Classic Police Organizational Arrangements: A Democratic Model," *Criminology*, no. 1 1971, pp. 185–206.

**27** National Advisory Commission, *Police*, p. 156.

**28** Samuel Walker, "Does Anyone Remember Team Policing? Lessons of the Team Policing Experience for Community Policing," *American Journal of Police* 12, no. 1 (1993): 33–55.

**29** Lawrence W. Sherman, Catherine H. Milton, and Thomas V. Kelly, *Team Policing: Seven Case Studies* (Washington: The Police Foundation, 1973). U.S. Department of Justice, *Neighborhood Team Policing* (Washington: Government Printing Office, 1977).

**30** Sherman, Milton, and Kelly, *Team Policing*, p. 7.

**31** U.S. Department of Justice, *Neighborhood Team Policing*, p. 40.

**32** Alfred I. Schwartz and Sumner N. Clarren, *The Cincinnati Team Policing Experiment* (Washington: The Police Foundation, 1977), p. 9.

**33** Ibid. p. 7.

**34** Walker, "Does Anyone Remember Team Policing?"

**35** Jack R. Greene, "Organizational Change in Law Enforcement," *Journal of Criminal Justice* 9, no. 1 (1981): 79–91.

**36** Marvin Weisbord, Howard Lamb, Allan Drexler, *Improving Police Department Management Through Problem–Solving Task Forces* (Reading, Mass.: Addison-Wesley, 1974).

**37** Sherman, Milton, and Kelley, *Team Policing*.

**38** George L. Kelling et al., *The Kansas City Preventive Patrol Experiment: A Summary Report* (Washington: The Police Foundation, 1974), pp. 6–7.

**39** Wesley G. Skogan and Susan Hartnett, *Community Policing, Chicago Style* (New York: Oxford University Press, 1997).

**40** Walker, "Does Anyone Remember Team Policing?"

**41** Dorothy Guyot, "Bending Granite: Attempts to Change the Rank Structure of American Police Departments," *Journal of Police Science and Administration* 7, no. 3 (1979): 253–284.

**42** Mary Ann Wycoff and George L. Kelling, *The Dallas Experience: Organizational Reform* (Washington: The Police Foundation, 1978).

**43** William A. Geller, "Suppose We Were Really Serious about Police Departments Becoming Learning Organizations'?" *National Institute of Justice Journal*, no. 234 (December 1997): 2–8.

**44** Herman Goldstein, *Policing a Free Society* (Cambridge, Mass.: Ballinger, 1977), pp. 307–333.

**45** Skogan and Hartnett, *Community Policing*, Chicago Style.

**46** Gary W. Cordner, Craig B. Fraser, and Chuck Wexler, "Research, Planning, and Implementation," in *Local Government Police Management* ed., W. A. Geller, (Washington: International City Management Association, 1991), pp. 333–362.

**47** Geller, "Suppose We Were Really Serious," p. 4.

**48** Ibid.

**49** David H. Bayley, *Police for the Future* (New York: Oxford University Press, 1994), p. 101.

**50** Mark H. Moore and Darrel W. Stephens, *Beyond Command and Control: The Strategic Management of Police Departments* (Washington: Police Executive Research Forum, 1991).

**51** Bayley, *Police for the Future*, pp. 123–142.

**52** Moore and Stephens, *Beyond Command and Control*.

**53** George W. Griesinger, Jeffrey S. Slovak, Joseph J. Molkup, *Civil Service Systems: Their Impact on Police Administration* (Washington: Government Printing Office, 1979).

**54** Ibid.

**55** Guyot, "Bending Granite."

**56** Bureau of Justice Statistics, *Law Enforcement Management and Administrative Statistics, 1993* (Washington: Government Printing Office, 1995), p. x.

**57** Bureau of the Census, *Statistical Abstract of the United States, 1997* (Washington: Government Printing Office, 1997), pp. 438–442.

**58** Hervey A. Juris and Peter Feuille, *Police Unions* (Lexington, Mass.: Lexington Books, 1973), pp. 26–39.

**59** International Association of Chiefs of Police, *Guidelines and Papers from the National Symposium on Police Labor Relations* (Washington: IACP, 1974).

**60** Michael T. Leibig and Robert B. Kliesmet, *Police Unions and the Law: A Handbook for Police Organizers* (Washington: Institute for Police Research, 1988).

**61** Jack Steiber, *Public Employee Unionism: Structure and Growth* (Washington: The Brookings Institution, 1973), pp. 159–192.

**62** Margaret Levi, *Bureaucratic Insurgency* (Lexington, Mass.: Lexington Books, 1977), pp. 91–130.

**63** William J. Bopp, "The San Francisco Police Strike of 1975: A Case Study," *Journal of Police Science and Administration* 5, no. 1 (1977): 32–42.

**64** Bureau of the Census, *Statistical Abstract of the United States, 1997*, p. 439.

**65** Stephen C. Halpern, *Police-Association and Department Leaders* (Lexington, Mass.: Lexington Books, 1974).

**66** Juris and Feuille, *Police Unions*, pp. 103–117.

**67** John P. Crank and Robert Langworthy, "An Institutional Perspective on Policing," *Journal of Criminal Law and Criminology* 83, no. 2 (1992): 338–363.

**68** Peter K. Manning, *Police Work* (Cambridge: MIT Press, 1977), pp. 89–126.

# NAME INDEX

## A

Aaronson, David E., 122n
Abrahamse, Allan, 139, 153n
Adams, Kenneth, 238n, 288n
Albrecht, Stan, 218, 236n
Alex, Nicholas, 302–303, 318n, 329, 334, 351n, 352n
Alpert, Geoffrey P. 84, 93n, 94n, 151n, 183n, 196, 203, 208n, 209n, 216, 223, 230, 234, 236n, 237n, 239n, 241n, 263n, 273, 287n, 288n, 316, 321n
Amendola, Karen, 265n
Amsterdam, Anthony, 66n
Anderson, Deborah, 44n, 334, 352n
Anechiarico, Frank, 263, 266n
Angell, John E., 375n
Antunes, George E., 18n, 77, 92n, 93n, 94n, 140, 151n, 153n, 183n, 185n
Aone, Sucre, 350n, 351n
Austin, Thomas, 352n
Avery, Michael, 289n

## B

Baker, Ralph, 240n, 351n
Baldwin, Lola, 29

Bannon, James, 352n
Bard, Morton, 105, 121n
Barker, Thomas, 175, 185n, 186n, 243, 251–252, 256, 264n, 265n
Barlow, David, 321n, 241n
Bates, Ronald, 152n
Baumgartner, M.P., 208n
Bayley, David H., 12, 15, 17n, 18n, 21, 40, 41n, 45n, 76, 79, 92n, 93n, 100, 120n, 151n, 176, 183, 185n, 186n, 220, 222, 226, 236n, 237n, 238n, 240n, 264, 268, 287n, 296, 302, 316n, 318n, 327, 336, 340, 342, 350n, 352n, 353n, 366–367, 375n
Bechtel, H. Kenneth, 42n
Bell, James, 153n
Berg, Bruce L., 314, 320n
Berk, Richard A., 121n
Berk, Sara Fenstermaker, 105, 121n
Berman, Jay Stuart, 42n, 264n
Berrill, Kevin T., 235n
Biegel, Herbert, 266n
Bittner, Egon, 10, 17n, 43n, 99, 109–110, 116, 119n, 122n, 123n, 154n, 208n, 218, 236n, 326, 350n, 374n
Black, Donald, 35, 36, 101, 104–105, 116–117, 120n, 121n, 123n, 130,

133, 151n, 152n, 190, 194–195,
206n, 207n, 220, 226, 238n, 239n,
288n, 333, 350n, 351n, 352n
Blakemore, Jerome L., 241n, 321n
Bloch Peter B., 44n, 153n, 222, 237n,
334, 352n
Blomberg, Thomas G., 124n
Blum, Karen, 289n
Blumberg, Abraham, 218, 236n
Bobb, Merrick J., 239n, 240n
Bobo, Lawrence, 235n
Bogen, Phil, 124n
Boger, John Charles, 235n
Bopp, William J., 43n, 376n
Bordua, David J., 123n, 138, 152n,
318n
Borsage, B., 123n
Bouza, Anthony V., 305, 319n
Boyd, Julian P., 41n
Boydstun, John E., 92n, 123n, 239n
Brancato, Gilda, 292n, 354n
Brandeau, Margaret L., 93n
Brandl, Steven G., 138, 177, 183n, 185n,
236n, 240n
Bratton, William, 18n, 172, 272, 184n,
288n
Briar, Scott, 117, 220, 226, 237n, 238n
Broderick, J. J., 336–337, 352n
Brooks, Laure, 120n
Brown, Dale K., 93n
Brown, Lee P., 54, 65n, 172, 184n, 240n
Brown, Michael K., 191, 200, 204, 206n,
209n
Brown, Richard Maxwell, 41n
Browning, Sandra Lee, 236n, 239n
Brueger, Michael E., 92n, 93n, 180,
184n, 186n
Bumphus, Vic, 282
Burnham, David, 244, 247, 262, 264n,
266n, 292n
Butler, Smedley, 28
Buzawa, Eva, 107, 121n, 352n, 353n
Bynum, Timothy S., 82, 93n, 177, 183n,
185n

# C

Calvert, Geoffrey N., 353n
Campbell, Michael S., 320n
Cao, Liqun, 236n
Carte, Elaine H., 42n, 43n
Carte, Gene E., 42n, 43n
Carter, David L., 44n, 208n, 243, 256,
264n, 317n, 320n, 329, 331, 351n,
352n
Cassell, Paul G., 275–276, 289n
Castellano, Thomas C., 147, 154n
Chaiken, Jan M., 65n, 94n, 305–306,
319n
Chaiken, Marcia, 65n
Chambliss, William, 228–229, 239n, 249,
251, 264n, 265n
Chermak, Steven M., 17n
Chevigny, Paul, 43n
Clark, John P., 349n, 351n
Clarren, Summer N., 185n, 210n, 288n,
375n
Clemmer, Elizabeth, 103, 120n
Cohen, Bernard, 304–306, 319n
Cohen, Marica, 93n, 94n
Cohn, Ellen G., 121n, 223, 238n, 240n
Coles, Catherine, 14, 18n, 45n, 122n,
184n, 185n
Colton, Kent W., 93n
Conley, John A, 44n
Connors, Edward F., III, 93n, 94n, 266n
Coolidge, Calvin, 30
Cordner, Gary W., 61, 66n, 82, 90, 93n,
95n, 184n 375n
Cosgrove, Colleen A., 18n, 45n, 151n,
184n
Couzens, Michael, 151n
Cox, John Stuart, 43n
Cox, Sarah J., 153
Cox, Stephen M., 62n, 76, 186n
Cramer, James A., 94n
Crank, John P., 64n, 145, 154n, 183n,
373, 376n
Critchley, T. A., 41n

Culbertson, Robert G., 351n
Cullen, Francis T., 236n, 240n
Cumming, Elaine, 80, 93n
Cumming, Ian, 80
Cunningham, William C., 65n
Currie, Elliot, 154n
Curring, Ian, 93n
Curtis, Edwin U., 30
Cushing, Michael A., 92n, 350n, 354n

# D

Daley, Robert, 155n, 247, 258, 264n,
    266n
Dantzker, M. L., 299, 317n
Daughtry, Sylvester, Jr., 151n
Davidson, Laura A., 117, 123n, 133,
    152n, 195, 196, 207n, 208n, 238n
Davis, Kenneth Culp, 191, 194, 197, 199,
    201, 204–205, 206n, 207n, 208n,
    209n
Decker, Scott, 233, 240n
DeGeneste, Henry I., 235n, 374n
Dellatre, Edwin J., 266n
DeLone, Miriam, 92n, 212–215, 223,
    235n, 236n, 239n, 320n
Dienes, C. Thomas, 122n
Dinkins, David, 172
Doerner, William, 304, 306, 348, 319n,
    320n, 353n, 354n
Donziger, Steven R., 239n
Dowd, Michael, 243, 257, 260, 280, 340
Drexler, Allan, 375n
Dulaney, W. Marvin, 42n
Dunford, Franklyn W., 120n, 121n
Dunham, Roger, 84, 93n, 94n, 209n, 216,
    223, 236n, 237n, 273, 288n
Durk, David, 258, 262

# E

Eastman, W. E., 66n, 291n
Eck, John E., 18n, 45n, 152, 138, 182,
    184n

Edell, Laura, 80, 93n
Eisenberg, Terry, 240n, 266n
Elliott, Delbert S., 120n, 121n
Emmett, Susan T., 124n, 155n
Erez, Edna, 152n
Ermer, Virginia B., 301–302, 318n
Esbensen, Finn–Aage, 124n
Ezell, Mark, 124n

# F

Fagan, Jeffrey, 108, 120n, 122n
Fairchild, E. S., 155n
Falcone, David N., 47, 64n, 66n,
    94n
Feeney, Floyd, 152n
Felkenes, George, 320n
Feuille, Peter, 44n, 376n
Figlio, Robert, 153n
Finn, Peter E., 119n, 122n, 354n
Flanagan, Timothy J., 123n, 236n,
    318n
Flewelling, Robert L., 124n
Floyd, Pretty Boy, 33
Fogelson, Robert M., 36, 44n
Forst, Brian, 153n
Fox, James Alan, 123n
Frank, James, 76, 92n, 138, 177, 183n,
    185n, 236n, 240n
Fraser, Craig B., 375n
Freels, Sally, 153n
Fridell, Lorie A., 230, 239, 291n
Friedman, Lucy N., 352n
Friedrich, Robert, 238n, 333, 351n,
    352n
Frost, Thomas M., 320n, 240n
Furstenburg, Frank F., Jr., 83, 93n, 229,
    239n
Fyfe, James J., 38, 44n, 63, 64n, 66n,
    95n, 196, 202–203, 207n, 208n,
    209n, 223, 232, 334, 235n, 237n,
    238n, 240n, 289n, 291n, 318n, 321n,
    350n, 352n, 353n

# G

Galliher, John, 64n
Gardiner, John A., 142, 153n, 190, 206n
Garner, Joel, 103, 120n
Garofalo, James, 76, 79, 92n, 93n, 100,
    120n, 336, 340, 342, 352, 353
Gartin, Patrick R., 92n, 93n, 121n,
    184n
Geis, Gilbert, 154n
Geller, William A., 44n, 206n, 224, 207n,
    237n, 238n, 287n, 292n, 350n,
    365–366, 375n
Gelles, Richard J., 101–103, 120n
Gentry, Curt, 42n, 43n, 65n
Giacopassi, David, 143, 152n, 154n,
    208n, 237n, 354n
Gifis, Steven H., 152n
Gilsinan, James F., 93n
Giocomazzi, Andrew, 124n
Girard, Charles M., 65n
Giuliani, Rudolph, 172, 272
Glazer, Nathan, 235n
Glick, Barry D., 152n, 269, 288n
Goldman, Nathan, 190–191, 206n
Goldman, Roger, 66n, 320n, 321n
Goldsmith, Andrew, 44n
Goldstein, Herman, 6, 9, 11, 13, 17n,
    18n, 39, 44n, 64n, 93n 119, 124n,
    132, 151n, 157–158, 161, 163, 169,
    171, 177, 180, 183, 185n, 186n, 197,
    201–202, 205, 206n, 207n, 208n,
    209n, 243, 252, 254, 260, 263n,
    264n, 268, 279–280, 287n, 288n,
    290n, 375n
Goldstein, Joseph, 199, 207n, 209n,
    265n, 266n
Goolkasian, Gail A., 354n
Gottfredson, Don, 152n
Graham, Fred P., 43n, 289n
Gray, Thomas, 288n
Green, Lorraine, 14, 155n, 170, 155n,
    184n

Green, Miles, 218, 236n
Greenberg, Douglas, 41n
Greene, Jack R., 18n, 44n, 65n, 89, 93n,
    151n, 169, 175, 183n, 184n, 185n,
    352n, 353n, 375n
Greene, Lorraine, 18n
Greenwood, Peter W., 43n, 152n
Griesinger, George W., 317n, 318n, 321n,
    350n, 375n
Grinc, Randolph, 184n
Groeger, John A., 237n
Groger, John A., 349n
Groves, W. Eugene, 236n,
Guyot, Dorothy, 353n, 361, 365, 368,
    374n, 375n

# H

Haarr, Robin N., 45n, 328, 330–331,
    351n,
Hacker, Andrew, 212, 235n
Haller, Mark, 26, 42n
Halpern, Stephen C., 376n
Hamilton, Edwin E., 63n, 64n, 291n
Hammett, Theodore M., 123n
Hanewicz, Wayne, 120n, 121n
Hannon, Martin, 65n
Harring, Sidney L., 27, 42n
Harris, David a., 239n
Hart, Barbara J., 122n
Hart, William, 243
Hartnett, Susan, 18n, 164, 166–167, 18n,
    184n, 185n, 317n, 375n
Hawkins, Keith, 208n
Hayman, Bret S., 275–276, 289n
Heaphy, John F., 18n, 139, 153n
Heidingsfield, Michael, 317n
Heininger, Bruce L., 64n
Hepburn, John, 227, 238n
Herbert, Bob, 18n
Herek, Gregory M., 235n
Hernandez, Eusevio, 151n
Heussenstamm, F.K., 239n

Hochstedler, Ellen, 301, 312, 318n, 320n, 352n, 336–337
Hofstadter, Richard, 41n
Holmes, Oliver Wendell, 347
Homat, Robert J., 354n
Hoover, J. Edgar, 33, 57
Howard, Gwendolyn, 350n, 351n
Huang, W. S. Wilson, 123n, 216, 236n, 318n
Hudson, James R., 284, 291n
Hughes, Thomas, 317n, 318n, 319n, 320n, 321n
Huizinga, David, 120n, 121n
Hunter, Ronald D., 175, 185n, 186n
Husansky, Tamar, 320n

**J**

Jacob, Herbert, 119n
Jacobs, James B., 153n, 263, 266n, 317n
Janowitz, Morris, 10, 18n, 95n
Jencks, Christopher, 110, 122n
Johnson, Guy, 237n
Johnson, James H., Jr., 235n
Johnson, Lyndon, 35
Jones, Mark, 264n
Jurik, Nancy C., 235n, 331, 340, 351n, 352n, 353n, 354n
Juris, Hervey A., 44n, 376n

**K**

Kaminski, Robert J., 303, 318n
Kania, Richard, 264n, 265n
Kaplan, Edward H., 94n
Kappeler, Victor E., 208n, 263n, 352n
Karales, Kevin, 224, 238n
Kelley, Clarence, 255, 365
Kelling, George L., 14, 17n, 18n, 39–40, 43n, 44n, 45n, 93n, 94n, 122n, 151n, 158, 160–161, 172, 180, 182, 183n, 184n, 185n, 186n, 375n
Kelly, Thomas V., 375n

Kennedy, Daniel B., 354n
Kennedy, David M., 92n, 183n
Kenney, Dennis J., 172, 184n
Kerstetter, Wayne A., 284, 291n
Key, V.O., 150, 265n
King, Rodney, 53, 172, 212–213, 217, 224, 231, 234, 278
Kinlock, Timothy W., 146, 154n
Klein, Malcolm W., 124n, 152n
Kliesmet, Robert B., 376n
Klinger, David, 117, 124n, 195, 207n, 226, 238n
Klockars, Carl B., 238n
Klyman, Fred A., 151n, 185n, 240n
Knoblach, Peter, 184n
Knobler, Peter, 18n, 288n
Kobetz, R., 123n
Koepsell, Terry W., 65n
Kopache, Renee, 236n
Kopers, Christopher S., 104, 120n
Kornblum, Allan, 262, 264n, 266n
Krantz, Sheldon, 275, 289n
Kreisel, Betsy, 210n, 291n
Kruckenberg, Joanna, 151n, 185n, 240n
Kuhns, Joseph B., 186n

**L**

LaFave, Wayne R., 18n, 154n, 191, 193, 206n, 207n, 221, 237n
LaFree, Gary, 131, 151n, 195, 207n
Lamb, Howard, 375n
Landy, Frank J., 207n, 353n
Lane, Roger, 41n, 42n
Langworthy, Robert 64n, 145, 154n, 327, 318n, 319n, 320n, 321n, 327, 351n, 373, 376n
Larson, Richard C., 18n, 93n, 94n, 95n
Lefkowitz, Joel, 327, 350n
Leibig, Michael T., 376n
Leinen, Stephen, 351n
Lempert, Richard E., 121n
Lent, Cynthia J., 241n

Leo, Richard, 275–276, 289n
Leuci, Robert, 258
Levi, Margaret, 376n
Levine, Margaret J., 95n
Levy, Paul R., 65n
Lewis, Diane, 154n
Lewis, William, 309
Lincoln, Abraham, 23
Lipsky, Michael, 91n, 206n
Littlejohn, Edward, 277, 288n, 289n
Loeske, Donileen, 105, 121n
Loftus, Elizabeth, 138, 152n
Longmire, Dennis R., 123n, 236n, 318n
Lott, John, 312, 320n
Louima, Abner, 173
Loving, Nancy, 121n
Lucianovic, Judith, 153n
Luirgio, Arthur J., Jr., 241n, 321n, 349n
Lumb, Richard C., 320n
Luna, Eileen, 65n, 289n, 290n, 291n
Lundman, Richard J., 117, 123n, 226,
    238n, 239n

# M

Magdovitz, Samuel B., 317n
Maguire, Edward R., 182, 186n
Manili, Barbara, 266n
Manning, Peter K., 5, 17n, 78–79, 92n,
    93n, 145, 151n, 154n, 204, 209n,
    376n
Martin, Susan E., 44n, 66n, 153n, 235n,
    298, 303, 312, 316, 317n, 318n,
    319n, 320n, 321n, 328–331, 339,
    340, 348, 351n, 352n, 353n, 354n
Marvell, Thomas B., 64n, 91n
Marx, Gary T., 150, 155n
Mastrofski, Stephen D., 17n, 18n, 40,
    41n, 44n, 45n, 63, 66n, 90, 95n, 98,
    100, 104, 119n, 120n, 133, 151n,
    152n, 169, 175, 183n, 184n, 185n,
    205, 210n, 226, 238n, 240n,
    317n

Mayo, Katherine, 42n
McCoy, Candace, 277–278, 289n
McDonald, William F., 209n
McElroy, Jerome E., 18n, 45n, 151n,
    184n, 185n, 291n
McEwen, J. Thomas, 93n, 94n, 95n, 266n
McGinniskin, Barney, 24
McGowan, Carl, 289n
McLaren, Roy C., 91n, 92n, 94n, 128,
    151n, 374n
McMullen, M., 251, 265n
McNamara, John H., 302, 315, 318n,
    321n, 323, 327, 349n, 351n, 353n
McNamara, Robert P., 154n
Meagher, M. Steven, 318n
Meier, Robert F., 154n 265n
Melekian, Barney, 122n
Mendelsohn, Harold, 220, 222, 236n,
    237n, 264n, 296, 302, 318n, 327,
    350n
Menzies, Robert J., 122n
Meyer, Fred A., 240n, 351n
Meyer, John C., 99, 120n
Miller, Jerome G., 154n, 212, 235n
Miller, Susan L., 121n
Miller, Wilbur R., 26, 42n
Milner, Neal, 52, 64n, 276, 289n, 332,
    351n
Milton, Catherine E., 352n,
    375n
Moelter, Nicholas P., 92n
Mokkonen, Eric H., 42n
Molkup, Joseph J., 317n, 350n, 375n
Moody, Carlisle E., 64n, 91n
Moore, Mark H., 17n, 92n, 151n, 154n,
    183n, 185n, 287n, 288n, 367, 375n
Moore, Wilbert E., 18n, 209n, 291n, 374n
Morash, Merry, 352n
Morris, Norval, 93n, 150n
Moulder, Evelina R., 320n
Muir, William K., 76, 92n,328, 336–337
    350n, 352n
Mulcahy, Aogan, 266n, 290n

Murphy, Patrick V., 181, 186n, 252, 255–258, 281
Musheno, Michael C., 122n
Myrdal, Gunnar, 237n, 221, 237n

# N

Narr, Ortwin A., 95n, 122n
Newell, Charldean, 289n
Niederhoffer, Arthur, 11, 18, 218, 236n, 316n, 342, 350n, 351n, 353n
Nielsen, Marianne O., 235n
Nimmer, Raymond T., 122n, 124n, 207n
Novak, C.A., 288n

# O

Oaks, Dallin J., 209n
Oettmeier, Timothy N., 207n, 288n, 290n, 353n
O'Neill, James L., 92n, 350n, 354n
Orfield, Myron W., Jr., 276, 289n, 351n
Osgood, D. Wayne, 124n
Ostrom, Elinor, 63n, 64n, 66n, 153n, 374

# P

Packer, Herbert, 350n
Padgett, Deborah L., 241n 321n
Parker, William, 35, 252, 255–256
Parks, Roger B. , 63n, 64n, 66n, 226, 374n
Pate, Anthony M., 63n, 64n, 87, 94n, 184n, 185n, 230, 239n, 291n
Patterson, E. Britt, 320n
Paulson, Monrad G., 43n, 289n
Pearson, Jack, 66n, 291n
Pepinsky, Harold E., 134, 152n, 204, 209n, 287n
Perez, Douglas, 291n
Perrott, Stephen B., 350n
Perrow, Charles, 374n

Petersilia, Joan, 139, 153n, 238n, 352n, 353n
Piliavin, Irving, 116–117, 123n, 220, 226, 237n, 238n
Plotkin, Martha R., 95n, 122n
Polebaum, Eliot E., 292n, 354n
Pollitz, Alissa A., 105, 121n
Pollock, Janay, 289n
Poole, Eric D., 351n
Poveda, Tony, 65n
Powers, Richard G., 43n
Puro, Steven, 66n, 320n, 321n

# Q

Quint, Janice C., 352n

# R

Rasinski, Kenneth A., 284, 291n
Reasons, Charles E., 240n
Regoli, Robert M., 327, 351n
Reiss, Albert, 35, 36, 43n, 71, 76–80, 91n, 92n, 93n, 116–117, 119n, 121n, 129, 131, 138, 151n, 152n, 186n, 195–196, 198, 207n, 208n, 209n, 225, 228, 231–232, 237n, 238n, 239n, 240n, 288n, 333–334, 349n, 351n, 352n, 354n
Reuss-Ianni, Elizabeth, 332, 351n
Riccio, Lucius J., 139, 153n
Richardson, James F., 41n
Ringwalt, Christopher, 124n
Robin, Gerald, 223, 237n
Rogan, Dennis P., 155n
Romero, Leo M., 235n
Roosevelt, Theodore, 27, 31
Rosenbaum, Dennis P., 18n, 151n, 184n, 185n, 241n, 321n, 349n
Rosensweig, Susan Labrin, 152n
Ross, H. Lawrence, 152n, 153n
Rossi, Peter H., 236n, 334, 352n

Rubenstein, Jonathan, 42n, 94n, 150, 153n, 155n
Rubin, Paula N., 319n
Rudovsky, David, 289n
Russell, Francis, 42n

# S

Sadd, Susan, 18n, 45n, 151n, 184n
Sanders, Beth, 317n, 318n, 319n, 320n, 321n
Sanders, William B., 132, 138, 151n, 152n
Sapp, Allen D., 44n, 208n, 317n, 320n, 351n, 352n
Schmidt, Wayne, 205, 210n
Schulman, Mark A., 120n, 121n
Schulz, Dorothy Moses, 42n
Schwartz, Alfred I., 64n, 185n, 210n, 288n, 375n
Scott, Eric J., 17, 77, 17n, 92n, 93n, 94n, 119n
Scott, Michael, 44n, 206n, 237n
Seamon, Thomas M., 65n
Seidman, David, 151n
Sellin, Thorsten, 153n
Seltzer, Richard, 350n, 351n
Seng, Magnus J., 240n, 320n
Serpico, Frank, 258, 262
Shaw, James W., 155n
Shell, Cudore L., 154n
Sherman, Lawrence W., 18n, 44n, 86, 92n, 93n, 94n, 95n, 98, 103, 107–108, 120n, 121n, 122n, 150n, 151n, 152n, 153n, 154n, 155n, 181, 184n, 185n, 208n, 223, 234, 235n, 236n, 238n, 240n, 241n, 243, 248, 251, 253–254, 257, 262, 263n, 264n, 265n, 266n, 269, 288n 290n, 317n, 320n, 350n, 352n, 375n
Sherry, Michael E., 92n
Shtull, Penny, 184n, 185n
Sichel, Joyce L., 208n, 352n

Silver, Allan, 21, 41n
Silverman, Robert A., 235n
Skogan, Wesley G., 18n, 94n, 140, 151n, 153n, 160, 164, 166–167, 183n, 184n, 185n, 186n, 317n, 375n
Skolnick, Jerome, 4, 17, 36, 43, 150, 154n, 155n, 183, 186n 191, 207n, 219–220, 227, 235n, 236n, 237n, 238n, 239n, 240n, 268, 287n, 288n, 317n, 321n, 326–327, 332, 350n, 351n, 354n
Sloan, John J., 65n
Slovak, Jeffrey S., 317n, 350n, 375n
Sluder, Richard D., 263n
Smith, Bruce, 359
Smith, Douglas A., 17, 123n, 133, 152n, 195–196, 207n, 230, 234, 238n, 316
Smith, Michael E., 352n
Smith, Ralph Lee, 264n
Smith, Russell, 233, 240n, 241n
Smith, William C., 239n, 320n, 321n
Snipes, Jeffrey B., 17n, 100, 104, 120n, 133, 152n, 205, 210n
Sparger, Jerry R., 143, 152n, 154n, 208n, 237n, 354n
Sparling, Pat, 320n
Sparrow, Malcolm K., 92n, 176, 183n, 185n
Speir, John C., 319n
Spelman, William, 18n, 45n, 93n, 153n, 194n
Spohn, Cassia, 92n, 212–215, 223, 235n, 236n, 239n, 320n
Steadman, Henry J., 122n
Steiber, Jack, 376n
Steinberg, Allen, 41n
Steinmetz, Suzanne K., 101, 120n
Stelzner, Luis G., 235n
Stephens, Darrell W., 44n, 317n, 320n, 351n, 367, 375n
Stevenson, Thomas J., 236n
Stewart, James K., 180, 185n
Stichman, Amy, 236n, 240n

Stinchcombe, Arthur L., 93n
Stoddard, Ellwyn R., 265n
Storms, Lowell, 374n
Strauchs, John J., 65n
Straus, Murray, 101–103, 120n
Sullivan, John P., 235n, 374n
Sullivan, Monique, 119n, 122n
Sulton, Cynthia G., 319n
Supina, Anne E., 17n, 100, 104, 120n,
  133, 152n
Sviridoff, Michele, 291n
Sweatwood, Harvey, 374n
Sylvester, Richard, 28

## T

Taylor, Donald M., 350n
Teilman, Kathie S., 124n
Tenzel, James H., 374n
Teplin, Linda, 122n, 190, 206n, 207n
Terrill, Richard J., 64n, 66n
Theoharis, Athan G., 43n
Thurman, Quint C., 124n, 182, 186n
Tien, James M., 18n, 93n, 95n
Tillman, Robert, 226, 238n
Tobler, Nancy, 124n
Toch, H., 207n, 237n, 238n, 350n
Tomz, Julie Esselman, 354n
Tonry, Michael, 93n, 150n, 186n
Torres, Donald A., 65n
Townsey, Roi D., 319n
Trojanowica, Robert, 241n
Tuch, Steven, 215, 217, 236n, 264n
Turner, K. B., 44n, 239n, 240n, 319n
Tweedy, Jerry, 289n

## U

Uchida, Craig, 104, 120, 147, 120n,
  154n, 186n, 374n
Uhlman, Thomas, 233, 240n
Unsinger, Peter Charles, 320n

Urbanek, Janine, 64n
Uviller, Richard, 198, 208n

## V

van Maanen, John, 92n, 209n, 336, 350n,
  352n
Van Meter, Clifford W., 65n
Vaughn, Alease M., 64n
Vaughn, Michael S., 123n, 216, 236n,
  318n
Vernon, Wyman, 252, 255
Visher, Christy A., 28–29, 33, 123n, 133,
  152n, 195–196, 207n, 208n, 238n,
  358

## W

Wagner, Judith Welch, 235n
Walker, Samuel, 18n, 41n, 42n, 43n, 44n,
  66n, 92n, 119n, 121n, 123n, 183n,
  185n, 191, 205, 206n, 207n, 209n,
  210n, 212–215, 223, 235n, 236n,
  238n, 239n, 240n, 266n, 282, 287n,
  288n, 289n, 290n, 291n, 292n, 309,
  319n, 320n, 351n, 374n, 375n
Wallace, Michael V., 41n
Waller, John D., 64n
Walsh, James Leo, 336, 352n
Walsh, William F., 354n
Ward, Carolyn M., 238n, 239n
Warren, Earl, 274
Wasby, Stephen, 276, 289n
Watters, Daniel, 230, 239n, 234, 241n,
  316, 321n
Webb, Vincent J., 155n, 240n, 320n
Weisbord, Marvin, 375n
Weisburd, David, 86, 94n, 95n, 374n
Weisheit, Ralph A., 64n, 66n
Weiss, Alexander, 153n
Weitzer, Ronald, 215, 217, 236n, 264n
Wellford, Charles, 83, 229, 239n
Wells, Alice Stebbins, 29

Wells, Edward, 47, 64n, 66n, 94n
Wells, Robert, O. 264n
Werthman, Carl, 116, 123n
Westley, William A., 36, 43, 74, 92, 151n,
    152n, 153n, 209n, 219, 236n, 252,
    264n, 265n, 290n, 302, 318n, 320n,
    323–327, 349n, 350n, 353n, 362,
    374n
Wexler, Chuck, 375n
Whitaker, Gordon P., 63n, 64n, 66n, 93n,
    121n, 374n
Wholey, Joseph S., 64n
Wilford, Charles F., 93n
Williams, Hubert, 181, 186n
Williams, Margo, 319n
Wilson, James Q., 39, 44n, 70, 76, 91n,
    92n, 94n, 139, 142, 153n, 158,
    160–161, 180, 183n, 186n, 190, 192,
    200, 206n, 207n, 209n, 219, 236n,
    251, 265n, 302, 318n, 363, 374n
Wilson, O. W., 33, 43n, 70, 88, 91n, 92n,
    128, 151n, 256, 359, 374n
Wintersmith, Robert F., 41n
Wirth, Bernard A., 240n

Wolfgang, Marvin E., 141, 153n
Woods, Arthur, 28
Worden, Alissa, 197, 208n, 225
Worden, Robert E., 89, 94n, 105, 121n,
    177, 183n, 185n, 195, 205, 207n,
    210n, 237n, 238n, 299, 317n, 350n
Wright, Benjamin S., 319n
Wright, Betsy, 44n
Wycoff, Mary Ann, 153n, 184n, 207n,
    204n, 288n, 290n, 353n, 375n

# Y

Yearwood, Douglas L., 123n
Yentes, Nancy, 318n
Yinger, J. Milton, 17n
Young, Ken, 235n

# Z

Zhao, Jihong, 182, 186n
Zimmer, Lynn, 154n
Zorza, Joan, 122n

# SUBJECT INDEX

## A

ABA; *see* American Bar Association

Academy of Criminal Justice Sciences, 301, 304, 313

Accountability, of police, 11, 16, 180, 267–292

Accreditation, 284–285; *see also* Commission on Accreditation for Law Enforcement

ACJS; *see* Academy of Criminal Justice Sciences

ACLU; *see* American Civil Liberties Union

Acquired Immune Deficiency Syndrome, 114

ADA; *see* Americans with Disabilities Act (1990)

Administrative rule making, 197, 200–206, 256

Advisory Committee on Intergovernmental Relations, 54

Affirmative Action, 230, 231, 307, 311–313, 348

African-Americans, 34, 37, 108, 117, 129, 147, 162, 168, 181, 190–191, 212, 215–218, 220–221, 223–224, 226–228, 230, 302, 303, 305, 308–310; *see also* Discrimination

communities, 30, 31, 166, 213, 222, 273

police officers, 24, 30, 34–35, 40, 195–196, 225, 231–232, 301, 311–312, 329, 330–331, 333–334, 340

AIDS; *see* Acquired Immune Deficiency Syndrome

Albany, NY, 303

Albuquerque, NM, 277–278, 284

American Bar Association (ABA), 6, 10, 230

Standards, 6, 35–36, 157, 197, 285

Survey of Criminal Justice, 157

American Civil Liberties Union, 35, 228, 277, 286, 347

American Telephone and Telegraph Company, 78

Americans With Disabilities Act, 113, 308

Ann Arbor, MI, 103–104

Arrest, 4–6, 10, 29, 31, 36, 49, 50, 76, 82, 84, 104–105, 107, 110–111, 114–117, 126, 129, 131–133, 136,

138–139, 141, 143–145, 150, 157, 190, 194–197, 225–227, 269
definition of, 136–137
factors influencing, 105, 117, 133, 194–195
mandatory, 105, 107–108, 195, 196, 201
rate, 147
Asian-Americans, 213
Assembly, freedom of, 10
Assignment, of police officers, 338–339
Atlanta, GA, 37, 309
AT&T; *see* American Telephone and Telegraph Company
Attitudes
of citizens, 215–219
of police chiefs, 255–256
of police officers, 36, 174, 197, 205, 220, 232, 234, 252, 323, 325–328, 332–334
Attorney General, 49
Attrition, of cases, rate, 51, 139, 140, 348
Australia, 39
Automobile, patrol, 31–32, 74–75

**B**

Background investigations, 304–305
Badge, 24
Baltimore, MD, 89, 176, 217, 229, 371
County Police, 101, 169
BCS; *see* California Bureau of Criminal Statistics
Beatlink Program, 167
Beats, patrol 21, 24, 26, 75, 79, 83, 85, 87, 164–167, 171
*Behind the Shield*, 327
Benefits, fringe, 337–338
BFOQ; *see* Bona Fide Occupational Qualifications
Berkeley, CA, 28–29, 273
BIA; *see* Bureau of Indian Affairs

Bill of Rights, 20, 176
police officers', 372
Birmingham Police Department, 113, 298
Birth Cohort Study, 141
BJA; *see* Bureau of Justice Assistance
BJS; *see* Bureau of Justice Statistics
Black Panthers, 229
"Blue Curtain," 258–259, 280
Blue-ribbon Commissions, 285–286
"Bobbies," 21
Bona Fide Occupational Qualifications, 307–308
Boston, MA, 22–24, 30, 53, 190, 227, 275, 301
Bribes, 247
"Broken Windows," 39, 158, 160, 170, 172, 180
*Bruno v. Codd (1978)*, 106
Brutality, police, 32, 34, 173, 213, 232, 245, 248; *see also* Force, police use of
Buffalo, NY, 32, 75
Bureau of Indian Affairs, 56
Bureau of Justice Statistics, 150, 168, 220, 225
Bureaucracy, 11, 14, 29–30, 40, 77, 180, 198–199, 357–359, 361–363; *see also* Organizations, police
*Burner v. Washington, D.C.*, 222

**C**

Cadets, police 89–90
CALEA; *see* Commission on Accreditation for Law Enforcement
California, 33, 37, 49, 62, 227, 312, 314
Bureau of Criminal Statistics, 137
Division of Law Enforcement, 56
Health and Safety Code, 170
Highway Patrol, 56
police departments, 118, 139
State College, 229
Call boxes, 25

Calls for Service, 6–8, 14, 16, 53–54,
  72–74, 77–80, 82–83, 89–91, 98,
  129, 141, 157–158, 162–163,
  165–166, 168, 171, 174, 229, 233
Campus police, 55
Canada, 39
CAPS; *see* Chicago Alternative Policing
  Strategy
Career criminals, 141
Careers of police officers, 296, 337–339
Case
  criminal, attrition of, 139
  enhancement programs, 141
  screening, 134, 139–140
CCRB; *see* Civilian Complaint Review
  Board
Certification, of police officers, 314
*Challenge of Crime in a Free Society,*
  *The,* 35
Charleston, SC, 22
Charlotte, NC, 60, 107
Chicago, IL, 14, 25, 29–30, 33, 36, 47,
  53, 168, 175, 181, 191, 232, 256,
  301–302, 309, 311, 332
  community policing in; *see* Chicago
    Alternative Policing Strategy
  police department, 114, 131, 164, 228
  police officers, 129, 165, 180, 223,
    224, 247, 276
Chicago Alternative Policing Strategy,
  14, 164–168, 175, 365
Chiefs of police, 5, 28, 32–33, 35, 38–40,
  53, 176, 201
Child Abuse and Neglect Unit, 116
Christopher Commission, 227–228,
  279–281, 283, 305, 326, 340
Cincinnati, OH, 23, 24, 27, 29, 173, 180,
  217, 227, 274, 364
Citizen complaints, 35, 282–284
Citizen reports, 10–11, 129–130, 131
Citizen review of police, 16, 39, 282–284
Citizen's arrest, 49
Civil commitment, 112

Civil liberties, 58
Civil service, 367–378
Civil remedies, 171
Civil rights
  groups, 37–39
  law, 33
  movement, 28, 34
Civil Rights Act (1964), 34, 37, 62, 230,
  306, 309–312
Civil Rights Commission, U.S. 229,
  281–282
Civilian Complaint Review Board, 35
Civilian oversight, of police, 282–284
Civilian review; *see* Citizen review of
  police
Civilianization of police, 51–52
Clearance rates, 82, 135–138, 140,
  269–270
Cleveland, OH, 24, 37, 51, 217, 230, 301,
  309–310
Coercive force, 6, 10
Cognitive dissonance, 143
"Cold" crimes, 13, 82, 89
Collective bargaining, 369; *see also*
  Unions, police
Colonial Era, 21–23
Colorado Springs, CO, 107
Commission on Accreditation for Law
  Enforcement, 38, 63, 71, 149–150,
  200, 203, 205, 230, 280, 284–285,
  309, 339–340
Commission to Combat Police
  Corruption, 244, 259
Common law, 20, 49
Communications
  center, 77–78, 88
  systems, 25, 28–29, 88, 158, 174
  technology, 31–32, 77, 84, 99
Community control, 273–274
Community cooperation model, of
  policing, 98
Community Organizing Response Team,
  161

Community Patrol Officer Program, 14, 40, 171–173, 176–177, 180
Community police stations, 161
Community policing, 4, 11, 14–15, 39–40, 61, 88, 90–91, 98, 127–128, 140, 150, 156–186, 205–206, 234, 270, 299, 339–340, 342, 364–365, 373; *see also* Chicago Alternative Policing Strategy
*Community Policing: Rehetoric or Reality,* 169
Community Sector Policing, 173–174, 364
Community service officer, 12–13, 89–90, 111, 161
COMSEC; *see* Community Sector Policing
Consolidation, of police agencies, 60–61
Constable, 21–22, 52, 54
Constitutional rights, 10, 33–34, 40, 57, 115, 347
Contracting, for police services, 61
Convictions, 36
Coproduction, of police services, 177
COPS; *see* Office of Community Oriented Police Services
COPY Kids Program, 118
Coroner, 49, 55
Corruption, 16, 20, 22–27, 29, 35, 40, 132, 145, 150, 180, 221, 242–266, 269, 278
  definition of, 243
  political, 11, 26
CORT; *see* Community–Organizing Response Team
County police, 53
CPOP; *see* Community Patrol Officer Program
Crack cocaine, 145
Crackdowns, 90, 146
Crime, police and, 125–155
Crime Commission, President's 12, 35, 36, 50, 58, 75, 89, 111–118,

197, 215, 227, 230–231, 233, 245, 250, 285, 298, 301, 325, 333, 339
Crime control, role of police, 6, 33, 35, 36, 39–40, 76, 80, 91, 98–99, 125–155, 158, 163, 169, 172, 269, 275
Crime fighter image of police, 4–5
Crime lab, 57
Crime mapping, 168
Crime prevention, role of police, 12, 14, 16–17, 21, 24, 49, 115–119, 127–128
Crime prophylactic model, 98
Crime rates, 52, 72, 270
Criminal investigation, 36, 49, 56, 126, 128, 131–138, 140–141, 149–150, 157, 161, 192–193; *see also* Detectives
Criminal Justice System, 11, 20, 32, 38, 52, 54, 70, 111, 118, 127, 129, 145, 147, 161, 171, 191, 194, 198–199, 212, 221, 243, 324
Criminal law, 4, 22, 131, 193–194, 201, 203, 250–251, 262, 278
  and corruption, 250–251
  and discretion, 193–194
  enforcement, 5, 6, 35, 80
Criminalistics, 138–139
Criminals, career, 141
Crisis management, 204
CSO; *see* Community service officer
Cultural diversity training, 234, 315

**D**

Dallas, TX, 142, 190, 279, 299, 306, 365
Damages, civil, 277–278
Danger, to police officers, 103–104
D.A.R.E.; *see* Drug Abuse Resistance Education Program
DAT; *see* Desk Appearance TicketPolicy
*Davis v. City of Dallas,* 308

Dayton, OH, 142
DEA; *see* Drug Enforcement Agency
Deadly force, use of, 6, 10, 20, 34, 38,
    190–191, 196, 200–205, 223–224,
    232, 285
Decentralization, of police departments,
    12, 14, 173–174, 180, 205
of law enforcement, 20, 47
Defense of life policy, 38, 200, 201, 223
Delicensing, of police officers, 63
Delinquency, juvenile, 11, 114–119
Demeanor, 117, 195, 225, 226
Demographic variables, 217
Denver, CO, 217, 220, 247, 296, 302, 327
Dependent persons, 6
Desk Appearance Ticket Policy, 146
Detective work, 5, 36, 39, 131–134, 138;
    *see also* Criminal investigation
Detectives, 135, 139–140, 145, 157
Deterrence of crime, 10, 21, 22, 39, 70,
    85, 86, 90, 106, 128, 142, 144–146,
    149, 157, 167, 174
Detroit, MI, 23, 37, 47, 52–53, 58–59,
    218, 230–234, 243, 272, 277, 298,
    309, 312, 315, 323, 342
Differential response, to calls for service,
    88–89
Directed patrol, 90
Disabilities, people with, 113–114
Discretion, 6, 16, 35, 36–40, 77, 80,
    83–84, 99, 106, 112, 116–117,
    129–134, 189–210, 256, 274, 361
definition of, 190
Discrimination, 30, 34, 114, 117, 191,
    195, 198, 212–215, 223, 230–231,
    235, 302, 306–307, 310–312,
    330–331
definition of, 214–215
sex, 197, 303, 314
Disorder, 158, 160–161, 163, 166, 170
Disparity, racial, 147, 212–215, 227, 299
definition of, 214–215
Dispatch, 77–79, 84, 88, 90, 165

Displacement of crime, 85, 146, 148–149
District of Columbia, 28, 108; *see also*
    Washington, DC
Diversion programs, 118
Domestic violence, 38, 98, 100–108, 133,
    190, 201–204
by police officers, 109
Drug Abuse Resistance Education
    Program, 115–119, 145, 148
Drug enforcement, 145–148
Drug Enforcement Agency, 48, 57
Drunk driving, enforcement, 142–143
Due process, 40, 180, 191, 198, 274, 276,
    347
Durham, NC, 114

# E

EAP; *see* Employee assistance program
Early warning system, 260, 277,
    281–282
EEO; *see* Equal employment opportunity
EEOC; *see* Employment Opportunity
    Commission
Effectiveness
of patrol, 85–88, 107, 128
of police, 127, 135–137
El Paso, TX, 231
Employee assistance program, 347
Employment practices
of police, 293–354
as source of racial tensions, 230–232
England, 39, 47, 49, 60, 61, 142, 222
English heritage, 20–21
Entertainment media, 5, 131
Entrapment, 144, 259
Equal employment opportunity, 306–311
Equal Employment Opportunity
    Commission, 230, 300, 306, 311
Equal Employment Opportunity Index,
    309, 310–311
Equal protection, of the law, 40, 105,
    108, 144, 180, 191, 198

Ethnicity, 213–219, 221, 224, 228, 308–309, 333–335; *see also* Police–community relations categories, 214
Evasion of duty, 84
Evidence, 133, 195
EW; *see* Early warning system
Excessive force; *see* Brutality, police; Force, police use of
Exclusionary rule, 202–203, 274–275, 332
Eyewitness identification, 138

# F

Family Crisis Intervention, 105
FBI; *see* Federal Bureau of Investigation
FCI; *see* Family Crisis Intervention
Fear Reduction Experiment, 140–141, 161–162, 233
Federal Bureau of Investigation, 31, 33–34, 48, 57, 103, 130, 135, 137, 164
Federal Bureau of Prisons, 57
Federal Communications Commission, 89
Federal law enforcement, 31, 33–34, 57
Female police officers; *see* Women, as police officers
Field interrogation, 223–229
San Diego study, 117, 227–228
Field training, 314
Field training officer, 314
Fifth Amendment, 274–275
Fingerprints, 139
Fish and Wildlife Service, U.S., 57
First Amendment, 6, 115, 347
Fleeing felons, 38, 200, 203, 205, 223
Florida, 63, 84, 306, 315
Follow-up investigations, 133–134
Foot patrol, 75, 87–88, 128, 160–161, 217

FOP; *see* Fraternal Order of Police
Force, police use of 6, 10, 26, 34, 40, 195–196, 203, 212–218, 224–226, 230, 253, 285–286, 334; *see also* Brutality, police; Deadly force, use of
use of force continuum, 224
Ford Foundation, 37
Forest Service, U.S. 57
Fourteenth Amendment, 191, 275, 312
Fourth Amendment, 274
Fragmentation of law enforcement, 20, 50, 58–61, 148
Fraternal Order of Police, 369
Fringe benefits, 337–338
FTO; *see* Field training

# G

Galveston County Sheriff's Department, 113
Gambling, 144–145
Gang Resistance Education and Training Program, 119
Gang units, 116
Gangs, 116, 146, 160, 180
GAO; *see* General Accounting Office
GAOL; *see* Gay Officer Action League
*Garrity*, 258, 347
Gay Officer Action League, 330
General Accounting Office, 275
Gratuities, 245–246, 253, 256
GREAT; *see* Gang Resistance Education and Training Program
Greensboro, NC, 88
Grievance procedures, 369–371
Guns; *see* Weapons

# H

Harassment
by police, 146, 160, 191, 227, 229
sexual, 309–310

Harvard University, Kennedy School of
Government, 161
Hawaii, 53, 56
Hayward, CA, 168
Highway Patrol, 31, 56
Hispanic Americans, 162, 168, 181, 190,
215–216, 221, 223, 230, 273, 302,
305, 308–310
communities, 213
police officers, 196, 231, 311, 329,
331, 340; *see also* Discrimination;
Ethnicity
History of police, 19–45
of accountability, 269
HIV-Positive Individuals, 114
Homeless, policing of, 108–111
Homosexuals as police officers, 330
discrimination against, 213
Honest law enforcement, 15
Hot Spots, 74, 90, 126, 148, 170–171
Housing and Urban Development, U.S.
Department of, 300
Houston, TX, 37, 50, 53, 140, 161–162,
177–179, 270–271, 342–345
Fear Reduction Experiment, 161–162,
181, 233
Operation Siege, 169
HUD; *see* Housing and Urban
Development, U.S. Department of
Human relations training, 233–234; *see
also* Cultural diversity training
Husband-beating controversy, 101–102


# I

IACP; *see* International Association of
Chiefs of Police
ICMA; *see* International City
Management Association
Imprisonment, 141
Incident-based policing, 158–159
Index crimes, 5, 114, 131, 135, 139,
269

Industry perspective, on policing , 47–48
Inefficiency, in policing, 24–29
Informants, 150, 258
Injunctions, 278
Innovative Neighborhood Oriented
Policing, 168, 175
INOP; *see* Innovative Neighborhood
Oriented Policing
In-service time, 83
INSLAW Study, 140
Institute for Liability Management, 278
Institute of Law and Society, 139
Interior, U. S. Department of, 56
Internal affairs units, 201, 257–258,
279–281
International Association of Chiefs of
Police, 28, 105, 115, 205, 256, 260,
261, 284, 314
International Association of
Policewomen, 29
International City Management
Association, 33, 311
International perspective on policing
48–49
on police-community relations, 222
International Union of Police
Associations, 369
Interpersonal conflict, 7
Interrogations, 38, 117
Investigation; *see* Criminal investigation
Involuntary civil commitment, 112
Iowa, 49, 102, 108
IUPA; *see* International Union of Police
Associations


# J

Jails, 54, 61
Job satisfaction, 342–347
Job stress, 342–347
Justice, U. S. Department of, 56, 58, 62,
113–114, 161, 263, 277, 281, 300,
311, 348, 364

Justice of the Peace, 21
*Justice Without Trial*, 268
Juvenile units, 29, 116
Juveniles, policing of, 114–119

# K

Kansas City, 103, 255, 281–283
  Gun Experiment, 148–149
  Preventive Patrol Experiment, 36–37,
    83, 85–87, 107, 128, 142, 157, 365
Kennedy School of Government, 161
Kentucky, 101–104
Kerner Commission, 34, 36–37, 220, 230
Knapp Commission, 149, 221, 245,
    248–250, 258, 261–262, 281, 286

# L

Labeling theorists, 118
Labor markets, 181
Labor relations, 27
Lansing, MI, 89
LAPD; *see* Los Angeles CA, Police
    Department
Lateral entry, 339
Law enforcement
  cost of, 52
  number of agencies, 50–51
  role of police, 10, 14, 16–17, 33, 48,
    52, 54, 56, 80, 127, 144–145
Law Enforcement Assistance
    Administration, 36
Law Enforcement Education Program,
    37, 298
Law Enforcement Management and
    Administrative Statistics, 74–75,
    116, 308, 368
LEAA; *see* Law Enforcement Assistance
    Administration
Learning organizations, 365–366
LEEP; *see* Law Enforcement Education
    Program

LEMAS; *see* Law Enforcement
    Management and Administrative
    Statistics
Local control, of police, 20
London, England, 21, 26, 40, 48, 183,
    222
London Metropolitan Police, 21, 26, 356
  model of policing, 23–24
Long Beach, CA, 139
Los Angeles, CA, 29, 34, 37, 110, 145,
    172, 204, 224, 228, 232, 255–256,
    259, 277, 286
  County Sheriff, 61
  Police Commission, 272–273
  Police Department, 35, 47, 53–54, 113,
    119, 137, 148, 204, 212, 217, 227,
    231, 234, 252, 277–283, 305, 311,
    326
  riot, 212
Louisville, KY, 169

# M

Madison, WI, 113
Management, police, 38, 367, 373
Mandatory arrest, 38, 105–108, 195, 196,
    201; *see also* Domestic violence
*Mapp v. Ohio*, 34, 62, 274, 276, 286
Marxist historians, 27
Maryland, 61, 127, 228
Mayor's Office of Inquiry and
    Information, 166
Mecklenburg County Sheriff's
    Department, 60
Media, 5, 33, 53, 80, 131, 262, 286
Mediation, 104, 107
Memphis, TN, 196, 223, 229, 349
Mental health
  commitment, 112, 190
  services, 112–113, 346
  system, 111
Mentally ill, policing of, 110–113
Metro-Dade, FL, 84, 196

Miami, FL, 37, 107, 196, 203, 216, 260, 281, 309
Military-style structure, of police organizations, 21, 24, 29, 31
Milwaukee, WI, 24, 29, 103, 107, 359
Minneapolis, MN, 81, 90, 181, 220, 281, 283
    Domestic Violence Experiment, 106–108
    Police Department, 74
    RECAP Program, 180
Minority, racial and ethnic
    citizens, 39, 89, 140, 147, 157, 162, 166, 168, 175, 181, 191, 212, 216–221, 224, 227, 230, 279, 308–309
    communities, 37, 40, 73, 117, 166, 212–213, 222–223, 234–235, 273
    police officers, 165, 225, 230–232, 260, 302, 311, 329, 340; *see also* African Americans; Discrimination; Hispanic Americans; Race
*Miranda v. Arizona*, 34, 58, 62, 204, 274–276, 286, 332
Misconduct, police, 32, 212, 276–278, 361; *see also* Corruption
Missing Children Unit, 116
Mississippi River, 111
MO; *see* Modus Operandi
MOII; *see* Mayor's Office of Inquiry and Information
Modus Operandi, 139
Mollen Commission, 243–249, 252–261, 278–280, 340
Moral careers, of police officers, 253–254
Municipal police, 52–54
*Municipal Police Administration*, 33
Myths
    about detective work, 131–132
    about police, 4–5, 12, 20, 50, 131–132

# N

NAACP; *see* National Association for the Advancement of Colored People
Nassau County Police, 53
National Academy of Sciences, 212
National Advisory Commission on Civil Disorders; *see* Kerner Commission
National Advisory Commission on Criminal Justice Standards and Goals, 60, 70, 199, 230, 285, 363
National Association for the Advancement of Colored People, 35, 286
National Black Police Officers Association, 232, 329
National Commission on Law Observance and Enforcement, 32
National control of police, 21
National Crime Information Center, 134
National Crime Victimization Survey, 72, 76, 86, 102–103, 129–130, 215, 217
National Criminal Justice Commission, 227
National Household Survey, 147, 227, 300
National Institute of Justice, 36
National Labor Relations Act, 369
National Law Enforcement Policy Center, 205
National Organization of Black Law Enforcement Executives, 284
National Police Academy, 33
National Sheriff's Association, 284
Native Americans, 144 , 213; *see also* Tribal police
NBPOA; *see* National Black Police Officers Association
NCIC; *see* National Crime Information Center
NCVS; *see* National Crime Victimization Survey
Nebraska, 48, 72–73

Neighborhood Oriented Policing,
168–169
Neighborhood police officers, 12
precincts, 29
Net-widening, 118
New Briarfield Apartments, 13, 162, 164
New Jersey Department of Public Safety,
56
New Orleans, LA, 251, 259, 371
New York City, NY, 14–15, 23–29, 34,
37–40, 105, 139, 145–146, 168–172,
176, 180, 197–198, 203, 221, 223,
225, 231–232, 244–246, 249, 251,
254–261, 272, 282, 284, 301, 304,
342
police department, 38, 47, 53, 85,
149–150, 196, 201–202, 243, 248,
252–253, 262–263, 278, 280–281,
286, 305, 335, 340
riot, 34
New York Civil Liberties Union, 258
New York Commission to Combat Police
Corruption, 244, 259
New York State, 27, 62, 314
*New York Times*, 244, 262
New Zealand, 39
Newark, NJ, 217
Foot Patrol Experiment, 75, 87– 88,
128, 160–161
Newport News, Virginia, 13, 14, 39,
162–165, 170
News media, 5, 53, 286
NIJ; *see* National Institute of Justice
911 Calls, 40, 57, 60, 61, 72, 77–78,
80–81, 88, 90, 126, 158, 165, 174,
220, 248, 364
NOBLE; *see* National Organization
of Black Law Enforcement
Executives
Noncrime calls for service, 98
Noncrime incidents, 81, 99
Nonsworn personnel, 51, 89
Nonviolent crimes, 6

Norfolk, VA, 168
North Carolina, 246
NPO; *see* Neighborhood Police Officers
NSA; *see* National Sheriff's Association
NYCLU; *see* New York Civil Liberties
Union

## O

Oakland, CA, 14, 38, 105, 106, 148,
170–171, 251–252, 255, 309, 326,
367
OCOPS; *see* Office of Community-
Oriented Police Services
Office of Community-Oriented Police
Services, 62, 89, 163
Office of Professional Standards, 256,
280–281
Office of Tribal Justice, 56
Officers, police; *see* Police officers
Ohio Bureau of Criminal Investigation,
56
Ohio Highway Patrol, 56
Omaha, NE, 72–3, 103–104, 107, 196,
201–203, 230, 243–244, 247, 256,
280, 283, 312
One-officer patrol, 75
Operation 25, 85
Operation Beat Feet, 166
Operation Pressure Point, 146
OPP; *see* Operation Pressure Point
OPS; *see* Office of Professional
Standards
Oral interviews, 304
Order maintenance, role of police, 5, 6,
10, 16, 17, 22, 26–27, 40, 49, 53, 57,
80, 97–124, 132, 144, 158, 192
Oregon, 256
Organizations, police; *see also*
Bureaucracy
hierarchy, 190, 358–359
structure, 21, 70
style, 76

Organized labor, 31
Out of service, time, 83, 143
Outside employment, of officers, 348

# P

PAB; *see* Police Advisory Board
PACE Program, 168
Part I crimes, 137, 225
Part II crimes, 107
Patrol, 69–95, 322–376
    effectiveness of, 85–88
    functions, of, 70–71
    officer use of time, 83–84
    organization of, 71–77
    response time, 82–83
Peacekeeping, 5, 35, 80, 91, 97–124, 132
Pennsylvania State Constabulary, 31
*People v. Cahan*, 274
People with AIDS, 114
PERF; *see* Police Executive Research
    Forum
Performance evaluation, 339–342
    measures, 127, 135, 139–140
Personnel, 16, 26, 49–52, 71, 83,
    296–297, 367
    management, 192
    nonsworn, 51, 89
    recruitment, 260–261, 297–304
    security, 58
    standards, 24, 26, 29, 40, 244, 256,
    313
    turnover, 26
*Perspectives on Policing*, 161, 176, 181
Phantom effect, 86
Police Advisory Board, 34
Philadelphia, PA, 23, 28, 47, 53, 58,
    72–75, 215, 221, 231, 244, 247–278,
    282, 284, 316
Phoenix, AZ, 224, 316
Physical force; *see* Force, police use of
Pittsburgh, PA, 277
Plea bargaining, 199

Police
    academy, 24
    brutality, 32, 34, 173, 213, 232, 245,
    248
    commissions, 27, 48
    commissioners, 26–30, 255
    discretion, 6, 35–37, 40, 80, 99, 105,
    112, 116, 130, 132–134, 189–210,
    256
    field practices, 223–229
    force, police use of 202, 252,
    255–256, 272
    officers, 293–376
    organizations, 36, 142, 252–254,
    355–376
    recruitment, 29, 35, 58, 60, 200,
    260–261, 297–304, 373
    strikes, 30, 371
    subculture, 36, 70, 176–177, 252–253,
    280, 313, 325–329
    supervision of, 25–26, 32, 35, 191,
    194, 252, 260, 279–280
    training, 24, 29, 33, 35, 37, 108, 200,
    313–316
    unions, 30, 34, 38, 368–373
    work, 5, 6, 33, 36, 40, 51, 67–187,
    251–252, 295–321, 335–337
    working personality, 220, 326
*Police Administration*, 33, 359
Police-community relations, 16, 20,
    30–31, 34–38, 75, 128, 157, 166,
    169, 173–175, 177, 191, 211–241,
    244, 315, 356, 359, 373; *see also*
    Race
Police Executive Research Forum, 37,
    72, 74, 82, 110, 113, 133–135, 140,
    150, 163, 182, 205, 213, 222, 280,
    282, 284, 299, 312
Police Foundation, 37, 53, 75, 82, 85,
    103, 105, 136, 141, 256, 273, 339,
    340, 363–365
*Police For the Future*, 12, 15, 367
*Police Integrity*, 281

Police officers, 322–376; *see also specific subjects (e.g., turnover)*
attitudes of, 86, 174, 197, 205, 220,
232, 234, 252, 323, 325–328,
332–334; *see also* Subculture,
police officer
definition of, 49
delicensing, of, 63
morale, 173
productivity, of, 139
recruitment of, 29, 35, 58, 60, 200,
260–261, 297–304, 373
rank and file, 30, 165, 328–332
training of, 24, 29, 33, 35, 37, 108,
200, 313–316
Police-population ratio, 52, 71–72
Police Services Study, 6, 61, 78, 81, 83,
98, 100, 112, 225–226
Policies, departmental, 84, 130, 142, 192,
196, 200, 221–223, 256; *see also*
Corruption; Discretion; Deadly
force; Domestic violence
Policing, community; *see* Community
policing
*Policing a Free Society*, 157
*Policing a Multicultural Community*, 213
Political machines, 24, 26, 29
Politics, influence on police,11, 22,
23–24, 53, 176, 200, 251, 262–263,
269–274
Polygraph Protection Act, 347
Pontiac, MI, 90
Portland, OR, 29, 77, 168, 270, 278,
281–283
Precinct stations, 29, 165
Predatory crimes, 110
Pregnancy, 309
Pregnancy Discrimination Act, 310
Preliminary investigation, 133
President's Commission on Law
Enforcement and Administration of
Justice; *see* Crime Commission,
President's

Press, freedom of, 10
*Preventing Crime*, 162, 181
Preventive patrol, 16, 21–22, 36, 107,
126, 157
Prince George County, 168
*Prince of the City*, 247, 258
Private security, 57–58
Proactive policing, 13, 85, 91, 126, 129,
132, 147
Probationary period, 316
Problem-oriented policing, 13–15, 39,
90–91, 98, 119, 128, 140, 146, 148,
150, 157–163, 170, 173, 180, 183,
206, 299
Problem-solving, 5, 39, 162–166, 168,
180, 182
Productivity, 139
Professional judgement, 199–200
Professionalism, 24–30, 33, 36, 82, 244,
269, 362–363, 373
Professionalization, 4, 27–29, 30, 33, 35,
234
Progressivism, 28
Promotion, 337
Prosecution, of police officers, 278
Prostitution, 144, 160, 171
PSA; *see* Public service aides
PSS; *see* Police Services Study
Public interest groups, 286
Public opinion about the police,
215–219
and corruption, 262
Public service aides, 13, 90
Pursuits, by police, 84, 201, 203
PWA; *see* People with AIDS

## Q

Quasi-military, style of organization,
12, 21, 24, 29, 356–357, 362,
368
Quotas, 76, 142, 311–313
hiring, 311–313

# R

Race, 16, 23, 34–35, 40, 133, 138, 162, 165–166, 180–182, 197, 206, 213–218, 226, 233–234, 273, 333–335, 340; *see also* African-Americans; Native Americans; Police community relations
  categories, 214
  discrimination, 30, 34, 117, 191, 195, 198, 212–215, 223, 230–231, 235, 302
  disparities, 147, 212–215, 227, 299
  relations 16, 23, 35, 40, 181, 233–234
Rand Corporation, 134, 227
  criminal investigation study, 36, 138
Rapid response, 36, 166
Reactive, patrol, 22, 132
Reality shock, 323–324
RECAP Program, 180
Recruitment, 29, 35, 58, 60, 200, 260–261, 297–304, 373
  standards, 297–300
Reform, police 26–27, 32, 36
Reformers, 26–30
Repeat offender program, 141
Report, police, 133, 136, 202
*Report on Lawlessness in Law Enforcement*, 32
*Report on Police*, 28
Reporting, of crimes, 82, 129–131
Republicans, 24
Resources, police, 194, 198
Response time, 39, 82–83, 86, 88–89, 157
Responsibilities, of police, 6, 9–10, 115, 171
Reverse discrimination, 311–313; *see also* Affirmative Action
Rhode Island, 53
Richmond, VA, 205–206
Ride-along programs, 161, 232–233

*Rights of Police Officers*, 286, 347
Riots, 23, 232, 234
  race, 30, 34–35, 38, 212, 230
*Rizzo v. Goode*, 278
Rochester, NY, 140
Role
  of federal government, 62
  of police, 9, 12, 17, 27, 115, 157–158, 172, 176
  of state governments, 62–63
Role conflict, 5–6, 98, 115
ROP; *see* Repeat offender program
Rotten apple theory, 248–249
Rotten pockets, 248–249
Rule-making, administrative, 200–206, 256; *see also* Policies, departmental

# S

St. Louis, MO, 24, 30, 83, 111, 229
Salaries, 337–338
San Antonio, TX, 231
San Diego, CA, 52, 75, 83, 86, 171, 283
  Field Interrogation Study, 117, 227–228
  Police Department, 163, 298
San Francisco, 234, 272, 283, 371
San Jose, CA, 197, 225, 232, 281–283, 314, 348
San Jose State College, 33
Santa Monica, CA, Police Department, 110
SARA; *see* Scanning, Analysis, Response, Assessment
Satisfaction, job, 342–347
*Scandal and Reform*, 251
Scandinavia, 142
Scanning, Analysis, Response, Assessment, 162–163
Scarman Report, 222
*Scott v. Hart (1979)*, 106
Search and Seizure, 34, 38

Seattle, WA, 90, 149
  police department, 111
Segregation, racial, 30
Selection, of police officers, 303–306
Self-incrimination, 34, 274
Seniority, 70, 74, 231, 324–325
Service calls, workload, 80–81, 89
Service style, of policing, 76
Sexual orientation, 330
Sheriff
  county, 21, 22, 47, 53–54, 60, 113–114
  responsibilities of, 22
  role of, 54
SIU; *see* Special Investigative Unit
Sixth Amendment, 275
Slave patrol, 22
SMART; *see* Specialized Multi-Agency
  Response Team
Social control, 10, 11, 22
Social problems, 11, 27
Social welfare system, 11, 25
Social Work Model, of policing, 98
SOP; *see* Standard operating procedure
  manuals
Special District Police, 55
Special Investigative Unit, 149
Specialization, 12–13, 29, 40
Specialized Multi-Agency Response
  Team, 14, 148, 170–171, 367
Specialized units, 29, 30, 132–133,
  143–145, 149, 164
Speech, freedom of, 10, 347
Spokane, WA, police department, 118
SRI; *see* Stanford Research Institute
Standard operating procedure manuals,
  38, 84, 202, 204, 359
*Standards for Criminal Justice*, 285
*Standards Relating to the Urban Police
  Function*, 35
Stanford Research Institute, 140
State police, 31, 56–57
Stereotypes, of police, 296
Stop and frisk, 35, 76, 191, 227–228

Strategic management, 367
Street-level bureaucrats, 71, 191
*Streetcorner Politicians*, 325
Stress, job, 342–347
Steubenville, OH, 277
Strikes, by police, 30, 31, 371
Subculture, police officer, 70, 252–253,
  280, 313, 325–329
Subpoena, 54
Subprofessionals, 89
Substance abuse, 11, 26, 90, 104,
  109–111, 118–119, 145, 160, 261,
  346
Suffolk County Police, 53, 257
Supervision of police, 25–26, 32, 35, 76,
  191, 194, 252, 260, 279–280
Supreme Court, U.S., 34, 52, 202, 269,
  274–278
  decisions, 37–38, 58, 62, 205, 223,
  312–313, 347

# T

Tallahassee, FL, 305, 348
Tammany Hall, 24
Task forces, 364–365
*Task Force Report: The Police*, 35
Team policing, 15, 39, 140, 164,
  173–175, 180, 205, 274, 363–364
Technology, 31–32, 77, 84, 99
Telephone, 31–32, 77–80
Telephone Reporting Units, 89
Tempe, AZ, 168
*Tennessee v. Garner*, 62 , 205, 223
Texas, 113
  Rangers, 31
311 phone systems, 89, 100
Toronto, Canada, 113
Traffic
  enforcement, 141–143, 228–229
  problems, 7
  units, 29
Training academy, 29, 60, 313–316

Tribal police, 55
Tribal Self Government Act, 1994, 56
TRUs; *see* Telephone, reporting units
Turnover among police officers,
    348–349
*Two Nations: Black and White, Separate,
    Hostile, Unequal*, 212
Two-officer patrol, 75
Two-way radio, 31–32

# U

UCR; *see* Uniform Crime Reports
Undercover police work, 149
Underrepresentation, of minority police
    officers, 37, 230, 311
Unfounding, of crimes, 130–131, 135
Uniform Crime Reports, 33, 85,
    130–131, 135–137, 158, 269
Uniforms, police 23, 29
Unions, police, 30, 34, 38, 368–373
University of California, 28
    School of Criminology, 33
University of Maryland, 127, 162, 181

# V

Vandalism, 160
*Varieties of Police Behavior*, 251
Vera Institute, 284
Verbal abuse, 228
Vice Unit, 29, 132–133, 143–145
Victimization survey, 85, 86
Victimless crimes, 143, 145, 150, 193, 258
Victims, crime, 5, 22, 82, 105, 126, 130,
    133, 140, 157, 161, 195, 221; *see
    also* Domestic violence
Victim/witness program, 139
Violence, domestic, 100–108, 133
*Violence and the Police*, 325
Violent Crime Act, 1994, 50, 163, 277
Violent crimes, 7, 80, 138

# W

War on Crime, 4, 33, 227, 356
War on Drugs, 147
Warrant, arrest, 141
Washington, D.C., 37, 52–53, 72, 131,
    141, 145, 172, 222, 228, 231, 260,
    301, 305, 313, 316, 324, 334, 342
Watch, the, 21–23
Watchman, style of policing, 76
Watts Riot, 34
Weapons, 5, 15, 24, 26, 29, 50, 79, 115,
    148–149, 172, 196, 201–203, 223,
    313, 334
*Weeks v. United States*, 274
Whorehouse riots, 23
Wickersham Commission, 28, 32, 285
Wilmington, DE, 83
Wisconsin, police departments, 52, 276
Wichita, KS, 33
Women
    as crime victims; *see* Domestic
        violence
    as police officers, 24, 29, 37, 40, 197,
        230, 301–302, 309–310, 314,
        328–331, 334–335, 346
Worchester, MA, 13, 90
Working environment of policing, 36,
    194, 196
Working personality of police officers,
    220, 326
*Working the Street*, 204
Workload, police, 33, 71–74, 88–89,
    222
    of criminal justice system, 191
World War I, 30, 31

# Z

Zero-tolerance policing, 14–15, 40,
    171–173